Royal Lives

Selected by **Frank Prochaska**

OXFORD
UNIVERSITY PRESS

OXFORD

UNIVERSITY PRESS

Great Clarendon Street, Oxford OX2 6DP

Oxford University Press is a department of the University of Oxford.
It furthers the University's objective of excellence in research, scholarship,
and education by publishing worldwide in

Oxford New York

Auckland Bangkok Buenos Aires Cape Town Chennai
Dar es Salaam Delhi Hong Kong Istanbul Karachi Kolkata
Kuala Lumpur Madrid Melbourne Mexico City Mumbai Nairobi
São Paulo Shanghai Singapore Taipei Tokyo Toronto
with an associated company in Berlin

Oxford is a registered trade mark of Oxford University Press
in the UK and in certain other countries

Published in the United States
by Oxford University Press Inc., New York

© Oxford University Press 2002

Database right Oxford University Press (maker)

First published 2002

British Library Cataloguing in Publication Data
Data available

Library of Congress Cataloging in Publication Data
Data available

ISBN 0-19-860530-7

10 9 8 7 6 5 4 3 2 1

Typeset in DanteMT
by Alliance Phototypesetters, Pondicherry, India
Printed in Great Britain
by T. J. International, Padstow, Cornwall

Preface

'The best record of a nation's past that any civilization has produced': G. M. Trevelyan's view in 1944 of the *Dictionary of National Biography* highlights the achievement of its first editor Leslie Stephen. Between 1885 and 1900 quarterly volumes rolled out from the presses in alphabetical order by subject. A national institution had come into existence, making its distinctive contribution to the national aptitude for the art of biography.

In his initial prospectus for the *DNB*, Stephen emphasized the need to express 'the greatest possible amount of information in a thoroughly business-like form'. Dates and facts, he said, 'should be given abundantly and precisely', and he had no patience with the sort of 'style' that meant 'superfluous ornament'. But he knew well enough that for 'lucid and condensed narrative', style in the best sense is essential. Nor did he content himself, in the many longer memoirs he himself contributed to the *DNB*, with mere dates and facts: a pioneer in the sociology of literature, he was not at all prone to exaggerate the individual's impact on events, and skilfully 'placed' people in context. Stephen's powerful machine was carried on by his work-horse of a successor Sidney Lee, who edited the first of the ten supplements (usually decennial) which added people who died between 1901 and 1990.

Memoirs were often written soon after the subject died and their authors were frequently able to cite 'personal knowledge' and 'private information'. In such cases there is always a balance to be struck between waiting for written sources to appear and drawing upon living memory while still abundant and fresh. Stephen had no doubts where he stood: he published book-length biographies of his Cambridge friend Henry Fawcett and of his brother Fitzjames within a year of their deaths, and cited Boswell's *Johnson* and Lockhart's *Scott* as proof that the earliest biographies are often the best. Furthermore, memoirs of the recently dead were included in the *DNB* right up to the last possible moment, the press often being stopped for the purpose. Roundell Palmer, for example, died on 4 May 1895 and got into the 43rd volume published at the end of June.

Preface

So the memoirs published in this series are fully in line with what was *DNB* policy from the outset. Furthermore, all have the virtue of reflecting the attitudes to their subjects that were taken up during their lifetimes. They may not always reflect what is now the latest scholarship, but as G. M. Young insisted, 'the real, central theme of history is not what happened, but what people felt about it when it was happening'. So they will never be superseded, and many are classics of their kind—essential raw material for the most up-to-date of historians. They have been selected by acknowledged experts, some of them prominent in helping to produce the new *Oxford Dictionary of National Biography*, which will appear in 2004. All are rightly keen that this ambitious revision will not cause these gems of the *DNB* to be lost. So here they are, still sparkling for posterity.

Brian Harrison
Editor, *Oxford Dictionary of National Biography*

Royal Lives—selections from the DNB

Introduction

In the *Rights of Man* that great anti-royalist Thomas Paine said that the monarchy was 'something kept behind a curtain', but when the curtain happens to be drawn people 'burst into laughter'. Paine would not be amused by reading the lives of royalty in the *Dictionary of National Biography*, for even when the curtains are open there is little hilarity on offer. This is not surprising, for the *DNB* was a high-minded Victorian enterprise. Many of the entries on royalty were written during Queen Victoria's reign by contributors who, if not monarchists to their fingertips, lived in a society in which the monarchy was seen as a constitutional anchor and royalty the fixed, if not magical, point of the social hierarchy. In the late nineteenth century, unlike today, anti-monarchists were an endangered species in Britain, comparable to atheists in a world of religious convention.

Unlike the trades and professions, royalty is not something one can choose as a career, which made the selection of entries for this volume automatic. Few were called to royal status and virtually all have been chosen. The focus is on members of the royal family since the reign of George III, over fifty entries. In order to fill out the picture of royalty in national life, I have complemented these by the inclusion of twenty further entries: private secretaries, palace servants, royal mistresses, and Wallis Simpson. Both members and non-members of the royal family have been integrated into the text, which is organized along chronological lines by date of birth. It should be said that several members of the royal family from the late eighteenth century onwards do not appear in the *DNB*, including children of George III and Queen Charlotte. Diana, Princess of Wales, is also missing, but will feature in the new *Oxford DNB*.

Because of the exalted station of the royal family, great care was taken over their entries. The Victorian editors of the *DNB*, Leslie Stephen and Sidney Lee, were men of exacting scholarship, and they ensured that

Introduction

Britain's kings and queens and their offspring received serious attention from reliable contributors. Indeed, Lee wrote the lives of Queen Victoria and Edward VII himself. The former was a prodigious effort, which he later transformed into the first full-scale biography of Victoria (1902). It remains a most useful guide to the queen's reign by a contemporary. His work on Edward VII formed the basis for his later life of the king, which was undertaken at the request of Edward's son, George V. Lee, knighted in 1911, was a safe pair of hands. Even so he had to tone down the initial memoir because it pained Queen Alexandra. He did manage to say that the king 'somewhat suffered in moral robustness', but his article on Edward VII is long on royal service and short on royal misdemeanour.

Several of the biographies offered here suffer from the sin of omission or undue deference. Would the future of the British monarchy have been secure had Edward VII's eldest son, the dissipated Albert Victor, Duke of Clarence, become king and not his dutiful younger brother? The distinguished historian A. F. Pollard, who treated Clarence perfunctorily, with academic propriety, and without warts, dodges the issue. John Gore's decorous life of Queen Mary fails to mention that the queen was highly charged politically and hostile to the Labour Party. Such discretion was in keeping with that widely observed by those who move in royal circles. The combination of social distinction and political sensitivity can make palace employment scary and uncomfortable. Sir Philip Hunloke, George V's sailing master, once confided to colleagues: 'there is a blackbird on the lawn. But for God's sake don't quote me.'

The royal lives in the *DNB* were typically written by people outside the limelight: palace insiders, the Royal Librarian, scholars like Lee and Pollard, or reliable hacks, who could be counted upon to meet a deadline in exchange for ready cash. Every editor knows the virtue of the last sort. Lee found one in John Andrew Hamilton, one of his contemporaries at Balliol, who supplemented a meagre Oxford fellowship with writing *DNB* articles, 288 in all. A man of 'cynical acidity' according to his own *DNB* entry (he became a judge), Hamilton wrote a colourful piece on George IV, notable for a lack of deference that may have made Lee shudder. (George IV, like Edward VIII, is a monarch who became fair game to the Establishment, partly because he had no surviving offspring.) Hamilton summed up the king:

> That he was a dissolute fop, a spendthrift and a gamester, 'a bad son, a bad husband, a bad father, a bad subject, a bad monarch, and a bad friend', that his word was worthless and his courage doubtful, are facts which cannot be denied. ... All that can be said in his favour is this. The fact that his character was one which not even his own

partisans could respect or defend caused the personal power of the monarchy . . . to dwindle almost to a shadow years before he died.

More recent scholarship on George IV has discovered redeeming qualities of charm, taste, and charity, but the political case against the king largely stands. In a sense, political weakness was George IV's greatest contribution to the British monarchy, for royal ineptitude contributed mightily to the institution's survival. A powerful theme running through the lives that are presented in these pages is the decline in royal political power, a trend that George IV accelerated through profligacy and in-attention. Kingly incapacity also runs through the critical entry on George III by the Victorian historian and cleric William Hunt, a sub-editor of the *DNB*. Whether through negligence or design, most monarchs in modern British history have had little inclination to recapture lost powers, while their reactionary counterparts on the Continent bit the proverbial dust. Reading these disparate royal biographies, one can only agree with that most subtle of palace advisers, Lord Esher, who said that over the years the monarchy exchanged 'authority' for 'influence'. Put differently, we can discern in the articles on successive monarchs that Britain was being transformed into a crowned republic, that is, a democracy that happened to retain a hereditary head of state.

The essay on Reginald Brett, Lord Esher, who masterminded much of the royal ceremonial at the end of Victoria's reign and pulled strings for Edward VII and George V, is full of those nicely turned phrases for which the *DNB* is notable: 'Inheriting marked ability, great social gifts, and in-fluential connexions, Esher possessed all the qualifications for success in public life except the conviction that it was worth while.' We are told that Esher exercised his own influence 'behind a curtain' (Paine's metaphor). This is a revealing phrase, for much of the monarchy's adjustment to social democracy, which has been its greatest challenge in modern history, has been the result of advice from private secretaries, palace insiders like Esher, and outsiders who happened to come into the royal orbit. Perhaps most notably in the reign of George V, such aides and confidants deeply influenced palace policy. Arthur Bigge, Lord Stamfordham, who steered the inexperienced king through a 'period of strong civil ferment', was arguably the most important palace official in modern history. Owen Morshead, the Royal Librarian, gives us a glimpse of Bigge's importance in a quote from George V's diary: 'Dear Bigge passed peacefully away at 4:30 today. I shall miss him terribly. His loss is irreparable.'

Intriguingly, there was no diminution in royal administration with the decline of the sovereign's political power in Britain. This was the result not only of royal incapacity (the first private secretary, Herbert Taylor, was appointed because of George III's blindness), but also because of the weight of business and the ever-growing demands on royalty to perform public services, from opening bridges and bazaars to reviewing sailors and undertaking overseas tours. Gradually, the private secretary took over as the pre-eminent palace official, the spider at the centre of the palace web. As the intermediary between the Crown and the politicians, the private secretary serves as the 'eyes and ears' of the sovereign, the adviser most responsible for setting the tenor of the reign. Sadly, one of the most influential private secretaries, Sir Henry Ponsonby, who served Queen Victoria, received such cursory treatment in the *DNB* that his entry was not worth including in this volume. But one can trace the transformation of the office through the entries on, among others, Herbert Taylor, Arthur Bigge, and Michael Adeane. Tellingly, all the private secretaries in the *DNB* had military associations, often with backgrounds in the empire.

It is one of the curiosities of British life that the politicians transformed the Crown into a political rubber stamp, only to perpetuate a belief that the Crown's first duty had to do with high politics. The monarchy has retained a residual political role, but the obsession with this role on the part of the politicians and the palace has been blinkered and atavistic. In its treatment of the extended royal family the *DNB*, despite its high political focus, provides a corrective. Running through these pages we see not only the decline in the political importance of the Crown, but the growth of a popular function for the royal family as patron, promoter, and fundraiser for deserving causes and the underprivileged. As power shifted to ministers, the monarchy could no longer be blamed for failed policies, while the growth of royal civic work created enduring links with all the social classes. Indeed, the loss of political power purified the monarchy for social purposes, and this was in keeping with a burgeoning democracy.

Those who think that Diana, Princess of Wales, was the first member of the royal family engaged in charity will be disabused by reading the entries on, among others, George III's daughters, Prince Albert, Queen Mary, or Marina, Duchess of Kent. Queen Adelaide, who contributed vast sums to good causes, 'won universal esteem by her blameless life and royal munificence in charity'. Charity defined Queen Alexandra, according to her biographer: 'All who gave their service to the sick or the sorrowful, who tried to help children, who cared for birds or animals, could rely on her practical sympathy and eager—sometimes perhaps too eager—readiness to help.' It is worth comparing such beneficent labours with the lifestyle of Wallis Simpson, the Duchess of Windsor, who, as Philip Ziegler notes, preferred shopping to hospital visiting. But then the duchess, not being royal, did not see social service as an inescapable vocation.

Introduction

As the Crown's political-cum-warrior traditions gave way to charitable patronage and civic duty, kings and princes, rather reluctantly, took off their uniforms and donned middle-class dress to open bazaars and visit hospitals. In his biography Sidney Lee pays considerable attention to Edward VII's charitable rounds, which were often prompted by Queen Alexandra, not to mention his mistress, Frances Greville, Countess of Warwick. Philanthropy did as much as anything else to change his image from youthful reprobate to benign patriarch. (Something similar seems to be happening to Prince Charles!) As the *DNB* suggests, the monarchy lost its political authority but discovered a promising career in social work. Now that the magic of monarchy has largely vanished, it is this civic purpose, more than anything else, which is likely to open the 'curtain' further, let in the daylight, and keep the royal family in business.

FRANK PROCHASKA

January 2002

Contents

Contents

Contents

Contents

Contents

King of England, eldest son of Frederick Louis, prince of Wales, and Augusta, daughter of Frederick II, duke of Saxe-Gotha, was born on 4 June (N.S.) 1738, in Norfolk House, St. James's Square, London. When he was in his seventh year, Dr. Francis Ayscough, afterwards dean of Bristol, was appointed his preceptor, but his early education was hindered by the quarrel between his father and grandfather, George II (*Life of Hardwicke*, ii. 312). In common with his brothers and sisters he acted in some plays which were performed by children at Leicester House (*Letters of Lady Hervey*, p. 147; Dodington, p. 31). In October 1750 Francis, Lord North, was appointed his governor. He was much attached to his father, and was deeply affected at his death in March 1751. By the death of the Prince of Wales he succeeded to the titles of Electoral-prince of Brunswick-Lüneburg, Duke of Edinburgh, and other honours. His grandfather showed a kindly interest in him; on 18 April his household was declared, and on the 19th he was created Prince of Wales and Earl of Chester. Lord Harcourt was appointed his governor in the place of Lord North, Dr. Hayter, bishop of Norwich, his preceptor, and Stone and Scott his sub-governor and sub-preceptor. The next year a feud broke out among these officers. Stone, who was a man of learning, was suspected of Jacobitism, and Scott, who had been recommended by Bolingbroke, was also offensive to the whigs. Harcourt and Bishop Hayter declared that they would resign unless Stone and Scott were dismissed, and Harcourt accused them of instilling Jacobite and arbitrary principles into the mind of their pupil (Dodington, p. 193). In the end Harcourt and Bishop Hayter retired, and their places were taken by Lord Waldegrave and Dr. Thomas, bishop of Peterborough (for George's judgment of his preceptors in after life see Rose, *Diaries*, ii. 187). The prince passed his youth in an atmosphere of intrigue and jealousy. Waldegrave found him 'full of prejudices which were fostered by women and pages;' he was completely under his mother's influence, and knew nothing of the outside world. Except his brother Edward, he had no young companions, for the princess was afraid lest his morals should be corrupted, and he was shy and did not like company. He was, his mother used to say, an 'honest boy,' good-natured and cheerful, but he was obstinate, and apt when displeased to be sullen. From his youth he seems to have been high-principled and religious. Although he was fairly intelligent he was not quick; he was idle, and, according to Scott, used to sleep all day. At the age of thirteen he was remarkably backward (Waldegrave, pp. 8, 9; Dodington, pp. 171, 255, 289,

325, 355; Walpole, *George II*, ii. 94). George II, anxious to prevent the princess marrying him to any of her Saxe-Gotha relations, proposed in 1755 that he should marry Sophia Caroline Maria, elder daughter of the Duke of Brunswick-Wolfenbüttel. The princess set her son against the marriage, telling him that his grandfather's only motive in proposing it was to advance the interest of Hanover. The scheme failed, and the prince imbibed undutiful feelings towards the king (Waldegrave, pp. 39–41; Dodington, p. 354; Walpole, *Letters*, ii. 475). He attained his majority on his eighteenth birthday (1756); Harcourt resigned his office, and a new household was appointed. The king and his ministers were anxious to remove him from his mother's influence, and George II offered him 40,000l. a year, and requested him to set up a separate establishment. He took the money, but refused to leave his mother. At his request the Earl of Bute was appointed his groom of the stole, and at once became his chief instructor. The princess, used to the royalty of a petty German court, taught him to hold exaggerated ideas about prerogative, and her constant exhortation to him was 'George, be king' (Nicholls, *Recollections*, p. 11). Bute procured him the manuscript of Blackstone's 'Commentaries,' the substance of which was delivered as lectures at Oxford in 1758 and succeeding years, to raise his view of the prerogative of the crown (Adolphus, i. 12), while he seems to have gained from Bolingbroke's works the idea of exalting the royal authority through the overthrow of party distinctions. To this period belongs the scandal about the prince's attachment to a certain Hannah Lightfoot, the 'fair quaker,' daughter or niece of a linendraper, whose shop was in St. James's Market. It is said that through the intervention of Elizabeth Chudleigh, who became Duchess of Kingston, he persuaded her to leave her home, and go through the form of marriage with one Axford, and that he frequently met her afterwards, and it is even pretended that he secretly married her, and had a daughter by her, who became the wife of a man named Dalton. It is probable that he showed some admiration for this girl, or at least for some one of her rank (Wraxall, i. 305), but the story rests merely on anonymous letters of a late date, and certain vile publications (*Monthly Magazine*, li. 532, lii. 110, 197; *Authentic Records of the Court*, pp. 2–7, revised as *Secret Hist.* i. 26–30; *Notes and Queries*, 1st ser. x. 228, 328, 430; the worthlessness of the story is exposed by Thoms, *Hannah Lightfoot*, &c., 1867). In July 1759 the prince wrote to the king offering his services in the war (Hardwicke, iii. 182). He succeeded to the throne on the death of George II on 25 Oct. 1760.

Up to the time of his accession George had been kept in perfect seclusion by his mother and Bute, in London at Carlton House or Leicester House, and in the country at Kew (Chesterfield, *Works*, ii. 472). He had no knowledge of public business, but shook off his youthful indolence, and became an industrious, and indeed an exceedingly managing, king. He was fairly tall, and had a florid and good-natured countenance. Although he bore himself with dignity on all public occasions, and spoke impressively and with a naturally fine voice, his bearing in private was homely and undignified; his utterance was rapid, he swung himself to and fro as he talked, asked numbers of questions, had a trick of ending each with 'what? what?' and often repeated his words. Generally affable in manner, he was often rude to those who offended him. He set a high value on small points of ceremony, never talked to a minister except standing and keeping the minister standing however long the interview might last, and refused to allow the judges to dispense with their wigs when not on the bench: 'I will have no innovations,' he said, 'in my time' (*Life of Eldon*, i. 340). He spoke French and German, and knew something of Italian, but had little Latin and less Greek, a slight acquaintance with history, and a very slender stock of general information; he wrote English ungrammatically, and always spelt badly. Although, perhaps owing to Bute's instructions, he encouraged genius where it took a form which he liked and understood, his taste was execrable. Shakespeare he thought wrote much 'sad stuff' (Madame d'Arblay, *Diary*, ii. 398), and though he took interest in the foundation of the Royal Academy and liked pictures, he preferred West to Reynolds. He was fond of music, had a good ear, and at one period of his life was constantly at the opera; Handel was his favourite composer. (For notices of the king's concerts see Mrs. Papendiek, *Court and Private Life*, passim.) Mechanics and agricultural science pleased him, and he took delight in models of ships and dockyards. He had a liking for books, and in 1762 bought the library of Consul Smith, who resided at Venice (Nichols, *Lit. Anecd.* viii. 230). This was the nucleus of a collection which grew into the 'King's Library,' now in the British Museum. Shortly after he came to the throne he appears to have studied experimental philosophy (*Life of Hardwicke*, iii. 291). He was sincerely pious, his morality was strict, and he invariably acted according to the dictates, erroneous or otherwise, of his conscience. He was always remarkably calm in moments of danger. The sullenness of his youth appeared in later life in the form of an implacable disposition. Conscious of the rectitude of his intentions, and with an overweening opinion of his own wisdom and dignity, he considered all opposition as an affront to himself and an evidence of moral turpitude. Some of his petulancy must be attributed to the morbid excitability of his brain, which broke out from time to time in attacks of insanity. His leading characteristic was described by himself as firmness, and by those who were opposed to him as obstinacy.

Although slow and prejudiced, George was not without ability; he had considerable insight into men's characters, and no small knowledge of kingcraft. He carried on, certainly with some peculiar advantages, a long and bitter conflict with the most powerful party in the state, and was on the whole successful, though at a terrible cost both to himself and the country. This conflict was waged with the great whig families and their political adherents. Ever since the accession of the house of Hanover the crown had leant on the support of the whigs. The first two Georges were foreigners, and the right of both was disputed. The weakness of the crown increased the importance of its supporters; political power was vested exclusively in a few noble families which claimed to represent the principles of the revolution. The affairs of the nation were thus controlled by a party which had almost wholly ceased to represent principles, was held together by connection, and was strengthened by bribery and other corrupt practices, while the crown was fast becoming a mere ornament, adding lustre to a powerful oligarchy. The power of the people at large was as yet non-existent; the House of Commons was not, except in name, a representative body, and the dominant faction had the advantage of distributing the patronage of the crown. George began his reign with a determination to break the yoke of the whig oligarchy, and to recover for the crown the power which it had lost since 1688. There was no need for him to depend on whig support; he was an Englishman, and his title was undisputed. He had been taught that the royal authority could be best asserted by disregarding ties of connection, and breaking up parties, and that a king should choose his ministers without yielding to the dictates of a faction. He had seen in the success of Pitt the triumph of a statesman who disregarded party connection. He therefore resolved to overthrow the system of exclusion, to open office to the tories, and not to allow any party to dictate to him. In his struggle with the whigs and his work of building up the prerogative he used the services of a number of politicians who attached themselves to him personally, rather than to any minister or faction, and were called by those who opposed his policy the 'king's friends.' He thus renounced the proper sphere of a constitutional monarch in favour of that of a party leader. The king's friends do not seem to have been an organised body or kind of secret cabinet, as Burke believed, but they were not the less a formidable party. They were recruited and bound to their master by self-interest, for George took the crown patronage out of the hands of his ministers, and dispensed it himself, and by this means maintained a crown influence in parliament which was apart from, and often opposed to, the ministerial influence. For the first ten years of his reign George was engaged in a struggle, which was often unsuccessful, to break down the whig factions, and find a minister who would, and could, carry out his political views.

The accession of the young king was popular, and a proclamation against immorality which he caused to be published was generally approved. He found the ministry of Newcastle and Pitt in office, but he told Newcastle at his first interview that Bute would inform him 'of my thoughts at large,' and wrote his declaration to the council without reference to Pitt; it contained words which threw a slight on the conduct of the war, and Pitt had some trouble to persuade Bute to allow alterations to be made before it was printed (*ib.* iii. 215, 216). The speech for the opening of parliament was drawn up by Lord-chancellor Hardwicke, and was sent back by the king, with the insertion in his own writing, 'Born and educated in this country, I glory in the name of Britain;' the word Britain was thought to denote the influence of Bute, who was a Scot (*ib.* p. 231), and whom the king had made a privy councillor; but in 1804 George, in a private conversation, declared that the alteration was 'suggested to him by no one' (Rose, *Diaries*, ii. 189). The king surrendered the hereditary revenues, and his civil list was fixed at 800,000*l.* He acquired great popularity by recommending parliament to provide that judges' commissions should not expire on the demise of the crown. It was remarked that tories now attended the court, and that prerogative became a fashionable word (Walpole, *George III*, i. 16). George appears to have fallen in love with Lady Sarah Lennox, sister of the Duke of Richmond, and to have received some encouragement; for when he rode towards Hammersmith, as he often did in the summer of 1761, Lady Sarah would be making hay in the grounds of Holland House, the residence of her brother-in-law (*ib.* p. 62; Wraxall, *Memoirs*, i. 302; *Grenville Papers*, iv. 209). However, the affair came to nothing, and Colonel David Graeme was sent to visit the protestant courts of Europe to look out a suitable wife for him. The result of his mission was that on 8 Sept., at about ten in the evening, George married Charlotte Sophia, younger sister of Adolphus Frederick IV, reigning duke of Mecklenburg-Strelitz, in the chapel of St. James's. On the 22nd he and his queen were crowned. In returning to Westminster Hall, the great diamond fell out of the king's crown, which was afterwards held to have been ominous (*Annual Register*, 1761, pp. 205–42). George was a model of domestic virtue. He and his queen lived much in private, sometimes at Windsor, where he used to take great interest in the doings of the Eton boys, who still celebrate his birthday, sometimes at Richmond Lodge, and when in London at Buckingham House, then often called the 'queen's house,' for it was bought for the queen's use. The king indulged in no public amusement except the theatre, did not dine with his nobles, and was accused of affecting the privacy of an 'Asiatic prince.'

Great discontent prevailed at the elevation of Bute and the influence which he and the princess exercised over the king, and many coarse jeers were levelled at them, and some at the king also. George, however, was determined to give Bute high ministerial office, to get rid of his present ministers, and to bring about a peace with France, a step which Bute strongly recommended. A scheme was arranged, according to which Lord Holderness, a secretary of state, was persuaded, or rather bribed, to resign in March 1761, and the king appointed Bute as his successor. George dismissed Legge, chancellor of the exchequer, in favour of William Wildman Barrington, Lord Barrington. Negotiations were opened with France, and it became evident that the king and Bute designed to get rid of Pitt, who was likely to oppose the terms of peace (*Bedford Correspondence*, iii. 19, 20, 2 July). George was encouraged in this resolve by the jealousy with which Pitt was regarded by the majority of the cabinet ministers, and also probably by a pamphlet attributed to Lord Bath and written by his chaplain, John Douglas (1721–1807), entitled 'Seasonable Hints from an Honest Man on the New Reign,' which defended the new theory of government (Lecky, iii. 22). Pitt, who was convinced that Spain was preparing to join France, urged a declaration of war, and highly disapproved of the concessions which the king, Bute, and other members of the cabinet were proposing to make. George every day grew more offended with him, and plainly showed that he 'wanted to get rid of him at all events' (*Life of Hardwicke*, iii. 256). On 5 Oct. Pitt felt constrained to resign the seals. The king treated him with extreme graciousness, and pressed rewards upon him, with the intention, it may fairly be surmised, of lessening his popularity (*Rockingham Memoirs*, i. 47). Pitt accepted a reward, which for the moment roused popular indignation. He quickly regained his popularity, and when, on 9 Nov., the king and queen dined in state at the Guildhall, he was received with enthusiasm, while the king's reception, though magnificent, was extremely chilling, and Bute's carriage was attacked in the streets. George had from the first treated Newcastle with extreme coldness (*Life of Hardwicke*, iii. 230), but the duke still clung to office. Although first lord of the treasury, he complained that, with a trifling exception, the king had never attended to a single recommendation he had made; all patronage was taken out of his hands, and seven peers were created without his having been told of the king's intention. On 14 May 1762 he told the king that he must resign. George merely replied, 'Then, my lord, I must fill your place as I can;' but when he was at last forced to resign on the 26th, George condescended to solicit his support (*Bedford Correspondence*, iii. 115). The king made Bute first minister, and gave him the Garter; other changes of office had already taken place, and in spite of the general clamour George gained his point. In June he was attacked with a serious illness, which set in with a cold and cough; drastic remedies were used, and by the 20th he had begun to recover (*Life of Hardwicke*, iii. 283; Walpole, *Letters*, iv. 1). In the hope of dividing the whigs, he persuaded Henry Fox to desert his party, and take the management of the commons, acting in this as in all else on Bute's suggestion (*Bedford Correspondence*, iii. 134). Persons about the court said that the 'king would now be king indeed,' and that the 'prerogative was to shine out.' The whigs were now to feel the royal displeasure. The Duke of Devonshire whom the princess-dowager bitterly called the 'prince of the whigs,' and who had refused to take part in the discussions about the peace, was lord chamberlain. He called at St. James's in October, but the king sent him out a message by a page, 'Tell the duke I will not see him.' The duke resigned his office; his brother, Lord George Cavendish, a member of the household, also resigned, and the king accepted his resignation in person, and with marked discourtesy. Lord Rockingham remonstrated with the king, resigned his office in the bedchamber on 4 Nov., and was treated in the same manner. The same day the king with his own hand erased Devonshire's name from the list of privy councillors. Newcastle, Grafton, and Rockingham were deprived of their lieutenancies, and with the king's approval a general proscription of the whigs was carried out, which extended to inferior officials, such as clerks, and even to pensioners (*Rockingham Memoirs*, i. 135–60). When the king went to open parliament on the 25th, he was not cheered in the streets. The royal influence, however, was strong in parliament, and the preliminaries of peace were approved. This was a signal triumph. 'Now,' the princess said, 'my son is king of England.' George was delighted, and when the peace of Paris was concluded in February 1763, declared that 'England never signed such a peace before' (*Bedford Corr.* iii. 199).

Meanwhile a storm of indignation rose against Bute, and the king himself did not wholly escape it; for the minister was held to be a 'favourite.' Favouritism in its special sense was not one of George's weaknesses; while he had of course personal preferences, he showed favour to Bute, and in later times to other ministers not for personal, but for political, reasons. The influence which Bute exercised over him was jeered at in many ways, and among them by a caricature entitled 'The Royal Dupe' (Wright, p. 285). Although the ministerial majority was strong in parliament—for, in addition to the practice of intimidation, 52,000*l.* a year was spent in maintaining it—Bute felt himself unable to brave the popular indignation, and resigned on 8 April. George received his resignation with unexpected alacrity; he considered him 'deficient in political firmness,' and seems to have been rather glad to get rid of him as a minister (Malmesbury, *Diaries*, iii. 163; Rose, *Diaries*, ii. 192; Walpole, *George III*, iv. 133). By Bute's advice he appointed George Grenville to the treasury, laying down as a basis of the administration which he was to form, that none of the Newcastle and Pitt ministry were ever to return to office during his reign, but that favour might be shown to those whigs who would support his government (*Bedford Corr.* iii. 224). The speech with which the king closed parliament on 19 April was scurrilously commented on by Wilkes in No. 45 of the 'North Briton,' where it was treated not as the king's, but as the minister's speech. George ordered that Wilkes should be prosecuted, urged forward the violent measures taken against him, treated the matter as a personal quarrel, and dismissed Temple from his lord-lieutenancy for sympathy with Wilkes (*Grenville Papers*, ii. 162, 192; Walpole, *George III*, iii. 296; Lecky, iii. 71). Grenville took office with the intention of shielding the king from dictation, but George found him masterful. The administration was bad, and the king was anxious to make some change in it. In August he offered cabinet office to Hardwicke, and even spoke of giving a court office to Newcastle, but Hardwicke would not come in alone, and George would not submit to take in a party in gross.

On the 21st George was much disturbed by the death of Lord Egremont, which weakened the tory side of the cabinet. By the advice of Bute he sent for Pitt, and on 27 Aug. requested him to state his opinions. Pitt dilated on the defects of the peace and the dismissal of the whigs, whom, he said, he should restore. George listened graciously, but said that his 'honour must be consulted.' He was in a difficult position; he wanted to get rid of his present ministers, and hoped that Pitt would have consented to be his minister without bringing with him any of the party which he hated. A decision was to be made on the 29th. The day before, Sunday, the 28th, Grenville saw the king, who was confused and flustered. The result of their conversation was that when Pitt the next day stated his terms, which were the treasury for Temple, and the restoration of the great whig families, the king refused them. 'My honour is concerned,' he said, 'and I must support it.' He asked Grenville to continue in office. The minister lectured him, and received the king's promise that Bute should not interfere. A few days later Bute made an attempt to win Pitt over. Grenville was indignant, and reproached the king, and when George promised that nothing of the sort should happen again, dryly answered that he hoped not. He insisted on Bute's retirement from London, and refused to allow the king to give the office of keeper of the privy purse, which Bute vacated, to one of Bute's friends. 'Good God! Mr. Grenville,' exclaimed the humiliated king, 'am I to be suspected after all I have done?' Bedford joined the administration; Bute left London, and for a time the king and his ministers were on better terms (*Grenville Papers*, ii. 197, 205, 210; *Life of Hardwicke*, iii. 278). George approved of their depriving military officers of their commands for voting against the government on the question of general warrants. 'Firmness and resolution,' he said, 'must be shown, and no one saved who dared to fly off.' He was much annoyed by the hereditary Prince of Brunswick, who came over in January 1764 to marry his sister Augusta, and who openly sympathised with the opposition. The king's unpopularity was shown by the enthusiasm with which the prince was received, and king and prince behaved rudely to each other. George disliked his ministers more and more; the administration was thoroughly bad, and was marked by want of concert, slackness, and haste. Grenville did his duty, but made himself personally hateful to the king by lecturing and thwarting him. Still George agreed with the chief measures taken by the ministers, and fully concurred in the Stamp Act, which became law on 22 March 1765. Meanwhile on 12 Jan. he was attacked by a serious illness, which lasted more or less until early in April, and during which symptoms of derangement appeared (Mrs. Papendiek, i. 33; *Quarterly Review*, cxxxi. 240).

On the king's recovery he wished that parliament should make provision for a regency in case of his death or incapacity, and proposed that he should be empowered to name from time to time the person he desired, keeping the nomination secret to 'prevent faction' (*Grenville Papers*, iii. 126). The ministers brought in a bill limiting his choice to the queen or any other person of the royal family. Bedford, out of dislike to Bute, was anxious to shut the king's mother out of any chance of power, and Halifax and Sandwich told George that unless this was done the bill would not pass the commons. He yielded to the representations of his ministers, apparently without grasping the full import of their proposal, and the princess was pointedly excluded. He soon became conscious of what he had done, had an interview with Grenville, in which he was much agitated, and even shed tears, and besought the minister to replace her name. Grenville would only promise to yield if pressed in the commons, and the king's mortification was increased when, after a ludicrous exhibition of his ministers' weakness, the house insisted on replacing his mother's name. On 6 May, the day after his interview with Grenville, he asked his uncle, the Duke of Cumberland, who had considerable influence with the opposition, and whom he had from his boyhood treated with neglect and suspicion, to negotiate with Pitt, Temple, and the great whig families as to the formation of a 'strong and lasting administration' (Duke of Cumberland's Statement, *Rockingham Memoirs*, i. 189). On the 18th he cavalierly announced to Grenville his intention of dismissing his ministers (*ib.* p. 203). Bedford, who believed that Bute was at the bottom of the intended change, scolded the king (*Bedford Corr.* iii. 280). Meanwhile Pitt refused the offer of the court, and the king sent Cumberland to Lord Lyttelton, who also refused to attempt to form an administration. During these negotiations the Spitalfields weavers were raising riots, on account of the rejection of a bill intended to benefit their industry. They marched to the king's lodge, and not finding him there followed him to Wimbledon, where he listened to their complaints, and persuaded them to return to their homes. But disorders broke out afresh, and were perhaps only checked by the vigorous action of the king, who personally gave orders that troops should be in readiness to prevent disturbance. He was anxious not to appear to avoid the rioters, and declared his willingness to 'put himself at the head of the army, or do anything else to save his country' (*Grenville Papers*, iii. 177). When Lyttelton refused the king's offer, Cumberland advised George to recall his ministers. He had a humiliating interview with Grenville on the 21st. The ministers compelled the king to promise that he would neither see Bute nor retain Bute's brother, Stuart Mackenzie, as privy seal in Scotland, though George had promised that he should keep the office (*ib.* p. 187). Although the king was in after days constantly suspected of acting by Bute's advice, it seems perfectly certain that he kept his word, and that he never willingly saw Bute again, or had any direct or indirect consultation with him after this. Grenville used his power mercilessly. 'When he has wearied me for two hours,' George once said, 'he looks at his watch to see if he may not tire me for one hour more.' The king allowed his dislike of his ministers to be seen, and on 12 June Bedford scolded him for not allowing his authority and his favour to go together, and accused him of listening to the misrepresentations of Bute. George heard him in silence, though he certainly was shamefully treated (*Bedford Corr.* iii. 288, 289). He again sent Cumberland to Pitt, who had two interviews with the king, and undertook to form an administration; but his arrangements were brought to an end on 25 June 1765 by Temple's refusal to accept the treasury. In his distress the king again turned to his uncle, who, with Newcastle's help, formed an administration under the Marquis of Rockingham, and on 10 July George at last got rid of Grenville. The humiliation of turning to the Rockingham whigs was a less evil than the retention of the old ministry. 'I would rather,' he said, 'see the devil in my closet than George Grenville' (*Rockingham Memoirs*, ii. 50).

George, though outwardly civil, thwarted his new ministers, and would not create peers on their recommendation. Indeed he probably from the first intended to get rid of them as soon as he could find others more subservient to himself. George saw with concern the abuses of the government in Ireland, and when Lord Hertford accepted the viceroyalty in October 1765, wrote him a paper of instructions, which was probably his own composition. It shows remarkable knowledge of the secret sources of mischief, and contains straightforward directions for destroying them by an honourable and decided policy (Froude, *English in Ireland*, ii. 39–43). Rockingham pressed to be allowed to treat with Pitt in January 1766. The king did not like the idea, probably because he did not wish to see the administration strengthened, and also because he did not want Pitt unless as, in a special sense, his own minister. He yielded, but Pitt was impracticable. George did not approve the repeal of the Stamp Act, though he was willing to modify it; but he asserted that he had all along preferred repeal to force, if one or the other was necessary. As Rockingham found that he was opposed by the king's friends, he obtained the king's sanction to the repeal in writing (*Rockingham Memoirs*, i. 301). George acted a double part, pretending to be pleased when his ministers were in a majority, but allowing the court party to see that his sympathies were really on the other side. Rockingham seems to have taxed him with this conduct (*ib*. pp. 299, 321; *Bedford Corr*. iii. 327). The repeal of the Stamp Act received the royal assent on 18 March. The retirement in May of the Duke of Grafton, one of the secretaries of state, was due to underhand negotiations carried on by Lord-chancellor Northington, who was one of the king's party. In July Northington openly quarrelled with his colleagues, and by his advice the king sent for Pitt. George received Pitt with pleasure, put all arrangements under his control, and dismissed his ministers ungraciously. Pitt was created Earl of Chatham, and formed an administration of which he was the real, and Grafton the ostensible, head. George thus won a decided success. He got rid of the administration of the great whig families, and was delighted at securing Pitt, who, he had good reason to believe, would 'destroy all party distinctions,' and 'root out the present method of parties banding together' (*Chatham Corr*. iii. 21, 127). Chiefly through the king's policy the whigs were now divided into hostile sections. He was personally gratified by the restoration of Stuart Mackenzie to his former office.

The new administration fell at once into a state of weakness and division. Against his own will the king allowed Chatham to treat with Bedford, and when the negotiation failed told his minister that 'due firmness would show the Bedfords of what little consequence they were' (*ib*. p. 137). The administration became more tory in character, and derived what little strength it had from the support of the king's friends. Chatham's illness reduced it to incapacity. The king was almost in despair, for he was afraid of being forced to receive Grenville. On 2 March 1767 he entreated Chatham to see his messenger if only for a quarter of an hour, in order that the 'world might know' that he was still advising him; on 30 May that Chatham would see Grafton, if only for five minutes; and on 2 June, when the administration seemed about to break up, that he would lay a plan before him (*ib*. pp. 137, 227, 267). He earnestly begged him to retain office. 'Your name,' he wrote, 'has been sufficient to enable my administration to proceed;' he hoped that his minister would recover, and help him 'in resisting the torrent of factions.' Chatham resigned on 14 Oct. 1768 (*ib*. pp. 318, 338–44). On 28 March, when Wilkes was elected for Middlesex, it was thought that the mob would attack the queen's house.

George declared that he wished that they 'would make the attempt, that he might disperse them at the head of his guards' (*Grenville Papers*, iv. 268). He took an active part in the arrangements for preserving order, urged the expulsion of Wilkes from the house, insisted that 'due firmness' should be used in resisting riots, approved the firing on the mob in St. George's Fields, and required the Westminster justices to show firmness in using the military. In 1769 he followed a similar course as regards Wilkes. On 22 March, after Wilkes had been declared incapable of sitting in the 'present parliament,' while the king was talking with his ministers in St. James's Palace, a mob beset the gates, and a hearse was driven into the courtyard decorated with insulting emblems, and having on the roof a man dressed as an executioner, masked, and with an axe in his hand. A sharp though short struggle took place before the rioters were dispersed. During the whole time the king remained perfectly unruffled, and talked as calmly as usual (*ib.* p. 416; Wraxall, *Memoirs*, i. 333). In July the lord mayor presented a petition to the king from the livery against the ministers, complaining specially of the employment of soldiers in repressing disturbances, and of the late affair in St. George's Fields; other petitions, one from ten thousand freeholders of Yorkshire, were also presented against the violation of the right of electors in the Wilkes case, and on 19 Dec. was published Junius's 'Address to the King,' which was made the subject of legal proceedings (*Ann. Register*, 1769, pp. 200–5; *Letters of Junius*, i. 225; May, *Const. Hist.* ii. 252). The speech with which George opened parliament on 9 Jan. 1770 began with a reference to a distemper then prevailing 'among horned cattle;' it was bitterly and unjustly ridiculed by Junius as containing 'nothing but the misery of a ruined grazier, and the whining piety of a methodist' (*Letters*, i. 272; Stanhope, *History*, v. 246). Chatham's return to parliament had been welcomed by the king the previous July, but the earl attacked the administration with such vigour that its fall became imminent. When it was necessary to dismiss Lord-chancellor Camden, George urged Charles Yorke to accept the great seal. Yorke refused, for he shrank from deserting his party, the 'Rockinghams.' On the next day, 17 Jan. 1770, the king at the levee called him into his closet, charged him on his loyalty to accept the office, and declared that if he did not do so it should never be offered to him again. Thus pressed Yorke yielded, and his acceptance caused his death on the 20th (*Life of Hardwicke*, iii. 465–79). Grafton resigned on the 28th, and the king gave the treasury to Lord North, at that time chancellor of the exchequer. Chatham renewed his attacks, and reflected on the king by inveighing against the 'invisible counsels of a favourite,' meaning that George allowed Bute to direct his policy, which was certainly not the case. Grafton defended the king, but Chatham renewed his accusation. On 14 March George received a petition from the lord mayor (Beckford) and the livery, declaring that the House of Commons did not represent the people, praying for a dissolution, and referring to a 'secret and malign influence which under each administration had defeated every good, and suggested every bad intention' (*Ann. Register*, 1770, p. 200). He made a short and not undignified reply, which seems to throw great doubt on the story that when the lord mayor was leaving the presence, he 'turned round to his courtiers and burst out a laughing' (Junius, i. 284). He was determined not to dissolve, for he knew that a new house would force him to part with his ministers, and perhaps to receive the whig families back into power. 'I will have recourse to this,' he said, laying his hand upon his sword, 'sooner than yield to a dissolution.' On 23 May he received another petition from the common council of much the same kind. After he had made a short answer the lord mayor addressed him in a magniloquent and impertinent speech, to which he returned no answer. The increase of the ministerial majority in parliament gratified him. Beckford's death (21 June 1770) brought the active hostility of the city to an end, and the distrust which existed between the followers of Chatham and of Rockingham strengthened the position of the administration. George had gained a signal success, for he had found in North a minister of considerable sagacity, courage, and parliamentary tact. His scheme of government was fully realised; parties were broken up; the 'power of the crown, almost dead and rotten as prerogative, [had] grown up anew, with more strength and far less odium under the name of influence' (Burke). George had succeeded in setting up a system of personal rule through a minister who commanded a large majority in parliament, and consented to shape his policy in accordance with commands given him in the closet. During the next twelve years he carried out his own system of government, and the affairs of the country were directed by an irresponsible king acting through responsible ministers.

George continued to indulge his love for a retired and simple life. He still lived much at Kew, and while there enjoyed domestic pleasures and homely pursuits (for a courtly account of his life at Kew during the summer see *Annual Register*, 1775, ii. 1); he took much interest in farming, a taste which increased as time went on, and in later days wrote some letters to Young on agriculture (Young, *Annals of Agriculture*, vii. 65, 332); was said to have farmed for profit, and to have looked sharply after it, and was made fun of in satires and caricatures as 'Farmer George.' He liked trifling mechanical occupations, and was at this time constantly ridiculed as the 'royal button-maker' (Wright). While not illiberal in his charities, he and his queen were extremely economical. His health was at this time good; he was afraid of becoming fat, and was therefore very abstemious and took much exercise without regard to weather, sometimes riding from Windsor to London in the rain, and after he had dressed holding a levee, and, when that was over, giving audience to his ministers and setting off for Windsor in his carriage about 6 p.m., without having taken anything but a little tea and bread and butter, which he would often eat as he walked up and down (Wraxall, *Memoirs*, i. 282). He never missed a drawing-room or a levee. The graciousness of his manners to men whom he respected is recorded by Dr. Johnson, whose well-known interview with him took place in February 1767. Johnson afterwards said: 'They may talk of the king as they will, but he is the finest gentleman I have ever seen' (Boswell, *Life*, ii. 37–43, ed. 1807). He worked hard, and was inspired by a genuine desire to do good to his people, and a belief that what he thought right necessarily was so. His letters to North, for whom at this time he felt a strong affection, show the deep interest which he took in the progress of affairs. The distribution of the crown patronage was now entirely in his hands, and he gave orders about every appointment, whether it was to the place of housekeeper at one of his palaces, or to a colonelcy of the guards, or to an episcopal see. Patronage was one of the chief means by which he maintained and managed his party in parliament. Another of these means was the manifestation of his feelings by word or manner when people who had either satisfied or displeased him presented themselves at court; and a third was the disposal of the civil list revenues. The income settled on the crown, swelled as it was by the profits of the duchies of Cornwall and Lancaster and revenues from Scotland, Ireland, and other sources, was sufficient for all ordinary needs, and far more than sufficient for a king who lived so simply, yet in 1769 the ministers were forced to ask parliament for 513,511*l.* for payment of debts; inquiry was demanded, but in the end the money was granted without investigation. Much waste went on, as was abundantly proved in 1777, but large sums were no doubt spent in corruption of various kinds (May, *Const. Hist.* i. 237, 341). George was now thoroughly acquainted with political business. He identified himself with North's administration, and wrote his minister constant letters, sometimes two or three in a day, with his own hand. These letters he used to date according to the minute of writing, a custom which illustrates the importance which he attached to trifles, and possibly also his feeling that everything connected with himself was of special moment. He was at all times ready to listen to suggestions from men who were not his constitutional advisers, and from 1770 to 1782 Charles Jenkinson, afterwards Lord Hawkesbury and Earl of Liverpool, is said to have exercised an influence which was 'sometimes paramount to, or subversive of, the measures proposed by his first minister' (Wraxall, *Memoirs*, i. 416). When the new parliament met in 1771, the result of the elections and the disorganisation of the whigs secured the success of the king's policy.

George saw with some alarm the rise of the quarrel between the House of Commons and the printers, and, while writing of the printers as 'miscreants,' hoped that matters would not be allowed to grow serious. On 17 March, however, he considered it necessary for the commons to commit the Lord-mayor Crosby and Alderman Oliver, but was glad that the ministers were content to leave alone so dangerous an antagonist as Wilkes (*Letters to North*, i. 64, 67). He also took an active interest in the opposition to Savile's 'Nullum Tempus' Bill, which was designed to protect the subject against the dormant claims of the crown, such as that revived to the prejudice of the popular whig magnate the Duke of Portland. Family troubles crowded on the king. In November 1770 he was forced to find, not without difficulty, 13,000l. to pay damages and expenses incurred by his brother, the Duke of Cumberland, in a divorce case, and early in 1772 was much troubled at the news of the disgrace of his sister, the queen of Denmark. On 8 Feb. he lost his mother; she had probably long ceased to influence his political conduct, but this was not generally believed, and the mob followed her body to the grave with insults (Walpole, *Last Journals*, i. 17). Shortly before this event he heard with indignation of the marriage of the Duke of Cumberland to Mrs. Horton, and soon afterwards of the marriage of his favourite brother, William Henry, duke of Gloucester, to the widow of Earl Waldegrave. The two dukes were forbidden the court, and it was announced that the king would not receive those who called on them. It was some years before he forgave the Duke and Duchess of Gloucester. These marriages and the scandals connected with them called forth a message from the king to parliament recommending the Royal Marriage Bill, which prohibited descendants of George II, except the issue of foreign princesses, from marrying before the age of twenty-five without the king's consent. After that age they might marry provided that no objection was raised by parliament to the proposed match, of which a year's notice had to be given to the privy council. All marriages contracted contrary to the act were to be null, and the parties to incur the penalties of præmunire. This bill was the king's own work, and he made it a personal matter. 'I expect every nerve to be strained,' he wrote, 'to carry the bill with becoming firmness, for it is not a question that immediately relates to administration, but personally to myself,' adding that he should 'remember defaulters.' Nevertheless the bill was violently opposed. Chatham pronounced it 'new-fangled and impudent,' and the king heard with anxiety that there was a strong feeling against it in the commons. He asked North for a list of 'those that went away and those that deserted to the minority; that,' he added, 'would be a rule for my conduct in the drawing-room to-morrow' (*Letters to North*, i. 97; *Chatham Corr.* iv. 199, 203; Lecky, *Hist.* iii. 463; Stanhope, *Hist.* v. 311). The bill was carried by considerable majorities. He expressed strong dislike to the motion for abolishing compulsory subscription to the articles of religion by clergymen, physicians, and others, observing that 'presbyterians often resembled Socinians rather than Christians.' Affairs in the north of Europe directly and indirectly conduced to set Great Britain in opposition to France. During the war between Russia and the Porte a French fleet would have entered the Baltic had not England interfered. George was anxious to prevent a war, and recommended his ministers to 'speak out' as to their determination not to allow France to take part against Russia. The policy he recommended was successful; France was forced to leave the Turk to his fate, and Russia obtained substantial gains by the treaty of Kainardji. He was hostile to Lord Clive, who was supported generally by the opposition, and on 22 May 1773 expressed his amazement 'that private interest could make so many individuals . . . approve of Lord Clive's rapine' (*Letters to North*, p. 135).

On 16 Dec. 1773 the irritation of the American colonists at the retention of the tea duty broke out in a riot at Boston. George shared the opinion of most of his people that the colonists might safely be despised, and that if firmness was used they would soon submit. Accordingly in 1774 he felt much satisfaction at the Boston Port Bill, and the bill for regulating the government of Massachusetts Bay. He had no wish to see fresh taxes laid on the colonists, but considered it necessary to maintain the duty in order to keep up the right of taxation. The meeting of congress in September convinced him that the colonists must 'either triumph or submit,' and he declared in November that blows must decide whether they were to be his subjects or independent (*ib.* pp. 202, 215). Meanwhile in the spring he was annoyed at the awkward predicament in which North was placed in the debate on the matter of the printer Woodfall, and insisted on the dismissal of Fox for his conduct in the affair. Although he was mortified at the return of Wilkes for Middlesex, the general result of the elections to the new parliament delighted him. In spite of the eloquence of the opposition, the ministers had a majority of 190 to 200 in the commons in favour of their American policy. War actually broke out on 19 April 1775, and in August the king as elector of Hanover arranged for the employment of Hanoverian troops to garrison Gibraltar and Minorca. He received no subsidy for lending these troops, but asked to be reimbursed for expenses and levy-money. He also busied himself about the hire of other German forces and recruiting matters at home. A proposal for the hire of Russian troops made in a letter written with his own hand called forth a rebuff from the empress Catherine which greatly annoyed him. (For the part taken by George in the negotiations for the hire of foreign troops see a chapter by E. J. Lowell in 'History of America,' ed. Winsor, vii. 16–23, 74–7.) He was indignant at the attacks which Chatham made in the course of the session on the policy of the ministers with respect to the colonists. Chatham was, he said, the 'trumpet of sedition;' his political conduct was 'abandoned.' For himself, he was 'fighting the battle of the legislature' (*Letters to North*, p. 267); and not only the legislature but the nation at large upheld his determination. At the same time he was not so embittered against the colonists as to refuse proposals of accommodation, for his influence was certainly exercised in February 1775 on behalf of North's Conciliation Bill. He did not believe that the war would be of long duration, and rejected Howe's advice that it should be carried on by sea only. As the war continued, his feelings became more bitter, and though the opposition in parliament and outside it gathered strength, the nation widely shared in them. The city of London disapproved of the ministerial policy; the royal proclamation for the suppression of rebellion was received with hisses on the Exchange, and the city tried to provoke a quarrel with the king by refusing to present an address, except to him on the throne. 'I am ever ready,' the king said, 'to receive addresses and petitions, but I am the judge where.' He was pleased at the capture of New York in September 1776, and believed it to have been 'well planned and executed with alacrity,' which was perhaps rather too high praise (*ib.* ii. 39). He was now thoroughly embittered against the rebels; he warmly approved of the bill passed in February 1777 for securing and detaining persons suspected of high treason in America, and of the employment of Indians in the war; 'every means of distressing America must,' he wrote, 'meet with my concurrence,' and he hoped that 'Howe would turn his thoughts to the mode of war best calculated to end the contest' (*ib.* i. 274, ii. 84). At no time probably in the course of the war was the country at large more fully in sympathy with his policy than during this year. The news of Burgoyne's surrender on 17 Oct. deeply affected him; the disaster was, he wrote on 4 Dec., 'very serious, but not without remedy;' the cause could not be given up.

On 9 April of this year (1777) the king through North made the commons acquainted with his debts, which on 5 Jan. preceding amounted to 600,000*l*. Although part of this deficit was no doubt due to relief given to the loyalist refugees, by far the larger part arose from corrupt practices, and from the waste which prevailed in every department of the household; highly paid sinecure offices abounded, the king's turnspit was a member of the house, there had been scandalous mismanagement, and while the 'lustre of the crown was tarnished' by the king's economical and almost sordid mode of life, the wages of his menial servants were six quarters in arrear, and his tradesmen were almost ruined. The accounts laid before the house were unsatisfactory, and there were neither vouchers nor audit-books. Enormous sums had been spent in pensions and in various other ways which extended and maintained the influence of the crown. The excess in pensions and annuities during the last eight years, as compared with the last eight years of the reign of George II, amounted to 194,144*l*., while, although the last years of the last reign included the great period of the seven years' war, the excess in secret service money during the same number of years just past was 63,559*l*. Indeed it is not unlikely that something like a million had already been spent during the reign on purposes which could not conveniently be avowed. All these matters were freely discussed in parliament (*Parl. Hist.* xix. 103, 160, 187; *Annual Register*, 1777, pp. 71–88; Massey, *Hist.* ii. 230–2). Nevertheless the house granted 618,340*l*. for discharge of arrears, and an addition of 100,000*l*. to the annual 800,000*l*. of the civil list. When at the close of the session the speaker, Sir Fletcher Norton, brought up the bill, he dilated on the magnificence of the gift, 'great beyond example, great beyond your majesty's highest expense.' The court party were grievously offended, and an attempt was made to censure the speaker, but Fox brought forward a resolution approving his conduct, which was carried nem. con.

As the king was going to the Haymarket Theatre on 25 July 1777, a mad woman attacked and did some damage to his chair. In September he pressed North to accept from him the payment of his debts, offering, if needful, as much as 20,000*l*., and expressing his love for him as a man and his esteem for him as minister, adding, 'I shall never forget your conduct at a critical minute'—on the retirement of Grafton (*Letters to North*, ii. 83). North had begun to disapprove of the colonial policy forced upon him by the king. War with France, declared in May 1778, was imminent. He felt that he could not conciliate the colonies and that conciliation was necessary, and on 31 Jan. he begged the king to accept his resignation and send for Chatham. He repeated his request in March. Men of every rank and political section looked on Chatham as the only hope of the country, and this was made known to George from various sides. He was immovable—not, as it would seem, so much from motives of public policy as from private feelings. He appealed to North's personal affection and sense of honour not to desert him. With Chatham he would hold no direct communication; but if he liked to serve under North 'he would receive him with open arms.' North might address him on this basis, with the distinct understanding that Chatham was not to bring in any member of the opposition. The administration must remain with North at its head, and include Thurlow, Sandwich, Gower, and others of its present members. He 'would rather lose his crown' than submit to the opposition, who, he declared, would 'make me a slave for the remainder of my days.' His conduct was chiefly governed by this and similar personal considerations; for he did not refuse to allow North to bring in conciliatory measures, and Chatham was as fully convinced as he was of the necessity of preventing American independence. North's negotiations were fruitless. That the king's conduct was culpable admits of no question (*ib.* ii. 149–56; *Memorials of Fox*, i. 180–7; Lecky, *Hist.* iv. 82). George declared on 18 March 1778 that he was 'fairly worn down,' but would not change his administration or receive 'that perfidious man.' Chatham's fatal illness made him hope that North would be more inclined to retain office. He was 'rather surprised' at the vote about the earl's funeral and monument; if it expressed admiration of his general conduct, 'it is,' he said, 'an offensive measure to me personally.' North renewed his entreaties to be allowed to resign, but was overpersuaded, and continued to carry out the king's policy. George showed his gratitude by giving him the lucrative post of warden of the Cinque ports. During the spring he made visits of inspection to Chatham and Portsmouth; on 28 Sept. he made a tour for the purpose of holding reviews at Winchester, Salisbury, and Warley in Essex, and on 22 Nov. reviewed the troops encamped on Coxheath, near Maidstone (*Annual Register*, 1778, p. 232 sq.). During 1779 he gave several proofs of his determination to uphold the administration. Referring to the debates on the manifesto of the king of Spain, who declared war in June, he wrote that he must know how members voted, and spoke of what might happen 'if the prerogative is not soon brought into effect' (Letter to Weymouth, 17 June, Jesse, ii. 243). A protest of the opposition lords against the conduct of the war seemed to him 'very wicked' (*Letters to North*, ii. 259). He was strongly opposed to Keppel, whose cause was maintained by the opposition. The feeling of the nation seems to have begun to change about this time, and the opposition, though numerically weak in parliament, grew more popular. North urged his former entreaties again and again without success, until in November 1779 George allowed him to negotiate with Camden and Shelburne for a coalition under a new first minister. In February 1780 the king, who was watching the debates on Burke's economic reform bills with painful intensity, was annoyed at the smallness of the ministerial majority on the proposal to regulate the pension list, and, as usual, recommended 'firmness' to North (*ib.* p. 305). Dunning carried his famous resolution concerning the influence of the crown in April 1780; George attributed the rising discontent of the commons to 'factious leaders and ruined men, who wish to overturn the constitution' (*ib.* p. 314). He allowed North to make some overtures to the Rockingham party in June, but objected to receive Fox or the Duke of Richmond on account of some personal displeasure. The overtures were abortive. It seems that the king felt keenly the humiliation which was gradually coming upon him; for it is said that he seriously contemplated retiring to Hanover, and that liveries were ordered and other preparations made for his departure (*Memorials of Fox*, i. 287 *n.*).

George, however, had other causes for uneasiness. On 6 June 1780 the 'no popery' riots reached a serious height, in consequence of the feebleness of the attempts to check them at an earlier stage. All responsible authority seemed paralysed, and the king himself came forward to supply its place. He wrote to North blaming the supineness of the magistrates, and called a special privy council for the next day. At the council it was alleged that the reading of the riot act and other formalities were necessary before the military could be called upon to act. George declared that if there was further hesitation he would lead the guards in person to disperse the rioters. It was 'black Wednesday,' and London was almost at the mercy of an infuriate mob. 'I lament,' George said, 'the conduct of the magistrates; but I can answer for one who will do his duty.' Attorney-general Wedderburn upheld, and had indeed suggested, the king's opinion that soldiers might in cases of necessity act against rioters without the civil power. The council at last agreed, and George promptly sent to the ad-jutant-general bidding him issue a proclamation that officers were at once to order their men to act (Twiss, *Life of Eldon*, i. 293; *Annual Register*, 1780, p. 266). His intrepidity, firmness, and good sense saved London from further havoc. On the 19th his action was declared by Lord Mansfield to have been in strict conformity with the common law. The feeling of the country was now against the administration. This change, though partly due to the failure of the war, must mainly be attributed to the exposure which the opposition made of the enormous and corrupt expenditure of the crown. The majority in the commons which had so long supported the royal policy was broken up, and the fruitless attempt at negotiation with the Rockinghams was followed by an unexpected dissolution. George used every means to influence the result of the general election. He was startled when the bill came in. It amounted to about 50,000*l.*, besides some pensions. 'The sum,' he wrote, 'is at least double of what was expended on any other general election since I came to the throne' (*Letters to North*, ii. 423). He was anxious to get Keppel unseated at Windsor, and to secure the election of the court candidate, and is said to have canvassed in person against the admiral, going into the shop of a silk mercer, one of Keppel's supporters, and saying in his usual hurried way, 'The queen wants a gown, wants a gown. No Keppel; no Keppel' (*Rockingham Memoirs*, ii. 425). The elections improved the prospects of the administration. They were ruined by the capitulation of Cornwallis on 19 Oct. 1781. George bore the blow with fortitude, though the fact that his reply to Lord George Germain's announcement of the news was not, as usual, dated according to the hour and minute of writing shows that he was much moved. In his speech in opening parliament on 25 Nov. 1781 he spoke of the necessity of 'most active exertions.' During the early part of 1782 he was much distressed by the constant decrease of the majority. The separation of the colonies would, he was convinced, 'annihilate (sic) the European position of the kingdom.' On 11 March he commissioned Lord-chancellor Thurlow to treat with Rockingham for an administration 'on a broad bottom;' but though he was willing to concede the demands for peace and economy, the negotiation failed on the 18th, because he would not pledge himself to accept Rockingham's selection of ministers. He wished to put Rockingham at the head of an administration partly formed by himself (*ib.* pp. 451–9). On the 20th North persuaded him to acknowledge that his administration could not stand any longer, and Thurlow renewed the negotiation with Rockingham. But the king would not consent to a reform of the household, and sent for Shelburne on the 21st, after North's resignation had been announced. Shelburne was bound to Rockingham, and on the 22nd George sent for Lord Gower, who refused his offer. He was then advised by Shelburne to accept Rockingham, and was forced to again bow his head to the yoke (Lecky). Nevertheless, he refused to see Rockingham personally until after the administration was formed, and by employing Shelburne as an intermediary sowed the seeds of discord among his new ministers. He delivered the seals to Rockingham on 27 March 1782. When North's resignation was imminent, and during the crisis which followed, he again entertained the idea of retiring to Hanover. His humiliation was notorious, and the triumph of the whigs was caricatured in the 'Captive Prince.'

The new administration included the Chatham section of the whigs under Shelburne as well as the Rockinghams, and the king, with the help of Thurlow, whom Rockingham had consented to retain as chancellor, set himself to weaken it by division. While he withheld his confidence from Rockingham, he gave it freely to Shelburne, and by bringing Dunning into the cabinet, without consulting his first minister, secured the Shelburne party an equal number of votes with the followers of Rockingham. George was annoyed at being forced by Rockingham to recommend the reform of the civil establishment, and would not speak to him on the subject, though he wrote his objections to Shelburne, telling him not to show his letter to any one except Thurlow (*Life of Shelburne*, iii. 157–9). Burke's efforts to reduce the expenditure of the crown were followed by some petty and apparently unworthy measures of economy in the king's household arrangements (Papendiek, i. 161–3). Rockingham died on 1 July 1782, and his death was followed by a disruption of the whigs, brought about, in part at least, by the king's management. This disruption made so great a change in the balance of power that Fox said that on Rockingham's death 'the crown devolved on the king.' Fox recommended the king to send for the Duke of Portland, and on finding that Shelburne was appointed to the treasury, gave up office with other members of the Rockingham party. On 5 Dec. the king, in his speech on opening parliament, announced that he had offered to declare the American colonies free and independent. 'Did I,' he afterwards asked, 'lower my voice when I came to that part of my speech?' (Walpole, *Journals*, ii. 577). George seems, like most other people, to have disliked Shelburne, and the minister thought that the king plotted against him. This was probably untrue, but George had by this time given people occasion to suspect him; 'by familiarity of intercourse he obtained your confidence and availed himself of his knowledge to sow dissension' (Nicholls, i. 342). He was certainly wholly on Shelburne's side when on 18 Feb. 1783 the combined parties led by Fox and North were in a majority in the commons (*Court and Cabinets*, i. 156). Shelburne's resignation on the 24th caused him much annoyance (*ib*. p. 303), for he could not endure the idea of falling into the hands of the coalition. The next day he pressed Pitt to take Shelburne's place, but he refused on the 27th. He made proposals in vain to Gower, and then tried to persuade North to leave the coalition, offering him the treasury if he would desert Fox, whom he regarded with vehement personal hatred. His distress of mind was great, and he again thought of retiring to Hanover. At length he yielded to Fox's demand, and sent for the Duke of Portland, but finding that Fox insisted on the dismissal of Thurlow, and that Portland treated him cavalierly, and refused to show him the list of proposed appointments to inferior offices, he broke off the negotiation (*ib*. p. 206). William Grenville, who was at this time admitted to his confidence, was impressed by his mental agitation; he spoke with 'inconceivable quickness.' On 23 March 1783 he again applied to Pitt. He was indignant at North's desertion; 'after the manner I have been personally treated by both the Duke of Portland and Lord North,' he wrote on the 24th, 'it is impossible that I can ever admit either of them into my service' (*Life of Pitt*, i. App. ii.). But Pitt again refused, and on 2 April the long interministerium ended in George's acceptance of the coalition administration. During this period George constantly resided at Kew from May to November, though he was sometimes at Windsor. He lived in great retirement, going into London on Wednesdays and Fridays to hold levees and talk with his ministers. His chief amusements were hunting and walking; and he occasionally had artists to play or recite before him. His life was quiet and respectable, and his court intensely dull (for particulars see authorities stated below).

The king hated his new ministers, and told Temple that he meant to take the first opportunity of getting rid of them, expressing his 'personal abhorrence' of North, who had, he considered, betrayed him (*Court and*

Cabinets, i. 303). He thwarted them as much as he could, and used to wish that he 'was eighty, or ninety, or dead.' The proposal of the ministers to grant the Prince of Wales 100,000l. a year greatly angered him, and he would probably have openly quarrelled with them had not Temple advised him not to do so on a private matter. The ill conduct of the prince caused him much uneasiness. Bad as the prince was, his father was not blameless in his treatment of him. George's temper was sullen and unforgiving, and it is probable that his eldest son was not lying when he said that he knew that his father hated him (Malmesbury, ii. 129). Fox's India bill gave the king the opportunity he wanted. Thurlow roused his jealousy by presenting him on 1 Dec. with a paper pointing out the effect which the bill would have on the royal authority (*Court and Cabinets*, i. 288). On 11 Dec., after the bill had passed the commons, he gave Temple a paper stating that 'whoever voted for the bill was not only not his friend, but would be considered by him as his enemy' (*ib.* p. 285). The bill was thrown out by the lords on 17 Dec.; on the same day the king's action was commented on in the commons, and a resolution was passed declaring that to 'report any opinion or pretended opinion of his majesty upon any bill' depending in parliament to influence votes was a 'high crime and misdemeanor.' The next day the king dismissed the ministers, and at once sent for Pitt. He took the deepest interest in Pitt's struggle against the hostile majority in the commons, and steadily refused to dismiss his new ministers, or to dissolve parliament before the opposition had lost its majority in the house and its popularity in the country. He prorogued parliament in person on 24 March 1784, with a view to its dissolution the next day.

In one sense Pitt's success, which was completed by the result of the general election, was a victory for the king. George got rid of the ministers whom he hated, he gained a minister who as long as he lived proved himself able to preserve him from again falling into the hands of the whigs, and he found himself more popular than he had been since his accession. But he had, on the other hand, to give up the system of personal government for which he had hitherto struggled. The result of the crisis was a diminution of the direct influence of the crown, and an immense increase in the power of the first minister. For many years George could not have afforded to quarrel with Pitt, for he was his one hope of salvation from Fox whom he hated (Lecky). The 'king's friends' consequently disappeared as a party, most of them becoming supporters of the minister whom he wished to keep in office. George never expressed the same personal affection for Pitt that he had for North, and he did not always like his measures. He disapproved of the Westminster scrutiny and of Pitt's plan for parliamentary reform (*Life of Pitt*, i. App. xv.), but refrained from opposing it, and appears to have disliked the proceedings against Warren Hastings, from whom he allowed the queen to accept an ivory bed (*ib.* p. 296); the court took its tone on this question from him and the queen, but he did not interfere in the matter. Although on 7 Aug. 1783 he had virtually refused to receive a minister from the United States (*Memorials of Fox*, ii. 140), he consented to receive John Adams on 1 June 1785. He behaved with dignity during the interview, though he showed that he was affected by it, and assured the minister that as he 'had been the last to consent to the separation,' so he 'would be the first to meet the friendship of the United States as an independent power' (Adams to Jay, Adams, *Works*, viii. 257, ed. 1853). On 2 Aug. 1786 an attempt was made to stab him at the gate of St. James's by a mad woman named Margaret Nicholson; he behaved with perfect composure (*Annual Register*, 1786, p. 233; Papendiek, i. 260).

In the spring of 1788 the king suffered much from bilious attacks, supposed to have been brought on by the worry and fatigue of business, combined with exhaustion produced by the violent exercise which he was in the habit of taking to prevent corpulence (*ib.* pp. 297, 298, 303). On 12 June he went to Cheltenham to drink the waters, and while there resided at Lord Fauconberg's house, Bays Hill Lodge (D'Arblay, *Diary*, iv. 214). He returned to Windsor on 16 Aug., and on 16 Oct. got wet while walking. The next day he was taken ill, and on the 22nd signs of derangement appeared. However, he got better, and on the 24th held a levee, in order, he said, 'to stop further lies and any fall of the stocks' (*Life of Pitt*, i. 385). His mind dwelt on the loss of the American colonies (Malmesbury, iv. 20). While at Windsor on 5 Nov. he became delirious, and for a while it was thought that his life was in imminent danger. He suffered from intense cerebral irritation, which showed itself in sleeplessness and increasing garrulity. On the 29th he was removed by his physicians to Kew, the removal being effected by deception (D'Arblay, *Diary*, iv. 341). On 5 Dec. his physicians stated to the privy council that his disease was not incurable, but that it was impossible to say how long it might last. He was then put under the charge of Dr. Willis. It is said that before this date he was treated with brutality (Massey, *Hist.* iii. 199, 207). The stories are probably greatly exaggerated, for they all seem to refer to a period of only five days, during which he was at Kew before Dr. Willis came there. (Mrs. Papendiek's account of the king's illness in 'Court and Private Life,' ii. 7–31, goes far to disprove, with one exception, p. 20, the stories of harsh usage; her narrative differs in some respects from that given by Madame d'Arblay.) He was, however, subjected to unnecessary restraints which tended to increase his mental irritation. Willis, who declared that his recovery at an early date was certain, changed this system, and soon gained complete control over him (*Court and Cabinets*, ii. 35). During his illness violent debates took place on the regency question. On 19 Feb. 1789 the chancellor announced that he was convalescent, and on 10 March he resumed his authority. His recovery was hailed with delight, and London was illuminated. He attended a public thanksgiving at St. Paul's on 23 April (*Annual Register*, 1789, p. 249; Papendiek, ii. 83–90), but was still suffering from dejection and lassitude on 5 May. The undutiful conduct of the Prince of Wales and Frederick Augustus, duke of York, caused much unhappiness in the royal family. On 25 June George, by his physicians' advice, left Windsor for Weymouth, where he resided at Gloucester Lodge. He was greeted with acclamations everywhere. In after years he constantly spent either the whole or some weeks of the summer at Weymouth. His life there was very simple. He bathed, yachted, rode, and made excursions, going this year to Lord Morley's at Saltram, 15–27 Aug., and visiting the ships at Plymouth. On 18 Sept. he returned to Windsor in complete health. On 21 Jan. 1790 an insane man threw a stone at him as he was going in state to open parliament (*Annual Register*, 1790, pp. 194, 205). During the summer, when there was some unusually hot weather (*ib.* p. 209), the state of the king's health caused some anxiety to his physicians, who endeavoured to keep him from dozing during the day and brooding over French affairs, and told the queen that she must devote herself entirely to him (Papendiek, ii. 214–16). A signal proof of his determination to uphold Pitt was given in 1792, when he reluctantly agreed to dismiss Thurlow from the chancellorship, because Pitt found it impossible to work with him (*Life of Pitt*, ii. 149, 150).

The proceedings of the 'Friends of the People' and other revolutionary societies strengthened the king's feelings against Fox and the parliamentary section which sympathised with the French revolution (*ib.* App. xiv.). The general feeling of the country was with him, and was signified and excited by caricatures, one of which, by Gillray, published in July 1791, and entitled 'The Hopes of the Party,' represented the king as brought to the block by Fox and Sheridan, with Priestley assisting at his execution. He was gratified by the declaration of war against France in 1793 (*ib.* xvii.; Nicholls, i. 136, 400), and received with 'infinite pleasure' the reports of the defeats of motions for peace. On 30 Jan. 1794 he held a review of Lord Howe's fleet at Spithead. He struggled hard to keep his son the Duke of York in command in the Low Countries, but Pitt insisted so strongly on the evils attending a division of command that, though 'very much hurt,' he at last agreed to his recall (*Life of Pitt*, iii. App. xxi.). Lord Fitzwilliam's Irish policy highly displeased him; it was overturning the 'fabric that the wisdom of our forefathers esteemed necessary;' the admission of Roman catholics to vote and office would be 'to adopt measures to prevent which my family was invited to mount the throne in preference to the House of Savoy,' and the proposal must have been instigated by a 'desire to humiliate the old friends of the English government,' or to pay 'implicit obedience to the heated imagination of Mr. Burge' (*ib.* xxx.). He thought that Fitzwilliam should be recalled. He consulted Lord Kenyon and Sir John Scott as to whether it would be consistent with his coronation oath to assent to an Irish Roman catholic relief bill; they answered that his oath did not prevent his doing so, but Lord Loughborough, whom he also consulted, was on the other side, and gave his reasons in writing (Campbell, *Lives of the Chancellors*, vi. 296–8). The year (1794) was one of scarcity and of much discontent among the lower classes, and as the king proceeded to open parliament on 29 Oct. his carriage was surrounded by a mob shouting 'Bread!' 'Peace!' and 'Down with George!' A missile was shot through the window of his coach, and as he returned stones were thrown; he behaved with great coolness, and the next evening was much cheered on appearing in Covent Garden Theatre (*Annual Register*, 1795, ii. 39). This attack led to the enactment of the Treasonable Attempts Bill. On 1 Feb. 1796 a stone was thrown at his carriage and hit the queen, as they were returning from Drury Lane Theatre. He was strongly opposed to negotiations with France in 1797, and wrote his opinion to Pitt on 9 April; Pitt answered in a decided tone. The next day George sorrowfully acquiesced, and negotiations were opened at Lille (*Life of Pitt*, iii. 52, App. ii–vi.). On 19 Dec. he went in state to St. Paul's to give thanks for the victories of Cape St. Vincent and Camperdown. As he was entering his box in Drury Lane Theatre on 15 May 1800, he was shot at by a madman named James Hadfield. He showed great unconcern, and slept as quietly as usual during the interval between the play and the afterpiece (Kelly, *Reminiscences*, ii. 156; Wraxall, *Memoirs*, ii. 29).

The homeliness of the king's manners, his lack of dignity in private life, and the minute economy of his domestic arrangements became more conspicuous as he grew older. They were ridiculed in caricatures chiefly by Gillray, and in verse by Dr. Wolcot (Peter Pindar) and others. In 1791 the king is represented in a print as toasting muffins, and in 1792 as applauding the happy thought of the queen, who is instructing her daughters to drink tea without sugar to save 'poor papa' expense. He is said while at Weymouth to have had household necessaries sent from Windsor to avoid the high prices of the watering-place, and Peter Pindar describes 'Great Cæsar' as handling the soap and candles which came by the mail. In a caricature of 1795 Gillray ridicules his 'affability,' or love of gossiping and asking questions, in a print representing him as chattering to a cottager who is carrying food to his pigs. The most famous story of George's eccentric and undignified habits is preserved by Peter Pindar in verse, and by Gillray in a caricature of November 1797, and records how he stopped while hunting at an old woman's cottage and learnt from her how the apple got inside the dumpling (see Gillray, *Caricatures*; Wolcot, *Works of Peter Pindar*, i. 337; Wright, *Caricature History*, pp. 458–65). He was, however, decidedly popular, especially with the middle class; the court was not fashionable, and a certain number of the working class were discontented, though the nation was as a whole strongly loyal. The king's virtues and failings alike were such as won the sympathy of average Englishmen of the middle class, and the affliction from which he had lately suffered greatly increased his subjects' affection for him.

George was fully persuaded of the necessity for a legislative union with Ireland, and took much interest in the progress of the scheme. At the same time he did not forget the proposals for Roman catholic relief which had caused him uneasiness in 1795, and saw that it was possible that the Irish union might cause their renewal in one shape or other. 'I only hope,' he said to Dundas in the autumn of 1799, 'that the government is not pledged to anything in favour of the Roman catholics,' and on Dundas replying that it would be a matter for future consideration, and pointing out that the coronation oath only applied to the sovereign in his 'executive capacity, and not as part of the legislature,' he angrily broke in with 'None of your Scotch metaphysics, Mr. Dundas—none of your Scotch metaphysics' (Mackintosh, *Life of Sir James Mackintosh*, i. 170). While he was at Weymouth on 27 Sept. 1800, the chancellor, Loughborough, who happened to be staying with him, showed him a private letter which he had received from Pitt summoning him to a cabinet council on the subject of catholic emancipation, and thus betrayed to him the minister's design before Pitt had thought fit to say anything to him about it. The news caused him great anxiety (Campbell, *Lives of the Chancellors*, vi. 306, 322). He further received letters from Dr. Moore, archbishop of Canterbury, and Dr. Stuart, archbishop of Armagh, condemning the design. On 13 Dec. he also received a paper from Loughborough, stating the objections to emancipation (*Life of Sidmouth*, i. 500–12). Meanwhile no communication took place between the king and his ministers on the subject. At the levee on 28 Jan. 1801, one of the days on which the speaker was swearing-in the members of the new parliament, George asked Dundas what the ministers were 'going to throw at his head,' and declared that it was the 'most Jacobinical thing he ever heard of,' adding, 'I shall reckon any man my personal enemy who proposes any such measure' (Wilberforce, *Life of Wilberforce*, iii. 7). The next day he wrote to the speaker, Addington, desiring him to 'open Mr. Pitt's eyes' as to the danger of the proposal, though he speaks of Pitt's approval of it as not absolutely certain (*Life of Sidmouth*, i. 285). On 1 Feb. 1801 he received a letter from Pitt, written the night before, which contained the first intimation from his minister as to the course he intended to adopt. In this letter Pitt stated that he should be forced to resign unless the measure could be brought forward with the king's 'full concurrence, and with the whole weight of government.' In reply George offered that if Pitt would abstain from bringing forward the measure, he, for his part, would be silent on the subject, adding, 'further I cannot go, for I cannot sacrifice my duty to any consideration.' On 5 Feb. 1801 the king sorrowfully accepted his minister's resignation (*Life of Pitt*, iii. App. xxiii–xxxii.). During the progress of the correspondence he received a letter from Loughborough written with the object of ingratiating himself. George showed Pitt, in a letter written on 18 Feb., that his esteem for him was unabated. He sent for Addington, who succeeded in forming an administration, but before the new ministers received their seals the worry and excitement of the crisis caused the king another attack of insanity. For some days he dwelt with much agitation on the sacredness of his coronation oath (*Life of Sidmouth*, i. 286; Malmesbury, iv. 22). On the 15th he took a severe cold; on the 22nd his mental alienation was unmistakable, and on the 23rd he was unconscious until evening, when he said, 'I am better now, but I will remain true to the church' (*Life of Pitt*, iii. 294). On 2 March his disease reached a crisis (Rose, *Diaries*, i. 325), and from that day he continued to get better. He ordered his physician Willis to write to Pitt on the 6th. 'Tell him,' he said, 'I am now quite well—quite recovered from my illness, but what has he not to answer for who is the cause of my having been ill at all?' Pitt sent the king an assurance 'that during his reign he would never agitate the catholic question,' on which George said, 'Now my mind will be at ease' (*ib.* p. 360; *Life of Pitt*, iii. 304). On 14 March he received Pitt's resignation with many expressions of kindness, and handed the seals to Addington, whom he styled the next day 'his own chancellor of the exchequer.' He also gave the great seal to Eldon, from, as he said, 'my heart' (*Life of Sidmouth*, i. 353; *Life of Eldon*, i. 368). The excitement of these interviews occasioned a relapse, and he was forced to live for some time in complete seclusion at Kew, under the care of the Willises; he was not sufficiently recovered to be out of their hands until 28 June, when he left for Weymouth. This illness aged him considerably, and it was observed that he stooped more and was less firm on his legs (Malmesbury, iv. 62). In the course of the summer he offered to pay 30,000*l.* from the privy purse for the settlement of Pitt's debts; this offer was gratefully declined (Rose, *Diaries*, ii. 214). A wild plot to overturn the government and assassinate the king was discovered in October 1802.

George did not expect much from the negotiations with France, and spoke of the peace as 'experimental' (Malmesbury, iv. 63, 69; *Life of Eldon*, i. 398). It is doubtful whether he cordially approved of the tone adopted by his ministers towards France, but the rumour that he regretted Pitt in October was an exaggeration; he was personally fond of Addington, whose character and opinions were in many points like his own; though two years later, after Addington had left office, he came to believe that he had parted with him feeling that he 'was not equal to the government of the country' (Rose, ii. 156). Nothing was told him about the negotiations between Pitt and Addington in 1803 until they were ended; then on 20 April Addington informed the king of them, evidently making his own story good, for George was indignant at Pitt's conduct, talked of his 'putting the crown in commission,' and said that Pitt 'carried his plan of removals so extremely far, and so high, that it might reach him' (Malmesbury, iv. 185). He attributed the attacks made upon the administration to 'faction.' On 13 June he heard of the surrender of Hanover to the French, and received the news 'with great magnanimity and a real kingliness of mind' (*ib.* p. 270). During the alarm of invasion on 26 Oct. he held a review of twenty-seven thousand volunteers in Hyde Park; he declared that if the French landed he would meet them at the head of his troops, and drew up a scheme of arrangements to be adopted in case of invasion (*Auckland Correspondence*, iv. 184). About the middle of January 1804 he caught a severe cold; he had been much annoyed by the conduct of the Prince of Wales in publishing the correspondence of 1803 on the subject of his offer to serve in the army, and this may have made his attack more serious; at all events his mind became again deranged, and for a while his life was in danger. The disease fluctuated a good deal; on 27 Feb. he was sensible, but perfect quiet was necessary for some time longer. His condition prolonged the existence of the administration; the opposition could not let matters continue as they were, and yet a change seemed impossible while he remained incompetent. On 26 April Addington came to him in company with Eldon, the chancellor, and announced that he must resign. The next day Eldon gave him a letter which Pitt had written a few days before, stating his political views; it appears to have been received graciously. On 2 May, Addington having resigned, Eldon, in whom the king placed perfect confidence, gave him another letter from Pitt offering to form an administration on a broad basis. To this the king returned an irritable reply, which he evidently hoped would put an end to Pitt's offer (*Life of Pitt*, iv. 296, App. viii.; *Life of Eldon*, i. 440–3; Malmesbury, iv. 296–8; Rose, ii. 113). Eldon, however, arranged matters, and on 7 May the king saw Pitt; he assented to the inclusion of the Grenvilles in the new administration, but refused to allow him to invite Fox to join it. George is said to have considered the proposal of Fox's name as merely 'ostensible' (Colchester, *Diary*, i. 539), but he expressed his determination in strong terms to Addington, and later declared that he would not admit Fox 'even at the hazard of a civil war' (Rose, ii. 156). During the change of ministers he was occasionally excitable, and showed an excessive love of talking (*Life of Eldon*, i. 445). In May, though collected when talking of business, he was flighty in private life, was harsh and irritable, made sudden changes in the household, and caused the queen much distress (Malmesbury, iv. 310, 319). The slowness of his recovery is said to have been due to the employment of another physician in place of the Willises, against whom he had strong feelings. Discussions about the Prince of Wales seem to have added to the discomfort at the palace, for the queen was anxious on her son's behalf, while the king declared that he 'could never forgive him' for publishing his letters (Rose, ii. 168). Somewhat ungraciously he consented to give his son an interview, but the prince failed to keep his appointment. Meanwhile the king had determined to support Pitt and was displeased when Addington opposed a government measure (*Life of Pitt*, iv., App. xvi.). He set out for Weymouth on 24 Aug. 1804, and while there regained his health. On his return he stayed at Mr. Rose's house, Cuffnells, in Hampshire, 29 Oct. to 2 Nov. (see the account of his conversation with Rose, *Diary*, ii. 155–196). He told his host that he had nearly lost the sight of his right eye, and could scarcely read a newspaper by candle-light with any spectacles. Family disputes troubled him, and he and the queen, who feared an outbreak of madness, lived entirely apart (Malmesbury, iv. 336; *Auckland Correspondence*, iv. 213, 220). During the autumn he took much interest in arrangements for the education of his granddaughter, Princess Charlotte, but was annoyed by the manner in which the prince treated him with reference to the matter. The reconciliation between Pitt and Addington delighted him. Addington's approaching return to office enabled George to renew his intercourse with him, and on 29 Dec. he was invited to share the king's dinner, which consisted of mutton chops and pudding (*Life of Sidmouth*, ii. 342).

The king's health improved during the early part of 1805, though for a time he still showed some signs of flightiness, insisting on 'wearing a flowing brigadier wig on state occasions' (Horner, *Memoirs*, i. 283). His speech at the opening of the session was the last which he delivered in parliament, and was printed before it was delivered to enable him to read it with more ease (*Court and Cabinets*, iii. 411). By July he had become almost entirely blind; he had a cataract in his right eye, and could see but little with his left. Although he got on well with Pitt, he still liked to have his own way, especially with regard to church appointments. He had laid great stress on his 'personal nomination' of Dr. Stuart to the archbishopric of Armagh in 1800. He knew that Pitt intended to recommend Bishop Tomline for the archbishopric of Canterbury, which was likely to become vacant during the year (1805). As soon, therefore, as the king heard of the archbishop's death, he walked from the castle to the deanery at Windsor, called the dean, Manners Sutton, out from dinner, and congratulated him as archbishop. When Pitt came with his recommendation, George insisted on his acquiescing in his nomination; the interview was stormy, but he carried his point (*Life of Pitt*, iv. 252, App. xxi.; Rose, ii. 67). In July, after the secession of Sidmouth (Addington), Pitt tried to induce the king to consent to an invitation to Fox to join the ministry, but he refused. Pitt followed him to Weymouth in September and again pressed his request in a long interview, and only desisted through fear of disturbing his mind (*Life of Pitt*, iv. 334; Rose, ii. 199; Lewis, *Administrations*, p. 260). He was much affected by Pitt's death on 23 Jan. 1806, and could not see his ministers for two days. He then sent for Lord Hawkesbury (Jenkinson), who declined attempting to form an administration. By the advice of his ministers he sent for Lord Grenville on the 26th, and when Grenville said that he must consult Fox, answered, 'I thought so and meant it so;' he would have no 'exclusions' (Horner, *Memoirs*, i. 331; Colchester, *Diary*, ii. 32). The only difficulty arose from his wish that the army should be under the direct control of the crown, while the incoming ministers contended that the control should belong to a ministerial department. It was settled by their promise that they would introduce no changes in the army without his approval (*Life of Sidmouth*, ii. 415). He received Fox graciously, expressing a wish to forget 'old grievances,' and when Fox died on 13 Sept., said that the country could ill afford to lose him, and that he little thought that he should ever live to regret his death (Lewis, *Administrations*, p. 292; *Life of Sidmouth*, ii. 435). Grenville's proposals as to the changes of office consequent on Fox's death were accepted by the king with satisfaction (*Court and Cabinets*, iv. 77). His sight grew worse, and at the beginning of 1807 it was remarked that he was becoming apathetic, and only wished to 'pass the remainder of his days in rest and quiet' (Malmesbury, iv. 358). He was roused on 9 Feb. 1807 by the proposal of his ministers to introduce a clause in the Mutiny Bill removing a restriction on Roman catholics, and at once expressed his strong dissent. A further communication from the cabinet led him to imagine that the proposal did not go beyond the Irish act of 1793; he therefore, on 12 Feb., promised his assent, declaring that he could not go one step further. On finding on 3 March that he was mistaken as to the scope of the act, which would have admitted English Roman catholics to hold commissions in the army and navy, without the re- strictions of the Irish act, he was much disturbed, and on 11 March declared that he was surprised at the extent of the proposal which Lord Howick then laid before him, informing Lords Grey and Howick that he would not go beyond the act of 1793. On the 15th he received a note from the cabinet agreeing to drop the bill, but adding that, in view of the present state of Ireland, they should feel at liberty to propose 'from time to time' such measures respecting that country 'as the nature of the circumstances shall appear to require.' In answer he wrote requiring a 'positive assurance from them that they would never again propose to him any concessions to catholics.' He was informed on 18 March that his ministers considered that it would be inconsistent with their duty as his 'sworn counsellors' to give him such an assurance. The king then said that it was impossible for him to keep his ministers; that between dismissing them and 'forfeiting his crown he saw no medium,' and he accepted their resignation. He had on 13 March received a letter from the Duke of Portland advising him to refuse his assent to the bill, and offering to form an administration (*ib.* iv. 358–72; Rose, ii. 318–33; *Colchester Diary*, ii. 96, 99; *Memoirs of the Whig Party*, ii. 173–205). On 19 March 1807 he commissioned Eldon and Hawkesbury to request the duke to do so, remarking that he had no restrictions, no engagements or promises to require of him. During this interview he was calm and cheerful. A resolution condemning the acceptance by ministers of pledges which should bind them as regards offering advice to the crown was moved in both houses; it conveyed a distinct censure on the king's conduct; in the lords it was supported by 90 against 171, and in the commons by 226 against 258 (Lewis, *Administrations*, p. 296).

During 1808 the king, who was now quite incapacitated from reading or writing, led a quiet and cheerful life. He was much distressed by the scandal about the Duke of York in 1809. The conduct of the Prince of Wales with reference to this affair added much to his trouble (*Court and Cabinets*, iv. 291, 325). He supported his ministers, who were quarrelling among themselves, and his influence is said to have enabled them to retain office (*ib.* pp. 234, 288). Early in June (1808) he sanctioned Canning's proposal that Lord Wellesley should be substituted for Lord Castlereagh as war minister, but in September, when Portland's resignation was imminent, he by no means approved of Canning's pretensions to the position of first minister, and was in a perfect agony of mind lest he should be forced to admit Grenville and Grey to office (*Memoirs of Castlereagh*, i. 18; *Life of Eldon*, ii. 80–94). He wrote a dignified paper to the cabinet on the impropriety of the duel between Canning and Castlereagh. Having offered Perceval the headship of the administration, which was now disorganised by the retirement of the two secretaries as well as of Portland, he with much reluctance allowed Perceval on 22 June to make overtures to Grenville and Grey for the purpose of forming an extended administration (*Life of Eldon*, ii. 98; Rose, ii. 390, 394). He was much relieved by their refusal. At Perceval's request he exacted no pledge on the catholic question from his new ministers, though he assured them that he 'would rather abandon his throne' than 'consent to emancipation.' On 25 Oct. the jubilee of the reign was kept with great rejoicings (*Jubilee Year of George III*, 1809, reprinted 1887). For some months after this George, who was then blind, lived in seclusion; he still rode out, and walked on the terrace of Windsor

Castle accompanied by his daughters. His temper was gentle and his manner quiet; he attended daily morning service at chapel. In the autumn of 1810 he was much distressed by the illness of his favourite daughter Amelia. On 24 Oct. he showed signs of approaching derangement of mind (Rose, ii. 447), and on the 29th Perceval found him incapable of transacting business. His malady continuing, the Regency Bill was passed in January 1811, but on 5 Feb. Eldon, who went to see him in order to ascertain that it was necessary to put the great seal in commission for the purpose of giving the royal assent to the bill, found him so much better that he was embarrassed (ib. p. 481). The king spoke of the regency with resignation, and almost with cheerfulness. The bill gave the care of the king's person to the queen. On 21 May 1811 he was able to ride through the Little Park at Windsor, a groom leading his horse. Soon after this, however, he became worse (Auckland Correspondence, iv. 66), and the remainder of his life was spent in mental and visual darkness, with very few momentary returns of reason. His bodily health was good. On the death of the queen in 1818 the guardianship of his person was entrusted by parliament to the Duke of York. Early in January 1820 his bodily powers decayed, and on the 29th he died very quietly in his eighty-second year, six days after the death of his fourth son, Edward, duke of Kent. After lying in state on 15 Feb. he was buried on the night of the 16th in St. George's Chapel, Windsor. He had fifteen children by his queen, Charlotte—nine sons (the first christian name only is given in each case): George, who succeeded him (1762–1830); Frederick, duke of York (1763–1827); William, duke of Clarence, afterwards William IV (1765–1837); Edward, duke of Kent (1767–1820); Ernest, duke of Cumberland and king of Hanover (1771–1851); Augustus, duke of Sussex (1773–1843); Adolphus, duke of Cambridge (1774–1850); Octavius (1779–1783); and Alfred (1780–1782); and six daughters: Charlotte, queen of Würtemberg (1766–1828); Augusta (1768–1840); Elizabeth, princess of Hesse-Homburg (1770–1840); Mary, duchess of Gloucester (1776–1857); Sophia (1777–1848); and Amelia (1783–1810).

At Windsor Castle are portraits of George by Dupont, Gainsborough, and Beechey. At Hampton Court is a family picture by Knapton, including George as a boy, besides portraits by West and Beechey. Portraits by Richard Wilson (as a boy) and by Allan Ramsay are in the National Portrait Gallery. A colossal equestrian statue by Westmacott terminates the long walk in Windsor Park.

[Jesse's Memoirs of the Life and Reign of George III, 3 vols. 2nd edit. 1867, contains many personal details, but is greater in gossip than in weightier matters; Adolphus's History of England during reign, 7 vols. 1840, has the merits and defects of a nearly contemporary work; Massey's History, 4 vols. 2nd edit. 1865, ends at 1802, dispassionate, though judging George rather severely; Mahon's

(Stanhope's) Hist. vols. iii–vii. 3rd edit. 1853, ends at 1783, clear and trustworthy, though dull; May's Const. Hist. 3 vols. 5th edit. 1875; Lecky's Hist. of England during the Eighteenth Century, vols. iii–vi. 1882–7. For early years Earl Waldegrave's Memoirs, 1821, 4to, ends 1758; Bubb Dodington's Diary, 1785, ends 1761; Lady Hervey's Letters, 1821; Harris's Life of Lord-chancellor Hardwicke, 3 vols. 1847, especially useful for 1760; Walpole's Memoirs of Reign of George II, 2 vols. 4to, 1822; Earl of Chesterfield's Letters, 5 vols. ed. Mahon, 1845. Monthly Magazine, vols. li. lii., Notes and Queries, 1st ser. vol. x., Authentic Records, 1832, and Thoms's Hannah Lightfoot, &c., 1867, contain the 'Fair Quaker' scandal. Walpole's Memoirs of reign, 4 vols. 1845, Last Journals, 2 vols. 1859, and Letters, ed. Cunningham, 9 vols. 1880, must be taken with allowance for the writer's love of gossip and personal hostility to the king. Political correspondence and memoirs, representing party views, chiefly valuable down to 1783, are: Russell's Bedford Correspondence, vols. ii. and iii. 1842, ends 1770; Grenville Papers, vols. ii. iii. and iv., ed. W. J. Smith, 1852, valuable to 1770; Albemarle's Memoirs of the Marquis of Rockingham, 2 vols. 1852; Chatham Correspondence, 4 vols. 1838; Albert von Ruville's Life of Pitt, Earl of Chatham, 3 vols. Stuttgart, 1905, English translation, 1907; Corresp. of George III with Lord North, 1768–83 (from originals at Windsor), ed. Donne, 2 vols. 1867, with good introd. and notes; Fitzmaurice's Earl of Shelburne, 3 vols. 1875; Russell's Memorials and Correspondence of C. J. Fox, 4 vols. 1862, down to Fox's death in 1806; Nicholls's Recollections, 2 vols. 1820; Justin Winsor's Narrative and Critical Hist. of America, 1888, vol. vii. chaps. i. and ii. Letters of Junius, 2 vols. ed. Bohn. Authorities chiefly valuable after 1783 are: Lewis's Administrations of Great Britain, 1864; for personal details, court, &c.: Autobiography and Correspondence of Mrs. Delany, ed. Lady Llanover, 6 vols. 1861–2, vols. ii. and iii. 2nd ser.; Diary and Letters of Madame d'Arblay, 7 vols. 1842–6; Mrs. Papendiek's Journals, or Court and Private Life in the Time of Queen Charlotte, ed. Mrs. Broughton, 2 vols. 1887; Jubilee Year of George III, an Account of the Celebration of 25 Oct., reprinted 1887; Quarterly Review, vols. xxxvi. cxxxi. Memoirs and correspondence, chiefly political: Wraxall's Historical and Posthumous Memoirs, 5 vols. 1884, of no great value for the king's life; Duke of Buckingham's Court and Cabinets, 4 vols. 1853, begins 1782, contains the correspondence of the Grenville family; Earl of Malmesbury's Diaries and Correspondence, 4 vols, 1844, for domestic affairs vol. iv. is chiefly valuable; Malmesbury seceded from Fox in 1793, and was fully in the confidence of Pitt and Portland; Earl Stanhope's Life of Pitt, 4 vols. 1862, has many letters written by the king in the appendixes; Campbell's Life of Loughborough, Lives of the Chancellors, vol. vi. 1847, for Loughborough's intrigue on catholic question; Lord Auckland's Journal and Correspondence, 4 vols. 1861; Rose's Diaries, 2 vols. 1860, of the highest value, for Rose was an intimate friend of Pitt, held office in both his administrations, and in 1804 had some interesting conversations with the king; Twiss's Life of Eldon, 3 vols. 1844 (from 1801 (i. 364) on to the time of his final derangement (ii. 165) the king treated Eldon with implicit confidence); Pellew's Life of Sidmouth, 3 vols. 1847, a strong ex parte statement (see Lewis's Administrations), and should be read along with Rose, Malmesbury, and Stanhope's Pitt; Lord Castlereagh's Memoirs and Correspondence, vols. i–v. 1849; Lord Holland's Memoirs of the Whig Party, 2 vols. 1854; Lord Colchester's Diary, 3 vols. 1861; Memoirs of F. Horner, 2 vols. 1853. Thackeray's Four Georges is of no historical value. For caricatures see Gillray in British Museum; Wright's Caricature Hist. of the Georges, 2nd edit. 1867; and satires, Wolcot's Works of Peter Pindar, 4 vols. 12mo, 1809.]

WILLIAM HUNT

published 1889

CHARLOTTE Sophia

(1744–1818)

Queen of George III, king of England, was the youngest daughter of Charles Lewis, brother of Frederic, third duke of Mecklenburg-Strelitz. When a young girl she was so distressed at the ravages of the Prussian troops on a relative's territory, that she wrote a letter to their king begging him to restrain them. This letter found its way to England, and is said to have done something to direct the attention of the English court to her as a suitable consort for George (Mahon, *History of England*, iv. 331, 1846). The inquiries made resulted in a formal proposal, which was accepted, and the princess set off for England. The voyage from Cuxhaven to Harwich took ten days, for the ship was delayed by contrary winds. Charlotte beguiled the time by practising English tunes on the harpsichord. On 7 Sept. 1761 she landed in England. The next day she saw George for the first time at St. James's. From that moment till the king's illness she said that she never knew real sorrow. They were married late that same evening. Their coronation took place on 22 Sept. of that year (a minute description is given in Richard Thomson's *Faithful Account*, &c., 1820). Her appearance at this time is briefly described by Horace Walpole: 'She is not tall nor a beauty. Pale and very thin; but looks sensible and genteel. Her hair is darkish and fine; her forehead low, her nose very well, except the nostrils spreading too wide. The mouth has the same fault, but her teeth are good. She talks a great deal, and French tolerably' (*Letters*, iii. 434). The records of Charlotte's life are entirely of a domestic nature. She was merely a lay figure in the numerous state pageants in which her position obliged her to take part, and she had no interest in nor influence over English politics, which she probably scarcely understood. The king, though a devoted husband, never discussed affairs of state with her. She was a woman of little ability, but she certainly acted up to her own standard of duty. Court life during this long reign was perfectly decorous, and it must be added very dull and colourless. Scandal could only say of her that she was somewhat mean in money matters; but this was probably from early training (the story of an intrigue with the Chevalier d'Eon hardly requires serious mention; see Thom, *Queen Charlotte and the Chevalier d'Eon*, reprinted from *Notes and Queries*, 1867). In 1788, when the king became ill, the care of his person and the disposition of his household were placed in her hands, and in 1810, when, on the death of the Princess Amelia, George became permanently insane, much the same arrangements were made. The queen died at Kew 17 Nov. 1818, and was buried in St. George's Chapel, Windsor. Of the fifteen children born of her marriage, the last three, Octavius, Alfred, and Amelia, predeceased their mother.

[There are Lives of Queen Charlotte (with portraits) by W. C. Oulton, 1819, and T. Williams, 1819, but they are merely external. In the numerous memoirs of the period there is much information about the queen's private life. Walpole's Letters, Miss Burney's Memoirs, and Mrs. Delany's Autobiography are the chief of these; others will be found quoted in Jesse's Memoirs of Life and Reign of George III, 3 vols. 1867. In Brit. Mus. Cat. under this heading is a list of funeral sermons, satires, &c., relating to the queen, and among the manuscripts are a number of her official papers.]

Francis Watt

published 1887

FITZHERBERT Maria Anne

(1756–1837)

Wife of George IV, born in July 1756, was the youngest daughter of Walter Smythe, esq., of Brambridge, Hampshire, second son of Mr. John Smythe of Acton Burnell, Shropshire. Little is known of her childhood beyond the fact that she visited Paris, and was taken to see Louis XV at dinner. When the king pulled a chicken to pieces with his fingers she burst out laughing, upon which his majesty presented her with a box of sugar-plums. She married in 1775 Edward Weld, esq., of Lulworth Castle, Dorsetshire, who died in the same year. In 1778 his widow married Thomas Fitzherbert of Swynnerton in Staffordshire, by whom she was left a widow a second time in 1781. Mrs. Fitzherbert, with a jointure of 2,000*l.* a year, now took up her abode at Richmond, where she soon became the centre of an admiring circle. In 1785 she first saw the Prince of Wales (born 1762). He fell, or thought he fell, desperately in love with her at first sight, and on one occasion pretended to stab himself in despair. On this occasion she was induced to visit him at Carlton House in company with the Duchess of Devonshire, but soon after went abroad to escape further solicitations. After remaining some time in Holland and Germany, she received an offer of marriage from the prince, which she is said to have accepted with reluctance. They were married on 21 Dec. 1785 in her own drawing-room, by a clergyman of the church of England, and in the presence of her brother, Mr. John Smythe, and her uncle, Mr. Errington. By the Marriage Act of 1772 every marriage contracted by a member of the royal family under twenty-five years of age without the king's consent was invalid; and by the Act of Settlement if the heir-apparent married a Roman catholic he forfeited his right to the crown. It was argued, however, that a man could not be said to marry when he merely went through a ceremony which he knew to be invalid. According to one account, repeated by Lord Holland in his 'Memoirs of the Whig Party,' Mrs. Fitzherbert took the same view, said the marriage was all nonsense, and knew well enough that she was about to become the prince's mistress. The story is discredited by her well-known character, by the footing on which she was always received by other members of the royal family, and by the fact that, even after the marriage of the prince regent with Caroline of Brunswick, she was advised by her own church (Roman Catholic) that she might lawfully live with him. Nobody seems to have thought the worse of her; she was received in the best society, and was treated by the prince at all events as if she was his wife.

In April 1787, on the occasion of the prince applying to parliament for the payment of his debts, Fox, in his place in the House of Commons, formally denied that any marriage had taken place. It is unknown to this day what authority he had for this statement. Common report asserted that 'a slip of paper' had passed between the prince and his friend; and Lord Stanhope, in his 'History of England,' declares his unhesitating belief that Fox had the best reasons for supposing the statement to be true. The prince himself, however, affected to be highly indignant. The next time he saw Mrs. Fitzherbert he went up to her with the words, 'What do you think, Maria? Charles declared in the House of Commons last night that you and I were not man and wife.' As the prince was now approaching the age at which he could make a legal marriage, the curiosity of parliament on the subject is perfectly intelligible. But after a lame kind of explanation from Sheridan, who tried to explain away Fox's statement, without contradicting it, the subject dropped, and the prince and the lady seem to have lived happily together till the appearance of the Princess Caroline. At the trial of Warren Hastings in 1788 Mrs. Fitzherbert, then in the full bloom of womanly beauty, attracted more attention than the queen or the princesses. On the prince's marriage (8 April 1795) to Caroline she ceased for a time to live with him. But being advised by her confessor, who had received his instructions from Rome, that she might do so without blame, she returned to him; and oddly enough gave a public breakfast to all the fashionable world to celebrate the event. She and the prince were in constant pecuniary difficulties, and once on their return from Brighton to London they had not money enough to pay for the post-horses, and were obliged to borrow of an old servant, yet these, she used to say, were the happiest years of her life. As years passed on, however, the prince appears to have fallen under other influences; and at last at a dinner given to Louis XVIII at Carlton House, in or about 1803, she received an affront which she could not overlook, and parted from the prince for ever. She was told that she had no fixed place at the dinner-table, and must sit 'according to her rank,' that is as plain Mrs. Fitzherbert. She was not perhaps sorry for the excuse to break off a connection which the prince's new ties had already made irksome to her; and resisting all further importunities she retired from court on an annuity of 6,000l. a year, which, as she had no children, was perhaps a sufficient maintenance. She was probably the only woman to whom George IV was ever sincerely attached. He inquired for her in his last illness, and he died with her portrait round his neck.

Mrs. Fitzherbert survived him seven years, dying at Brighton on 29 March 1837. From George III and Queen Charlotte, the Duke of York, William IV, and Queen Adelaide she had always experienced the greatest kindness and attention, and seems never to have been made to feel sensible of her equivocal position. The true facts of the case were long unknown to the public.

[In 1833 a box of papers was deposited with Messrs. Coutts, under the seals of the Duke of Wellington, Lord Albemarle, and a near connection of Mrs. Fitzherbert, Lord Stourton. Among other documents the box contained the marriage certificate, and a memorandum written by Mrs. Fitzherbert, attached to a letter written by the clergyman by whom the ceremony was performed, from which, however, she herself had torn off the signature, for fear it should compromise him. At her death she left full powers with her executors to use these papers as they pleased for the vindication of her own character. And on Lord Stourton's death in 1846 he assigned all his interest in and authority over them to his brother, the Hon. Charles Langdale, with a narrative drawn up by himself, from which all that we know of her is derived. On the appearance of Lord Holland's Memoirs of the Whig Party in 1854, containing statements very injurious to Mrs. Fitzherbert's reputation, Mr. Langdale was anxious to avail himself of the contents of the sealed box. But the surviving trustees being unwilling to have the seals broken, and thinking it better to let the whole story be forgotten, Mr. Langdale made use of the narrative entrusted to him to compose a Life of Mrs. Fitzherbert, which was published in London early in 1856, and is so far our only authority for the facts above stated. In an article in the Quarterly Review in 1854 a hope was expressed that the contents of the box will soon be given to the public; but it has not at present been fulfilled.]

Thomas Edward Kebbel

published 1889

JORDAN Dorothea or Dorothy
(1762–1816)

Actress, was born near Waterford, Ireland, in 1762. Her mother, Grace Phillips, is said to have been one of three daughters of the Rev. Dr. Phillips, all of whom took to the stage. Grace Phillips, who appears at one time to have been called Mrs. Frances, was an actress at Smock Alley Theatre, Dublin, where she captivated, and is stated to have married, a Captain Bland. Bland (it is said) was consequently disowned by his family, took to acting, and ultimately agreed to an annulment of his marriage, which was obtained by his father on the ground of nonage. These statements, given in all biographies of Mrs. Jordan, have grave inherent improbability. There is some reason to suppose that Bland, Mrs. Jordan's father, was merely a stage underling. In 1777 she was assistant to a milliner in Dame Street, Dublin, and the same year she appeared at Crow Street Theatre as Phœbe in 'As you like it.' Here, or at the theatre in Cork, in which her father is said to have been engaged as scene-shifter, and at Waterford, she played Lopez, a male character in 'The Governess,' a pirated version of 'The Duenna,' Priscilla Tomboy in 'The Romp,' and Adelaide in Captain Jephson's 'Count of Narbonne.' Afraid of her manager, Richard Daly, a man of infamous reputation, who, after lending her money and rendering her *enceinte*, strove to get her wholly in his power, she ran off with her mother, brother, and sister to Leeds, where the party arrived poorly clad and almost penniless. Tate Wilkinson, manager of the circuit, recognising in her mother 'his past Desdemona' in Dublin in 1758, asked the daughter what she could play, tragedy, comedy, or opera, to which she replied laconically 'All.' A few days later, 11 July 1782, under the name of Miss Frances, she appeared as Calista in the 'Fair Penitent,' and sang with great success 'The Greenwood Laddie,' wearing a frock and a mob-cap. Wilkinson engaged her at fifteen shillings a week. Changing her name to Mrs. Jordan, as suited the matronly condition in which she found herself, she played, in one or other of the various towns comprised in the York circuit, Rutland, The Romp, Arionelli, in which Wilkinson says she was excellent, Rachel in the 'Fair American,' in which she had a narrow escape of being killed by the roller of a curtain, William in 'Rosina,' Lady Racket, Lady Teazle, Lionel in the 'School for Fathers,' Zara, Jane Shore, Indiana, &c. Daly soon renewed his persecution, and proceeded against her for money lent and for breach of engagement. The money, some two or three hundred pounds, was paid for her by a Mr. Swan. Indolent, capricious, imprudent, and at times refractory, she made less way than might have been expected. Yates, who saw her, pronounced her 'a mere piece of theatrical mediocrity.' When, on the recommendation of 'Gentleman' Smith, she was engaged for Drury Lane Theatre, Mrs. Siddons gravely mistrusted the wisdom of the step. She bade farewell to the Yorkshire stage at Wakefield, 9 Sept. 1785, in the 'Poor Soldier,' and appeared at Drury Lane, 18 Oct. 1785, as Peggy in the 'Country Girl,' a part in which she had watched Mrs. Brown.

No conspicuous success attended her début. But before the close of her first season, in which she played Viola, Imogen, Priscilla Tomboy, Bellario in 'Philaster,' Miss Hoyden, Hypolita in 'She would and she would not,' Mrs. Brady in the 'Irish Widow,' Miss Lucy in the 'Virgin Unmasked,' and was the original Rosa in Cobb's 'Strangers at Home,' she was established in public favour. The 'European Magazine' for December 1785, p. 465, remarked that, while in tragedy little beyond mediocrity was to be expected, as Miss Tomboy 'she excelled every performer ... at present on the English stage, and almost equalled the celebrated Mrs. Clive.' Mrs. Jordan was counselled by the critic to confine herself to the characters within her range, and told that she would be, in her line, as great an ornament to the stage as Mrs. Siddons, then at the same theatre. As the original Matilda in Burgoyne's 'Richard Cœur de Lion' she obtained much popularity. During her long engagement at Drury Lane, lasting, with a break due to a temporary retirement from the stage in 1806–7 till 1809, she played many sentimental, imaginative, or tragic parts: Roxalana, Rosalind, Beatrice, Helena in 'All's well that ends well,' Juliet, Ophelia, and was the original Angela in 'Monk' Lewis's 'Castle Spectre,' 14 Dec. 1797, Flavia in 'Vortigern,' Cora in 'Pizarro,' 24 May 1799, and Imogen in Lewis's 'Adelmorn the Outlaw,' 4 May 1801. Gradually, however, a sense of her unparalleled excellence in comedy dawned on the management, and Sir Harry Wildair, Mrs. Woffington's great part, Miss Prue, Letitia Hardy, Lady Teazle, Miss Hardcastle, Mrs. Sullen, Bisarre, Lydia Languish, Nell in the 'Devil to Pay,' and most leading comic parts were assigned to her, as well as William in 'Rosina' and other 'breeches' parts. The retirement from the stage of Elizabeth Farren in 1797 led to the assumption by Mrs. Jordan of some characters outside her supposed range.

Her original parts were numerous, but, as a rule, unimportant (see for full list Genest, *Hist. Stage*). Most conspicuous among her 'creations' are: Beatrice in the 'Pannel,' an alteration by John Kemble of Bickerstaffe's ''Tis well it's no worse,' 28 Nov. 1788; Aura in the 'Farm House,' a version by Kemble of the 'Country Lasses' of Charles Johnson, 2 May 1789, second representation; Helena in 'Love in Many Masks,' Kemble's alteration of Mrs. Behn's 'Rover,' 8 March 1790; Little Pickle, a schoolboy, in the farce of the 'Spoiled Child,' 22 March 1790, the authorship of which has been assigned to her; Augusta in 'Better late than never,' by Reynolds and Andrews, 17 Nov. 1790; a character (?Celia) in the 'Greek Slave,' an adaptation of the 'Humorous Lieutenant' of Beaumont and Fletcher, 22 March 1791. During the rebuilding of Drury Lane she was with the company at the King's Theatre in the Haymarket, where she played the heroine of the 'Village Coquette,' an unprinted adaptation from the French by Simons, 16 April 1792; Julia Wingrove in the 'Fugitive,' by Richardson, 20 April 1792; and Clara in the 'French Duellist,' 22 May 1792. Returning to Drury Lane, she was Lady Contest in Mrs. Inchbald's 'Wedding Day,' 4 Nov. 1794 (third time); Miss Plinlimmon in the 'Welsh Heiress,' by Jerningham, 17 April 1795; Sabina Rosny in Cumberland's 'First Love,' 12 May 1795; Albina Mandeville in Reynolds's 'Will,' 19 April 1797; Letitia Manfred in Cumberland's 'Last of the Family,' 8 May 1797; Sir Edward Bloomly, a boy, in 'Cheap Living,' by Reynolds, 21 Oct. 1797; Susan in Holcroft's 'Knave or not;' Rosa in Morris's 'Secret,' 2 March 1799; Zorayda in Lewis's 'East Indian,' 22 April 1799; Julia in Hoare's 'Indiscretion,' 10 May 1800; Eliza in 'Hear both Sides,' by Holcroft, 29 Jan. 1803; Emma in Allingham's 'Marriage Promise,' 16 April 1803; Widow Cheerly in Cherry's 'Soldier's Daughter,' 7 Feb. 1804; Louisa Davenant in Cumberland's 'Sailor's Daughter,' 7 April 1804; Lady Lovelace in Holt's 'Land we live in,' 29 Dec. 1804; Lady Bloomfield in Kenney's 'World,' 31 March 1808; and Helen in Arnold's 'Man and Wife,' 5 Jan. 1809. After playing for some benefits at Covent Garden, she made her first appearance there as a member of the company in the part of Widow Cheerly on 2 July 1811. Here she played her last original part, 20 April 1814, that of Barbara Green in Kenney's 'Debtor and Creditor,' and here, as Lady Teazle, she made, 1 June 1814, her last appearance on the London stage. She is said to have played at the English theatre in Brussels in September 1814, and her final performances were given at Margate ten nights in July and August 1815. She grew stout in later life, but declined to play matronly parts.

In the summer she had visited regularly the principal country towns, reaping everywhere a golden harvest. Upon her revisiting, in 1786, Leeds, where she had previously been no special favourite, it was necessary to turn seven rows of the pit into boxes. In Edinburgh, where, as Hypolita in

'She would and she would not,' she appeared 22 July 1786, and in Glasgow, medals were struck in her honour. In these towns she delivered occasional addresses, in the composition of which she had some facility.

As an actress in comedy Mrs. Jordan can have had few equals. Genest says that she had never a superior in her line, and adds that her Hypolita will never be excelled. Rosalind, Viola, and Lady Contest were among her best characters (viii. 431–2). Hazlitt, in unwonted rapture, speaks of Mrs. Jordan, 'the child of nature whose voice was a cordial to the heart . . . to hear whose laugh was to drink nectar . . . who "talked far above singing," and whose singing was like the twang of Cupid's bow. Her person was large, soft, and generous, like her soul. . . . Mrs. Jordan was all exuberance and grace' (*Dramatic Essays*, pp. 49–50, ed. 1851). Leigh Hunt, after praising her artless vivacity, says: 'Mrs Jordan seems to speak with all her soul; her voice, piquant with melody, delights the ear with a peculiar and exquisite fulness and with an emphasis that appears the result of perfect conviction' (*Critical Essays*, p. 163). Though admitting that she is not sufficiently ladylike, he holds her 'not only the first actress of the day,' but, judging from what he reads, the first that has adorned our stage (*ib*. p. 168). Lamb's praise is not less high. Haydon spoke of her acting as touching beyond description. Byron declared her superb, and Mathews the elder called her 'an extraordinary and exquisite being, as distinct from any other being in the world as she was superior to all her contemporaries in her particular line of acting.' Campbell speaks of her beating Mrs. Siddons out of the character of Rosalind, and regards the instance as unique. Sir Joshua Reynolds delighted in a being 'who ran upon the stage as a playground, and laughed from sincere wildness of delight.' He preferred her to all actresses of his time. Boaden, her biographer, goes into ecstasies over her.

Mrs. Jordan's domestic life was brilliant rather than happy, and caused much scandal. By Daly, her first manager, she had a daughter who was known as Miss Jordan, married a Mr. Alsop, came out at Covent Garden 18 Oct. 1816 as Rosalind, was a good actress, and was praised by Hazlitt, but does not appear to have remained very long on the stage; she left her husband, and died a premature and deplorable death in America. By Richard (afterwards Sir Richard) Ford, whose name she bore for some years, she had four children. One daughter married a Mr. March in the ordnance office, and a second Colonel (afterwards General) Hawker. This connection was broken off before 1790, when she became the mistress of the Duke of Clarence, subsequently William IV. During her long connection with him she bore him ten children, all of whom took the name of Fitzclarence. Two sons, Adolphus Fitzclarence and George Augustus Frederick Fitzclarence, are separately noticed. Lord Frederick Fitzclarence (1799–1854) was lieutenant-general, and colonel of 36th foot; Lord Augustus (1805–1854) was rector of Mapledurham; Henry died a captain in India. Of the daughters, Sophia married Lord De l'Isle and Dudley; Mary married General Fox; Elizabeth married the Earl of Erroll; Augusta married, first, the Hon. John Kennedy Erskine, and, secondly, Lord John Frederick Gordon, who took the name of Halyburton; and Amelia married Viscount Falkland. Her liaison and the frequent absences from the stage attributable to the calls of maternity were noticed in the press, and sometimes led to noisy demonstrations in the theatres. In 1790, a period of great political ferment, her intrigue was specially unpopular. In the December of that year she came forward, and, addressing the public, said that the slightest mark of public disapprobation affected her very sensibly, and that she had never absented herself one minute from the duties of her profession except from real indisposition. 'Thus having invariably acted, I do,' she concluded, 'consider myself under the public protection.' This speech, printed in various quarters, arrested the complaint. Mrs. Jordan was earning at the time as much as 30*l.* a week. The duke allowed her 1,000*l.* a year, but at George III's suggestion is said to have subsequently proposed by letter a reduction to 500*l.* Mrs. Jordan sent by way of reply the bottom part of a playbill, bearing 'No money returned after the rising of the curtain.' To the objections of her lover is ascribed the absence of Mrs. Jordan from the stage in the seasons of 1806–7 and 1809–1810. Her late appearances were due to her anxiety to make provision for her earlier brood of children. She looked upon 10,000*l.* as requisite for the portion of each of her daughters by Ford. In 1811 she received, while acting at Cheltenham, a letter from the duke asking her to meet him at Maiden-head, with a view to a final separation. From her letters at the time we gather that want of money was the cause of separation. She acquits the duke of all blame, states that his letters are full of the most unqualified praise of her conduct, and wishes to shield him from unfair abuse. The terms allowed her were liberal. For the maintenance of herself, her daughters, and her earlier family an income of 4,400*l.* was secured to her; but in case of her returning to the stage the care of the duke's daughters and the allowance for their maintenance were to revert to the duke (cf. letter from Mr. Barton, master of the mint, January 1824).

Curious mystery envelopes her last days. She is said to have been in danger of imprisonment in consequence of liabilities which she had incurred in behalf of Alsop, then a civil magistrate at Calcutta, who had married her eldest daughter. But, according to Sir Jonah Barrington, she was really affluent, having made by her acting in 1814 as much as 7,000*l.* On 3 Dec. 1814 she wrote: 'When everything is adjusted it will be impossible for me to remain in England. I shall therefore go abroad, appropriating as much as I can spare of the remainder of my income to pay my debts.' This appears inconceivable, as her debts, due to personal friends, did not much exceed 2,000*l.*; but, according to Boaden (*Life of Jordan*, ii. 310), 'all her connections of *every* degree were her *annuitants.*' In one of her letters, dated Bath, 22 April 1809, she says: 'My professional success through life has, indeed, been *most extraordinary*, and consequently attended with *great emoluments*. But from my first starting in life, at the early age of fourteen, I have always had a large family to support. My mother was a duty. But on *brothers* and *sisters* I have lavished more money than can be supposed.' In August 1815, taking with her a Miss Sketchley and, according to Barrington, her son-in-law, Colonel Hawker, she went to France. Strange and apparently visionary alarms took possession of her. She passed as a Mrs. James, and her place of residence was kept a secret. She first established herself at Boulogne-sur-Mer. This place she quitted for Versailles, and thence, in still greater secrecy, proceeded to St. Cloud. Here, in complete seclusion and under the name of Johnson, in a large, dilapidated, and shabby house in 'the square adjoining the palace,' she remained from morning to night, 'sighing upon the sofa,' and waiting for news from England. On 3 July 1816, after sending for letters and being told there were none, she fell back on the sofa, and, sobbing deeply, died. She left no will, and letters of administration were taken out at Doctors' Commons by the treasury solicitor on 24 May 1817, and the property sworn to be under 300*l.* She was buried in the cemetery of St. Cloud, Mr. Forster, the chaplain to the English ambassador, officiating. Ireland, the Shakespearean forger, asserts that he attended the funeral (*Vortigern*, 1832, Preface). Her personal effects, including her body-linen, were sold in France under dishonouring circumstances. After a delay of years a stone was put on her grave, with a Latin epitaph, in the composition of which Genest says he assisted. Every circumstance connected with her death, which was generally said to be due to heartbreak, was calculated to arouse public sympathy, and a notice in the 'Morning Post,' 8 Dec. 1823, that a dividend of 5*s.* in the pound was to be paid to her creditors caused much outcry, which was met by a declaration that this was not a composition. It was long before the controversy to which these things gave rise was closed. Further mystery remains. A report that she was not dead long prevailed. Various persons, including her daughter, Mrs. Alsop, declared they saw her after she was supposed to have been buried, and Boaden, who knew her well, asserts that he saw her in Piccadilly after 1816, and that she dropped a long white veil over her face.

Many stories are current, all to the credit of her generosity and her good-heartedness, including one in which she effected a complete conquest of a Wesleyan minister, who left her with a warm blessing. Her brother, as Mr. Bland, was engaged by Kemble, and more than once played Sebastian to her Viola. Mrs. Inchbald is among those who spoke highly of her, and Kemble, quoting from Sterne, said: 'I could have taken her into my arms, and cherished her, though it was in the open street, without blushing.' A portrait of her by Romney, as the Country Girl, was in the possession of Colonel Fitzclarence, afterwards first Earl of Munster. The Garrick Club possesses two portraits of her by De Wilde, one as Phædra in 'Amphytrion,' a second as the Country Girl. A statue of her by Chantrey, executed for William IV, was in 1851 at Mapledurham, Oxfordshire, then the seat of one of her sons. She usually signed her name 'Dora.'

[The chief source of information is the Life of Mrs. Jordan by James Boaden, 2 vols. 1831. 'The Great Illegitimates: a Public and Private Life of that celebrated Actress, Miss Bland, otherwise Mrs. Ford, or Mrs. Jordan, late Mistress of H.R.H. the D. of Clarence, now King William IV, etc., by a confidential Friend of the Departed,' was published, s.d., by J. Dunscombe, 19 Little Queen Street, London, 12mo, about 1830, with portraits. It is a somewhat scandalous production, exceedingly rare, of which a reprint, probably with some excisions, has recently appeared. The latter only is in the British Museum. Jordan's Elixir of Life and Cure for the Spleen, 1789, 8vo, a collection of the songs in her various pieces, had a portrait of her as Sir Harry Wildair and an untrustworthy biography, in which it is said that she was born in St. Martin's, London, 1764. Tate Wilkinson, in the Wandering Patentee, gives a long and animated account of her. For one or two scandals, Memoirs and Amorous Adventures by Sea and Land of King William IV, London, 1830, is responsible. See also Personal Sketches of his own Time, by Sir Jonah Barrington; Personal Memoirs of P. L. Gordon; Georgian Era; Genest's Account of the Stage; the Era Almanack for 1876.]

JOSEPH KNIGHT

published 1891

GEORGE IV (1762–1830)

King of England, eldest son of George III and of Queen Charlotte of Mecklenburg-Strelitz, was born at St. James's Palace about half-past seven on the morning of 12 Aug. 1762. On the 17th he was created by patent Prince of Wales and Earl of Chester, and on 8 Sept. was baptised by Archbishop Secker under the names of George Augustus Frederick, his sponsors being the Dukes of Cumberland and Mecklenburg-Strelitz and the Princess Dowager of Wales. He was inoculated and handed over to the care of a retinue of nurses, under the control of Lady Charlotte Finch. On

26 Dec. 1765 he was created a knight of the Garter, and was presented to the public in October 1769 at a drawing-room formally held in his name. In the main, however, he was brought up along with his brother, Frederick Augustus duke of York, with strict and almost excessive plainness and seclusion, at the Bower Lodge at Kew. In 1771 his regular education began under Markham, bishop of Chester, Dr. Cyril Jackson, a Swiss gentleman, M. de Sulzas, and Lord Holdernesse. In 1776 these tutors were replaced by Hurd, bishop of Lichfield, Mr. Arnold, and Lord Bruce, and the latter was soon succeeded by the Duke of Montague. The prince's education was extensive, and included classics, modern languages, elocution, drawing, and husbandry. He learnt readily, and showed some taste for Tacitus, but he soon displayed a troublesome disposition. He was headstrong with his tutors and disrespectful to the king. He was addicted to lying, tippling, and low company.

As he approached his nineteenth birthday he pressed his father for a commission in the army and greater personal liberty, but the king refused the request. In 1780, however, he was provided with a small separate establishment in a portion of Buckingham House; the arrangement took effect on 1 Jan. 1781, and he was forthwith launched upon the town. He immediately became closely attached to Fox and the whigs, and though Fox advised him not to identify himself with any political party (*Diary of Lord Malmesbury*, ii. 75), his partisanship was undisguised, and at times indecent (Walpole, *Last Journals*, ii. 599, 600). He was at this time stout, of a florid complexion, with gracious and engaging manners, considerable social facility, and some accomplishments. He sang agreeably, played on the violoncello, dressed extravagantly, quoted poetry, and conversed in French and Italian. He fell under the influence of the Duke of Cumberland and the Duc de Chartres; he gamed and drank, and was so extravagant that he spent 10,000l. on his clothes in a year. In 1780 he became involved in an intrigue with Mary Robinson, a beautiful actress, by whose performance of Perdita at Drury Lane he was captivated. He provided for her a splendid establishment, and when after two years the connection terminated, she obtained from him his bond for 20,000l., which she afterwards surrendered. He left her to want in her latter days (see Mary Robinson, *Memoirs of Perdita*). When the Rockingham ministry came in, he shared the triumph of Fox and the enmity of the king. In June 1783 it became necessary to consider his future allowance. The ministry proposed 100,000l. a year, charged on the civil list. The king thought this an extravagant sum, and offered to provide 50,000l. a year himself. After a ministerial crisis upon the question, it was ultimately decided that the prince, now harassed with debts, should receive from parliament a vote of 30,000l. to liquidate them, and 50,000l. a year from the king. To this the duchy of Cornwall added

13,000*l.* per annum. He came of age in August, established himself at Carlton House, and took his seat in the House of Lords on 11 Nov. 1783.

The prince's first vote in parliament was given for Fox in one of the India Bill divisions on 15 Dec., and he assisted Fox in his Westminster election. Fox had fallen (18 Dec.), and the prince shared his unpopularity. For some time he lived in the closest alliance with the whig leaders, and sought amusement in an endless round of routs and masquerades, boxing matches, horse races, and drinking bouts. He lavished vast sums on alterations and decorations at Carlton House. He spent 30,000*l.* a year on his stud. By the end of 1784 he was 160,000*l.* in debt. He appealed to the king for aid, and talked of living incognito on the continent in order to retrench. The king refused either to help him or to allow him to travel. With every month he became more and more embarrassed. In 1786 he opened negotiations with the ministry for a parliamentary vote of 250,000*l.* He endeavoured to put pressure on the king by proposing to devote 40,000*l.* a year, two-thirds of his income, to paying his debts; broke up his establishment, shut up part of Carlton House, and sold his horses and carriages at auction. He lived in borrowed houses, travelled in borrowed chaises, and squandered borrowed guineas. At length a meeting of his friends was held at Pelham's house, and early in 1787 it was decided to appeal to parliament, and accordingly Alderman Newenham, member for the city of London, gave notice of a motion on the subject for 4 May.

The prince's friends were embarrassed by the allegation that, in breach of the Royal Marriage Act of 1772, he was secretly married without the king's consent, and to a Roman catholic. In 1784 he had become acquainted at Richmond with the widow of Mr. Fitzherbert of Swinnerton, Staffordshire, then a beautiful and accomplished woman of eight-and-twenty. He fell violently in love with her. She resisted his importunities. To work upon her feelings he stabbed himself so as to draw abundance of blood without risking his life, and sent complaisant friends to bring her to see him in this state of despair. She withdrew to Holland, where he persecuted her with endless couriers and correspondence. His ardour passed all bounds. He would go to Fox's mistress, Mrs. Armstead, to tell her of his love, cry by the hour, beat his brow, tear his hair, roll on the floor, and fall into fits of hysterics (see for his use of phlebotomy on these occasions, Holland's *Memoirs of the Whig Party*, ii. 68). At length in December 1785 Mrs. Fitzherbert was prevailed upon to return, on condition that a formal ceremony of marriage should be gone through. Fox, suspecting what was intended, wrote to the prince advising him to have nothing to do with a marriage. The prince replied that he was not going to marry, but on 21 Dec. he secretly went through the ceremony of marriage, by a clergyman of the church of England, with Mrs. Fitzherbert in her drawing-room in Park Lane, in the presence of her brother, John Smythe, and her uncle, Henry Errington. They thenceforth lived together openly, and in the society of his friends, male and female, she was treated with the respect due to his wife. The rumour of this union seriously endangered his chance of obtaining parliamentary assistance in 1787. The leading whigs, headed by the Duke of Portland, had declined to injure their party by espousing his cause. At the meeting at Pelham's the prince denied that he was married to Mrs. Fitzherbert, but Fox alone was eager to support him. Newenham's notice of motion was at once followed by dark hints from Rolle, M.P. for Devonshire, of an inquiry into the supposed marriage. On 30 April Fox, authorised and instructed by the prince, rose to deny that any marriage had been entered into, or form of marriage gone through. To the prince the announcement was of inestimable value; it encouraged his friends, and disarmed his enemies; but having obtained his end by throwing over Mrs. Fitzherbert, he found it necessary to pacify Mrs. Fitzherbert by throwing over Fox. Next day he owned to Grey that a ceremony had been gone through, and asked him to say something in the House of Commons to modify what Fox had said, but Grey haughtily declined (Holland, *Memoirs of the Whig Party*, ii. 139; Russell, *Memorials of Fox*, ii. 289). He told Mrs. Fitzherbert that Fox had 'exceeded his instructions.' Fox found his mouth closed. To vindicate himself was to charge the prince with lying, and for a whole year he refused to speak to him. Mrs. Fitzherbert had to console herself for her husband's slight with the increased respect which she received from the Duchesses of Portland and Devonshire, and all the leaders of whig society. Pitt now saw that no ground remained for refusing assistance which could creditably be brought forward. On 21 May a royal message was brought down, recommending an increase in the prince's income, and promising 10,000l. a year from the civil list; 161,000l. was voted to pay the debts, which amounted to that sum, and 20,000l. for the completion of Carlton House. The prince promised to be more careful in future.

The reconciliation which followed with the king was short-lived. In August the Duke of York returned from abroad, and the prince, in his company and that of Fox, Sheridan, Brummell, and Lord Rawdon, soon fell into new extravagance. Resenting the exclusion from Brooks's of his henchmen, Payne and Tarleton, he founded a new club under the management of his German cook, Weltjie, where boundless drinking and gaming went on. Here, when he was sober enough to play at all, he lost thousands of pounds a night. His I O U's became a speculative security among usurers. To add to these follies, he began in 1784 to build his costly absurdity, the Brighton Pavilion, decorated in the oriental, especially the Chinese, style. He had taken a fancy to Brighton since his first visit in 1782, and soon made it equally fashionable and dissolute. It was from Brighton that he was summoned post haste to Windsor in November 1788 by the news of the king's insanity.

The king's madness was in part brought on by distress at the prince's irregularities. On catching sight of his son, the unhappy father flew at him, clutched him by the collar, and threw him against the wall. The prince was overcome, and could only shed tears. Next day, however, he recovered himself, and assumed the direction of affairs in the castle. It was thought the king would die, and already Thurlow, the chancellor, began to ingratiate himself with the prince. The prince accepted his overtures, but also made overtures of his own through Payne to Lord Loughborough. Soon, however, it became plain that a regency would have to be provided for, and a warfare of intrigue between the prince and the queen, the whigs and the Pittites, began, first for the regency, and then for the custody of the king's person. Finding that the ministry proposed to fetter the regent with many restrictions to be imposed by parliament, the whigs put forward on behalf of the prince a claim to an indefeasible title in right of his birth to a regency without any restrictions at all. On Lord Loughborough's advice a plan was prepared by which the prince was to assume power and summon parliament by a sort of *coup d'état*. When parliament met on 20 Nov. 1788, the day to which it had been prorogued, an adjournment took place for a fortnight. The arrival of Fox from the continent gave greater consistency to the policy of the whigs, and on his advice the prince became reconciled to the Duke of Portland. By 29 Nov. matters had so far progressed that Loughborough was prevailed upon to waive his claims to the great seal in favour of Thurlow, and the prince was in a fair way to have his new ministry settled. Parliament met on 4 Dec., and a series of debates followed, in which Pitt easily exposed the inconsistency and unconstitutionality of the whig theory of the prince's right to the regency. The prince wrote to the chancellor complaining of Pitt for want of respect to him in general, and in particular for settling his proposals for the regency without any communication to himself. On 16 Dec. Pitt introduced his three resolutions as a preliminary to bills to provide for the exercise of the powers of the crown. Though the prince had openly canvassed for votes against them, the second was carried by 268 to 204, and the others were passed also. They were carried in the House of Lords by 99 to 66, and a bill was prepared. Meantime the dissensions between the queen and the prince had grown very grave. He was charged with exhibiting his mad father to visitors in the most unfeeling manner, and with insulting the queen by sealing up the king's papers and jewels which had been left at Windsor on his removal to Kew. The prince retaliated with bitter complaints of the queen, and permitted his henchmen to speak of her in his presence in a ribald manner. On 30 Dec. Pitt communicated to him the heads of the bill: the queen was to have the custody of the king and the control of his household, and although the prince, as regent, was to exercise the royal powers generally, he was not to create peerages, except in the case of his brothers as they came of age, or to convey away the king's real or personal property, or to grant pensions or offices, except during pleasure. The prince, having consulted Burke and Fox, replied on 2 Jan. 1789 in a letter, which was also revised by Loughborough and Sheridan, complaining of the restrictions as a plan for dividing the royal family, and for dislocating all the royal powers. On 16 Jan. Pitt's proposals were brought forward in the form of resolutions, and these having been passed by both houses the bill was introduced. It passed the commons on 12 Feb., and reached the lords, but in the beginning of February the king's health had begun to improve, and the progress of the bill was now suspended. Meantime the Irish parliament, on Grattan's motion on 11 Feb., had agreed to an address to the prince praying him to assume the royal powers unrestricted, and despatched a deputation of six members to London to offer him the regency in Ireland entirely unfettered. It arrived on 25 Feb., only to find the king all but restored to health. By the end of the month the king was tolerably sane again. The prince, suspecting that his recovery was exaggerated, desired to see him; but the queen, in spite of long written remonstrances, excluded him from the king's presence, so that the meeting did not take place till 23 Feb. The conversation at this interview was guarded and general, and the king suffered no relapse; but the queen contrived to prevent further interviews, and on 7 March the king was induced practically to decline to see his son. On 23 April, when the king returned thanks at St. Paul's for his recovery, the prince attended the service, but his indecorous levity on the occasion was much remarked. He also addressed to the king in writing long remonstrances against the animosity shown by the queen in the affair of Colonel Lenox's duel with the Duke of York, and a memorial explanatory of his conduct during the king's insanity, but the father and son continued to be estranged.

By 1789 the prince was again almost as deeply in debt as ever. More than double the amount granted by parliament had been spent upon Carlton House. His creditors were clamorous and dunned him in the streets. During the king's illness he and his brother, the Duke of York, with the assistance of Weltjie, the cook, had begun raising money abroad upon their joint post-obits, conditioned for payment when either should ascend the throne. Some 30,000l. was obtained in this way upon most usurious terms, but with the king's recovery these bonds lost their attraction to speculators. The prince had also, in 1788, endeavoured to raise 350,000l. in Holland upon the security of the bishopric of Osnaburg. It was brought out as a formal loan; Thomas Hammersley, a banker of Pall Mall, was to receive subscriptions and pay dividends. The loan was taken up abroad, and large sums were obtained in this way through persons named Boas, De Beaume, and Vaucher. Interest at six per cent. was paid till 1792, but when the bonds at maturity were presented for payment the prince's agents repudiated their liability. Importunate claimants were expelled the kingdom under the Alien Act. The affair began to wear the aspect of a deliberate fraud. Mrs. Fitzherbert, too, had brought her jointure into the common stock of her own and the prince's funds, and was soon almost penniless. To pay the bailiffs out of her house, the prince pawned his diamonds. Yet mere want of money was not allowed to interfere with his numerous amusements. Faro at Mrs. Hobart's, cricket at Brighton, private theatricals at Richmond House, and masked balls at Wargrave engrossed his attention. He became an ardent patron of the turf till an imputation of swindling fell at least upon his jockey, and drove him from it in dudgeon. In 1788 he won the Derby, and in the four years following took 185 prizes. His jockey, Sam Chifney, was suspected of spoiling the prince's horse, Escape, for his first race at Newmarket on 20 Oct. 1791, in order to affect the betting upon the next day's race, which the horse was allowed to win. The Jockey Club censured Chifney, and sent Sir Charles Bunbury to warn the prince that if he suffered Chifney to ride for him no gentleman's horse would start against him. The prince took deep offence. He never revisited Newmarket, but he continued racing for at least twenty years longer. He bought seven horses one after another in hopes of winning the Ascot Cup, and even so late as 1829 attended the Ascot meeting (see *Greville Memoirs*, 1st ser.). After 1792 he retired into the country, and for some time lived principally at Bagshot Park, at Kempshott Park, near Basingstoke, and at Critchill House in Dorsetshire.

At last he became so involved that for the sake of an increase of income he consented to a marriage as the only condition upon which the king could be induced to assist him. In June 1793 he employed Lord Malmesbury to arrange his affairs for him. He owed 370,000*l.*, and had executions in his house. He talked of going abroad; he sold five hundred horses and shut up Carlton House; he proposed to live in the country and devote three-fourths of his income to the payment of his debts. By August 1794 matters had proceeded so far that he had promised the king to give up Mrs. Fitzherbert and to marry the Princess of Brunswick. A reconciliation was all the more easy because, since the disunion among the leading whigs in 1792, the prince had nearly severed himself from his old friends. In November Lord Malmesbury was despatched to the court of Brunswick with a formal proposal for the princess's hand, and the prince, though he had then only seen her portrait, displayed in his correspondence with the emissary the impatience and ardour of a lover. None the less he was at the same time wholly under the influence of Lady Jersey, whose husband he appointed his master of the horse, and this person after the wedding was thrust upon the princess as her principal lady in waiting. When the Princess Caroline arrived at St. James's on 5 April 1795, she and the prince met for the first time, and he found the shock of his emotions upon that occasion so severe that, having kissed her in silence, he was obliged to drink a dram of brandy in a corner of the room. The ceremony of marriage took place on the evening of 8 April at the Chapel Royal, St. James's, and the prince was only brought through it with decorum by the prompting of his father, who was more familiar than he was with the prayer-book. Long afterwards the princess accused him of having been dead drunk most of the wedding night (*Diary of the Times of George IV*). The honeymoon was spent partly at Windsor, partly at Kempshott, but very shortly a quasi-separation took place between the prince and his wife. The marriage had been entirely without affection on either side, and he treated her without respect or even decorum. On 27 April his pecuniary position came before parliament and was debated in May. His total income was then about 73,000l. His debts since the last grant amounted to 639,890l., 500,000l. being on bonds or I O U's bearing interest. Pitt proposed to give the prince a total income of about 140,000l., with 28,000l. down for jewels and 26,000l. for Carlton House. His debts were to be liquidated by setting aside 25,000l. per annum. Even the whigs were no longer close allies of the prince, and, to his lasting displeasure, Grey moved to limit the parliamentary income to 100,000l., and Fox doubted whether it was wise after the pledges of 1787 again to apply to parliament for aid. It was said on the prince's behalf that he had never received the arrears of revenue of his duchy of Cornwall, which had accumulated during his minority to the enormous amount of 233,764l., exclusive of interest; the whole of it had been retained by the king. Pitt's proposals eventually passed the House of Commons by 93 to 68, and received the royal assent on 26 June; and a commission, consisting of the speaker, the chancellor of the exchequer, the master of the rolls, the master of the king's household, the accountant of the court of chancery, and the surveyor of the crown lands for the time being respectively, was appointed to investigate and compromise his creditors' claims. This produced much dissatisfaction, and one creditor, Jeffreys, a jeweller, who found himself almost ruined, published a series of pamphlets attacking the prince and Mrs. Fitzherbert.

The prince meantime was occupying himself with public affairs. He was persuaded by Grattan that he ought to be appointed viceroy of Ireland, and he addressed to Pitt two long memorials, dated 8 Feb. and 29 Aug. 1797, urging his claims to that post, but Pitt declined so much as to bring the subject before the king. Subsequently, in June 1798, the prince was prevailed upon to exert himself actively to obtain a pardon or commutation of sentence for Lord Edward Fitzgerald (Moore, *Life of Lord Edward Fitzgerald*, 1875, p. 203), and in the same year he again applied to the king to be sent abroad on active service with his regiment, the 10th light dragoons, of which he had been appointed colonel in 1793; his request was refused on the ground that 'military command was incompatible with the situation of the Prince of Wales.'

Meantime the Princess of Wales had been delivered of a daughter on 7 Jan. 1796. As soon as the princess recovered, a final separation took place. On 30 April, after some negotiation through Lord Cholmondeley, he wrote to her a coldly insulting letter, dated 30 April 1796, renouncing further cohabitation. The princess continued for some time to have rooms reserved for her at Carlton House, while the prince lived principally at Windsor and at Brighton. After the princess had removed to Blackheath he returned to Carlton House, and presently resumed his intimacy with Mrs. Fitzherbert.

For some time the prince concerned himself but little with public affairs. He amused himself with letters and with art. He inspected Ireland's Shakespeare forgeries, and was disposed to believe them genuine; he despatched the Rev. John Hayter to Naples to unroll papyri, at great expense and with no result; he practised music and played at faro. In 1801 he again was brought into political prominence. Under Lord Moira's influence he for the time being entertained opinions favourable to catholic emancipation. Accordingly, when the king became temporarily insane in February, the prince on 23 Feb. willingly made overtures to Pitt. Pitt insisted that if a regency should be found necessary it must be on the terms of the bill of 1789. The prince acquiesced and was in high spirits. The king, however, recovered early in March, and, in spite of a relapse a few weeks later, was able to continue to occupy the throne much as before.

After the peace of Amiens the question of the heavy arrears of the civil list came before parliament, and advantage was taken of the opportunity by the prince's friends to press his claims to the proceeds of the duchy of Cornwall during his minority. Addington desired to get rid of this inconvenient claim by a compromise, and proposed a grant of 60,000l. to the prince for three years from the previous January; this was in addition to the augmented grant of 1795 and to a further augmentation of 8,000l. a year which had been arranged by Addington in 1801; and, in spite of the fact that, as Pitt wrote to Rose on 8 March, 'these debts have been contracted in the teeth of the last act of parliament, and in breach of repeated and positive promises,' the further arrangement was carried out in February 1803. Having found Addington complaisant in money matters, the prince renewed his claim to military rank and employment. He addressed himself first to the minister on 18 July 1803, and subsequently a long correspondence took place with the king. The king, however, was resolute. He met his son's impassioned prayer to be allowed 'to shed the last drop of my blood in support of your majesty's person, crown, and dignity' with the cool reminder that 'should the implacable enemy so far succeed as to land, you will have an opportunity of showing your zeal at the head of your regiment;' nor could the prince enlist the assistance of the commander-in-chief, his brother the Duke of York. The publication of some correspondence on this subject with the prince's connivance still further embittered his relations with the king.

All through 1804 the king's health was again uncertain, and a regency appeared to be imminent. Addington, on the pretence of saving the king trouble, proposed that a council of regency should be named, of which the prince should be a member. The prince accordingly endeavoured to balance himself dexterously between the ministry and the opposition, depending on the advice of his favourite, the Earl of Moira, and communicating through Sheridan with Addington. Though he still occasionally communicated with Fox, all intimacy had ceased between them. Yet, little as he had maintained his old relations with the whig leaders, when Erskine consulted him as to the acceptance of the proffered attorney-generalship, he expressed his astonishment that such a suggestion should have been brought before him. At the same time, on his own behalf he was willing to approach Pitt, and sent Moira to the lord advocate in March 1804 with a message, intended for Pitt, saying that he had informed Fox and Grey that he would not consult them in the event of a regency, but would leave himself in Moira's hands, and suggesting a union of Fox and Pitt under Moira's moderating leadership. Pitt declined to commit himself, and when he returned to office the prince found that his elaborate strategy had failed (Russell, *Memorials of Fox*, iv. 63; Stanhope, *Pitt*, iv. 137; Moore, *Sheridan*, ii. 321–6).

During the next three years the prince's relations with his wife and daughter grew more critical. The king, who always remained friendly to his daughter-in-law and devoted to his grandchild, was desirous of providing satisfactorily for the Princess Charlotte's education. Owing to recent events, the prince had been studiously uncivil to his father. He had absented himself from the birthday drawing-room on 4 June, though he knew that the king especially desired the attendance of all his family on that day; and to show that his absence was not due to indisposition he ostentatiously showed himself in the streets all day. However, in the summer of 1804 negotiations for a reconciliation were begun by Pitt and Eldon on the king's part, and Moira and Tierney on the prince's. As a first step, an interview between the king and the prince was arranged on 12 Nov., and they became, outwardly at least, reconciled, though the prince's ill-humour was so visible that it was not thought the reconciliation could be lasting (Buckingham, *Courts and Cabinets of George III*, p. 366). Moira saw Pitt on behalf of the prince, and the king and his minister understood the prince to consent to provision being made by the king for the Princess Charlotte's education at Windsor. The prince, however, declared that he had given no such consent. Negotiations were resumed in December between the lord chancellor, acting for the king, and the prince; and at the end of the year it was arranged to place the princess under the care of Lady de Clifford and the Bishop of Exeter. Deprived of his own child, the prince interested himself in a protégée of Mrs. Fitzherbert's, Miss Mary Seymour, daughter of Lady Horace Seymour, even canvassing the House of Lords for votes when the chancery suit about the guardianship of the child came before that tribunal. He was successful in procuring a decision that the child should be placed under care of Lord Hertford, who transferred her to Mrs. Fitzherbert. It was in the course of this suit that the prince became intimately acquainted with Lady Hertford, who ultimately supplanted Mrs. Fitzherbert in his affections.

In November 1805 the Duke of Sussex took up the scandalous charges which Sir John and Lady Douglas had made against the Princess of Wales, and laid them before the prince. Actuated solely by a sense of duty, the prince consulted Thurlow and Romilly upon them in December. They advised him that the present charges were inadequately supported, and recommended further inquiry. Ultimately a commission was constituted by the king on 29 May 1806 to examine the princess's conduct. During this inquiry the prince seems to have remained passive as soon as he had obtained its institution, but the princess was ultimately exonerated by the commissioners on 14 July.

In the various changes of ministry of 1805 and 1806 the prince played a very subordinate part. He had let it be known on Pitt's return to office that, though still generally favourable to catholic emancipation, he did not wish to press the question forward at present. When Fox succeeded Pitt the prince stood aloof, and although in September, after Fox's death, he wrote effusively about it to Grey, still from this time, thinking himself not sufficiently consulted by the whig leaders, he practically severed himself from that party. In effect all that he really desired was profit for himself and place for his friends, and he saw no great prospect of obtaining either from the whigs. His friends, Moira, Erskine, and Romilly, were provided for in the 'Talents' administration, but he was not favourably disposed to Howick's Army Bill, and when the ministry fell he was gratified at the event, and announced that he had ceased to be a party man. He now extended his long-standing dislike of Grey to Lord Grenville, and when next he appeared prominently before the public was carried by these feelings of personal hostility into an opposition to them both unconstitutional and dangerous. In October 1810 the king again became deranged. The prince at first thought it wise to remain passive. Perceval determined to follow the precedents of Pitt. Parliament met on 1 Nov., and was successively adjourned till 12 Dec. The prince gave out that he would continue the present ministry subject to the admission to it of a friend of his own. Perceval, however, communicated to him on 19 Dec. that the restrictions to be proposed upon the regency were to be as before: restrictions from making peers, from granting offices in reversion or pensions, from dealing with the king's property, and from having the custody of the king's person. The prince replied evasively; but having assembled his brothers prevailed upon them to sign a protest against the restrictions, and the Duke of Sussex spoke against them in the House of Lords on 27 Dec. During the first days of 1811 the ministry met with more than one defeat in parliament, and the prince at once veered towards Lords Grenville and Grey. He consulted them upon the answer which he was to return to the address of the two houses, and they submitted to him a draft of his reply. The prince, however, then privately submitted it to Adam and Sheridan, and, following their counsel, decided to reject it and to prepare another. With this Lord Grey, who disapproved of it altogether, would have nothing to do, and on 11 Jan. he and Grenville addressed a brief note to the prince to the effect that they understood they had been applied to as his public and responsible advisers, expressing their 'deep concern' at his treatment, and declining to be in any way responsible for his letter. Sheridan's own account of the transaction did not get rid of the inference that Grey and Grenville had been both foolishly and uncivilly treated, but rather convicted himself and the prince of duplicity (see Sheridan's 'Letter to Lord Holland,' 15 Jan., in Moore's *Sheridan*). Amends were eventually made to the two lords, and they undertook the task of considering what administration they could form, stipulating, however, with the prince that he was not to call into council any secret advisers. By 21 Jan. the general outlines of arrangements were settled, but when they came to the distribution of particular offices they found that the prince had already made promises of the chancellorship to Erskine, the Irish secretaryship to Sheridan, and similar dispositions. These they rather unceremoniously overrode. But at this point, about the end of the month, the king seemed in a fair way of recovery, and the prince oscillated again towards his father's ministers. He consulted his friends Lady Hertford and Mrs. Fitzherbert, who used their powerful influence with him in favour of Perceval, and through Sir Henry Halford he was in communication with the queen, and through her with the ministers. He yielded at last to these advisers, and on 1 Feb. announced to Lords Grenville and Grey that he should not require their services, and on the 4th to Perceval his intention of continuing his father's servants in office. The disappointment of the whigs was great, but they hoped for future favour when the period of restriction upon the regent's powers should have expired.

The Regency Bill having passed on 5 Feb. 1811, the prince took the oaths as regent, and virtually, though not in form, began his reign. But although, contrary to general expectation (Romilly, *Diary*, ii. 365; *Life of Wilberforce*, iii. 492), he had decided not to dismiss the ministry, he took care to let them feel that his favour was not to be counted upon. He placed busts of Fox and the Duke of Bedford in the privy council chamber; he communicated with his ministers through his servants, Macmahon and Turner. On 20 Feb. he held his first levee, and he celebrated his accession to power by a costly entertainment of the most tasteless and extravagant kind at Carlton House on 19 June. He made use of this occasion to break with Mrs. Fitzherbert, by refusing her at his table any precedence above that to which her own position entitled her. In his political sympathies he showed a curious vacillation. He sanctioned the suppression of the Irish 'catholic committee' on the one hand, and, on the other, caused a radical address in favour of reform, which had been presented to him, to be printed in the 'Gazette.' He occupied himself with the plans for laying out the Regent's Park and surrounding terraces, and, having returned to Brighton for the recess, amused himself by giving a number of concerts. As, however, the time for the expiry of the restrictions approached, signs appeared of an intention to reconsider the constitution of his ministry. He began about September to cultivate close relations with one member of the cabinet, the Marquis Wellesley. That the prince had before him any definite plan would be too much to assume; he wavered in his preferences almost from day to day; but as time went on two facts became apparent: his close reliance on Wellesley, and his personal dislike of Grey and Grenville. Yet his liking for Eldon and his objection to the catholic claims were a barrier to complete confidence in Wellesley, and public opinion was steadily growing in favour of some combination which would restore the whig leaders to the service of their country. The prince's principal interest in the arrangements seems to have been to secure the best terms that he could for himself. To his indignation Perceval had withdrawn from his original proposal of 150,000l. to defray the extra expenses of the regency, and had reduced it to 100,000l. The prince employed Wellesley to urge upon the cabinet that the king should have a suitable but modest establishment, the queen and princesses separate allowances, and that he should himself take over the entire civil list and state of the sovereign. To this Perceval would not consent (see *Life of Perceval*, ii. 227; *Wellington's Supplementary Despatches*, iii. 257; McCullagh Torrens, *Marquis Wellesley*, p. 465).

When parliament met on 7 Jan. 1812 the public mind was in an excited condition. The catholic question was brought forward by the opposition, and this was inconvenient alike to the prince and his ministers; it produced a division between Wellesley and the rest of the cabinet, and placed the prince, who had on many occasions expressed his agreement with the catholic claims, in the difficult position of having to choose between his preferences and his consistency. To add to his troubles he was out of health. He had become very fat; he suffered from symptoms in the head that seemed to threaten paralysis; and in the previous November, while teaching his daughter the highland fling at the Duchess of York's ball at Oatlands, he had struck against a sofa and severely sprained his ankle and broken two tendons. He bore his pain with little fortitude, refusing to attend to business, and resorting to laudanum every three hours to such an extent that he took as much as seven hundred drops a day. Naturally, therefore, in January 1812 he was in a state of body highly disordered. With some dexterity, however, he induced the cabinet to agree to treat the catholic question as an open one. The defeat of the catholics being thus assured, the Marquis Wellesley resigned on 17 Jan. The prince now had to consider how to deal with Lords Grenville and Grey, and he appears to have conceived an adroit plan to fulfil popular expectations by inviting them to enter his service, and yet so to frame the invitation that they must necessarily refuse it on grounds which would appear punctilious and unaccommodating. He addressed a letter to his brother the Duke of York, dated 13 Feb. 1812, intended to be communicated to the two lords, in which he expressed the gratification he should feel 'if some of those persons with whom the early habits of my public life were formed would strengthen my hands and constitute a part of my government.' The two lords wrote to the duke two days later to say that on grounds of 'honour and duty' they were unable to unite with the present government. They insisted upon a total change in the system of administration and upon concession to the catholic claims. For the present Perceval and his colleagues remained undisturbed, as indeed, secure in the support of the Marchioness of Hertford, they had all along felt certain of being. But the regent was very unpopular. As he went in state on 23 Feb. to the Chapel Royal, his first appearance as sovereign, 'not a huzza was heard, not a hat was raised.' The ministerial negotiations were brought before the House of Lords on 19 March, and Lord Grey openly accused the prince of having broken express promises made to the catholics, and of being dominated by the influence of his favourite. Among other lampoons upon him was the attack in the

'Examiner,' describing him as a 'libertine' and a 'corpulent gentleman of fifty,' for which the Hunts were indicted and imprisoned. But unexpectedly the whole imbroglio was revived after the lapse of only a few weeks by the assassination of Perceval on 11 May 1812.

Personally the prince was anxious to retain in office a ministry which would follow the lines of Perceval's policy, and he asked the cabinet whether they would be willing to go on under a prime minister whom he would choose from among them. They returned a doubtful assent, and wished overtures to be made either to Wellesley and Canning or to Grenville and Grey. On 17 May Lord Liverpool opened communications with Canning. But on the 21st the prince's hand was forced. Matters being still unsettled, Stuart Wortley moved an address to the prince regent praying him to cause a firmer administration to be formed, and carried it against ministers by a majority of four. It was presented to the prince next day by Lord Milton and Stuart Wortley, and the ministry resigned. They remained, however, during the ensuing crisis in temporary discharge of their duties, and were in so little doubt that with the assistance of the Hertford influence they would retain their places, that Eldon did not trouble himself to pronounce judgment in a single one of the many cases pending before him. The prince sent for Lord Wellesley, who, though he had thought himself betrayed in January, now proposed to form an administration upon the basis of catholic emancipation and the vigorous prosecution of the Peninsular war. After some negotiations with the whigs, on 23 May, which were met by Grenville's well-founded doubt of the prince's sincerity, the prince, on 25 May, gave Wellesley full liberty in forming an administration. Although he had vacillated upon Grattan's motion in favour of emancipation earlier in the year, at one time desiring his friends to oppose it, at another to support it, he now promised the marquis his full support on the catholic question, but bitterly opposed the inclusion of any of the opposition in the ministry. As a body he said he would rather abdicate the regency than come in contact with them, and, when Wellesley pointed out to him that no ministry founded on a principle of exclusion could be honourable or permanent, the conflict between his antipathy to Grey and the necessity in which his situation placed him was so acute that for the time being he became almost deranged with irritation (see Buckingham, *Courts and Cabinets of the Regency*). Wellesley's efforts failing, the prince had recourse on 27 May to Moira, who endeavoured to reconcile the regent to Grey by sending the Duke of York on 31 May to remonstrate with his brother. The result merely was that the prince quarrelled with the duke. What rankled in his mind was Grey's phrase used in the House of Lords on 19 May, that there was 'an unseen and pestilent secret influence behind the throne, which it would be the duty of parliament to brand with some signal mark of condemnation.' On 1 June he again had recourse to Wellesley, who came to Grey authorised to form an administration in conjunction with him. But Grey found that it was already settled with the prince that Moira, Erskine, and Canning were to be in the cabinet, and that only four places were to be open to the nominees of himself and Grenville. He refused to negotiate on the principle of disunion and jealousy and the supposed balance of contending interests, and on 3 June Wellesley announced to the House of Lords that, owing to the 'dreadful animosities' with which he met, he had failed to form any administration.

Though not very openly talked of, the last remaining point upon which the prince would not give way was the household, where Lady Hertford's son, Lord Yarmouth, held high office. Grey and Grenville required that the household should go out with the other ministers. The regent now began to be frightened. He invested Moira with authority to form a government. Moira asked if this included the filling up of the household, and although the prince consented, Moira, for some inexplicable reason, undertook that the existing household should not be dismissed. Accordingly he found, on again applying to Grey and Grenville, that he had effectually prevented the success of his attempts, and after three weeks of negotiations the crisis came to an end by Lord Liverpool becoming first lord of the treasury on 9 June 1812.

The prince next came into conflict with his wife and with the Princess Charlotte, who showed herself warmly attached to her mother's cause. At the beginning of 1813 she intimated to her father that she would no longer submit to be under governesses; but under the pressure which, with the assistance of Eldon, he put upon her, she gave way. The prince, always jealous of his wife, conceived that she had incited the Princess Charlotte to this resistance, and brought the intercourse of mother and child before the privy council, which decided that the restrictions upon it ought to continue as before. Upon the pretext that the Princess of Wales had caused the publication in the 'Morning Chronicle' on 10 Feb. of the letter she had addressed to George on 14 Jan.—a letter of strong remonstrance composed by Brougham—the prince refused to allow her to see her daughter. Later on he made a pretext of himself requiring Kensington Palace, in order to deprive his wife of her residence there. To relieve himself of the embarrassment of managing the Princess Charlotte, he decided to procure her marriage, and selected the Prince of Orange as her husband, but after a few months the princess's resistance baffled his design. When the exiled king of France came up to London before the restoration in 1814, the prince carefully excluded his wife and daughter from any share in the festivities, and when the allied sovereigns visited England he sent Sir

Thomas Tyrwhitt to the czar requesting him not to carry out his intention of visiting the Princess of Wales. The ceremonies attending their reception were entirely after the regent's own heart, and he played his part in the pageants with a satisfaction alloyed only by the marked disfavour with which the public, even at that juncture, received him. When he endeavoured to induce the committee of White's Club to exclude the Princess of Wales from their ball, they took such offence that they abandoned their ball altogether. At length his difficulties cleared away. The Princess Charlotte was allowed to become betrothed to Prince Leopold in January 1816. In the previous August the Princess of Wales had finally left England. The regent, whose excesses had impaired even his constitution, and brought him to the verge of death in September 1816, obtained an opportunity of recruiting his health and his reputation by living a quiet life, and attracting as little public attention as possible.

Unfortunately, he continued to come before the public in the most unpopular way. Tierney brought to light the enormous extravagance of his expenditure since he had become regent. The 100,000*l.* then provided by Perceval as his outfit had been diverted to the payment of pressing debts. 160,000*l.* had since been lavished on furniture for Carlton House. His silversmith's bill was 130,000*l.*, and, in spite of the scheme for liquidating his debts which had now been many years in operation, they still amounted to 339,000*l.* It is hardly surprising that after these revelations a populace, impoverished and almost starving after so long a war, wrote ominously upon his walls, 'Bread, or the Regent's head.' He had retired to the less conspicuous publicity of Brighton; but his very unpopularity made residence in London important, and Lord Liverpool strongly insisted upon the inconvenience and even danger of his absence. He appeared in public surrounded by troops, and in vain attempted to elude the hatred of the crowd by stealing across the park to the Chapel Royal in a private carriage. The mob hung hissing upon his carriage-wheels. As he returned from opening parliament in January 1817 they stoned his coach, and were said to have fired on him with air-guns. For his protection the act of 1795, for the security of the king's person, was extended to cover the person of the regent. His unpopularity increased, and his hold on the people diminished, after the death of the Princess Charlotte on 6 Nov. 1817, an event by which he was himself as a father so deeply affected that he sought relief for his feelings by being cupped and bled. He diverted himself by yachting and attending regattas; and as soon as, by his mother's death on 17 Nov. 1818, Buckingham House, the old 'Queen's House,' fell into his hands, he threw himself with ardour into the congenial extravagance of reconstructing it. Nash, the architect, was taken under his patronage, and the quarter of London about the Regent's Park, together with Regent Street, the

Quadrant, and Waterloo Place, was erected during the regency with his sanction and encouragement.

George III died on 29 Jan. 1820. The new king nearly died in the hour of his accession to the throne. He had been too ill to attend his father's deathbed, and the inflammation, due to a chill, from which he suffered was, on the night of 1 Feb., so acute that he was in danger of suffocation, and was saved only by a bleeding so severe that it alone almost killed him. No less than 130 oz. of blood was taken from him (Colchester, *Diary*, iii. 111). On recovering his first step was, on 6 Feb., to consider how to deal with the prayer in the Book of Common Prayer which prays for 'our most Gracious Queen' (*Croker Papers*). His next was to employ the servant whom he most relied upon, Sir William Knighton, to compromise, buy up, or pay off his outstanding and long-overdue debts, bonds, and notes of hand, and during the next ten years Knighton was constantly and successfully engaged in delicate and secret negotiations with this object. He then pressed his ministry to attack the queen, against whom he had since 1818 been collecting evidence; and now, upon her determination to return to England and assert her claims, he resolved to take steps for a divorce. His ministers were at first loth to assist him, and in a cabinet minute of 10 Feb. 1820 recorded their opinion that the evidence was inadequate. 'The cabinet,' writes Croker, 'offer all but divorce. The king will have divorce or nothing.' As the queen drew nearer to England, George urged Lord Liverpool to endeavour to come to some compromise with Brougham, by which she would be induced to remain on the continent; but the queen reached England in the first days of June. On the 6th the king sent to the House of Lords a message recommending to their attention the evidence which had been collected against her, and the divorce proceedings began. During the remainder of the year, though the king remained inexorably resolved that they should go on to the end, his hand did not openly appear in the matter. The Divorce Bill was a ministerial bill, and the proceedings went on in the House of Lords without the king's intervention. Even after it had been withdrawn he bore himself with outward indifference to its failure.

In the spring of 1821 he was engrossed with the preparations for his coronation, the outlay on which was on the most profuse and elaborate scale. Sheltered by his ministers he was able to refuse the queen's request to be present at the ceremony, and even carried this affectation of indifference so far as to return her letters unopened to Lord Liverpool (1 May 1821), 'in conformity to a resolution adopted more than twenty years ago, and since invariably adhered to by the king, that the king would never again receive or open any letter or paper addressed to him personally by the queen'. The ceremony took place with great pomp, but the expense was so enormous and the exclusion of the public so complete that it produced only unpopularity. The royal robes alone cost 24,000*l.*, the crown 54,000*l.* The king next made preparations for visiting Ireland, and landed at Howth, from the Lightning packet, on 12 Aug., undeterred by the news of his wife's death (7 Aug.), which he had just received. 'The king was uncommonly well during his passage and gayer than it might be proper to tell,' but in deference to his bereavement he postponed his entry into Dublin until the 17th. He quitted Ireland on 3 Sept., after a series of festivities, to which all parties contributed with enthusiastic loyalty; but the weather was so unfavourable that it was not till the 13th, after considerable peril, that he landed at Milford. He next arranged to visit Hanover. He left England 24 Sept., and, travelling via Calais and Brussels, in about a week reached Osnaburg and Hanover, where he remained till the end of October. It was on this journey that he encountered his old friend Brummell, almost destitute, at Calais, and passed him by without recognition or relief. To complete the tour of his dominions he next visited Scotland, and landed at Leith on 14 Aug. 1822, remaining in Edinburgh till the 29th. Lord Londonderry's death occurred during his absence, and on his return to town he was engaged in the arrangements for a reconstitution of the ministry. He resisted as long as he could the introduction of Canning into the cabinet, but at length he yielded on 8 Sept. When Canning had retired in 1820 the king had parted from him with expressions of goodwill, but subsequently he took offence because Canning's friends in the House of Lords opposed the Divorce Bill, as he supposed at Canning's instigation. Greville also reports that Canning had insisted that the expense of the Milan commission should be defrayed by the king and not by the state (see this exclusion of Canning from office 1820–2, discussed in Stapleton, *Correspondence of Canning*, vol. i.). For some time after Canning became foreign secretary he found himself thwarted by the king, who derived from some of the other ministers, especially Lord Westmorland, private information and advice, and even communicated directly with the foreign ambassadors. Now, however, and for the remainder of his life, he withdrew himself almost completely from the public view. Except to open and prorogue parliament, he made no public appearance in London after his visit to the two theatres in 1823. He spent his time, attended, without any concealment, by his mistress, Lady Conyngham, at Brighton, and latterly almost entirely at Windsor, where he built a pagoda at Virginia Water and established a menagerie. Signs of dropsy had begun to appear, and, apprehensive of being ridiculed for his unwieldy bulk, he took extraordinary precautions to prevent himself from being seen even while driving in Windsor Park. As the catholic question grew more pressing his opposition to emancipation became more decided, and it was also with great reluctance that he was brought to consent to the recognition of the Spanish-American republics (see Stapleton, *Correspondence of Canning*). In 1825 it was known that he supported the Duke of York in his almost passionate denunciation of the measures for the relief of the catholics. At the end of the year he came to an understanding with Canning, that his objections to catholic relief were to be respected, and thenceforward their relations became more amicable. Upon the retirement of Lord Liverpool (February 1827) he was at first desirous of keeping Canning out of the first place, making some peer, to be selected by the cabinet, Liverpool's successor, and retaining the existing ministry; but this proving impracticable, and the delay in the formation of a ministry being now serious, he commissioned Canning on 10 April to form a ministry. During this crisis his health was bad, and excitement and indecision rendered it worse. In a long interview with the Duke of Buckingham he explained that his chief anxiety had been to keep together a cabinet which would let the catholic question rest. Next the Duke of Wellington resigned his position of commander-in-chief, and the king was with difficulty convinced that it would be unconstitutional for him to assume the direct command of the army himself. After Canning's death (8 Aug. 1827) all the troubles of the spring began again. Contrary to expectation the king, instead of selecting a 'protestant' premier, commissioned Lord Goderich to form an administration. He was very anxious to have Herries included as chancellor of the exchequer, and after considerable pressure induced him to accept the seals. It was thought that he desired this because Herries was intimate with Knighton, his confidential servant, and was consequently, though wrongly, supposed to be likely to yield to the king's wishes on money matters. During the existence of Lord Goderich's weak ministry in 1827–8 the king assumed considerable freedom in disposing of patronage and appointments without consulting his ministers. By the end of the year 1828 dissensions had broken out in the cabinet, and Lord Goderich resigned. The Duke of Wellington was sent for and formed a strong protestant administration. The only person whom the king had refused to accept as a minister was Grey, but the duke had no difficulty in forming a tory ministry. For twelve months the king enjoyed comparative peace, though it was with reluctance that he accepted the Test and Corporation Acts; but when the ministry was compelled in 1829 to face the necessity for catholic emancipation, he offered a resistance which not even his habitual awe of the firm management of the Duke of Wellington could overcome, and he was all the less fitted for a contest by the fact that he suffered from chronic inflammation of the bladder, and his dropsical and gouty swellings were increasing, both preventing him from taking any wholesome exercise and necessitating the use of large quantities of laudanum. All through the autumn of 1828, in proportion as Peel and Wellington became favourable to emancipation, the king became more suspicious of them and more determined against it. Lord Anglesey's encouragement of the catholic association in December threw him into a fury, and early in January 1829 his agitation was so great that it was thought that the family tendency to insanity might break out in him. He talked freely of laying his head on the block rather than yield. On 26 Jan. the duke went to Windsor with a cabinet minute, stating the intentions of the ministry to introduce a Catholic Relief Bill, and the grounds on which they were acting. This he carefully got signed by his majesty. Thus pinned down, the king assented to the speech with which the session was opened, announcing that the ministry would propose a measure of catholic relief. Soon, however, influenced by the Duke of Cumberland, he began to waver. The Duke of Wellington was obliged to see him again on 26 and 27 Feb., and after an interview of five hours he was again brought to acquiesce in the policy of his ministers. But the defeat of Peel at Oxford revived his hopes. On 1 March he obstinately refused to direct his household to vote for the Relief Bill, and protested he would rather abdicate. A cabinet was then held, and he was reminded that he had signed a memorandum of his adhesion to this policy. On 4 March he sent for the duke, the chancellor, and Peel, and said he must have a clearer explanation of their policy. He was told the oaths of supremacy were to be repealed. He protested he had never understood that, and could never consent to it, and after five hours of discussion the resignation of his ministers was tendered and accepted. Next day, however, he repented, and wrote to the duke that he would yield, and the ministry was allowed to proceed with its bill. For some time he continued to complain to his visitors of the violence done to his feelings, and the injudicious provision which compelled O'Connell to undergo a second election in Clare was inserted to gratify his resentment; but his resistance to his ministers, except in a few matters of patronage, and indeed his political activity of any kind, was now at an end. His health began clearly to fail. No one but Knighton could induce him even to sign the necessary documents of state. He lay all day in bed and passed his nights in restless wakefulness. He kept his room at a high temperature and drank excessive quantities of cherry brandy. By February of 1830 he had become partially blind, and his singular delusions, such as that he had commanded a division at Waterloo and ridden a winning race at Goodwood, were in high force. On 12 April he drove out for the last time. Those about him knew, though he did not, that he was sinking. In May the Duke of Wellington caused the Bishop of Winchester to attend on him to prepare him for his end. Though Knighton thought he might rally, Halford and Tierney had given him over. On the 23rd he signed a request to parliament that a stamp might be substituted for the sign-manual. On 8 June he learned with fortitude that his end was near. In the night of the 25th he suddenly died. He was buried in St. George's Chapel, Windsor.

When his affairs came to be looked into, a curious condition of things was revealed. He seemed to have had a mania for misplaced hoarding. All the coats, boots, and pantaloons of fifty years were in his wardrobe, and to the end he carried the catalogue of them all in his head, and could call for any one of them at any moment. He had five hundred pocket-books, and all contained small sums of money laid by and forgotten; 10,000*l*. in all was thus collected. There were countless bundles of women's love letters, of women's gloves, of locks of women's hair. These were destroyed. In 1823 Lord Eldon had made the king's will, and the executors were Lord Gifford and Sir W. Knighton, but his private effects were of comparatively small value.

The character of George IV was a singular mixture of good talents and mean failings. Undoubtedly he was clever and versatile, and, lazy though he was, he acquired a fair dilettante knowledge of many things. When he chose he could prove himself a capable man of business, nor could a person who associated with all the distinguished men of two generations, and won the regard of not a few of them, have been either without natural merit of his own, or incapable of profiting by their society. He had considerable mimetic talent (see *Macvey Napier's Correspondence*, p. 276; Campbell, *Chief Justices*, iii. 245), and could assume a most gracious and winning manner at will, which accounted for, if it did not justify, his title of the 'first gentleman in Europe.' Undoubtedly he was master of that art which is called 'deportment.' 'Louis XIV himself,' says Wraxall, 'could scarcely have surpassed the son of George III in a ballroom, or when doing the honours of his palace, surrounded by the pomp and attributes of luxury and royal state.' But he often chose to be coarse, gross, and rude in his own demeanour, and the tone of manners of which he set the fashion was unrefined and vulgar. His flatterers called him a good musician, but Croker, who knew him well, says in 1822: 'His voice, a bass, is not good, and he does not sing so much from notes as from recollection. He is therefore as a musician very far from good.' In conversation he was very amusing and talkative, and passionately fond of gossip, and what he most sought for in his companions was deference without awe, and a capacity for keeping him amused. But his memory was very inaccurate, and his word wholly untrustworthy. The long statement which he dictated to Croker in 1825 for publication, which is given in the 'Croker Papers,' purported to correct the errors in the account given in Moore's 'Life of Sheridan' of the negotiations for a change of ministry in 1811 and 1812; but as an authority for the events of those years it is not to be relied upon. It is rather a political apology and a statement of the view which he would have desired the world should take of his conduct down to 1812, than a statement of fact. He was extraordinarily dissolute. In addition to his five more or less historic connections with Mrs. Robinson and Mrs. Fitzherbert, and Ladies Jersey, Hertford, and Conyngham, Lloyd and Huish, who devote much curious industry to this topic, enumerate eleven other persons by name and two others unnamed who were at one time or other his mistresses, and intimates the existence of very many other more temporary intrigues. Greville, who knew him well, and had no reason to judge him unfairly, says of him: 'This confirms the opinion I have long had, that a more contemptible, cowardly, unfeeling, selfish dog does not exist than this king.' In substance this is likely to be the judgment of posterity. There have been more wicked kings in English history, but none so unredeemed by any signal greatness or virtue. That he was a dissolute and drunken fop, a spendthrift and a gamester, 'a bad son, a bad husband, a bad father, a bad subject, a bad monarch, and a bad friend,' that his word was worthless and his courage doubtful, are facts which cannot be denied, and though there may be exaggerations in the scandals which were current about him, and palliation for his vices in an ill-judged education and overpowering temptations, there was not in his character any of that staple of worth which tempts historians to revise and correct a somewhat too emphatic contemporary condemnation. All that can be said in his favour is this. The fact that his character was one which not even his own partisans could respect or defend caused the personal power of the monarch, which was almost at its highest when he became regent, to dwindle almost to a shadow years before he died.

Three portraits by Sir Thomas Lawrence and a marble statue by Chantrey are at Windsor. Portraits by West as a boy (with the Duke of York), and by Owen after Hoppner, are at Hampton Court. An unfinished portrait by Lawrence is in the National Portrait Gallery.

[Duke of Buckingham's Courts and Cabinets of George III, the Regency, and George IV, 1853; Lord John Russell's Memorials of Fox, 1862; Lord Holland's Memoirs of the Whig Party, 1854; Moore's Sheridan; Moore's Diary; Memoirs of Lord Malmesbury; Memoirs and Correspondence of Lord Auckland, 1861; Cornwallis Correspondence; Stanhope's Pitt; Life and Letters of Sir Gilbert Elliot, first lord Minto, 1874; Lord Colchester's Diary, 1861; Croker Papers, ed. Jennings; Greville Memoirs, 1st ser.; Twiss's Life of Eldon, 1844; Life of Sir J. Romilly; Lady Bury's Diary of Times of George IV; Cobbett's History of the Regency; Lives of George IV, by G. Croly, P. Fitzgerald, R. Huish, H. L. Lloyd, and Wallace; Langdale's Memoirs of Mrs. Fitzherbert; Jesse's George III; Horace Walpole's Journals and Correspondence; Gronow's Reminiscences; Massey's History of England, 1865, ending in 1802; Thackeray's Four Georges;

Mrs. Delany's Autobiography, ed. Lady Llanover, 1861–2; Wraxall's Memoirs, 1884.]

JOHN ANDREW HAMILTON

published 1889

FREDERICK Augustus

(1763–1827)

Duke of York and Albany

Second son of George III and Queen Charlotte, was born at St. James's Palace on 16 Aug. 1763, and on 27 Feb. 1764 he was elected to the valuable bishopric of Osnaburg through the influence of his father as elector of Hanover. He was educated with the greatest care at Kew, and became the constant companion of his elder brother, afterwards George IV. In 1767 he was invested a knight of the Bath, and in 1771 a knight of the Garter. On 1 Nov. 1780 he was gazetted a colonel in the army, and in the following year was sent to Hanover to study French and German. He studied not only tactics but the minutiæ of regimental discipline, and varied his studies by visits to the Austrian and Prussian military manœuvres. He created a favourable impression in every court he visited, and in 1782 was presented to Frederick the Great. Meanwhile the Bishop of Osnaburg, as he was generally styled, was appointed colonel of the 2nd horse grenadier guards, now the 2nd life guards, on 23 March 1782; promoted major-general on 20 Nov. 1782, and lieutenant-general on 27 Oct. 1784, on which day he succeeded the Duke of Richmond as colonel of the 2nd or Coldstream guards. On 27 Nov. 1784 Prince Frederick was created Duke of York and Albany in the peerage of Great Britain, and Earl of Ulster in the peerage of Ireland. He retained the bishopric of Osnaburg till 1803.

In 1787 the Duke of York returned to England, where he was received with enthusiasm by all classes (see *Gent. Mag.* lvii. 734). He was the favourite of his father, and the Prince of Wales was devotedly attached to him. His kindly manners, generous disposition, and handsome face made him popular in society. He took his seat in the House of Lords on 27 Nov. 1787, and on 15 Dec. 1788 he made, on the question of the regency in opposition to Pitt's Regency Bill, a speech which attracted attention, as it was held to convey the sentiments of the Prince of Wales. On 26 May 1789 he fought a duel on Wimbledon Common with Colonel Lennox, afterwards Duke of Richmond, who was aggrieved by some of the duke's remarks. The duke coolly received the fire of Colonel Lennox, and then fired in the air. His coolness and his refusal to avail himself of his rank to decline the challenge were much applauded. In January 1791 a marriage was arranged for him with Princess Frederica Charlotte Ulrica Catherina (*b* 7 May 1767), eldest daughter of Frederick William II, king of Prussia, whose acquaintance he made during his visits to Berlin. Parliament granted him an additional income of 18,000*l.* a year, and the king gave him 7,000*l.* a year on the Irish revenue, which sums, with the revenues of the bishopric of Osnaburgh, raised his income to 70,000*l.* a year. The marriage was celebrated at Berlin on 29 Sept. 1791, and at the queen's house, London, on 23 Nov. The princess was received with enthusiasm in London, where it is noted among other demonstrations of respect that a great sale was found even for imitations of the princess's slipper. The husband and wife soon separated, and the Duchess of York retired to Oatlands Park, Weybridge, Surrey, where she amused herself with her pet dogs, and died 6 Aug. 1820, being buried in Weybridge church.

On the outbreak of war in 1793 George III insisted that York should take command of the English contingent despatched to Flanders to co-operate with the Austrian army under the Prince of Coburg. The campaigns of 1793, 1794, and 1795 in Flanders served to prove that the English army was unable to cope with the enthusiastic French republicans, and that York was not a born military commander. His staff, and especially his adjutant and quartermaster-generals, Craig and Murray, were chiefly responsible; the duke showed himself brave but inexperienced, and there is much truth in Gillray's caricatures and Peter Pindar's squibs, which represented him as indulging too freely in the prevalent dissipation of his officers. In 1793 the allied army drove the French army out of Belgium, defeated it at Tournay and Famars, and took Valenciennes on 26 July. Then came a difference between the generals; the Prince of Coburg wished to march on Paris, while York was ordered to take Dunkirk. The armies separated, and Carnot at once concentrated all the best French troops and attacked the duke in his lines before Dunkirk. After severe fighting at Hondschoten on 6 and 8 Sept. the English had to fall back, and, after the defeat of the Austrians at Wattignies, finally joined them at Tournay, where both armies went into winter quarters. In February 1794 the duke joined the head-quarters of the army in Flanders, and the new campaign opened with some slight successes at Cateau Cambrésis, Villiers-en-Cauche, and Troixville. But on 10, 14, and 18 May the French army under Pichegru attacked the English army at Tournay. In the last engagement the English were entirely defeated, and would have been destroyed but for the conduct of Generals Ralph Abercromby and Henry Edward Fox. York himself was nearly taken prisoner. After this defeat the English army steadily fell back, in spite of the arrival in July of ten thousand fresh troops under the Earl of Moira. The duke was, in fact, driven out of Belgium after several severe engagements. There followed the terrible winter retreat of 1794–5, which concluded the unsuccessful campaign. York shared the perils of the retreat up to the beginning of December, in which month he returned to England.

The duke's reputation had not been raised. Nevertheless George III promoted him to be a field-marshal on 18 Feb. 1795, and made him commander-in-chief of the army 3 April 1798. Amherst, the retiring commander-in-chief, was an old man, who had allowed countless abuses in the discipline and administration of the army. The duke by his high rank could be considered as belonging to no party, and he was able from his position to put down much of the jobbery which had disgraced his predecessor's tenure of office. He was not a man of brilliant parts, but he determined to remove some of the abuses which he had seen in Flanders.

In 1799 he was appointed to command an army destined to invade Holland in conjunction with a Russian corps d'armée. The vanguard of this army, under Sir Ralph Abercromby and Admiral Sir Charles Mitchell, performed an important duty in capturing the Dutch ships in the Helder; but when the main force arrived under the duke on 13 Sept. nothing but disaster followed. Generals Brune and Daendaels collected an army, which, though defeated on 19 Sept., 2 Oct., and 9 Oct., managed to keep the English and Russians penned on the narrow strip of land seized by Abercromby, and on 17 Oct. the duke signed the disgraceful convention of Alkmaer, by which the victors were allowed to leave Holland on condition that eight thousand French prisoners of war should be surrendered to the republic. This failure confirmed the general opinion that the duke was unfit for the command of an army in the field.

The attention of the public was now turned to the state of the army; money was not spared by parliament, and while Abercromby was engaged in the Mediterranean in restoring the true spirit of discipline in the field, the duke devoted himself to the task of weeding out incapable officers, and encouraging those who did their duty. It was nothing short of a disaster that York was on 18 March 1809 forced to retire from his post of commander-in-chief. He had become entangled with a handsome adventuress, Mary Anne Clarke, who made money out of her intimacy with the commander-in-chief, by promising promotion to officers, who paid her for her recommendations. This matter was raised in the House of Commons by Colonel Wardle on 27 Jan. 1809, and referred to a select committee, which took evidence on oath. The inquiries of this committee proved that York had shown most reprehensible carelessness in his dealings with Mrs. Clarke, but he could not be convicted of receiving money himself, and the House of Commons acquitted him of any corrupt practices by 278 votes to 196. Sir

David Dundas, who succeeded the duke at the Horse Guards, continued his policy, and the action of the prince regent in replacing his brother at the head of the army in May 1811 was received with almost unanimous satisfaction. The House of Commons rejected Lord Milton's motion censuring the ministry for allowing the appointment by 296 votes to 47.

No other scandal marked the duke's career. He was twice thanked by the houses of parliament, in July 1814 and July 1815, after the battle of Waterloo, for the benefits he had bestowed on the army and his unremitting attention to his duties as commander-in-chief; and in 1818, on the death of Queen Charlotte, he was appointed guardian of the person of the king, with an allowance of 10,000l. a year. The death of George III made York heir to the throne, but he continued to hold his post at the Horse Guards. The real affection which George IV entertained for him made him an important personage, but he never interfered much with politics. He opposed catholic emancipation, and on 25 April 1825, in a speech in the House of Lords, declared his opinions in opposition to it in a speech which was held to embody the ideas of his royal brother. In July 1826 York was attacked with dropsy, and after a long illness, borne with exemplary fortitude, he died at the Duke of Rutland's house in Arlington Street on 5 Jan. 1827. His body lay in state in St. James's Palace, and on 19 Jan. 1827 he was buried in St. George's Chapel, Windsor, his brother, the Duke of Clarence, acting as chief mourner.

The conduct of York as commander-in-chief had the greatest influence on the history of the British army. He supported the efforts successfully to revive military spirit made by commanders in the field, and by his own subordinates, above all by his military secretary, Sir Henry Torrens. Without his strenuous support the regulations of Sir David Dundas could not have been successful, nor the quartermaster-general's department purified. He looked well after the soldiers and their comforts, but it was with the officers that he was most successful. He set apart every Tuesday as a levée day, in which any officer might have an audience. He sternly put down the influence of personal favouritism. The purchase system was in force during his tenure of office, but a certain amount of military service in every rank was required before an officer could purchase a step, and it was impossible for boys at school to hold rank as colonels. The duke did much to eradicate political jobbery in military appointments, and set his face against systematic corruption. Though he had himself failed on the field, he generously recognised the superior merits of Wellington and his subordinates.

York was good-tempered and affable; he was a sportsman, and kept a racing stable, which was superintended by Greville, the diarist, and he possessed the open, if unintellectual, features common to his brothers. His name is better commemorated by his foundation of the Duke of York's School for the sons of soldiers, Chelsea, London, than by the column which bears his name at the end of Waterloo Place, St. James's Park, London.

> [Annual Register for 1827, pp. 436–67, contains the best contemporary memoir of the Duke of York, and embodies all the pith of the obituary notices in the various newspapers and magazines, as well as the biography written by Sir Walter Scott for the Edinburgh Weekly Journal; for his military career see Philippart's Royal Military Calendar and Sir F. W. Hamilton's Hist. of the Grenadier Guards; for the campaigns of 1793–5 see Jones's Hist. of the late War in Flanders (London, 1796); for the expedition of 1799, Sir H. Bunbury's Narrative of some Passages in the late War; and for his character see especially the Greville Memoirs, 1st series, and numerous allusions in Thomas Wright's Gillray the Caricaturist.]

Henry Morse Stephens

published 1889

WILLIAM IV (1765–1837)

King of Great Britain and Ireland, third son of George III and of his queen, Charlotte Sophia of Mecklenburg-Strelitz, was born in Buckingham Palace on the morning of 21 Aug. 1765, and was baptised by the archbishop of Canterbury (Thomas Secker) as William Henry. On 5 April 1770 he was nominated a knight of the Thistle. His early years were passed for the most part at Kew, where he was educated under the charge of Dr. John James Majendie and Major-general Budé, a Swiss with a commission in the army of Hanover. While William was still a child the king, his father, determined that he should serve in the navy, and on his visit to Portsmouth in May 1778 had arranged with Captain Robert Digby that he should, in due time, go to sea with him. He also talked the matter over with Sir Samuel (afterwards Viscount) Hood, then commissioner in the dockyard, to whom he wrote, 12 July 1778, asking him 'to write down what clothes, necessaries, and books he ought to take. . . . He has begun geometry, and I shall have an attention to forward him in whatever you may hint as proper to be done before he enters into that glorious profession.' In May 1779 it was arranged that the boy should embark on board the Prince George, Digby's flagship, and on the 27th the king wrote to Hood that he had 'sent an hair-trunk, two chests, and two cots done up in one mat to be delivered unto you for the use of my young sailor. . . . I flatter myself you will be pleased with the appearance of the boy, who neither wants resolution nor cheerfulness, which seem necessary ingredients for those who enter into that noble profession.' On 11 June the king wrote again, introducing Mr. Majendie, 'who is to attend my son on board of the Prince George, to pursue his classical studies. The young midshipman will be at the dockyard between one and two on Monday (14th). I desire he may be received without the smallest marks of parade. I trust the admiral will order him immediately on board. . . . The young man goes as a sailor, and as such, I add again, no marks of distinction are to be shown unto him; they would destroy my whole plan.' It had, however, been provided that he should be allowed 'a small place made with light sufficient for following his studies.'

As soon as he arrived he was sent on board the Prince George, on whose books he was borne as an 'able seaman;' Henry Majendie being borne as a midshipman. In the Prince George he took part in the August cruise of the Channel fleet under Sir Charles Hardy (1716?–1780), and in the relief of Gibraltar in January 1780. On 18 Jan. 1780 he was rated midshipman. The familiar story of his having been seen doing duty as a midshipman by the Spanish admiral, Don Juan de Langara, belongs to this time. Langara, who had been taken prisoner in the action off Cape St. Vincent, was, while at Gibraltar, paying a visit to Digby on board the Prince George, and is said to have exclaimed, when the prince reported his boat ready, 'Well does Great Britain merit the empire of the sea, when the humblest stations in her navy are supported by princes of the blood' (Drinkwater, *Siege of Gibraltar*). The broad facts of the story are probably historical; but it may be doubted if any Spanish admiral in 1780 would have spoken of Great Britain as meriting the empire of the sea. Other stories told of the same time—the prince's quarrel with a midshipman named Sturt, and his fight with Lieutenant Moodie of the marines—are probable enough; that Sturt and Moodie were his shipmates is shown by the Prince George's pay-book.

Rodney's success of itself was sufficient to excite the popular enthusiasm, which was much increased by the young prince's share in it, and by his return to London bringing to his father the flag of Langara and a plan of Gibraltar drawn by himself. When he visited Drury Lane Theatre a tremendous crush welcomed him; but when the king found that he was being initiated by his elder brothers in the dissipations of the town, and had been carried off to the watch-house for brawling at Vauxhall or Ranelagh, he promptly sent him back to his ship, in which he was present in the cruise of the Channel fleet under (Sir) Francis Geary. In August Geary retired from the command, and in doing so gave a farewell dinner to the captains, to which he invited Prince William, who is said to have surprised both host and guests by replying to the toast of 'The King' in a long-winded, rambling speech, the first of a very great many similar speeches which he made during a long life. In a visit to London after this he is said to have fallen deeply in love with a Miss Fortescue, described as a girl of sixteen, whom he would have married but for 'the iniquitous Royal Marriage Act,' for which the king was entirely responsible (Huish). That his father thought the boy was behaving like a young fool and cut short his holiday by sending him back to his ship is extremely probable. In the Prince George, William was present at the second relief of Gibraltar under Darby, and afterwards went out to New York, where, in March–April 1782, he narrowly escaped being kidnapped by an agent of Washington's (Watkins, pp. 66–71; Sparks, *Washington's Writings*, viii. 261). After this it was probably thought that he would be safer in a sea-going ship, and he was lent to the Warwick, then commanded by Captain George Keith Elphinstone (afterwards Lord Keith). On 19 April he was nominated a K.G. On 4 Nov. he was moved to the Barfleur, the flagship of Lord Hood, with whom he went to the West Indies. It was at this time, while still at New York, that he made the acquaintance of Nelson, then captain of the Albemarle, whose intense loyalty gave him, it may be, a too favourable opinion of the son of his king. In the West Indies they saw a good deal of each other, and the prince even then formed a high opinion of Nelson's character and ability. On the other hand, Nelson wrote of the prince: 'He is a seaman, which you could hardly suppose. He will be a disciplinarian, and a strong one. He says he is determined every person shall serve his time before they shall be provided for, as he is obliged to serve his. A vast deal of notice has been taken of him at Jamaica; he has been addressed by the Council, and the House of Assembly were to address him the day after I sailed. He has his levees at Spanish Town. They are all highly delighted with him. With the best temper and great good sense, he cannot fail of being pleasing to every one' (Nicolas, i. 72). In the end of April 1783, when the Barfleur left Jamaica for England, it was thought well that the prince should accept the invitation of the governor of Havana and visit that place. He accordingly went on board the Fortunée frigate, and, in company with the Albemarle, arrived off Havana on the forenoon of 9 May. The prince immediately landed, under a royal salute, and was received on shore with royal honours. On the morning of the 11th Prince William re-embarked in the Fortunée, and before noon rejoined the Barfleur, which arrived at Spithead on 27 June, when the royal midshipman was discharged to the shore.

After this for nearly two years he travelled in Germany and Italy, getting into many scrapes, quarrels with gamblers, and entanglements with young women, till, on his return to England in the summer of 1785, he passed his examination, and was at once, 17 June, promoted to be lieutenant of the Hebe, carrying the broad pennant of Commodore John Leveson-Gower, and commanded by Captain Edward Thornbrough, who had the reputation of being one of the smartest seamen in the navy. In the following March he was appointed to the Pegasus frigate, and on 10 April was promoted to be her captain. In the Pegasus he went to the West Indies, where he was again associated with Nelson, and formed a considerable degree of intimacy with him. The two were constantly together. When Nelson was married the prince gave away the bride, and Nelson's affectionate and loyal nature was completely won. 'In every respect, both as a man and a prince, I love him,' he wrote to his brother on 9 Feb. 1787; and to Captain William Locker, on the same day: 'His Royal Highness keeps up strict discipline in his ship; and, without paying him any compliment, she is one of the first ordered frigates I have seen. He has had more plague with his officers than enough; his first lieutenant will, I have no doubt, be broke' (Nicolas, i. 214–15). The prince's quarrel with his first lieutenant was perhaps a natural result of appointing an officer of experience to control or keep out of scrapes a self-willed and opinionated young captain. But Schomberg was not the only officer of the Pegasus who found the prince's rule intolerable. So far from considering it an honour and a privilege to serve under his command, the lieutenants made what interest they could to get out of the ship. They said openly that 'no officer could serve under the prince but that sooner or later he must be broke.'

In consequence of the prince's dispute with his first lieutenant, Nelson sent the Pegasus to Jamaica, where the commodore smoothed matters by appointing Schomberg to another ship; after which the Pegasus went to Quebec and thence to England, where she arrived in the end of December. 'I returned from Plymouth three days ago,' Nelson wrote on 27 Jan. 1788, 'and found Prince William everything I could wish—respected by all. . . . The Pegasus is allowed by every one to be one of the best disciplined ships that ever came into Plymouth. But the great folks above now see he will not be a cipher, therefore many of the rising people must submit to act subordinate to him, which is not so palatable; and I think a lord of the admiralty—Gower, presumably—is hurt to see him so able, after what he has said about him' (Nicolas, i. 266). On 1 March 1788 Prince William commissioned the Andromeda, attached to the Channel fleet during the summer and afterwards sent out to the West Indies; she arrived at Port Royal on 15 Nov. At this time the prince assumed more of the state of royalty than he had hitherto been allowed. On 25 Nov. he held a levee on board the Europa, Commodore Gardner's flagship, the royal standard being hoisted, the ships firing a royal salute, manning yards and cheering. On 6 Dec. he landed at Port Royal with the standard in the bow of his boat, and was received on shore 'as a prince of the blood.' His order-book, too, is very precise and detailed as to dress, conduct, &c.; and though the several instructions were not uncommon, taken all together they give the idea of a more stringent etiquette than was customary, especially in a frigate. On 20 May 1789 the prince was created Earl of Munster and Duke of Clarence and St. Andrews. On 3 June the Andromeda was paid off at Portsmouth. In the following May the prince was appointed to command the Valiant in the fleet got together in consequence of the dispute with Spain relative to Nootka Sound. The Valiant was paid off on 27 Nov., and on 3 Dec. the Duke of Clarence was specially promoted to be rear-admiral. The promotion marked the end of his service afloat, successive admiralties and the king being determined that he should not be employed. That during the eleven years since he had entered the navy, nine of them in active service, he had learnt his business, there is no reason to doubt; but, notwithstanding the eulogies of Nelson, there is great reason to doubt his ability as an officer, nor does anything in his whole history suggest that he could possibly have made an efficient admiral. That the admiralty recognised this would seem certain; but to the king they probably represented it as unfitting that a prince of the blood should be exposed to the risks and dangers inseparable from naval warfare.

The period of his command of the Valiant, and the certainty thus afforded that he was in England or in English waters during the summer and autumn of 1790 (cf. Nicolas, i. 288–9), are interesting as establishing the falsehood of a romance published in Leipzig in 1880; this purported to be the confessions of Caroline von Linsingen, of an amour with William beginning in April 1790, continued, with much sentimental love-making, through 1790 to August 1791, when the love-sick pair married, and till August 1792, when the marriage was consummated. It was shown at once that the whole story, which has been received in Germany as historical (*Allgemeine Deutsche Biographie*, s.n. 'Linsingen, Caroline von'), is utterly unsupported and incredible (*Times*, 24 June 1880; *Westminster Review*, October 1880); but a reference to the dates shows that it is impossible, and that, whether intentionally or an hysteric hallucination, it is wholly untrue.

It was in the end of 1790 or the beginning of 1791 that the Duke of Clarence formed the connection with Mrs. Jordan, which continued for rather more than twenty years, and gave rise to much scandal and public ill-feeling. The duke was appointed ranger of Bushey Park, and at Bushey Mrs. Jordan lived in the intervals of her theatrical engagements, and was there recognised as the mistress of the duke's household, taking the head of the table at dinner parties, with the Prince of Wales—when present—at her right hand. The duke is said to have allowed her 1,000l. a year, and Mrs. Jordan spoke of his unfailing liberality; but the facts that during these years she continued on the stage, in receipt of large sums (7,000l. was named as her professional income), and that on separating from the duke in 1811 she was reported to be in very needy circumstances, gave rise to the popular belief that the duke had been living on her earnings; that she kept him, not he her. This appears incorrect, but the matter was and still is veiled in mystery. It was, however, admitted that want of money led to the separation. There was no quarrel; and, indeed, Mrs. Jordan's letters refer to the duke as generous and affectionate, but obliged, much against his will, to leave her. It was said that he intended to marry an heiress—any heiress; two were particularly named; and his supposed rejection by them formed the subject of numerous ballads, more or less scurrilous, by 'Peter Pindar' and others.

But it was only when some scandalmongers could make capital out of the duke's errors or eccentricities that he appeared as a public character. In the beginning of the war he earnestly desired to serve afloat, if only as a volunteer; but his applications for employment were ignored or refused. Later on he resided pretty constantly at Bushey 'and brought up his numerous children with very tender affection; with them, and for them, he seemed entirely to live' (Greville, iv. 2). He is said also to have been well read in naval history, even in minute details (Barrow, *Life of Anson*, pp. iii–iv), and his correspondence with naval officers—Nelson more especially—is a proof that he continued to take very great interest in the navy, and followed the course of events with attention. These letters tell of professional intelligence, but on other matters his incapacity was often painfully apparent, the more so as then and throughout his life he had a mania for making speeches without any regard to the fitness of things; as when in 1800–1 he delivered a course of lectures on the wickedness of adultery to the House of Lords; and in presence of his elder brothers, described an adulterer as 'an insidious and designing villain, who would ever be held in disgrace and abhorrence by an enlightened and civilised society' (*Parl. Hist.* vol. xxxv.). There was, indeed, very often a rude commonsense in his remarks; but the rambling manner in which they were tacked together and uttered made them sound like foolishness; and the total disregard of times and seasons and the feelings or prejudices of his hearers excited an antagonism which took its revenge in nicknaming him 'Silly Billy.'

In such circumstances his promotions in the navy were little more than nominal. He was made a vice-admiral on 12 April 1794; an admiral on 14 April 1799; and, on the death of Sir Peter Parker (1721–1811), admiral of the fleet on 24 Dec. 1811. This last promotion, though to the Duke of Clarence little more than an empty honour, was a material wrong to his brother officers; for the rule was then, as it always had been, that there could be only one admiral of the fleet, or, as he was called in his commission, commander-in-chief; so that, the post being filled by the duke, it could not reward the services of any other admiral. It was not till 1821 that George IV remedied the grievance by introducing the apparent anomaly of two commanders-in-chief, and promoted the Earl of St. Vincent. As admiral of the fleet, however, the Duke of Clarence, with his flag on board the Jason frigate, commanded the escort of Louis XVIII on his return to France in April 1814; and in June, with his flag in the Impregnable, commanded the fleet at Spithead when reviewed by the prince regent and the allied sovereigns.

The death of the Princess Charlotte in 1817, the flutter among the king's younger sons, and the duke's marriage on 18 July 1818 to Adelaide, eldest daughter of George, duke of Saxe-Coburg Meiningen, brought him momentarily before the public eye. The year after his marriage he spent in Hanover; but in 1820 he returned to Bushey, where he continued to reside in social obscurity till the death of the Duke of York in January 1827, which left him heir to the throne (the joint income of the duke and duchess, which had hitherto been 26,500l., was after considerable opposition raised by parliament to 38,500l.), and his acceptance in April of the office of lord high admiral in the Canning administration again brought him into notice.

In making this appointment there was no intention to revert to the government of the navy by one man, vested with all the power and prerogatives attached to the office of lord high admiral, and this was clearly stated in the patent. The Duke of Clarence, with no individual authority apart from his 'council,' was to be virtually first lord of the admiralty, under a different name, and with an exceptionally strong board, now called the 'duke's council,' at the head of which was Sir George Cockburn. It was supposed that the duke, who had not been in active service for nearly forty years—years, too, of great events and changes— would readily acquiesce in this arrangement, but this he absolutely refused to do, just as when a young captain he had refused to be dry-nursed by an old lieutenant. He wished to be lord high admiral in fact as well as in name, with the result that between him and his council there were continual differences which could not always be quietly settled. It does not, indeed, appear that he ever acted counter to the decisions of the cabinet on questions of policy, though the freedom of his speech and the eccentricity of his conduct gave rise to many reports; such as that in September 1827 he wrote to Sir Edward Codrington in three words, 'Go it, Ned,' or at greater length, 'Go in, my dear Ned, and smash these damned Turks,' a story which a knowledge of the duke's correspondence is sufficient to refute, even without the specific contradiction given it by Sir William Codrington (Fitzgerald, i. 170). It was out of matters of detail and administration that difficulties arose. He refused to be bound by the limitations of the patent. He ordered departmental commissions without consulting his colleagues; if he acquainted them with it afterwards, it was rather as a matter of courtesy than of obligation. He ordered promotions on the whim of the moment (Wellington, iv. 652, 680; cf. Buckingham, i. 4), and expected them to be made. 'You're a damned fine fellow,' he said to one lieutenant who had spun him a yarn of adventure; 'go and tell Sir George he's to promote you at once.' Cockburn refused. 'We know quite as much about you,' he said, 'as his royal highness does, perhaps more, but if we were to promote all the "damned fine fellows" in the service, we should be very short of lieutenants.'

On comparatively small points like these there was a great deal of friction; but matters came to a head in the summer of 1828, when the duke went on board the Royal Sovereign yacht, hoisted the lord high admiral's flag, and assumed military command. Cockburn remonstrated in a letter which the duke pronounced 'disrespectful and impertinent.' The Duke wrote to Wellington, who had succeeded as prime minister, desiring him to ask the king to remove Cockburn from the council and appoint Sir Charles Paget in his room. Wellington and, afterwards, the king both took Cockburn's view, that the duke had no authority to exercise military command; and the duke seemed to yield the point; but a few days later he went round to Plymouth in the yacht, again hoisted the lord high admiral's flag, and put to sea in command of the Channel fleet. This brought on him very strong letters from both the king and the prime minister, and on 11 Aug. he resigned, 'conceiving that, with the impediments thrown and intended to have been thrown in the way of the execution of my office, I could not have done justice either to the king or to my country' (*ib*. i. 193). During his short term of office he had 'distinguished himself by making absurd speeches, by a morbid official activity, and by a general wildness which was thought to indicate incipient insanity' (Greville, ii. 2).

For a time he dropped back into something like his former obscurity, but George IV died on 26 June 1830, and the Duke of Clarence succeeded as William IV. He is said to have expressed a wish that the 'old-fashioned' and expensive coronation ceremony might be pretermitted; it took place eventually on 8 Sept. 1831, the outlay, which amounted in the case of his predecessor to 240,000*l*., having been cut down by laborious economy to 30,000*l*. The new king 'threw himself into the arms of the Duke of Wellington—who was still prime minister—with the strongest expressions of confidence and esteem.' Wellington, who had not been able to tolerate him as lord high admiral, was delighted with him as king, and told Greville 'that he was so reasonable and tractable that he had done more business with him in ten minutes than with George IV in as many days.' He presided at the council 'very decently, and looked like a respectable old admiral' (*ib*. ii. 3). 'He began immediately to do good-natured things, to provide for old friends and professional adherents. There was never anything like the enthusiasm with which he was greeted by all ranks; though he has trotted about both town and country for sixty-four years and nobody ever turned round to look at him, he cannot stir now without a mob, patrician as well as plebeian, at his heels. But in the midst of all this success and good conduct certain indications of strangeness and oddness peep out which are not a little alarming, and he promises to realise the fears of his ministers that he will do and say too much, though they flatter themselves that they have muzzled him' (*ib*. ii. 4). He had, in fact, all his life, when on shore, affected the manners and language of the rough and hearty tar; and this, added to much natural *bonhomie*, led him to do kindly things, and to set the etiquette of the court at defiance. 'The king's good nature, simplicity, and affability to all about him are certainly very striking, and in his elevation he does not forget any of his old friends and companions. He was in no hurry to take upon himself the dignity of king, nor to throw off the habits and manners of a country gentleman. When Lord Chesterfield went to Bushey to kiss his hand and be presented to the queen, he found Sir John and Lady Gore there lunching, and when they went away the king called for their carriage, handed Lady Gore into it, and stood at the door to see them off. When Lord Howe came over from Twickenham to see him, he said the queen was going out driving, and should "drop him" at his own house' (*ib*. ii. 6). Greville is full of stories of a similar kind, and adds, 'he ought to be made to understand that his simplicity degenerates into vulgarity, and that without departing from his natural urbanity he may conduct himself so as not to lower the character with which he is invested, and which belongs not to him but to the country' (*ib*. ii. 12).

But he never did learn this, and continued to the end the same garrulous, homely, kind-hearted old man, fond of making speeches, which were generally uncalled for, and frequently absurd; fierce in his dislikes but not vindictive, and liable to wild bursts of passion, when what little dignity remained was thrown utterly to the winds. One of the most extraordinary of these happened within a year of his death. He had always disliked the Duchess of Kent, who, on her side, had not endeavoured to conciliate him. Of the duchess's daughter, the Princess Victoria, he was extremely fond, and one of his grievances was that her mother would not allow her to come to see him as often as he wished. The dislike came to a head in August 1836, when he discovered that the duchess had appropriated a suite of rooms in Kensington Palace, which he had categorically refused to allow her; and at Windsor, on the 21st, at a dinner of over a hundred people, to celebrate his birthday, he broke out in one of the wildest and most outrageous speeches that even he ever uttered; and that, with the duchess sitting next to him, in the post of honour, at his right hand. The Princess Victoria, who was present, burst into tears; the company broke up in dismay, and the duchess ordered her carriage. A sort of reconciliation was, however, patched up, and she consented to remain till the next day (*ib.* iii. 374–6).

Politically the conduct of affairs was, of course, in the hands of the successive administrations; and though it might have been supposed that he would resent the control which they exercised, quite as strongly as he had resented interference on board his frigate or at the admiralty, he did not do so. It would appear that in this case he really understood that the control was, in the very essence of the thing, inseparable from the position. He had, too, lived so long apart from politics that he can scarcely have had any very strong feeling, even on reform, which was the engrossing question of the early years of his reign. It would indeed appear that his personal opinion was in favour of it; he had, from his youth, interested himself in the condition of the poor (Nicolas, i. 294), and parliamentary reform may very well have seemed to him a step towards its amelioration. Thus, when, in November 1830, the Duke of Wellington resigned, the king accepted Lord Grey and the whigs, and their stipulation that reform should be a cabinet measure. The Reform Bill, brought in on 1 March 1831, passed the second reading in the House of Commons by a majority of one (302 to 301) on the 22nd; and when, in committee, a hostile amendment was carried by a majority of eight, 19 April, Grey proposed an appeal to the country. The opposition, assuming that the king must be adverse to reform, deplored his weakness in 'neglecting the opportunity to emancipate himself from the thraldom of the whigs.' The king, however, considered that in calling on Grey to form a ministry, he had pledged himself to accept reform, and that the virtual dismissal of them would be a dishonest violation of an implied compact.

Parliament was dissolved on 22 April, and in the new House of Commons the Reform Bill was passed by a large majority on 22 Sept. It was, however, thrown out by the lords on 8 Oct.; but was brought in again and passed by the commons early in the next session, 22 March 1832. It was again rejected by the lords, and on the king's refusal to swamp the hostile majority by the creation of a large batch of peers, Grey resigned. The king appealed to Wellington, who was unable to form a ministry, and Grey returned to office on the understanding that the king would make the new peers if it should be found necessary. A circular letter from the king to the tory peers did away with the necessity; a hundred of them absented themselves from the divisions, and the bill became law. In other points in which, at the time, the king was blamed as having shown weakness or ignorance, it appears by later lights and, in particular by his own

'Statement of his majesty's general proceedings, and of the principles by which he was guided from the period of his accession, 1830, to that of the recent change in the administration, 14 Jan. 1835' (Stockmar, i. 314; Fitzgerald, ii. 331), drawn up for Sir Robert Peel, that he was really guided by constitutional principles and the feelings of an honourable gentleman; while his exposition of foreign policy and his forecast of the course of affairs in the east, which was pretty exactly verified in 1840—three years after his death—serve to show that though unused to public life, unversed in courtly etiquette and the conventionalities of London society, and grievously wanting in reticence and self-command, he had still the instincts of a statesman, and was very far from the fool, or imbecile, which it became the fashion to reckon him.

He had repeatedly expressed a wish, dictated by his hatred of the Duchess of Kent, that he might live till the Princess Victoria came of age—24 May 1837—so that the duchess might not be regent. His wish was just accomplished. He was taken seriously ill on 20 May, and—though with occasional rallies—grew gradually worse, till his death on the early morning of 20 June 1837. He was buried at Windsor on 8 July. By the queen he had issue two daughters, both of whom died in infancy; his niece, the Princess Victoria, thus succeeded to the throne. By Mrs. Jordan he had ten children, whom from the first he recognised, and to whom he gave the name of FitzClarence. He regarded his connection with Mrs. Jordan as fully sanctioned by custom, and society made no difficulty about accepting the numerous 'bastards,' as Greville always calls them. His eldest son was George Augustus Frederick FitzClarence, earl of Munster. Once settled at Bushey, he led a regular life which—at any rate in comparison with that of his elder brothers—might be called moral. In old age, and influenced, perhaps, by the queen, he was certainly impressed by a feeling of religion which comforted and sustained his dying hours.

Of the very numerous portraits of William IV, the most worthy of note are: 1. As a boy on the Prince George by Benjamin West, engraved by V. Green. 2. A portrait as Duke of Clarence by Gainsborough, of which there is a very rare mezzotint by G. Dupont. 3. By Sir M. A. Shee, engraved by C. Turner. 4. By Sir Thomas Lawrence, engraved by J. E. Coombs. 5. By Sir David Wilkie (cf. *Cat. Guelph Exhib.* p. 112). The National Portrait Gallery has a watercolour half-length, painter unknown (purchased July 1898).

[The several Lives of William IV by John Watkins, G. N. Wright, and Robert Huish are of very slender authority, being for the most part mere compilations of gossip and scandal; that by Mr. Percy Fitzgerald (1884) is better, but its value is seriously impaired by the almost total want of dates and references. The small impartial Life by W. Harding is of greater value than its unpretentious form would suggest. The naval part of the king's life may be read in Marshall's Roy. Nav. Biogr. i. 1, and Ralfe's Nav. Biogr. i. 339; ships' logs and pay-books, &c., in the Public Record Office; the Hood Papers, by favour of Viscount Hood; Nicolas's Despatches and Letters of Viscount Nelson (see Index in vol. vii.). See also Boaden's Life of Mrs. Jordan; Walpole's Hist. of England since 1815; Molesworth's Hist. of England from 1830; Maley's Historical Recollections of the Reign of William IV; The Greville Memoirs; Memoirs of Baron Stockmar, vol. i.; Duke of Buckingham's Memoirs of the Courts and Cabinets of William IV and Victoria; Journal kept by Thomas Raikes, 1831–47; Corresp. of Earl Grey with William IV; Torrens's Life of Viscount Melbourne; Despatches, &c., of Arthur, Duke of Wellington, 2nd ser. edited by his son, vols. iv–viii.]

JOHN KNOX LAUGHTON

published 1900

CHARLOTTE AUGUSTA Matilda

(1766–1828)

Princess Royal of Great Britain and Ireland and Queen of Würtemberg

The eldest daughter of George III and Queen Charlotte, was born at Buckingham House, London, on 29 Sept. 1766—a 'Michaelmas goose,' according to her mother's homely wit. The 'Diary' of Madame d'Arblay contains many reminiscences besides this of the princess royal in her early womanhood from 1786 to 1791; and all are to the credit of her temper and disposition. She is described as writing German with perfect facility, and drawing is mentioned as one of her occupations, while music appears to have been an art 'which she even professes to have no taste for, and to hear almost with pain.' To Miss Burney she was always kind and condescending, and for Mrs. Delany she cherished a warm affection. She seems to have been loved in the quiet domestic circle of her father's court, and to have behaved as a dutiful daughter to the king himself, whose companion she was during a drive on the morning (5 Nov. 1788) when his delirium declared itself. When in July 1796 Madame d'Arblay (as she now was) paid a visit to the royal family at Windsor, she learned that the princess was betrothed to the hereditary prince of Würtemberg. Madame d'Arblay's 'Diary' furnishes a lively though respectful account of the wooing, and subsequently of the wedding, which took place 18 May 1797 at the Chapel Royal St. James's. The princess royal was not altogether unwilling to leave home; as Madame d'Arblay puts it, 'she adored the king, honoured the queen, and loved her sisters, and had much kindness for her brothers; but her style of life was not adapted to the royalty of her nature any more than of her birth; and though she only wished for power to do good and confer favours, she thought herself out of her place in not possessing it.'

If the tattle of Sir N. W. Wraxall is in any degree to be trusted, the negotiations as to this marriage had not been altogether smooth. He relates that when in 1796 overtures were first made on the subject by the Würtemberg court, George III was so prepossessed against the prince, who was suspected of having been privy to the death of his first wife, a Brunswick-Wolfenbüttel princess, eight years previously in Russia, that he would not listen to the proposal. Wraxall adds, however, that the prince sent over an agent to London to disprove the accusation, and that it was refuted to the king's satisfaction. A few months after his marriage, in December 1797, Prince Frederick William Charles succeeded to the government of Würtemberg on the death of his father, Duke Frederick Eugene. He was a prince of considerable ability and tact, strengthened by experience in both the Prussian and the Russian service; and he showed extraordinary skill in apprehending the signs of the times, averting difficulties, and seizing opportunities before it was too late. A fugitive at Vienna (1799–1801), an elector of the empire (1803), king by the grace of Napoleon (1806), and a member of the Confederation of the Rhine, he ultimately contrived to make his peace with the allies soon after the battle of Leipzig. At home he ruled from 1806 as an absolute monarch, having abolished the ancient Würtemberg constitution, of which in 1771 Great Britain had virtually become a guaranteeing power. The new constitution which he offered in 1815 was rejected by his estates and people, and while the discussions on the subject were in progress he died, 30 Oct. 1816. There is no evidence that Charlotte Augusta played a part in any of these transactions, which must, however, have largely added to the anxieties of her life. Her marriage with Frederick, who had had three children by his first wife, remained childless, with the exception of a stillborn daughter. During her later years the Dowager Queen of Würtemberg was much afflicted by dropsy, and her size increased abnormally. In 1827 she visited England, to obtain, if possible, relief from the skill of Sir Astley Cooper and other physicians. But her journey was made in vain, for on 6 Oct. 1828 she died, rather suddenly, at Ludwigsburg, near Stuttgart.

[Annual Register for 1828. For reminiscences of the early life of Charlotte Augusta see the Diary and Letters of Madame d'Arblay, vols. iii–vi. (7 vol. edition, London, 1854). Of the career of her husband a good account is given in Pfaff's Geschichte des Fürstenhauses and Landes Wirtemberg (Stuttgart, 1839), vol. iii. pt. 2, and in Allgemeine Deutsche Biographie, vol. viii. For the gossip concerning the fate of his first wife see Wraxall's Memoirs of my own Time, i. 203–15; cf. Preface to his Posthumous Memoirs (2nd ed. 1836), v–viii.]

ADOLPHUS WILLIAM WARD

published 1887

KENT AND STRATHERN Edward Augustus

(1767–1820)

Duke of

Prince, fourth son of George III, by Queen Charlotte, born on 2 Nov. 1767 at Buckingham House, had his early education in England under John Fisher, successively bishop of Exeter and Salisbury, and completed it on the continent under Baron Wangenheim, with whom he spent two years (1785–7) at Luneburg and Hanover, and two years more at Geneva. On 30 May 1786 he was gazetted brevet-colonel. Wangenheim treated him with needless rigour, allowed him only a guinea and a half a week pocket-money out of the annuity of 6,000l. provided for his maintenance, and intercepted his letters home. The prince accordingly borrowed largely, and the debts thus contracted were a burden to him throughout life. In June 1790 he came home from Geneva without leave. The king was much displeased, gave him peremptory orders to embark for Gibraltar, and saw him for only five minutes on the night before he sailed (1 Feb.). At Gibraltar he was put in command of the 7th regiment of foot (royal fusiliers). A thorough martinet, he became so unpopular with his men that in May 1791 he was sent to Canada.

He was now in receipt of an income of 5,000l. a year, but out of this he had to pay the interest on his debts. In October 1793 he was advanced to the rank of major-general, and received at his own request orders to join Sir Charles (afterwards Lord) Grey's force in the West Indies. He arrived on 4 March 1794 at Martinique. In command of a brigade of grenadiers he took part in the reduction of that island, and also of St. Lucia, was honourably mentioned in despatches, and received the thanks of parliament. On the close of the operations he returned to Canada; on 16 Jan. 1796 was promoted lieutenant-general, and in October 1798, being invalided, returned to England.

In March 1799 parliament granted him an annual income of 12,000l., and on 23 April he was raised to the peerage as Duke of Kent and

Strathern and Earl of Dublin. On 10 May he was gazetted general, and on 17 May commander-in-chief of the forces in British North America. He sailed in July, but was compelled by ill-health to return to England in the autumn of the following year. On 27 March 1802 he was appointed governor of Gibraltar, where he arrived on 10 May with express instructions from the Duke of York, then commander-in-chief, to restore the discipline of the garrison, which was seriously demoralised. He accordingly issued a general order, forbidding any but commissioned officers to enter the wine-shops, half of which—there were ninety on the Rock—he summarily closed at a personal sacrifice of 4,000*l.* a year in licensing fees. The incensed wine-sellers plied the soldiers with liquor gratis, and a mutiny, to which it was thought some of the officers were privy, broke out on Christmas eve 1802. The mutiny was promptly quelled, three of the ringleaders were shot, discipline was thoroughly restored, and in the following March the duke was recalled. On his return to England he demanded a formal investigation of his conduct, which was refused. He then asked to be permitted to return to Gibraltar; this also was refused. He still remained nominally governor, but without pay; the standing orders he had issued while in command were set aside by the lieutenant-governor, Sir Thomas Trigge, and the garrison relapsed into its former condition. On 7 Sept. 1805 the duke was gazetted field-marshal, and on 25 Nov. following keeper and paler of Hampton Court. For some years he resided at Castle Hill, near Ealing, taking little part in state affairs. He was, however, the confidant and adviser of the Prince of Wales in his matrimonial difficulties. In 1810 he opposed the Regency Bill as unconstitutional. In 1812 he spoke in favour of catholic emancipation, and became a patron of the British and Foreign School Society, the Anti-Slavery Society, the Society for Promoting Christianity among the Jews, and the Bible Society. In 1815 and 1816 he took the chair at the Literary Fund dinner. Finding his pecuniary embarrassments increasing, and getting no relief from government, he made in 1815 an assignment of the bulk of his property in favour of his creditors, and retired to Brussels, where he lived in the simplest possible style. In 1818 he married, for reasons of state, Victoria Mary Louisa, widow of Emich Charles, prince of Leiningen. The marriage was solemnised on 29 May at Coburg, and on 13 July following at Kew. Returning with his bride to the continent, he resided with her at her palace of Amorbach, Leiningen, until the spring of 1819, when he brought her to England for her confinement. After the birth of the child (Queen Victoria) on 24 May, at Kensington Palace, he took the duchess and the princess to Sidmouth, Devonshire, and applied to parliament for authority to dispose of his establishment at Ealing by lottery, a sale being unadvisable, for the benefit of his creditors. The petition was refused, and the duke had made up his mind to return to Amorbach, when he died suddenly of inflammation of the lungs at Sidmouth on 23 Jan. 1820. During his illness he was attended with the utmost devotion by the duchess, to whom he left his entire property. He was buried in St. George's Chapel, Windsor, on 11 Feb.

As a soldier the duke never had an opportunity of gaining high distinction, and his pedantic, almost superstitious, insistence upon minutiæ of military etiquette, discipline, dress, and equipments, made him unpopular in the army. He was, however, the first to abandon flogging and to establish a regimental school. He was extremely regular in his habits, a model of punctuality and despatch in the discharge of duty, and sincerely pious. He was a knight of the orders of the Garter, Bath, and St. Patrick, and a knight grand cross of the Bath and of the order of the Guelphs. There is a portrait of the duke, together with his elder brother the Duke of Clarence (afterwards William IV), at Hampton Court Palace, dated 1779. A bronze statue by Gahagon is in Park Crescent, Portland Place.

[Life by Erskine Neale, 1850; obituary notices in the Gent. Mag. and European Mag. for 1820; Sidney Lee's Life of Queen Victoria, 1902. See also Nicolas's Hist. of British Knighthood; Smeeton's The Unique, vol. i. (with portrait); London Gazette for 1793, 1796, 1799, 1802, 1805; Annual Register, 1767, p. 170, and 1794 App. 68 et seq.; Commons' Journals, liv. 311; Gent. Mag. 1790 p. 80, 1818 pt. i. p. 562, pt. ii. p. 79, 1819 pt. i. p. 479; and the Duke of Buckingham's Memoirs of the Regency, ii. 390.]

JAMES McMULLEN RIGG

published 1892

CAROLINE Amelia Elizabeth, of Brunswick-Wolfenbüttel

(1768–1821)

Queen of George IV, second daughter of Duke Charles William Ferdinand of Brunswick and the Princess Augusta of England, sister of George III, was born 17 May 1768.

The few anecdotes told of her childhood show that she was kind, good-hearted, and charitable. The court of Brunswick-Wolfenbüttel was one of the gayest in Germany, and it had very little of the stiff etiquette which was characteristic of the other North German courts. She was extremely fond of children, and would stop in her walks to notice them. The Duke of York had, during the campaign, seen much of his uncle, the Duke of Brunswick, and he was so charmed with the Princess Caroline, that he mentioned her to his brother the king and the Prince of Wales as a suitable bride for the latter. There was no prospect of the Duke and Duchess of York having any family, and the king was naturally most anxious that the succession to the throne should be indubitably settled by heritage in the direct line. Hard pressed on all sides, the prince consented, on condition of the liquidation of his debts, and a large addition to his income, to marry his cousin, then twenty-six years old. He stipulated that his income was to be raised from 60,000*l*, to 125,000*l*. per annum, of which 25,000*l*. per annum was to be set aside to pay his debts, which at that time amounted to 630,000*l*. Besides this he was to receive 27,000*l*. for preparations for the marriage, 28,000*l*. for jewels and plate, 26,000*l*. for the completion of Carlton House, and 50,000*l*. per annum as a jointure to her royal highness, of which, however, she would only accept 35,000*l*.

She left Brunswick on 30 Dec. 1794, but on her way was met by a messenger from Lord St. Helen's, telling her that the squadron sent to escort her had been obliged to return to England. For a few weeks she stayed at Hanover until her embarkation, which took place at Cuxhaven on 28 March 1795. She arrived at Greenwich about noon on 5 April, where she dressed, and then drove to St. James's, accompanied by Lady Jersey, who had been sent to meet her. Lady Jersey naturally became her most implacable enemy, and probably did more than any one else to estrange the prince from his consort. The marriage took place at 8 p.m. on 8 April in the Chapel Royal, St. James's. The prince's relations with Mrs. Fitzherbert and Lady Jersey—especially the latter—soon led to quarrels, and an appeal was made to the king to act as arbiter between them. Their matrimonial relations continued in this state until the birth of the Princess Charlotte Augusta, on 7 Jan. 1796, when the prince deliberately forsook his wife. A formal separation between them was agreed on three months later, and it was only through the kind offices of the king that the princess was to have free access to her child during the first eight years of its life.

She left Carlton House and went to reside in strict privacy at an unpretentious residence, Shrewsbury House, near Shooter's Hill. In 1801 she removed to Montague House, Blackheath, where she entertained her friends, among whom were Sir John and Lady Douglas, Sir Sidney Smith, Captain Manby, &c. Hitherto there had been nothing against her moral character. But becoming very intimate with Lady Douglas, she foolishly talked some nonsense as to her being about to give birth to a child, which she intended to account for by saying she had adopted it. She already had several young protégés, and one named William Austin was singled out as being her own son. This rumour was spread by Lady Douglas, and in 1806 the king granted a commission, consisting of Lords Erskine, Grenville, Spencer, and Ellenborough, to investigate the matter. This was called 'the delicate investigation,' and at the conclusion of their labours they unhesitatingly repudiated the charge made against the princess, although they censured her levity of manners on several occasions. For this also the king gently rebuked her, but he allotted her apartments in Kensington Palace, and often passed a whole day at Blackheath with her and his grandchild, the Princess Charlotte, a proceeding which certainly tended to widen the breach between him and the Prince of Wales. Still, although on friendly relations with the king, she never recovered her former footing at court, and when, after the death of the Princess Amelia in 1810, the king's health gave way, the intercourse between her and her daughter was much restricted. Her position suffered still more when, in 1811, the Prince of Wales was proclaimed regent, an accession of rank which brought to her no corresponding dignity.

Princess Caroline felt deeply the separation from her child. On 4 Oct. 1812 she went to Windsor with the intention of paying her daughter a visit, but was not permitted to see her, whereon she demanded an audience of the queen, which was immediately granted, but no satisfaction could be obtained. Her indignation knew no bounds, and she wrote a long and most impassioned letter of remonstrance to the regent on 12 Jan. 1813. This letter was laid before the privy council, and in their report they 'were of opinion that, under all the circumstances of the case, it is highly fit and proper, with a view to the welfare of her royal highness the Princess Charlotte, in which are equally involved the happiness of your royal highness in your parental and royal character, and the most important interests of the state, that the intercourse between her royal highness the Princess of Wales and her royal highness the Princess Charlotte should continue to be subject to regulation and restraint.' The princess then addressed a letter to the speaker of the House of Commons on the subject, which was read to the house, and a debate was raised, but the sense of the house was that the regent was the sole judge of the conduct to be observed in the education of his daughter. On 8 March the princess received an intimation that her restricted visits to her daughter were to be discontinued, but by accident the mother and child met when out driving, and had some ten minutes' conversation; and on the death of the Duchess of Brunswick (who was living in England) on 23 March 1813, the regent permitted his daughter to visit her mother, and they passed two hours together. When, on 12 July, the Prince of Wales visited his daughter, and informed her that he was going to dismiss all her household, and that she must take up her residence at Carlton House, she fled at once to her mother at Connaught House, only to find that the princess had gone to

Blackheath. A messenger was despatched after her, and she immediately returned to comfort her daughter, but the counsels and advice of Brougham prevailed, and the princess obeyed her father's will.

Indignant at being excluded from court, and debarred from the society of her daughter, the Princess of Wales resolved to travel abroad, and she sailed for the continent, with the regent's sanction, in the Jason frigate on 9 Aug. She started with a suite mainly composed of English men and women, but from one cause or another they all shortly left her, and she did not fill their places worthily. After visiting her brother, Duke Frederick William of Brunswick-Wolfenbüttel, she turned her steps to Italy, and at Milan she engaged one Bartolomeo Bergami as her courier. Some infatuation led her to lavish upon this man every kind of favour it was in her power to bestow. He had served in some capacity on the *état major* of the force commanded by General Count Pino in the campaign of 1812–1814, and was offered the brevet rank of captain by Joachim, king of Naples, but refused it in order to remain in the service of the princess. His looks were in his favour, for his portraits show him as a handsome man. She raised him to be her equerry, her chamberlain, her constant companion, even at dinner; procured for him a barony in Sicily and the knighthood of Malta, besides several other orders, among which was one which she instituted, that of St. Caroline. She took his relatives into her service. Louis Bergami directed her household, Vallotti Bergami kept her purse, the Countess Oldi, Bergami's sister, was her lady of honour, and Bergami's child Victorine also travelled in her suite.

After living some time at Como, she visited many places, among others Tunis, Malta, Athens, Constantinople, Ephesus, and Jerusalem. Here she made her entry in somewhat theatrical style, and behaved with such levity that secret commissioners were sent from England to investigate her conduct. She was surrounded by spies, and, after her return to Italy, an attempt was made to seize her papers by surreptitious means.

On 6 Nov. 1817 the Princess Charlotte died, and the following year the Princess of Wales much desired to return to England, but she remained abroad for the next year and a half, and wintered at Marseilles in 1819. On hearing of the death of George III, 29 Jan. 1820, she proceeded to Rome, where, although queen consort, she was refused a guard of honour. She was never officially informed of the old king's death, and her name was omitted in the prayers of the church of England. On her way to England early in 1820 she received at St. Omer a letter on behalf of the king, in which it was proposed to allow her 50,000*l.* per annum, subject to such conditions as the king might impose, which were that she was not to take the title of queen of England, or any title attached to the royal family of England, and that she was to reside abroad, and never even to visit England. It was not likely that these terms could be accepted, and she at once set out for Calais, and embarked the same night for England. She set sail next morning, 5 June 1820, and landed at Dover the same day at 1 p.m., being received with a royal salute, no instructions to the contrary having been given. She was welcomed most enthusiastically, and her journey to London was an ovation. On her arrival she went to live at the house of her friend Alderman Wood, in South Audley Street. Her unexpected arrival filled the king and his party with consternation, and next day he sent a message to the House of Lords, accompanied by the evidence collected by the Milan commission, requesting their lordships to give the matter their serious consideration. A committee was appointed, which reported, with regard to the charges made against the queen, that 'it is indispensable that they should become the subject of a solemn inquiry,' and on 5 July the Earl of Liverpool proposed the introduction of 'a bill entitled an Act to deprive her Majesty, Caroline Amelia Elizabeth, of the Title, Prerogatives, Rights, Privileges, and Exemptions of Queen Consort of this Realm, and to dissolve the Marriage between his Majesty and the said Caroline Amelia Elizabeth.' It was read a first time, and appointed to be read a second on 19 Aug. 1820, but this was only a preliminary sitting, the examination of the witnesses not taking place until 21 Aug. Brougham defended the queen. On 6 Nov. the House of Lords divided on the second reading of the bill—contents 123, non-contents 95; majority in favour of second reading, 28. On 8 Nov. the divorce clause was carried in committee by 67. On 10 Nov., the date of the third reading, the Earl of Liverpool suddenly announced that he was prepared to move that it be read that day six months. If the witnesses were not all perjured, the queen's relations with Bergami admitted only of the conclusion that she was guilty, and even her own friends and apologists were fain to admit that her conduct was open to the charge of grave indiscretion. Her friends claimed it as a triumphant acquittal, and Brougham's defence of the queen raised him to the summit of his profession. There can be but little doubt that had the queen been found guilty, and divorced, George IV's position as king would have been imperilled. As it was, the popular feeling in her favour found a safety-valve in the presentation of addresses of sympathy, which poured in from all parts of the kingdom.

Her majesty was then living at Brandenburgh House, near Hammersmith, but on the abandonment of the bill she demanded a palace and establishment suited to her rank; the reply to which was that it was 'not possible for his majesty, under all the circumstances, to assign any of the royal palaces for the queen's residence,' and that until parliament met 'the allowance which has hitherto been enjoyed by the queen will be continued to her.' When parliament met, they voted her 50,000l. per annum.

On Wednesday, 30 Nov. 1820, she went in state, although unaccompanied by soldiers, to St. Paul's to return public thanks for her acquittal. 'The Queen's Guards are the People' was inscribed on one banner. According to the procedure prescribed for royal visits to the city, the gates of Temple Bar were closed, and opened on her arrival by the civic authorities, who accompanied the queen in procession to the cathedral. Addresses continued to pour in on her, but two attempts in parliament to restore her name in the liturgy failed.

The king was to be crowned with great pomp and ceremony at Westminster Abbey on 19 July 1821. The queen declared her intention to be present, and demanded that a suitable place should be provided for her, which was peremptorily refused. She persisted in presenting herself for admission, but was most firmly repulsed, and, not wishing to force an entrance, which would most assuredly have led to a riot, she returned home. This was her death-blow. She was taken ill at Drury Lane Theatre on the evening of 30 July, and died on the night of 7 Aug.

Yet not even with her death came peace. She desired in her will that she should be buried beside her father at Brunswick. The king ordered soldiers to escort the body. The city desired to show their respect to the royal corpse. The king decided that it should not go through the city; but through the city the people determined it should go, and through the city it ultimately went, not before a bloody encounter with the Life Guards at Hyde Park Corner, where they fired on the mob with fatal effect. The coffin duly arrived at Harwich, and Queen Caroline was laid to rest in the royal vault at Brunswick on 26 Aug. 1821.

[Nightingale's Memoirs of Queen Caroline, 1820; Adolphus's ditto, 1821; Wilks's ditto, 1822; Clerke's Life of Her Majesty Caroline, &c., 1821; Huish's Memoirs of George IV, 1830; Duke of Buckingham's Memoirs of the Court of George IV, 1859; Works of Henry, Lord Brougham, vols. ix. and x. 1873; Journal of an English Traveller from 1814 to 1816, 1817; The Book, 1813; The Trial at Large of her Majesty Caroline, &c., 1821; Hansard's Parliamentary Debates, contemporary newspapers, and numerous political tracts.]

JOHN ASHTON

published 1886

AUGUSTA Sophia

(1768–1840)

Princess, daughter of George III and his sixth child, was born at Buckingham House, London, 8 Nov. 1768. The public reception on her birth took place on Sunday, 13 Nov., when two young girls, discovered carrying away the cups in which their caudle had been served, and secreting cake, were reprimanded on their knees (*George III, his Court and Family*, vol. i. p. 317). Princess Augusta is several times mentioned in Mme. d'Arblay's diary; she was sprightly enough in her manner to endure considerable banter from 'Mr. Turbulent' 1 March 1787, and to be called 'la Coquette corrigée' by him, on her supposed attachment to the Prince Royal of Denmark, then visiting at the castle (*ibid.* pp. 281 et seq.). She was partner to her brother, the Duke of York, in the historical country dance on the evening of the day, 1 June, 1789, when the duke had fought the duel with Colonel Lennox, and the Prince of Wales had resented the colonel's presence amongst his sisters by breaking up the ball (*Annual Register*, 1827, p. 438). She accompanied the king and queen later in the month to Weymouth, joining in the chorus of 'God save the King' at Lyndhurst (*Diary of Royal Tour*, 1789). In 1810 she was in attendance on her father, helping him to take exercise at Windsor. In 1816, 2 May, she was at Carlton House at the marriage of her niece, the Princess Charlotte. In May 1818 she gave 50l. to the National Society for the Education of the Poor. On 15 July 1819, she played and sang some of her own musical compositions to Mme. d'Arblay (*Diary*, vol. vii. p. 270). In 1820 she was again at Windsor attending to her father, whose death in that year was the occasion of her being supplied with residences of her own at Frogmore, and at Clarence House, St. James's. In this position of head of an establishment the princess showed the same pleasantness and patience she had shown in her parents' homes; and died at Clarence House 22 Sept. 1840 in her 72nd year (*Annual Register*, 1840, p. 176). She was buried at Windsor 2 Oct.

[Gent. Mag. lxxxvi. i. 462; lxxxvii. i. 559; ii. 270, 333, 334; lxxxviii. i. 462.]

JENNETT HUMPHREYS

published 1885

Landgravine of Hesse-Homburg

Artist, seventh child and third daughter of George III and Queen Charlotte, was born at the queen's palace, Buckingham House, on 22 May 1770. She had the usual allowance of 2,000*l.* a year from the king, but was by her own report a bad economist. She early began to use her pencil, and was called 'The Muse.' In 1795 she designed a series of pictures entitled 'The Birth and Triumph of Cupid,' which were engraved by Tomkins, and published by the king at his own expense. In 1796 this series was reissued as 'The Birth and Triumph of Love,' dedicated to the queen, with poetical letterpress by Sir J. B. Burges. Dean Vincent made the pictures the theme of his election verses at Westminster School. In 1804 the princess produced, with a frontispiece, 'Cupid turned Volunteer,' 4to, dedicated to Princess Augusta, with a poetical description by Thomas Park, F.S.A. In 1806 appeared 'The Power and Progress of Genius,' in twenty-four sketches, folio, each sketch signed 'Eliza, invt and sculpt,' and the princess says in her dedication to the queen that she is venturing before the public alone. In 1808 she established a society at Windsor for giving marriage portions to virtuous girls; shortly after she had her own residence assigned her, The Cottage, Old Windsor. She was always busy in philanthropic work, the patronage of literature, and attendance upon her father.

In 1818, on the evening of 7 April, at Buckingham House, she was married to Frederick Joseph Louis, the hereditary prince of Hesse-Homburg. Parliament voted her 10,000*l.* a year. In June she and her husband left for Germany, where in 1820, on the death of the prince's father, they succeeded as landgrave and landgravine, and established themselves at the family castle. There the princess devoted 6,000*l.* a year of her allowance to the settlement of the difficulties in which the public funds of Hesse-Homburg had become involved. She produced in seven subjects 'The New Doll, or Birthday Gift,' 8vo, and in four subjects 'The Seasons' (the Flower Girl, Milk Girl, Hop Girl, Wood Girl), her work being generally announced as that of 'an illustrious personage.' In 1822, and again in 1823, appeared fresh editions of her 'Love' in octavo, still with Burges's poetry. William Combe, or 'Doctor Syntax', also co-operated with her. In 1829 the landgrave died, and the princess, then dowager landgravine, took up her residence in Hanover, where, by one of the first acts of William IV, a palace was made over to her. In 1831 she paid a visit to England. In 1834, to benefit the poor of Hanover, she permitted a new issue of her 'Genius,' engraved (and considerably altered) by Ramberg, and illustrated by the poetry, in German, of Minna Witte, afterwards Maedler. This work was dedicated by the princess to the Duke of Cambridge in a lithographed autograph letter. The princess's health obliged her to pass many winters at Frankfort-on-the-Maine, and there she died on 10 Jan. 1840, aged 70. She was buried in the mausoleum of the landgraves of Hesse-Homburg. Her library was sold in London by Sotheby & Wilkinson in April 1863. A collection of her 'Letters,' addressed for the most part to Miss L. Swinburne, was edited by P. A. Yorke, 1898.

[Jesse's Memoirs of George III, ii. 531, iii. 134, 280–2, 452; Dict. of Living Authors; Hutton's Bland-Burges Papers, 277, 279, 294, 297, 298; Russell's Moore, ii. 99, vi. 206, viii. 203; Gent. Mag. for 1770, 1788, 1818, 1829, 1840.]

JENNETT HUMPHREYS

published 1888

ERNEST Augustus

(1771–1851)

Duke of Cumberland and *King of Hanover*

Fifth son of George III and Queen Charlotte, born at Kew on 5 June 1771, was baptised at St. James's Palace by Archbishop Cornwallis on 1 July following. His sponsors were Prince Ernest of Mecklenburg-Strelitz, from whom he received his name, Prince Maurice of Saxe-Gotha, and the Hereditary Grand Duchess of Hesse-Cassel. He was educated at Kew with his younger brothers, and his first tutors were the Rev. G. Cookson, afterwards canon of Windsor, and Dr. Hughes, who regarded him as a far more promising lad than his brothers. He was destined by his father from the first to be the commander-in-chief of the Hanoverian army, and in 1786 he was sent to the university of Göttingen with his younger brothers. Among his teachers at Göttingen were Heyne, the classical scholar, and General Malortie, who was his tutor in military subjects.

Before leaving England Prince Ernest was installed a knight of the Garter on 2 June 1786, and on completing his education in 1790 he was gazetted a lieutenant in the 9th Hanoverian hussars, of which regiment he was appointed lieutenant-colonel in 1793. His military training was superintended by Lieutenant-general Baron Linsingen, and on the outbreak of war in 1793 his regiment was sent to the front with a division of

95

the Hanoverian army under the command of General Walmoden. Prince Ernest served with the Hanoverians through the campaigns of 1793 and 1794 in Belgium and the north-west of France. In the campaign of 1793 the Hanoverians were generally kept in reserve, but in 1794 the Duke of York was obliged to make use of all the troops under his command. In February 1794 Prince Ernest was gazetted to the rank of a major-general in the Hanoverian army, and when the campaign opened he was appointed to the command of the first brigade of Hanoverian cavalry in charge of the outposts. In this capacity he was constantly engaged with the enemy, and in the first battle of Tournay, 10 May 1794, he lost his left eye and was severely wounded in the right arm in a hand-to-hand conflict. Recuperating in England, he hurried back to the army in the November of the same year before his wounds were thoroughly healed. Again conspicuous in the field, he in the sortie from Nimeguen on 10 Dec. 1794 lifted a French dragoon off his horse and carried him prisoner into the English camp. Prince Ernest then commanded the Hanoverian cavalry of the rear guard through the winter retreat before the French army, until the troops returned to England and Hanover respectively in February 1795.

In 1796 Prince Ernest returned to England with a high military reputation for courage, and in July 1799 he was made lieutenant-general in the English service, his first rank in the English army; his commission was antedated May 1798. In 1799 also he became governor of Chester. On 4 April 1799 George III created his four younger sons peers of the realm. Prince Ernest became Duke of Cumberland and of Teviotdale in the peerage of Great Britain, and Earl of Armagh in the peerage of Ireland. Parliament also granted him 12,000l. a year, which was in 1804 increased to 18,000l. In the same year (1799) the duke was appointed to command the division of cavalry which was to support the expedition of the Duke of York to the Helder, but owing to the immediate failure of the campaign the cavalry never embarked. On 28 March 1801 he was appointed colonel of the 15th light dragoons, afterwards hussars, and in April 1808 he was gazetted general (commission antedated September 1803); he also received some lucrative military commands, such as that of the Severn district, which he held from 1801 to 1804, and of the south-western district, from 1804 to 1807. Far more important than these military commands was the commencement of Cumberland's political career. He soon gained an important influence over the mind of the Prince of Wales, and in the House of Lords he showed himself a clear, if not very eloquent, speaker and a ready debater. He was a constant attendant at debates, and soon obtained much weight in the councils of his party. From the first he took his place as a tory partisan and a supporter of the protestant religion. His first speech in parliament was delivered in opposition to the Adultery

Prevention Bill in 1800, and in 1803 he seconded an address from the House of Lords in reply to an address from the crown, in a speech vigorously attacking the ambition of Napoleon. He was elected chancellor of Trinity College, Dublin, in 1805 and grand master of the Orange lodges of Ireland two years later. In 1808 he presented a petition from the Dublin corporation to the House of Lords with a speech in which he declared his undying opposition to any relief of the penal laws against the catholics. In 1810 the tory ministry introduced a regency bill, intended to limit the prerogatives of the Prince of Wales on account of his supposed sympathy with the whigs, when Cumberland at once told the ministers that they were filled with a false idea of his eldest brother's character, and both spoke and voted against them. This conduct strengthened his influence alike over the prince regent and the Duke of York. When his prophecy came true, and the prince regent maintained the tory ministry in power in 1812, the ministers too felt the perspicuity of Cumberland, and admitted him freely to their councils. This alliance with the tories exasperated both the whig leaders and the radical agitators and journalists.

On the night of 31 May 1810 the duke was found in his apartments in St. James's Palace with a terrible wound on his head, which would have been mortal had not the assassin's weapon struck against the duke's sword. Shortly afterwards his valet, Sellis, was found dead in his bed with his throat cut. On hearing the evidence of the surgeons and other witnesses, the coroner's jury returned a verdict that Sellis had committed suicide after attempting to assassinate the duke. The absence of any reasonable motive (see, however, Col. Willis's 'Diary MS.,' quoted in Jesse, *Life of George III*, iii. 545, 546) caused this event to be greatly discussed, and democratic journalists did not hesitate to accuse the duke of horrible crimes, and even to hint that he really murdered Sellis. In 1813 Henry White was sentenced to fifteen months' imprisonment and a fine of 200l. for publishing this rumour.

In the short campaign of 1806, under Lord Cathcart (1755–1843), the duke commanded a Hanoverian division, and after the battle of Leipzig, at which he was present as a spectator, he took over the electorate of Hanover in his father's name, and raised a fresh Hanoverian army, at the head of which he served during the campaigns of 1813 and 1814 in France. At the opening of the campaign of 1813 Cumberland was promoted to be a field-marshal in the British army, and in January 1815 he was made a G.C.B. on the extension of the order of the Bath. It now became apparent that the duke might possibly succeed to the throne of England. He accordingly married at Strelitz on 29 May 1815 his cousin, Frederica Caroline Sophia Alexandrina, daughter of the Duke of Mecklenburg-Strelitz, and widow of Prince Frederick of Prussia and of Prince Frederick of Solms-Braunfels.

This marriage, solemnised according to the rites of the English church on 29 Aug. 1815 at Carlton House, received the consent of the prince regent, but was most obnoxious to Queen Charlotte, who until the end of her life absolutely refused to receive the Duchess of Cumberland. It was not popular among the English people, who were prejudiced against the duke, and even the tory House of Commons refused to grant him the increase in his income, from 18,000l. to 24,000l. a year, which was subsequently granted to the Dukes of Clarence, Kent, and Cambridge.

The accession of the prince regent as George IV greatly increased Cumberland's power. His influence over the king was only rivalled by that of the Marchioness of Conyngham, and Greville's 'Journals' show how that influence was consistently maintained. The duke had the power of a strong mind over a weak one, and this influence, always exercised in the tory interest, caused him to be absolutely loathed by the radical journalists. Yet he sought no wealth or honour for himself, and the only appointment he received was in January 1827, the colonelcy of the royal horse guards (the blues). The death of the Princess Charlotte, and then that of the Duke of York, brought him nearer to the throne, and his policy was closely watched. He opposed the repeal of the Test and Corporation Acts with vigour, and when the Catholic Emancipation Bill was introduced into the House of Lords he said: 'I will act as I believe my sainted father would wish me to act, and that is to oppose to the utmost the dangerous measure, and to withdraw all confidence from the dangerous men who are forcing it through parliament.'

The accession of William IV put an end to Cumberland's influence on English politics. One of the first measures of the new reign was the placing of the royal horse guards under the authority of the commander-in-chief of the army. This measure was contrary to old precedent. Cumberland regarded it as a personal insult to himself, and at once resigned the colonelcy of the blues. He continued to attend regularly in the House of Lords, and energetically opposed the Reform Bill of 1832, the Municipal Corporations Reform Bill, and the new poor law. This conduct made the duke still more obnoxious to the radical press and to the whig statesmen, and in 1832 a pamphleteer named Joseph Phillips published the statement that 'the general opinion was that his royal highness had been the murderer of his servant Sellis.' The duke prosecuted the pamphleteer, who was immediately found guilty by the jury without retiring, and sentenced to six months' imprisonment. Lord Brougham in the House of Lords went nearly as far, and deliberately called him to his face 'the illustrious duke—illustrious only by courtesy.' William IV did not hesitate to insult his brother also, and in 1833, full of reforming ardour, he granted a liberal constitution to his Hanoverian dominions, which was drawn up by

Professor Dahlmann. This constitution was submitted by the king to his brothers, the Duke of Sussex and the Duke of Cambridge, who was governing Hanover as viceroy, but it was not even laid before Cumberland, the heir presumptive to the throne of Hanover. A further accusation was made openly in the House of Commons. The duke had been since 1817 grand master of the Irish Orangemen, and he was accused of making use of this position to pose as the defender of protestantism, and to tamper with the loyalty of the army. These accusations were only set at rest by the duke's categorical denial, and by the assistance he rendered in suppressing the whole of the Orange societies at the request of the government.

Upon the accession of Queen Victoria to the throne of England, the duke, under the regulations of the Salic law, succeeded to the German dominions of his family as King Ernest I of Hanover. He first took the oath of allegiance to the queen as an English peer, and then started for Hanover, where he took over the administration of his new kingdom from the Duke of Cambridge, who had acted as viceroy during the two preceding reigns. He at once cancelled the constitution, which had been granted by William IV, and assumed absolute power, a proceeding which drew down upon him the hatred of the liberal parties, both in England and in Hanover. The Hanoverian radicals conspired against him and projected open rebellion, and in the English House of Commons Colonel Perronet Thompson proposed that he should be deprived of his right to succeed to the throne if Queen Victoria should die. The fact that he was the next heir to the throne was the reason which urged the whig cabinet to hurry on the queen's marriage; and King Ernest, who had commenced his reign by quarrelling with the queen about the Hanover crown jewels, loudly protested against her marriage, and refused to be present at it. He preserved an implacable attitude for many years later, and when he visited Queen Victoria's court in the summer of 1843, gave many proofs of his surliness (Lee, *Queen Victoria*, p. 149).

The reign of King Ernest was popular in Hanover. The personal interest which he took in the affairs of his people, compared with the absenteeism of his three immediate predecessors, compensated to a great extent for his unbending toryism. In 1840, when his power was firmly established, he granted his subjects a new constitution, which was based upon modern ideas, and, while maintaining the privileges of the aristocracy, recognised the right of the people to representation. The care which he took of the material interests of his people, his accessibility, and the way in which he identified himself with Hanover, made up for his roughness of manner and confidence in himself. In 1848 he was supported by his people, and was able to suppress with ease the beginnings of revolt. In England he became yet more unpopular owing to his conduct with regard to the Stade tolls

Ernest

(see *The Stade Duties Considered*, by William Hutt, M.P., London, 1839). The king continued his interest in English politics, and constantly corresponded with his old friends and the leaders of the tory party. He had many domestic misfortunes; in 1841 he lost his wife, and his only son, afterwards George V of Hanover, was totally blind.

An interesting account of the court of Ernest of Hanover has been published by his English domestic chaplain ('The Court and Times of King Ernest of Hanover,' by the Rev. C. Allix Wilkinson), from which it appears that the character of the monarch remained the same throughout his life. He was always a plain, downright man, and his manners are well summed in the words of William IV, which were quoted to Mr. Wilkinson by Dean Wellesley: 'Ernest is not a bad fellow, but if any one has a corn he is sure to tread on it.' Of all the sons of George III he was the one who had the strongest will, the best intellect, and greatest courage (cf. 'Tales of my Father' [equerry to Ernest before his accession to Hanover], by A. M. F., 1902).

King Ernest died on 18 Nov. 1851 at his palace of Herrenhausen, at the age of eighty, and was buried on the 26th amidst the universal grief of his people. 'I have no objection to my body being exposed to the view of my loyal subjects,' he wrote in his will, 'that they may cast a last look at me, who never had any other object or wish than to contribute to their welfare and happiness, who have never consulted my own interests, while I endeavoured to correct the abuses and supply the wants which have arisen during a period of 150 years' absenteeism, and which are sufficiently explained by that fact.' The inscription affixed to the statue of King Ernest in the Grande Place of Hanover bears the words, 'Dem Landes Vater sein treues Volk.'

[There is no good biography of King Ernest of Hanover extant; of the obituary notices the most valuable are those in the Times, the Examiner, and in the Gent. Mag. for January 1852; for his military career see Jones's Narrative of the War in the Low Countries (London, 1795), the biographies in Philippart's Royal Military Calendar, and the record of the 15th hussars; for the attack on his life by Sellis, Jesse's Life of George III, iii. 541–6, and Rose's Diaries and Correspondence, ii. 437–46; for his quarrel with William IV see Stocqueler's Hist. of the Royal Horse Guards; for his political career the memoirs and journals, especially Pellew's Life of Lord Sidmouth and the Greville Journals; and for his later life Queen Victoria's Letters [1837–1861], 1907, and Reminiscences of the Court and Times of King Ernest of Hanover, by the Rev. C. A. Wilkinson.]

HENRY MORSE STEPHENS

published 1888

AUGUSTUS Frederick

(1773–1843)

Duke of Sussex

Sixth son and ninth child of King George III and Queen Charlotte, was born at Buckingham Palace 27 Jan. 1773. He was made K.G. in 1786. From the time he entered the university of Göttingen until 1804 he mostly resided abroad, on account of delicate health. Probably his lengthened sojourn on the Continent tended to foster his intellectual tastes, and undoubtedly the opportunity it afforded for diversified social intercourse assisted to liberalise his sentiments and to impart a genial facility to his manner. While resident in Rome in the winter of 1792, Prince Augustus made the acquaintance of Lady Augusta Murray, second daughter of the fourth Earl of Dunmore, and after four months' intimacy offered her his hand. The lady, who was some years older than the prince, at first declined the proposal, from regard to his interests; but on 21 March, 1793, they pledged eternal constancy to each other in a solemn written engagement. This was followed on 4 April by a marriage ceremony, performed by a clergyman of the Church of England named Gunn. To guard against the possibility of objections to the marriage from the fact that it had taken place in Roman jurisdiction, the ceremony was repeated at St. George's, Hanover Square, on 5 Dec. following, under the disguised names of Augustus Frederick and Augusta Murray. Shortly after the birth of a son on 13 January, 1794, news of the marriage reached the king, who, in accordance with the regulations of the Royal Marriage Act of 1772 (12 George III, c. 11), declared it void in August 1794. There were two children born of the marriage, Augustus Frederick, 13 Jan. 1794, and Ellen Augusta, 11 Aug. 1801, who married Sir Thomas Wilde, afterwards Lord Truro, and Lord Chancellor of England. They took the surname of d'Este, which belonged to common Italian ancestors of the father and mother, for Lady Augusta Murray was also of royal descent. For some years the prince ignored the decision of the court, but ultimately he acquiesced, and even in 1809 applied for the custody of his children, because he had heard that their mother was bringing them up in the idea that 'they were princes and princesses.' In 1806 Lady Augusta received royal licence to assume the name of D'Ameland instead of Murray. The son, Sir Augustus Frederick d'Este, made various efforts to get his claims recognised, and in 1831 filed a Bill in chancery, 'to prove the marriage good and valid' (see *Papers elucidating the Claims of Sir Augustus d'Este, K. C. H.*, 1831, and *A Letter to a Noble Lord explanatory of a Bill in the Court of Chancery*, 1831).

Augustus

It was not till 1801 that Prince Augustus was raised to the peerage by the title of Baron Arklow, Earl of Inverness and Duke of Sussex. His adoption of liberal political views estranged him from his father and the court, and excluded him from lucrative employments similar to those enjoyed by the other royal dukes. Indeed, he had incurred the resentment of his father for political contumacy as early as his seventh year, when 'he was by order of the king locked up in his nursery, and sent supperless to bed, for wearing Admiral Keppel's election colours' (Earl of Albemarle, *Fifty Years of my Life*, vol. ii. p. 103). The Duke of Sussex gave an energetic support to all the progressive political policy of his time, including the abolition of the slave trade, catholic emancipation, the removal of the civil disabilities of Jews and dissenters, the abolition of the corn laws, and parliamentary reform. His interest in the advancement of art and science was also genuine and enlightened, and he readily lent his influence to promote schemes of benevolence. In his later years he was in great request as chairman at anniversary dinners. When his eldest brother became Prince Regent in 1811, he succeeded him as grand master of the freemasons. He was elected president of the Society of Arts in 1816, and from 30 Nov. 1830 to 30 Nov. 1838, was president of the Royal Society. In the latter capacity he gave brilliant receptions in his apartments at Kensington Palace to men of science, but the expense they incurred induced him to resign the presidentship, as he preferred to employ the money in making additions to his library. This collection, which amounted in all to over 50,000 volumes, included about 1,000 editions of the Bible, and many Hebrew and other ancient manuscripts, the duke being specially interested in the study of Hebrew and of biblical subjects. The Duke of Sussex contracted a second marriage with Lady Cecilia, ninth daughter of the Earl of Arran, and widow of Sir George Buggin. In 1840 the lady was created Duchess of Inverness. There was no issue by the marriage, and the duke died from erysipelas 21 April 1843. By his will he directed that his remains should not be interred with the royal family at Windsor, but in the public cemetery at Kensal Green. As was the case with his brothers, there was in his character a strong vein of eccentricity and waywardness; but this was tempered by intentions which, on the whole, were well meant, by liberal and benevolent sympathies, and by genuine intellectual tastes. Most of the addresses delivered by the Duke of Sussex as president of the Royal Society have been published in pamphlet form, as has also his speech on the Roman Catholic Relief Bill in 1829.

[Gentleman's Magazine, New Series, vol. xix. pp. 645–652; S. L. Blanchard, The Cemetery at Kensal Green, 1844; Glück-Rosenthal, Memoir of the Duke of Sussex, 1846; Fitzgerald, Dukes and Princes of the Family of George III., 1882, vol. ii. pp. 40–96; Catalogue of Collection of Manuscripts and Music of the Duke of Sussex, 1846; Catalogue of Collections in Oil of the Duke of Sussex, 1843; Pettigrew, Bibliotheca Sussexiana.]

THOMAS FINLAYSON HENDERSON

published 1885

ADOLPHUS FREDERICK (1774–1850)

Duke of Cambridge

The tenth child and seventh son of King George III and Queen Charlotte, was born at the Queen's Palace, St. James's Park (now Buckingham Palace) in the evening of 24 Feb. 1774. On 2 June 1786 he was made a knight of the Garter, with three of his elder brothers; and on that occasion a new statute was read enlarging the number of the order, and ordaining that it should 'in future consist of the sovereign and twenty-five knights, exclusive of the sons of his majesty or his successors.' Having received his earlier education at Kew under Dr. Hughes and Mr. Cookson, he was sent, with his brothers Ernest and Augustus—afterwards severally Dukes of Cumberland and Sussex—to Göttingen, at the university of which they were entered on 6 July 1786. The three members of the 'little colony' sent by the king were 'highly delighted and pleased' with their academical pursuits and associations. 'I think,' writes the king to Bishop Hurd under date 30 July, 'Adolphus for the present seems the favourite of all, which, from his lively manners, is natural; but the good sense of Augustus will in the end prove conspicuous' (Jesse's *Memoirs of the Life and Reign of George III*, ii. 531).

In 1793 Prince Adolphus Frederick, who had visited the court of Prussia to perfect his knowledge of military tactics, was appointed colonel in the Hanoverian army, and, after serving for a short time as a volunteer with the British forces before Dunkirk, arrived in England in September of the same year, towards the close of which he was appointed colonel of the Hanoverian guards. He served in the campaign of 1794–5 as colonel and major-general in General Walmoden's corps, and on 24 Aug. 1798 was promoted to be lieutenant-general in the Hanoverian service, from which he was transferred, 18 June 1803, with the same rank, to the British army. On 17 November following he was appointed to be colonel-in-chief of the king's German legion, a force in British pay, and destined for the relief of Hanover, then menaced, together with the rest of eastern and northern Europe, by the French armies. Disappointed, however, at the indifference of the Hanoverians to the honour and advantage of their connection with England, the prince presently returned to this country, leaving the British forces under the command of Count Walmoden, who soon afterwards surrendered.

Peerages fell comparatively late to the younger sons of George III, and were conferred simultaneously on the Princes Augustus—whose principal creation was that of Duke of Sussex—and Adolphus on 24 Nov. 1801, when the latter was created Baron of Culloden, Earl of Tipperary, and Duke of Cambridge. On 3 February following, 1802, the Duke of Cambridge was sworn a member of the privy council, and took his place at the board on the left hand of the king.

In 1804 the Duke of Cambridge was nominated to the military command of the home district, and on 5 Sept. 1805 received the colonelcy of the Coldstream guards, to which was added, 22 Jan. 1827, the colonelcy-in-chief of the 60th, or the King's Royal rifle corps. Several years previously, on 26 Nov. 1813, he had been promoted, with his brother, the Duke of Cumberland, to be field-marshal in the British army.

The Duke of Cambridge again took the command in the electorate of Hanover on the recovery of its independence after its sometime annexation to the kingdom of Westphalia; and after the treaty of Vienna, October 1814, had elevated the electorate into a kingdom, the Duke of Cambridge was, in November 1816, appointed to the viceroyalty. He continued to discharge the important functions of the office until the year 1837, when the death of King William IV opened the throne of Hanover to the Duke of Cumberland. The administration of Hanoverian affairs by the Duke of Cambridge was characterised by wisdom, mildness, and discretion, and by the introduction of timely and conciliatory reforms. He successively weathered the storms, whether popular or academical, of the revolutionary period of 1831, and his prudent management of affairs is said to have gone 'a great way to preserve the Hanoverian crown for his family.'

In July 1811 the Duke of Cambridge had been elected chancellor of the university of St. Andrews in succession to Viscount Melville; but held office only till April 1814, when he was succeeded by Lord Melville, the son of his predecessor, who accepted the distinction 'vice the Duke of Cambridge resident in Germany' (Gent. Mag. April 1814). After his return to this country the Duke of Cambridge acquired great popularity; and he was recognised as 'emphatically the connecting link between the throne and the people' (United Service Gazette, 13 July 1850). He was an indefatigable supporter of public charities. In committee meetings he was accustomed to act as a peacemaker and healer of divisions, or else as a thorough and fearless investigator, who was determined to 'put the burden and disgrace of the dispute on the right shoulders' (Times, 9 July 1850). He was president of at least six hospitals, and the patron or vice-patron of more than a score of other beneficent corporations. 'He was also a supporter of almost every literary and of scientific institution of importance in the empire' (*United Service Gazette*, 13 July 1850); and in the various manifestations of his devotion to the fine arts, especially painting and music, achieved in his day a fair reputation in the latter among amateur performers.

In politics the Duke of Cambridge was on the conservative side, having in early life withstood, not without being sensibly affected by their influence, the attractive overtures of the leaders of the whigs, Fox, Sheridan, the Prince of Wales, the Duke of Sussex, and the Duchess of Devonshire. The duke's partisanship was modified, however, by a constant desire to support, whenever he could do so conscientiously, the measures of any government which for the time represented the choice of the sovereign. He was not an orator, either in the House of Lords or in any other place; but his earnestness and sincerity won from his audiences the tribute of attention and respect. He died at Cambridge House, Piccadilly, on the evening of Monday, 8 July 1850, and was buried at Kew, amidst the scenes of his childhood, and near his favourite suburban retreat.

The Duke of Cambridge married at Cassel on 7 May, and on 1 June 1818 in London, the Princess Augusta Wilhelmina Louisa, third daughter of Frederick, landgrave of Hesse-Cassel, by whom he left a son and two daughters—the present Duke of Cambridge, the Princess Augusta Caroline, married to Frederick William, reigning grand duke of Mecklenburg Strelitz, and the Princess Mary Adelaide, the wife of the Prince and Duke of Teck.

The Duke of Cambridge was a prince of Brunswick-Luneberg; G.C.B. 2 Jan. 1815; G.C.M.G., 1825; G.C.H. (grand cross of the royal Hanoverian Guelphic order); knight of the Prussian orders of the black and the red eagle; a commissioner of the Royal Military College and the Royal Military Asylum; ranger of Richmond Park 29 Aug. 1835; ranger of St. James's Park and Hyde Park 31 May 1843; warden and keeper of the New Forest 22 Feb. 1845; and honorary LL.D. of Cambridge, 4 July 1842.

[Jesse's Memoirs of the Life and Reign of George III; Gent. Mag. Aug. 1850, N.S. xxiv. 204; Annual Register; Times, 9 July 1850; United Service Gazette, 13 July 1850.]

ARTHUR HENRY GRANT

published 1885

(1775–1839)

Sir

Lieutenant-general, second son of the Rev. Edward Taylor (1734–1798), of Bifrons, Kent, rector of Patricksbourne, by his wife, Margaret, daughter of Thomas Payler of Ileden, Kent, was born on 29 Sept. 1755 at Bifrons. A younger brother, Sir Brook Taylor 1776–1846, was in the diplomatic service, and acted as British minister successively at the courts of Hesse-Cassel, Wurtemberg, and Munich, and as ambassador at Berlin from 1828 to 1831; he was created G.C.H. in 1822, and was admitted to the privy council in 1828 (*Gent. Mag.* 1847, pt. i. p. 82).

During the wanderings of his family on the continent between 1780 and 1790 Herbert received private tuition, and became a good linguist. In Rome he made the acquaintance of Lord Camelford, by whom he was introduced to Lord Grenville, who gave him a place in the foreign office under Mr. (afterwards Sir) James Bland Burgess. Taylor's knowledge of foreign languages made him very useful, and Lord Grenville occasionally employed him on confidential work at his own house. In December 1792 he accompanied Sir James Murray (afterwards Murray-Pulteney) on a special mission to the Prussian headquarters at Frankfort. After a few weeks Murray left Frankfort to take up his military duties as adjutant-general to the Duke of York's army at Antwerp, and Taylor remained behind for a short time in charge of the mission. In April 1793, on Murray's application, Taylor joined the army headquarters. Murray presented him to the Duke of York, to whom he became greatly attached. He was employed as Murray's secretary, and was present as a volunteer at the action of St. Amand (8 May), the battle of Famars (23 May), and the sieges of Valenciennes and Dunkirk.

On 25 March 1794 Taylor was given a commission as cornet in the 2nd dragoon guards, and on 17 July following he was promoted to be lieutenant. Upon the return of Murray to England, Taylor remained with the Duke of York as assistant secretary. He generally joined his regiment when in the field, and was present at the actions of 17, 22, and 26 April, near Cateau; of 10 and 22 May, near Tournay, and at other operations of the campaign, including the retreat into Holland. On 6 May 1795 he was promoted to be captain in the 2nd dragoon guards. On the return of the Duke of York to England, Taylor remained with the army as assistant secretary to the commander-in-chief of the British forces on the continent, and served in that capacity successively with Lieutenant-general Harcourt and Sir David Dundas.

On 16 Sept. 1795 Taylor returned to England, having been appointed on 1 Aug. of that year aide-de-camp to the commander-in-chief, the Duke of York. He was soon afterwards nominated assistant military secretary in the commander-in-chief's office.

In July 1798 Taylor accompanied Lord Cornwallis to Ireland on his appointment as lord-lieutenant, in the threefold capacity of aide-de-camp, military secretary, and private secretary. He returned to England in February 1799 to take over the duties of private secretary to the Duke of York. He went to Holland as aide-de-camp to the duke in the expedition to the Helder in September, and was present at the battles of 19 Sept. and of 2 and 6 Oct.

On 22 Jan. 1801 Taylor was promoted to be major in the 2nd dragoon guards, and on 26 Dec. of the same year to be lieutenant-colonel in the 9th West India regiment. On 25 June 1802 he was placed on half-pay, and on 25 May was brought into the Coldstream guards, of which the Duke of York was colonel. He continued in the appointment of private secretary and aide-de-camp to the Duke of York until 13 June 1805, when he was appointed private secretary to the king. The king placed every confidence in him, so that his position was one of great delicacy, but his straightforwardness secured the good opinion of all. On the establishment of the regency he was continued in the same office to the queen, who was appointed by act of parliament guardian of the king's person. By the same act Taylor was appointed one of the three commissioners of the king's real and personal estate. He was promoted to be brevet colonel on 25 July 1810, and to be major-general on 4 June 1813.

In November 1813 he was appointed to command a brigade in the army of Sir Thomas Graham (afterwards Lord Lynedoch), which was besieging Antwerp. He returned to England in March 1814, when he was sent on special military missions to Bernadotte, crown prince of Sweden, then commanding the Swedish force in Germany, and to The Hague. During these absences from the court his place was taken by his brother (afterwards Sir) Brook Taylor. He resumed the duties of private secretary to Queen Charlotte on his return, and continued in this office until her death in November 1818. In 1819 he was made a knight of the royal Guelphic order. From 1820 to 1823 he represented Windsor in parliament, resigning his seat because he found he could not satisfactorily fulfil both his parliamentary and other duties. On 25 March 1820 Taylor was appointed military secretary at the Horse Guards. On 23 April 1823 he was made colonel of the 85th foot, in 1824 a knight grand cross of the royal Guelphic order, and on 27 May 1825 was promoted to be lieutenant-general. On the death of the Duke of York in January 1827, he was appointed military secretary to the new commander-in-chief, the Duke of Wellington; but on the duke resigning the command-in-chief in July 1827, Taylor was nominated by Lord Palmerston, then secretary at war, to be a deputy secretary at war in the military branch of the war office; the king had already made him his first and principal aide-de-camp on 1 May 1827. On 19 March 1828 Taylor was appointed master surveyor and surveyor-general of the ordnance of the United Kingdom. On 25 Aug. of the same year he became adjutant-general of the forces, an appointment which he held until the accession of William IV, to whom he became private secretary, and continued in the office during the whole of his reign. On 16 April 1834 the king conferred upon him the grand cross of the order of the Bath. On the death of William IV in 1837 Taylor retired into private life, but was continued by the young queen in the appointment of first and principal aide-de-camp to the sovereign. He had already received from George III a pension of 1,000l. a year on the civil list, with remainder to his widow. In the autumn of 1837 he went with his family to Cannes. In the spring of 1838 he went on to Italy, and he died at Rome on 20 March 1839. His body was embalmed for conveyance to England, but was buried in the protestant cemetery at Rome. In the middle of April his remains were exhumed and sent to England, and on 13 June were deposited in a vault of the chapel of St. Katherine's Hospital, Regent's Park, to the mastership of which he had been appointed in 1818.

Taylor married, in 1819, Charlotte Albina, daughter of Edward Disbrowe of Walton Hall, Derbyshire, M.P. for Windsor, vice-chamberlain to Queen Charlotte, and granddaughter of the third Earl of Buckinghamshire. By her he left two daughters, who, with their mother, survived him.

Taylor, who was a confidential friend of the Duke of York, and who was nominated one of the duke's executors, wrote the 'Memoirs of the last Illness and Decease of H.R.H. the Duke of York,' London, 1827, 8vo (three editions). In 1838, in a pamphlet ('Remarks,' &c.) he defended his patrons George III and George IV from some strictures in an article in the 'Edinburgh Review,' No. 135.

A portrait by W. J. Newton was engraved by W. Ward.

[War Office Records; Despatches; Annual Register, 1839; Gent. Mag. 1839; United Service Journal, 1839 (contains a very complete memoir); Naval and Military Mag. vols. i–iii. 1827–1828; The Royal Military Calendar, 1820; Correspondence of Earl Grey, 1867; Nichols's Lit. Illustr. vi. 755; Edinb. Rev. October 1838; Evans's Cat. of Engraved Portraits, vol. ii.; Carmichael Smyth's Chronological Epitome of the Wars in the Low Countries.]

ROBERT HAMILTON VETCH

published 1898

Princess, youngest daughter, and last and fifteenth child of George III, was born 7 Aug. 1783. Always delicate, and the successor of two delicate little brothers who died shortly before her birth, this princess was the object of most careful and affectionate concern to all around her, and was especially the pet and companion of her father (Mme. D'Arblay's *Diary*, iii. 25). The child understood the dignity of her position even at three years old (*ibid.* iii. 51, iv. 3, &c.); she would remember her sick friends in her prayers (*ibid.* iii. 202); yet she was childlike enough to refuse to go to bed unless Miss Burney undressed her (*ibid.* pp. 172 and 185), and to insist on Miss Burney and Mr. Smelt playing at phaeton-driving with her, with all the fun of a frisky horse (*ibid.* p. 178). The delicacy of the princess's health continuing as she grew up, she did not become so proficient in accomplishments as her sisters, though her skill at the piano was considerable, and she was comely and graceful, full of all a girl's attractiveness and charm. She was warmly disposed to be charitable, and imposed upon herself the expense of three little girls, chosen from necessitous homes, whom she educated and brought up to trade, and who were allowed, upon occasions, to visit her. One of these, Mary, the princess apprenticed to her own dressmaker, Mrs. Bingley, of Piccadilly; and on Mrs. Bingley having to inform her royal highness of the unhappy fall of the girl, the princess wrote a touching letter to her, exhorting her to consider her position and return to a virtuous life (Hone's *Every-Day Book*, i. 1074). As early as 1798, when the princess was only fifteen years old, she suffered from painful lameness in her knee, and her health began to break up. She went to Worthing for sea-bathing (Mme. D'Arblay's *Diary*, 1 Dec. 1798, vi. 178), which gave much benefit, and on a return of the malady from time to time the same remedy was tried again. In 1808, however, all means began to fail, and the princess had to pass most of her hours amidst all the restraints of an invalid. In 1809 she could occasionally take short walks in the garden. This improvement was but temporary, however, and in August 1810 her sufferings grew sharper, whilst in the October of that year she was seized with St. Anthony's fire (erysipelas), which cut off all hope, confined her to her bed on the 25th, when all the world was celebrating her father's jubilee (*Annual Register*, 1810, appendix, p. 406), and made it manifest that her death was rapidly approaching. The king's distress was intense. Himself part-blind then, and having only intervals of sanity, he summoned his daughter's physicians to him at seven o'clock every morning, and three or four other times during the day, questioning them minutely as to her condition. The dying princess had a mourning ring made for the king, composed of a lock of her hair, under crystal, set round with diamonds; and saying to him, 'Remember me,' she herself pressed it on his finger, thereby throwing him into such poignant grief that he passed into that last sad condition of madness from which he was never restored. Mercifully the princess was never informed of this terrible effect of her gift (*Gent. Mag.* lxxx. part ii. p. 487); and lingering a few days more, waited upon to the last by her favourite and devoted sister, the Princess Mary, she died, at Augusta Lodge, Windsor, on 2 Nov. 1810, aged 27; and was buried at Windsor, Tuesday evening, 13 Nov. 1810, with full pageantry of pages, ushers, knights, equerries, and grooms (see *State Ceremonial*). Her royal highness left the Prince of Wales her residuary legatee, desiring him to sell her jewels to pay her debts and realise enough for a few small legacies; but the prince gave the jewels to the Princess Mary, and took upon himself all the other charges.

The untimely death of the Princess Amelia evoked warm sympathy throughout the country, many sermons and elegies being published on the occasion, and the incident of her gift of the ring was commemorated in verse by Peter Pindar and others. The stanzas beginning 'Unthinking, idle, wild, and young,' were attributed to the Princess Amelia, and appeared in most publications of the day as her undoubted composition. The authorship has been questioned, however (see *George III, his Court*, &c., ii. 357, where the stanzas are given in full; also *Gent. Mag.* for 1810, and the monthly magazines).

[Gent. Mag. Supplement to, 1810, 646; ibid. 1810, 565; European Magazine, iv. part ii. p. 159; Annual Register.]

Jennett Humphreys

published 1885

(c. 1784–1870)

Baroness

Royal governess, was born c.1784 in Hanover, a younger child among the two sons and seven daughters of a Lutheran pastor and his wife, Melusine Palm, herself the child of a clergyman. Lehzen came to England, after service in the aristocratic family of von Marenholtz, in December 1819 as governess to Princess Féodore, daughter (by her first marriage) of Princess Victoria of Leiningen, since 1818 Duchess of Kent, to whom was born, shortly before Lehzen's arrival, the future Queen Victoria. In 1824 Lehzen was appointed governess to the young princess. When in 1830 the Duchess of Northumberland was appointed official governess, Lehzen stayed as lady in attendance and Victoria's constant attendant, without an official appointment, until 1842, acting latterly as her secretary in private matters. Lehzen made it a condition of her appointment that the princess should never see strangers except in her presence. She herself was never to receive her own acquaintances in her quarters. Though she encouraged the princess to keep a journal, she never kept one herself, thinking it inappropriate to her position.

The accession of William IV in 1827 brought serious friction between the Duchess of Kent and the new king. William resented the mother's influence over the heir presumptive, while the duchess asserted, not always successfully, her own and the princess's position. In the quarrels arising from the 'Kensington system' established by Sir John Conroy, comptroller of the duchess's household, the princess was an unhappy pawn. Until her accession her only true, constant, and ever-present friend and champion was Lehzen. When, ill with typhoid in October 1835, Victoria was pressed hard by Conroy to nominate him as her personal secretary on her accession, she persistently and successfully resisted, with Lehzen's support. By this time Lehzen 'occupied the first place in her pupil's thoughts and affections' (Esher). After Victoria's accession Lehzen, never skilled in personal relationships, failed to adjust to changed circumstances and her charge's coming of age. Jealousy, first of William Lamb, second Viscount Melbourne, and then, more seriously, of Prince Albert, whom the queen married in 1840, led to serious tensions in the royal household. Lehzen was blamed, probably wrongly, for the queen's ineptness in the Lady Flora Hastings affair, and fear of losing Lehzen was a major contribution to the queen's stubbornness in the 'bedchamber crisis' of 1839.

In September 1842, after quarrels about the management of the royal nursery, Lehzen left the royal service on Albert's insistence, with the gift of a carriage from the queen and a pension of £800 p.a. She lived out her life unmarried in Bückeburg in Hanover, first with her remaining sister, who died within the year, and then alone. She saw the queen occasionally on royal visits to Germany. 'My dearest, kindest Lehzen' died 9 September 1870 in Bückeburg.

Though not lettered, Lehzen read (and read aloud to the princess) and imparted to the child a love of history. She provided the affection and discipline which the princess never received from her mother. The princess was taught to curb her natural impetuous temper and to own her mistakes to all she had wronged, regardless of rank. 'She was very strict', the queen remembered, 'and the Princess had great respect and even awe of her, but with that the greatest affection.' Lehzen was the greatest single influence, and that for good, in the formative period of the character of the lonely, little-loved princess. 'That Lehzen handed over to the nation a potentially great queen must be to her credit' (Longford).

There is a miniature of Lehzen by Koepke in royal possession. She was made a baroness on the Hanover establishment by George IV in 1827.

[Elizabeth Longford, *Victoria R.I.*, 1964; R. B. Brett (Viscount Esher), *The Girlhood of Queen Victoria*, 2 vols., 1912; C. Woodham-Smith, *Queen Victoria, her Life and Times, 1819–1861*, 1972; Philip W. Wilson (ed.), *The Greville Diary*, 2 vols., 1927, vol. i, p. 27; Royal Archives, Windsor, Y 203/80, Y 203/79.]

H. G. Pitt

published 1993

CONROY Sir John Ponsonby

(1786–1854)

First baronet

Courtier, was born 21 October 1786 in Caehrun, Caernarfonshire, the eldest in the family of five sons and one daughter of John Ponsonby Conroy, barrister, and his wife Margaret Wilson, who were both Irish-born. Commissioned in the Royal Artillery in 1803, he became equerry to the Duke of Kent when Edward married Princess Victoire of Leiningen in 1818 to ensure the succession, Princess (later Queen) Victoria being born in 1819. Conroy was an organizer of genius. He made it possible for the duke and his eight-months pregnant duchess to rush back from Germany to Kensington Palace for the birth, putting up the royal cavalcade at his home in Shooter's Hill on the way. When the duke died suddenly in 1820, Conroy became comptroller of the Duchess of Kent's household. In 1822 he retired from the army as captain on half pay.

At first Conroy shared his influence on the duchess with her brother, Prince Leopold of Saxe-Coburg, but after Leopold ascended the Belgian throne in 1830, Conroy ruled supreme. He survived the 'Cumberland plot' in 1829, when a rumour said to have been started by Ernest, Duke of Cumberland, circulated, saying that the Duchess of Kent was Conroy's mistress. This was intended to discredit the duchess and have Princess

Victoria removed from her care, and even, Conroy feared, killed. William IV angrily called him 'King John'. He established the 'Kensington system', by which Victoria should be suitably educated as heir presumptive to the Crown, her mother should be created regent if the king died before Victoria was eighteen, Conroy should be appointed Victoria's private secretary with a peerage, and a rival court should develop at Kensington, cut off from William IV's Tory politics and morals. Victoria had no youthful companionship except Conroy's daughters and no personal champion but her German governess, Baroness Lehzen, Conroy's implacable foe. In order to make Victoria known to the people, Conroy would run her around the country on semi-royal tours, after the last of which, in 1835, she succumbed to typhoid. While still on her sick-bed, Conroy tried to force her to appoint him as her personal secretary when she became queen. Afterwards she told Lord Melbourne: 'I resisted in spite of my illness.'

As William IV lay dying, Conroy's final desperate attempt to coerce Victoria failed. Succeeding to the throne on 20 June 1837, she dismissed him from her household. But he continued to serve her mother, being partly responsible for the tragedy of the duchess's lady-in-waiting, Lady Flora Hastings, who died of a tumour while suspected of being pregnant by Conroy. The duchess, too, was reported to be Conroy's mistress, though without evidence. However, he cannot be absolved of mismanaging her funds and those of Princess Sophia, Victoria's aunt and Conroy's 'spy', from whom he also received gifts.

In 1839 Wellington persuaded him to resign from the Duchess of Kent's household and go abroad for a time. He had a Guelphic knighthood, an honorary DCL from Oxford, and foreign honours. He was created baronet in 1837, but Sir Robert Peel refused him the Irish peerage promised him by Melbourne. 'JC' was not the arch-villain Victoria painted, but the victim of his own inordinate ambition. In 1808 he married Elizabeth, daughter of Major-General Benjamin Fisher and niece of Dr John Fisher, bishop of Salisbury, who had tutored Prince Edward, Duke of Kent. They had four sons, one of whom died young, and two daughters. Conroy believed his wife to be the Duke of Kent's natural child. This fantasy may have accounted for the arrogance of Conroy towards Queen Victoria. He died at Arborfield Hall, Berkshire, 2 March 1854. He was succeeded in the baronetcy by his eldest son, Edward (born 1809).

[Conroy papers in Balliol College, Oxford; Elizabeth Longford, *Victoria R.I.*, 1964; 'All Sir John's Invention', MS life of Conroy, 1990, by Katherine Hudson (in her possession).]

ELIZABETH LONGFORD

published 1993

(1786–1861)

Duchess of

Fourth daughter of Francis Frederic Antony, hereditary prince (afterwards duke) of Saxe-Saalfeld-Coburg, by Augusta Carolina Sophia, daughter of Henry, count Reuss-Eberstadt, was born at Coburg on 17 Aug. 1786, and married on 21 Dec. 1803 to Emich Charles, hereditary prince, afterwards prince of Leiningen-Dachsburg-Hardenburg, a widower twenty-three years her senior. The marriage was happy, and on the death of the prince (4 July 1814) he left his widow guardian of their only son, Charles Frederick William Ernest (1804–1856), and regent of the principality. Her only other child by the prince was Anne Feodorowna Augusta Charlotte Wilhelmina (1807–1872), who resided with her mother till her marriage on 18 Feb. 1828 to Ernest Christian Charles, prince of Hohenlohe-Langenburg.

Princess Victoria Mary married in 1818 a second husband, Edward Augustus, duke of Kent, fourth son of George III. The marriage ceremony took place at Coburg on 29 May, and was repeated at Kew on 13 July. By the Duke of Kent she had an only daughter, Alexandrina Victoria, queen of England. On the duke's death on 23 Jan. 1820 the duchess was in straitened circumstances, having only a jointure of 6,000*l.* and an allowance of 3,000*l.* made her by her brother Leopold. In 1825, however, parliament voted her an annuity of 6,000*l.* towards the support and education of her daughter Victoria, and a further annuity of 10,000*l.* was granted her in 1831. In the previous year she had been appointed regent of the realm in the event of her daughter succeeding to the throne while yet a minor. She resided at Kensington Palace, devoting herself to the education of her daughter, and during the reign of George IV saw little society; but as the Princess Victoria grew up she took her from time to time to visit most of the places of interest in England, and gathered round her at Kensington a small highly intellectual coterie. She regretted the princess's accession to the throne in 1837 as depriving her of her one interest and occupation. Thenceforward she accompanied the court on its periodical migrations.

She died of cancer at Frogmore on 16 March 1861, and was buried in St. George's Chapel, Windsor on 25 March, whence her remains were transferred to the Frogmore mausoleum.

[Queen Victoria's Letters, 1837–61, 3 vols. 1907; S. Lee's Life of Queen Victoria, 1902; Almanach de Gotha for 1790, 1805–6, 1817, 1829; Commons' Journals, lxxx.

471, lxxxvi. pt. ii. p. 727; Greville Memoirs, 1837–52, i. 15; Gent. Mag. 1861, pt. i. p. 456; Sir Theodore Martin's *Life of the Prince Consort.*]

JAMES MCMULLEN RIGG

published 1892

STOCKMAR Christian Friedrich

(1787–1863)

Baron Stockmar

Adviser of Prince Albert, was born 22 August 1787 in Coburg of German parentage and Swedish descent, the eldest son and second child in the family of two sons and two daughters of Johann Ernest Gotthelf Stockmar, a scientific lawyer. A quiet, unobtrusive youth, Stockmar was educated at Coburg Gymnasium and from 1805 to 1810 studied medicine at the universities of Würzburg, Erlangen, and Jena.

In 1812 Stockmar opened a military hospital in Coburg. Favourably noticed by Prince Leopold of Saxe-Coburg-Saalfeld, Stockmar was invited in 1816 to be Leopold's physician-in-ordinary. Leopold made Stockmar promise never to leave him after his wife, Princess Charlotte, died in childbirth in 1817 at Claremont near Windsor. Prudently, 'Stocky' had not attended her, just held her hand. He was promoted to be Leopold's private secretary and in 1831, when his master became king of the Belgians, a Bavarian baron. He helped organize Leopold's court, devised the constitution, and inspired the Coburg–Portuguese marriage of 1835; above all he promoted the marriage between Queen Victoria and Prince Albert, Leopold's nephew, in 1840. Stockmar's royal career was well under way.

On 20 June 1837 Victoria had ascended the British throne. Sixteen days earlier 'the Baron' (as Victoria and Albert called him) had been sent to England by her 'Uncle Leopold' as his *alter ego*, and was Victoria's guest at breakfast on her first day as queen. He was soon working on a valuable theory of the Crown as above party politics. He left England in 1838 to vet the suitability of Prince Albert of Saxe-Coburg and Gotha for Victoria's consort, returning when they married. For the next seventeen years he spent only the summers in Germany, saying of Albert, 'I love him as if he were my own son.' With Albert he planned the royal children's education and systematized the royal household. Before their reforms all footmen, livery-porters, and under-butlers were under the master of the horse. Stockmar took care not to get involved in court favours, such as the bribe offered by an MP of £10,000 to obtain him a peerage. Stockmar's political views were sometimes absurd. 'The omnipotence of the House of Commons,' he wrote, 'is revolution itself and death to the true old English constitution'—of which he fancied himself the best judge. He distrusted British statesmen: Sir Robert Peel was 'myopic', the third Viscount Palmerston (Albert's opponent) 'insane'. He advised the monarch to avoid being 'a Mandarin figure' but to become a 'Permanent Premier'. The European revolutions of 1848 he saw as a golden opportunity for introducing constitutional monarchies and a united Germany in alliance with Britain.

By 1855 his health was failing. In the past he had settled several disputes between Victoria and Albert. Now his 'nerves' were too weak to make his advice effective. He returned to Germany for good in 1857, moving for a time to Berlin to be near Prince and Princess Frederick William of Prussia ('Fritz' and 'Vicky'). When Prince Albert died in 1861, Stockmar's hopes were shattered. His absence may even have contributed to the tragedy, for on his deathbed Albert lamented, 'if only Stockmar were here...' It was not until his last years that Stockmar enjoyed a real home life, though married in 1821 in Coburg to a cousin, Fanny Sommer, the daughter of a physician. They had two sons and one daughter. Stockmar died 9 July 1863 in Coburg. His son, Ernest, wrote Stockmar's *Memoirs*, describing them as lifting the veil 'but a little'. An angry Queen Victoria, however, felt it had been lifted far too much, particularly over the clashes between Palmerston as foreign secretary and the prince consort.

[F. Max Müller (ed.), *Memoirs of Baron Stockmar*, 2 vols., 1872; E. Longford, *Victoria R.I.*, 1964; Roger Fulford (ed.), *Darling Child: Private Correspondence of Queen Victoria and the Crown Princess of Prussia 1871–1878*, 1976.]

ELIZABETH LONGFORD

published 1993

ADELAIDE (1792–1849)

Queen Dowager

Amelia Adelaide Louisa Theresa Caroline, eldest child of George, duke of Saxe-Coburg Meiningen, and of Louisa, daughter of Christian Albert, prince of Hohenlohe-Langenburg, was born 13 Aug. 1792. Brought up by a widowed mother (her father died 1803), her reputation for amiability determined Queen Charlotte to select her as a wife for William Henry, duke of Clarence, whose marriage, with that of his three brothers, took place when the death of the Princess Charlotte made it desirable to provide heirs for the crown. A temporary difficulty, caused by the refusal of parliament to raise the duke's allowance of 18,000l. a year by more than 6,000l. instead of the 10,000l. demanded, was got over, and the princess and her mother arrived in London for the marriage, 4 July 1818. It took place at Kew, simultaneously with that of the Duke of Kent, on 18 July, and proved a happy one, despite the disparity in years (the bride was in her twenty-sixth, the bridegroom in his fifty-third year) and the absence of any preliminary courtship.

The Duke and Duchess of Clarence passed the first year of their marriage in Hanover, where, in 1819, a daughter was born to them, to live only a few hours. Their second child, the Princess Elizabeth Georgina Adelaide, born 10 Dec. 1820, died in the following year. Their principal English residence was Bushey Park, where they lived in comparative retirement until the accession of William to the throne on the death of George IV, 26 June 1830. By a bill passed in the following November, the queen was nominated as regent, in case a child of hers should survive the king, and provision was made for her widowhood by a settlement of 100,000l. a year, with Marlborough House and Bushey Park, of which she was immediately constituted perpetual ranger. The royal coronation took place on 8 Sept. 1831.

Her supposed interference in politics rendered the queen very unpopular during and after the reform agitation, and her carriage was once assailed in the streets by an angry mob, who were only beaten off by the canes of her footmen. On the dismissal of the whig (Lord Melbourne's) ministry in 1834, the words of the 'Times,' 'The queen has done it all,' were placarded over London. The dismissal of her chamberlain, Lord Howe, for a vote adverse to the ministry, caused her much annoyance, and she refused to accept any one in his place, which he continued to fill unofficially.

In the spring of 1837, Queen Adelaide was summoned to Germany to her mother's deathbed, and had not long returned, when the commencement of the king's last illness entailed a long and arduous attendance. He died in her arms on 20 June, and was buried at Windsor on 8 July, the queen, contrary to precedent, assisting at the funeral service. Her health was shattered by the fatigues she had undergone, and her subsequent life was that of an invalid seeking relief by change of climate. She spent a winter in Malta (1838–39), where the church of Valetta, erected by her at a cost of 10,000l., remains a permanent memorial of her stay, visited Madeira in 1847, and died from the rupture of a blood-vessel in the chest at Bentley Priory, near Stanmore, 2 Dec. 1849. Her written requests that she should be buried simply, and her remains borne to the grave by sailors, were complied with at her interment at Windsor on 13 Dec. She had long lived down her unpopularity, and won universal esteem by her blameless life and royal munificence in charity. She subscribed about 20,000*l.* yearly to public institutions, and her private donations were equally liberal. Her domestic life was overshadowed by the loss of her children, a blow no less to ambition than to affection.

[Doran's Memoir of Queen Adelaide, London, 1861; Maley's Historical Recollections of the Reign of William IV, London, 1860; Molesworth's History of England from 1830 to 1874, London, 1874; Greville Memoirs, ed. by H. Reeve, 4th ed., London, 1875.]

ELLEN MARY CLERKE

published 1885

CHARLOTTE Augusta

(1796–1817)

Princess

Was born at Carlton House, London, on 7 Jan. 1796. She was the only daughter of George, prince of Wales, afterwards George IV, and Caroline of Brunswick. Before her birth differences between her parents had widened to an irreparable breach, and a formal separation was agreed upon when she was but a few months old. The effect of this was to consign her in childhood to the care of governesses, the chief superintendent being Lady Elgin, who, until 1804, watched over her, and acted as the medium of communication between her and her parents. According to the report of those who knew her as a girl, she was bright and intelligent, very merry, but 'pepper-hot, too.' 'Princess Charlotte,' says Miss Hayman, her sub-governess, 'is very delightful, and tears her caps with showing me how Mr. Canning takes off his hat as he rides in the park.' Her home at this time was Carlton House, the then town residence of the Prince of Wales. Letters from the Duchess of Würtemberg, formerly princess royal, not only bear witness to her own high principle, but also disclose the plan of education adopted for her niece. Among other things, Lady Elgin was to show her bible pictures, and hopes are expressed that her English master has, 'by dint of pains and patience, got the better of the hesitation in her speech, which is unfortunately very common on all sides in the Brunswick family.' The child, the duchess trusted, might ultimately be the means of a reconciliation between her father and mother. But, as time wore on, things grew worse instead of better. In 1805 she was removed to the Lower Lodge, Windsor. For reasons probably connected with his alienation from his wife, the Prince of Wales avoided acknowledging his daughter as heir presumptive; and Queen Charlotte sided with him in concluding that the best training for a girl of the princess's high spirit was seclusion. Her mother she met for two hours a week at the house of the Duchess of Brunswick, mother of the Princess of Wales. The establishment of the regency in 1811 confirmed the regent's estrangement from his daughter, and offered further opportunity for ignoring her. On the resignation of her governess, Lady de Clifford, when the princess was nearly seventeen, a petition that a lady of the bedchamber should take her place resulted in her being transferred to the care of Miss Cornelia Knight, and her position at this juncture may be said to have been that of a naughty child in disgrace. But neither her loneliness nor the constraints of ceremony seem to have effaced her native simplicity or her personal charm, and some of her letters to her few friends are delightfully fresh and genuine. In December 1813 Princess Charlotte became engaged to William, hereditary prince of Orange. Having served under Wellington, and been educated in England, he was ostensibly a not ineligible husband. But his residence in Holland, owing to his father's return from exile to the throne, became a necessity; and this fact, though it attracted the prince regent to the match, was not equally welcome to the princess herself. Her sympathy for her mother was distasteful to her father, and he was anxious to get rid of her; she, on the other hand, desired to live among, and endear herself to, the people she might be called upon to govern. She did not hesitate to express her desire that the marriage treaty should contain a clause to the effect that she should never be obliged to leave England against her will. 'My reasons,' she wrote to the Duke of York, 'arise not less from personal feelings than from a sense of personal duty. Both impose on me the obligation to form my first connexions and habits in the country at the head of which I may one day be placed.' To Prince William she stated even yet more plainly that the sense of duty which attached her to England was 'such as to make even a short absence inconvenient and painful,' and finding that she could not carry her point, she broke off her engagement. It was renewed under fresh conditions, but a want of real sympathy between the pair ultimately put an end to it in 1814. When the princess, to whose act this result was due, announced it to her father, she was met by an abrupt order for the dismissal of every member of her household. Thereupon she rushed from the house, threw herself into a hackney coach, and sought refuge with

Charlotte

her mother in Connaught Place. But the Princess of Wales, long goaded by indignities, had by this time grown callous, and when Charlotte's friend Miss Mercer, Miss Knight, Lord Liverpool, the Bishop of Salisbury, Lord Eldon, and the Duke of York, all in turn arrived and tried to persuade her to return, her mother also joined her voice to theirs. She consequently returned to Carlton House, whence, in a few days, she was transferred to Cranbourn Lodge at Windsor. Here, surrounded by a new set of attendants, she was kept in the strictest retirement, allowed to receive visits from none of her friends, forced to send her letters under cover to her new lady in waiting, Lady Ilchester, and, as a passage in one of her letters seems to imply, even deprived of pocket-money. That her health suffered is scarcely to be wondered at, or that she herself should consider 'six months got over of the dreadful life she led, six months gained.'

The spring of 1816 brought another suitor, Prince Leopold of Saxe-Coburg, who proposed and was accepted. He had many good qualities in addition to good looks, and the wedding, which took place on 2 May 1816, at Carlton House, seemed to promise a future of unmixed happiness. Claremont was bought for a country residence, and Marlborough House was prepared as their home in town. At the former the princess spent most of her brief but cloudless wedded life. On 5 Nov. 1817 she gave birth to a stillborn son, dying herself a few hours later. Some strictures were made upon the management of the case by the accoucheur, Sir Richard Croft. The nation received the intelligence of her death with an outburst of grief which is well expressed in the school-book jingle—

> Never was sorrow more sincere
> Than that which flowed round Charlotte's bier.

She was buried in St. George's Chapel, Windsor, on 19 Nov. 1817.

The Princess Charlotte was rather above middle height, and, although slightly pitted with small-pox, possessed considerable personal attractions. Her pale complexion and fair eyebrows and lashes, however, gave a want of colour to her face. In her later portraits the likeness to George IV is plainly discoverable. She had many fine and noble qualities, to which her warmth of heart and enthusiastic temperament lent an additional charm.

[The chief authority for the life of the Princess Charlotte is the excellent Brief Memoir published in 1874 by Lady Rose Weigall, which was reprinted from the Quarterly Review by the queen's desire, and extended by material supplied by her majesty herself. In 1885 an illustrated monograph supplementing this was published by Mrs. Herbert Jones. It contains, inter alia, reproductions of a series of miniatures of the princess by Miss Charlotte Jones, a pupil of Cosway.]

AUSTIN DOBSON

published 1887

PHIPPS Charles Beaumont

(1801–1866)

Sir

Court official, second son of Henry Phipps, first earl of Mulgrave and viscount Normanby, was born at Mulgrave Castle, Yorkshire, on 27 Dec. 1801, and educated at Harrow. He entered the army as an ensign and lieutenant in the Scots fusilier guards on 17 Aug. 1820, and ultimately became lieutenant-colonel (26 May 1837). On 22 Jan. 1847 he was placed on half-pay. He retired from active service on 11 Nov. 1851, and was thenceforth a colonel unattached. Meanwhile Phipps acted as secretary to his brother, Constantine Henry, first marquis of Normanby, when governor of Jamaica, 1832–4, and in that capacity went from plantation to plantation, announcing to the slaves that they were to be free. When his brother went to Ireland as lord lieutenant in 1835, Phipps became steward of the viceregal household, and held the office until 1839. For a short time he was secretary to the master-general of the ordnance. On 1 Aug. 1846 he became equerry to Queen Victoria, and on 1 Jan. 1847 private secretary to the prince consort. He soon was appointed the prince's treasurer. On the death of George Edward Anson he was made keeper of her majesty's purse, 10 Oct. 1849. His integrity and zeal were highly appreciated by the queen and the prince consort. He became treasurer and cofferer to the Prince of Wales on 10 Oct. 1849, was nominated C.B. on 6 Sept. 1853, and K.C.B. on 19 Jan. 1858. He was made receiver-general of the duchy of Cornwall on 26 May 1862, and one of the council to the Prince of Wales in January 1863. On 8 Feb. 1864 he was appointed secretary to the Prince of Wales as steward of Scotland. He died of bronchitis at his apartments, Ambassadors' Court, St. James's Palace, on 24 Feb. 1866. As a testimony of the high esteem in which he was held, the court appointed for 27 Feb. was postponed to 9 March, and, in obedience to the desire of her majesty, he was buried in the catacombs of St. George's Chapel, Windsor, on 2 March. He married, on 25 June 1835, Margaret Anne, second daughter of Henry Bathurst, archdeacon of York. She was granted a civil list pension of 150*l.* on 23 March 1866, and died on 13 April 1874. The issue of the marriage were two sons and two daughters, the eldest son being Charles Edmund, born in 1844, a captain in the 18th regiment of foot.

[Gent. Mag. April 1866, pp. 587–8; Men of the Time, 1865, p. 660; Illustr. London News, 1862, xlii. 399–400, with portrait.]

GEORGE CLEMENT BOASE

published 1895

GREY Charles

(1804–1870)

General, second surviving son of Charles, second Earl Grey, K.G., was born at Howick Hall, Northumberland, on 15 March 1804. In after life he spoke with emotion of the happy, judicious freedom of his boyhood passed at home under his father's eye (*Life and Opinions*, pp. 404–5). He entered the army in 1820 as second lieutenant in the rifle brigade, and rose rapidly by purchasing unattached steps and exchanging. In this way he became lieutenant in the 23rd royal Welch fusiliers in 1823, captain in the 43rd light infantry in 1825, major in the 60th rifles in 1828, lieutenant-colonel unattached in 1830, exchanging to the 71st highland infantry in 1833, of which regiment he was lieutenant-colonel from 1833 to 1842. He became brevet-colonel in 1846, a major-general in 1854, lieutenant-general in 1861, general in 1865, and was colonel of the 3rd buffs in 1860–3, and afterwards of his old corps, the 71st light infantry.

He was for some time private secretary to his father when first lord of the treasury, 1830–4; was one of Queen Victoria's equerries almost from her accession, and acted as private secretary to Prince Albert from 1849 until the prince's death in December 1861. He then served her majesty in the same capacity up to his death, and also as joint keeper of the privy purse from 1866. He sat in parliament in the liberal interest in 1831 for High Wycombe, and represented the same constituency in the first two re-formed parliaments. On the second occasion in 1834 he was opposed by Benjamin Disraeli, who then held radical views, and polled 128 votes against Grey's 147. Grey supported Lord John Russell's motion on Irish church temporalities (1833), and opposed Sir Robert Peel's motion to divide into two bills the ministerial motion for the reform of the Irish church. He also voted against the motion of Sir William Follett to protect from the operation of the Corporation Bill such freemen as had their rights secured to them under the Reform Act. He retired from parliamentary life at the general election consequent on the queen's accession in 1837, after which he was in almost constant attendance on the sovereign. Grey was author of 'Some Account of the Life and Opinions of Charles, second Earl Grey,' London, 1861, and of 'Early Years of his Royal Highness the Prince Consort,' London, 1867, compiled under direction of the queen, and translated into the French, German, and Italian languages. He is described by those who knew him well as a man of masculine mind, of great readiness and sound sense, and highly independent character, who faithfully discharged the duties of his important and delicate post.

Grey married, in July 1830, Caroline Eliza, eldest daughter of the late Sir Thomas Farquhar, second baronet, by whom he had two sons, of whom the elder died young, the second, Albert Henry George, is heir to his uncle, the present Earl Grey, and four daughters. A paralytic seizure caused his death, which took place in London on 31 March 1870, in his sixty-seventh year.

[Foster's Peerage, under 'Grey of Howick;' Life and Opinions of Charles, second Earl Grey, K.G.; Army Lists; Parl. Debates, 1831–4; Times, 1 April 1870, 12 April 1870 (reproduction of an article in Sat. Review, 9 April 1870), 31 May 1870 (will, personalty sworn under 5,000l.).]

HENRY MANNERS CHICHESTER

published 1890

BIDDULPH Thomas Myddleton

(1809–1878)

Sir

General, born 29 July 1809, was the second son of Robert Biddulph, Esq., of Ledbury; his mother was Charlotte, the daughter of Richard Myddleton, Esq., M.P., of Chirk Castle, of the old Welsh family of Myddleton of Gwaynenog. He became a cornet in the 1st life guards 7 Oct. 1826, lieutenant 23 Feb. 1829, captain 16 May 1834, and brevet-major 9 Nov. 1846. On 31 Oct. 1851 he was major in the 7th light dragoons, and lieu-tenant-colonel unattached. He had been gazetted 16 July 1851 as master of Queen Victoria's household, for which office he had been selected by Baron Stockmar (Martin, *Life of the Prince Consort*, ii. 382–3). On 16 July 1854 he was appointed an extra equerry to the queen, and became colonel 28 Nov. 1854. Colonel Biddulph married, 16 Feb. 1857, Mary Frederica, only daughter of Mr. Frederick Charles W. Seymour, who was at one time maid of honour, and afterwards honorary bedchamber woman to the queen. He was created, 27 March 1863, a knight commander of the order of the Bath for his civil services, and was appointed, 3 March 1866, one of the joint keepers of her majesty's privy purse, in succession to the Hon. Sir C. B. Phipps, and in conjunction with General the Hon. Charles Grey. On Grey's appointment to be private secretary to Queen Victoria, 30 April 1867, Sir Thomas Biddulph became sole keeper of the privy purse. He became major-general 31 May 1865, and lieutenant-general 29 Dec. 1873, and he was gazetted, 1 Oct. 1877, to the brevet rank of general, as one of a large number of officers who obtained promotion under the provisions of article 137 of the royal warrant of 13 Aug. 1877. Later in the same year he was sworn of the privy council. From 1866 till death he was receiver-general of the duchy of Cornwall, and from 1873 of the duchy of Lancaster. The official duties of Sir Thomas Biddulph involved close attendance on the queen. He died at Abergeldie Mains, near Balmoral, after a short illness, during which he was daily visited by her majesty, 28 Sept. 1878, and was buried at Clewer. Sir Theodore Martin says of Biddulph that 'he was the last survivor of the three very able men—Sir Charles Phipps and General Grey being the other two—who had been intimately associated with the prince from their position as leading members of her majesty's household' (*Life of the Prince Consort*, iv. 12).

[Aberdeen Free Press, 30 Sept. 1878; Times, 30 Sept. and 3 and 8 Oct. 1878; Army List; London Gazette; Illustrated London News, 5 Oct. 1878; Martin's Life of the Prince Consort, 1875–80; Queen Victoria's More Leaves from the Journal of a Life in the Highlands, 1884.]

ARTHUR HENRY GRANT

published 1885

ALBERT Francis Charles Augustus Emmanuel

(1819–1861)

Prince Consort of England

Was the second of the two sons of Ernest, duke of Saxe-Coburg-Gotha, and of his wife Louise, daughter of Augustus, duke of Saxe-Gotha-Altenburg. He was born at the Rosenau, a summer residence of his father's near Coburg, 26 Aug. 1819, rather less than a year after his brother Ernest, now duke of Saxe-Coburg-Gotha. They were the only children of the marriage, which terminated in 1824 by a separation, followed in 1826 by a divorce. Although thus early deprived of his mother's care, the prince always retained a vivid recollection of her sweet and fascinating manners and her great beauty. She died at St. Wendel, in Switzerland, in 1831, at the age of thirty-two, after a long and painful illness, never having seen her sons after her separation from their father.

The mother's place in watching over the childhood and youth of the young princes was admirably filled by their grandmothers on both father's and mother's side. Albert was a beautiful child, and as winning by his intelligence and playful humour as he was handsome. In 1820 his uncle, Prince Leopold, when on a visit to Coburg, saw him for the first time. The boy formed an extraordinary attachment to him, was 'never happy except when near him.' His uncle shared the feeling, and thus began an intimacy which deepened into a lifelong affection on both sides.

The grandmothers were both remarkable women, accomplished, gifted with strong sense and warm hearts. They vied with each other who should show most attention to the two boys, but were careful not to spoil them. In their earliest years they were most under the eye of their maternal grandmother, and, their riotous spirits having become rather oppressive to the good old lady, they were placed, while at the respective ages of four and five, under the guardianship of a Mr. Florschütz as their tutor. The maternal grandmother dreaded evil from the care of children so young being entrusted to a man. But though he was still so young that he liked to be carried up and down stairs, the Prince Albert hailed the change with delight, having from infancy shown a great dislike to being in the charge of women. The young princes could not have been better placed. Mr. Florschütz was a thoroughly competent tutor. He loved the boys, and they loved and respected him. Albert was his favourite. 'Every grace,' are his own words, 'had been showered by nature on this charming boy. Every eye rested on him with delight, and he won the hearts of all.' From the first his love for acquiring knowledge was remarkable. He learned quickly and retained what he learned. Though far from strong, he carried the same ardour into his sports as into his studies, and in both established a superiority over his companions. To excel in all he undertook was his aim. Sweetness was combined in his character with force then as in his more mature years. His great earnestness and purity of disposition, together with a cheerful joyous spirit, and a keen sense of the ludicrous, became more marked as he grew up from boyhood into youth, as well as a great consideration for the feelings of others, by no means usual at that age. His education covered a range of subjects well fitted to prepare him for the practical business of life. The study of history, geography, mathematics, philosophy, religion, Latin, and the modern European languages was relieved by practice in music and drawing, for both of which the prince showed a decided talent. He was an eager and exact observer of natural objects, for which the country round Coburg presented a rich field, and together with his brother he formed a collection of birds, butterflies, stones, and shells, which subsequently formed the nucleus of the 'Albert-Ernest Museum,' now deposited in the Festung at Coburg. In his boyish rambles he acquired the habit of accurate observation, and delight in the sights and sounds of a country life, for which in after years he was distinguished.

'Nothing,' we are told, 'could exceed the intense enjoyment with which a fine or commanding view inspired the young prince.' So it was with him to the last. No feature of a fine landscape, no fluctuation of a fine sky escaped his notice. And as he saw outward objects in their just proportion and relations, so in dealing with the facts and phenomena of history, of politics, or social life, the same keenness of insight and the same precision of estimate were apparent. When old enough to join in the field sports which in his native country are the prescriptive pastime of his class, he proved to be an excellent shot; but, as in after life, he cared for the pursuit of game chiefly for the exercise and the open-air life as a tonic and the recreation of a few hours. As he often said in later life, he could never understand people 'making a business of shooting and going out for the whole day.' To him the mixture of active exercise with the severe studies to which he gave himself in youth, with the definite purpose, as he wrote (1830) to his father, of making himself 'a good and useful man,' proved of great value. The delicate child grew up a strong, active, thoroughly healthy youth.

The young princes remained at home till 1832, when they made a short visit to their uncle, now King Leopold, at Brussels. In 1835 they visited the court of Mecklenburg-Schwerin, and afterwards that of Berlin, and produced at both places a most favourable impression. They then made a tour to Dresden, Prague, Vienna, Pesth, and Ofen, and returned to Coburg, where Prince Albert resumed his studies with fresh enthusiasm.

Meanwhile the development of the prince's character was being watched by anxious and observant eyes. The idea that his brother or himself would be a fitting mate for the young Princess Victoria of England had been from the first entertained in the family. The Dowager Duchess of Coburg had settled in her own mind that both by mental and moral qualities Prince Albert would prove well fitted to enable her grandchild to bear 'the dangerous grandeur of royalty,' and on the duchess's death in November 1831 her views were adopted by her son King Leopold.

In 1836 it became a certainty that the Princess Victoria would succeed to the throne at no very distant date. Of the several aspirants for her hand, King Leopold, who, since the death of the Duke of Kent, had fulfilled the duties of a father to the young princess, thought that none was so qualified to make her happy as her cousin Albert. But in a matter of such grave importance he would not trust his own judgment. He therefore called to his assistance his old and tried friend, Baron Christian Friedrich von Stockmar, on whose penetrating judgment of men and things, as well as fearless independence, the king knew by long experience that he might place implicit trust. Stockmar, after seeing Leopold fairly established as king of the Belgians, had retired to his native town of Coburg. Stockmar knew and loved the young princess. He had hoped to see the Princess

Charlotte filling the throne by the side of his master and friend Prince Leopold, and to aid them in making monarchy in England a model of what a monarchy might be. That hope was extinguished by the untimely death of the princess in 1817. But now it seemed as though it might be revived by the union of the cousins, if the high qualities required to satisfy Stockmar's austere judgment should be found in the young Prince Albert. Writing to King Leopold in the beginning of 1836, Stockmar speaks of the prince 'as a fine young fellow, well grown, with agreeable and valuable qualities,' with an English look, prepossessing in person, and with 'a kindly, simple, yet dignified demeanour.' As to mind he has heard much to the prince's credit; but he must observe him longer before he can form a judgment upon his capacity and the probable development of his character. 'He is said to be circumspect, discreet, and even now cautious. But all this is not enough. He ought to have not merely great ability, but a right ambition and great force of will as well. To pursue for a lifetime a political career so arduous demands more than energy and inclination; it demands also that earnest frame of mind which is ready of its own accord to sacrifice mere pleasure to real usefulness.'

Within the next few months Stockmar had the opportunity of observing the prince closely, and he satisfied himself that his mind and character were such that time and training were alone wanted to develop in him the qualities which Stockmar demanded as essential for the high vocation for which the prince's uncle designed him. But in the selection of her future consort he stipulated that the Princess Victoria must be left wholly un-fettered, and, before any claim for her hand was preferred, an impression in the prince's favour must first have been produced. The cousins must meet, and neither must be aware of the object of their meeting, 'so as to leave them completely at their ease.'

In May 1836 the Duke of Coburg came to England with his two sons, and remained there for about four weeks. The secret was kept, but the desired impression was produced. Finding this to be the case, King Leopold, almost simultaneously with the prince leaving England, made his niece aware of what his wishes were. The Princess Victoria's answer showed that these were in accordance with her own. The prince was, however, still kept in the dark, but a plan for his education was laid out, with a view to the possibility of his becoming the prince consort of the Queen of England. Brussels was selected by Baron Stockmar as the place most favourable for the requisite personal training and political study. The prince would there be under the eye and influence of his uncle, who was working out the problem of constitutional government in a country where it had been previously unknown. To Brussels accordingly the prince and his brother went in 1836, and here they remained for ten months, closely occupied with the study of history and European languages. To these the Prince Albert added the higher mathematics and the application of the law of probabilities to social and natural phenomena. His guide in these was M. Quetelet, the eminent statist and mathematician, to whose instructions the prince always acknowledged himself to be deeply indebted.

From Brussels the princes went in April 1837 to Bonn, where they continued to prosecute their studies for the next eighteen months. 'Amongst all the young men of the university,' writes his friend Prince William of Löwenstein, 'Albert was distinguished by his knowledge, his diligence, and his amiable bearing in society. He liked above all things to discuss questions of public law and metaphysics, and constantly, during our many weeks, juridical principles or philosophical doctrines were thoroughly discussed.' At the same time the prince excelled in all manly exercises. In a fencing match he carried off the prize from about thirty competitors. To music he was passionately devoted, and had already shown considerable skill as a composer. He entered with eagerness, again to quote the same friend, 'into every study in which he engaged, whether belonging to science or art. He spared no exertion, either of mind or body; on the contrary, he rather sought difficulties in order to overcome them. The result was such an harmonious development of his powers and faculties as is very seldom arrived at.'

Soon after the prince had settled in Bonn the death of William IV (20 June 1837) opened the succession to the throne to the Princess Victoria, then only eighteen. To this event the prince could not be indifferent, and he heard with great satisfaction of the 'astonishing self-possession' shown by the young queen in the difficult and trying position to which she had been so suddenly called. 'Now,' he writes to her (26 June), 'you are queen of the mightiest land of Europe, in your hand lies the happiness of millions. May Heaven assist you and strengthen you with its strength in that high but difficult task! I hope that your reign may be long, happy, and glorious, and that your efforts may be rewarded by the thankfulness and love of your subjects.'

The autumn vacation of 1837 was spent by the two young princes in a walking tour through Switzerland and the north of Italy. On their return to Bonn the prince applied himself to his studies with renewed energy. By this time he must have been well aware of the possible great, but most responsible, future before him, and he set himself strenuously to prepare for its duties. The subject was not, however, broached to him by his uncle, King Leopold, till the beginning of 1838, during a visit of the prince to Brussels. In a letter from the king to Baron Stockmar, recounting what had passed, he says: 'If I am not very much mistaken, Albert possesses all the qualities required to fit him for the position which he will occupy in

England. His understanding is sound, his apprehension clear and rapid, and his heart in the right place. He has great powers of observation and possesses singular prudence, and there is nothing about him that can be called cold or morose.' He also already displayed that 'remarkable power of self-control' which, often tested in his later life, never failed him under the most trying circumstances.

On leaving the university of Bonn it was arranged that the prince should make a tour in Italy, accompanied by Baron Stockmar. Up to this time the prince had known very little of Stockmar, and he was therefore a little surprised at being thus sought out by a comparative stranger. But Stockmar had been more than once through Italy with King Leopold, and this appeared the natural explanation. Florence, Rome, and Naples were visited in succession, and in each the prince left no object of interest unnoticed. He was naturally much courted in society, but showed a marked disinclination to its dissipations, grudging the time it abstracted from his graver studies, or from intercourse with the distinguished men of the country. From Naples he turned back towards Coburg, taking Rome, Tivoli, Viterbo, Sienna, Leghorn, Lucca, Genoa, and Milan on the way. The prince felt that this tour had been of great service to him in extending his range of observation and increasing his power of forming right judgments. He had found Stockmar's society to be 'most precious and valuable,' while, on the other hand, he had established a hold upon that austere but invaluable mentor's heart, which grew closer and dearer with every future year.

In a memorandum by Baron Stockmar of the estimate formed by him of the prince's character during the Italian tour he notes that 'his constitution cannot be called strong, but that with proper dietetic management it might easily gain strength and stability.' He adds that 'great exertion is repugnant to him, and his tendency is to spare himself both morally and physically,' a tendency of which the prince most effectually cured himself within a very short period. More remarkable was his other peculiarity, which was no less signally overcome, that the prince showed 'not the slightest interest in politics. Even while the most important events are in progress, and their issues undecided, he does not care to look into a newspaper;' and this at the time was no doubt true of the man who, as the years advanced, allowed no incident of domestic or foreign politics to escape his notice, and concentrated the whole force of his mind upon their changing phases and possible eventualities. Stockmar's lessons on these points sank deeply into the prince's mind, and on his return to Coburg he set himself the task of making himself master of English history and language.

But the progress of events had now made it desirable that the Princess Victoria's marriage should not be much longer delayed. She was herself by no means inclined to hurry it on; but the prince having, by his uncle's desire, come to England with his brother (10 Oct. 1839), his presence quickly produced a very altered feeling. 'Albert's beauty,' said the queen, in writing her first impressions to King Leopold, 'is most striking, and he is most amiable and unaffected—in short, fascinating.' On 14 Oct. the queen made Lord Melbourne aware that the conquest of her heart was complete, much to the satisfaction of her prime minister. Not less was the delight of King Leopold on hearing from the queen that the wish he had cherished for years was about to be realised: 'I had,' he writes to her (24 Oct. 1839), 'when I learned your decision, almost the feeling of old Simeon: "Now lettest Thou thy servant depart in peace!" Your choice has been for some years my conviction of what might and would be best for your happiness.'

On the prince's side it was no less clear that his heart was deeply engaged. 'Victoria,' he wrote (16 Oct.) to Baron Stockmar, 'is so good and kind to me, that I am often puzzled to believe that I should be the object of so much affection. I know the interest you take in my happiness, and therefore pour out my heart to you.' Stockmar heard the news with pleasure, but accompanied his congratulations with earnest counsels as to the future conduct of the prince. They accorded with the principles which the prince had thought out for himself. 'An individuality,' he wrote in reply, 'a character which shall win the respect, the love, and the confidence of the queen and of the nation, must be the keystone of my position.' He foresaw the many difficulties which must inevitably surround his position. But, as he wrote to his stepmother, 'life has its thorns in every position, and the consciousness of having used one's powers and endeavours for an object so great as that of promoting the welfare of so many will surely be sufficient to support me.' Prophetic words, because they were spoken from the settled conviction which never afterwards wavered or slept. Not less prophetic were the words of Stockmar (15 Dec.): 'If the prince really possess the love of the queen and the respect of the nation, I will answer for it that after every storm he will come safely into port.'

Meanwhile the prince was the happiest of lovers; his joy was tempered by the humility which enters into all noble love. 'What am I,' he writes to the queen (21 Nov.), 'that such happiness should be mine? For excess of happiness it is for me to know that I am so dear to you.' Not all the splendour of the alliance could reconcile the grandmother at Gotha to losing the idol of her affection. 'I cannot rejoice,' she wrote to the prince's father. To his brother it was no less hard to part with him. 'I love and esteem him more than any one on earth,' he wrote to the queen (19 Dec.). 'Guided by his own clear sense,' he added, 'Albert always walked calmly and steadily in the right path. In the greatest difficulties that may meet you in your eventful life, you may repose the most entire confidence in him. And then only will you feel how great a treasure you possess in him.'

The prince left Gotha on 28 Jan. 1840, followed by the earnest good wishes, but also by the regrets, of his countrymen of all classes. He reached Dover on 6 Feb., and was met with the heartiest welcome, which attended him all along the route till he reached Buckingham Palace on the 8th. The announcement of the marriage had given general satisfaction. Some absurd doubts as to the prince's protestant convictions had in the meantime been raised, only to be swept away, and a movement had been made in the House of Commons to reduce his annuity from 50,000l., the sum proposed by Lord Melbourne, to 21,000l. This motion had been negatived, but another, moved by Colonel Sibthorp and supported by Sir Robert Peel and his friends, was carried, reducing it to 30,000l. This seemed for the moment not to augur well for the prince's popularity; but if any feeling of this kind rested in his mind, it vanished before the cordiality with which he was hailed by the crowds who turned out to give him welcome from the moment he set his foot on the English shore.

His demeanour at the marriage in the chapel of St. James's Palace (10 Feb.) deepened the favourable impression which his appearance had produced—young and handsome as he was, and bearing himself with a quiet grace and dignity quite exceptional. The morning had been wet and dark, but before the sovereign and her husband left Buckingham Palace the sun had broken out with peculiar brilliancy, so that they were well seen by the thousands who lined the roads from the one palace to the other. 'There cannot exist a dearer, purer, nobler being in the world than the prince,' were the queen's words in writing to Baron Stockmar the next day. Of this faith he was to prove himself eminently worthy.

A man of a character so marked and a disposition so resolute was sure to find it no easy matter to obtain the independence and power with which alone he could be satisfied. There were naturally in the royal household some who were reluctant to surrender the control which had hitherto been in their hands; there were others who scarcely concealed their disappointment that the queen had selected her husband from abroad. All was happiness between the queen and himself, but so early as the following May the prince wrote to his friend, Prince von Löwenstein: 'The difficulty in filling my place with the proper dignity is that I am only the husband, and not the master in the house.' Such a state of things could not last long, when the queen herself was determined that in all matters, save those of state, the paramount authority was to be conceded to the husband whom she had vowed to obey as well as to love. Her example was enough to quell resistance; and the prince's own tact, forbearance, and superior grasp of mind were not long in removing every obstacle to his legitimate authority.

His position with regard to public affairs was more delicate and difficult. Being what he was, it was impossible he should not engage in the study of politics domestic and foreign, so as to be in a position to assist the queen in forming just conclusions in regard to all matters affecting the welfare of her kingdom, as well as upon those which affected her family and home. So late as October 1838 Baron Stockmar had been struck with the prince's indifference to politics. This indifference was no longer possible, and he at once devoted himself to the study of them with as much conscientious zeal as if he had himself been the head of the state. At the same time he fully appreciated the just jealousy with which any active intervention in affairs of state would be regarded, and he laid it down as a rule never to expose himself to the charge of interference with the machinery of the state, or of encroachment on the functions or privileges of the sovereign. The principles on which he acted were thus expressed by himself ten years later, in a letter to the Duke of Wellington: 'to sink his own individual existence in that of his wife—to aim at no power by himself or for himself—to shun all ostentation—to assume no separate responsibility before the public—to make his position entirely a part of hers—to fill up every gap which, as a woman, she would naturally leave in the exercise of her regal functions—continually and anxiously to watch every part of the public business, in order to be able to advise and assist her at any moment in any of the multifarious and difficult questions brought before her, political, social, or personal'—to place all his time and powers at her command 'as the natural head of her family, superintendent of her household, manager of her private affairs, her sole confidential adviser in politics, and only assistant in her communications with the officers of the government, her private secretary, and permanent minister.'

To fit himself for accomplishing all this was the work of time, and the prince had to feel his way cautiously, and to inspire confidence in his ability and tact, no less than in his freedom from personal ambition. In Stockmar's fearless independence and great knowledge of the working of the English constitution, as well as of the forces at work throughout all the continental states, he knew that he should find the best support. To him, therefore, he appealed 'to sacrifice his time to him for the first year of his life in England.' Stockmar loved the prince and queen so well; he felt so strongly of what supreme importance to England the right action of the prince might be, that he yielded to this request; and not only for this first year, but for many years afterwards, he was always ready to give to the prince the benefit of his great political sagacity and wide experience. As

Stockmar, according to Lord Palmerston, was 'one of the best political heads he had ever met with,' and as, according to Bunsen, he was 'honoured as one of the first' statesmen of Europe, the gain to the prince was very great, and it was prized by him as inestimable. It was the condition of Stockmar's friendship that he should speak his mind freely. To none was candour, combined with clear insight, so precious as to the sovereign and her husband. The condition was therefore frankly accepted, and never infringed, for Stockmar's noble sincerity made him more and more dear to both as the years—years of great anxiety and political disturbance—advanced. His first lesson was to inculcate the necessity of entire neutrality as between the rival parties in the state. The queen, much under the influence of Lord Melbourne, her first minister, had previously to her marriage shown too marked a leaning towards the party of which he was the leader. Its fall was obviously not far off. The prince, who shared Stockmar's views as to the necessity for the crown maintaining absolute neutrality between whig and tory, had no difficulty in persuading the queen to hold out the olive branch to the party whose advent to power could not be much longer delayed.

The impression produced by the prince on those who came into contact with him in those early days was generally favourable. 'The prince is liked,' wrote the watchful Stockmar (14 Feb.), and a few days later: 'Those who are not carried away by party feelings like him greatly.' His love of art, and his knowledge and skill in music, gave him occupation for his leisure hours, and led to his being called on to take a prominent part in the encouragement of both arts. In March he became one of the directors of the Ancient Concerts, and in arranging the programmes of these concerts, as well as those of the Philharmonic Society down to 1860, he did much to raise the standard of public taste in music. He took an active interest in all that was being done in painting and sculpture; he also let it be seen that he shared the public interest in the questions of the day. One of the most urgent of these was the abolition of the slave trade, and he presided at a meeting called to promote it, where he made the first of the compact and suggestive speeches for which he afterwards became distinguished. He never spoke in public without careful preparation, his view being that, as his utterances would be regarded as practically those of the sovereign, no word should be left to the chance of the moment.

By this time the opposition had in a great measure died down which had at first sprung up against the prince in the tory ranks. When, therefore, the queen being *enceinte*, a regency bill, to provide against the casualty of her death, became necessary, the bill appointing the prince as regent (introduced 13 July 1840) passed through both houses, the Duke of Sussex alone dissenting. This, Lord Melbourne told the queen, was entirely due to the prince's own character. 'Three months ago they would not have done it for him.'

Having thus seen public acknowledgment made of the status of the prince, whom he had come to 'love as a son,' Stockmar retired to his quiet home at Coburg, addressing to him before he left (4 Aug.) the admonition, 'Never lose self-possession or patience; but, above all, at no time, and in no way, fail in princely worth and nobleness.' The words were but the voice of the prince's own resolution, as his whole after life proved.

During the summer he went through a course of reading on the laws and constitution of England with Mr. Selwyn, author of the standard work on Nisi Prius, and at the same time read with the queen Hallam's 'Constitutional History of England.' Acting on Lord Melbourne's advice, the queen communicated all foreign despatches to him. The Eastern question, on which England seemed likely to come into collision with France, was then pressing, and it was a good introduction to the study of foreign politics, of which the prince ultimately became thorough master. His Mentor, Stockmar, with whom he kept up a close correspondence, heard of this with pleasure, and urged him to study the despatches thoroughly, as 'besides the great knowledge thus conveyed they would beget in him a taste for general politics, which, he added, was quite indispensable for the duties of his vocation.'

In November Stockmar came back to London on the urgent solicitation of the prince, who wished to have him near on the first accouchement of the queen, Stockmar being a skilled physician as well as a politician of the highest order. The Princess Charlotte had died with her hand in his twenty-four years before, when, had his warnings to her physicians been taken, her life might have been saved. All went happily now at the birth (21 Nov.) of the princess royal, for the wise old physician's injunctions against excitement of every kind were rigidly enforced by the prince.

Stockmar remained in England till May 1841, assisting the prince with his counsels, and watching the development of his character with loving but sternly critical eyes. 'Your royal highness's conduct,' he wrote (7 May 1841), 'should always be regulated by conviction, based upon a clear perception of what is true.' He must be on his guard against whatever was false or mistaken in sentiment, and 'never be satisfied with mere talk where action is alone appropriate.' This was the task the prince must set before him, hard as it was; 'it was worthy of him, within his power to achieve, and, unless achieved, it was idle for him to hope for any genuine triumph as a man or as a prince.'

When the letter containing these words reached the prince, the Melbourne administration was tottering to its fall. This event had been for some time apparent to the queen and prince, and he used his influence to prepare the way with the queen for a change which could not be contemplated by her majesty without some degree of pain, attached as she was to Lord Melbourne and his friends. Party spirit ran high. The tories thought that on a former occasion they had not been fairly treated by Lord Melbourne's party, and it was important that they should have no room for complaint should the turn of events place Sir Robert Peel in power. A debate on a vote of no confidence, which left the ministry in a minority of ninety-one (28 Aug. 1841), brought about this result. In Lord Melbourne the queen lost not only a first minister, but also a very dear friend, and to her the separation was necessarily most painful. At this moment the kindness and tact of the prince smoothed every difficulty. It was a source of great satisfaction, both to Lord Melbourne and the queen, that in resigning his position he was able to assure her majesty that he had 'formed the highest opinion of the prince's judgment, temper, and discretion;' that his 'advice and assistance would be of inestimable advantage' to the queen, and that she could not 'do better than have recourse to it, whenever it was needed, and rely on it with confidence.'

The change of ministry was effected with satisfaction on all sides. Sir R. Peel used afterwards to say that, on first coming into official contact with the prince, he felt no slight embarrassment, remembering that the curtailment of the prince's income was in a great measure due to the support he had given to Colonel Sibthorp's motion the previous year. But the prince at once removed this feeling by the way he met him. Peel quickly formed a very high idea of the prince's powers, and in 1841 told Mr. Pemberton, afterwards Lord Kingsdown, that he would 'find him one of the most extraordinary young men he had ever met with.' This Lord Kingsdown records he found to be more than verified: 'His aptitude for business was wonderful; the dullest and most intricate matters did not escape or weary his attention; his judgment was very good,' and his temper admirable.

Peel placed the prince at the head of the royal commission appointed (October 1841) to inquire whether advantage might not be taken of the rebuilding of the houses of parliament to promote and encourage the fine arts in the United Kingdom. The commission included men of the first distinction in politics, art, and literature; and this was regarded by the prince himself as his real initiation into public life, by bringing him into intimate relations with so many leading public men. The secretary of the commission was Sir Charles Eastlake, who was surprised at the wide and accurate practical knowledge as well as the highly cultivated taste of the prince.

On 9 Nov. 1841 the Prince of Wales was born. King Frederick William of Prussia, who was one of his sponsors, came to England to attend the christening on 25 Jan., and during his stay the foundation was laid of a friendship with the queen and prince, which was cemented by the confidential correspondence of future years.

The prince very early impressed Sir Robert Peel and Lord Aberdeen, as he had impressed Lord Melbourne, with the idea that his capacity and strong practical judgment would make his assistance to the queen in her political duties of the utmost value. This assistance her majesty showed that she thoroughly appreciated, and they saw with pleasure that the prince was determined to use the influence which he had gained with extreme modesty and within strictly constitutional limits. To secure his services to the state seemed to the ministry so important, that even at this early period (1842) his appointment as commander-in-chief, in the event of the Duke of Wellington's death, was privately contemplated by them. On the project being mooted by them to Baron Stockmar he decidedly set his face against it, for much the same reasons as were advanced by the prince when the acceptance of the office was pressed upon him by the duke himself in 1850. Stockmar seems to have known the English people better than their rulers did, and to have understood with what jealousy the appointment of a prince of foreign blood, of whom as yet they knew so little, to such an office would have been regarded.

The prince himself knew well that time and accumulated evidence of what he was were needed to win for him the confidence of the nation. Among his first objects was to establish order, economy, and integrity in the royal household, where, under the loose administration of former sovereigns, these qualities had been too much neglected. At the same time he set himself, in concert with the queen, to raise the character of the court. It was not enough that his life was pure and blameless. He took care to make it impossible for gossiping malignity to throw a semblance of suspicion upon it. He never stirred abroad unless in company with an equerry. He paid no visits in general society. All his leisure was given to visits to the studios of artists, to museums of science or art, to institutions for good and benevolent purposes, or to rides to parts of London where either improvements were in progress or were chiefly needed, especially such as might ameliorate the condition or minister to the pleasure of the labouring classes. The life of unintermitting study and toil which was henceforth to be his was already entered upon, and in the palace, as well as in the outer world, the presence of a strong master hand was steadily making itself felt.

His study of politics was unremitting, and, availing himself of the rare advantage of having at command all the information which is accessible to the sovereign, his judgment upon men and things very early placed him on an equality with the most experienced observers and statesmen of his time. In April 1843 Baron Stockmar writes of him: 'He is rapidly showing what is in him. He is full of practical talent, which enables him at a glance to seize the essential points of a question, like the vulture that pounces on his prey and hurries off with it to his nest.' This practical talent was ever at work, whatever the subject. Speaking, for example, of the education of the poor, he writes thus to warn the Duchess of Saxe-Coburg of the danger of giving an education not in accordance with the circumstances and probable future of the child, and tells her not to forget 'that education is the preparation for the future life, and that, if it be not consistent with the pupil's prospects, he may have to pay for the pleasure which his education gives you with the happiness of his whole life, as nothing is more certain to insure an unhappy future than disappointed expectations.'

In this year (1843–4) the prince was mainly instrumental in obtaining an amendment of the Articles of War which had for its object to put an end to duelling. Public attention had been painfully called to the subject by the death of Colonel Fawcett in a duel with his brother-in-law, Lieutenant Munro, who had been compelled to challenge Colonel Fawcett under circumstances of gross provocation, which, according to the prevailing code of honour, left him no alternative. The intimate relations of the two men gave prominence to the hatefulness of a system by which a man who had been insulted must, at the peril of being branded as a coward, expose himself to be shot, and, if the issue proved fatal to his adversary, be punished as a criminal. Feeling that the reform must begin in the army in order to be effectual, the prince opened a correspondence with the Duke of Wellington, which ended in the amendment above mentioned, declaring it to be 'suitable to the character of honourable men to apologise and offer redress for wrong or insult committed, and equally so for the party aggrieved to accept frankly and cordially explanation and apologies for the same.' This proved to be the death-blow to 'affairs of honour.'

In the end of August of this year (1843) the prince accompanied the queen on a visit to King Louis-Philippe at the Château d'Eu. The reception of the English royal family by the French was most cordial, and even enthusiastic. A six days' tour in Belgium followed in September. The country put itself into holiday array to welcome the royal visitors, and the people were everywhere warm in their demonstrations of satisfaction at this visit to their king, while the queen was delighted to be once again under the roof of one who had ever been a father to her, and to whom she owed it that she was so happily mated.

In October the queen and prince visited Cambridge, where the prince received the degree of LL.D. from the university of which he was not long afterwards to be the chancellor. 'The enthusiasm of the students,' the prince writes to Stockmar (30 Oct.), 'was tremendous, and I cannot remember that we were ever received anywhere so well as upon the road to Cambridge (to which 2,000 horsemen accompanied us), and in Cambridge itself.' In the same letter the prince mentions with satisfaction that he has netted a good return from the sale by auction of his farm stock, a subject in which he took the greatest interest, having established a model farm at Windsor in 1840 for the purpose of breeding stock and introducing agricultural improvements. To the last nothing that tended to make farming more efficient and more economical escaped his notice.

During a visit of the queen to Sir Robert Peel at Drayton Manor in November, the prince went to Birmingham to inspect some of its chief manufactories. Birmingham was at this time the stronghold of chartism, and some of the ministry sought to prevent him from going there, being alarmed lest his presence might provoke some unpleasant demonstration. But the prince overruled their scruples, and the result showed that he had rightly understood the temper of the people. He was received by crowds that thronged the streets to excess with admirable good humour and the warmest demonstrations of loyalty. 'The people,' he wrote (17 Dec.), 'regarded the visit as a great proof of confidence, and did all they could to give assurance of their loyalty.' The prince visited five of the principal manufactories, the town hall, and King Edward VI's school, where he was much pleased to find that, although it was strictly a church of England foundation, there were 400 dissenters among the boys, and that the system pursued there worked most harmoniously. From Drayton Manor the royal party went first to Chatsworth and then to Belvoir Castle. At the latter place the prince carried off the honours of the hunting-field to the amazement of most, who were not prepared to find him so bold and skilful a rider. This sport was one, however, in which, in compliance with her majesty's wish, he rarely indulged, and in a few years he gave it up altogether.

On 29 Feb. 1844 Prince Albert's father died at Gotha. To his father the prince was devotedly attached, and his grief was consequently very great. With his death the prince felt that a great and important chapter of his life was closed, and that thenceforth he must put behind him the cherished associations with his old home. 'From that world,' he wrote to Stockmar, 'I am forcibly torn away, and my whole thoughts are diverted to my life here and my own separate family. For these I will live wholly from this time forth, and be to it the father whose loss I mourn for myself.'

In June of this year the Russian emperor Nicholas visited the queen. His visit was unexpected, and was probably made with the view of ascertaining whether England could be detached from the French alliance in the event of his making any move upon Turkey. He professed not 'to covet an inch of Turkish soil for himself,' while asserting that he would not allow anybody else to have one. The prince was not to be hoodwinked as to the real aims of Russian policy in the East. He spoke out to the emperor firmly and frankly on the same lines as Sir R. Peel and Lord Aberdeen, letting it be seen that England would not look calmly on at any attempt to interfere with Turkey, or at any movement which might close the free passage across Egypt of English commerce or English mails. As to France it would be the policy of England to continue to cultivate a close and friendly alliance with that kingdom. By his political sagacity and his courage the prince produced a deep impression on the emperor, who said of him to Sir R. Peel 'that he wished any prince in Germany had as much ability and sense.'

A visit of the Prince of Prussia (now Emperor of Germany) to the queen in August of this year resulted in the establishment of a very cordial and intimate relation between Prince Albert and himself, which was cemented by four subsequent visits of the Prince of Prussia to England, and by the marriage, in 1858, of his son to the Princess Royal of England.

In October King Louis-Philippe paid a return visit to her majesty at Windsor Castle. The visit was of political importance, as it smoothed down the jealous and angry feelings which had been roused by the recent high-handed conduct of the French in the island of Tahiti. While the prince made the strength of his character and his remarkable abilities felt with Louis-Philippe and the other royal personages with whom he had recently been brought into contact, he was gradually increasing in popularity at home. This was shown whenever he appeared in public with the queen, who, in writing to King Leopold (28 Oct. 1844) of her opening of the Royal Exchange, said: 'My beloved Albert was most enthusiastically received by the people. . . . The papers say "No sovereign was ever more loved than I am" (I am bold enough to say), and this because of our happy domestic home and the good example it presents.' Soon afterwards the prince wrote to Baron Stockmar: 'You always said that if monarchy was to rise in popularity it could only be by the sovereign leading an exemplary life and keeping quite aloof from and above party. Melbourne called this "nonsense." Now Victoria is praised by Lord Spencer, the liberal, for giving her constitutional support to the tories.'

In 1845 the queen and prince were able to gratify a long-cherished desire to possess a place of their own, 'quiet and retired, and free from all Woods and Forests and other charming departments, which really are the plague of one's life,' by purchasing the estate of Osborne in the Isle of Wight. The prince's genius for landscape gardening and for agricultural improvement was exercised with the best results in laying out the grounds, and generally in improving the estate. It was his pride that he made his farming pay, and he lived to see, in the growth of his plantations, how well his plans for beautifying the property had been devised. What Scott said of Abbotsford the prince might have said of Osborne: 'My heart clings to the place I have created. There is scarce a tree in it that does not owe its existence to me.' Here his passionate love for the country found scope for its gratification. The woods and shrubberies were a favourite haunt of the nightingale. Of all birds he loved its song the most, and the queen notes in her journal that he would listen for it 'in the happy peaceful walks he used to take with her in the woods, and whistle to them in their own long peculiar note, which they invariably answered.' One of the attractions of Osborne for the prince was its proximity to Portsmouth, which gave him the ready means of watching the condition of the fleet, a subject to him of the most vital interest. In this year much progress in strengthening it had been made, and on 18 July he writes with great satisfaction to Stockmar: 'Since the war no such fleet has been assembled on the English coast; and it has this additional interest, that every possible new invention and discovery in the naval department will be tried.'

Watching the current of home politics with keen and anxious eyes, the prince saw that, although Peel was able to carry his measures with very large majorities, his hold over his party was by this time slipping from his grasp. To the prospect of the confusion likely to ensue upon the breaking up of the conservative party the prince looked forward with no small apprehension, as, to use his own words, 'the opposition had as many different opinions and principles as heads.' For the moment, however, the country seemed, at the close of the parliamentary session, to Sir R. Peel, to be both prosperous and happy, and Ireland tranquillised by the measures which he had carried through. The queen and prince, therefore, felt themselves free to carry out a cherished project of paying a visit to Germany, in which the prince might show the queen the scenes where his youth had been passed. Three weeks of August were devoted to this object. After spending some days on the Rhine, during which Bonn was visited, while the prince's old friends and masters were introduced to the queen, Coburg was reached on the 19th. 'How happy, how joyful,' the queen writes in her journal next day, 'we were, on awaking, to feel ourselves here, at the dear Rosenau, my Albert's birthplace, the place he most loves! He was so happy to be here with me. It is like a beautiful dream.' On 2 Sept. they left Gotha on their return. Here the prince saw for the last time his grandmother, the Dowager Duchess of Gotha, whose motherlike affection for him he had requited with all a son's love. 'When at last,' writes the queen, 'we were obliged to leave, she clasped him in her arms, and kissed him again and again, saying "Gott segne Dich, mein Engel!" (God bless you, my angel!) in such a plaintive voice.' She died on 7 Feb. 1848.

The return to England was made by way of Antwerp, where the King and Queen of the Belgians met the royal visitors. In fulfilment of an old promise Tréport was taken on the way back to England. Here a very cordial reception was given to the queen and prince by King Louis-Philippe. It was during this visit that the king, in conversation with the queen, the prince, and Lord Aberdeen, volunteered the declaration, subsequently violated, that he entertained no designs which could have the effect of placing any of his sons upon the Spanish throne.

Meanwhile the state of affairs in England had become critical. A wet season had blighted the prospects of the farmers, while the potato disease made famine imminent in Ireland. Peel, convinced that free trade in corn was inevitable, but that it was unmeet he should initiate the change, resigned; but, on the failure of Lord John Russell to form a ministry, consented to remain in office, and to face the hostility of the party which had originally placed him there. The prince could not but admire Peel's courage in adopting this resolution. So important was the crisis that he went to the House of Commons (29 Jan. 1846) to hear the debate upon Peel's financial statement. Such, however, was the heated state of men's minds, that this innocent wish to hear a great debate was construed by the party led by Lord George Bentinck into a manœuvre of the minister to give the semblance of royal sanction to his measures. The prince felt that he must never again expose himself to the risk of similar misconstruction, and was thus deprived of the satisfaction of being present at any of the debates of either house. During this stormy session and the ministerial crisis which ensued on the fall of Peel's ministry at the end of June, the queen writes, the prince's 'use to me and to the country by his firmness and sagacity is beyond all belief.' He had by this time made himself fully master of the political situation at home and abroad, and his judgment and sagacity were daily making themselves more and more felt by the statesmen whose position at the head of affairs brought them into more immediate contact with him. Politics had now indeed become his favourite study. In the painful controversy which arose on the subject of the Spanish marriages in the autumn of 1846, and especially in the correspondence to which it led between the royal family of France and Queen Victoria, his advice was of the greatest service to her majesty. He foresaw, what was proved by the event, that Louis-Philippe's conduct in the affair would give a shock not only to his reputation throughout Europe, but to the stability of his government in the troublous epoch of revolutionary change which seemed to the prince to be fast approaching. The days of despotic and aristocratic supremacy, he felt, had gone by, and changes were inevitable, which should make rulers feel that their people did not live for them, but that they must live for their people.

In February 1847 the prince was elected chancellor of Cambridge University after a keen contest in competition with Lord Powis. The ceremony of installation took place at Cambridge on 5 July in the presence of the queen. 'Never,' writes the prince to Stockmar, 'have I seen people in such good humour. There was a great gathering of bishops, scholars, royal personages, nobles, and political men, and all seemed well pleased. My Latin, too, proved a success.' The prince was much gratified by this event, as one among many significant indications that, while he was gaining by degrees the confidence of the country, the queen was growing in popularity and establishing a firmer hold upon the loyalty of her people.

This was no unimportant gain, for the times were rapidly becoming more and more critical for crowned heads in Europe. Portugal, Spain, Germany, Austria, Italy, were all penetrated by a revolutionary spirit. Wherever the prince was free to use his influence abroad to induce such changes in the prevailing systems as might avert the dangers of resistance to legitimate reforms, he did not fail to express his opinions, and these were already coming to be recognised throughout the Continent as those of a sagacious statesman. But the lessons he inculcated were only to be learned under a sterner pressure. By the end of 1847 the cry for independence had been raised throughout the north of Italy. Sicily was in full revolt, Naples had extorted a liberal constitution from its sovereign, Tuscany and Sardinia had done the same, and on 24 Feb. 1848 a revolution in Paris drove Louis-Philippe and his family into exile. England had its own troubles from bad harvests and great commercial and financial depression. 'Here,' the prince writes to Stockmar (27 Feb.), 'they refuse to pay the income tax, and attack the ministry; Victoria will be confined in a few days'—Princess Louise was born 18 March following—'our poor good grandmama is taken from this world. I am not cast down, still I have need of friends and of counsel.' Now the fruits of his past years of political study and reflection were apparent in the calm courage with which the prince met the startling events that were crowded into the next few months, and in which he was sustained by a similar spirit in the queen. 'My only thoughts and talk,' she writes to King Leopold (4 April) 'were politics; but I was never calmer and quieter, or less nervous. Great events make me calm; it is only trifles that irritate my nerves.'

While Italy, Austria, and Germany were convulsed with revolutionary outbreaks which followed on the example of France, England and Belgium remained unshaken. A threatened movement of the chartists on 10 April, in such numbers as to create anxiety, evoked a spirit amid the general population which showed how deeply attached the country was to its constitution. 'We,' the prince wrote next day, 'had our revolution yesterday, and it ended in smoke. How mightily will this tell over the world!'

Ireland alone was dangerous. The Russell ministry had been compelled to adopt even more severe measures of coercion than those which their party had displaced Sir Robert Peel for attempting. England continued to suffer greatly from stagnation of trade and general financial depression, but the prince never lost heart. 'Albert,' the queen writes to King Leopold (2 May 1848), 'is my constant pride and admiration, and his cheerfulness and courage are my great comfort and satisfaction.'

On 18 May the prince presided at a meeting of the Society for improving the Condition of the Working Classes, and made the first of his many expressions of the sympathy and interest which he felt 'for that class of our community which has most of the toil and least of the enjoyments of this world.' His speech attracted great notice. Its main idea was, that while the rich were bound to help, yet that 'any real improvement must be the result of the exertion of the working people themselves.' The favourable impression thus produced was deepened by the appearance of the prince at a meeting of the Royal Agricultural Society at York in July, when he surprised those who knew most about agriculture and the machinery employed in it by showing that he was thorough master of the knowledge which their whole lives had been spent in acquiring. At this meeting, writes the queen to Stockmar, 'he made another most successful speech, and he is himself quite astonished at being such an excellent speaker, as he says it is the last thing he ever dreamt he should have success in. He possesses one other great quality, which is "tact;" he never says a word too much or too little.'

The close of the session (5 Sept.), which had been unusually protracted, set the queen and prince free to go, for the first time, to Balmoral, a property in Aberdeenshire which the queen had recently acquired on the recommendation of Sir James Clark, the court physician, because of its fine air, dry climate, and beautiful situation. Even in this secluded retreat the prince was absorbed in the tidings of fresh disturbances which reached him from all parts of Europe, as well as from India, where the war against the Sikhs was causing the English government great anxiety. He was much engaged, too, in maturing, in communication with many of the most distinguished and influential members of the Cambridge University, a plan for giving a wider scope to the course of study there, which was successfully carried through in the course of this autumn. 'The nation,' the 'Times' wrote, 'owed a debt of gratitude to the prince consort for having been the first to suggest, and the most determined to carry out, the alteration in the Cambridge system.' The example thus set was soon afterwards followed by Oxford.

While the countries of the Continent were still agitated by revolutionary movements, and by the reaction, due less to conviction than to overbearing military force, which followed upon the violence by which these had been marked, trade and manufacture in England had been gradually recovering, wages were rising, and the popular discontent of which the chartists had taken advantage was dying out. Ireland, too, had regained a temporary tranquillity. Sedition had for the time been crushed, and the people were doing their best to retrieve their losses from the ruined harvests and agitation of the last four years. The queen seized the opportunity to visit the country (August 1849), and her presence evoked an exuberant display of loyalty natural to the demonstrative temperament of the Celtic race. The prince was everywhere received with enthusiasm. He showed, as usual, the keenest interest in all local institutions, especially those for the improvement of agriculture. The peculiar aptitude of the country in soil and climate for the rearing of cattle was urged strongly by him as a certain source of future prosperity. His counsels were appreciated and acted upon with the best results; so also his suggestions for the improvement of the system of education at the Queen's Colleges were elaborated with great care, and were gratefully acknowledged.

In this year (1849) the prince projected the idea of the great International Exhibition, which was ultimately carried out in 1851, and which up to that time engaged much of his attention, and called into play all the resources of his intelligence and tact. The strain upon his strength caused by his ceaseless activity and the incessant demands upon his time in every movement of public interest were now beginning to tell upon a constitution never very strong, and we find the queen writing to Stockmar (25 Jan. 1850) that 'the prince's sleep is again as bad as ever, and he looks very ill of an evening.' Change of air, and of life and scene, was urged by his doctor, but of this the prince would not hear. The tasks which he had set himself must be carried through, especially that of organising the Great Exhibition. Of this Lord Granville writes (8 March): 'The whole thing would fall to pieces if he left it to itself.' The scheme encountered great opposition, and chiefly from those who feared, not without cause, that the sight which it would present of what had given to England's manufactures pre-eminence throughout the world would stimulate a competition among other nations, which might in the end tell formidably upon the prosperity of the kingdom. But the prince had so much faith in the energy and resources of the British race, that he did not fear their being able to hold their own in the future as in the past, and, in any case, he deemed it to be 'England's mission, duty, and interest, to put herself at the head of the diffusion of civilisation and the attainment of liberty.' His views were developed in a speech at the Mansion House (21 March 1850) which raised him higher than before in the public estimation. 'People,' the queen writes to King Leopold (26 March), 'are much struck by his great power and energy, by the great self-denial and constant wish to work for others, which are so striking in his character. But this is the happiest life.'

The death of Sir Robert Peel (2 July 1850) was deeply felt by the prince, who had long admired his sagacity and courage, and whom, in the first impulse of his grief, he writes of to the Duchess of Kent as 'the best of men, our truest friend, the strongest bulwark of the throne, the greatest statesman of his time.' Sorrow at his loss brought on a fresh attack of sleeplessness, which, in the state of tension to which his mind was wrought by his anxiety about the Great Exhibition and other matters, caused the queen considerable uneasiness. Not the least of these was the necessity which had arisen for putting a check upon Lord Palmerston's habit of sending away official despatches on foreign affairs without their having previously been submitted for the queen's consideration, by which she had on several occasions found herself committed to a policy on which she had had no opportunity of expressing an opinion. The now historical memorandum by the queen (12 Aug. 1850), defining what her majesty would in future expect on this point, led Lord Palmerston to request an interview with the prince. In this he had his first experience of the prince's clearness of view, firmness, and tact, which he learned in after years to look up to with such genuine admiration, that he regarded the prince's early death as the greatest calamity which could have befallen the nation.

The demands of the Exhibition year upon the prince were such as to try the severest constitution. His influence had become by this time so great in all questions of social interest, that his presence at great public meetings to advocate the advancement of art, science, and philanthropy, was eagerly sought. Of the impression he produced, the best and truest record is found in the words of the queen, writing to Stockmar (17 Aug.): 'He has such large views of everything, and such extreme lucidity in working all these views out. His greatness is wonderfully combined with abnegation of self, with humility, with great courage, with such kindness, too, and goodness, and such a love for his fellow-creatures. And then there is such a desire to do everything without shining himself. But he does shine, and every word which falls from his lips is listened to with attention.' The success which everywhere attended the prince's efforts helped to carry him through them. His reward for all his toils was the inward conviction that he had done, and was doing, work which would bear good fruits for the country of his adoption and for mankind.

When the Duke of Wellington pressed the prince personally in 1850 to accept the office of commander-in-chief, he probably did so because he recognised in him the foresight, the mastery of details, the power of organisation, and the force of character which are essential for such a post.

Added to these was a clear perception of the necessity that England should always be in a position to keep what she had won, and to hold her own against insult or aggression. How this was to be done was a subject which occupied much of the prince's thoughts; and the seizure of the sovereignty of France by Louis Napoleon's *coup d'état* of 2 Dec. 1851, and the hazard of a French invasion, made this a matter of urgent anxiety. From this time onwards he made himself intimately acquainted with every detail both of the naval and military resources of the kingdom, and used every effort to have them put upon a satisfactory footing. Earnestly as he loved and had wrought for peace, the condition of Europe was such that he knew well it could not settle down into a state of enduring tranquillity until after many questions had been settled by the arbitrament of the sword. When a rupture might take place, or how it might affect England, it was impossible to foresee, but safety could lie only in the consciousness that it was well prepared. On the death of the great duke (14 Sept.) he made the measures for insuring this safety his peculiar care, and his counsels were eagerly sought by Lord Hardinge, the duke's successor, from the consciousness that no one had stored up such exact information as the prince, or was more skilful in suggesting how defects might be remedied or existing resources turned to the best account.

Apprehension of danger on the side of France soon died out before the evident anxiety of its new emperor to cultivate the friendship of England. This was so obviously his interest, and the assurance of internal peace was of such vital moment to France at this moment, that credit was given, if not to his good will, at least to his necessities. But already an uneasy feeling was abroad as to the hostile intentions of Russia towards Turkey, to which England could not be indifferent. The country, therefore, was well pleased when a government combining apparently all the elements of strength was formed under Lord Aberdeen, and it saw with satisfaction the efforts which were made to put both the forces upon a more satisfactory footing. On the prince's suggestion a camp for the training of troops to the incidents of life in the field was formed at Chobham Common. He also pressed on the government the idea of a permanent camp of instruction, which ultimately led to the establishment of the camp at Aldershot. The prince paid frequent visits during 1853 to the camp at Chobham, and watched the training of the troops for the work of actual warfare, in which its preparatory discipline was soon afterwards to be tested. The spectacle also (11 Aug. 1853) of a review at Spithead of 'the finest fleet, perhaps, which England ever fitted out, forty ships of war of all kinds, all moved by steam except three,' gave him intense satisfaction. 'I speak of it,' he writes to Stockmar (16 Aug.), 'because last autumn we were bewailing our defenceless state, and because I must rejoice to see that achieved which I had struggled so long and hard to effect.' The feeling was natural, as he saw that England was at this time drifting into war with Russia. He had never been deceived, as Lord Aberdeen had been, into trusting Russia's protestations. 'We must deal with our enemies as honourable men,' he writes to Stockmar (27 Sept.), 'and deal honourably towards them; but that is no reason why we should think they are so in fact; this is what Aberdeen does, and maintains that it is right to do.' The prince was alive to the danger of not letting the Emperor Nicholas see betimes that his designs of aggrandisement were seen through, and, if persisted in, would bring England into the field. The vacillating policy of Lord Aberdeen pained him; but so little was the prince's character then understood that the most bitter attacks were made against him as sympathising with the schemes of Russian ambition, and as an evil influence working behind the throne to thwart the policy of her majesty's government. So far were these carried that it was for a time currently believed that he had been impeached for treason and committed to the Tower. These calumnies had the good effect of forcing from ministers, both past and present, on the meeting of parliament (31 Jan. 1854), the fullest vindication of the way in which the prince had used his position as the nearest friend and private secretary of the queen, not only within strictly constitutional limits, but also to the great advantage of the nation. From this time that position was rightly understood, and successive governments eagerly availed themselves of his information, experience, and sagacity on questions of great national importance.

Throughout the Crimean war and in the arrangement of the terms of peace these were found to be of the greatest value. By none were they more frankly recognised than by Lord Palmerston, who had been at one time by no means predisposed to regard the prince with favour. 'Till my present position,' he said to a friend some time after he had become premier in 1855, 'gave me so many opportunies of seeing his royal highness, I had no idea of his possessing such eminent qualities as he has, and how fortunate it has been for the country that the queen married such a prince.' In the remaining years of the prince's life Lord Palmerston found increasing reasons for the opinion thus expressed. They were years of great anxiety, in consequence of the state of affairs upon the Continent, the restless and vague ambition of the Emperor of the French, the struggles of Italy, ultimately triumphant, for independence, and the growing antagonism between Prussia and Austria in their struggle for supremacy in Germany. On the prince the government could at all times rely for valuable information, which was not always to be obtained through the ordinary official channels, and for the conclusions of a calm and penetrating judgment unswayed by political or party bias.

Nor was his influence less available in every movement for promoting the interests of art and science, for developing the education and improving the material welfare of the people. His speeches at meetings for promoting these objects were eagerly studied, and carried into the people's homes ideas which have since borne the best fruits. He always lifted his subject to a high level, and his life was felt to be impregnated by a noble sense of duty and a determination to do always what was right. So he won by degrees a hold upon the hearts of the English people much stronger than he was himself aware of.

His toil was unremitting. Rising at seven every morning, the day was never long enough for what he had to do. Imperceptibly the strain was undermining his health; but to the last he preserved his natural vivacity and cheerfulness. 'At breakfast and luncheon,' the queen writes (1862), 'and also at our family dinners, he sat at the top of the table, and kept us all enlivened by his interesting conversation, by his charming anecdotes, and droll stories without end of his childhood, of people at Coburg, of our good people in Scotland, which he would repeat with a wonderful power of mimicry, and at which he would himself laugh most heartily. Then he would at other times entertain us with his talk about the most interesting and important topics of the present and former days, on which it was ever a pleasure to hear him speak.'

In the strongest man there is only a limited power of endurance. If he puts the work of eighty years into forty years, there can be but one result. So it was with the prince. While yet young in years he had done the work of a long life. During the three or four last years of his life signs were not wanting, in recurring attacks of illness, that he was using up his physical resources too rapidly. He had doubtless an inward feeling that this was so, and that the end might not be far off. Shortly before his last illness he said to the queen, 'I do not cling to life. I set no store by it. If I knew that those I love were well cared for, I should be quite ready to die to-morrow.' Very significant were the words which followed: 'I am sure if I had a severe illness I should give up at once, I would not struggle for life.' His old friend Stockmar had said many years before that any severe fever would kill him. The prediction proved true. Early in November 1861 the prince showed signs of serious indisposition. Persistent sleeplessness was one of the worst symptoms. With his usual energy he struggled on at his multifarious pursuits. The last of his political acts was one which will always be remembered to his honour, for it was probably instrumental in preventing a war with America, which threatened to arise out of the unwarrantable seizure of Messrs. Mason and Slidell, the confederate envoys, on the English steamer Trent. The draft of the despatch to be sent to the American government on the subject was submitted to the queen for consideration on the night of 30 Nov. Its terms seemed to the prince likely to cause perilous irritation. Ill as he was, he was up by seven next morning and wrote the draft of a memorandum for the queen, pointing out his objections, and brought it to her, telling her he could scarcely hold his pen while writing it. His suggestions were adopted by Lord John Russell, and the disaster of a war was averted.

From this time onward the prince grew steadily worse. Typhoid fever was developed, and by the night of 14 Dec. 1861 his strength had run down, and calmly and gently his noble spirit was released from its burden of 'world-wearied flesh.' The event, wholly unexpected by the nation, filled it with profound sorrow. Much as it had seen in the prince to admire, it had yet to learn how much it owed to him of which it knew nothing, how deep and loyal had been his devotion to his adopted country, how pregnant for good had been his example to his family and to those on whom rest the responsibilities of governing the state, of which he had for many years been the silent stay. As this has from time to time been brought to light, the country has not been slow to acknowledge its debt of gratitude, and to assign to him a foremost place among its most honoured worthies.

[For fuller details see Sir Theodore Martin's Life of the Prince Consort.]

THEODORE MARTIN

published 1885

VICTORIA (1819–1901)

Queen of the United Kingdom of Great Britain and Ireland

Was granddaughter of George III, and only child of George III's fourth son Edward, duke of Kent, K.G., G.C.B., field-marshal. Princess Charlotte Augusta of Wales, only child of the Prince Regent (George III's heir), having married Prince Leopold of Saxe-Coburg on 2 May 1816, died after the birth of a stillborn son on 6 Nov. 1817. The crown was thereby deprived of its only legitimate representative in the third generation. Of the seven sons of George III who survived infancy three, at the date of Princess Charlotte's death, were bachelors, and the four who were married were either childless or without lawful issue. With a view to maintaining the succession it was deemed essential after Princess Charlotte's demise that the three unmarried sons—William, duke of Clarence, the third son; Edward, duke of Kent, the fourth son; and Adolphus Frederick, duke of Cambridge, the seventh and youngest son—should marry without delay. All were middle-aged. In each case the bride was chosen from a princely family of Germany. The weddings followed one another with rapidity. On 7 May 1818 the Duke of Cambridge, who had long resided in Hanover as the representative of his father, George III, in the government there, married, at Cassel, Augusta, daughter of Frederick, Landgrave of Hesse-Cassel. On 11 June 1818 the Duke of Clarence married in his fifty-third year Adelaide, eldest daughter of George Frederick Charles, reigning duke of Saxe-Meiningen. In the interval, on 29 May, the Duke of Kent, who was in his fifty-first year, and since 1816 had mainly lived abroad, took to wife a widowed sister of Prince Leopold of Saxe-Coburg, the widowed husband of that Princess Charlotte whose death had induced so much matrimonial activity in the English royal house. The Duke of Kent's bride, who was commonly known by the Christian name of Victoria, although her full Christian names were Mary Louisa Victoria, was nearly thirty-two years old. She was fourth daughter and youngest of the eight children of Francis Frederick Antony (1750–1806), reigning duke of Saxe-Coburg and Saalfeld. (In 1825 Saalfeld, by a family arrangement, was exchanged for Gotha.) Her first husband was Ernest Charles, reigning prince of Leiningen, whose second wife she became on 21 Sept. 1803, at the age of seventeen; he died on 4 July 1814, leaving by her a son and a daughter. For the son, who was born on 12 Sept. 1804, she was acting as regent and guardian when the Duke of Kent proposed marriage to her. Her responsibilities to her first family and to the principality of Leiningen made her somewhat reluctant to accept the duke's offer. But her father's family of Saxe-Coburg was unwilling for her to neglect an opportunity of reinforcing those intimate relations with the English reigning house which the Princess Charlotte's marriage had no sooner brought into being than her premature death threatened to extinguish. The Dowager Princess of Leiningen consequently married the Duke of Kent, and the ceremony took place at the ducal palace of Coburg. The princess was a cheerful woman of homely intellect and temperament, with a pronounced love of her family and her fatherland. Her kindred was exceptionally numerous; she maintained close relations with most of them, and domestic interests thus absorbed her attention through life. Besides the son and daughter of her first marriage, she had three surviving brothers and three sisters, all of whom married, and all but one of whom had issue. Fifteen nephews and three nieces reached maturity, and their marriages greatly extended her family connections. Most of her near kindred allied themselves in marriage, as she in the first instance had done, with the smaller German reigning families. Her eldest brother, Ernest, who succeeded to the duchy of Saxe-Coburg, and was father of Albert, prince consort of Queen Victoria, twice married princesses of small German courts. A sister, Antoinette Ernestina Amelia, married Alexander Frederick Charles, duke of Würtemberg. At the same time some matrimonial unions were effected by the Saxe-Coburg family with the royal houses of Latin countries—France and Portugal. One of the Duchess of Kent's nephews married the queen of Portugal, while there were no fewer than five intermarriages on the part of her family with that of King Louis Philippe: two of her brothers and two of her nephews married the French king's daughters, and a niece married his second son, the Duc de Nemours. Members of the Hanoverian family on the English throne had long been accustomed to seek husbands or wives at the minor courts of Germany, but the private relations of the English royal house with those courts became far closer than before through the strong family sentiment which the Duchess of Kent not merely cherished personally but instilled in her daughter, the queen of England. For the first time since the seventeenth century, too, the private ties of kinship and family feeling linked the sovereign of England with rulers of France and Portugal. The Duke of Kent brought his bride to England for the first time in July 1818, and the marriage ceremony was repeated at Kew Palace on the 11th of that month. The duke received on his marriage an annuity of 6,000l. from parliament, but he was embarrassed by debt, and his income was wholly inadequate to his needs. His brothers and sisters showed no disposition either to assist him or to show his duchess much personal courtesy. He therefore left the country for Germany and accepted the hospitality of his wife, with whom and with whose children by her former marriage he settled at her dower-house at Amorbach in her son's principality of Leiningen. In the spring of 1819 the birth of a child grew imminent. There was a likelihood, although at the moment it looked remote, that it might prove the heir to the English crown; the duke and duchess hurried to England so that the birth might take place on English soil. Apartments were allotted them in the palace at Kensington, in the southeast wing, and there on Monday, 24 May 1819, at 4.15 in the morning, was born to them the girl who was the future Queen Victoria. A gilt plate above the mantelpiece of the room still attests the fact. The Duke of Kent, while describing his daughter as 'a fine healthy child,' modestly deprecated congratulations which anticipated her succession to the throne, 'for while I have three brothers senior to myself, and one (i.e. the Duke of Clarence) possessing every reasonable prospect of having a family, I should deem it the height of presumption to believe it probable that a future heir to the crown of England would spring from me.' Her mother's mother, the Duchess of Saxe-Coburg-Saalfeld, wrote of her as 'a Charlotte—destined perhaps to play a great part one day.' 'The English like queens,' she added, 'and the niece [and also first cousin] of the ever-lamented beloved Charlotte will be most dear to them.' Her father remarked that the infant was too healthy to satisfy the members of his own family, who regarded her as an unwelcome intruder. The child held, in fact, the fifth place in the succession. Between her and the crown there stood her three uncles, the Prince Regent, the Duke of York, and the Duke of Clarence, besides her father the Duke of Kent. Formal honours were accorded the newly born princess as one in the direct line. The privy councillors who were summoned to Kensington on her birth included her uncle, the Duke of Sussex, the Duke of Wellington, the Marquis of Lansdowne, and two leading members of Lord Liverpool's tory ministry, Canning and Vansittart. On 24 June her baptism took place in the grand saloon at Kensington Palace. The gold font, which was part of the regalia of the kingdom, was brought from the Tower, and crimson velvet curtains from the chapel at St. James's. There were three sponsors, of whom the most interesting was the tsar, Alexander I, the head of the Holy Alliance and the most powerful monarch on the continent of Europe. The regent and the tory prime minister, Lord Liverpool, desired to maintain friendly relations with Russia, and the offer of Prince Lieven, Russian ambassador in London, that his master should act as sponsor was accepted with alacrity. The second sponsor was the child's eldest aunt, the queen of Würtemberg (princess royal of England), and the third her mother's mother, the Duchess of Saxe-Coburg-Saalfeld. The three were represented respectively by the infant's uncle, the Duke of York, and her aunts, the Princess Augusta and the Duchess of Gloucester. The rite was performed by Dr. Manners Sutton, archbishop of Canterbury, assisted by the bishop of London. The prince regent, who was present, declared that the one name of 'Alexandrina,' after the tsar, was sufficient. The Duke of Kent requested that a second name should be added. The prince regent suggested 'Georgina.' The Duke of Kent urged 'Elizabeth.' Thereupon the regent brusquely insisted on the mother's name of Victoria, at the same time stipulating that it should follow that of Alexandrina. The princess was therefore named at baptism Alexandrina Victoria, and for several years was known in the family circle as 'Drina.' But her mother was desirous from the first to give public and official prominence to her second name of Victoria. When only four the child signed her name as Victoria to a letter which is now in the British Museum (Addit. MS. 18204, fol. 12). The appellation, although it was not unknown in England, had a foreign sound to English ears, and its bestowal on the princess excited some insular prejudice.

When the child was a month old her parents removed with her to Claremont, the residence which had been granted for life to her uncle,

Prince Leopold, the widowed husband of the Princess Charlotte, and remained his property till his death in 1865. In August the princess was vaccinated, and the fact of her being the first member of the royal family to undergo the operation widely extended its vogue. Before the end of the month the Duchess of Kent learned from her mother of the birth on the 26th, at Rosenau in Coburg, of the second son (Albert) of her eldest brother, the reigning Duke of Saxe-Coburg-Saalfeld (afterwards Gotha). Madame Siebold, the German accoucheuse, who had attended Princess Victoria's birth, was also present at Prince Albert's, and in the Saxe-Coburg circle the names of the two children were at once linked together. In December 1819 the Duke and Duchess of Kent went with their daughter to Sidmouth, where they rented a small house called Woolbrook Cottage. The sojourn there did not lack incident. The discharge of an arrow by a mischievous boy at the window of the room which the infant was occupying went very near ending her career before it was well begun. After a few weeks at Sidmouth, too, the child's position in the state underwent momentous change.On 29 Jan. 1820 her grandfather, King George III, who had long been blind and imbecile, passed away, and the prince regent became king at the age of fifty-eight. Nine days earlier, on 20 Jan. 1820, her father, the Duke of Kent, fell ill of a cold contracted while walking in wet weather; inflammation of the lungs set in, and on the 23rd he died. Thus the four lives that had intervened between the princess and the highest place in the state were suddenly reduced to two—those of her uncles, the Duke of York, who was fifty-seven, and the Duke of Clarence, who was fifty-five. Neither duke had a lawful heir, or seemed likely to have one. A great future for the child of the Duchess of Kent thus seemed assured.The immediate position of mother and daughter was not, however, enviable. The Duke of Kent appointed his widow sole guardian of their child, with his friends General Wetherall and Sir John Conroy as executors of his will. Conroy thenceforth acted as major-domo for the duchess, and lived under the same roof until the accession of the princess, by whom he was always cordially disliked. The duchess was obnoxious to her husband's brothers, especially to the new king, to the Duke of Clarence, and to their younger brother, the Duke of Cumberland, the next heir to the throne after her daughter. Speaking later of her relations with the heads of the royal family, she said that on her husband's death she stood with her daughter 'friendless and alone.' Not the least of her trials was her inability to speak English. Although the duke had made a will, he left no property. He only bequeathed a mass of debts, which the princess, to her lasting credit, took in course of time on her own shoulders and discharged to the last penny. Parliament had granted the duchess in 1818 an annuity of 6,000l. in case of her widowhood; apartments were allowed her in Kensington Palace, but she and her daughter had no other acknowledged resources. Her desolate lot was, however, not without private mitigation. She had the sympathy of her late husband's unmarried sisters, Sophia and Augusta, who admired her self-possession at this critical period; and the kindly Duchess of Clarence, who, a German princess, like herself, conversed with her in her mother-tongue, paid her constant visits. But her main source of consolation was her brother Leopold, who proved an invaluable adviser and a generous benefactor. As soon as the gravity of the duke's illness declared itself he had hurried to Sidmouth to console and counsel her. Deprived by death some four years before of wife and child, he had since led an aimless career of travel in England and Scotland, without any recognised position or influence. It was congenial to him to assume informally the place of a father to the duke's child. Although his German education never made him quite at home in English politics, he was cautious and far-seeing, and was qualified for the rôle of guardian of his niece and counsellor of his sister. He impressed the duchess with the destiny in store for her youngest child. Her responsibilities as regent of the principality of Leiningen in behalf of her son by her first marriage weighed much with her. But strong as was her affection for her German kindred, anxious as she was to maintain close relations with them, and sensitive as she was to the indifference to her manifested at the English court, she, under Leopold's influence, resigned the regency of Leiningen, and resolved to reside permanently in England. After deliberating with her brother, she chose as 'the whole object of her future life' the education of her younger daughter, in view of the likelihood of her accession to the English throne. Until the princess's marriage, when she was in her twenty-first year, mother and daughter were never parted for a day.

Of her father the princess had no personal remembrance, but her mother taught her to honour his memory. Through his early life he had been an active soldier in Canada and at Gibraltar, and he was sincerely attached to the military profession. When his daughter, as Queen Victoria, presented new colours to his old regiment, the royal Scots, at Ballater on 26 Sept. 1876, she said of him: 'He was proud of his profession, and I was always told to consider myself a soldier's child.' Strong sympathy with the army was a main characteristic of her career. Nor were her father's strong liberal, even radical, sympathies concealed from her. At the time of his death he was arranging to visit New Lanark with his wife as the guests of Robert Owen, with whose principles he had already declared his agreement (Owen, *Autobiography*, 1857, p. 237). The princess's whiggish proclivities in early life were part of her paternal inheritance. It was in the spring of 1820 that the Duchess of Kent took up her permanent abode in Kensington Palace, and there in comparative seclusion the princess spent most of her first eighteen years of life. Kensington was then effectually cut off from London by market gardens and country lanes. Besides her infant daughter the duchess had another companion in her child by her first husband, Princess Féodore of Leiningen, who was twelve years Princess Victoria's senior, and inspired her with deep and lasting affection. Prince Charles of Leiningen, Princess Victoria's stepbrother, was also a frequent visitor, and to him also she was much attached. Chief among the permanent members of the Kensington household was Louise Lehzen, the daughter of a Lutheran clergyman of Hanover, who had acted as governess of the Princess Féodore from 1818. Princess Victoria's education was begun in 1824, when Fräulein Lehzen transferred her services from the elder to the younger daughter. Voluble in talk, severe in manner, restricted in information, conventional in opinion, she was never popular in English society; but she was shrewd in judgment and whole-hearted in her devotion to her charge, whom she at once inspired with affection and fear, memory of which never wholly left her pupil. Long after the princess's girlhood close intimacy continued between the two. At Lehzen's death in 1870 the queen wrote of her: 'She knew me from six months old, and from my fifth to my eighteenth years devoted all her care and energies to me with most wonderful abnegation of self, never even taking one day's holiday. I adored, though I was greatly in awe of her. She really seemed to have no thought but for me.' The need of fittingly providing for the princess's education first brought the child to the formal notice of parliament. In 1825 parliament unanimously resolved to allow the Duchess of Kent an additional 6,000l. a year 'for the purpose of making an adequate provision for the honourable support and education of her highness Princess Alexandrina Victoria of Kent' (*Hansard*, new ser. xiii. 909–27). English instruction was needful, and Fräulein Lehzen, whose position was never officially recognised, was hardly qualified for the whole of the teaching. On the advice of the Rev. Thomas Russell, vicar of Kensington, the Rev. George Davys, at the time vicar of a small Lincolnshire parish— from which he was soon transferred to the crown living of All Hallows-on-the-Wall, in the city of London—became the princess's preceptor. He was formally appointed in 1827, when he took up his residence at Kensington Palace. To reconcile Fräulein Lehzen to the new situation, George IV in 1827, at the request of his sister, Princess Sophia, made her a Hanoverian baroness. Davys did his work discreetly. He gathered round him a band of efficient masters in special subjects of study, mainly reserving for himself religious knowledge and history. Although his personal religious views were decidedly evangelical, he was liberal in his attitude to all religious opinions, and he encouraged in his pupil a singularly tolerant temper, which in after life served her in good stead. Thomas Steward, the writing-master of Westminster school, taught her penmanship and arithmetic. She rapidly acquired great ease and speed in writing, although at the sacrifice of elegance. As a girl she was a voluble correspondent with her numerous kinsfolk, and she maintained the practice till the end of her life. Although during her girlhood the duchess conscientiously caused her daughter to converse almost entirely in English, German was the earliest language she learned, and she always knew it as a mother-tongue. She studied it and German literature grammatically under M. Barez. At first she spoke English with a slight German accent; but this was soon mended, and in mature years her pronunciation of English was thoroughly natural, although refined. As a young woman she liked to be regarded as an authority on English accent (Lady Lyttelton, *Letters*). She was instructed in French by M. Grandineau, and came to speak it well and with fluency. At a later period, when she was fascinated by Italian opera, she studied Italian assiduously, and rarely lost an opportunity of speaking it. Although she was naturally a good linguist, she showed no marked aptitude or liking for literary subjects of study. She was not permitted in youth to read novels. First-rate literature never appealed to her. Nor was she endowed with genuine artistic taste. But to the practical pursuit of the arts she applied herself as a girl with persistency and delight. Music occupied much time. John Bernard Sale, organist of St. Margaret's, Westminster, and subsequently organist of the Chapel Royal, gave her her first lessons in singing in 1826. She developed a sweet soprano voice, and soon both sang and played the piano with good effect. Drawing was first taught her by Richard Westall the academician, who in 1829 painted one of the earliest portraits of her, and afterwards by (Sir) Edwin Landseer. Sketching in pencil or water-colours was a lifelong amusement, and after her marriage she attempted etching. In music and the pictorial arts she sought instruction till comparatively late in life. To dancing, which she was first taught by Mdlle. Bourdin, she was, like her mother, devoted; and like her, until middle age, danced with exceptional grace and energy. She was also from childhood a skilful horsewoman, and thoroughly enjoyed physical exercise, taking part in all manner of indoor and outdoor games. The princess grew up an amiable, merry, affectionate, simple-hearted child—very considerate for others' comfort, scrupulously regardful of truth, and easily pleased by homely amusement. At the same time she was self-willed and often showed impatience of restraint. Her memory was from the first singularly retentive. Great simplicity was encouraged in her general mode of life. She dressed without ostentation. Lord Albemarle watched her watering, at Kensington, a little garden of her own, wearing 'a large straw hat and a suit of white cotton,' her only ornament being 'a coloured fichu round the neck.' Charles Knight watched her breakfasting in the open air when she was nine years old, enjoying all the freedom of her years, and suddenly darting from the breakfast table 'to gather a flower in an adjoining pasture.' Leigh Hunt often met her walking at her ease in Kensington Gardens, and although he was impressed by the gorgeous raiment of the footman who followed her, noticed the unaffected playfulness with which she treated a companion of her own age. The Duchess of Kent was fond of presenting her at Kensington to her visitors, who included men of distinction in all ranks of life. William Wilberforce describes how he received an invitation to visit the duchess at Kensington Palace in July 1820, and how the duchess received him 'with her fine animated child on the floor by her side with its playthings, of which I soon became one.' On 19 May 1828 Sir Walter Scott 'dined with the duchess' and was 'presented to the little Princess Victoria—I hope they will change her name (he added)—the heir apparent to the crown as things now stand. ... This little lady is educating with much care, and watched so closely, that no busy maid has a moment to whisper, "You are heir of England." ' But Sir Walter suggested 'I suspect, if we could dissect the little heart, we should find that some pigeon or other bird of the air had carried the matter.'

According to a story recorded many years afterwards by Baroness Lehzen, the fact of her rank was carefully concealed from her until her twelfth year, when after much consultation it was solemnly revealed to her by the baroness, who cunningly inserted in the child's book of English history a royal genealogical tree in which her place was prominently indicated. The princess, the baroness stated, received the information, of which she knew nothing before, with an ecstatic assurance that she would be 'good' thenceforth. But there were many opportunities open to her previously of learning the truth about her position, and on the story in the precise form that it took in the Baroness Lehzen's reminiscence the queen herself threw doubt. Among the princess's childish companions were the daughters of Heinrich von Bülow, the Prussian ambassador in London, whose wife was daughter of Humboldt. When, on 28 May 1829, they and some other children spent an afternoon at Kensington at play with the princess, each of them on leaving was presented by her with her portrait—an act which does not harmonise well with the ignorance of her rank with which Baroness Lehzen was anxious to credit her (*Gabriele von Bülow*, a memoir, English transl. 1897, p. 163). The most impressive of the princess's recreations were summer and autumn excursions into the country or to the seaside. Visits to her uncle Leopold's house at Claremont, near Esher, were repeated many times a year. There, she said, the happiest days of her youth were spent (Grey, p. 392). In the autumn of 1824 she was introduced at Claremont to Leopold's mother, who was her own godmother and grandmother, the Duchess Dowager of Saxe-Coburg, who stayed at

Claremont for more than two months. The old duchess was enthusiastic in praise of her granddaughter—'the sweet blossom of May' she called her— and she favoured the notion, which her son Leopold seems first to have suggested to her, that the girl might do worse than marry into the Saxe-Coburg family. Albert, the younger of the two sons of her eldest son, the reigning Duke of Saxe-Coburg—a boy of her own age—was seriously considered as a suitor. Thenceforth the princess's uncle Leopold was as solicitous about the well-being of his nephew Albert as about that of his niece Victoria. A little later in the same year (1824) the child and her mother paid the first of many visits to Ramsgate, staying at Albion House. Broadstairs was also in early days a favourite resort with the duchess and her daughter, and on returning thence on one occasion they paid a first visit to a nobleman, the Earl of Winchilsea, at Eastwell Park, Ashford. In 1826 the princess and her mother were invited for the first time to visit the king, George IV, at Windsor. He was then residing at the royal lodge in the park while the castle was undergoing restoration, and his guests were allotted quarters at Cumberland Lodge. The king was gracious to his niece, and gave her the badge worn by members of the royal family. Her good spirits and frankness made her thoroughly agreeable to him. On one occasion she especially pleased him by bidding a band play 'God save the King' after he had invited her to choose the tune. On 17 Aug. 1826 she went with him on Virginia Water, and afterwards he drove her out in his phaeton.

Next year there died without issue her uncle the Duke of York, of whom she knew little, although just before his death, while he was living in the King's Road, Chelsea, he had invited her to pay him a visit, and had provided a punch-and-judy show for her amusement. His death left only her uncle the Duke of Clarence between herself and the throne, and her ultimate succession was now recognised. On 28 May 1829 she attended, at St. James's Palace, a court function for the first time. The queen of Portugal, Maria II (da Gloria), who was only a month older than the princess, although she had already occupied her throne three years, was on a visit to England, and a ball was given in her honour by George IV. Queen Maria afterwards (9 April 1836) married Princess Victoria's first cousin, Prince Ferdinand Augustus of Saxe-Coburg, and Queen Victoria always took an extremely sympathetic interest in her career, her descendants, and her country. In June 1830 the last stage but one in the princess's progress towards the crown was reached. Her uncle George IV died on 26 June, and was succeeded by his brother William, duke of Clarence. The girl thus became heir-presumptive. Public interest was much excited in her, and in November 1830 her status was brought to the notice of parliament. A bill was introduced by the lord chancellor, Lord Lyndhurst, and was duly passed, which conferred the regency on the Duchess of Kent, in case the new king died before the princess came of age. This mark of confidence was a source of great satisfaction to the duchess. Next year William IV invited parliament to make further 'provision for Princess Alexandrina Victoria of Kent, in view of recent events.' The government recommended that 10,000*l.* should be added to the Duchess of Kent's allowance on behalf of the princess. Two influential members, Sir Matthew White Ridley and Sir Robert Inglis, while supporting the proposal, urged that the princess should as queen assume the style of Elizabeth II, and repeated the old complaint that the name Victoria did not accord with the feelings of the people. The princess had, however, already taken a violent antipathy to Queen Elizabeth, and always deprecated any association with her. An amendment to reduce the new allowance by one half was lost, and the government's recommendation was adopted (*Hansard*, 3rd ser. v. 591, 654 seq.). Greater dignity was thus secured for the household of the Duchess of Kent and her daughter, although the duchess regarded the addition to her income as inadequate to the needs of her position. The Duchess of Northumberland (a granddaughter of Clive) was formally appointed governess of the princess, and her preceptor Davys was made dean of Chester. She was requested to attend court functions. On 20 July 1830, dressed in deep mourning with a long court train and veil reaching to the ground (Bülow, p. 191), she followed Queen Adelaide at a chapter of the order of the Garter held at St. James's Palace. A few months later she was present at the prorogation of parliament. On 24 Feb. 1831 she attended her first drawing-room, in honour of Queen Adelaide's birthday. The king complained that she looked at him stonily, and was afterwards deeply offended by the irregularity of her attendances at court. She and her mother were expected to attend his coronation on 8 Sept. 1831, but they did not come, and comment on their absence was made in parliament.

With the apparent access of prosperity went griefs and annoyances which caused passing tears, and permanently impressed the princess's mind with a sense of the 'sadness' of her youth. In 1828 her constant companion, the Princess Féodore of Leiningen, left England for good, on her marriage, 18 Feb., to Prince von Hohenlohe-Langenburg, and the separation deeply pained Victoria. In 1830 alarm was felt at Kensington at the prospect of Prince Leopold's permanent removal to the continent. Both mother and daughter trusted his guidance implicitly. The princess was almost as deeply attached to him as to her mother. Although he declined the offer of the throne of Greece in 1830, his acceptance next year of the throne of Belgium grieved her acutely. As king of the Belgians, he watched her interests with no less devotion than before, and he was assiduous in correspondence; but his absence from the country and his subsequent marriage with Louis Philippe's daughter withdrew him from

159

that constant control of her affairs to which she and her mother had grown accustomed. Two deaths which followed in the Saxe-Coburg family increased the sense of depression. The earlier loss did not justify deep regrets. The Duchess of Kent's sister-in-law, the mother of Prince Albert, who soon after his birth had been divorced, died in August 1831. But the death on 16 Nov. of the Duchess Dowager of Saxe-Coburg, the Duchess of Kent's mother and the princess's godmother and grandmother, who took the warmest interest in the child's future, was a lasting sorrow.

The main cause of the Duchess of Kent's anxieties at the time was, however, the hostile attitude that William IV assumed towards her. She had no reason to complain of the unconventional good humour which he extended to her daughter, nor would it be easy to exaggerate the maternal solicitude which the homely Duchess of Clarence, now become Queen Adelaide, showed the princess. But the king resented the payment to the duchess of any of the public consideration which the princess's station warranted. The king seems to have been moved by a senile jealousy of the duchess's influence with the heiress presumptive to the crown, and he repeatedly threatened to remove the girl from her mother's care. When the two ladies received, in August 1831, a royal salute from the ships at Portsmouth on proceeding for their autumn holiday to a hired residence, Norris Castle, Isle of Wight, William IV requested the duchess to forgo such honours, and, when she refused, prohibited them from being offered. Incessant wrangling between him and the duchess continued throughout the reign.

From a maternal point of view the duchess's conduct was unexceptionable. She was indefatigable in making her daughter acquainted with places of interest in England. On 23 Oct. 1830 the princess opened at Bath the Royal Victoria Park, and afterwards inaugurated the Victoria Drive at Malvern. From 1832 onwards the duchess frequently accompanied her on extended tours, during which they were the guests of the nobility, or visited public works and manufacturing centres, so that the princess might acquire practical knowledge of the industrial and social conditions of the people. William IV made impotent protests against these 'royal progresses,' as he derisively called them. The royal heiress was everywhere well received, took part for the first time in public functions, and left in all directions a favourable impression. Municipal corporations invariably offered her addresses of welcome; and the Duchess of Kent, in varying phraseology, replied that it was 'the object of her life to render her daughter deserving of the affectionate solicitude she so universally inspires, and to make her worthy of the attachment and respect of a free and loyal people.' The first tour, which took place in the autumn of 1832, introduced the princess to the principality of Wales. Leaving Kensington in

August, the party drove rapidly through Birmingham, Wolverhampton, and Shrewsbury to Powis Castle, an early home of her governess, the Duchess of Northumberland; thence the princess went over the Menai Bridge to a house at Beaumaris, which she rented for a month. She presented prizes at the Eisteddfod there; but an outbreak of cholera shortened her stay, and she removed to Plas Newydd, which was lent them by the Marquis of Anglesea. She laid the first stone of a boys' school in the neighbourhood on 13 Oct., and made so good an impression that 'the Princess Victoria' was the topic set for a poetic competition in 1834 at the Cardiff Bardic Festival. The candidates were two hundred, and the prize was won by Mrs. Cornwell Baron Wilson. Passing on to Eaton Hall, the seat of Lord Grosvenor, she visited Chester on 17 Oct., and opened a new bridge over the Dee, which was called Victoria Bridge. From 17 to 24 Oct. she stayed with the Duke of Devonshire at Chatsworth, and made many excursions in the neighbourhood, including a visit to Strutt's cotton mills at Belper. Subsequently they stayed at a long series of noblemen's houses—Shugborough, the house of Lord Lichfield; Pitchford, the seat of the third earl of Liverpool, half-brother of the tory statesman, and himself a politician of ability and insight, for whom the queen cherished affection; Hewell Grange, the seat of Lord Plymouth; and Wytham Abbey, the seat of the Earl of Abingdon. From Wytham she and her mother twice went over to Oxford (8–9 Nov.), where they received addresses from both town and university; Dean Gaisford conducted them over Christ Church; they spent some time at the Bodleian Library and at the buildings of the university press. Robert Lowe (afterwards Viscount Sherbrooke), then an undergraduate, described the incidents of the visit in a brilliant macaronic poem (printed in Patchett Martin's *Life of Lord Sherbrooke*, i. 86–90). Leaving Oxford the royal party journeyed by way of High Wycombe and Uxbridge to Kensington. Throughout this tour the princess dined with her mother and her hosts at seven o'clock each evening.

Every year now saw some increase of social occupation. Visitors of all kinds grew numerous at Kensington. In November 1832 Captain Back came to explain his projected polar expedition. In January 1833 the portrait painters David Wilkie and George Hayter arrived to paint the princess's portrait. On 24 April the Duchess of Kent, with a view to mollifying the king, elaborately entertained him at a large dinner party; the princess was present only before and after dinner. In June two of her first cousins, Princes Alexander and Ernest of Würtemberg, and her half-brother, the prince of Leiningen, were her mother's guests. On 24 May 1833 the princess's fourteenth birthday was celebrated by a juvenile ball given by the king at St. James's Palace. A summer and autumn tour was arranged for the south coast in July 1833. The royal party went a second time to

Norris Castle, Isle of Wight, and made personal acquaintance with those parts of the island with which an important part of the princess's after-life was identified. She visited the director of her mother's household, Sir John Conroy, at his residence, Osborne Lodge, on the site of which at a later date Queen Victoria built Osborne Cottage, and near which she erected Osborne House. She explored Whippingham Church and East Cowes; but the main object of her present sojourn in the island was to inspect national objects of interest on the Hampshire coast. At Portsmouth she visited the Victory, Nelson's flagship. Crossing to Weymouth on 29 July she spent some time at Melbury, Lord Ilchester's seat. On 2 Aug. she and her mother arrived at Plymouth to inspect the dockyards. Next day the princess presented on Plymouth Hoe new colours to the 89th regiment (royal Irish fusiliers), which was then stationed at Devonport. Lord Hill, the commander-in-chief, who happened to be at the barracks, took part in the ceremony. The Duchess of Kent on behalf of her daughter addressed the troops, declaring that her daughter's study of English history had inspired her with martial ardour. With the fortunes of the regiment the princess always identified herself thenceforth. It was at a later date named the Princess Victoria's Royal Irish Fusiliers, and twice again, in 1866 and 1889, she presented it with new colours (cf. Rowland Brinckman's *Hist. Records of the Eighty-ninth (Princess Victoria's) Regiment*, 1888, pp. 83–4). The princess afterwards made a cruise in the yacht Emerald to Eddystone lighthouse, to Torquay, whence she visited Exeter, and to Swanage. While she was responding to the calls of public duty she was enjoying enlarged opportunities of recreation. She frequently visited the theatre, in which she always delighted. But it was the Italian opera that roused her highest enthusiasm. She never forgot the deep impressions that Pasta, Malibran, and Grisi, Tamburini and Rubini made on her girlhood. Grisi was her ideal vocalist, by whom she judged all others. All forms of music, competently rendered, fascinated her. Her reverence for the violinist Paganini, after she had once heard him, never waned. In June 1834 she was a deeply interested auditor at the royal musical festival that was given at Westminster Abbey. During her autumn holiday in the same year, when she first stayed at Tunbridge Wells, and afterwards at St. Leonards-on-Sea, she spent much of her time in playing and singing, and her instrument was then the harp (cf. *Memoirs of Georgiana Lady Chatterton*, by E. H. Dering, 1901, p. 29). In 1836 Lablache became her singing master, and he gave her lessons for nearly twenty years, long after her accession to the throne. During 1835, when she completed her sixteenth year, new experiences crowded on her. In June she went for the first time to Ascot, and joined in the royal procession. The American observer, N. P. Willis, watched her listening with unaffected delight to an itinerant ballad singer, and thought her 'quite unnecessarily pretty and interesting,' but he regretfully anticipated that it would be the fate of 'the heir to such a crown of England' to be sold in marriage for political purposes without regard to her personal character or wishes (Willis, *Pencillings by the Way*, 1835, iii. 115). On 30 July 1835 the princess was confirmed at Chapel Royal, St. James's. The archbishop of Canterbury's address on her future responsibilities affected her. She 'was drowned in tears and frightened to death.' Next Sunday, at the chapel of Kensington Palace, the princess received the holy sacrament for the first time. The grim archbishop (Howley) again officiated, together with her preceptor, Davys, the dean of Chester. After a second visit to Tunbridge Wells, where she stayed at Avoyne House, she made a triumphal northern progress. At York she remained a week with Archbishop Harcourt at Bishopsthorp, and visited Lord Fitzwilliam at Wentworth House, whence she went over to the races at Doncaster. She was the guest of the Duke of Rutland at Belvoir House, was enthusiastically received by the people of Stamford, and was next entertained by the Marquis of Exeter at Burghley. A great ball at Burghley was opened by a dance in which the marquis was the princess's partner. When she reached Lynn on her way to Holkham, the Earl of Leicester's seat, navvies yoked themselves to her carriage and drew it round the town. Her last sojourn on this tour was at Euston Hall, the residence of the Duke of Grafton. After returning to Kensington, she spent the month of September at Ramsgate, making excursions to Walmer Castle and to Dover. In 1836, when the princess was seventeen, her uncle Leopold deemed that the time had arrived to apply a practical test to his scheme of uniting her in marriage with her first cousin, Prince Albert of Saxe-Coburg. Accordingly, he arranged with his sister, the Duchess of Kent, that Albert and his elder brother Ernest, the heir-apparent to the duchy, should in the spring pay a visit of some weeks' duration to aunt and daughter at Kensington Palace. In May Princess Victoria met Prince Albert for the first time. William IV and Queen Adelaide received him and his brother courteously, and they were frequently entertained at court. They saw the chief sights of London, and lunched with the lord mayor at the Mansion House. But the king looked with no favour on Prince Albert as a suitor for his niece's hand. At any rate, he was resolved to provide her with a wider field of choice, and he therefore invited the prince of Orange and his two sons and Duke William of Brunswick to be his guests at the same period that the Saxe-Coburg princes were in England, and he gave the princess every opportunity of meeting all the young men together. His own choice finally fell on Alexander, the younger son of the prince of Orange. On 30 May the Duchess of Kent gave a brilliant ball at Kensington Palace, and found herself under the necessity of inviting Duke William of Brunswick and the prince of Orange with his two sons as well as her own protégés. Among the general guests was the Duke of Wellington. Some days later the Saxe-Coburg princes left England. Albert had constantly sketched and played the piano with his cousin; but her ordinary language, like that of those about her, was English which placed him at a disadvantage, for he had but recently begun to learn it. The result of their visit was hardly decisive. Prince Albert wrote of his cousin as 'very amiable,' and astonishingly self-possessed, but parted with her heart-whole. The princess, however, had learned the suggested plan from her uncle Leopold, whose wishes were law for her, and on 7 June, after Albert had left England, she wrote ingenuously to Leopold that she commended the youth to her uncle's special protection, adding, 'I hope and trust that all will go on prosperously and well on this subject, now of so much importance to me.' Her views were uncoloured by sentiment. It was natural and congenial to obey her uncle.

In the early autumn of 1836 she paid a second visit to the retired tory statesman, Lord Liverpool, who was then living at Buxted Park, near Uckfield, and afterwards spent a quiet month at Ramsgate. The old king was at the moment causing the Duchess of Kent renewed disquietude. The princess had consequently absented herself from court, and the king complained that he saw too little of her. On 20 Aug. 1836, the king's birthday, mother and daughter dined with him at a state banquet, when he publicly expressed the hope that he might live till his niece came of age, so that the kingdom might be spared the regency which parliament had designed for the Duchess of Kent. He described his sister-in-law as a 'person' 'surrounded by evil counsellors,' and unfitted 'to the exercise of the duties of her station.' He asserted that, contrary to his command, she was occupying an excessive number of rooms—seventeen—at Kensington Palace. He would not 'endure conduct so disrespectful to him.' The princess burst into tears. The breach between the king and her mother was complete. William IV's hope of living long enough to prevent a regency was fulfilled. Although his health was feeble, no serious crisis was feared when, on 24 May 1837, the princess celebrated her eighteenth birthday, and thus came of age. At Kensington the occasion was worthily celebrated, and the hamlet kept holiday. The princess was awakened by an *aubade*, and received many costly gifts. Addresses from public bodies were presented to her mother. To one from the corporation of London the duchess made, on behalf of her daughter, an elaborate reply. She pointed out that the princess was in intercourse with all classes of society, and, after an indiscreet reference to the slights put on herself by the royal family, spoke volubly of the diffusion of religious knowledge, the preservation of the constitutional prerogatives of the crown, and the protection of popular liberties as the proper aims of a sovereign. The king was loth to withdraw himself from the public rejoicing. He sent his niece a grand piano, and in the evening gave a state ball in her honour at St. James's Palace. Neither he nor the queen attended it, owing, it was stated, to illness. The princess opened the entertainment in a quadrille with Lord FitzAlan, grandson of the Duke of Norfolk, and afterwards danced with Nicholas Esterhazy, son of the Austrian ambassador. In the same month she paid two visits to the Royal Academy, which then for the first time held its exhibition in what is now the National Gallery, Trafalgar Square. She was the centre of attraction. On the first visit she shook hands and talked with Rogers the poet, and, hearing that the actor, Charles Kemble, was in the room, desired that he should be introduced to her. A few days later the king, in a letter addressed personally to her, offered to place 10,000*l.* a year at her own disposal, independently of her mother. She accepted the offer to her mother's chagrin.

No sooner had the celebrations of the princess's majority ended than death put her in possession of the fullest rights that it could confer. Early in June it was announced that the king's health was breaking. On Tuesday, 20 June 1837, at twelve minutes past two in the morning, he died at Windsor Castle. The last barrier between Princess Victoria and the crown was thus removed. The archbishop of Canterbury, who had performed the last religious rites, at once took leave of Queen Adelaide and with Lord Conyngham, the lord chamberlain, drove through the early morning to Kensington to break the news to the new sovereign. They arrived there before 5 a.m. and found difficulty in obtaining admission. The porter refused to rouse the princess. At length the Baroness Lehzen was sent for, and she reluctantly agreed to warn the princess of their presence. The girl came into the room with a shawl thrown over her dressing-gown, her feet in slippers, and her hair falling down her back. Lord Conyngham dropped on his knee, saluted her as queen, and kissed the hand she held towards him. The archbishop did the like, addressing to her 'a sort of pastoral charge.' At the same time she was informed of the king's peaceful end. The princess clasped her hands and anxiously asked for news of her aunt (Bunsen, i. 272). The prime minister, Lord Melbourne, arrived before nine o'clock, and was at once received in audience. The queen's uncle, the Duke of Sussex, and the Duke of Wellington, the most popular man in the state, also visited her. But, in accordance with the constitution, it was from the prime minister, Lord Melbourne, alone that she could receive counsel as to her official duties and conduct. The privy council was hastily summoned to meet at Kensington at 11 a.m. on the day of the king's death. On entering the room the queen was met by her uncles, the Dukes of Cumberland and Sussex, and having taken her seat at once read the speech which Lord Melbourne had written for her some days before in consultation with Lord Lansdowne, the veteran president of the council. She was dressed very plainly in black and wore no ornaments. She was already in mourning for the death of Queen Adelaide's mother. She spoke of herself as 'educated in England under the tender and enlightened care of a most affectionate mother; she had learned from her infancy to respect and love the constitution of her native country.' She would aim at securing the enjoyment of religious liberty and would protect the rights of all her subjects. She then took the oath, guaranteeing the security of the church of Scotland; the ministers gave up their seals to her and she returned them; they then kissed hands on reappointment, and the privy councillors took the oaths. Although she was unusually short in stature (below five feet), and with no pretensions to beauty, her manner and movement were singularly unembarrassed, modest, graceful, and dignified, while her distinct and perfectly modulated elocution thrilled her auditors. 'She not merely filled her chair,' said the Duke of Wellington, 'she filled the room.' Throughout the ceremony she conducted herself as though she had long been familiar with her part in it (cf. Poole, *Life of Stratford Canning*, 1888, ii. 45; *Croker Papers*, ii. 359; Ashley, *Life of Palmerston*, i. 340). The admirable impression she created on this her first public appearance as queen was fully confirmed in the weeks that followed. Next day she drove to St. James's Palace to attend the formal proclamation of her accession to the throne. While the heralds recited their announcement she stood in full view of the public between Lord Melbourne and Lord Lansdowne, at the open window of the privy council chamber, looking on the quadrangle nearest Marlborough House. The crowd cheered vociferously, and prominent in the throng was Daniel O'Connell, who waved his hat with conspicuous energy. 'At the sound of the first shouts the colour faded from the queen's cheeks,' wrote Lord Albemarle, her first master of the horse, who was also an onlooker, 'and her eyes filled with tears. The emotion thus called forth imparted an additional charm to the winning courtesy with which the girl-sovereign accepted the proffered homage' (Albemarle, *Fifty Years of my Life*, p. 378).

After the proclamation the queen saw Lord Hill, the commander-in-chief, the lord-chancellor, and other great officers of state. At noon her second council was held at St. James's Palace, and all the cabinet ministers were present. Later in the day the proclamation was repeated at Trafalgar Square, Temple Bar, Wood Street, and the Royal Exchange. Although the queen signed the privy council register at her first council in the name of Victoria only, in all the official documents which were prepared on the first day of her reign her name figured with the prefix of Alexandrina. In the proclamation she was called 'Her Royal Majesty Alexandrina Victoria, Queen of the United Kingdom.' But, despite the sentiment that had been excited against the name Victoria, it was contrary to her wish to be known by any other. Papers omitting the prefix 'Alexandrina' were hastily substituted for those in which that prefix had been introduced, and from the second day of the new reign the sovereign was known solely as Queen Victoria. Thenceforth that name was accepted without cavil as of the worthiest English significance. It has since spread far among her subjects. It was conferred on one of the most prosperous colonies of the British empire in 1851, and since on many smaller settlements or cities, while few municipalities in the United Kingdom or the empire have failed to employ it in the nomenclature of streets, parks, railway-stations, or places of public assembly. Abroad, and even in some well-informed quarters at home, surprise was manifested at the tranquillity with which the nation saw the change of monarch effected. But the general enthusiasm that Queen Victoria's accession evoked was partly due to the contrast she presented with those who had lately occupied the throne. Since the century began there had been three kings of England—men all advanced in years—of whom the first was an imbecile, the second a profligate, and the third little better than a buffoon. The principle of monarchy was an article of faith with the British people which the personal unfitness of the monarch seemed unable to touch. But the substitution for kings whose characters could not inspire respect of an innocent girl, with what promised to be a long and virtuous life before her, evoked at the outset in the large mass of the people a new sentiment—a sentiment of chivalric devotion to the monarchy which gave it new stability and rendered revolution impossible. Although the play of party politics failed to render the sentiment universal, and some actions of the queen in the early and late years of the reign severely tried it, it was a plant that, once taking root, did not readily decay. Politicians—of the high rank of Lord Palmerston, the foreign secretary in the whig ministry, and Sir Robert Peel, leader of the tories in the House of Commons—deplored the young queen's inexperience and ignorance of the world; but such defects were more specious than real in a constitutional monarch, and, as far as they were disadvantageous, were capable of remedy by time. Sydney Smith echoed the national feeling when, preaching in St. Paul's Cathedral on the first Sunday of her reign, he described the new sovereign as 'a patriot queen,' who might be expected to live to a ripe old age and to contribute to the happiness and prosperity of her people. 'We have had glorious female reigns,' said Lord John Russell, the home secretary under Melbourne, a few weeks later. 'Those of Elizabeth and Anne led us to great victories. Let us now hope that we are going to have a female reign illustrious in its deeds of peace—an Elizabeth without her tyranny, an Anne without her weakness' (Walpole, *Life of Lord John Russell*, i. 284). Owing to her sex, some changes in the position and duties of a British sovereign were inevitable. The Salic law rendered her incompetent to succeed to the throne of Hanover, which British sovereigns had filled since George the elector of Hanover became George I of England in 1714. Hanover had been elevated from an electorate to a kingdom by the congress of Vienna in 1814, and the kingdom now passed to the queen's uncle, the next heir after her to the English throne, Ernest, duke of Cumberland. The dissolution of the union between England and Hanover was acquiesced in readily by both countries. They had long drifted apart in political sentiments and aspirations. The new king of Hanover was altogether out of sympathy with his royal niece. He proved an illiberal and reactionary ruler; but she, in whom domestic feeling was always strong, took a lively interest in the fortunes of his family, and showed especial kindness to them in the trials that awaited them. At home the main alteration in her duty as sovereign related to the criminal law. Death was the punishment accorded to every manner of felony until William IV's parliament humanely reduced the number of capital offences to four or five, and it had been the custom of the sovereign personally to revise the numerous capital sentences pronounced in London at the Old Bailey. At the close of each session these were reported to the sovereign by the recorder for final judgment. A girl was obviously unfitted to perform this repugnant task. Accordingly the queen was promptly relieved of it by act of parliament (7 William IV and 1 Vict. cap. 77). Outside London the order of the court to the sheriff had long been sufficient to insure the execution of the death penalty. To that practice London now conformed, while the home secretary dealt henceforth by his sole authority with petitions affecting offenders capitally convicted, and was alone responsible for the grant of pardons, reprieves, or respites. Whenever capital sentences were modified by the home secretary, he made a report to that effect to the queen, and occasionally it evoked comment from her; but his decision was always acted on as soon as it was formed. Thus, although the statute of 1837 formally reserved 'the royal prerogative of mercy,' the accession of a woman to the throne had the paradoxical effect of practically annulling all that survived of it. But, while the queen was not called on to do everything that her predecessors had done, she studied with ardour the routine duties of her station and was immersed from the moment of her accession in pressing business. The prime minister, Melbourne, approached his task of giving her political instruction with exceptional tact and consideration, and she proved on the whole an apt pupil. Melbourne was the leader of the whig party, whose constitutional principles denied the sovereign any independence; but it was with the whigs that her father had associated himself, and association with them was personally congenial to her. None the less, she was of an imperious, self-reliant, and somewhat wilful disposition; she was naturally proud of her elevation and of the dignified responsibilities which nominally adhered to the crown. While, therefore, accepting without demur Melbourne's theories of the dependent place of a sovereign in a constitutional monarchy, she soon set her own interpretation on their practical working. She was wise enough at the outset to recognise her inexperience, and she knew instinctively the need of trusting those who were older and better versed in affairs than herself. But she never admitted her subjection to her ministers. From almost the first to the last day of her reign she did not hesitate closely to interrogate them, to ask for time for consideration before accepting their decisions, and to express her own wishes and views frankly and ingenuously in all affairs of government that came before her. After giving voice to her opinion, she left the final choice of action or policy to her official advisers' discretion; but if she disapproved of their choice, or it failed of its effect, she exercised unsparingly the right of private rebuke. The first duty of her ministers and herself was to create a royal household. The principles to be followed differed from those which had recently prevailed. It was necessary for a female sovereign to have women and not men as her personal attendants. She deprecated an establishment on the enormous scale that was adopted by the last female sovereign in England—Queen Anne. A mistress of the robes, eight ladies-in-waiting, and six women of the bedchamber she regarded as adequate. Her uncle Leopold wisely urged her to ignore political considerations in choosing her attendants. But she was without personal friends of the rank needed for the household offices, and she accepted Lord Melbourne's injudicious advice to choose their first holders exclusively from the wives and daughters of the whig ministers. She asked the Marchioness of Lansdowne to become mistress of the robes, and although her health did not permit her to accept that post, she agreed to act as first lady-in-waiting. The higher household dignity was filled (1 July 1837) by the Duchess of Sutherland, who was soon one of the queen's intimate associates. Others of her first ladies-in-waiting were the Countess of Mulgrave, afterwards Marchioness of Normanby, and Lady Tavistock. The Countess of Rosebery declined to join them. In accord with better established precedent, the gentlemen of her household were also chosen from orthodox supporters of the whig ministry. The queen only asserted herself by requesting that Sir John Conroy, the master of her mother's and her own household, whom she never liked, should retire from her service; she gave him a pension of 3,000*l.* a year, but refused his request for an order and an Irish peerage. Graver perplexities attached to the question of the appointment of a private secretary to the new sovereign. Although former occupants of the throne had found such an officer absolutely essential to the due performance of their duties, the ministers feared the influence that one occupying so confidential a relation with a young untried girl might gain over her. With admirable self-denial Melbourne solved the difficulty by taking on himself the work of her private secretary for all public business. As both her prime minister and private secretary it was thus necessary for him to be always with the court. For the first two years of her reign he was her constant companion, spending most of the morning at work with her, riding with her of an afternoon, and dining with her of an evening. The paternal care which he bestowed on her was acknowledged with gratitude by political friends and foes.

Melbourne's acceptance of the office of private secretary best guaranteed the queen's course against pitfalls which might have involved disaster. Members of the family circle in which she had grown up claimed the right and duty of taking part in her guidance when she began the labour of her life, and, owing to their foreign birth, it was in her own interest that their influence should be permanently counterbalanced by native counsel. King Leopold, the queen's foster-father, who had hitherto controlled her career, and remained a trusted adviser till his death, had, as soon as she reached her majority, sent his confidential friend and former secretary, Baron Stockmar, to direct her political education. The baron remained in continuous attendance on her, without official recognition, for the first fifteen months of her reign, and when the question of a choice of private secretary was first raised, the queen expressed an infelicitous anxiety to appoint him. A native of Coburg, who originally came to England with Leopold in 1816 as his medical attendant, Stockmar was now fifty years old. Sincerely devoted to his master and to the Saxe-Coburg family, he sought no personal advantage from his association with them. Even Lord Palmerston, who bore him no affection, admitted that he was the most disinterested man he ever met. Intelligently read in English history, he studied with zeal the theory of the British constitution. There was genuine virtue in the substance of his reiterated advice that the queen should endeavour to maintain a position above party and above intrigue. But, although sagacious, Stockmar was a pedantic and a sententious critic of English politics, and cherished some perilous heresies. The internal working of the British government was never quite understood by him. His opinion that the sovereign was no 'nodding mandarin' was arguable, but his contention that a monarch, if of competent ability, might act as his own minister was wholly fallacious. The constant intercourse which he sought with Melbourne and other ministers was consequently felt by them to be embarrassing, and to be disadvantageous to the queen. An impression got abroad that he exerted on her a mysterious anti-national influence behind the throne. Abercromby, speaker of the House of

Commons, threatened in very early days to bring the subject to the notice of parliament. But when it was rumoured that Stockmar was acting as the queen's private secretary, Melbourne circulated a peremptory denial, and public attention was for the time diverted. The queen's openly displayed fidelity to her old governess, the Baroness Lehzen, did not tend to dissipate the suspicion that she was in the hands of foreign advisers. But the baroness's relations with her mistress were above reproach and did credit to both. She had acted as her old pupil's secretary in private matters before she came to the throne, and she continued to perform the same functions after the queen's accession. But public affairs were never brought by the queen to her cognisance, and the baroness loyally accepted the situation. With the Duchess of Kent, who continued to reside with her daughter, although she was now given a separate suite of apartments, the queen's relation was no less discreet—far more discreet than the duchess approved. She was excluded from all share in public business—an exclusion in which she did not readily acquiesce. For a long time she treated her daughter's emancipation from her direction as a personal grievance (Greville). There was never any ground for the insinuation which Lord Brougham conveyed when he spoke in the House of Lords of the Duchess of Kent as 'the queen-mother.' Melbourne protested with just indignation against applying such a misnomer to 'the mother of the queen,' who was wholly outside the political sphere.Public ceremonials meanwhile claimed much of the queen's attention. On 27 June she held her first levee at Kensington to receive the credentials of the ambassadors and envoys. She was dressed in black, but, as sovereign of the order of the Garter, wore all its brilliant insignia—ribbon, star, and a band bearing the motto, in place of the garter, buckled on the left arm (Bunsen, ii. 273). There followed a long series of deputations from public bodies, bearing addresses of condolence and congratulation, to all of which she replied with characteristic composure. On 17 July she went in state to dissolve parliament in accordance with the law which required a general election to take place immediately on the demise of the crown. For the first time she appeared in apparel of state—a mantle of crimson velvet lined with ermine, an ermine cape, a dress of white satin embroidered with gold, a tiara and stomacher of diamonds, and the insignia of the garter. She read the speech with splendid effect. Fanny Kemble, who was present, wrote: 'The queen's voice was exquisite. . . . The enunciation was as perfect as the intonation was melodious, and I think it is impossible to hear a more excellent utterance than that of the queen's English by the English queen.' A more disinterested visitor, the American orator, Charles Sumner, used very similar language: 'Her voice was sweet and finely modulated. . . . I think I have never heard anything better read in my life than her speech.' On 19 July the queen held her first levee at St. James's Palace, and next day her first drawing-room. On both occasions the attendance was enormous. A few days before (13 July) the queen left the home of her girlhood at Kensington for Buckingham Palace, the new official residence in London appointed for the sovereign. The building had been begun by the architect John Nash for George IV, but was not completed until William IV became king. He, however, disliked it, and preferred to remain at St. James's Palace. No monarch occupied Buckingham Palace before Queen Victoria, for whom it was for the first time put in order. A contemporary wag in the 'Times' declared it was the cheapest house ever built, having been built for one sovereign and furnished for another. But the inconvenience with which William IV credited it proved real, and it underwent radical alterations and additions at the instance of the queen and Prince Albert before it was deemed to be adapted for its purpose. An east front was erected to form a quadrangle; the ground behind the house, to the extent of forty acres, was laid out as a pleasure-garden; a conservatory was converted into a chapel, and a ballroom was added as late as 1856. One of the first entertainments which were given at Buckingham Palace was a grand concert on 17 Aug. 1837, under the direction of Signor Costa. In honour of the occasion the queen ordered the court to go out of mourning for the day. The vocalists were Madame Grisi, Madame Albertazzi, Signor Lablache, and Signor Tamburini. The queen's first official appearance in public out of doors took place on 21 Aug., when she opened the new gate of Hyde Park on the Bayswater Road, and conferred on it the name of Victoria. On 22 Aug. she drove to Windsor to assume residence at the castle for the first time. On 28 Sept. she had her earliest experience of a military review, when the guards in Windsor garrison marched before her in the Home Park. After remaining at Windsor till 4 Oct. she made acquaintance with the third and last of the royal palaces then in existence, the pretentious Pavilion at Brighton, which George IV had erected in a foolish freak of fancy. Lord John Russell, the home secretary, together with his wife, stayed with her there. On 4 Nov. she returned to Buckingham Palace. The queen took a girlish delight in the sense of proprietorship: she actively directed her domestic establishments, and the mode of life she adopted in her palaces was of her own devising. She exercised a constant and wide hospitality which had been long unknown in the royal circle. The entertainments were somewhat formal and monotonous; but, although she was zealous for rules of etiquette, she was never indisposed to modify them if she was thereby the better able to indulge the kindly feeling that she invariably extended to her guests. Most of her mornings were spent at work with Melbourne. In the early afternoon when at Windsor she rode in the park or neighbouring country with a large cavalcade often numbering thirty persons. Later she romped with children, some of whom she usually contrived to include among her guests, or played at ball or battledore and shuttlecock with ladies of the court—a practice which she continued till middle age—or practised singing and pianoforte playing. Dining at half-past seven, she usually devoted the evening to round games of cards, chess, or draughts, while the Duchess of Kent played whist. One of her innovations was the institution of a court band, which played music during and after dinner. When she was settled at Buckingham Palace she gave a small dance every Monday. She found time for a little serious historical reading, one of the earliest books through which she plodded as queen being Coxe's 'Life of Sir Robert Walpole' (Lady Lyttelton), and for the first time in her life she attempted novel-reading, making trial of three books by Sir Walter Scott, Fenimore Cooper, and Bulwer Lytton respectively (Bunsen, i. 296). A little later she struggled with Hallam's 'Constitutional History' and St. Simon's 'Memoirs.' Relatives from the continent of Europe were in the first days of her reign very frequent guests. With them she always seemed most at ease, and she showed them marked attention. Vacant garters were bestowed on two of her German kinsmen, who came on early visits to her—the first on her half-brother, the Prince of Leiningen, in July 1837, the next on her uncle, Prince Albert's father, in the year following. The king of the Belgians and his gentle Queen Louise spent three weeks with her at Windsor (August-September 1837), and the visit was repeated for years every autumn. Her first cousin Victoria, daughter of Duke Ferdinand of Saxe-Coburg, who in 1840 married the Duc de Nemours, was also often with her, and shared in her afternoon games. But she was not at the same time neglectful of her kinsfolk at home. Nothing could exceed the tenderness with which she treated the Dowager Queen Adelaide. On the day of her accession she wrote a letter of condolence, addressing it to 'the Queen' and not to 'the Dowager Queen,' for fear of adding to her grief. A very few days later, before the late king's funeral, she visited the widowed lady at Windsor, and she forbade, of her own motion, the lifting of the royal standard, then at half-mast, to mast-high, as was customary on the arrival of the sovereign. When Queen Adelaide removed from Windsor Castle ultimately to settle at Marlborough House, her royal niece bade her take from the castle any furniture that her residence there had especially endeared to her, and until the old queen's death the young queen never relaxed any of her attentions. To all her uncles and aunts she showed like consideration. She corresponded with them, entertained them, visited them, read to them, sang to them; and she bore with little murmuring her uncles' displays of ill-temper. The Duchess of Cambridge, the last survivor of that generation, died as late as 1889, and no cares of family or state were ever permitted by the queen to interfere with the due rendering of those acts of personal devotion to which the aged duchess had been accustomed. Even to the welfare of the FitzClarences—William IV's illegitimate children by Mrs. Jordan—she was not indifferent, and often exerted her influence in their interests. At the same time domestic sentiment was rarely suffered to affect court etiquette. At her own table she deemed it politic to give, for the first time, precedence to foreign ambassadors—even to the American envoy, Mr. Stephenson—over all guests of whatever rank, excepting only Lord Melbourne, who always sat at her left hand. For years she declined to alter the practice in favour of the royal dukes and duchesses, but ultimately made some exceptions. Meanwhile the first general election of the new reign had taken place, and the battle of the rival parties mainly raged round the position and prospects of the queen. The tories, who were the attacking force, bitterly complained that Melbourne and the whigs in power identified her with themselves, and used her and her name as party weapons of offence. Lord John Russell, in a letter to Lord Mulgrave, lord-lieutenant of Ireland, had written of her sympathy with the whig policy in Ireland. Croker, a tory spokesman, in an article in the 'Quarterly Review' (July 1837), denounced the policy of surrounding her with female relatives of the whig leaders. Sir Robert Peel argued that the monarchy was endangered by the rigour with which she was ruled by Melbourne, the chief of one political party. Release of the sovereign from whig tyranny consequently became a tory cry, and it gave rise to the epigram:

> 'The Queen is with us,' Whigs insulting say;
> 'For when *she found us in* she let us stay.'
> It may be so, but give me leave to doubt
> How long she'll keep you when *she finds you out.*
> (*Annual Register*, 1837, p. 239).

Whig wire-pullers, on the other hand, made the most of the recent conduct of the next heir to the throne, the new king of Hanover, the queen's uncle Ernest, who had signalised his accession by revoking constitutional government in his dominions. They spread a report that the new king of Hanover was plotting to dethrone his niece in order to destroy constitutional government in England as well as in Hanover, and a cartoon was issued entitled 'The Contrast,' which represented side by side portraits of the queen and her uncle, the queen being depicted as a charming *ingénue*, and her uncle as a grey-haired beetle-browed villain. The final result of the elections was not satisfactory to either side. The tories gained on the balance thirty-seven seats, and thus reduced their opponents' majority; but in the new House of Commons the whigs still led by thirty-eight, and Melbourne and his colleagues retained office. Before the new parliament opened, the queen made a formal progress through London, going from Buckingham Palace to the Guildhall to dine in state with the lord mayor. Her passage through the streets evoked an imposing demonstration of loyalty. Fifty-eight carriages formed the procession, in which rode many of the foreign ambassadors. The lord mayor, Sir John Cowan, with the sheriffs, George Carroll and Moses Montefiore, and members of the corporation of London, received the queen at Temple Bar. The banquet lasted from 3.30 in the afternoon till 8.30 in the evening, when the city was ablaze with illuminations. A medal was struck from a design by William Wyon, and the queen's arrival at Temple Bar was pictured in a bas-relief on the monument that now marks the site of the old gate. On 20 Nov. the queen opened her first parliament, reading her own speech, as was her custom until her widowhood whenever she attended in person. The opening business of the session was a settlement of the royal civil list. Financially the queen's position since her accession had been a source of anxiety. She inherited nothing, and the crown had lost the royal revenues of Hanover. She had complained to Melbourne of her lack of money for immediate private expenses. He had done little but listen sympathetically, but Messrs. Coutts, who had been bankers to various members of the royal family, came to her rescue with temporary advances. The main question for the government to consider was not merely the amount of the income necessary to maintain the throne in fitting dignity, but the proportion of that income which might be prudently derived from the hereditary revenues of the crown, i.e. revenues from the crown lands. In return for a fixed annuity George III had surrendered a large portion of these revenues, and George IV yielded a further portion, while William IV surrendered all but those proceeding from the duchies of Cornwall and Lancaster, which were held to belong to a different category. At the same time it was arranged, on the accession of William IV, that the general expenses of civil government, which had been previously defrayed out of the king's civil list, should henceforth be discharged by the consolidated fund, and that of the income allotted to King William only a very small proportion should be applied to aught outside his household and personal expenses; the sole external calls were 75,000l. for pensions and 10,000l. for the secret service fund. On these conditions King William was content to accept 460,000l. instead of 850,000l. which had been paid his predecessor, while an annuity of 50,000l. was bestowed on his queen consort. His net personal parliamentary income (excluding pensions and the secret service fund) was thus 375,000l., with some 25,000l. from the duchies of Lancaster and Cornwall. Radical members of parliament now urged Melbourne to bring the whole of the crown lands under parliamentary control, to deprive the crown of the control and income of the duchies of Lancaster and Cornwall, and to supply the sovereign with a revenue which should be exclusively applied to her own purposes, and not to any part of the civil government. Treasury officials drew out a scheme with these ends in view, but Melbourne rejected most of it from a fear of rousing against his somewhat unstable government the cry of tampering with the royal prerogative. In the result the precedent of William IV's case was followed, with certain modifications. The queen resigned all the hereditary revenues of the crown, but was left in possession of the revenues of the duchies of Lancaster and Cornwall, of which the latter was the lawful appanage of the heir-apparent. The duchy of Cornwall therefore ceased to be the sovereign's property as soon as a lawful heir to the throne was born. It and the duchy of Lancaster produced during the first years of the reign about 27,500*l.* annually, but the revenues from both rose rapidly, and the duchy of Lancaster, which was a permanent source of income to the queen, ultimately produced above 60,000*l.* a year. (The duchy of Cornwall, which passed to the prince of Wales at his birth in 1841, ultimately produced more than 66,000*l.*) Parliament now granted her, apart from these hereditary revenues, an annuity of 385,000*l.*, being 10,000*l.* in excess of the net personal income granted by parliament to her predecessor. Of this sum 60,000*l.* was appropriated to her privy purse, 131,260*l.* to the salaries of the household, 172,500*l.* to the expenses of the household, 13,200*l.* to the royal bounty, while 8,040*l.* was unappropriated. The annual payment from the civil list of 75,000*l.* in pensions and of 10,000*l.* secret service money was cancelled, but permission was given the crown to create 'civil list' pensions to the amount of 1,200*l.* annually, a sum which the treasury undertook to defray independently of the royal income; this arrangement ultimately meant the yearly expenditure of some 23,000*l.*, but the pensions were only nominally associated with the sovereign's expenditure. Repairs to the sovereign's official residences and the maintenance of the royal yachts were also provided for by the treasury apart from the civil list revenues. Joseph Hume, on the third reading of the civil list bill, moved a reduction of 50,000*l.*, which was rejected by 199 votes against 19. Benjamin Hawes vainly moved a reduction of 10,000*l.*, which was supported by 41 members and opposed by 173. Lord Brougham severely criticised the settlement on the second reading of the bill in the House of Lords. He made searching inquiries respecting the incomes from the crown duchies, and objected to the arrangement being made for the queen's life. Although numerous additional grants, approaching a total of 200,000*l.* a year, were afterwards allotted to the queen's children, the annual sum allowed her by parliament on her accession was never altered during her reign of nearly sixty-four years, and proved amply sufficient for all her needs. At the same time as the civil list bill passed through parliament, the queen's mother, at the sovereign's instance, was granted an annuity of 30,000*l*.; she formerly received 22,000*l*. a year, of which 10,000*l*. was appropriated to the care of her daughter while princess. On 23 Dec. 1837 the queen went to parliament to return thanks in person for what had been done. Christmas was spent at Buckingham Palace, and next day the court withdrew to Windsor. The liberal allowance enabled the queen to fulfil at once her resolve to pay off her father's debts. By the autumn of next year she had transferred to the late duke's creditors from her privy purse nearly 50,000*l*., and on 7 Oct. 1839 she received their formal thanks. Meanwhile the queen's sympathy with her ministers increased. Through 1838–9 she followed their parliamentary movements with keen anxiety lest their narrow majority might prove inadequate to maintain them in office. Disturbances in Canada during the early months of 1838 roused differences of opinion in the House of Commons, which imperilled their position, but the crisis passed. 'The queen is as steady to us as ever,' wrote Palmerston on 14 April 1838, 'and was in the depth of despair when she thought we were in danger of being turned out. She keeps well in health, and even in London takes long rides into the country, which have done her great good' (Ashley, *Life of Palmerston*, i. 344). Under Melbourne's guidance, and in agreement with her own wish, she daily perused masses of despatches and correspondence with exemplary diligence.Outside politics her chief interest lay in the preparations that were in progress for her coronation and for the festivities accompanying it. Three state balls—one on 18 June, the day of Waterloo, a choice of date which offended the French—two levees, a drawing-room, a state concert, a first state visit to Ascot, and attendance at Eton 'montem' immediately preceded the elaborate ceremonial, which took place on 28 June 1838, eight days after the anniversary of her accession. The ministers resolved to endow it with exceptional splendour. For the expenses of William IV's coronation 50,000*l*. had been allowed. No less a sum than 200,000*l*. was voted by parliament for the expenses of Queen Victoria's coronation. Westminster Abbey was elaborately decorated in crimson and gold. The royal procession to the abbey was revived for the first time since the coronation of George III in 1761, and four hundred thousand persons came to London to witness it, many bivouacking in the streets the night before. At 10 a.m. on the appointed day, in magnificent weather, the queen left Buckingham Palace in full panoply of state, passing up Constitution Hill, along Piccadilly, down St. James's Street, and across Trafalgar Square, which had just been laid out in Nelson's memory. The abbey was reached by way of Parliament Street at 11.30. Among foreign visitors, who went thither in advance of the queen, was Marshal Soult, the representative of France, whom the crowds received with hardly less enthusiasm than her majesty. The great company of her German relatives included her uncle the Duke of Saxe-Coburg and her half-brother and half-sister of Leiningen. When the queen entered the abbey, 'with eight ladies all in white, floating about her like a silvery cloud, she paused, as if for breath, and clasped her hands' (Stanley). A ray of sunlight fell on her head as she knelt to receive the crown, and the Duchess of Kent burst into tears. The brilliance of the scene impressed every one, but there were some drawbacks. Harriet Martineau, who was present, wrote: 'The brightness, vastness, and dreamy magnificence produced a strange effect of exhaustion and sleepiness.' The queen, too, suffered not only from natural emotion and fatigue, but from the hesitation of the officiating clergy as to the exact part she was to play in many parts of the long ritual, and from the insufficient training that had been accorded her. 'Pray tell me what I am to do, for they [i.e. the clergy] don't know,' she said at one solemn point to a lay official who stood near her. She complained that the orb which was unexpectedly put into her hand was too heavy for her to hold; and when the ruby ring, which had been made for her little finger, was forced by the archbishop on to her fourth, she nearly cried out with the pain. For the first time at a coronation, the commons were allowed to acclaim her after the peers. The latter had enjoyed the privilege from time immemorial. The commons now cheered their sovereign nine times (*Gent. Mag.* 1838, ii. 198); but Dean Stanley, who, then a boy, sat in a gallery, thought all the responses and acclamations were feebly given. Towards the close of the ceremony a singular accident befell Lord Rolle, a peer, eighty years old, as he was endeavouring to offer his homage. He 'fell down as he was getting up the steps of the throne.' The queen's 'first impulse was to rise, and when afterwards he came again to do homage she said, "May I not get up and meet him?" and then rose from the throne and advanced down one or two of the steps to prevent his coming up, an act of graciousness and kindness which made a great sensation' (Greville, 2nd ser. i. 107). While the peers were doing homage, the lord-chamberlain and his officers flung medals, specially designed by Pistrucci, for the spectators to scramble for, and the confusion was not dignified. At length the ceremonial, which lasted more than five hours, ended, and at a quarter past four the queen returned to Buckingham Palace. She then wore her crown and all her apparel of state, but she looked to spectators pale and tremulous. Carlyle, who was in the throng, breathed a blessing on her: 'Poor little queen!' he added, 'she is at an age at which a girl can hardly be trusted to choose a bonnet for herself; yet a task is laid upon her from which an archangel might shrink.' But despite her zeal to fulfil the responsibilities of her station, she still had much of the child's lightness and simplicity of heart. On returning to the palace she hastily doffed her splendours in order to give her pet spaniel, Dash, its afternoon bath (Leslie). She then dined quietly with her relatives who were her guests, and after sending a message of inquiry to the unfortunate Lord Rolle, concluded the day by witnessing from the roof of the palace the public illuminations and fireworks in the Green and Hyde Parks. Next morning a great 'coronation' fair was opened by permission of the government for four days in Hyde Park; and on the second day the queen paid it a long visit. The coronation festivities concluded with a review by her of five thousand men in Hyde Park (9 July), when she again shared the popular applause with Marshal Soult. A month later (16 Aug.) she prorogued parliament in person, and, after listening to the usual harangue on the work of the session from the speaker of the House of Commons, read her speech with customary clearness. A few months later the queen was to realise that her popularity was not invulnerable, and that, despite Melbourne's parental care, her position was fraught with difficulty and danger, with which she was as yet hardly fitted to cope. With both the crises through which the queen and her court passed in the first half of 1839, her youth and inexperience prevented her from dealing satisfactorily. In January 1839 Lady Flora Hastings, daughter of the Marquis of Hastings, was lady-in-waiting to the Duchess of Kent at Buckingham Palace. On account of her appearance, she was most improperly suspected by some of the queen's attendants of immoral conduct. Neither the queen nor her mother put any faith in the imputation, but Lady Tavistock informed Melbourne of the matter, and the queen assented to his proposal that the unfortunate lady should be subjected by the royal physician, Sir James Clark, to a medical examination. Clark afterwards signed a certificate denying all allegations against Lady Flora (17 Feb. 1839). The incident was soon noised abroad. The lady's family appealed directly to the queen to make fitting reparation. Lady Flora's brother, the Marquis of Hastings, obtained an interview with her. Lady Flora's mother wrote her passionate letters and begged for the dismissal of Sir James Clark. The queen made no reply. Melbourne stated that she had seized the earliest opportunity of personally acknowledging to Lady Flora the unhappy error, but that it was not intended to take any other step. Lady Hastings published her correspondence with the queen and Melbourne in the 'Morning Post,' and Clark circulated a defence of his own conduct. A general feeling of disgust was roused, and the reputation of the court suffered, especially with the conservative section of the nobility to which the Hastings family belonged. The situation was rendered worse by the tragic ending of the episode. Lady Flora was suffering from a fatal internal disease—the enlargement of the liver. On 4 July she was announced to be dying at Buckingham Palace. A royal banquet which was to take place that evening was countermanded (Malmesbury's *Memoirs*, p. 77). The lady died next day. The queen was gravely perturbed. Society was depressed and shocked. The blunder which the queen's advisers had committed was bad enough to warrant an unmistakable expression of her personal regret, and her innocent supineness, for which the blame was currently laid on the Baroness Lehzen, was a calamity. The second court crisis of 1839 was due to a precisely opposite cause—to the queen's peremptory exercise of her personal authority without consulting any one. During the session of 1839 the whig ministry finally lost its hold on the House of Commons. The recent emancipation of the slaves in Jamaica had led the planters into rebellion, and the government was driven to the disagreeable necessity of inviting parliament to suspend the constitution. The proposal was carried by a majority of only five (7 May). Melbourne felt the position to be hopeless, and placed the resignation of himself and his colleagues in the queen's hands. The queen was deeply distressed. When Lord John, leader of the House of Commons, visited her to discuss the situation, she burst into tears. But she soon nerved herself fully to exert for the first time the sovereign's power of choosing a successor to the outgoing prime minister. Her grief at parting with Melbourne was quickly checked. She asked him for no advice, but, after consulting Lord Spencer, she sent for the Duke of Wellington, and startled him by her self-possession (8 May). He declined her offer to form a ministry on the ground of his age and of the desirability of the prime minister being in the House of Commons. Accordingly she summoned Sir Robert Peel, the leader of the conservative opposition in the lower house. She feared his coldness and severity of manner, but her personal demeanour at their first interview was dignified, although very frank. She deprecated a dissolution of parliament at so early a date in the life of the existing parliament. Peel vaguely expressed sympathy with her view, but declined to pledge himself not to advise a dissolution. He, however, accepted without demur her commission to form the government, and, on leaving her, set about selecting members of the cabinet. There was already a strong feeling among the conservatives that the queen, who had hitherto shrunk from association with conservatives, was hedged in on all sides of her household by the female relatives of her whig ministers. Peel, in consultation with his friends, decided that the ladies holding the higher posts in the household must be displaced if conservative ministers were to receive adequate support from the crown. He had no intention of interfering with the subordinate offices, but deemed it essential to remove some at least of the ladies from such posts as those of mistress of the robes or of lady-in-waiting. Peel formed a high conception of his responsibility, and was willing to consult the queen's wishes in filling all appointments that might fall vacant. Unfortunately he did not define at the outset the precise posts or the number of them which were affected by his proposals. The subject was broached in a personal interview (9 May).

The queen feared that she was to be deprived of the companionship of her closest friends, and suspected—quite incorrectly—that the Baroness Lehzen was aimed at. She declined point blank to entertain any suggestion of change in the female constitution of her household. After Peel left her she wrote to Melbourne that they wanted to deprive her of her ladies; they would rob her next of her dressers and housemaids; they thought to treat her as a girl; she would show them she was queen of England. Finally she requested her old minister to draft a reply of refusal to Peel's demands. Melbourne expressed no opinion, but did as he was asked. The queen's letter to Peel ran: 'Buckingham Palace, May 10, 1839.—The Queen, having considered the proposal made to her yesterday by Sir Robert Peel to remove the ladies of her bedchamber, cannot consent to adopt a course which she conceives to be contrary to usage, and which is repugnant to her feelings.' Peel answered that he feared there was some misunderstanding, and declined to proceed to the formation of a government. Peel's decision was received by the queen with immense relief, which she made no endeavour to conceal at a state ball that took place the same evening. With every sign of satisfaction she appealed to Melbourne to resume power. Although her action was her own, Melbourne had given it a tacit approval by not resisting it, when she first informed him of her intention. The old cabinet met on 11 May; some members argued for advising the queen to withdraw from the attitude that she had assumed. But Lord Spencer insisted that as gentlemen they must stand by her. Palmerston declared that her youth and isolation should have protected her from the odious conditions that Peel sought to impose. At length the good-natured Melbourne acquiesced in that opinion, and the whigs returned to office. The episode formed the topic of animated debate in both houses of parliament. Peel defended his action, which Lord John Russell lamely endeavoured to prove to be without precedent. Melbourne thoroughly identified himself with the queen, and was severely handled from different points of view by both the Duke of Wellington and Lord Brougham. In point of fact Peel's conduct was amply warranted, and subsequently Melbourne, Lord John Russell, and the queen herself admitted as much. In 1853 she confided to Lord John that she had taken no advice in the matter. 'No,' she said, 'it was entirely my own foolishness!' Melbourne afterwards remarked characteristically: 'You should take care to give people who are cross time to come round. Peel's fault in that business, when he failed to form a government, was not giving the queen time to come round.'

The momentary effect of the queen's act was to extend by more than two years the duration of Melbourne's ministry, and to embitter the personal hostility of the tories towards her. James Bradshaw, the tory M.P. for Canterbury, made in July so violent an attack upon her at a conservative meeting that the whig M.P. for Cockermouth, Edward Horsman, challenged him to a duel, which was duly fought. But the permanent outcome of the crisis was to the good. The queen never repeated her obduracy, and although she often asserted her authority and betrayed her personal predilection when a new ministry was in course of creation, the nineteen changes of government that followed during her reign were effected with comparatively little friction. The 'household' difficulty never recurred. Ladies-in-waiting at once ceased to be drawn from the families of any one political party, and as early as July 1839 the queen invited Lady Sandwich, the wife of a tory peer, to join the household. It became the settled practice for the office of mistress of the robes alone to bear a political complexion, and for its holder to retire from office with the party to which she owed her appointment. Increase of years and the good counsel of a wise husband were to teach the queen to exercise with greater tact that habit of command which was natural to her, and to bring under firmer control the impatience and quickness of her temper. Absorption in the sovereign's work, the elation of spirit which accompanied the major part of her new experiences, the change from dependence to independence in her private affairs, put marriage out of her mind during the first two years of her reign. But King Leopold had no intention of quietly allowing his choice of her cousin Albert for her husband to be thwarted. Early in 1838 he reminded her of the suggestion. She replied that she and the prince, who was of her own age, were too young to think of marriage yet, and she claimed permission to defer a decision till the end of three years. King Leopold summoned Prince Albert to Brussels in March and explained the situation. Albert assented with some hesitation to the queen's proposal of delay. He assumed that in her proud elevation she would ultimately seek in marriage a partner of more exalted rank than a younger son of a poor and undistinguished German duke. But Stockmar was as zealous in Albert's cause as his uncle Leopold. He had left the queen's side at the end of 1838 for the first time since her accession, and accompanied Prince Albert on a tour in Italy with a view to keeping him faithful to the plan and to instructing him betimes, in case of need, in the duties of the consort of a reigning English monarch. Among the English courtiers doubts of the success of the innocent conspiracy were freely entertained. Such members of the large Coburg family as visited the queen at this period were too 'deutsch' in manner to recommend themselves to her English attendants (Lady Lyttelton). 'After being used to agreeable and well-informed Englishmen, I fear she will not easily find a foreign prince to her liking,' Lord Palmerston wrote in April 1838. Several names besides Prince Albert's were, too, freely canvassed as those of suitable candidates for her hand (cf. *Stafford House Letters*, p. 223).

Another first cousin, Prince George of Cambridge (now Duke of Cambridge), was often in her society. The Duc de Nemours (brother of the queen of the Belgians and son of Louis Philippe) and a prince of the Prussian reigning family were believed to possess attractions, both in her sight and in that of some of her advisers. In May 1839 she entertained at Windsor the tsarevitch of Russia (afterwards Tsar Alexander II) and Prince William Henry, younger son of King William II of the Netherlands; and both the young men were reported to aspire to her hand. The social and political embarrassments of the first half of 1839 gave the queen a sense of isolation, which rendered the prospect of marriage more congenial to her than it was before. At the same time she suffered much annoyance from a number of offers of marriage made to her by weak-minded subjects, several of whom forced themselves personally on her notice when she was riding out, or even gained entrance to her palaces. King Leopold, who was her guest at Windsor in September 1839, was not slow to use the opportunity. He arranged that Prince Albert and his elder brother Ernest should stay at the English court next month. Nothing was said to the queen of the objects of the mission. On 10 Oct. the young men arrived at Windsor, bearing a letter from King Leopold commending them to her notice. Many guests were there, besides Lord Melbourne. For four days the princes joined the queen and her crowded retinue in the ordinary routine of afternoon rides, evening banquets, and dances, but during the entertainments she contrived to have much talk with Albert, and suddenly a genuine and overpowering affection between them declared itself. On 15 Oct. she summoned the prince to her room, and, taking full advantage of her royal station, offered him marriage. It was 'a nervous thing' to do, she afterwards told her aunt, the Duchess of Gloucester; but, she added, it would not have been possible for him to propose to the queen of England (*Peel Papers*, ii. 414). Melbourne, who took the wise view that in the choice of a husband it was best for the queen to please herself, thought Prince Albert too young and untrained for the position, but hoped for the best and was warm in his congratulations.

The queen sent the information at once to King Leopold, but the public announcement was delayed for more than a month. During that period the queen and her affianced lover were rarely separated either in public or private. The prince was conspicuously at her side at a review of the rifle brigade which she held in the Home Park on 1 Nov. On the 14th the visit of Albert and his brother came to an end. Next day the queen wrote with delightful naïveté to all members of the royal family announcing her engagement. Sir Robert Peel saw the communication she sent to Queen Adelaide, and, although he regarded the match with little enthusiasm, said she was 'as full of love as Juliet' (*Croker Papers*). On 20 Nov. she left

Windsor for Buckingham Palace, where on 23 Nov. she made the official declaration, which Melbourne had drawn up, to an extraordinary meeting of the privy council. No less than eighty-three members were present. The queen wore on her arm a bracelet enclosing the prince's miniature; although her hand shook, she read her short and simple speech without hesitation, and accepted the congratulations of her councillors with composure. The news was received by the public with mixed feeling. Daniel O'Connell, when he spoke of it at a meeting at Bandon, gave vent to ludicrous hyperboles of joy. But there were ominous murmurs amid the popular applause. Little was definitely known of the prince, excepting that he was German and very young. The tories took for granted that he was of 'liberal' opinions—an assumption which did not please them—and while some agreed that he owed his good fortune to his distaste for affairs of state and his fondness for empty amusement, others credited him with perilously stirring ambitions (*Peel Papers*, ii. 408–9). Although it was notorious that the Saxe-Coburg house was staunchly Lutheran, two of its members, King Leopold and Prince Ferdinand, had lately married catholics, and a foolish rumour circulated that Albert was a papist. At foreign courts, and even in his own domestic circle, it was felt that the prize the prince had won was above his station. The queen, who saw the situation only through the haze of true womanly affection, deplored the sacrifice of family and country which she regarded the prince as making for her sake. She pressed her ministers to secure for him wellnigh every honour that she enjoyed, in order to compensate him for his expatriation. Like Queen Mary, she entreated that her husband should be created a king consort. The ministers pointed out that Prince Albert's rank, as well as his household and emoluments, must correspond with those accorded the last prince consort, Prince George of Denmark, and she was galled by the comparison of her lover with 'the stupid and insignificant husband of Queen Anne,' as she called him. The final decision rested with parliament, and Melbourne made no effort to force its hand. The session opened on 16 Jan. 1840, and the queen, in the speech which she read from the throne, spoke of her approaching marriage. Melbourne found himself in a critical situation. While the queen demanded a fare higher status for her future husband than precedent warranted, a majority in both houses of parliament showed signs of a resolve to grant far less. Stockmar, who had resumed residence with the queen in order to watch the position of affairs and give her private advice, wisely recommended a consultation between whigs and tories so as to avoid public disputes, but he gained no hearing. The ministers proposed to grant Prince Albert an annuity of 50,000*l*., the sum granted to the queen consorts of George II, George III, and William IV. Joseph Hume moved an amendment to reduce the sum to 21,000*l*. on his favourite ground of economy. This was negatived by 305 to 38; but Colonel Sibthorp, a tory of a very pronounced kind, who echoed the general sentiment of dissatisfaction, moved another amendment to reduce the sum to 30,000l. He received exceptionally powerful support. Sir Robert Peel spoke in his favour. Sir James Graham denied that the parallel with the position of the queen consorts could be sustained; the independent status of the queen consort, he said, not very logically, was recognised by the constitution, but the prince consort stood in no need of a separate establishment. On a division the reduction was carried by the large majority of 104, the votes being 262 to 158. Sir Robert Peel and his friends made emphatic protests against insinuations of disloyalty, and denied that the tories were 'acting from a spiteful recollection of the events of last May.' Lord John Russell insisted that the vote was an insult to the sovereign. Colonel Sibthorp further proposed in committee that, should the prince survive the queen, he should forfeit the annuity if he remarried a catholic, or failed to reside in the United Kingdom for at least six months a year. This motion was disavowed by Peel, who agreed that it implied a want of confidence in the prince, and it was rejected. But the whole proceedings deeply incensed the queen, and King Leopold wrote that the action of the commons was intolerable.

The House of Lords was in no more amiable mood. The Duke of Wellington carried an amendment to the address censuring ministers for having failed to make a public declaration that the prince was a protestant and able to take the holy communion in the form prescribed by the church of England—a point on which Stockmar had already given the ministers satisfactory assurances in private. When, on 27 Jan., the bill for the naturalisation of the prince was introduced into the upper chamber, it contained a clause giving him precedence next after the queen. The royal dukes of Sussex and Cambridge had agreed to accept a position below the queen's husband; but the king of Hanover, who was still Duke of Cumberland, bluntly declined to give way to any 'paper royal highness;' and his protest found much sympathy in the lords. Melbourne argued that he was following the precedent set in the case of Philip and Mary, but was willing to modify the clause so as to give the heir-apparent, when he should arrive, precedence of his father. The concession was deemed inadequate, and the clause was withdrawn. Thereupon the naturalisation bill passed without further opposition. Subsequently Greville, the clerk of the council, issued a paper proving that the queen could grant her husband by royal warrant what precedence she chose without any appeal to parliament, and she acted accordingly, giving him the next place to her. But, to the queen's chagrin, foreign courts declined to recognise in him any rank above that of his hereditary honours. Another difficulty arose with regard to the choice of his personal attendants. It was deemed inadvisable to allow him to appoint a private secretary for himself. A German was not reckoned fit for the post. Melbourne nominated his own private secretary, George Anson. Meanwhile the marriage was fixed for 10 Feb. Before the parliamentary wrangle ended, Lord Torrington and Colonel Grey had been sent to Coburg to invest the prince with the insignia of the Garter, and to conduct him to England. On 28 Jan. the prince with his father and brother left Coburg. At Brussels he met his uncle Leopold. On 7 Feb. he was at Dover. Next day he was received with much enthusiasm in London, and on reaching Buckingham Palace the oaths of naturalisation were administered to him by the lord chancellor. On the 10th the wedding took place in the chapel of St. James's Palace, and after an elaborate breakfast at Buckingham Palace the bride and bridegroom drove to Windsor amid vociferous acclamations. Two days later they were visited by the Duchess of Kent, the Duke of Coburg, and others, and on 14 Feb. returned to London. On 19 Feb. the queen held a levee, and the prince stood at her left hand. With her marriage a new era in the queen's life and reign began. From a personal point of view the union realised the highest ideal of which matrimony is capable. The queen's love for her husband was without alloy, and invested him in her sight with every perfection. He, on his part, reciprocated her affection, and he made her happiness the main object of his life. Intellectually and morally he was worthy of his position. He was admirably educated; his interests were wide; he was devoted to art, science, and literature; his life was scrupulously well ordered; he was sagacious, philanthropic, conscientious, and unselfish. His example and influence gave new weight and stability to the queen's character and temperament, and her knowledge and experience grew. But outside the domestic circle the prince was not liked. He was cold and distant in manner, and his bearing, both mental and physical, was held to be characteristically German. It was out of harmony with the habitual ease and levity of the English aristocracy. He had no active sense of humour, no enthusiasm for field sports, no vices; he abhorred late hours, and did not conceal his disdain for many of the recreations in which the English leisured classes indulged. His public position was at the same time ill-defined. There was a jealous fear that his private influence with the queen and his foreign prejudices might affect her public action. Resentment at any possible interference by him in affairs of state quickly spread abroad. Although Melbourne gave the queen permission to show him official papers, he was during the first two years of his settlement in England excluded from her interviews with ministers. He felt his position to be one of humiliation. He was 'the husband, not the master of the house,' he wrote in May 1840 to his friend, Prince William of Löwenstein.

It was never with the queen's concurrence that he filled a rank in her household subordinate to herself. On 28 Dec. 1841 she wrote in her journal: 'He ought to be, and is above me in everything really, and therefore I wish that he should be equal in rank with me.' As his abilities came to be recognised by ministers, they gradually yielded to her persuasion to take him fully into their counsels. He was allowed to act as her private secretary. The cares of maternity were soon to distract her on occasion from the details of public duty, and her dependence on her husband in all relations naturally increased. Ultimately Prince Albert assumed in behalf of his wife in reality, although not in form, most of her responsibilities, and his share in the rule of the country through most of the twenty-one years of their married life is indistinguishable from hers. 'Lord Melbourne was very useful to me,' she said many years afterwards, 'but I can never be sufficiently thankful that I passed safely through those two years to my marriage. Then I was in a safe haven, and there I remained for twenty[-one] years,' (Prothero, *Life of Dean Stanley*, ii. 127). As soon as the prince finally settled down to his new life he regarded it as his duty (as he wrote in 1850 to the Duke of Wellington) to 'fill up every gap which, as a woman, she would naturally leave in the exercise of her regal functions, continually and anxiously to watch every part of the public business, in order to be able to advise and assist her at any moment, in any of the multifarious and difficult questions or duties brought before her, sometimes international, sometimes political, or social, or personal.' He claimed to be of right 'the natural head of her family, superintendent of her household, manager of her private affairs, sole *confidential* adviser in politics, and only assistant in the communications with the officers of the government.' At the same time he was, he pointed out, 'the husband of the queen, the tutor of the royal children, the private secretary of the sovereign, and her permanent minister.' The defect and danger of such a claim lay, according to the constitution of the country, in the fact that the prince was under no parliamentary control, and his description of himself as the queen's 'permanent minister' was inexact. Substantially, however, the statement truthfully represented the prince's functions and occupation during his career as Queen Victoria's consort. But a large section of the public never willingly acquiesced in his exercise of so much activity and authority. Until his death he had to run the gauntlet of a galling and unceasing public criticism, and the queen, despite her wealth of domestic happiness, was rarely free from the sense of discomfort and anxiety which was bred of a consciousness that many of her subjects viewed her husband with dislike or suspicion. But from 1841 to 1861, the date of his death, the fact is unassailable that Prince Albert had as good a right as the queen to be regarded as the ruler of the British realm. On the queen's marriage the

Duchess of Kent at once removed from the royal palace, and the Baroness Lehzen soon afterwards retired from the queen's service. These changes in the royal household disposed of checks which might have seriously limited the development of Prince Albert's influence. The supersession of both mother and *gouvernante* was effected without friction. The curmudgeonly king of Hanover declined the queen's request to give up to the Duchess of Kent his apartments in St. James's Palace which he never occupied, and thereupon the queen rented for her mother Ingestre House, Belgrave Square, at 2,000*l.* a year; but on the death of the Princess Augusta in September, Clarence House, St. James's Palace, was made over to her, together with Frogmore Lodge at Windsor. Hardly a day passed without the exchange of visits. As a rule, the duchess both lunched and dined with her daughter. The Baroness Lehzen left England in October 1842 for her native country of Hanover, finally settling with a sister at Bückeburg (cf. Bloomfield, *Reminiscences*, i. 215). For many years the queen found time to write her a letter once a week, an interval which was subsequently lengthened to a month at the baroness's own considerate request; the correspondence was maintained until the baroness's death in 1870. Stockmar alone of the queen's early confidential attendants retained his position after her marriage; until 1857 he spent the autumn, winter, and spring of each year with the queen and Prince Albert, and occupied rooms in their palaces. On every domestic or public question that arose both the queen and prince looked to him for private guidance. Amid the festivities which celebrated the early days of married life general alarm was caused by an attack on the queen's life. The outrage had no political significance, and served to increase her popularity. On 10 June a brainless potboy, Edward Oxford, fired two shots at her from a pistol as she was driving through the Green Park from Buckingham Palace to Hyde Park Corner. She was unhurt, and to all appearance unmoved, and after making a call at her mother's house to assure her of her safety, she continued her customary drive in Hyde Park. The lad was arrested and was mercifully pronounced to be insane. Addresses of congratulation were presented by both houses of parliament. On 12 June 1840—two days after the incident— a concert was given at Buckingham Palace under Costa's direction, and the queen herself took part in no less than five numbers, singing in a duet with Prince Albert, and in a trio with Signors Rubini and Lablache, and in three choruses. A week or two later a magnificent reception was accorded her at Ascot. Next month the approaching birth of an heir to the throne was announced, and, in accordance with the queen's wish, a bill was passed constituting Prince Albert regent in case of her death, provided that he did not remarry a catholic and that he resided in the country. Prince Albert, by the advice of Stockmar, and with the full concurrence of

Melbourne, had already given proofs of an anxiety to relieve the strained relations between the court and the tories. Their leaders had been entertained by the queen, and she had shown them marked civility. With the Duke of Wellington every effort was made to maintain cordial relations, and he reciprocated the advances with alacrity. The Duke of Sussex, whose critical attitude to the queen still caused her discomfort, was partially conciliated by the bestowal of the title of Duchess of Inverness on his morganatic wife, and in April, when the queen and Prince Albert attended a great ball at Lansdowne House, she permitted the new duchess to sup at the royal table. The pacific atmosphere which was thus engendered had the agreeable effect of stifling opposition to the nomination of Prince Albert to the regency. In the House of Lords the Duke of Sussex alone resisted it on the ground that the rights of 'the family' were ignored. On 11 Aug., when the queen prorogued parliament in person, the prince sat in an arm-chair next the throne, and, although objection was feared, none was raised. His predominance was treated as inevitable. On 28 Aug. he received the freedom of the city. On 11 Sept. he was admitted to the privy council. On 5 Feb. 1841 the queen ordered his name to be inserted in the liturgy. Meanwhile, on 21 Nov., the queen's first child, a daughter, was born at Buckingham Palace. Her recovery from the confinement was rapid, and she removed to Windsor for the Christmas holidays. On 10 Feb., the anniversary of her marriage, the child, the princess royal of England, was baptised at Buckingham Palace in the names of Victoria Adelaide Mary Louisa. The sponsors were the prince's father, the queen's mother, and her uncle Leopold, besides the Dowager Queen Adelaide, the Duchess of Gloucester, and the Duke of Sussex. The Duke of Saxe-Coburg was unable to attend in person, and the queen by her own motion chose the Duke of Wellington to represent him. The last trace of animosity in regard to Wellington on account of his open objections to the queen's marriage was now removed. 'He is,' the queen wrote in her journal, 'the best friend we have.' Meanwhile politics were casting clouds on the joys of domestic life. The queen was to suffer, for the first of many times, that conflict of feeling between her private obligations to her foreign kindred and her public obligations to her country, which, despite an instinctive repugnance to unworthy concessions in the sphere of foreign diplomacy, was liable to involve her in difficulties with her advisers. Under Prince Albert's guidance and in accordance with her own predisposition, the queen regarded foreign affairs as peculiarly within the sovereign's province, and the prince, who with Melbourne's assent now enjoyed access to foreign despatches, claimed in behalf of the queen the full right to a voice in consultation before any action was taken by the government abroad. Palmerston, the masterful minister of foreign affairs, was reluctant to recognise the existence outside parliament of any check on his independence. This attitude at once caused vexation in the royal circle, and after prolonged heartburnings ultimately led to an open rupture. The immediate cause of divergence between the queen and her foreign minister was due to affairs in the east of Europe, which threatened a breach in the friendly relations of France and England. Egypt under her viceroy, Mehemet Ali, was seeking to cast off her allegiance to the sultan of Turkey. France encouraged the act of rebellion, while England and the rest of the great powers took Turkey under their protection. The queen and Prince Albert loathed the prospect of war with France, with whose sovereign, Louis Philippe, they had, through repeated intermarriages, close domestic relations; and the added likelihood that the dominions of her uncle and political ally, King Leopold, would, in case of war between England and France, be invaded by a French army filled the queen with alarm. Divisions in the cabinet encouraged resolute intervention on her part. In opposition to Lord John Russell's views, Palmerston, minister of foreign affairs, decided that the best way of dissipating all risk of French predominance in Egypt was to crush Mehemet Ali at once by force of English arms. The queen entreated Melbourne to reconcile his divided colleagues, to use his influence against Palmerston, and to seek a pacific settlement with France. But Palmerston stood firm. By his orders the British fleet forced Mehemet Ali to return to his allegiance to the sultan (November 1840). The minister's victory was more complete than he anticipated. Louis Philippe, to the general surprise, proved too pusillanimous to take the offensive in behalf of his friend in Egypt, and he finally joined the concert of the powers, who in July 1841 pledged themselves by treaty to maintain Turkey and Egypt in statu quo. The incident evoked in the French king, in his ministers, and in King Leopold a feeling of bitterness against Palmerston which found a ready echo in the minds of Queen Victoria and the prince. Before this foreign crisis terminated, the retirement of Melbourne's ministry, which the queen had long dreaded, took place. The prospect of parting with Melbourne, her tried councillor, caused her pain. But, in anticipation of the event, hints had been given at Prince Albert's instance by the court officials to the tory leaders that the queen would interpose no obstacle to a change of government when it became inevitable, and would not resist such reconstruction of her household as might be needful. The blow fell in May. The whig ministers introduced a budget which tended towards free trade, and on their proposal to reduce the duty on sugar they were defeated by a majority of 36. Sir Robert Peel thereupon carried a vote of confidence against them by one vote. Moved by the queen's feelings, Melbourne, instead of resigning, appealed to the country. Parliament was dissolved on 29 June.

In June, amid the political excitement, the queen paid a visit to Archbishop Harcourt at Nuneham, and thence she and Prince Albert proceeded to Oxford to attend commemoration. The Duke of Wellington, the chancellor of the university, presided, and conferred on the prince an honorary degree. The queen was disturbed by the hisses which were levelled at the whig ministers who were present, but she was not the less willing on that account to give further proof of her attachment to them, and she seized the opportunity to pay a series of visits among the whig nobility. After spending a day or two with the Duke of Devonshire at Chatsworth, the royal party next month were entertained by the Duke of Bedford at Woburn Abbey and by Lord Cowper, Melbourne's nephew, at Panshanger. From Panshanger they went to lunch with Melbourne himself at his country residence, Brocket Park. The general election was proceeding at the time, and the whigs made the most out of the queen's known sympathy with them and of her alleged antipathy to their opponents. But, to the queen's dismay, a large tory majority was returned. The new parliament assembled on 19 Aug. 1841. For the first time in her reign the queen was absent and her speech was read by the lord chancellor, an indication that the constitution of the House of Commons was not to her liking. Melbourne's ministry remained in office till the last possible moment, but on 28 Aug. a vote of confidence was refused it by both houses of parliament; the same evening Melbourne saw the queen at Windsor and resigned his trust. She accepted his resignation in a spirit of deep dejection, which he helped to dissipate by an assurance of the high opinion he had formed of her husband. In conformity with his advice she at once summoned Sir Robert Peel, and although she spoke freely to him of her grief in separating from her late ministers, she quickly recovered her composure and discussed the business in hand with a correctness of manner which aroused in Peel enthusiastic admiration. He promised to consult her comfort in all household appointments. The Duchess of Buccleuch replaced the Duchess of Sutherland as mistress of the robes, and the Duchess of Bedford and Lady Normanby voluntarily made way for other ladies-in-waiting. By September the new government was fully constituted, and the queen had the tact to treat her new ministers with much amiability. Peel adapted himself to the situation with complete success. He and the queen were soon the best of friends. Accepting Melbourne's hint, he fully yet briefly explained to her every detail of affairs. He strictly obeyed her request to send regularly and promptly a daily report of proceedings of interest that took place in both the houses of parliament. Melbourne was thenceforth an occasional and always an honoured guest at court, but the queen accustomed herself without delay to seek political guidance exclusively from Peel. The queen's absence at the prorogation of parliament on 7 Oct., after a short autumn session, was due to personal affairs and to no want of confidence in her new advisers. On 9 Nov. 1841 her second child, a son and heir, was born at Buckingham Palace. The confinement was imminent for several weeks, and, though she hesitated to appear in public, she, with characteristic spirit, continued 'to write notes, sign her name, and declare her pleasure up to the last moment, as if nothing serious were at hand' (Sir James Graham, ap. *Croker Papers*, ii. 408). Sir Robert Peel had accepted an invitation to dine with her on the night of the child's birth. Much public and private rejoicing followed the arrival of an heir to the throne. Christmas festivities were kept with great brilliance at Windsor, and on 10 Jan. the christening took place in St. George's Chapel with exceptional pomp. Vague political reasons induced the government to invite Frederick William, king of Prussia, to be the chief sponsor; the others were the Duke of Cambridge, Princess Sophia, and three members of the Saxe-Coburg family. To the king of Prussia, who stayed with her from 22 Jan. to 4 Feb., the queen paid every honour (Bunsen, ii. 7). Subsequently he took advantage of the good personal relations he had formed with the queen to correspond with her confidentially on political affairs. Adverse criticism was excited by the bestowal on the prince of Wales of the title of Duke of Saxony, and by the quartering of the arms of Saxony on his shield with those of England. Such procedure was regretted as a concession by the queen to her husband's German predilections. On 3 Feb. 1842, when the queen opened parliament and the king of Prussia accompanied her, there was no great display of popular loyalty (Fanny Kemble's *Records*, ii. 181), but she impressed her auditors by referring in the speech from the throne to the birth of her son as 'an event which has completed the measure of my domestic happiness.' When a week later she went with her young family to stay a month at the Pavilion at Brighton, her presence excited more public demonstration of goodwill than was convenient (Lady Bloomfield's *Reminiscences*), and the queen and Prince Albert, conceiving a dislike for the place, soon sought a more sequestered seaside retreat.

The season of 1842 combined agreeable with distasteful incidents. The first of a brilliant series of fancy dress balls took place to the queen's great contentment at Buckingham Palace on 12 May; the prince appeared as Edward III and the queen as Queen Philippa. Some feeling was shown in France at what was foolishly viewed as the celebration of ancient victories won by the English over French arms. The entertainment was charitably designed to give work to the Spitalfields weavers, who were then in distress. A fortnight later the queen and court went in state to a ball at Covent Garden theatre, which was organised in the interest of the same sufferers. In June the queen had her first experience of railway travelling, an event of no little interest to herself and of no little encouragement to the pioneers of a mechanical invention which was to revolutionise the social economy of the country. She went by rail from Windsor to Paddington. Court etiquette required that the master of the horse and the coachmen under his control should actively direct the queen's travels by land, and it was difficult to adapt the old forms to the new conditions of locomotion. The queen, who thoroughly enjoyed the experiment, thenceforth utilised to the fullest extent the growing railway systems of the kingdom. Unhappily two further senseless attempts on her life, which took place at the same time, marred her sense of security, and rendered new preventive legislation essential. In her attitude to the first attempt the queen and Prince Albert showed a courage which bordered on imprudence. On Sunday, 29 May, Prince Albert noticed that a man pointed a pistol at the queen as she drove past him in her carriage through the Green Park. She and the prince resolved to pass the same spot on the following afternoon in order to secure the arrest of the assailant. The bold device succeeded. 'She would much rather,' she said, 'run the immediate risk at any time than have the presentiment of danger constantly hovering over her.' The man, whose name was found to be John Francis, fired at her, happily without result, and, being captured, was condemned to death, a sentence which was commuted to transportation for life. On the evening following the outrage the queen visited the opera to hear the 'Prophète,' and was cheered rapturously. But the danger was not past. On 3 July, when the queen was driving in the Mall with the king of the Belgians, who happened to be her guest, a crippled lad, John William Bean, sought in an aimless, halfhearted way to emulate the misdeeds of Francis and Oxford. Such contemptible outrages could, according to the existing law, be treated solely as acts of high treason. Now Peel hastily passed through parliament a 'bill for providing for the further protection and security of her majesty's person,' the terms of which made the offence to attempt to hurt the queen a misdemeanour punishable by either transportation for seven years or imprisonment for three with personal chastisement. In the autumn Peel organised for the queen a holiday in Scotland. Chartist riots were distracting the country, but Peel and Sir James Graham, the home secretary, believed that the expedition might be safely and wisely made. It was the first visit that the queen paid to North Britain, and it inspired her with a lifelong regard for it and its inhabitants. The first portion of the journey, from Windsor to Paddington, was again made by rail. At Woolwich the royal party embarked on the Royal George yacht on 29 Aug., and on 1 Sept. they arrived at Granton pier. There Sir Robert Peel, at the queen's request, met them. Passing through Edinburgh they stayed with the Duke of Buccleuch at Dalkeith, where on 5 Sept. the queen held a drawing-room and received addresses. Next day they left for the highlands, and, after paying a visit to Lord Mansfield at Scone, were accorded a princely reception by Lord Breadalbane at Taymouth. A brief stay with Lord Willoughby at Drummond Castle was followed by their return to Dalkeith, and they left Scotland by sea on the 15th. Not only was the queen enchanted with the scenery through which she passed, but the historic associations, especially those connected with Mary Stuart and her son, deeply interested her, and she read on the voyage with a new zest Sir Walter Scott's poems, 'The Lady of the Lake' and 'The Lay of the Last Minstrel' (*Leaves from the Queen's Journal*, 1877, pp. 1–28). Before embarking she instructed Lord Aberdeen to write to the lord advocate an expression of her regret that her visit was so brief, and of her admiration of the devotion and enthusiasm which her Scottish subjects had 'evinced in every quarter and by all ranks' (Greville, *Memoirs*). On 17 Sept. she was again at Windsor. In November the Duke of Wellington placed Walmer Castle at her disposal, and she and her family were there from 10 Nov. to 3 Dec. With Peel the queen's relations steadily improved. On 6 April 1842 Peel described his own position thus: 'My relations with her majesty are most satisfactory. The queen has acted towards me not merely (as every one who knew her majesty's character must have anticipated) with perfect fidelity and honour, but with great kindness and consideration. There is every facility for the despatch of public business, a scrupulous and most punctual discharge of every public duty, and an exact understanding of the relation of a constitutional sovereign to her advisers' (*Peel Papers*, ii. 544). In January 1843 the queen was deeply concerned at the assassination of Peel's secretary, Edward Drummond, in mistake for himself, and she shrewdly denounced in private the verdict of insanity which the jury brought in against the assassin at his trial (Martin, i. 27; *Peel Papers*, ii. 553). Among Peel's colleagues, Lord Aberdeen, minister of foreign affairs, came after Peel himself into closest personal relations with the queen and the prince, and with him she found herself in hardly less complete accord. At the same time she never concealed her wish to bring the foreign office under the active influence of the crown. She bade Aberdeen observe 'the rule that all drafts not mere matters of course should be sent to her before the despatches had left the office.' Aberdeen guardedly replied that 'this should be done in all cases in which the exigencies of the situation did not require another course.' She prudently accepted the reservation, but Lord Aberdeen's general policy developed no principle from which the queen or the prince dissented, and the harmony of their relations was undisturbed (Walpole, *Life of Lord John Russell*, ii. 54). Peel greatly strengthened his position by a full acknowledgment of Prince Albert's position. He permitted the prince to attend the audiences of ministers with the queen. He nominated him president of a royal commission to promote the fine arts of the United Kingdom in connection with the rebuilding of the houses of parliament, and he encouraged the prince to reform the confused administration of the royal palaces. The prince's authority consequently increased. From 1843 onwards the queen, in announcing her decision on public questions to her ministers, substituted for the singular personal pronoun 'I' the plural 'we,' and thus entirely identified her husband's judgment with her own. The growth of his authority was indicated in the spring of 1843 by his holding levees in the queen's behalf in her absence— an apparent assumption of power which was ill received. Domestic incidents occupied much of the queen's attention, and compelled the occasional delegation of some of her duties. The death of the Duke of Sussex on 21 April 1843 preceded by four days the birth of a third child, the Princess Alice. In order to conciliate her unfriendly uncle, the king of Hanover, the queen asked him to be a sponsor, together with the queen's half-sister, Countess Féodore, Prince Albert's brother, and Princess Sophia. With characteristic awkwardness the king of Hanover arrived too late for the christening (5 June). A large family gathering followed in July, when the queen's first cousin Augusta, elder daughter of the Duke of Cambridge, married at Buckingham Palace (28 July) Friedrich, hereditary grand duke of Mecklenburg-Strelitz. In August two of Louis Philippe's sons, the Prince de Joinville and the Duc d'Aumale, were the queen's guests. A month later, after proroguing parliament in person (24 Aug.), and making a short yachting tour on the south coast, the queen carried out an intention that had long been present in her mind of paying a visit to the king of the French, with whose family her own was by marriage so closely connected. This was an event of much historic interest. In the first place it was the first occasion on which the queen had trodden foreign soil. In the second place it was the first occasion on which an English sovereign had visited a French sovereign since Henry VIII appeared on the Field of the Cloth of Gold at the invitation of Francis I in 1520. In the third place it was the first time for nearly a century that an English monarch had left his dominions, and the old procedure of nominating a regent or lords-justices in his absence was now first dropped. Although the expedition was the outcome of domestic sentiment rather than of political design, Peel and Aberdeen encouraged it in the belief that the maintenance of good personal relations between the English sovereign and her continental colleagues was a guarantee of peace and goodwill among the nations—a view which Lord Brougham also held strongly. Louis Philippe and his queen were staying at the Château d'Eu, a private domain near Tréport. The queen, accompanied by Lord Aberdeen, arrived there on 2 Sept. in her new yacht Victoria and Albert, which had been launched on 25 April, and of which Lord Adolphus FitzClarence, a natural son of William IV, had been appointed captain. Her host met the queen in his barge off the coast, and a magnificent reception was accorded her. The happy domestic life of the French royal family strongly impressed her. She greeted with enthusiasm, among the French king's guests, the French musician Auber, with whose works she was very well acquainted, and she was charmed by two *fêtes champêtres* and a military review. Lord Aberdeen and M. Guizot, Louis Philippe's minister, discussed political questions with the utmost cordiality, and although their conversations led later to misunderstanding, everything passed off at the moment most agreeably. The visit lasted five days, from 2 to 7 Sept., and the queen's spirit fell when it was over. On leaving Tréport the queen spent another four days with her children at Brighton, and paid her last visit to George IV's inconvenient Pavilion. But her foreign tour was not yet ended. From Brighton she sailed in her yacht to Ostend, to pay a long promised visit to her uncle, the king of the Belgians, at the palace of Laeken, near Brussels. 'It was such a joy for me,' she wrote after parting with him, 'to be once again under the roof of one who has ever been a father to me.' Charlotte Brontë, who was in Brussels, saw her 'laughing and talking very gaily' when driving through the Rue Royale, and noticed how plainly and unpretentiously she was dressed (Gaskell, *Life of Charlotte Brontë*, 1900, p. 270). Her vivacity brought unwonted sunshine to King Leopold's habitually sombre court. She reached Woolwich, on her return from Antwerp, on 21 Sept. The concluding months of the year (1843) were agreeably spent in visits at home. In October she went by road to pay a first visit to Cambridge. She stayed, according to prescriptive right, at the lodge of Trinity College, where she held a levee. Prince Albert received a doctor's degree, and the undergraduates offered her a thoroughly enthusiastic reception. Next month she gave public proof of her regard for Peel by visiting him at Drayton Manor (28 Nov. to 1 Dec.). Thence she passed to Chatsworth, where, to her gratification, Melbourne and the Duke of Wellington were fellow-guests. The presence of Lord and Lady Palmerston was less congenial. At a great ball one evening her partners included Lord Morpeth and Lord Leveson (better known later as Earl Granville), who was afterwards to be one of her most trusted ministers. Another night there were a vast series of illuminations in the grounds, of which all traces were cleared away before the morning by two hundred men, working under the direction of the duke's gardener, (Sir) Joseph Paxton. The royal progress was continued to Belvoir Castle, the home of the Duke of Rutland, where she again met Peel and Wellington, and it was not till 7 Dec. that she returned to Windsor. On 29 Jan. 1844 Prince Albert's father died, and in the spring he paid a visit to his native land (28 March–11 April). It was the first time the queen had been separated from her husband, and in his absence the king and queen of the Belgians came over to console her. On 1 June two other continental sovereigns arrived to pay her their respects, the king of Saxony and the Tsar Nicholas I of Russia. To the tsar, who came uninvited at short notice, it was needful to pay elaborate attentions. His half-brother (Alexander I) had been the queen's godfather, and political interests made the strengthening of the personal tie desirable. He attended a great review at Windsor Park with the queen, and went with her to Ascot and to the opera. At a grand concert given in his honour at Buckingham Palace, Joseph Joachim, then on a visit to England as a boy, was engaged to perform. A rough soldier in appearance and manner, the tsar treated his hostess with a courtesy which seemed to her pathetic, and, although preoccupied by public affairs, civilly ignored all likelihood of a divergence of political interests between England and his own country. At the time domestic politics were agitating the queen. The spread of disaffection in Ireland during the repeal agitation distressed her, and her name was made more prominent in the controversy than was prudent. The Irish lord chancellor, Sir Edward Sugden, publicly asserted that the queen was personally determined to prevent repeal (May 1843). The repeal leader O'Connell, a warm admirer of the queen, promptly denied the statement. Peel mildly reprimanded Sugden, but truth forced him to admit that the queen 'would do all in her power to maintain the union as the bond of connection between the two countries' (*Peel Papers*, iii. 52). The obstructive policy of the opposition in parliament at the same time caused her concern. She wrote to Peel on 15 Aug. of 'her indignation at the very unjustifiable manner in which the minority were obstructing the order of business;' she hoped that every attempt would be made 'to put an end to what is really indecent conduct,' and that Sir Robert Peel would 'make no kind of concession to these gentlemen which could encourage them to go on in the same way' (*ib*. iii. 568). Worse followed in the month of the tsar's visit. On 14 June the government were defeated on a proposal to reduce the sugar duties. To the queen's consternation, Peel expressed an intention of resigning at once. Happily, four days later a vote of confidence was carried and the crisis passed. The queen wrote at once to express her relief (18 June). 'Last night,' she said, 'every one thought that the government would be beat, and therefore the surprise was the more unexpected and gratifying' (*ib*. iii. 153). Foreign affairs, too, despite the hospitalities of the English court to royal visitors, were threatening. The jealousy between the English and French peoples might be restrained, but could not be stifled, by the friendliness subsisting between the courts, and in the autumn of 1844 the maltreatment by French officials of an English consul, George Pritchard, in the island of Tahiti, which the French had lately occupied, caused in England an explosion of popular wrath with France, which the queen and her government at one time feared must end in war. Amid these excitements a second son, Prince Alfred, was born to the queen at Windsor on 6 Aug., and at the end of the month she entertained another royal personage from Germany, the prince of Prussia, brother of the king, and eventually first emperor of Germany. There sprang up between her and her new guest a warm friendship which lasted for more than forty years. A peaceful autumn holiday was again spent in Scotland, whither they proceeded by sea from Woolwich to Dundee. Thence they drove to Blair Athol to visit Lord and Lady Glenlyon, afterwards Duke and Duchess of Athol. Prince Albert engaged in deer-stalking, and the queen did much sketching. They thoroughly enjoyed 'the life of quiet and liberty,' and with regret disembarked at Woolwich on 3 Oct. to face anew official anxieties (*Journal*, pp. 29–42). Five days later Louis Philippe returned the queen's visit, and thus for the first time a French monarch voluntarily landed on English shores. The Tahiti quarrel had been composed, and the interchange of hospitable amenities was unclouded. On 9 Oct. the king was invested with the order of the Garter. On the 14th the visit ended, and the queen and Prince Albert accompanied their visitor to Portsmouth, though the stormy weather ultimately compelled him to proceed to Dover to take the short sea trip to Calais. Another elaborate ceremony at home attested the queen's popularity, which she liked to trace to public sympathy with her happy domestic life. She went in state to the city, 28 Oct., to open the new Royal Exchange. An elaborate coloured panoramic plate of the procession which was published at the time is now rare. Of her reception Peel wrote to Sir Henry Hardinge (6 Nov. 1844): 'As usual she had a fine day, and uninterrupted success. It was a glorious spectacle. But she saw a sight which few sovereigns have ever seen, and perhaps none may see again, a million human faces with a smile on each. She did not hear one discordant sound' (*Peel Papers*, iii. 264). On 12 Nov. the radical town of Northampton gave her a hardly less enthusiastic greeting when she passed through it on her way to visit the Marquis of Exeter at Burghley House. Other noble hosts of the period included the Duke of Buckingham at Stowe (14–16 Jan. 1845), and the Duke of Wellington at Strathfieldsaye (20–22 Jan.).

When the queen read her speech at the opening of parliament, 4 Feb. 1845, she referred with great satisfaction to the visits of the Tsar Nicholas and the king of the French, and Peel took an early opportunity of pointing out that the munificent receptions accorded those sovereigns and other royal visitors were paid for by the queen out of her personal income without incurring any debt. The session was largely occupied with the affairs of Ireland and the proposal of the government to endow the catholic priests' training college at Maynooth. The queen encouraged Peel to press on with the measure, which she regarded as a tolerant concession to the dominant religion in Ireland. But it roused much protestant bigotry, which excited the queen's disdain. On 15 April 1845 she wrote to Peel: 'It is not honourable to protestantism to see the bad and violent and bigoted passions displayed at this moment.'

Another *bal costumé* at Buckingham Palace on 6 June, when the period chosen for illustration was the reign of George II, was the chief court entertainment of the year; and in the same month (21 June) there was a review of the fleet, which was assembled at Spithead in greater strength than was known before. Next month the queen received the king of the Netherlands at Osborne. Again in the autumn the queen left England for a month's foreign travel, and Lord Aberdeen again bore the royal party company. The chief object of the journey was to visit Coburg and the scenes of Prince Albert's youth, but a subsidiary object was to pay on their outward road a return visit to the king of Prussia. Landing at Antwerp (6 Aug.), they were met at Malines by the king and queen of the Belgians, and at Aix-la-Chapelle by the king of Prussia; thence they journeyed through Cologne to the king of Prussia's palace at Brühl. They visited Bonn to attend the unveiling of the statue of Beethoven, and a great Beethoven festival concert, while at a concert at Brühl, which Meyerbeer conducted, the artists included Jenny Lind, Liszt, and Vieuxtemps. The regal entertainment was continued at the king's castle of Stolzenfels, near Coblenz on the Rhine, which they left on 16 Aug. The visit was not wholly without painful incident. The question of the prince's rank amid the great company caused the queen annoyance. Archduke Frederick of Austria, who was also a guest, claimed and, to the queen's chagrin, was awarded precedence of the prince. The refusal of court officials to give her husband at Stolzenfels in 1845 the place of honour next herself led her to refuse for many years offers of hospitality from the Prussian court.

On 19 Aug. the queen finally reached the palace of Rosenau, Prince Albert's birthplace, and thence they passed through Coburg, finally making their way to Gotha. There the queen was gratified by a visit from her old governess Lehzen, and many pleasant excursions were made in the Thuringian forest. On 3 Sept. they left for Frankfort, stopping a night at Weimar on the way. They reached Antwerp on the 6th, but on their way to Osborne they paid a flying visit to Tréport. The state of the tide did not allow them to land from the yacht, and Louis Philippe's homely wit suggested a debarkation in bathing machines. Next day (9 Sept.) they settled once again at Osborne. Writing thence (14 Sept. 1845) to her aunt, the Duchess of Gloucester, she said: 'I am enchanted with Germany, and in particular with dear Coburg and Gotha, which I left with the very greatest regret. The realisation of this delightful visit, which I had wished for so many years, will be constant and lasting satisfaction to me.' To her uncle Leopold she wrote to the same effect. Before the close of 1845 the queen was involved in the always dreaded anxiety of a ministerial crisis. The potato crop had completely failed in Ireland, and the harvest in England and Scotland was very bad. Great distress was certain throughout the United Kingdom during the winter. Thereupon Peel made up his mind that the situation demanded the repeal of the corn laws—a step which he and his party were pledged to oppose. His colleagues were startled by his change of view, many threatened resistance, but all except Lord Stanley ultimately agreed to stand by him. The rank and file of the party showed fewer signs of complacence. The queen was gravely disturbed, but straightway threw the whole weight of her influence into the prime minister's scale. On 28 Nov. 1845, after expressing her sorrow at the differences of opinion in the cabinet, she wrote without hesitation: 'The queen thinks the time is come when a removal of the restrictions on the importation of food cannot be successfully resisted. Should this be Sir Robert's own opinion, the queen very much hopes that none of his colleagues will prevent him from doing what it is right to do' (*Peel Papers*, iii. 237–8). But Peel, although greatly heartened by the queen's support, deemed it just both to his supporters and to his opponents to let the opposite party, which had lately advocated the reform, carry it out. On 5 Dec. 1845 he resigned. The queen was as loth to part with him as she had formerly been to part with Melbourne, but prepared herself to exercise, according to her wont, all the influence that was possible to her in the formation of a new government. By Peel's desire she sent for Lord John Russell, who was at the moment at Edinburgh, and did not reach Windsor till the 11th. In the meantime she asked Melbourne to come and give her counsel, but his health was failing, and on every ground prudence urged him to refuse interference. The queen's chief fear of a whig cabinet was due to her and her foreign kinsmen's distrust of Palmerston as foreign minister. No whig ministry could exclude him, but she promptly requested Lord John to give him the colonial office. Lord John demurred, and asked for time before proceeding further. In the extremity of her fear she begged Lord Aberdeen to support her objections to Palmerston; but since it was notorious in political circles that Palmerston would accept no post but that of foreign secretary, Aberdeen could give her little comfort. He merely advised her to impress Palmerston with her desire of peace with France, and to bid him consult her regularly on matters of foreign policy. On 13 Dec. the queen had a second interview at Windsor with Lord John, who was now accompanied by the veteran whig leader, Lord Lansdowne. Prince Albert sat beside her, and she let her visitors understand that she spoke for him as well as for herself. Lord John asked her to obtain assurances from Peel that the dissentient members of his cabinet were not in a position to form a new government, and to secure for him, if he undertook to repeal the corn laws, the full support of Peel and his followers. Peel gave her a guarded answer, which dissatisfied Lord John, who urged her to obtain more specific promise of co-operation. The queen, although she deemed the request unreasonable, politely appealed anew to Peel without result. At length, on 18 Dec., Lord John accepted her command to form a government. But his difficulties were only begun. There were members of his party who distrusted Palmerston as thoroughly as the queen. Lord Grey declined to join the government if Palmerston took the foreign office, and demanded a place in the cabinet for Cobden. Lord John felt unable either to accept Lord Grey's proposal or to forego his presence in the administration; and greatly to the queen's surprise he, on 29 Dec., suddenly informed her that he was unable to serve her. For a moment it looked as if she were to be left without any government, but she turned once more to Peel, who, at her earnest request, resumed power. To this result she had passively contributed throughout the intricate negotiation, and it was completely satisfactory to her. The next day, 30 Dec., she wrote: 'The queen cannot sufficiently express how much we feel Sir Robert Peel's high-minded conduct, courage, and loyalty, which can only add to the queen's confidence in him.'

Thenceforth the queen identified herself almost recklessly with Peel's policy of repeal. Melbourne, when dining at Windsor, told her that Peel's conduct was 'damned dishonest,' but she declined to discuss the topic. She lost no opportunity of urging Peel to persevere. On 12 Jan. 1846 she wrote of her satisfaction at learning of the drastic character of his proposed measures, 'feeling certain,' she added, 'that what was so just and wise must succeed.' On 27 Jan. Prince Albert attended the House of Commons to hear Peel announce his plan of abolishing the corn laws in the course of three years. Strong objection was raised to the prince's presence by protectionists, who argued that it showed partisanship on the part of the crown. The queen ridiculed the protest, but the prince never went to the lower house again. On 4 Feb. she told Peel that he would be rewarded with the gratitude of the country, which 'would make up for the abuse he has to endure from so many of his party.' She expressed sympathy with him in his loss of the support of Gladstone and Lord Lincoln, who had accepted his policy, but had withdrawn from the House of Commons because, as parliamentary nominees of the Duke of Newcastle, who was a staunch protectionist, they could not honourably vote against his opinions. The queen pressed Peel to secure other seats for them. On 18 Feb. She not only wrote to congratulate Peel on his speech in introducing the bill, but forwarded to him a letter from the Dowager Queen Adelaide which expressed an equally flattering opinion. Every speech during the corn-law debates she read with minute attention, and she closely studied the division lists.

The birth of the Princess Helena on 25 May was not suffered to distract the royal attention, and the queen watched with delight the safe passage of the bill through both houses of parliament. The sequel, however, disconcerted her. On 26 June, the night that the corn-law bill passed its third reading in the Lords, the protectionists and whigs voted together against the government on the second reading of a coercion bill for Ireland, and Peel was defeated by seventy-three. His resignation followed of necessity, and, at a moment when his services seemed most valuable to her, the queen saw herself deprived of them, as it proved for ever. She wrote of 'her *deep* concern' at parting with him. 'In whatever position Sir Robert Peel may be,' she concluded, 'we shall ever look on him as a kind and true friend.' Hardly less did she regret the retirement of Lord Aberdeen. 'We felt so safe with them,' she wrote of the two men to her uncle Leopold, who agreed that Peel, almost alone among contemporary English statesmen, could be trusted 'never to let monarchy be robbed of the little strength and power it still may possess' (*Peel Papers*, iii. 172). At the queen's request Lord John Russell formed a new government, and with misgivings the queen agreed to Palmerston's return to the foreign office. The ministry lasted nearly five years. Lord John, although awkward and unattractive in manner, and wedded to a narrow view of the queen's constitutional powers, did much to conciliate the royal favour. Closer acquaintance improved his relations with the queen, and she marked the increase of cordiality by giving him for life Pembroke Lodge in Richmond Park in March 1847, on the death of the Earl of Erroll, husband of a natural daughter of William IV. Some of Lord John's colleagues greatly interested the queen. Lord Clarendon, who was at first president of the board of trade, and in 1847 lord-lieutenant of Ireland, gained her entire confidence and became an intimate friend. She liked, too, Sir George Grey, the home secretary, and she admired the conversation of Macaulay, the paymaster-general, after he had overcome a feeling of shyness in meeting her. On 9 March 1850, when Macaulay dined at Buckingham Palace, he talked freely of his 'History.' The queen owned that she had nothing to say for her poor ancestor, James II. 'Not your majesty's ancestor, your majesty's predecessor,' Macaulay returned; and the remark, which was intended as a compliment, was well received (Trevelyan's *Life of Macaulay*, pp. 537–8). On 14 Jan. 1851, when he stayed at Windsor, he 'made her laugh heartily,' he said. 'She talked on for some time most courteously and pleasantly. Nothing could be more sensible than her remarks on German affairs' (*ibid.*

p. 549). But, on the whole, the queen's relations with her third ministry were less amicable than with her first or second, owing to the unaccommodating temper of the most prominent member of it— Palmerston, the foreign secretary. Between him and the crown a constant struggle was in progress for the effective supervision of foreign affairs. The constitution did not define the distribution of control between monarch and minister over that or any other department of the state. The minister had it in his power to work quite independently of the crown, and it practically lay with him to admit or reject a claim on the crown's part to suggest even points of procedure, still less points of policy. For the crown to challenge the fact in dealing with a strong-willed and popular minister was to invite, as the queen and prince were to find, a tormenting sense of impotence. At the outset monarch and minister found themselves in agreement. Although Palmerston realised anticipations by embroiling France and England, the breach was deemed, in the peculiar circumstances, inevitable even by the queen and the prince. A difference had for some years existed between the two countries in regard to the affairs of Spain. The Spanish throne was occupied by a child of sixteen (Queen Isabella), whose position sufficiently resembled that of the queen of England at her accession to excite at the English court interest in her future. It was the known ambition of Louis Philippe or of his ministers to bring the Spanish kingdom under French sway. English politicians of all parties were agreed, however, that an extension of French influence in the Spanish peninsula was undesirable. Perfectly conscious of the strength with which this view was held, Louis Philippe prudently announced in 1843 that his younger son, the Duc de Montpensier, was to be affianced, not to the little Spanish queen herself, but to her younger sister. Lord Aberdeen saw no objection to such a match provided that the marriage should be delayed till the Spanish queen had herself both married and had issue, and that no member of the French Bourbon house should become the royal consort of Spain. During each of the visits of Queen Victoria to the Château d'Eu the king of the French gave her a distinct verbal assent to these conditions. The Spanish queen had many suitors, but she was slow in making a choice, and her hesitation kept the Spanish question open. Unluckily for the good relations of France and England, the personal position of Prince Albert in England and his relations with Germany introduced a curious complication into the process of selecting a consort for the Spanish queen. Christina, the mother of the Spanish queen, had no wish to facilitate French ambition. With a view to foiling it she urged her daughter to follow the example alike of the English queen and of the queen of Portugal, and marry into the Saxe-Coburg family. In 1841, when the notion was first put forward, Prince Albert's elder brother Ernest, who was as yet unmarried, was suggested as a desirable suitor; but on his marriage to another in 1842, Queen Christina designated for her son-in-law Ernest and Albert's first cousin, Prince Leopold, whose brother was already prince consort of Portugal. Prince Albert, who had entertained the young man at Windsor, was consulted. He felt that his cousin should not be lightly deprived of the opportunity of securing a throne, but recognised a delicacy in urging English statesmen to serve Saxe-Coburg interests. France showed at once passionate hostility to the scheme, and at the instance of Guizot, who brusquely declared that he would at all hazards preserve Spain from England's and Portugal's fate of a Saxe-Coburg ruler, the Saxe-Coburg suit was before 1844 avowedly dropped by consent. On 2 May 1846 it was covertly revived by Queen Christina. That lady wrote to Duke Ernest of Saxe-Coburg, who was on a visit to his relatives in Portugal, bidding him seek the personal aid of Queen Victoria in marrying her daughter to Prince Leopold. With the embarrassing ignorance which prevailed in continental courts of English constitutional usages, Queen Christina desired her letter to reach Queen Victoria's hand alone, and not that of any of her ministers. Duke Ernest forwarded it to King Leopold, who communicated it to his niece. Both Duke Ernest and King Leopold came to England in August, and they discussed the Saxe-Coburg aspect of the question with the queen and Prince Albert. Reluctantly a decision adverse to the Saxe-Coburg prince was reached, on the ground that both English and French ministers had virtually rejected him. Duke Ernest at once wrote to that effect to the Queen-mother Christina, and advised the young queen to marry a Spanish prince (Duke Ernest of Saxe-Coburg, *Memoirs*, i. 190 seq.). At the same moment Palmerston returned to the foreign office, and in a despatch to the Spanish government which he wrote in haste and with half knowledge of the result of the recent Saxe-Coburg conclave, he pressed the Spanish queen to choose without delay one of three suitors, among whom he included Prince Leopold. The despatch was communicated to the French ministers, who saw in Palmerston's resuscitation of the Saxe-Coburg offer of marriage a special grievance against the English court. Retaliation was at once attempted. Without seeking further negotiations, the French ministers arranged at Madrid that the young queen should marry at once, that the bridegroom should be a Spanish suitor, the Duke of Cadiz, and that on the same day the Duc de Montpensier should marry her younger sister. On 8 Sept. the queen of the French, in a private letter to Queen Victoria, announced the approaching marriage of her son, Montpensier. The queen, in reply (10 Sept.), expressed surprise and regret. Louis Philippe sent an apologetic explanation to his daughter, the queen of the Belgians, who forwarded it to Queen Victoria. She replied that Louis Philippe had broken his word.

Bitter charges of breach of faith abounded on both sides, and the war of vituperation involved not merely both countries but both courts. The sinister rumour ran in England that the French ministers knew the Duke of Cadiz to be unfit for matrimony, and had selected him as husband of the Spanish queen so that the succession to the Spanish crown might be secured to the offspring of Montpensier. In any case, that hope was thwarted; for although the marriage of the Spanish queen Isabella proved unhappy, she was mother of five children, who were ostensibly born in wedlock. The indignation of the queen and Prince Albert was intensified by the contempt which was showered in France on the Saxe-Coburg family, and the efforts of Louis Philippe and his family at a domestic reconciliation proved vain. Palmerston, after his wont, conducted the official negotiation without any endeavour to respect the views of the queen or Prince Albert. In one despatch to Sir Henry Bulwer, the English minister at Madrid, he reinserted, to the queen's annoyance, a paragraph which Prince Albert had deleted in the first draft touching the relation of the issue of the Duc de Montpensier to the Spanish succession. King Leopold held Palmerston responsible for the whole imbroglio (Duke Ernest, i. 199). But the queen's public and private sentiments were in this case identical with those of Palmerston and of the English public, and, in the absence of any genuine difference of opinion, the minister's independent action won from the queen reluctant acquiescence. The English government formally protested against the two Spanish marriages, but they duly took place on 10 Oct., despite English execrations. 'There is but one voice here on the subject,' the queen wrote (13 Oct.) to King Leopold, 'and I am, alas! unable to say a word in defence of one [i.e. Louis Philippe] whom I had esteemed and respected. You may imagine what the whole of this makes me suffer. . . . You cannot represent too strongly to the king and queen [of the French] my indignation, and my sorrow, at what has been done' (Martin). Then the hubbub, which seemed to threaten war, gradually subsided. The effect of the incident on English prestige proved small, but it cost Louis Philippe the moral support of England, and his tottering throne fell an easy prey to revolution. At the opening of 1847 the political horizon was clouded on every side, but despite the political anxieties at home—threats of civil war in Ireland, and so great a rise in the price of wheat in England that the queen diminished the supply of bread to her own household—the 'season' of that year was exceptionally lively. Numerous foreign visitors were entertained, including the Grand Duke Constantine of Russia, the Tsar Nicholas's son, Prince Oscar of Sweden, and many German princes. On 15 June a state visit was paid to Her Majesty's Theatre in the Haymarket, during the first season of Jenny Lind, who appeared as Norma in Bellini's opera. The queen applauded eagerly

(Holland and Rockstro, *Jenny Lind*, ii. 113 seq.), and wrote to her uncle Leopold: 'Jenny Lind is quite a remarkable phenomenon.' In the spring the queen had been much gratified by the election of Prince Albert as chancellor of Cambridge University. The choice was not made without a contest—'the unseemly contest' the queen called it—and the prince won by a majority of only 117 votes over those cast for his opponent, the Earl of Powis. But the queen wisely concentrated her attention on the result, which she felt to be no gift of hers, but an honour that the prince had earned independently. In July she accompanied him to the Cambridge commencement, over which he presided as chancellor. From Tottenham she travelled on the Eastern Counties railway, under the personal guidance of the railway king, George Hudson. On 5 July 1847 she received from her husband in his official capacity, in the hall of Trinity College, an address of welcome. In reply she congratulated the university on their wise selection of a chancellor (*Life of Wilberforce*, i. 398; Dean Merivale, *Letters*; Cooper, *Annals of Cambridge*). Melbourne and three German princes, who were royal guests—Prince Waldemar of Prussia, Prince Peter of Oldenburg, and the hereditary Grand Duke of Saxe-Weimar—received honorary degrees from Prince Albert's hands. An installation ode was written by Wordsworth and set to music by T. A. Walmisley. On the evening of the 6th there was a levee at the lodge of Trinity College, and next morning the queen attended a public breakfast in Nevill's Court. For the third time the queen spent her autumn holiday in Scotland, where she had taken a highland residence at Ardverikie, a lodge on Loch Laggan, in the occupation of the Marquis of Abercorn. They travelled thither by the west coast from the Isle of Wight in the yacht Victoria and Albert (11–14 Aug.). Spending at the outset a night on the Scilly Isles, they made for the Menai Straits, where they transferred themselves to the yacht Fairy. Passing up the Clyde they visited Loch Fyne. On the 18th they arrived at Inveraray Castle, and afterwards reached their destination by way of Fort William. Palmerston was for the most part the minister in attendance, and, amid the deerstalking, walks, and drives, there was much political discussion between him and Prince Albert. The sojourn lasted three weeks, till 17 Sept., and on the return journey the royal party went by sea only as far as Fleetwood, proceeding by rail from Liverpool to London (*Journal*, pp. 43–61). Meanwhile a general election had taken place in August without involving any change of ministry. In the new parliament, which was opened by commission on 18 Nov. 1847, the liberals obtained a working majority numbering 325 to 226 protectionists and 105 conservative free traders or Peelites. Public affairs, especially abroad, abounded in causes of alarm for the queen. 1848, the year of revolution in Europe, passed off without serious disturbance in England, but the queen's equanimity was rudely shaken by rebellions in foreign lands. The dethronement of Louis Philippe in February shocked her. Ignoring recent political differences, she thought only of his distress. When his sons and daughters hurried to England, nothing for a time was known of the fate of Louis and his queen. On 2 March they arrived in disguise at Newhaven, and Louis immediately wrote to the queen, throwing himself on her protection. She obtained her uncle Leopold's consent to offer them his own royal residence at Claremont. There Prince Albert at once visited them. To all members of the French royal family the queen showed henceforth unremitting attention. To the Duc de Nemours she allotted another royal residence at Bushey. She frequently entertained him and his brothers, and always treated them with the respect which was due to members of reigning families. But it was not only in France that the revolution dealt havoc in the queen's circle of acquaintances. Her half-brother of Leiningen, who had been in Scotland with her the year before, her half-sister, the Duke of Saxe-Coburg-Gotha (Prince Albert's brother), and their friend, the king of Prussia, suffered severely in the revolutionary movements of Germany. In Italy and Austria, too, kings and princes were similarly menaced. Happily, in England, threats of revolution came to nothing. The great chartist meeting on Kensington Common, on 10 April, proved abortive. By the advice of ministers the queen and her family removed to Osborne a few days before, but they returned on 2 May. During the crisis the queen was temporarily disabled by the birth, on 18 March, of the Princess Louise; but throughout her confinement, she wrote to her uncle, King Leopold, 'My only thoughts and talk were politics, and I never was calmer or quieter or more earnest. Great events make me calm; it is only trifles that irritate my nerves' (4 April). When the infant Princess Louise was christened at Buckingham Palace on the 13th, the queen of the Belgians stood godmother, and the strain of anxiety was greatly lessened. A new perplexity arose in June 1848, when Lord John feared defeat in the House of Commons on the old question of the sugar duties, which had already nearly wrecked two governments. The queen, although her confidence in the ministry was chequered by Palmerston's conduct of the foreign office, declared any change inopportune, and she approached with reluctance the consideration of the choice of Lord John's successor. Demurring to Lord John's own suggestion of Lord Stanley, who as a seceder from Peel was not congenial to her, she took counsel with Melbourne, who advised her to summon Peel. But the government proved stronger than was anticipated, and for three years more Lord John continued in office. On 5 Sept. 1848 the queen prorogued parliament in person, the ceremony taking place for the first time in the Peers' Chamber in the new houses of parliament, which had been rebuilt after the fire of 1834. Her French kinsmen, the

Duc de Nemours and the Prince de Joinville, were present with her. Popular enthusiasm ran high, and she was in thorough accord with the congratulatory words which her ministers put into her mouth on the steadfastness with which the bulk of her people had resisted incitements to disorder. On the same afternoon she embarked at Woolwich for Aberdeen in order to spend three weeks at Balmoral House, then little more than a shooting lodge, which she now hired for the first time of Lord Aberdeen's brother, Sir Robert Gordon. Owing to bad weather the queen tried the new experiment of making practically the whole of the return journey to London by rail, travelling from Perth by way of Crewe. Thenceforth she travelled to and from Scotland in no other way. Later in the year a distressing accident caused the queen deep depression (9 Oct.). While she was crossing from Osborne to Portsmouth, her yacht, the Fairy, ran down a boat belonging to the Grampus frigate, and three women were drowned. 'It is a terrible thing, and haunts me continually,' the queen wrote. Every year the queen, when in London or at Windsor, sought recreation more and more conspicuously in music and the drama. Elaborate concerts, oratorios, or musical recitations were repeatedly given both at Windsor and at Buckingham Palace. On 10 Feb. 1846 Charles Kemble read the words of the 'Antigone' when Mendelssohn's music was rendered, and there followed like renderings of 'Athalie' (1 Jan. 1847), again of 'Antigone' (1 Jan. 1848), and of 'Œdipus at Colonos' (10 Feb. 1848 and 1 Jan. 1852). During 1842 and 1844 the composer Mendelssohn was many times at court. The great French actress Rachel was invited to recite on more than one occasion, and on 26 Feb. 1851, when Macready took farewell of the stage at Drury Lane, the queen was present. Meanwhile, to give greater brilliance to the Christmas festivities, the queen organised at the end of 1848 dramatic performances at Windsor. Charles Kean was appointed director, and until Prince Albert's death, except during three years—in 1850 owing to the queen dowager's death, in 1855 during the gloom of the Crimean war, and in 1858 owing to the distraction of the princess royal's marriage—dramatic representations were repeated in the Rubens room at the castle during each Christmas season. On 28 Dec. 1848, at the first performance, 'The Merchant of Venice' was presented, with Mr. and Mrs. Kean and Mr. and Mrs. Keeley in the cast. Thirteen other plays of Shakespeare and nineteen lighter pieces followed in the course of the next thirteen years, and the actors included Macready, Phelps, Charles Mathews, Ben Webster, and Buckstone. In 1857 William Bodham Donne succeeded Kean as director; and the last performance under Donne's management took place on 31 Jan. 1861. More than thirty years then elapsed before the queen suffered another professional dramatic entertainment to take place in a royal palace. The most conspicuous encouragement which the queen and her husband bestowed on art during this period was their commission to eight artists (Eastlake, Maclise, Landseer, Dyce, Stanfield, Uwins, Leslie, and Ross) to decorate with frescoes the queen's summer house in the gardens of Buckingham Palace. The subjects were drawn from Milton's 'Comus.' The work was completed in 1845. Under Prince Albert's guidance, the queen's domestic life was now very systematically ordered. The education of the growing family occupied their parents' minds almost from the children's birth. Prince Albert frequently took counsel on the subject with Stockmar and Bunsen, and the queen consulted Melbourne (24 March 1842) even after he had ceased to be her minister. In the result Lady Lyttelton, widow of the third Baron Lyttelton, and sister of the second Earl Spencer (Lord Althorp), who had been a lady-in-waiting since 1837, was in 1842 appointed governess of the royal children, and, on her retirement in January 1851, she was succeeded by Lady Caroline Barrington, widow of Captain the Hon. George Barrington, R.N., and daughter of the second Earl Grey; she held the office till her death on 28 April 1875. The office of royal governess, which thus was filled during the queen's reign by only two holders, carried with it complete control of the 'nursery establishment,' which soon included German and French as well as English attendants. All the children spoke German fluently from infancy. The queen sensibly insisted that they should be brought up as simply, naturally, and domestically as possible, and that no obsequious deference should be paid to their rank. The need of cultivating perfect trust between parents and children, the value of a thorough but liberal religious training from childhood, and the folly of child-worship or excessive laudation were constantly in her mind. She spent with her children all the time that her public engagements permitted, and delighted in teaching them youthful amusements. As they grew older she and the prince encouraged them to recite poetry and to act little plays, or arrange tableaux vivants. To the education of the prince of Wales as the heir apparent they naturally devoted special attention, and in every way they protected his interests. Very soon after his birth the queen appointed a commission to receive and accumulate the revenues of the Duchy of Cornwall, the appanage of the heir apparent, in their son's behalf, until he should come of age, and the estate was administered admirably. Although the queen abhorred advanced views on the position of women in social life, she sought to make her daughters as useful as her sons to the world at large, and, while causing them to be instructed in all domestic arts, repudiated the notion that marriage was the only object which they should be brought up to attain (*Letters to Princess Alice* (1874), p. 320). She expressed regret that among the upper classes in England girls were taught to aim at little else in life than matrimony. The queen and Prince Albert regulated with care their own habits and pursuits. Although public business compelled them to spend much time in London, the prince rapidly acquired a distaste for it, which he soon communicated to the queen. As a young woman she was, she said, wretched to leave London, but, though she never despised or disliked London amusements, she came to adopt her husband's view, that peace and quiet were most readily to be secured at a distance from the capital. The sentiment grew, and she reached the conclusion that 'the extreme weight and thickness of the atmosphere' injured her health, and in consequence her sojourns at Buckingham Palace became less frequent and briefer; in later life she did not visit it more than twice or thrice a year, staying on each occasion not more than two days. Windsor, which was agreeable to her, was near enough to London to enable her to transact business there without inconvenience. In early married life she chiefly resided there. The Pavilion at Brighton she abandoned, and, after being dismantled in 1846, it was sold to the corporation of Brighton in 1850 to form a place of public assembly. Anxious to secure residences which should be personal property and free from the restraints of supervision by public officials, she soon decided to acquire private abodes in those parts of her dominions which were peculiarly congenial to her—the Isle of Wight and the highlands of Scotland. Her residence in the south was secured first. Late in 1844 she purchased of Lady Isabella Blachford the estate of Osborne, consisting of about eight hundred acres, near East Cowes. Subsequent purchases increased the land to about two thousand acres. The existing house proved inconvenient, and the foundation-stone of a new one was laid on 23 June 1845. A portion of it was occupied in September 1846, although the whole was not completed until 1851. In the grounds was set up in 1854 a Swiss cottage as a workshop and playhouse for the children. In the designing of the new Osborne House and in laying out the gardens Prince Albert took a very active part. The queen interested herself in the neighbourhood, and rebuilt the parish church at Whippingham. In 1848 the queen leased of the Fife trustees Balmoral House, as her residence in the highlands; she purchased it in 1852, and then resolved to replace it by an elaborate edifice. The new Balmoral Castle was completed in the autumn of 1854, and large additions were subsequently made to the estate. The Duchess of Kent rented in the neighbourhood Abergeldie Castle, which was subsequently occupied by the prince of Wales. At Balmoral, after 1854, a part of every spring and autumn was spent during the rest of the queen's life, while three or four annual visits were paid regularly to Osborne. At both Osborne and Balmoral very homely modes of life were adopted, and, at Balmoral especially, ministers and foreign friends were surprised at the simplicity which characterised the queen's domestic arrangements. Before the larger house was built only two sitting-rooms were occupied by the royal family. Of an evening billiards were played in the one, under such cramped conditions that the queen, who usually looked on, had constantly to move her seat to give the players elbow-space. In the other room the queen at times would take lessons in the Scotch reel. The minister in attendance did all his work in his small bedroom, and the queen would run carelessly in and out of the house all day long, walking alone, visiting neighbouring cottages, and chatting unreservedly with their occupants. After identifying herself thus closely with Scotland, it was only right for her to make the acquaintance of Ireland, the only portion of the United Kingdom which she had not visited during the first decade of her reign. Peel had entertained a suggestion that the queen should visit the country in 1844, when she received an invitation from the lord mayor of Dublin, and a conditional promise of future acceptance was given. In the early autumn of 1849 the plan was carried out with good results. The social and political condition of the country was not promising. The effects of the famine were still acute. Civil war had broken out in 1848, and, although it was easily repressed, disaffection was widespread. In June 1849 the queen's attention was disagreeably drawn to the unsatisfactory condition of the country by a difficulty which arose in regard to recent convictions for high treason; commutation of capital sentences was resolved upon, but it was found to be impossible to substitute terms of imprisonment until a new statute had been hastily devised, giving the crown specific authority to that effect. The general distress precluded a state visit. But personal loyalty to the sovereign was still believed to prevail in Ireland. The queen went by sea from Cowes to the Cove of Cork, upon which she bestowed the new name of Queenstown in honour of her first landing there on Irish soil. She thence proceeded in her yacht to Kingstown, and took up her residence for four days at the viceregal lodge in Phœnix Park, Dublin. She held a levee one evening in Dublin Castle. Her reception was all that could be wished. It was 'idolatrous,' wrote Monckton Milnes, lord Houghton, 'and utterly unworthy of a free, not to say ill-used, nation' (Reid, *Lord Houghton*, i. 485–5). She received addresses and visited public institutions. Everything she saw delighted her, and she commemorated her presence in Dublin by making the prince of Wales Earl of Dublin (10 Sept. 1849). From the Irish capital she went by sea to Belfast, where her reception was equally enthusiastic. Thence she crossed to the Scottish coast, and after a public visit to Glasgow she sought the grateful seclusion of Balmoral. On 30 Oct. 1849 an attack of chicken-pox prevented the queen from fulfilling her promise to open the new coal exchange in Lower Thames Street, and she was represented by her husband. In two ways the incident proved of interest. The queen's two eldest children there first appeared at a public ceremonial, while the royal barge, which bore the royal party from

Westminster to St. Paul's wharf, made its last state journey on the Thames during the queen's reign. In the large circle of the queen's family and court, it was inevitable that death should be often busy and should gradually sever valued links with the queen's youth. Her aunt, Princess Sophia, died on 27 May 1848, and her old minister and mentor, Melbourne, on 24 Nov. 1848, while a year later George Anson, the prince's former secretary and now keeper of his privy purse, passed suddenly away, and his loss was severely felt by the queen. Another grief was the death, on 2 Dec. 1849 at Stanmore Priory, of the old Queen Adelaide, who was buried in St. George's Chapel, Windsor, beside William IV on 13 Dec. The summer of the following year (1850) was still more fruitful in episodes of mourning. On 3 July Peel succumbed to an accidental fall from his horse; in him the queen said she lost not merely a friend, but a father. Five days later there died her uncle, the Duke of Cambridge; on 26 Aug., Louis Philippe, whose fate of exile roused the queen's abiding sympathy; and on 10 Oct. the French king's gentle daughter, the queen of the Belgians, wife of King Leopold. Minor anxieties were caused the queen by two brutal attacks upon her person: on 19 May 1849, when she was returning from a drive near Constitution Hill, a blank charge was fired at her from a pistol by an Irishman, William Hamilton of Adare, and on 27 May 1850 one Robert Pate, a retired officer, hit her on the head with a cane as she was leaving Cambridge House in Piccadilly, where the Duke of Cambridge was lying ill.

The last outrage was the more brutal, seeing that the queen was just recovering from her confinement. Her third son, Arthur, was born on 1 May 1850. The date was the Duke of Wellington's eighty-first birthday. A few weeks before the duke had delighted the queen by the injudicious suggestion that Prince Albert should become commander-in-chief of the army in succession to himself. The prince wisely declined the honour. Apart from other considerations his hands were over full already and his health was giving evidence of undue mental strain. But, by way of showing her appreciation of the duke's proposal, the queen made him godfather to her new-born son. A second sponsor was the prince of Prussia, and the christening took place on 22 June. The infant's third name, Patrick, commemorated the queen's recent Irish visit. At the time, despite family and political cares, the queen's health was exceptionally robust. On going north in the autumn, after inaugurating the high-level bridge at Newcastle and the Royal Border Bridge on the Scottish boundary at Berwick, she stopped two days in Edinburgh at Holyrood Palace, in order to climb Arthur's Seat. When she settled down to her holiday at Balmoral, she took energetic walking exercise and showed a physical briskness enabling her to face boldly annoyances in official life, which were now graver than any she had yet experienced. The breach between the foreign minister (Palmerston) and the crown was growing wider each year. Foreign affairs interested the queen and her husband intensely. As they grew more complex the prince studied them more closely, and prepared memoranda with a view to counselling the foreign minister. But Palmerston rendered such efforts abortive by going his own way, without consulting the court or, at times, even his colleagues. The antagonism between Prince Albert's views, with which the queen identified herself, and those of Palmerston was largely based on principle. Palmerston consistently supported liberal movements abroad, even at the risk of exposing himself to the charge of encouraging revolution. Although the queen and the prince fully recognised the value of constitutional methods of government in England, and were by no means averse to their spread on the continent of Europe, their personal relations with foreign dynasties evoked strong sympathy with reigning monarchs and an active dread of revolution, which Palmerston seemed to them to view with a perilous complaisance. Through 1848, the year of revolution, the difference steadily grew. Palmerston treated with equanimity the revolutionary riots at Berlin, Vienna, and Baden in 1848–9, while they stirred in his royal mistress a poignant compassion for those crowned kinsmen or acquaintances whose lives and fortunes were menaced. When efforts were first made in Italy to secure national unity and to throw off the yoke of Austria, Palmerston spoke with benevolence of the endeavours of the Italian patriots. Although the prince strongly deprecated the cruelties which Italian rulers practised on their subjects, he and the queen cherished a warm sympathy with the Austrians and their emperor. In regard to Germany, on the other hand, the opposition between royal and ministerial opinions involved other considerations. The prince was well affected to the movement for national unity under Prussia's leadership. Palmerston's distrust of the weak reactionary Prussian king and his allies among the German princes rendered him suspicious of German nationalist aspirations. In the intricate struggle for the possession of the duchies of Schleswig-Holstein, which opened in 1848, Palmerston inclined to the claim of Denmark against that of the confederation of German states with Prussia at its head, whose triumph the English royal family hopefully anticipated.

In point of practice Palmerston was equally offensive to the prince and the queen. He frequently caused them intense irritation or alarm by involving the government in acute international crises without warning the queen of their approach. In 1848, before consulting her, he peremptorily ordered the reactionary Spanish government to liberalise its institutions, with the result that the English ambassador, Sir Henry

Bulwer, was promptly expelled from Madrid. In January 1850, to the queen's consternation, Palmerston coerced Greece into compliance with English demands for the compensation of Don Pacifico and other English subjects who had claims against the Greek government. Thereupon France, who was trying to mediate, and regarded Palmerston's precipitate action as insulting, withdrew her ambassador from London, and for the third time in the queen's reign—on this occasion almost before she had an opportunity of learning the cause—Palmerston brought France and England to the brink of war. The queen's embarrassments were aggravated by the habit of foreign sovereigns, who believed her power to be far greater than it was, of writing autograph appeals to her personally on political affairs, and of seeking privately to influence the foreign policy of the country. She was wise enough to avoid the snares that were thus laid for her, and frankly consulted Palmerston before replying. He invariably derided the notion of conciliating the good opinion of foreign courts, where his name was a word of loathing. The experience was often mortifying for the queen. In 1847, when the queen of Portugal, the queen's early playmate, was threatened by her revolutionary subjects, she appealed directly to Queen Victoria for protection. Palmerston treated the Portuguese difficulty as a 'Coburg family affair.' He attributed the queen's peril to her reliance on the absolutist advice of one Dietz, a native of Coburg, who stood towards the Portuguese queen and her husband, Prince Ferdinand of Saxe-Coburg, in a relation resembling that of Stockmar to Prince Albert and the queen. Palmerston insisted on Dietz's dismissal—a proceeding that was highly offensive to the queen and to her Saxe-Coburg kinsmen (Duke Ernest, *Memoirs*, i. 288 sq.). Afterwards he dictated a solemn letter of constitutional advice for his royal mistress to copy in her own hand and forward to her unhappy correspondent at Lisbon (Walpole, *Lord John Russell*). Later in the year the king of Prussia, in a private letter which his ambassador at St. James's, Baron Bunsen, was directed to deliver to the queen in private audience, invited her encouragement of the feeble efforts of Prussia to dominate the German federation. Palmerston learned from Bunsen of the missive, and told him that it was irregular for the English sovereign to correspond with foreign monarchs unless they were her relatives (Bunsen, *Memoirs*, ii. 149). In concert with Prince Albert he sketched a colourless draft reply, which the queen copied out; it 'began and ended in German, though the body of it was in English.' Prince Albert, in frequent private correspondence with the king of Prussia, had sought to stimulate the king to more active assertion of Prussian power in Germany, and the apparent discrepancy between the prince's ardour and the coolness which Palmerston imposed on his wife was peculiarly repugnant to both her and her husband.

Expostulation with Palmerston seemed vain. In June 1848 Prince Albert bade Lord John remind him that every one of the ten thousand despatches which were received annually at the foreign office was addressed to the queen and to the prime minister as well as to himself, and that the replies involved them all. In the following autumn Palmerston remarked on a further protest made in the queen's behalf by Lord John: 'Unfortunately the queen gives ear too easily to persons who are hostile to her government, and who wish to poison her mind with distrust of her ministers, and in this way she is constantly suffering under groundless uneasiness.' To this challenge she answered, through Lord John, 1 Oct. 1848: 'The queen naturally, as I think, dreads that upon some occasion you may give her name to sanction proceedings which she may afterwards be compelled to disavow' (Walpole, *Lord John Russell*, ii. 47). Unluckily for the queen, Palmerston's action was vehemently applauded by a majority in parliament and in the country, and his defence of his action in regard to Greece in the Don Pacifico affair in June 1850 elicited the stirring enthusiasm of the House of Commons. The queen, in conversation with political friends like Aberdeen and Clarendon, loudly exclaimed against her humiliation. Lord John was often as much out of sympathy with Palmerston as she, but he knew the government could not stand without its foreign secretary; and the queen, who was always averse to inviting the perplexities of a change of ministry, viewed the situation with blank despair. In March 1850 she and the prince drafted a statement of their grievance, but in face of the statesman's triumphant appeal to the House of Commons in June it was laid aside. In the summer Lord John recalled Palmerston's attention to the queen's irritation, and he disavowed any intention of treating her with disrespect. At length, on 12 Aug. 1850, she sent him through Lord John two requests in regard to his future conduct: 'She requires,' her words ran, '(1) that the foreign secretary will distinctly state what he proposes in a given case, in order that the queen may know as distinctly to what she has given her royal sanction. (2) Having once given her sanction to a measure, that it be not arbitrarily altered or modified by the minister. Such an act she must consider as failure in sincerity towards the crown, and justly to be visited by the exercise of her constitutional right of dismissing that minister. She expects to be kept informed of what passes between him and the foreign ministers before important decisions are taken, based upon that intercourse; to receive the foreign despatches in good time, and to have the drafts for her approval sent to her in sufficient time to make herself acquainted with their contents before they must be sent off' (Martin, ii. 51). Two days afterwards Prince Albert explained more fully to Palmerston, in a personal interview, the queen's grounds of complaint. 'The queen had often,' the prince said, 'latterly almost invariably, differed from the line of policy pursued by Lord Palmerston. She had always openly stated her objections; but when overruled by the cabinet, or convinced that it would, from political reasons, be more prudent to waive her objections, she knew her constitutional position too well not to give her full support to whatever was done on the part of the government. She knew that they were going to battle together, and that she was going to receive the blows which were aimed at the government; and she had these last years received several, such as no sovereign of England had before been obliged to put up with, and which had been most painful to her. But what she had a right to require in return was, that before a line of policy was adopted or brought before her for her sanction, she should be in full possession of all the facts and all the motives operating; she felt that in this respect she was not dealt with as she ought to be. She never found a matter "intact," nor a question, in which we were not already compromised, when it was submitted to her; she had no means of knowing what passed in the cabinet, nor what passed between Lord Palmerston and the foreign ministers in their conferences, but what Lord Palmerston chose to tell her, or what she found in the newspapers.' Palmerston affected pained surprise and solemnly promised amendment, but he remained in office and his course of action underwent no permanent change. A few months later he committed the queen, without her assent, to new dissensions with the Austrian government and to new encouragement of Denmark in her claims to Schleswig-Holstein. In the first case Palmerston, after threatening Lord John with resignation, endeavoured to modify his action in accordance with the royal wish, but he was still impenitent. In the winter of 1850 a distasteful domestic question distracted the queen's mind from foreign affairs. Lord John had identified the government with the strong protestant feeling which was roused by Cardinal Wiseman's announcement of the pope's revival of Roman catholic bishoprics in England. Hundreds of protests from public bodies were addressed to the queen in person, and she received them patiently. But she detested the controversy and regretted 'the unchristian and intolerant spirit' exhibited by the protestant agitators. 'I cannot bear to hear the violent abuse of the catholic religion, which is so painful and so cruel towards the many innocent and good Roman catholics.' When she opened parliament on 4 Feb. 1851 she resented the cries of 'no popery,' with which she was greeted; but the ministry determined actively to resist the 'papal aggression,' and the queen acquiesced. It was consequently with composure that she saw Lord John's government—partly through intestine differences on the religious question—outvoted in the House of Commons in February 1851. The immediate question at issue was electoral reform. Lord John at once resigned. The queen sent for the conservative leader, Lord Stanley, afterwards Lord Derby, who declined office without adequate support in the House of Commons. He advised a reconstruction of the existing ministry—a course congenial to the queen. On 22 Feb. she consulted Lord Aberdeen with a view to a fusion between whigs and Peelites, but the combination proved impracticable. Perplexed by the deadlock which the refusals of Derby and Aberdeen created, she turned for advice to the old Duke of Wellington. In agreement with the duke's counsel she recalled Russell after Prince Albert had sent him a memorandum of the recent negotiations. Lord John managed to get through the session in safety and secured the passage of his antipapal Ecclesiastical Titles Bill after completely emasculating it; it received the royal assent on 29 July 1851. Meanwhile the attention of the court and country had turned from party polemics to a demonstration of peace and goodwill among the nations which excited the queen's highest hopes. It was the inauguration of the Great Exhibition in the Crystal Palace which was erected in Hyde Park. In origin and execution that design was due to Prince Albert; and it had consequently encountered abundant opposition from high tories and all sections of society who disliked the prince. Abroad it was condemned by absolute monarchs and their ministers as an invitation to revolutionary conspiracy through the suggestion it offered to revolutionary agents in Europe to assemble in London on a speciously innocent pretext, and hatch nefarious designs against law and order. The result belied the prophets of evil. The queen flung herself with spirit into the enterprise. She interested herself in every detail, and she was rewarded for her energy by the knowledge that the realised scheme powerfully appealed to the imagination of the mass of her people. The brilliant opening ceremony over which she presided on 1 May 1851 evoked a marvellous outburst of loyalty. Her bearing was described on all hands as 'thoroughly regal' (Stanley, i. 424). Besides twenty-five thousand people in the building, seven hundred thousand cheered her outside as she passed them on her way from Buckingham Palace. It was, she said, the proudest and happiest day of her happy life. Her feelings were gratified both as queen and wife. 'The great event has taken place,' she wrote in her diary (1 May), 'a complete and beautiful triumph—a glorious and touching sight, one which I shall ever be proud of for my beloved Albert and my country. ... Yes! it is a day which makes my heart swell with pride and glory and thankfulness!' In her eyes the great festival of peace was a thousand times more memorable than the thrilling scene of her coronation. In spite of their censorious fears foreign courts were well represented, and among the queen's guests were the prince and princess of Prussia. Tennyson, who had been appointed poet laureate in November 1850, in succession to Wordsworth, in the address 'To the Queen,' which he prefixed to the seventh edition of his

'Poems' (March 1851), wrote of the Great Exhibition, in a stanza which was not reprinted:

> She brought a vast design to pass
> When Europe and the scatter'd ends
> Of our fierce world did meet as friends
> And brethren in her halls of glass.

The season of the Great Exhibition was exceptionally brilliant. On 13 June another *bal costumé* at Buckingham Palace illustrated the reign of Charles II. On 9 July the queen attended a ball at the Guildhall, which celebrated the success of the Exhibition. Everywhere her reception was admirably cordial. When at length she temporarily left London for Osborne, she expressed pain that 'this brilliant and for ever memorable season should be past.' Of the continuous display of devotion to her in London she wrote to Stockmar: 'All this will be of a use not to be described: it identifies us with the people and gives them an additional cause for loyalty and attachment.' Early in August, when the queen came to Westminster to prorogue parliament, she visited the Exhibition for the last time. In October, on her removal to Balmoral, she made a formal progress through Liverpool and Manchester, and stayed for a few days with the Earl of Ellesmere at Worsley Hall. She manifested intelligent interest in the improvements which manufacturing processes were making in these great centres of industry. Her visit to Peel Park, Salford (10 Oct.), was commemorated by a statue of her, the cost of which was mainly defrayed by 80,000 Sunday school teachers and scholars; it was unveiled by Prince Albert 5 May 1857. A month after the closing of the Exhibition the dream of happiness was fading. The death of her sour-tempered uncle, King Ernest of Hanover (18 Nov. 1851), was not a heavy blow, but Palmerston was again disturbing her equanimity. Kossuth, the leader of the Hungarian revolution, had just arrived in England; Palmerston openly avowed sympathy with him. Both the queen and Lord John remonstrated, and the queen begged the cabinet to censure his attitude unequivocally; but her appeal was vain. Relief from the tormenting attitude of Palmerston was, however, at hand. It came at a moment when the queen despaired of any alleviation of her lot. On 2 Dec. 1851 Prince Louis Napoleon by a *coup d'état* made himself absolute head of the French government. Palmerston believed in Napoleon's ability, and a day or two later, in conversation with the French ambassador, Walewski, expressed of his own initiative approbation of the new form of government in France. The queen and Lord John viewed Napoleon's accession to power, and the means whereby it had been accomplished, with detestation. Palmerston's precipitate committal of England to a friendly recognition of the new *régime* before he had communicated with the queen or his colleagues united the Gordian knot that bound him to the queen. This display of self-sufficiency roused the temper of Lord John, who had assured the queen that for the present England would extend to Napoleon the coldest neutrality. To the queen's surprise and delight, Lord John summarily demanded Palmerston's resignation (19 Dec.). Palmerston feebly defended himself by claiming that in his intercourse with Walewski he had only expressed his personal views, and that he was entitled to converse at will with ambassadors. Lord John offered to rearrange the government so as to give him another office, but this Palmerston declined. The seals of the foreign office were transferred to the queen's friend, Lord Granville.

The queen and the prince did not conceal their joy at the turn of events. To his brother Ernest, Prince Albert wrote without reserve: 'And now the year closes with the happy circumstance for us, that the man who embittered our whole life, by continually placing before us the shameful alternative of either sanctioning his misdeeds throughout Europe, and rearing up the radical party here to a power under his leadership, or bringing about an open conflict with the crown, and thus plunging the only country where liberty, order, and lawfulness exist together into the general chaos—that this man has, as it were, cut his own throat. "Give a rogue rope enough and he will hang himself" is an old English adage with which we have sometimes tried to console ourselves, and which has proved true again here. . . .' (*Duke Ernest's Memoirs*). As a matter of fact, Palmerston's dismissal was a doubtful triumph for the crown. It was, in the first place, not the queen's act; it was the act of Lord John, who was not greatly influenced by court feeling, and it was an act that Lord John lived to regret. Palmerston's popularity in the country grew in proportion to his unpopularity at court, and, in the decade that followed, his power and ministerial power generally increased steadily at the expense of the crown's influence in both home and foreign affairs. The genuine victory lay with the minister. Palmerston's removal did not, in fact, even at the moment diminish anxiety at court. 1852 opened ominously. The intentions of France were doubtful. The need of increasing the naval and military forces was successfully urged on the government, but no sooner had the discussions on that subject opened in the House of Commons than Palmerston condemned as inadequate the earliest proposals of the government which were embodied in a militia bill, and, inflicting a defeat on his former colleagues, brought about their resignation on 20 Feb. 1852, within two months of his own dismissal. The queen summoned Lord Derby, who formed a conservative government, with Disraeli as chancellor of the exchequer and leader of the House of Commons. It was not a strong ministry. Its members, almost all of whom were new to official life, belonged to the party of protection; but protection had long since vanished from practical politics, and the queen was disposed to reproach her new advisers with their delay in discerning the impracticability of their obsolete policy. A little more haste, she said, 'would have saved so much annoyance, so much difficulty.' But personal intercourse rapidly overcame her prejudices. Lord Derby proved extremely courteous. Lord Malmesbury, the foreign minister, kept her thoroughly well informed of the affairs of his office, and the personal difficulty that she and her friends had anticipated from Disraeli was held in check. Disraeli had won his first parliamentary repute by his caustic denunciations of the queen's friend Peel, and she was inclined to adopt the widespread view that he was an unprincipled adventurer. He was perfectly aware of her sentiment, and during the ministerial crisis of 1851 he expressed himself quite ready to accept a post that should not bring him into frequent relations with the court. But personal acquaintance with him at once diminished the queen's distrust; his clever conversation amused her. She afterwards gave signal proof of a dispassionate spirit by dismissing every trace of early hostility, and by extending to him in course of time a confidence and a devotion which far exceeded that she showed to any other minister of her reign. But her present experience of Disraeli and his colleagues was brief. A general election in July left the conservatives in a minority. In the same month the queen made a cruise in the royal yacht on the south coast, and a few weeks later paid a second private visit to King Leopold at his summer palace at Laeken. The weather was bad, but on returning she visited the chief objects of interest in Antwerp, and steered close to Calais, so that she might see it. When at Balmoral later in the autumn, information reached her of the generous bequest to her by an eccentric subject, John Camden Neild, of all his fortune, amounting to a quarter of a million. The elation of spirit which this news caused her was succeeded by depression on hearing of the death of the Duke of Wellington on 14 Sept. 'He was to us a true friend,' she wrote to her uncle Leopold, 'and most valuable adviser . . . we shall soon stand sadly alone. Aberdeen is almost the only personal friend of that kind left to us. Melbourne, Peel, [the third earl of] Liverpool, now the Duke—all gone.' The queen issued a general order of regret to the army, and she put her household into mourning. She went to the lying in state in Chelsea Hospital, and witnessed the funeral procession to St. Paul's from the balcony of Buckingham Palace on 18 Nov.

On 11 Nov. the queen opened the new parliament. Lord Derby was still prime minister, but the position of the government was hopeless. On 3 Dec. Disraeli's budget was introduced, and on the 17th it was thrown out by a majority of nineteen. Lord Derby promptly resigned. For six years the queen's government had been extraordinarily weak. Parties were disorganised, and no leader enjoyed the full confidence of any large section of the House of Commons. A reconstruction of party seemed essential to the queen and the prince. In November she had discussed with Lord Derby a possible coalition, and the chief condition she then imposed was that Palmerston should not lead the House of Commons. When Derby resigned she made up her mind to give her views effect. She sent for veteran statesmen on each side, Lord Aberdeen and Lord Lansdowne, both of whom she had known long and fully trusted. Lansdowne was ill, and Aberdeen came alone. On 19 Dec. she wrote to Lord John Russell (Walpole, *Life*, ii. 161): 'The queen thinks the moment to have arrived when a popular, efficient, and durable government could be formed by the sincere and united efforts of all parties professing conservative and liberal opinions.' Aberdeen undertook to form such a government, with the queen's assistance. Palmerston's presence was deemed essential, and she raised no objection to his appointment to the home office. The foreign office was bestowed on Lord John, who almost immediately withdrew from it in favour of the queen's friend, Lord Clarendon. On 28 Dec. Aberdeen had completed his task, and the queen wrote with sanguine satisfaction to her uncle Leopold of 'our excellent Aberdeen's success,' and of the 'realisation of the country's and of our own most ardent wishes.' Thus the next year opened promisingly, but it proved a calm before a great storm. On 7 April 1853 the queen's fourth and youngest son was born, and was named Leopold, after the queen's uncle, King Leopold, who was his godfather. George, the new king of Hanover, was also a sponsor, and the infant's third name of Duncan celebrated the queen's affection for Scotland. She was not long in retirement, and public calls were numerous. Military training, in view of possible warlike complications on the continent, was proceeding actively with the queen's concurrence. Twice—21 June and 5 August 1853—she visited, the first time with her guests, the new king and queen of Hanover, a camp newly formed on Chobham Common, and (on 5 Aug. 1901) a granite cross was unveiled to commemorate the first of these visits. In the interval between the two the queen, Prince Albert, the prince of Wales, Princess Royal, and Princess Alice had been disabled by an attack of measles, and Prince Albert, to the queen's alarm, suffered severely from nervous prostration. On 11 Aug. the navy was encouraged by a great naval review which the queen held at Spithead. Before the month ended the queen paid a second visit to Dublin, in order to inspect an exhibition of Irish industries which was framed on the model of the Great Exhibition of 1851. A million Irish men and women are said to have met her on her landing at Kingstown. The royal party stayed in Dublin from 30 Aug. to 3 Sept., and attended many public functions. As on the former occasion, the queen spent, she said, 'a pleasant, gay, and interesting time.' Throughout 1852 the queen continued her frank avowals of repugnance to personal intercourse with Napoleon III. Her relations with the exiled royal family of France rendered him an object of suspicion and dislike, and the benevolence with which Palmerston regarded him did not soften her animosity. But she gradually acknowledged the danger of allowing her personal feeling to compromise peaceful relations with France. On 2 Dec. 1852 the empire had been formally recognised by the European powers, and the emperor was making marked advances to England. The French ambassador in London sounded Malmesbury, the foreign minister (December 1852), as to whether a marriage between the emperor and Princess Adelaide of Hohenlohe, daughter of the queen's half sister, would be acceptable. The queen spoke with horror of the emperor's religion and morals, and was not sorry that the discussion should be ended by the emperor's marriage in the following January with Mlle. Eugénie de Montijo, a lady with whom the irony of fate was soon to connect the queen in a lasting friendship. Meanwhile the queen's uncle, King Leopold, realised the wisdom of promoting better relations between her and the emperor, whose openly expressed anxiety to secure her countenance was becoming a source of embarrassment. In the early months of 1853 Duke Ernest, Prince Albert's brother, after consultation with King Leopold, privately visited Paris and accepted the hospitality of the Tuileries. Emperor and empress outbid each other in their laudation of Queen Victoria's domestic life. The empress expressed a longing for close acquaintance with her, her husband, and children. A revolution had been worked, she said, in the conditions of court life throughout Europe by the virtuous examples of Queen Victoria and of her friend and ally the queen of Portugal. Duke Ernest promptly reported the conversation to his brother and sister-in-law. The queen, always sensitive to sympathy with her domestic experiences, was greatly mollified. Her initial prejudices were shaken, and the political situation soon opened the road to perfect amity.

Napoleon lost no opportunity of improving the situation. At the end of 1853 he boldly suggested a matrimonial alliance between the two families. With the approval of King Leopold and of Palmerston he proposed a marriage between his first cousin, Prince Jerome, who ultimately became the political head of the Bonaparte family, and the queen's first cousin, Princess Mary of Cambridge, afterwards Duchess of Teck. Princess Mary was a frequent guest at Windsor, and constantly shared in the queen's recreations. The queen had no faith in forced political marriages, and at once consulted the princess, whose buoyant, cheerful disposition endeared her to all the royal family. The princess rejected the proposal without hesitation, and the queen would hear no more of it. Palmerston coolly remarked that Prince Jerome was at any rate preferable to a German princeling.

But although Napoleon's first move led to nothing, an alliance between France and England was already at hand. It was not France among the countries of Europe that England under the queen's sway was first to meet in war. It was in conflict with Russia that her country, under the spell of Palmerston, in conjunction with France, was to break the peace of Europe for the first time in her reign. In the autumn of 1853 Russia pushed her claims to protect the Greek Christians of the Turkish empire with such violence as to extort from Turkey a declaration of war (23 Oct.). The mass of the British nation held that England was under an imperative and an immediate obligation to intervene by force of arms in behalf of Turkey, her protégé and ally. The English cabinet was divided in opinion. Aberdeen regarded the conduct of Russia as indefensible, but hoped to avert war by negotiation. Palmerston, then home secretary, took the popular view, that the inability of Turkey to meet Russia single-handed allowed no delay in intervention. On 16 Dec. Palmerston suddenly resigned, on the ostensible ground that he differed from proposals of electoral reform which his colleagues had adopted. The true reason was his attitude to the foreign crisis. Signs that he interpreted the voice of the country aright abounded. The ministry felt compelled to readmit him to the cabinet, with the certainty of destroying the peace of Europe. To the court the crisis was from every point of view distressing. The queen placed implicit trust in Aberdeen, and with him she hoped to avoid war. But Palmerston's restored predominance alarmed her. Abroad the situation was not more reassuring. The Emperor Napoleon promptly offered to join his army with that of England, and the king of Sardinia promised to follow his example. But other foreign sovereigns with whom the queen was in fuller sympathy privately entreated her to thwart the bellicose designs which they identified with her most popular minister's name. The tsar protested to her the innocence of his designs (November 1853). The nervous king of Prussia petitioned her to keep the peace, and even sent her an autograph note by the hand of General von Gröben. Clarendon, the foreign minister, gave her wise advice regarding the tenor of her replies. She reproached the king of Prussia with his weakness in failing to aid the vindication of international law and order (17 March 1854), and her attitude to all her continental correspondents was irreproachable. But the rumour spread that she and her husband were employing their foreign intimacies against the country's interest. Aberdeen's hesitation to proceed to extremities, the known dissensions between Palmerston and the court, the natural jealousy of foreign influences in the sphere of government, fed the suspicion that the crown at the instance of a foreign prince consort was obstructing the due assertion of the country's rights, and was playing into the hands of the country's foes. As the winter of 1853-4 progressed without any signs of decisive action on the part of the English government, popular indignation redoubled and burst in its fullest fury on the head of Prince Albert. He was denounced as the chief agent of an Austro-Belgian-Coburg-Orleans clique, the avowed enemy of England, and the subservient tool of Russian ambition. The tsar, it was seriously alleged, communicated his pleasure to the prince through the prince's kinsmen at Gotha and Brussels. 'It is pretended,' the prince told his brother (7 Jan. 1854), 'that I whisper [the tsar's orders] in Victoria's ear, she gets round old Aberdeen, and the voice of the only *English* minister, Palmerston, is not listened to—ay, he is always intrigued against, at the court and by the court' (Duke Ernest's *Memoirs*, ii. 46). The queen's husband, in fact, served as scapegoat for the ministry's vacillation. Honest men believed that he had exposed himself to the penalties of high treason, and they gravely doubted if the queen herself were wholly guiltless. The queen took the calumnies to heart, and Aberdeen, who was, she told Stockmar, 'all kindness,' sought vainly for a time to console her. 'In attacking the prince,' she pointed out to Aberdeen (4 Jan. 1854), 'who is one and the same with the queen herself, the throne is assailed, and she must say she little expected that any portion of her subjects would thus requite the unceasing labours of the prince.' The prime minister in reply spoke with disdain of 'these contemptible exhibitions of malevolence and faction,' but he admitted that the prince held an anomalous position which the constitution had not provided for. When the queen opened parliament on 31 Jan. she was well received, and the leaders of both sides—Lord Aberdeen and Lord Derby in the upper house and Lord John Russell and Spencer Walpole in the commons—emphatically repudiated the slanders on her and her husband. The tide of abuse thereupon flowed more sluggishly, and it was temporarily checked on 27 Feb. 1854, when the queen sent a message to the House of Lords announcing the breakdown of negotiations with Russia. War was formally declared next day, and France and Sardinia affirmed their readiness to fight at England's side. The popular criticism of the queen was unwarranted. Repulsive as the incidents of war were to her, and active as was her sympathy with the suffering that it entailed, she never ceased to urge her ministers and her generals, when war was actually in being, to press forward with dogged resolution and not to slacken their efforts until the final goal of victory was reached. Her attitude was characterised alike by dignity and common sense. She was generous in the encouragement she gave all ranks of the army and navy. For months she watched in person the departure of troops. On 10 March she inspected at Spithead the great fleet which was destined for the Baltic under Sir Charles Napier. At the opening of the conflict the government proposed a day of humiliation for the success of the British arms. The queen was not enthusiastic in favour of the proposal. She warned Aberdeen of the hypocrisy of self-abasement in the form of prayers, and at the same time she deprecated abuse of the enemy.

Some alleviation of anxiety was sought in the ordinary incidents of court life. On 12 May the queen, by way of acknowledging the alliance into which she had entered with the emperor, paid the French ambassador, Count Walewski, the high compliment of attending a *bal costumé* at the French embassy at Albert Gate. The queen alone wore ordinary evening dress. Next day she went to Woolwich to christen in her husband's honour a new battleship of enormous dimensions, the Royal Albert. In June the queen entertained for a month her cousin, the new king of Portugal, Pedro V, and his brother the Duke of Oporto, who afterwards succeeded to the throne. Their mother, in whom she was from her childhood deeply interested, had died in childbed seven months before (20 Nov. 1853). The queen showed the young men every attention, taking them with her to the opera, the theatre, and Ascot. A suggestion made to them that Portugal should join England in the Crimean war was reasonably rejected by their advisers. The chief spectacular event of the season was the opening by the queen at Sydenham, on 10 June, of the Crystal Palace, which had, much to the prince's satisfaction, been transferred from Hyde Park after the Great Exhibition. Through the summer the queen shared with a large section of the public a fear that the government was not pursuing the war with requisite energy. When Lord Aberdeen, in a speech in the House of Lords on 20 June, argumentatively defended Russia against violent assaults in the English press, the queen promptly reminded him of the misapprehensions that the appearance of lukewarmness must create in the public mind. Whatever were the misrepresentations of the tsar's policy, she said, it was at the moment incumbent on him to remember that 'there is enough in that policy to make us fight with all our might against it.' She and the prince incessantly appealed to the ministers to hasten their deliberations and to improve the organisation of the Crimean army. A hopeful feature of the situation was Napoleon III's zeal. In July the prince accepted the emperor's invitation to inspect with him the camp at St. Omer, where an army was fitting out for the Crimea. The meeting was completely successful, and the good relations of the rulers of the two countries were thus placed on a surer foundation. While at Balmoral in September the queen was elated to receive 'all the most interesting and gratifying details of the splendid and decisive victory of the Alma.' On leaving Balmoral (11 Oct.) she visited the docks at Grimsby and Hull, but her mind was elsewhere. From Hull (13 Oct.) she wrote to her uncle Leopold, 'We are, and indeed the whole country is, entirely engrossed with one idea, one anxious thought—the Crimea.' News of the victories of Inkermann (25 Oct.) and Balaclava (5 Nov.) did not entirely relieve her anxiety. 'Such a time of suspense,' she wrote on 7 Nov., 'I never expected to see, much less to *feel*.'

During the winter the cruel hardships which climate, disease, and failure of the commissariat inflicted on the troops strongly stirred public feeling. The queen initiated or supported all manner of voluntary measures of relief. With her own hands she made woollen comforters and mittens for the men. On New Year's day, 1855, she wrote to the commander-in-chief, Lord Raglan, expressing her sympathy with the army in its 'sad privations and constant sickness,' and entreated him to make the camps 'as comfortable as circumstances can admit of.' No details escaped her, and she especially called his attention to the rumour 'that the soldiers' coffee was given them green instead of roasted.' Although the queen and the prince grew every day more convinced of the defective administration of the war office, they were unflinchingly loyal to the prime minister, Lord Aberdeen, who was the target of much public censure. Before the opening of parliament in January 1855, by way of proof of their personal sympathy, she made him a knight of the garter. But it was beyond her power, had it been her wish, to prop the falling government. The session no sooner opened than Lord John insisted on seceding in face of the outcry against the management of the war. The blow was serious, and Lord Aberdeen was with difficulty persuaded by the queen to hold on. But complete shipwreck was not long delayed. On 29 Jan. the government was hopelessly defeated on a hostile motion for an inquiry into the management of the war. Aberdeen's retirement was inevitable, and it was obvious that the queen was face to face with the distasteful necessity of conferring the supreme power in the state on her old enemy, Palmerston. The situation called for all her fortitude. She took time before submitting. A study of the division lists taught her that Lord Derby's supporters formed the greater number of the voters who had destroyed Lord Aberdeen's ministry. She therefore, despite Aberdeen's warning, invited Lord Derby to assume the government. Derby explained to her that he could not without aid from other parties, and a day later he announced his failure to secure extraneous assistance. The queen then turned to the veteran whig, Lord Lansdowne, and bade him privately seek advice for her from all the party leaders. In the result she summoned Lord John Russell on the ground that his followers were in number and compactness second to Lord Derby's. But she could not blind herself to the inevitable result of the negotiations, and, suppressing her private feeling, she assured Lord John that she hoped Palmerston would join him. But she had not gone far enough. Lord John was not strong enough to accept the queen's commands. A continuance of the deadlock was perilous. The queen confided to her sympathetic friend Lord Clarendon her reluctance to take the next step, but he convinced her that she had no course but one to follow. He assured her that Palmerston would prove conciliatory if frankly treated. Thereupon she took the plunge and bade Palmerston form an administration. Palmerston's popular strength was undoubted, and resistance on the part of the crown was idle. As soon as the die was cast the queen with characteristic good sense indicated that she would extend her full confidence to her new prime minister. On 15 Feb. he wrote to his brother: 'I am backed by the general opinion of the whole country, and I have no reason to complain of the least want of cordiality or confidence on the part of the court.' To the queen's satisfaction Lord Aberdeen had persuaded most of his colleagues to serve temporarily under his successor, but within a few days the Peelite members of the old government went out, the unity of the government was assured, and Palmerston's power was freed of all restraint. Baseless rumours of the malign influence exerted by Prince Albert were still alive, but no doubt was permissible of the devoted energy with which the queen was promoting the relief of the wounded. In March she visited the hospitals at Chatham and Woolwich, and complained privately that she was not kept informed in sufficient detail of the condition and prospects of disabled soldiers on their return home. A new difficulty arose with the announcement on the part of Napoleon that he intended to proceed to the Crimea to take command of the French army there. His presence was certain to provoke complications in the command of the allied forces in the field. The emperor hinted that it might be well for him to discuss the project in person with the queen. She and her advisers at once acceded to the suggestion, and she invited him and the empress to pay her a state visit. On all sides she was thrown into association with men who had inspired her with distrust, but she cheerfully yielded her private sentiments at the call of a national crisis. The queen made every effort to give her guests a brilliant reception. She personally supervised every detail of the programme and drew up with her own hands the lists of guests who were to be commanded to meet them. On 16 April the emperor and empress reached Dover and proceeded through London to Windsor. Every elaborate formality that could mark the entertainment of sovereigns was strictly observed, and the emperor was proportionately impressed. The ordeal proved far less trying than the queen feared. At a great banquet in St. George's Hall on the evening of his arrival, the emperor won the queen's heart by his adroit flattery and respectful familiarity. She found him 'very quiet and amiable and easy to get on with.' There was a review of the household troops in Windsor Park next day, and on the 18th the queen bestowed on Napoleon the knighthood of the garter. A visit to Her

Majesty's opera house in the Haymarket on the 19th evoked a great display of popular enthusiasm, and amid similar manifestations the royal party went on the 20th to the Crystal Palace. On the 21st the visit ended, and with every sign of mutual goodwill the emperor left Buckingham Palace for Dover. Of 'the great event' the queen wrote: 'On all it has left a pleasant satisfactory impression.' The royal party had talked much of the war with the result that was desired. On 25 April the emperor wrote to the queen that he had abandoned his intention of going to the Crimea. But throughout the hospitable gaieties the ironies of fate that dog the steps of sovereigns were rarely far from the queen's mind. Three days before the emperor arrived, the widowed ex-queen of the French, who had fallen far from her high estate, visited her at Windsor, whence she drove away unnoticed in the humblest of equipages. After the great ball in the Waterloo room at Windsor, when she danced a quadrille with the emperor on the 17th, she noted in her diary, 'How strange to think that I, the granddaughter of George III, should dance with the Emperor Napoleon, nephew of England's great enemy, and now my nearest and most intimate ally, in the Waterloo room, and this ally, only six years ago, living in this country an exile, poor and unthought of!' Meanwhile peace proposals, which proved abortive, were under consideration at a conference of the powers at Vienna; but the queen was resolved that none but the best possible terms should be entertained by her ministers. Lord John represented England and M. Drouyn de Lhuys France, and when Lord John seemed willing to consider conditions that were to the queen unduly favourable to Russia she wrote peremptorily (25 April 1855) to Palmerston, 'How Lord John Russell and M. Drouyn can recommend such proposals for our acceptance is beyond her [our] comprehension.' In May the queen identified herself conspicuously with the national feeling by distributing with her own hands war medals to the returned soldiers on the Horse Guards' Parade (18 May). It was the queen's own suggestion, and it was the first time that the sovereign had performed such functions. 'The rough hand of the brave and honest private soldier came,' she said, 'for the first time in contact with that of their [his] sovereign and their [his] queen.' Later in the day she visited the riding school in Wellington barracks while the men were assembled at dinner. In the months that followed the queen and prince were indefatigable in exerting their influence against what they deemed unworthy concessions to Russia. From their point of view the resignation of Lord John on 16 July rendered the situation more hopeful. At the moment domestic distress was occasioned by an outbreak of scarlet fever in the royal household, which attacked the four younger children. On their recovery the queen and prince sought to strengthen the French alliance by paying the emperor a return visit at Paris. Following the example of Prince Albert, the emperor had organised a great 'Exposition,' which it was his desire that his royal friends should compare with their own. On 20 Aug., after parliament had been prorogued by commission, the queen travelled, with the prince, the prince of Wales, and the Princess Royal, from Osborne to Boulogne. There the emperor met them. By an accident they reached Paris rather late, but they passed through it in procession to the palace of St. Cloud, and Marshal Magnan declared that the great Napoleon was not so warmly received on his return from Austerlitz. The occasion was worthy of enthusiasm. It was the first time that an English sovereign had entered the French capital since the infant Henry VI went there to be crowned in 1422. The splendid festivities allowed the queen time for several visits, not merely to the Exposition, but to the historic buildings of Paris and Versailles. Their historical associations greatly interested her, especially those which recalled the tragedies— always fascinating to her—of Marie Antoinette or James II. Among the official celebrations were a review on the Champ de Mars of 45,000 troops, and balls of dazzling magnificence at the Hôtel de Ville and at Versailles. At the Versailles fête, on 25 Aug., the queen was introduced for the first time to Count (afterwards Prince) Bismarck, then Prussian minister at Frankfort, from whose iron will her host, and afterwards her daughter, were soon to suffer. The queen conversed with him in German with great civility. He thought that she was interested in him, but lacked sympathy with him. The impression was correct. On reaching Boulogne on her way to Osborne (27 Aug.) she was accorded a great military reception by the emperor, who exchanged with her on parting the warmest assurances of attachment to her, her husband, and her children. The anticipations of a permanent alliance between the two countries seemed at the moment likely to be fulfilled, but they quickly proved too sanguine. The political relations between Napoleon III and the queen were soon to be severely strained, and her faith in his sincerity to be rudely shaken. Yet his personal courtesies left an indelible impression on her. Despite her political distrust she constantly corresponded with her host in autograph letters in terms of a dignified cordiality until the emperor's death; and the sympathetic affection which had arisen between the queen and the Empress Eugénie steadily grew with time and the vicissitudes of fortune. The month (September–October) which was spent, as usual, at Balmoral was brightened by two gratifying incidents. On 10 Sept. there reached the queen news of the fall of Sebastopol, after a siege of nearly a year—a decisive triumph for British arms, which brought honourable peace well in sight. Prince Albert himself superintended the lighting of a bonfire on the top of a neighbouring cairn. The other episode appealed more directly to the queen's maternal feeling. The eldest son of the prince of Prussia (afterwards the Emperor Frederick I), who, attended by Count von Moltke, was at the time a guest at Balmoral, requested permission to propose marriage to the Princess Royal. She was barely sixteen, and he was twenty-four, but there were indications of a mutual affection. The manly goodness of the prince strongly appealed to the queen, and an engagement was privately made on 29 Sept. The public announcement was to be deferred till after the princess's confirmation next year. Prince Albert denied that the betrothal had any political significance. From the point of view of English politics it had at the instant little to recommend it. A close union between the royal families of London and Berlin was not likely to recommend itself to the queen's late host of Paris. To most English statesmen Prussia appeared to be on the downward grade; and although Prince Albert and the queen had faith in its future, they were personally disappointed by the incompetence of its present ruler, the uncle of their future son-in-law. He had deserted them in the recent war, but was still seeking their influence in Europe in his own interests in private letters to the queen, which he conjured her not to divulge in Downing Street or at the Tuileries. His pertinacity had grown so troublesome that, to avoid friction, she deemed it wisest to suppress his correspondence unanswered (Duke Ernest, vol. iii.). It was not surprising that, when the news of the betrothal leaked out, the public comments should be unpleasing to the court. The 'Times' on 3 Oct. denounced it with heat as an act of truckling 'to a paltry German dynasty.'

In November, when the court was again at Windsor, the queen extended her acquaintance among great kings and statesmen by receiving a visit from her second ally in the Crimea, Victor Emanuel, king of Sardinia, and his minister, Count Cavour, and the affairs of one more country of Europe were pressed upon her attention. The king's brother, the Duke of Genoa, had been her guest in 1852, and she had presented him with a riding-horse in words that he interpreted to imply sympathy with the efforts of Cavour and his master to unite Italy under a single king, and to purge the separate states of native tyranny or foreign domination (*ib.* iii. 22–3). Victor Emanuel had come to Windsor in effect to seek confirmation of his brother's version of the queen's sentiment, and to test its practical value. He had just been at the Tuileries, where Napoleon was encouraging, while Palmerston, now prime minister, was known to sympathise with the Italian aspiration. It was not opportune at the moment for Palmerston to promise material aid; while the prince, however deeply he deplored the misgovernment which it was sought to annul in Italy, deprecated any breach with Austria, which ruled in North Italy. He and the queen, moreover, dreaded the kindling of further war in Europe, in whatever cause. Victor Emanuel and Cavour therefore received from the queen cold comfort, but she paid the king every formal honour, despite his brusque and unrefined demeanour. He was invested with the garter on 5 Dec., and a great banquet was given him in St. George's Hall in the evening. When he departed the queen rose at four o'clock in the morning to bid him farewell. Meanwhile peace was arranged in Paris with Russia, and the queen opened parliament on 31 Jan. 1856 amid great rejoicing. On 30 March the treaty was signed and the encroachment of Russia on Turkey was checked. Napoleon had shown much supineness in the negotiations and seemed to be developing a tendency to conciliate the common enemy, Russia. But the queen exchanged hearty congratulations with him, and on 11 April she celebrated the general harmony by conferring the knighthood of the garter on Palmerston, to whom she acknowledged, with some natural qualifications, the successful issue to be mainly due. Henceforth the army, to a larger extent than before, was the queen's constant care. A visit to the military hospital at Chatham on 16 April was followed by a first visit to the newly formed camp at Aldershot. There the queen, for the first of many times, slept the night in the royal pavilion, and next day she reviewed eighteen thousand men. She was on horseback, and wore the uniform of a field-marshal with the star and riband of the garter. Shortly after she laid two foundation stones—of a new military (the Royal Victoria) hospital at Netley (19 May), and of Wellington College, Sandhurst, for the sons of officers (2 June). Much of the summer she spent in welcoming troops on their return from the war. On 7 and 8 June the queen, accompanied by her guests, the king of the Belgians and Prince Oscar of Sweden, inspected a great body of them at Aldershot, and addressed to them stirring words of thanks and sympathy. Thoroughly identifying herself with the heroism of her soldiers and sailors, she instituted a decoration for acts of conspicuous valour in war, to be known as the Victoria Cross (V.C.); the decoration carried with it a pension of 10l. a year. A list of the earliest recipients of the honour was soon drawn up, and the crosses were pinned by the queen herself on the breasts of sixty-two men at a great review in Hyde Park next year (26 June 1857). A melancholy incident had marked her visit to Aldershot on 8 June 1856. While the commander-in-chief, Lord Hardinge, was speaking to her he was seized by incurable paralysis, and had to vacate his post. An opportunity seemed thus presented to the queen of tightening the traditional bond between herself and the army, on which recent events had led her to set an enhanced value. Of no prerogative of the crown was the queen more tenacious than that which gave her a nominal control of the army through the commander-in-chief. It was a control that was in name independent of parliament, although that body claimed a concurrent authority over the military forces through the secretary of state for war. Parliament was in course of time, to the queen's dismay, to make its authority over the army sole and supreme, to the injury of her prerogative. But her immediate ambition was to confirm the personal connection between the army and herself. She therefore induced Palmerston to sanction the appointment of her cousin, George, duke of Cambridge, as commander-in-chief, in succession to Lord Hardinge (14 July 1856). The duke had held a command in the Crimea, and the queen's recent displays of attachment to the army rendered it difficult for her advisers to oppose her wish. But the choice was not in accord with public policy, and in practical effect ultimately weakened the military prerogative which she sought to strengthen. Public and private affairs justified a season of exceptional gaiety. The Princess Royal had been confirmed on 20 March and her betrothal became generally known, when in May Prince Frederick William, again accompanied by Von Moltke, paid the court another visit. The queen's spirits ran high. On 7 May she gave a great banquet to the leaders of both parties and their wives, and she was amused at the signs of discomfort which made themselves apparent. But Lord Derby told the prince that the guests constituted 'a happy family' (Malmesbury, *Memoirs*). Balls were incessant, and at them all the queen danced indefatigably. On 9 May the new ballroom and concert-room at Buckingham Palace, which Prince Albert had devised, was brought into use for the first time on the occasion of a ball in honour of the Princess Royal's *début*. On 27 May the queen attended a ball at the Turkish ambassador's, and, to the ambassador's embarrassment, chose him for her partner in the first country dance. At a ball in the Waterloo Gallery at Windsor on 10 June the queen danced every dance, and finally a Scottish reel to the bagpipes (Moltke, *Letters*, vol. i. passim; Malmesbury, *Memoirs*, pp. 380 sqq.). On 20 June she entertained Sir Fenwick Williams of Kars at Buckingham Palace. On 26 June the Duke of Westminster gave a great ball in her honour at Grosvenor House. On 9 July there was a state reception by her of the guards on their home-coming from the Crimea. From 10 to 28 Aug. the prince and princess of Prussia, the father and mother of her future son-in-law, were her guests, and later in the autumn the queen received at Balmoral Miss Florence Nightingale, to whom she had sent in the previous January a valuable memorial jewel. In November 1856 the family were plunged in mourning by the death of Prince Leiningen, the queen's half-brother and a companion of her youth.

The next year (1857) involved the queen in a new and great public anxiety, and the serious side of life oppressed her. Parliament was opened by commission on 3 Feb., and before the end of the month the country heard the first bitter cry of the Indian mutiny. Next month Palmerston was defeated in the House of Commons on Cobden's motion condemning his warlike policy in China. The queen, with characteristic reluctance, assented to his demand for a dissolution. His appeal to the country received a triumphant answer, and the new parliament assembled with a majority of seventy-nine in his favour—a signal tribute to his personal popularity. On 14 April the queen's youngest child, Princess Beatrice, was born at Buckingham Palace, and on the 30th the queen suffered much grief on the death of her aunt, the Duchess of Gloucester, the last surviving child of George III; 'we all looked upon her,' said the queen, 'as a sort of grandmother.' At the time the forthcoming marriage of her eldest daughter began to occupy her thoughts. On 16 May the betrothal was formally announced at Berlin, and on the 25th the queen sent a message to parliament asking for a provision for the princess. It was her earliest appeal to the nation for the pecuniary support of her children. The request was favourably entertained. The government proposed a dowry of 40,000*l.* and an annuity of 8,000*l.* Roebuck raised the objection that the marriage was an 'entangling alliance,' and opposed the grant of an annuity. Sir George Cornewall Lewis, the chancellor of the exchequer, called attention to the fact that the queen's recent expenses in connection with the French visits were defrayed out of her income, and that the eldest daughters of George II and George III each received a dowry of 80,000*l.* and an annuity of 5,000*l.* All parties finally combined to support the government's proposal, which found in its last stages only eighteen dissentients. The royal betrothal continued to be celebrated by brilliant and prolonged festivities. In June and July Prince Frederick William once more stayed at court, and Von Moltke, who was again his companion, declared the succession of gaieties to be overpowering. One day (15 June) there was a state visit to the Princess's Theatre to see Kean's spectacular production of Shakespeare's 'Richard II.' Next day the infant Princess Beatrice was baptised. On 11 June the Ascot ceremonies were conducted in full state, and among the royal guests was M. Achille Fould, the Paris banker and Napoleon III's minister of finance. On the 17th the whole court attended the first Handel festival at the Crystal Palace, when 'Judas Maccabeus' was performed; the royal company drove to and fro in nine four-in-hands. On the 18th a levee was followed by a state ball, in which the queen danced with unabated energy. Hardly a day passed without an elaborate ceremonial. On 26 June a military review took place in Hyde Park amid extraordinary signs of popular enthusiasm, and the first batch of Victoria crosses was distributed. From 29 June to 2 July the queen stayed with the Earl of Ellesmere at Worsley Hall to inspect the art treasures exhibition at Manchester. Next month she laid the foundation at Wandsworth Common of the Royal Victoria Patriotic Asylum for daughters of soldiers, sailors, and marines, and before the end of the month time was found for a visit to Aldershot. Royal personages from the continent thronged the queen's palaces. The king of the Belgians brought his daughter, the Princess Charlotte, and her *fiancé* the Archduke Maximilian of Austria, who was later to lay down his life in Mexico under heartrending circumstances. The prince of Hohenzollern, the queen of the Netherlands, and the Duke and Duchess of Montpensier all interested their royal hostess. She was gratified, too, on both personal and political grounds, by a short visit to Osborne of the Grand Duke Constantine of Russia, brother of the reigning tsar Alexander II. He had been invited to the Tuileries by Napoleon, who was ominously seeking every opportunity of manifesting goodwill to Russia, and the queen did not wish to be behind him in showing courtesies to her recent foes. The constant intercourse of the queen and the prince at this moment with the royal families of Europe led her to define her husband's rank more accurately than had been done before. On 25 June 1857, by royal letters patent, she conferred on him the title of prince consort. 'It was always a source of weakness,' the prince wrote, 'for the crown that the queen always appeared before the people with her *foreign* husband.' But it was doubtful whether this bestowal of a new name effectively removed the embarrassment. The 'Times' wrote sneeringly that the new title guaranteed increased homage to its bearer on the banks of the Spree and the Danube, but made no difference in his position anywhere else. Abroad it achieved the desired result. When on 29 July the prince attended at Brussels the marriage of the ill-fated Archduke Maximilian with the Princess Charlotte of Belgium, he was accorded precedence before the Austrian archdukes and immediately after the king of the Belgians. The English government still deemed it prudent to cultivate the French alliance, but the emperor's policy was growing enigmatic, and in the diplomatic skirmishes among the powers which attended the final adjustment, in accordance with the provisions of the treaty of Paris, of the affairs of the Balkan peninsula, he and the English government took opposite sides. The anxiety of the emperor to maintain good personal relations with the queen was the talisman which restored harmony. A few informal words with the queen, the emperor assured her ministers, would dissolve all difficulties. Accordingly he and the empress were invited to pay a private visit to Osborne, and they stayed there from 6 to 10 Aug. The French ministers, Walewski and Persigny, accompanied their master, and the queen was attended by Palmerston and Clarendon. The blandest cordiality characterised the discussion, but from the point of view of practical diplomacy advantage lay with the emperor. He had supported the contention of Russia and Sardinia that it was desirable to unite under one ruler the two semi-independent principalities of Wallachia and Moldavia. The English government supported Austria's desire to keep the two apart. Napoleon now agreed to the continued separation of the principalities; but in 1859, when they, by their own efforts, joined together and founded the dominion which was afterwards named Roumania, he insisted on maintaining the union. When the Osborne visit was ended affectionate compliments passed between the emperor and the queen in autograph letters, and the agreement was regarded as final. The queen wrote with ingenuous confidence of the isolation that characterised the position of a sovereign, but added that fortunately her ally, no less than herself, enjoyed the compensation of a happy marriage. The ostentatious activity with which the emperor was strengthening his armaments at Cherbourg hardly seemed promising for the continuance of such personal harmony, but the emperor paradoxically converted the warlike preparations which were going forward almost within hail of the English shore, into new links of the chain of amity which was binding the two royal families together. At his suggestion, within a fortnight of his leaving Osborne, the queen and the prince crossed in her yacht Victoria and Albert to Cherbourg on 19 Aug. in order to inspect the dockyard, arsenal, and fortifications. Every facility of examination was given them, but amid the civilities of the welcome the queen did not ignore the use to which those gigantic works might be put if England and France came to blows. The relations of the queen and emperor abounded in irony. Meanwhile the nation was in the throes of the Indian mutiny—a crisis more trying and harrowing than the recent war. Having broken out in the previous June, it was in August at its cruel height, and the queen, in common with all her subjects, suffered acute mental torture. She eagerly scanned the news from the disturbed districts, and, according to her wont, showered upon her ministers entreaties to do this and that in order to suppress the rebellion with all available speed. Palmerston resented the queen's urgency of counsel, and wrote (18 July) with unbecoming sarcasm, to which she was happily blind, how fortunate it was for him that she was not on the opposition side of the House of Commons. At the same time he reminded her that 'measures are sometimes best calculated to succeed which follow each other step by step.' The minister's cavils only stimulated the activity of her pen. She left Osborne for her autumn holiday at Balmoral on 28 Aug. Parliament was still sitting. Her withdrawal to the north before the prorogation excited adverse criticism, but throughout her sojourn at Balmoral little else except India occupied her mind. She vividly felt the added anxieties due to the distance and the difficulty of communication. Happily, just after the court left Scotland (on 16 Sept.) events took a more favourable turn. On 3 Dec., when the queen opened parliament in person, the mutiny was in process of extinction. The sudden death of the Duchess de Nemours in November at Claremont increased at the time the queen's depression. 'We were like sisters,' she wrote; 'bore the same name, married the same year, our children of the same age.' But the need of arranging for the celebration of her eldest daughter's marriage soon distracted her attention. As many as seventeen German princes and princesses accepted invitations to be present. The festivities opened on 19 Jan. 1858 with a state performance at Her Majesty's Theatre, when 'Macbeth' was performed, with Phelps and Miss Faucit in the chief parts, and was followed by Mr. and Mrs. Keeley's rendering of the farce of 'Twice Killed.' The wedding took place at St. James's Palace on the 25th, and eight days later the bride and bridegroom left England. The queen felt the parting severely, and dwelt upon her mixed feelings of joy and sorrow in her replies to the addresses of congratulation which poured in upon her. Before the queen quite reconciled herself to the separation from her daughter, she was suddenly involved in the perplexities of a ministerial crisis. The French alliance which Palmerston had initiated proved a boomerang and destroyed his government. On 15 Jan. an explosive bomb had been thrown by one Orsini, an Italian refugee, at the emperor and empress of the French while entering the Opera House in Paris, and though they escaped unhurt ten persons were killed and 150 wounded. It was soon discovered that the plot had been hatched in England, and that the bomb had been manufactured there. A strongly worded despatch from the French minister Walewski to Palmerston demanded that he should take steps to restrict the right of asylum in England which was hitherto freely accorded to foreign political malcontents. Addresses of congratulation to the emperor on his escape, which he published in the official 'Moniteur,' threatened England with reprisal. Palmerston ignored Walewski's despatch, but introduced a mild bill making conspiracy to murder, hitherto a misdemeanour, a felony. The step was approved by the queen, but it was denounced as a weak truckling to Palmerston's old friend Napoleon, and his bill was defeated on the second reading (19 Feb.). Thereupon he resigned. The queen begged him to reconsider the matter. Although she never derived much comfort from Palmerston, she had great faith in his colleague Clarendon, and it was on his account that she sought to keep the ministry in office; but Palmerston persisted in resigning, and she at once summoned Lord Derby. The queen, although she recognised the parliamentary weakness of a conservative government, was successful in urging him to attempt it. It gratified her that the brother of Sir Robert Peel, General Jonathan Peel, became secretary for war. 'His likeness to his deceased brother,' she wrote, 'in manner, in his way of thinking, and in patriotic feeling, is quite touching.' Friendly relations with France were easily re-established by the new ministry, and the queen was delighted by the emperor's choice of the eminent General Pélissier, Duc de Malakoff, to represent France at her court in place of Persigny, who was no favourite.

General Pélissier was constantly at court, and was much liked by all the royal family, and when he withdrew, on 5 March 1859, tears were shed on both sides. In June 1858 the prince consort paid a visit to his daughter and son-in-law in Germany, and on his return the queen, during exceptionally hot weather, which interfered with her comfort, made a royal progress to Birmingham to open the Aston Park. She and the prince stayed with Lord Leigh at Stoneleigh Abbey. The need of maintaining at full heat the French alliance again called them to France in August, when they paid a second visit to Cherbourg. The meeting of the sovereigns bore a somewhat equivocal aspect. The queen in her yacht was accompanied by a great escort of men-of-war, while nearly all the ships of the French navy stood by to welcome her. On landing at Cherbourg she joined the emperor in witnessing the formal opening of the new arsenal, and she climbed up the steep fort La Roule in order to survey the whole extent of the fortifications. The emperor pleasantly reminded the queen that a century before the English fleet had bombarded Cherbourg, but the cordiality between the two appeared unchanged, and the emperor repeated his confidence in the permanence of the Anglo-French alliance; the prince, however, thought the imperial ardour somewhat cooler than of old. From France the queen passed to Germany on a visit to her daughter. It was a long and interesting expedition, and she renewed personal intercourse with many friends and kinsmen. She and the prince landed at Antwerp, and at Malines met King Leopold, who travelled with them to Verviers. At Aix-la-Chapelle the prince of Prussia joined them. Thence they travelled to Hanover to visit the king and queen at Herrenhausen, where the queen delighted in the many memorials of her Hanoverian predecessors. Her daughter was residing at the castle of Babelsberg, about three miles from Potsdam, and there she arrived on 13 Aug. In the course of the next few days many visits were paid to Berlin, and the queen inspected the public buildings, the tomb of Frederick the Great, and the royal palaces of Sans Souci and Charlottenberg, and the Neues Palais. On the 27th she left for Cologne, and after a brief visit to places of interest she arrived at Osborne by way of Antwerp and Dover on the 31st. She and the prince soon left for the north, but they paused on the journey at Leeds to open the new town-hall. The foreign tour had not withdrawn the queen from important business at home. When she was setting out the country was excited by the completion of the laying of the first submarine cable between America and the United Kingdom, and the queen sent an elaborate message of congratulation over the wires to the president of the United States, James Buchanan. She described the enterprise as an additional link between nations whose friendship was founded upon common interest and reciprocal esteem. Unfortunately the cable soon ceased to work and the permanent connection was not established till 1861. During her stay in Germany, Indian affairs mainly occupied her government's attention. While the mutiny was in course of suppression parliament decided to abolish the old East India Company and to transfer its territories and powers to the crown. India was thenceforth to be administered by a secretary of state assisted by a council of fifteen. The queen set a high value on the new and direct connection which the measure created between India and herself. She felt that it added to the prestige of the monarchy, but in two details the queen deemed the bill to encroach on her prerogative. In the first place, the introduction of competitive examinations for appointments in the new Indian civil service cancelled the crown's power of nomination. In the second place, the Indian army was to be put under the authority of the Indian council. She insisted that her prerogative gave her control of all military forces of the crown through the commander-in-chief exclusively. She laid her objections before Lord Derby with her usual frankness, but the government had pledged itself to the proposed arrangements, and on Lord Derby threatening to resign if the queen pressed the points, she prudently dropped the first and waited for a more opportune moment for renewing discussion on the second. In 1860 it was decided to amalgamate the European forces in India with the home army. The act for the reorganisation of the Indian government received the royal assent on 2 Aug. 1858. Thereupon Lord Derby's cabinet drafted a proclamation to the people of India defining the principles which would henceforth determine the crown's relations with them. The queen was resolved that her first address to the native population should plainly set forth her personal interest in its welfare. She had thrown the whole weight of her influence against those who defended indiscriminate retaliatory punishment of the native population for the misdeeds of the mutiny. The governor-general, Lord Canning, who pursued a policy of conciliation, had no more sympathising adherent than the queen. 'The Indian people should know,' she had written to him in December 1857, 'that there is no hatred to a brown skin, none; but the greatest wish on their queen's part to see them happy, contented, and flourishing.' The draft proclamation which was forwarded to her at Babelsberg seemed to assert England's power with needless brusqueness, and was not calculated to conciliate native sentiment. Undeterred by the ill-success which had attended her efforts to modify those provisions in the bill which offended her, she now reminded the prime minister 'that it is a female sovereign who speaks to more than a hundred millions of eastern people on assuming the direct government over them, and after a bloody civil war, giving them pledges which her future reign is to redeem, and explaining the principles of her government. Such a document should breathe feelings of generosity, benevolence, and religious toleration, and point out the privilege which the Indians will receive in being placed on an equality with the subjects of the British crown, and the prosperity following in the train of civilisation' (Martin, iv. 49). She resented her ministers' failure to refer with sympathy to native religion and customs. The deep attachment which she felt to her own religion imposed on her, she said, the obligation of protecting all her subjects in their adherence to their own religious faith. She desired to give expression to her feelings of horror and regret at the mutiny, and her gratitude to God at its approaching end. She desired Lord Derby to rewrite the proclamation in what she described as 'his excellent language.'

The queen never brought her influence to bear on an executive act of government with nobler effect. The second draft, which was warmly approved by the queen, breathed that wise spirit of humanity and toleration which was the best guarantee of the future prosperity of English rule in India. Her suggestion was especially responsible for the magnificent passage in the proclamation the effect of which, from the point of view of both literature and politics, it would be difficult to exaggerate: 'Firmly relying ourselves on the truth of Christianity, and acknowledging with gratitude the solace of religion, we disclaim alike the right and the desire to impose our convictions on any of our subjects. We declare it to be our royal will and pleasure that none be in any wise favoured, none molested or disquieted by reason of their religious faith or observances, but that all shall alike enjoy the equal and impartial protection of the law; and we do strictly charge and enjoin all those who may be in authority under us that they abstain from all interference with the religious belief or worship of any of our subjects on pain of our highest displeasure.' Finally, the queen recommended the establishment of a new order of the star of India as a decorative reward for those native princes who were loyal to her rule, and such of her officials in the Indian government as rendered conspicuous service. The first investiture took place on 1 Nov. 1861. In the closing months of 1858 and the opening months of 1859 time forcibly reminded the queen of its passage. On 9 Nov. 1858 the prince of Wales, who had been confirmed on 1 April 1858, completed his eighteenth year. That age in the royal family was equivalent to a majority, and the queen in an admirable letter to her eldest son, while acknowledging that, in the interest of his own welfare, his discipline had been severe, now bade him consider himself his own master; she would always be ready to offer him advice if he wished it, but she would not intrude it. No sooner had she set her eldest son on the road to independence than she welcomed the first birth of that second generation of her family which before her death was to grow to great dimensions. On 27 Jan. 1859 a son and heir was born at Berlin to the Princess Royal. The child ultimately became the present

German emperor William II. For some time the princess's condition caused anxiety to her family, but the crisis happily passed. The queen thus became a grandmother at the age of thirty-nine. Congratulations poured in from every quarter. Among the earliest and the warmest greetings came one from Napoleon III, and the queen in her acknowledgment took occasion solemnly to urge him to abide in the paths of peace. The persistency with which he continued to increase his armaments had roused a widespread suspicion that he was preparing to emulate the example of his great predecessor. For a time it seemed doubtful in which direction he would aim his first blow. But when the queen's first grandson was born, she knew that her gentle-spoken ally was about to challenge the peace of Europe by joining the king of Sardinia in an endeavour to expel Austria from Lombardy and Venetia, and thereby to promote the unity of Italy under the kingship of the royal house of Sardinia. The emperor accepted the queen's pacific counsel in good part, but at the same time wrote to her in defence of the proposed war. On 3 Feb. she opened parliament in person and read with emphasis those passages in her speech which delared that England would be no party to the Emperor Napoleon's ambitious designs. Before the end of April the queen's hopes of peace were defeated by the unexpected action of Austria, which, grasping its nettle, declared war on Sardinia. Napoleon at once entered the field with his ally of Italy. The queen and the prince were harassed by fear of a universal war. Popular feeling in England in regard to the struggle that was in progress was entirely distasteful to them. English public sentiment regarded Sardinia as the courageous challenger of absolutist tyranny. Napoleon was applauded for rendering Sardinia assistance. The queen and the prince, on the other hand, while they deplored Austria's precipitancy, cherished sympathy with her as a German power, whose fortunes appeared to affect immediately those of her neighbour, Prussia. Affection for her newly married daughter redoubled the queen's desire for the safety of Prussia. Her son-in-law had risen a step nearer the Prussian throne in 1858, when the king, his uncle, had, owing to failing health, been superseded by his father, the prince of Prussia, who became prince-regent. The change of rule greatly increased the influence that Prince Albert could exert on Prussia, for the new ruler was an old friend of his and of the queen, and, having much faith in the prince's judgment, freely appealed to them for confidential counsel. It was now for the prince-regent of Prussia to decide whether the safety of his dominions required him to throw in his lot with Austria. The English court, mainly moved by a desire to protect their daughter from the consequences of strife, besought him to stand aside. He assented, and the queen turned to Napoleon to persuade him to keep hostilities within a narrow compass. When the empress of the French sent her birthday congratulations on 25 May, she in reply entreated her to persuade her husband to localise the war. The prompt triumph of the French arms achieved that result, and, to the queen's relief, although not without anxiety, she learned that the two emperors were to meet at Villafranca to negotiate terms of peace. The queen's fears of the sequel were greatly increased by the change of government which took place during the progress of the war. On 1 April Lord Derby's government, which in the main held her views in regard to the foreign situation, was defeated on its reform bill. She declined to accept the ministers' resignation, but assented to the only alternative, dissolution of parliament. The elections passed off quietly, but left the conservatives in a minority of forty-three. On 10 June the ministers were attacked and defeated, and, to the queen's disappointment, she saw herself compelled to accept Lord Derby's resignation. Again Palmerston was the conservative leader's only practicable successor. But it was repugnant to the queen to recall him to power at the existing juncture in foreign politics. His sympathy with Italy and his antipathy to Austria were alike notorious. Lord John Russell, too, had identified himself with Italian interests. On 11 June she therefore invited Lord Granville, a comparatively subordinate member of the party, to extricate her from her difficulties by forming a government. To him she was personally attached, and he was calculated to prove more pliable than his older colleagues. In autograph letters addressed to Palmerston and Lord John, which Granville was charged to deliver, she requested those veterans to serve under him. Her action was mortifying to both, and by accident involved her and them in even more embarrassment than could have been anticipated. Owing to some indiscreet talk of Lord Granville with a friend, a correct report of the queen's conversation with him appeared in the 'Times' next day (12 June). She was in despair. 'Whom am I to trust?' she said; 'these were my own very words.' In the result Palmerston genially agreed to accept Granville's leadership, but Lord John refused to hear of it; and Lord Granville withdrew from the negotiation. The queen was thus compelled to appeal to Palmerston, and to accept him as her prime minister for the second time. Before his ministry was constituted she suffered yet another disappointment. Lord John insisted on taking the foreign office, and, as a consequence, Lord Clarendon, her trusted friend, who had good claims to the post, was excluded from the government. Her forebodings of difficulties with her new ministers were justified. At the hands of Lord John, as foreign minister, she endured hardly fewer torments than Palmerston had inflicted on her when he held that office. Lord John and his chief at once avowed a resolve to serve the interests of Italy at the expense of Austria, and won, in the inner circle of the court, the sobriquet of 'the old Italian masters.' At the same time the course of the negotiations between Napoleon and the emperor of Austria was perplexing alike to the queen and to her ministers. Napoleon had at Villafranca arranged mysterious terms with the emperor of Austria which seemed to the friends of Italy far too favourable to Austria, although they gave France no advantage. Austria was to lose Lombardy, but was to retain Venetia. France protested unwillingness to take further part in the matter. Sardinia was recommended to rely on her own efforts to obtain whatever other changes she sought in the adjustment of Italy. So barren a result was unsatisfactory to all Italian liberals, and was deemed by Palmerston and Lord John to be grossly unjust to them. They opened diplomatic negotiations with a view to a modification of the proposed treaty, and to the encouragement of the Italians to fight their battle out to the end. The queen, who was relieved by the cessation of hostilities and by the easy terms offered to Austria, stoutly objected to her ministers' intervention. 'We did not protest against the war,' she told Lord John; 'we cannot protest against the peace.' She insisted that the cry 'Italy for the Italians,' if loudly raised by the government, would compel this country to join Sardinia in war. But Palmerston and Lord John were unmoved by her appeals. Palmerston declared that, if their advice were not acted on, their resignations would follow. In August, when the vacation had scattered the ministers, the queen insisted on the whole cabinet being summoned, so that they might realise her unconquerable determination to observe a strict neutrality. Palmerston affected indifference to her persistency, but Italian affairs were suffered to take their own course without English intervention. Yet the outcome was not agreeable to the queen. As soon as the treaty of Villafranca was signed, Sardinia, aided by Garibaldi, sought at the sword's point, without foreign aid, full control of the independent states of the peninsula outside Rome and Venetia. Although she was aware of the weakness of their cause, the queen could not resist sympathy with the petty Italian rulers who were driven by Sardinia from their principalities. The Duchess of Parma, one of the discrowned sovereigns, appealed to the queen for protection. Lord John, whose stolidity in such matters widened the breach between him and the queen, drew up a cold and bald refusal, which she declined to send. Lord Clarendon, however, was on a visit to her at the moment, and by his advice she gave her reply a more sympathetic tone, without openly defying her ministers. At the same time, with Sardinia's reluctant assent, Napoleon annexed Savoy and Nice to France as the price of his benevolent service to Italy in the past, and by way of a warning that he would tolerate no foreign intrusion while the internal struggle for Italian unity was proceeding. The queen viewed this episode with especial disgust. That Napoleon should benefit from the confusion into which, in her eyes, he had wantonly thrown southern

Europe roused her indignation to its full height. She bitterly reproached her ministers, whom she suspected of secret sympathy with him, with playing into his hands. Her complaint was hardly logical, for she had herself urged on them the strictest neutrality. On 5 Feb. 1860 she wrote to Lord John, 'We have been made regular dupes, which the queen apprehended and warned against all along.' Her hope that Europe would stand together to prevent the annexation was unavailing, and she wrathfully exclaimed against maintaining further intercourse with France. 'France,' she wrote to her uncle (8 May 1860), 'must needs disturb every quarter of the globe, and try to make mischief, and set every one by the ears. Of course this will end some day in a general crusade against the universal disturber of the world.' But her wrath cooled, and her future action bore small trace of it. In 1860 the ministry gave her another ground for annoyance by proposing to abolish the post of commander-in-chief, and to bring the army entirely under the control of parliament through the secretary of state. She protested with warmth against the change as an infringement of her prerogative, and for the moment the scheme was dropped. Apart from political questions her life still knew no cloud. Her public duties continued to bring her into personal relations with the army which were always congenial to her. On 29 Jan. 1859 she opened Wellington College for the sons of officers, an institution of which she had already laid the foundation-stone. On 6 June she once more distributed Victoria crosses. On 26 Aug. she inspected at Portsmouth the 32nd regiment, whence the heroes of Lucknow had been drawn. To meet surprises of invasion a volunteer force was called into existence by royal command in May 1859, and to this new branch of the service the queen showed every favour. She held a special levee of 2,500 volunteer officers at St. James's Palace on 7 March 1860, and she reviewed twenty thousand men in Hyde Park on 23 June. Her brother-in-law, Duke Ernest, who accompanied her on the occasion, did not conceal his contempt for the evolutions of her citizen soldiers, but she was earnest in her commendation of their zeal. On 2 July 1860 she personally inaugurated the National Rifle Association, which was a needful complement of the volunteer movement, and in opening its first annual meeting on Wimbledon Common she fired the first shot at the targets from a Whitworth rifle. She at once instituted the queen's prize of the value of 250l., which was awarded annually till the end of her reign. When on the way to Balmoral in August 1860 she stayed at Holyrood in order to review the Scottish volunteer forces.

Domestic life proceeded agreeably. Twice in 1859 her daughter, the Princess Royal, visited her, on the second occasion with her husband. During the autumn sojourn at Balmoral of that year the queen was exceptionally vigorous, making many mountaineering expeditions with her children. The prince consort presided over the meeting of the British Association at Aberdeen in September 1859, and afterwards invited two hundred of the members to be the queen's guests at a highland gathering on Deeside. On her way south she opened the Glasgow waterworks at Loch Katrine, and made a tour through the Trossachs. She also paid a visit to Colonel Douglas Pennant, M.P., at Penrhyn Castle, near Bangor, and was well received by the workmen at the Penrhyn slate quarries. During the season of next year, when she opened parliament in person (24 Jan., 1860), her guests included the king of the Belgians and the young German princes, Louis of Hesse-Darmstadt and his brother. She looked with silent favour on the attentions which Prince Louis paid her second daughter, the Princess Alice, who was now seventeen, and, although she deprecated so early a marriage, awaited the result with interest. At the same time the queen and prince were organising a tour for the prince of Wales through Canada and the United States, which promised well for the good relations of England and the United States. President Buchanan, in a letter to the queen, invited the prince to Washington, an invitation which she accepted in an autograph reply.

In the late autumn of 1860 the royal family paid a second visit to Coburg. A main inducement was to converse once more with Stockmar, who had since 1857 lived there in retirement owing to age and failing health. The queen and the prince were still actively corresponding with him, and were as dependent as ever on his counsel. On 22 Sept., accompanied by Princess Alice and attended by Lord John Russell, they embarked at Gravesend for Antwerp. On the journey they were distressed by the intelligence of the death of the prince consort's stepmother, with whom they had both cherished a sympathetic intimacy. While passing through Germany they were joined by members of the Prussian royal family, including their son-in-law. At Coburg they met their daughter and her first-born son, with whom his grandmother then made her first acquaintance. On 29 Sept. they removed to Rosenau. Among the guests there was Gustav Freytag, the German novelist, who interested the queen, and described in his reminiscences her 'march-like gait' and affable demeanour (Gustav Freytag, *Reminiscences*, Eng. Trans. 1890, vol. ii.). On 1 Oct. the prince met with an alarming carriage accident (cf. Lord Augustus Loftus, *Reminiscences*, 1st ser. ii. 89). The queen, though she suppressed her emotion, was gravely perturbed, and by way of thank-offering instituted at Coburg, after her return home, a Victoria-Stift (i.e. foundation), endowing it with 1,000l. for the assistance of young men and women beginning life. Happily the prince sustained slight injury, but the nervous depression which followed led his friend Stockmar to remark that he would fall an easy prey to illness. When walking with his brother on the day of his departure (10 Oct.) he completely broke down, and sobbed out that he would never see his native land again (Duke Ernest's *Memoirs*, iv. 55). On the return journey the prince and princess of Prussia entertained the queen and the prince at the palace of Coblenz, where slight illness detained the queen for a few days. Lord John Russell and Baron von Schleinitz, the German minister, spent the time in political discussion, partly in regard to a trifling incident which was at the moment causing friction between the two countries. An English traveller, Captain Macdonald, had been imprisoned by the mistake of an over-zealous policeman at Bonn. No settlement was reached by Lord John. Afterwards Palmerston used characteristically strong language in a demand for reparation. A vexatious dispute followed between the two governments, and the queen and the prince were displeased by the manner in which the English ministers handled it. The queen wisely avoided all open expression of opinion, but shrewdly observed that, 'although foreign governments were often violent and arbitrary, our people are apt to give offence and to pay no regard to the laws of the country.' The discussion was gradually dropped, and when, on 2 Jan. 1861, the death of the paralysed Frederick William IV placed the queen's friend, the prince-regent of Prussia, finally on the throne of Prussia as King William I, and her son-in-law and her daughter then became crown prince and princess, the queen believed that friendship between the two countries, as between the two courts, was permanently assured. Her wrath with Napoleon, too, was waning. A private visit to Windsor and Osborne from the Empress Eugénie, who had come in search of health, revived the tie of personal affection that bound her to the queen, and the new year (1861) saw the customary interchange of letters between the queen and Napoleon III. English and French armies had been engaged together in China. But the main burden of the queen's greeting to the emperor was an appeal for peace.

A further source of satisfaction sprang from the second visit which Prince Louis of Hesse paid to Windsor in November 1860, when he formally betrothed himself to Princess Alice (30 Nov.).Christmas and New Year 1860–1 were kept at Windsor with unusual spirit, although the death of Lord Aberdeen on 14 Dec. was a cause of grief. Among the many guests were both Lord Palmerston and Mr. Disraeli with his wife. The queen and prince had much talk with Disraeli, of whose growing influence they took due account, and they were gratified by his assurance that his followers might be relied on to support a national policy. On more personal questions he was equally complacent. He readily agreed to support the government in granting a dowry of 30,000*l*. and an annuity of 3,000*l*. to Princess Alice on her approaching marriage. On 4 Feb. 1861 the queen opened parliament in person, and herself announced the happy event. It was the last occasion on which she delivered with her own voice the speech from the throne. On 10 Feb. she kept quietly at Buckingham Palace the twenty-first anniversary of her marriage. 'Very few,' she wrote to her uncle Leopold, 'can say with me that their husband at the end of twenty-one years is not only full of the friendship, kindness, and affection which a truly happy marriage brings with it, but of the same tender love as in the very first days of our marriage.' But death was to destroy the mainspring of her happiness within the year. The queen passed to the crowning sorrow of her life through a lesser grief, which on its coming tried her severely. On 16 March her mother, who kept her youthful spirit and cheerfulness to the last, and especially delighted in her grandchildren, died at Frogmore after a brief illness. It was the queen's first experience of death in the inmost circle of her family. Princess Alice, who was with her at the moment, first gave proof of that capacity of consolation which she was often afterwards to display in her mother's future trials. Although she was much broken, the queen at once sent the sad news in her own hand to her half-sister, to the princess royal, and to King Leopold. Expressions of sympathy abounded, and the general sentiment was well interpreted by Disraeli, who said in his speech in the House of Commons, in seconding a vote of condolence: 'She who reigns over us has elected, amid all the splendours of empire, to establish her life on the principle of domestic love.'

The duchess's body was laid on 25 March in St. George's Chapel, Windsor. The queen resolved that a special mausoleum should be built at Frogmore for a permanent burial-place, and the remains were removed thither on 17 Aug. The queen's behaviour to all who were in any way dependent on her mother was exemplary. She pensioned her servants; she continued allowances that the Duchess of Kent had made to the Princess Hohenlohe and her sons Victor and Edward Leiningen. To the duchess's lady-in-waiting, Lady Augusta Bruce, sister of Lord Elgin, who had shown great devotion, the queen was herself much attached, and she at once made her her own bedchamber woman in permanent attendance upon her.

The mourning at court put an end for the time to festivities, and some minor troubles added to the queen's depression. In May, when Prince Louis of Hesse visited Osborne, he fell ill of measles. On 14 July the queen was shocked by news of the attempted assassination at Baden of her friend the king of Prussia. But she gradually resumed the hospitalities and activities of public life. Before the end of the season she entertained the king of the Belgians and the crown prince and princess of Prussia, the king and Prince Oscar of Sweden, and the ill-fated Archduke and Archduchess Maximilian. On 21 Aug. the queen, with the prince consort, the Princesses Alice and Helena, and Prince Arthur, set out from Osborne to pay Ireland a third visit. The immediate inducement was to see the prince of Wales, who was learning regimental duties at the Curragh camp. The royal party travelled by railway from Southampton to Holyhead, and crossed to Kingstown in the royal yacht. The queen took up her residence in the Viceregal Lodge in Phœnix Park on the 22nd. On Saturday the 24th she went to the Curragh to review a force of ten thousand men, among whom her eldest son held a place. On the 26th the queen and her family went south, travelling to Killarney and taking up their residence at Kenmare House. They were received by the people of the district with every mark of enthusiasm. Next day they explored the lakes of Killarney, and removed in the evening to Muckross Abbey, the residence of Mr. Herbert. Among the queen's guests there was James O'Connell, brother of Daniel O'Connell the agitator, with other members of the agitator's family. A stag hunt, which proved abortive, was organised for the enjoyment of the royal party. On the 29th the queen left Killarney for Dublin and Holyhead on her way to Balmoral. Nearly thirty-nine years were to pass before the queen visited Ireland again for the fourth and last time. At Balmoral she occupied herself mainly with outdoor pursuits. On 4 Sept., to her delight, she was joined by her half-sister, the Princess Leiningen, who came on a long visit. Near the end of October, on the journey south, a short halt was made at Edinburgh to enable the prince consort to lay the foundation-stones of a new post office and the industrial museum of Scotland (22 Oct.). Windsor Castle was reached the next morning. This was the last migration of the court which the prince consort was destined to share. As usual, guests were numerous at Windsor in November, but the deaths of Sir James Graham and of Pedro V of Portugal and his brother Ferdinand damped the spirits of host and hostess. In the middle of November signs that the prince's health was failing became obvious. A year before he had had an attack of English cholera, and he suffered habitually from low fever. Though the queen was solicitous, she, like most persons in robust health, was inclined to take a hopeful view of his condition, and not until the last did she realise that a fatal issue was impending. A serious political crisis suddenly arose to absorb her attention, and for the last time she, under her husband's advice, brought personal influence to bear on her ministers in the interests of the country's peace. In April the civil war in America had broken out, and the queen had issued a proclamation of neutrality. Public opinion in England was divided on the merits of the two antagonists, but the mass of the people favoured the confederation of the south. Palmerston, the prime minister, Gladstone, and many of their colleagues made no secret of their faith in the justice of the cause of the south. In November the prevailing sentiment seemed on the point of translating itself into actual war with the north. Two southern envoys, named respectively Mason and Slidell, had been despatched by the southern confederates to plead their cause at the English and French courts. They had run the federals' blockade of the American coast, and, embarking on the Trent, an English steamer, at Havana, set sail in her on 8 Nov. Next day a federal ship-of-war fired at the Trent. The federal captain (Wilkes) boarded her after threatening violence, and captured the confederate envoys with their secretaries. On 27 Nov. the Trent arrived at Southampton, and the news was divulged in England. On 30 Nov. Palmerston forwarded to the queen the draft of a despatch to be forwarded to Washington. In peremptory and uncompromising terms the English government demanded immediate reparation and redress. The strength of Palmerston's language seemed to place any likelihood of an accommodation out of question. The prince consort realised the perils of the situation. He did not share the prime minister's veneration of the southerners, and war with any party in the United States was abhorrent to him. He at once suggested, in behalf of the queen, gentler phraseology, and in spite of his rapidly developing illness wrote to Lord Palmerston for the queen (1 Dec.) urging him to recast the critical despatch so that it might disavow the belief that the assault on the Trent was the deliberate act of the government of the United States. Let the prime minister assume that an over-zealous officer of the federal fleet had made an unfortunate error which could easily be repaired by 'the restoration of the unfortunate passengers and a suitable apology.' This note to Palmerston 'was the last thing' the prince 'ever wrote,' the queen said afterwards, and it had the effect its author desired. The English government had a strong case. The emperor of the French, the emperor of Austria, the king of Prussia, and the emperor of Russia expressed themselves in full sympathy with England. But Palmerston and Russell willingly accepted the prince consort's correction. They substituted his moderation for their virulence, with the result that the government of Washington assented cheerfully to their demands. Both in England and America it was acknowledged that a grave disaster was averted by the prince's tact.But he was never to learn of his victory. He already had a presentiment that he was going to die, and he did not cling to life. He had none of the queen's sanguineness or elasticity of temperament, and of late irremovable gloom had oppressed him. During the early days of December he gradually sank, and on the 14th he passed away unexpectedly in the queen's presence. Almost without warning the romance of the queen's life was changed into a tragedy.

At the time of the prince's death, her daughter Alice and her stepsister the Princess Hohenlohe were with her at Windsor, and all the comfort that kindred could offer they gave her in full measure. Four days after the tragic event she drove with Princess Alice to the gardens at Frogmore, and chose a site for a mausoleum, where she and her husband might both be buried together. Her uncle Leopold took control of her immediate action, and at his bidding she reluctantly removed to Osborne next day. In the course of the 20th she mechanically signed some papers of state. At midnight her brother-in-law, Duke Ernest, reached Osborne, and, dissolved in tears, she at once met him on the staircase. On 23 Dec., in all the panoply of state, the prince's remains were temporarily laid to rest in St. George's Chapel, Windsor. The prince of Wales represented her as chief mourner. Early in January her uncle Leopold came to Osborne to console and counsel her. No heavier blow than the prince's removal could have fallen on the queen. Rarely was a wife more dependent on a husband. More than fifteen years before she had written to Stockmar (30 July 1846), in reference to a few days' separation from the prince: 'Without him everything loses its interest . . . it will always be a terrible pang for me to separate from him even for two days, and I pray God never to let me survive him.' Now that the permanent separation had come, the future spelt for her desolation. As she wrote on a photograph of a family group, consisting of herself, her children, and a bust of the prince consort, 'day for her was turned into night' (Lady Bloomfield, ii. 148).

Her tragic fate appealed strongly to the sympathies of her people, who mourned with her through every rank. 'They cannot tell what I have lost,' she said; but she was not indifferent to the mighty outburst of compassion. Personal sympathy with her in her bereavement was not, however, all that she asked. She knew that the exalted estimate she had formed of her husband was not shared by her subjects, and as in his lifetime, so to a greater degree after his death, she yearned for signs that he had won her countrymen's and countrywomen's highest esteem. 'Will they do him justice now?' she cried, as, in company with her friend the Duchess of Sutherland, she looked for the last time on his dead face. Praise of him was her fullest consolation, and happily it was not denied her. The elegiac eulogy with which Tennyson prefaced his 'Idylls of the King,' within a month of the prince's death, was the manner of salve that best soothed 'her aching, bleeding heart.' The memorials and statues that sprang up in profusion over the land served to illumine the gloom that encircled her, and in course of years she found in the task of supervising the compilation of his biography a potent mitigation of grief. Public opinion proved tractable, and ultimately she enjoyed the satisfaction of an almost universal acknowledgment that the prince had worked zealously and honestly for the good of his adopted country. But, despite the poignancy of her sorrow, and the sense of isolation which thenceforth abode with her, her nerve was never wholly shattered. Naturally and freely as she gave vent to her grief, her woe did not degenerate into morbid wailing. One of its most permanent results was to sharpen her sense of sympathy, which had always been keen, with the distresses of others, especially with distresses resembling her own; no widow in the land, in whatever rank of life, had henceforth a more tender sympathiser than the queen. As early as 10 Jan. 1862 she sent a touching message of sympathy with a gift of 200*l.* to the relatives of the victims of a great colliery explosion in Northumberland. In the days following the prince's death, the Princess Alice and Sir Charles Phipps, keeper of her privy purse, acted as intermediaries between her and her ministers, but before the end of the first month her ministers reminded her that she was bound to communicate with them directly. Palmerston at the moment was disabled by gout, and the cabinet was under the somewhat severe and pedantic control of Lord John Russell. The reproof awoke the queen to a sense of her position. Gradually she controlled her anguish, and resigned herself to her fate. She had lost half her existence. Nothing hereafter could be to her what it had once been. No child could fill the place that was vacant. But she did not seek to ease herself of her burden. She steeled herself to bear it alone. Hitherto the prince, she said, had thought for her. Now she would think for herself. His example was to be her guide. The minute care that he had bestowed with her on affairs of state she would bestow. Her decisions would be those that she believed he would have taken. She would seek every advantage that she could derive from the memory of his counsel. Nothing that reminded her of him was disturbed—no room that he inhabited, scarcely a paper that he had handled. The anniversary of his death was henceforth kept as a solemn day of rest and prayer, and the days of his birth, betrothal, and marriage were held in religious veneration. She never ceased to wear mourning for him; she long lived in seclusion, and took no part in court festivities or ceremonial pageantry. Now that the grave had closed over her sole companion and oracle of one-and-twenty years, she felt that a new reign had begun, and must in outward aspect be distinguished from the reign that had closed. But the lessons that the prince had taught her left so deep an impression on her, she clung so tenaciously to his spirit, that her attitude to the business of state and her action in it during the forty years that followed his death bore little outward sign of change from the days when he was perpetually at her side. In the 'two dreadful first years of loneliness' that followed the prince's death the queen lived in complete seclusion, dining often by herself or with her half-sister, and seeing only for any length of time members of her own family. But her widowhood rendered her more dependent than before on her personal attendants, and her intimacy with them gradually grew greater. Of the female members of her household on whose support she rested, the chief was Lady Augusta Bruce, and on her marriage to Dean Stanley on 23 Dec. 1863, congenial successors to Lady Augusta were found in Jane Marchioness of Ely, who had been a lady of the bedchamber since 1857 and filled that office till 30 April 1889, and in Jane Lady Churchill, who was a lady of the bedchamber from 4 July 1854 and remained in attendance on the queen till her sudden death on Christmas day 1900—less than a month before the queen herself died. Even from the lower ranks of her household she welcomed sympathy and proofs of personal attachment. She found Scotsmen and Scotswomen of all classes, but especially of the humbler, readier in the expression of kindly feeling than Englishmen and Englishwomen. When she paid, in May 1862, the first painful visit of her widowhood to Balmoral, her reception was a real solace to her. Her Scottish chaplain, Dr. Norman Macleod, gave her more real consolation than any clergyman of the south. She found a satisfaction in employing Scots men and women in her domestic service. John Brown, a son of a farmer on her highland estate, had been an outdoor servant at Balmoral since 1849, and had won the regard of the prince and herself. She soon made him a personal retainer, to be in constant attendance upon her in all the migrations of the court. He was of rugged exterior and uncourtly manners, but she believed in his devotion to her and in his strong common sense, and she willingly pardoned in him the familiarity of speech and manner which old servants are in the habit of acquiring. She took all his brothers into her service, and came to regard him as one of her trustiest friends. In official business she derived invaluable assistance in the early years of her widowhood from those who were filling more dignified positions in her household. The old objections to the appointment of a private secretary to the queen, now that the prince who had acted in that capacity was no more, were not revived, and it was at once conferred without debate on General the Hon. Charles Grey, a younger son of the second Earl Grey, who had been since 1846 private secretary to the prince, and whose sister, Lady Caroline Barrington, was since 1851 the governess of the royal children. Some differences of opinion were held outside court circles as to his tact and judgment, but until his death in 1870 his devotion to his work relieved the queen of much pressing anxiety. She also reposed full confidence in Sir Charles Phipps, keeper of the privy purse, who died in 1866, and in Sir Thomas Biddulph, who was master of her household from 1851, and after 1867 sole keeper of the privy purse until his death in 1878. No three men could have served her more single-mindedly than Grey, Phipps, and Biddulph. She was especially fortunate, too, in General Sir Henry Ponsonby, Grey's successor as private secretary, who, as equerry to the prince consort, had been brought within the sphere of influence which the queen deemed the best inspiration for her advisers. Sir Henry remained her secretary for the long period of a quarter of a century—8 April 1870 to May 1895, when he was succeeded by her last private secretary, Colonel Sir

Arthur Bigge. Outside her household she derived much benefit from the counsel of Gerald Wellesley, son of Lord Cowley, and nephew of the Duke of Wellington, who had been her domestic chaplain since 1849, and was dean of Windsor from 1854 until his death in 1882. She was often in consultation with him, particularly in regard to the church appointments which her ministers suggested to her. In one direction only did the queen relieve herself of any of her official work on the prince's death. It had been her custom to sign (in three places) every commission issued to officers in all branches of the military service, but she had fallen into arrears with the labour of late years, and sixteen thousand documents now awaited her signature. In March 1862 a bill was introduced into parliament enabling commissions to be issued without bearing her autograph, though her right of signing was reserved in case she wished to resume the practice, as she subsequently did.

Public business, in accordance with her resolve, occupied her almost as soon as her husband was buried. On 9 Jan. 1862 she received the welcome news that the authorities at Washington had solved the difficulty of the Trent by acceding to the requests of the English government. She reminded Lord Palmerston that 'this peaceful issue of the American quarrel was greatly owing to her beloved prince,' and Palmerston considerately replied that the alterations in the despatch were only one of innumerable instances 'of the tact and judgment and the power of nice discrimination which excited Lord Palmerston's constant and unbounded admiration.' A day or two later she assented to Palmerston's proposal to confer the garter on Lord Russell, though she would not hear of a chapter of the order being held, and insisted on conferring the distinction by warrant. On 11 Jan. she presided over a meeting of her privy council. Two plans of domestic interest which the prince had initiated she at once carried to completion. It had been arranged that the prince of Wales should make a tour to the Holy Land with Dr. A. P. Stanley, the late prince's chaplain. In January 1862 the queen finally settled the tour with Stanley, who visited her at Osborne for the purpose, and from 6 Feb. till 14 June her eldest son was absent from her on the expedition. There was some inevitable delay in the solemnisation of the marriage of Princess Alice, but it was quietly celebrated at Osborne on 1 July. The queen was present in deep mourning. Her brother-in-law, the Duke of Saxe-Coburg, gave the princess away. The queen felt acutely the separation from the daughter who had chiefly stood by her in her recent trial. During the autumn visit to Balmoral (21 Aug. 1862) the queen laid the foundations of a cairn 'to the beloved memory of Albert the Great and Good, Prince Consort, raised by his broken-hearted widow.' She and the six children who were with her placed on it stones on which their initials were to be carved. Next month (September 1862) negotiations were in progress for the betrothal of the prince of Wales. His choice had fallen on Princess Alexandra, daughter of Prince Christian of Schleswig-Holstein-Sonderburg-Glucksburg, the next heir to the throne of Denmark, to which he ascended shortly afterwards on 15 Nov. 1863. Her mother, Princess Louise of Hesse-Cassel, was niece of Christian VIII of Denmark, and sole heiress of the old Danish royal family. Princess Alexandra was already a distant connection of the queen by marriage, for the queen's aunt, the old Duchess of Cambridge, a member of the princely house of Hesse-Cassel, was also aunt of the princess's father. The queen readily assented to the match, and the princess was her guest at Osborne in November. Her grace and beauty fascinated the queen and the people of England from the first, and although the princess's connection with Denmark did not recommend the alliance to the Prussian government, which anticipated complications with its little northern neighbour, the betrothal had little political significance or influence. More perplexing was the consideration which it was needful to devote in December 1862 to a question affecting the future of her second son, Alfred, who, under the prince consort's careful supervision, had been educated for the navy. The popular assembly of the kingdom of Greece had driven their king, Otho, from the throne, and resolved to confer the vacant crown on Prince Alfred. The queen regarded the proposal with unconcealed favour, but her ministers declared its acceptance to be impracticable and to be contrary to the country's treaty obligations with the powers. Unhappily for the queen's peace of mind, the ministers' rejection of the invitation to her second son, in which she soon acquiesced, did not relieve her of further debate on the subject. A substitute for Alfred as a candidate for the Greek throne was suggested in the person of her brother-in-law, Duke Ernest of Saxe-Coburg. He at once came to England to take the queen's advice, and his conduct greatly harassed her. His attitude to the question threatened a breach between them. The duke had no children, and his throne of Saxe-Coburg would naturally devolve, should he die childless, on his only brother's eldest son, the prince of Wales; but it had already been agreed that, in view of the prince of Wales's heirship to the English throne, he should transfer to his next brother Alfred his claim to the German duchy. Duke Ernest was quite willing to ascend the Greek throne, but made it a condition that he should not immediately on his accession sever his connection with Coburg. This condition was treated as impossible of acceptance, alike by English ministers and by Greek leaders. For the duke to abandon Coburg meant its immediate assignment to Prince Alfred. Of this result the queen, who was deeply attached to the principality and was always solicitous of the future fortunes of her younger children, by no means disapproved. But it was congenial neither to Duke Ernest nor to their uncle Leopold, and the duke thought his sister-in-law's action ambiguous and insufficiently considerate towards his own interests. She endeavoured to soothe him, while resenting his pertinacious criticism, and on 29 Jan. 1863 she wrote to him: 'What I can do to remove difficulties, without prejudicing the rights of our children and the welfare of the beloved little country, you may rely upon. You are sure of my sisterly love, as well as my immense love for Coburg and the whole country. . . . I am not at all well, and this whole Greek matter has affected me fearfully. Much too much rests upon me, poor woman, standing alone as I do with so many children, and every day, every hour, I feel more and more the horrible void that is ever growing greater and more fearful' (Duke Ernest, iv. 99–100). Finally the duke's candidature for the Greek throne was withdrawn, and the crown was placed by England, in concert with the powers, on the head of George, brother of the Princess Alexandra, who was the affianced bride of the prince of Wales. The settlement freed the queen from the worry of family bickerings. Through all the ranks of the nation the marriage of the queen's eldest son, the heir to the throne, evoked abundant enthusiasm. There was an anticipation that the queen would make it the occasion of ending the period of gloomy seclusion in which she had chosen to encircle the court. At her request parliament readily granted an annuity of 40,000*l*. for the prince, which, added to the revenues of the duchy of Cornwall, brought his income to over 100,000*l*. a year, while his bride was awarded an immediate annuity of 10,000*l*. and a prospective one of 30,000*l*. in case of widowhood. In accordance with the marriage treaty, which was signed at Copenhagen on 15 Jan. 1863, the marriage took place on 5 March 1863 at St. George's Chapel, Windsor. The queen played no part in the ceremony, but witnessed it from a gallery overlooking the chancel. The sadness of her situation impressed so unsentimental a spectator as Lord Palmerston, who shed tears as he gazed on her. After the prince's marriage the court resumed some of its old routine; state balls and concerts were revived to a small extent, but the queen disappointed expectation by refusing to attend court entertainments herself. She entrusted her place in them to her eldest son and his bride, and to others of her children.

But while ignoring the pleasures of the court, she did not relax her devotion to the business of state. Her main energy was applied to foreign politics. While anxious that the prestige of England should be maintained abroad, she was desirous to keep the peace, and to impress other sovereigns with her pacific example. Her dislike of war in Europe now mainly sprang from family considerations—from her concern for the interests of her married daughters at Berlin and Darmstadt, and in a smaller degree for those of her brother-in-law at Coburg. The fortunes of all, and especially those of the crown princess of Prussia, seemed to her to be involved in every menace of the tranquillity of Europe. Into the precise merits of the difficulties which arose among the nations she did not enter with quite the same fulness as her husband. But the safety of existing dynasties was a principle that had appealed to him, and by that she stood firm. Consequently the points of view from which she and her ministers, Lord Palmerston and Lord John Russell, approached the foreign questions that engrossed the attention of Europe from 1863 to 1866 rarely coincided. But she pressed counsel on them with all her old pertinacity, and constantly had to acquiesce unwillingly in its rejection in detail. Nevertheless she fulfilled her main purpose of keeping her country free from such European complications as were likely to issue in war. And though she was unable to give effective political aid to her German relatives, she was often successful in checking the activity of her ministers' or her people's sympathies with their enemies. The different mental attitudes in which the queen and her ministers stood to current foreign events is well illustrated by the divergent sentiments which the Polish insurrection excited in them in 1863. Palmerston and his colleague Lord John sympathised with the efforts of Poland to release itself from the grip of Russia, and their abhorrence of the persecution of a small race by a great reflected popular English feeling. France, affecting horror at Russia's cruelty, invited English co-operation in opposing her. Prussia, on the other hand, where Bismarck now ruled, declared that the Poles were meeting their deserts. The queen sternly warned her government against any manner of interference. Her view of the situation altogether ignored the grievances of the Poles. She privately identified herself with their oppressors. The Grand Duke Constantine, who was governor-general of Poland when the insurrection broke out, had been her guest. His life was menaced by the Polish rebels, wherefore his modes of tyranny, however repugnant, became in her sight inevitable weapons of self-defence. The question had driven France and Prussia into opposite camps. Maternal duty called her to the side of Prussia, her eldest daughter's adopted country and future dominion. Early in the autumn of 1863 the queen visited Germany and examined the foreign situation for herself at close quarters. The main object of her tour was to revive her memories of the scenes of her late husband's youth. After staying a night at the summer palace of Laeken with her uncle Leopold, she proceeded to Rosenau, Prince Albert's birthplace, and thence passed on to Coburg. The recent death of her husband's constant counsellor, Stockmar, at Coburg, intensified the depression in which public and private anxieties involved her, but she took pleasure in the society of the crown prince and princess, who joined her at Rosenau. Their political prospects, however, filled her with fresh alarms. The sovereigns of Germany were meeting at Frankfort to consider a reform of the confederation of the German states. For reasons that were to appear later, Prussia declined to join the meeting, and Austria assumed the leading place in the conference. It looked probable that an empire of Germany would come into being under the headship of the emperor of Austria, that Prussia would be excluded from it, and would be ruined in its helpless isolation. The jealousy with which not only Austria, but the smaller German states, regarded Prussia seemed to the queen to render imminent its decay and fall. Domestic instincts spurred her to exert all her personal influence in Germany to set the future of Prussia and her daughter's fortunes on a securer basis. Her brother-in-law, Duke Ernest, was attending the German diet of sovereigns at Frankfort. From Rosenau she addressed to him constant appeals to protect Prussia from the disasters with which the Frankfort meeting threatened it. On 29 Aug., after drawing a dismal picture of Prussia's rapid decline, she wrote: 'All the more would I beg you, as much as lies in your power, to prevent a weakening of Prussia, which not only my own feeling resists—on account of the future of our children—but which would surely also be contrary to the interest of Germany; and I know that our dear angel Albert always regarded a strong Prussia as a necessity, for which therefore it is a sacred duty for me to work.' Two days later, on 31 Aug., the king of Prussia, at her request, paid her a visit. Bismarck, who had a year before assumed control of the policy of Prussia and understood the situation better than the queen, was in his master's retinue, but he was not present at the interview. The king's kindly tone did not reassure the queen. She thought he failed to realise his country's and his family's danger. But his apparent pusillanimity did not daunt her energies. A personal explanation with the ruler, from whom Prussia had, in her view, everything to fear, became essential. Early in September Francis Joseph, the emperor of Austria, was returning to Vienna from the diet at Frankfort. She invited him to visit her on the way at the castle of Coburg. On 3 Sept. he arrived there. It was her first meeting with him. She had been interested in him since his accession to the throne in the eventful year 1848. Ten years later, in August 1858, he had sent to her when at Babelsberg a letter regretting his inability to make her personal acquaintance while she was in the neighbourhood of his dominions; and when his son and heir was born a day or two later, on 22 Aug. 1858, she at once wrote a cordial note of congratulation. Now his interview with her lasted three hours. Only Duke Ernest was present with them. The queen prudently deprecated the notion that she desired to enter in detail into political questions, but her maternal anxiety for her children at Berlin impelled her (she said) to leave no stone unturned to stave off the dangers that threatened Prussia. She knew how greatly Prussia would benefit if she won a sympathetic hearing from the emperor. He heard her respectfully, but committed himself to nothing, and the interview left the situation unchanged (Duke Ernest, *Memoirs*, iv. 134). But the interest of the episode cannot be measured by its material result. It is a signal proof of the queen's courageous will and passionate devotion to her family. Soon after parting with Emperor Francis Joseph, the queen set her face homewards, only pausing at Darmstadt to see her daughter Alice in her own home. Arrived in England, she paid her customary autumn visit to Balmoral, and spent some days in September with her friends the Duke and Duchess of Athol at Blair Athol. Afterwards she temporarily issued from her seclusion in order to unveil publicly at Aberdeen, on 13 Oct. 1863, a bronze statue of the prince consort, which Marochetti had designed at the expense of the city and county. In reply to the address from the subscribers the queen declared through Sir George Grey, the home secretary, that she had come 'to proclaim in public the unbounded reverence and admiration, the devoted love that fills my heart for him whose loss must throw a lasting gloom over all my future life.' The occasion was one of severe and painful trial to her; but it proved the first of numerous occasions on which she presided over a like ceremony. She welcomed the multiplication of statues of the late prince with such warmth that by degrees, as Gladstone said, they 'covered the land.' Before the end of the year (1863) there broke out the struggle in central Europe which the conflicting claims of Germany and Denmark to the duchies of Schleswig-Holstein had long threatened. English ministers and the queen had always kept the question well in view. In 1852 a conference in London of representatives of the various parties had arranged, under the English government's guidance, a compromise, whereby the relation of the duchies to Germany and Denmark was so defined as to preserve peace for eleven years. The Danes held them under German supervision. But in the course of 1863 Frederick VII of Denmark asserted new claims on the disputed territory. Although he died just before he gave effect to his intentions, his successor, the princess of Wales's father, Christian IX, at once fully accepted his policy. Opinion in Germany, while at one in its hostility to Denmark and in its deliberate resolve henceforth to exclude her from the duchies, ran in two sharply divided currents in regard to their future status and their relation to Germany. In 1852 Denmark had bought off a German claimant to the duchies in the person of Duke Christian of Schleswig-Holstein-Sonderburg-Augustenburg, but his son Duke Frederick declined to be bound by the bargain, and had, in 1863, reasserted an alleged hereditary right to the territory, with the enthusiastic concurrence of the smaller German states and of a liberal minority in Prussia. Two of Duke Frederick's adherents, the kings of Saxony and Hanover, actually sent troops to drive the Danes from Kiel, the chief city of Holstein, in December 1863, and to put him in possession.

The government of Prussia, on the other hand, was indifferent to Duke Frederick's pretensions, and anticipating embarrassment from co-operation with the small German states, it took the matter entirely out of their hands. The king of Prussia induced the emperor of Austria to join him exclusively in expelling the Danes from the two duchies, and it was agreed that the two powers, having overcome the Danes, should hold the territories jointly until some final arrangement was reached. There were thus three parties to the dispute—the king of Denmark, Duke Frederick of Augustenburg with his German champions, and the rulers of Prussia and Austria. Two of the three litigants, the king of Denmark and Duke Frederick, each clamoured for the queen's support and the intervention of English arms. The queen, who narrowly watched the progress of events and surprised ministers at home and envoys from abroad with the minuteness and accuracy of her knowledge, was gravely disturbed. Her sympathies were naturally German and anti-Danish; but between the two sections of German opinion she somewhat hesitated. Duke Frederick was the husband of the daughter of her half-sister Féodore, and she had entertained him at Windsor. The crown prince of Prussia was his close friend, and his cause was also espoused by the queen's daughter Alice and her husband, Prince Louis of Hesse, as well as by her brother-in-law, Duke Ernest of Saxe-Coburg. But while regarding with benevolence the pretensions of Duke Frederick of Augustenburg, and pitying the misfortunes of his family, she could not repress the thought that the policy of Prussia, although antagonistic to his interests, was calculated to increase the strength and prestige of that kingdom, the promotion of which was for her 'a sacred duty.'

There were other grounds which impelled her to restrain her impulse to identity herself completely with any one party to the strife. Radical divergences of opinion were alive in her own domestic circle. The princess of Wales, the daughter of the king of Denmark, naturally felt acutely her father's position, and when, in December 1863, she and her husband were fellow-guests at Windsor with the crown prince and princess of Prussia, the queen treated Schleswig-Holstein as a forbidden subject at her table. To her ministers and to the mass of her subjects, moreover, the cause of Denmark made a strong appeal. The threats of Prussia and Austria to attack a small power like Denmark seemed to them another instance of brutal oppression of the weak by the strong. Duke Frederick's position was deemed futile. The popularity of the princess of Wales, the king of Denmark's daughter, tended to strengthen the prevailing popular sentiment in favour of the Danes.

In view of interests so widely divided the queen hoped against hope that peace might be preserved. At any rate she was resolved that England should not directly engage in the strife, which she wished to see restricted to the narrowest possible limits of time and space. It was therefore with deep indignation that she learned that active interference in behalf of Denmark was contemplated by her cabinet. Napoleon III was sounded as to whether he would lend his aid, but he had grown estranged from Palmerston, and answered coldly. The ministers' ardour in behalf of Denmark was not diminished by this rebuff. But the queen's repugnance to their Danish sentiment was strengthened. She made no endeavour to conceal her German sympathies, although they became, to her regret, the subject of reproachful comment in the press. Theodor von Bernhardi, the Prussian envoy, had an interview with her at Osborne on 8 Jan. 1864. She frankly deplored the strength of the Danish party in England, which had won, she said, the leading journalistic organs. She thought that Germany might exert more influence in the same direction. She was dissatisfied, she added, with the position of the crown prince, and lamented the depressed condition of the liberal party in Prussia (Bernhardi, *Aus dem Leben*, 1895, pt. v. 276–81). At the same time she turned a deaf ear to the urgent appeals of Duke Frederick's friends for material assistance. Within a few hours of her interview with Bernhardi she wrote to her brother-in-law at Coburg that she had come to see with her government that Duke Frederick's claim was unworkable. 'All my endeavours and those of my government,' she said, 'are only directed towards the preservation of peace.' When her ministers introduced what she regarded as bellicose expressions into the queen's speech at the opening of parliament (4 Feb. 1864), she insisted on their removal. A more critical stage was reached in the same month, when hostilities actually broke out between Austria and Prussia on the one hand and Denmark on the other. Although the Danes fought bravely, they were soon defeated, and the English government, with the assent of the queen, urged on the belligerents not merely an armistice, but a conference in London, so that an accommodation might be reached and the war abridged. The conference met on 20 April. The queen saw many of the envoys and talked to them with freedom. She recommended mutual concessions. But it was soon seen that the conference would prove abortive. To the queen's annoyance, before it dissolved, her government championed with new vehemence the cause of the Danes, and warlike operations in their behalf were again threatened. Palmerston told the Austrian ambassador, Count Apponyi, that if the Austrian fleet went to the Baltic it would meet the British fleet there. The queen, through Lord Granville, expressed dissatisfaction with the threat, and appealed to the cabinet to aid her against the prime minister. She invited the private support of the leader of the opposition, Lord Derby, in the service of peace, and hinted that, if parliament did not adopt a pacific and neutral policy, she would have to resort to a dissolution. Meanwhile her German relatives complained to her of the encouragement that her ministers and subjects were giving the Danes. But in her foreign correspondence, as the situation developed, she displayed scrupulous tact. She deprecated the rumours that she and her ministers were pulling in opposite directions, or that she had it in her power to take a course to which they were adverse. In May the London conference broke up without arriving at any decision. The war was resumed in June with triumphant results to the German allies, who quickly routed the Danes and occupied the whole of the disputed duchies. Throughout these operations England maintained the strictest neutrality, the full credit of which was laid in diplomatic circles at the queen's door (cf. Duke Ernest's *Memoirs*; Count von Beust's *Memoirs*; Count Vitzthum von Eckstadt's *Memoirs*).

Much of this agitation waged round the princess of Wales, and while it was at its height a new interest was aroused in her. On 8 Jan. 1864 she became, at Frogmore, the mother of a son (Albert Victor), who was in the direct line of succession to the throne. The happy event, which gave the queen, in the heat of the political anxiety, much gratification, was soon followed by her first public appearance in London since her bereavement. On 30 March she attended a flower show at the Horticultural Gardens, while she permitted her birthday on 24 May to be celebrated for the first time since her widowhood with state formalities. In the autumn Duke Ernest and his wife were her guests at Balmoral, and German politics continued to be warmly debated. But she mainly devoted her time to recreation. She made, as of old, many excursions in the neighbourhood of her highland home. For the second time in Scotland she unveiled a statue of the prince consort, now at Perth; and on her return to Windsor she paid a private visit to her late husband's foundation of Wellington College. A feeling was growing throughout the country that the queen's seclusion was unduly prolonged, and was contrary to the nation's interest. It was not within the knowledge of the majority of her subjects that she was performing the routine business of her station with all her ancient pertinacity, and she had never failed to give public signs of interest in social and non-political questions affecting the people's welfare. On New Year's Day 1865 she, on her own responsibility, addressed a letter to railway companies, calling their attention to the frequency of accidents, and to their responsibilities for making better provision for the safety of their passengers. In London, in March, she visited the Consumption Hospital at Brompton. The assassination of President Lincoln on 14 April called forth all her sympathy, and she at once sent to the president's widow an autograph letter of condolence, which excited enthusiasm on both sides of the Atlantic, and did much to relieve the tension that English sympathy with the Southern confederates had introduced into the relations of the governments of London and Washington. But it was obvious at the same time that she was neglecting the ceremonial functions of her office. On three occasions she had failed to open parliament in person. That ceremony most effectually brought into prominence the place of the sovereign in the constitution; it was greatly valued by ministers, and had in the past been rarely omitted. William IV, who had excused his attendance at the opening of parliament in 1837 on the ground of the illness of his sister, the Duchess of Gloucester, had been warned that his absence contravened a principle of the constitution; and Lord Melbourne, the prime minister, wrote to Lord John Russell that that was the first occasion in the history of the country on which a sovereign had failed to present himself at the opening of parliament, except in cases of personal illness or infirmity (Walpole's *Russell*, i. 275). The queen was known to be in the enjoyment of good health, and, despite her sorrow, had regained some of her native cheerfulness. When, therefore, early in 1865 the rumour spread that she would resume her place on the throne at the opening of parliament, signs of popular satisfaction abounded. But she did not come, and the disappointment intensified popular discontent. Radicals, who had no enthusiasm for the monarchical principle, began to argue that the cost of the crown was out of all proportion to its practical use. On 28 Sept. 1865 a cartoon in 'Punch' portrayed the queen as the statue of Hermione in Shakespeare's 'Winter's Tale,' and Britannia figuring as Paulina was represented as addressing to her the words: "'Tis time; descend; be stone no more' (v. iii. 99). On the other hand, chivalrous defenders pointed to the natural womanly sentiment which explained and justified her retirement. In the first number of the 'Pall Mall Gazette,' which appeared on 7 Feb. 1865, the day of the opening of the new parliament, the first article, headed 'The Queen's Seclusion,' sympathetically sought to stem the tide of censure. Similarly at a great liberal meeting at St. James's Hall on 4 Dec. 1866, after Mr. A. S. Ayrton, member of parliament for the Tower Hamlets, had denounced the queen in no sparing terms, John Bright, who was present, brought his eloquence to her defence and said: 'I am not accustomed to stand up in defence of those who are the possessors of crowns. But I think there has been, by many persons, a great injustice done to the queen in reference to her desolate and widowed position; and I venture to say this, that a woman, be she the queen of a great realm, or be she the wife of one of your labouring men, who can keep alive in her heart a great sorrow for the lost object of her life and affection, is not at all likely to be wanting in a great and generous sympathy with you.' Mr. Ayrton endeavoured to explain his words, but was refused a hearing. Nevertheless the agitation was unrepressed. A year later there was a revival of the rumour that court life was to resume its former brilliance under the queen's personal auspices. Unmoved by the popular outcry, she peremptorily denied the truth of the report in a communication to the 'Times' newspaper. She said 'she would not shrink from any personal sacrifice or exertion, however painful. She had worked hard in the public service to the injury of her health and strength. The fatigue of mere state ceremonies, which could be equally well performed by other members of the royal family, she was unable to undergo. She would do what she could—in the manner least trying to her health, strength, and spirits—to meet the loyal wishes of her subjects; to afford that support and countenance to society, and to give that encouragement to trade, which was desired of her. More the queen could not do, and more the kindness and good feeling of her people would surely not exact of her.' In the autumn of 1865 domestic matters largely occupied her. Accompanied by her family, she paid another visit to her husband's native country, in order to unveil, in the presence of all his relatives, a statue to him at Coburg (26 Aug.). While at Coburg she approved a matrimonial project affecting her third and eldest unmarried daughter, Helena, who had of late years been her constant companion. In view of recent events in Germany the match was calculated strongly to excite political feeling there. Largely at the instance of Duke Ernest, the princess was betrothed to Prince Christian of Schleswig-Holstein-Sonderburg-Augustenburg, the younger brother of that Duke Frederick whose claim to the duchies of Schleswig and Holstein had been pressed by the smaller German states on Denmark and on the Prussian-Austrian alliance with results disastrous to himself. After the recent Schleswig-Holstein war Bismarck had deprived Duke Frederick and his family of their property and standing, and the claimant's younger brother, Prince Christian, who had previously been an officer in the Prussian army, had been compelled to retire. The sympathy felt by the crown prince and princess for the injured house of Augustenburg rendered the match congenial to them; but it was viewed with no favour at Berlin, and the queen was freely reproached there with a wanton interference in the domestic affairs of Germany. She unmistakably identified herself with the arrangement, and by her private munificence met the difficulty incident to the narrow pecuniary resources of the young prince. She returned to England in good health and spirits, meeting at Ostend her uncle Leopold for what proved to be the last time. Events in the autumn unfortunately reinvigorated her sense of isolation. In the summer of 1865 a dissolution of parliament had become necessary, and the liberals slightly increased their majority in the new House of Commons. But, before the new parliament met, the death of Palmerston, the prime minister, on 18 Oct., broke for the queen another link with the past. In the presence of death the queen magnanimously forgot all the trials that the minister had caused her. She only felt, she said, how one by one her servants and ministers were taken from her. She acknowledged the admiration which Lord Palmerston's acts, even those that met with her disapproval, had roused in his fellow-countrymen, and, justly interpreting public sentiment, she directed that a public funeral should be accorded him. She afterwards paid Lady Palmerston a touching visit of condolence. Without hesitation she turned to Lord John, the oldest minister in her service, who in 1861 had gone to the House of Lords as Earl Russell, and bade him take Palmerston's place. The change was rendered grateful to her by the bestowal of the office of foreign secretary, which Lord Russell had hitherto held, on her trusted friend, Lord Clarendon. But at the same time Gladstone, the chancellor of the exchequer, became leader of the House of Commons in succession to Palmerston, and she was thus for the first time brought into close personal relations with one who was to play a larger part in her subsequent career than proved congenial to her. On 10 Dec. the queen suffered another loss, which brought her acute sorrow—the death of King Leopold. She had depended on him almost since her birth for advice on both public and private questions. There was no member of the Saxe-Coburg family, of which she was herself practically the head henceforth, who could take her uncle's place. Her brother-in-law Ernest, who was vain and quixotic, looked up to her for counsel, and in his judgment she put little faith. In her family circle it was now, more than before, on herself alone that she had to rely. The forthcoming marriage of Princess Helena coincided with the coming of age of her second son, Prince Alfred. For her son and daughter the queen was anxious that due pecuniary provision should be made by parliament. This circumstance, coupled with the fact that a new parliament was assembling, led her to yield to the request of her ministers and once more, after an interval of five years, open the legislature in person (10 Feb. 1866). She came to London from Windsor only for the day, and she deprived the ceremony of much of its ancient splendour. No flourish of trumpets announced her entrance. The gilded state carriage was replaced by one of more modern build, though it was drawn as of old by the eight cream-coloured horses. The queen, instead of wearing the royal robes of state, had them laid on a chair at her side, and her speech was read not by herself, as had been her habit hitherto, but by the lord chancellor. The old procedure was never restored by the queen, and on the six subsequent occasions that she opened parliament before the close of her reign, the formalities followed the new precedent of 1866. She was dressed in black, wearing a Marie Stuart cap and the blue riband of the garter. During the ceremony she sat perfectly motionless, and manifested little consciousness of what was proceeding. A month later she showed the direction that her thoughts were always taking by instituting the Albert medal, a new decoration for those endangering their lives in seeking to rescue others from perils of the sea (7 March 1866).

Later in the year she, for the first time after the prince's death, revisited Aldershot, going there twice to review troops—on 13 March and on 5 April. On the second occasion she gave new colours to the 89th regiment, which she had first honoured thus in 1833, and she now bestowed on the regiment the title 'The Princess Victoria's Regiment,' permitting the officers to wear on their forage caps the badge of a princess's coronet.

The summer was brightened by two marriages. Not only her daughter Helena but her cousin and friend, Princess Mary of Cambridge, had recently become engaged. The latter was betrothed to the Duke of Teck, who was congenial to the queen by reason of his Saxe-Coburg connections. He was her second cousin, being the son, by a morganatic marriage, of Duke Alexander Constantine of Würtemberg, whose mother, of the Saxe-Coburg family, was elder sister of the Duchess of Kent, and thus the queen's aunt. On 12 June, dressed in deep black, she was present at Princess Mary's wedding, which took place at Kew. On 5 July she attended the solemnisation of marriage at Windsor of her third daughter, Helena, with Prince Christian of Schleswig-Holstein. Parliament had been conciliatory in the matter of grants to her children. Princess Helena received a dowry of 30,000l. and an annuity of 6,000l., while Prince Alfred received an annuity of 15,000l., to be raised to 25,000l. in case of his marriage. There was no opposition to either arrangement. But throughout the session the position of the government and the course of affairs in Germany filled the queen with alarm. It was clear that the disputes between Prussia and Austria in regard to the final allotment of the conquered duchies of Schleswig-Holstein were to issue in a desperate conflict between the two powers. Not otherwise could their long rivalry for the headship of the German states be finally decided. The prospect of war caused the queen acute distress. The merits of the quarrels were blurred in her eyes by domestic considerations. The struggle hopelessly divided her family in Germany. The crown prince was wholly identified with Prussia, but her son-in-law of Hesse, her cousin of Hanover, and her brother-in-law of Saxe-Coburg were supporters of Austria. The likelihood that her two sons-in-law of Prussia and Hesse would fight against each other was especially alarming to her. Her former desire to see Prussia strong and self-reliant was now in conflict with her fear that Prussian predominance meant ruin for all the smaller states of Germany, to which she was personally attached. In the early months of 1866 she eagerly consulted Lord Clarendon with a view to learning how best to apply her influence to the maintenance of peace. She bade Lord Russell, the prime minister, take every step to prevent war; and in March 1866 her ministry, with her assent, proposed to the king of Prussia that she should act as mediator. Bismarck, however, brusquely declined her advances. Her perplexities were increased in May by her government's domestic difficulties. Lord Russell warned her of the probable defeat of the government on the reform bill, which they had lately introduced into the House of Commons. The queen had already acknowledged the desirability of a prompt settlement of the long-debated extension of the franchise. She had even told Lord Russell that vacillation or indifference respecting it on the government's part, now that the question was in the air, weakened the power of the crown. But the continental complication reduced a home political question to small dimensions in the queen's eye. She declined to recognise a reform bill as a matter of the first importance, and she wrote with some heat to Lord Russell that, whatever happened to his franchise proposals in the commons, she would permit no resignation of the ministers until the foreign crisis was passed. Her ministers begged her to remain at Windsor in May instead of paying her usual spring visit to Balmoral. She declined, with the remark that they were bound at all hazards to avert a ministerial crisis. In June the worst happened, alike at home and abroad. War was declared between Prussia and Austria, and Lord Russell's government was defeated while its reform bill was in committee in the House of Commons. On 19 June Lord Russell forwarded his resignation to Balmoral and deprecated dissolution. The queen wrote protesting that she was taken completely by surprise. 'In the present state of Europe,' she said, 'and the apathy which Lord Russell himself admits to exist in the country on the subject of reform, the queen cannot think it consistent with the duty which the ministers owe to herself and the country that they should abandon their posts in consequence of their defeat on a matter of detail (not of principle) in a question which can never be settled unless all sides are prepared to make concessions; and she must therefore ask them to reconsider their decision' (Walpole, *Lord John Russell*, ii. 415). Lord Russell retorted that his continuance in office was impracticable, and with his retirement he in effect ended his long public life. The queen in her anger regarded his withdrawal as amounting to desertion, and, failing to hasten her departure from Balmoral, suffered the government for some days to lie in abeyance. At length the conservative leader, Lord Derby, accepted her request to form a new ministry, with Disraeli as chancellor of the exchequer and leader of the House of Commons (6 July 1866). Meanwhile the Austro-Prussian war was waging in Germany, and many of the queen's relatives were in the field, the crown prince alone fighting for Prussia, the rest supporting Austria. She was in constant communication with her kindred on the two sides, and her anxiety was intense. She took charge of the children of Princess Alice of Hesse-Darmstadt, and sent her at Darmstadt much linen for the wounded. The result was not long in doubt. At the outset, the rapid invasion of Hanover by Prussian troops drove the queen's cousin the king from his throne, and blotted out the kingdom, converting it into a Prussian province. The queen felt bitterly the humiliation of the dissolution of a kingdom which had long been identified with England. She made urgent inquiries after the safety of the expelled royal family of Hanover. The king, who was blind, made his residence at Paris, and in the welfare of him and of his family, especially of his daughter Frederica, whom she called 'the poor lily of Hanover,' her affectionate interest never waned. Elsewhere Prussia's triumph in the war was as quickly assured, and the queen suffered more disappointments. Italy had joined Prussia against Austria. Austria was summarily deprived of Venetia, her last hold on the Italian peninsula, and the union of Italy under Victor Emanuel—a project with which the queen had no sympathy—was virtually accomplished. The Austrians were decisively defeated at the battle at Sadowa near Königgratz on 3 July 1866, and the conflict was at an end seven weeks after it had begun. Thus Prussia was finally placed at the head of the whole of North Germany; its accession to an imperial crown of Germany was in sight, and Austria was compelled to retire from the German confederation. It was with mixed feelings that the queen saw her early hopes of a strong Prussia realised. The price of the victory was abolition of the kingdom of Hanover, loss of territory for her son-in-law of Hesse-Darmstadt, and reduction of power and dignity for the other small German states with which she was lineally associated. The queen's withdrawal to the quiet of Balmoral in October gave welcome relief after such severe political strains. She repeated a short sojourn, which she had made the year before, with the lately widowed Duchess of Athol, a lady of the bedchamber, at Dunkeld, and she opened the Aberdeen waterworks at Invercannie (16 Oct. 1866), when for the first time in her widowhood she herself read the answer to the address of the lord provost. Another public ceremonial in which she took part after her return south revealed the vast store of loyalty which, despite detraction and criticism, the queen still had at her command. On 30 Nov. she visited Wolverhampton to unveil a statue of the prince consort in the market-place. She expressed a desire that her route should be so arranged as to give the inhabitants, both poor and rich, full opportunities of showing their respect. A network of streets measuring a course of nearly three miles was traversed. The queen acknowledged that 'the heartiness and cordiality of the reception' left nothing to be desired, and her spirits rose. But the perpetuation of her husband's memory was still a main endeavour of her life, and she now enlisted biography in her service.

Under her direction her private secretary, General Grey, completed in 1866 a very minute account of the early years of the prince consort. She designed the volume, which was based on confidential and intimate correspondence, and only brought the prince's life to the date of his marriage, for private distribution among friends and relatives. But in 1867 she placed the book at the disposal of the wider audience of the general public. The work was well received. At the queen's request Wilberforce reviewed it in the 'Quarterly.' He described it as a cry from the queen's heart for her people's sympathy, and he said that her cry was answered (Wilberforce, iii. 236). The queen resolved that the biography should be continued, and on General Grey's death in May 1870 she entrusted the task, on the recommendation of Sir Arthur Helps, clerk of the council, to Sir Arthur's friend, (Sir) Theodore Martin. Much of her time was thenceforth devoted to the sorting of her and her husband's private papers and correspondence, and to the selection of extracts for publication. Sir Theodore Martin's work was designed on an ample scale, the first volume appearing in 1874, and the fifth and last in 1880. Amazement was felt even by her own children at the want of reserve which characterised the prince's biography. The whole truth best vindicated him, she explained, and it was undesirable to wait before telling it till those who had known him had passed away. The German side of his character, which alienated sympathy in his lifetime, could only be apprehended in a full exposition. Both she and he would suffer, she said, were the work not carried through (*Princess Alice's Letters*, pp. 333–5). At the same time she deprecated indiscretion or levity in writing of the royal family, and in 1874 she was greatly irritated by the publication of the first part of the 'Greville Memoirs.' She judged the work, by its freedom of comment on her predecessors, to be disrespectful to the monarchy. Henry Reeve, the editor, was informed of her displeasure, and she was not convinced by his defence that monarchy had been injured by George IV's depravity and William IV's absurdity, and had only been placed on a sure footing by her own virtues (Laughton, *Memoir of Henry Reeve*). To illustrate the happy character of her married life, she privately issued in 1867 some extracts from her diary under the title of 'Leaves from a Journal of our Life in the Highlands from 1848 to 1861.' This, too, she was induced to publish at the beginning of the following year (1868). Its unaffected simplicity and naïveté greatly attracted the public, who saw in the book, with its frank descriptions of her private life, proof of her wish to share her joys and sorrows with her people. A second part followed in 1883, covering the years 1862 to 1882. The year 1867 abounded in political incidents which absorbed the queen's attention. With her new conservative ministers her relations were invariably cordial. Their views on foreign politics were mainly identical with her own, and there was none of the tension which had marked her relations with Palmerston and Lord Russell in that direction. As proof of the harmony existing between her advisers and herself, she consented to open parliament in person on 5 Feb. In May she again appeared in public, when she laid the foundation of the Royal Albert Hall, which was erected in her husband's memory. Her voice, in replying to the address of welcome, was scarcely audible. It had been with a struggle, she said, that she had nerved herself to take part in the proceedings. The chief event of the year in domestic politics was the passage of Disraeli's reform bill through parliament. The queen encouraged the government to settle the question. Although she had no enthusiasm for sweeping reforms, her old whig training inclined her to regard extensions of the franchise as favourable to the monarchy and to the foundations of her government. But foreign affairs still appealed to her more strongly than home legislation. The European sky had not grown clear, despite the storms of the previous year. The queen was particularly perturbed in the early months of 1867 by renewed fear of her former ally, Napoleon III. Although her personal correspondence with him was still as amiable as of old, her distrust of his political intentions was greater than ever, and she always believed him to be secretly fomenting serious disquiet. He now professed to detect a menace to France in the semi-independence of the frontier state—the duchy of Luxemburg—seeing that the new conditions which Prussian predominance created in north Germany gave that power the right to fortify the duchy on its French border. He therefore negotiated with the suzerain of the duchy, the king of Holland, for its annexation to his own dominions, or he was willing to see it annexed to Belgium if some small strip of Belgian territory were assigned to him. Prussia raised protests and Belgium declined his suggestion. The queen urgently appealed to her government to keep the peace, and her appeal had its effect. A conference met in London (11–14 May 1867) with the result that the independence of the duchy of Luxemburg was guaranteed by the powers, though its fortresses were to be dismantled. Napoleon was disappointed by his failure to secure any material advantage from the settlement, and he was inclined to credit the queen with thwarting his ambition. His relations with her endured a further strain next month when his fatal abandonment in Mexico of her friend and connection, the Archduke Maximilian, became known. In 1864 Napoleon had managed to persuade the archduke, the Austrian emperor's brother, who had married the queen's first cousin, Princess Charlotte of Belgium, and had frequently been the queen's guest, to accept the imperial throne which a French army was setting up in republican Mexico. Few of the inhabitants of the country acknowledged the title of the new emperor, and in 1866, after the close of the American civil war, the government at Washington warned Napoleon that, unless his troops were summarily withdrawn from the North American continent, force would be used to expel them. The emperor pusillanimously offered no resistance to the demand, and the French army was withdrawn, but the archduke declined to leave with it. His wife, Princess Charlotte of Belgium, as soon as she realised her husband's peril, came to Europe to beg protection for him, and to the queen's lasting sorrow her anxieties permanently affected her intellect. Meanwhile the inhabitants of Mexico restored the republic, and the archduke was shot by order of a court-martial on 20 June 1867. The catastrophe appalled the queen, whose personal attachment to its victims was great. She wrote a frank letter of condolence to the archduke's brother, the emperor of Austria, and for the time spoke of Napoleon as politically past redemption. But she still cherished private affection for the empress of the French, and privately entertained her as her guest at Osborne in July. Nor, when misfortune overtook the emperor himself in 1870, did she permit her repugnance to his political action to repress her sense of compassion. While the Mexican tragedy was nearing its last scene the second great exhibition was taking place at Paris, and Napoleon III, despite the universal suspicion that he excited, succeeded in entertaining many royal personages—among them the tsar Alexander II, the king of Prussia, Abdul Aziz, sultan of Turkey, Ismail Pasha, khedive of Egypt, and the prince of Wales. The queen's ministers recommended that she should renew the old hospitalities of her court and invite the royal visitors in Paris to be her guests. The queen of Prussia had spent several days with her in June, but she demurred to acting as hostess in state on a large scale. She however agreed, with a view to confirming her influence in Eastern Europe, to entertain Abdul Aziz, the sultan of Turkey, and to receive Ismail Pasha, the khedive of Egypt, who had announced his intention of coming, and was in the country from 6 to 18 July. No sultan of Turkey had yet set foot on English soil, and the visit, which seemed to set the seal on the old political alliance between the two governments, evoked intense popular excitement. The sultan was magnificently received on his arrival on 12 July, and was lodged in Buckingham Palace. Though the queen took as small a part as possible in the festivities, she did not withdraw herself altogether from them. Princess Alice helped her in extending hospitalities to her guest, who lunched with her at Windsor and highly commended her attentions. A great naval review by the queen at Spithead was arranged in his honour and he accompanied his hostess on board her yacht, the Victoria and Albert. The weather was bad, and amid a howling storm the queen invested the sultan with the order of the garter on the yacht's deck. When the sultan left on 23 July he exchanged with her highly complimentary telegrams.

At Balmoral, in the autumn, she showed more than her usual energy. On her way thither she made an excursion in the Scottish border country, staying for two days with the Duke and Duchess of Roxburgh at Floors Castle, near Kelso (21 to 23 Aug.). On the 22nd she visited Melrose Abbey, and thence proceeded to Abbotsford, where she was received by Mr. Hope Scott, and was greatly interested in the memorials of Sir Walter Scott. In the study, at her host's request, she wrote her name in Scott's journal, an act of which she wrote in her diary: 'I felt it to be a presumption in me to do.' Subsequently she unveiled with some formality a memorial to the Prince Albert at Deeside, and visited the Duke of Richmond at Glenfiddich (24–7 Sept.). Early in 1868 she accepted, for the seventh time in her experience, a new prime minister, and one with whom her intimacy was to be greater than with any of his six predecessors. In February Lord Derby resigned owing to failing health. The choice of a successor lay between Disraeli and Lord Derby's son, Lord Stanley. Disraeli's steady work for his party for a quarter of a century seemed to entitle him to the great reward, and the queen without any hesitation conferred it on him. Her relations with him had been steadily improving. Though she acknowledged that he was eccentric, his efforts to please her convinced her of his devotion to the crown. As her prime minister Disraeli from the first confirmed her good opinion of him, and by the adroitness of his counsel increased her sense of power and dignity. But his power in parliament was insecure, and she was soon brought face to face with a ministerial crisis in which he contrived that she should play not unwillingly an unwontedly prominent part. In April Gladstone brought forward his first and main resolution in favour of the disestablishment of the Irish church. The government resisted him, and on 1 May was sharply defeated by a majority of sixty-five. Next day Disraeli went to Windsor and tendered his resignation to the queen. Personally the queen disliked Gladstone's proposal. She regarded the established church throughout her dominions as intimately associated with the crown, and interference with it seemed to her to impair her prerogative. But as a constitutional sovereign she realised that the future of the church establishment in Ireland or elsewhere was no matter for her own decision; it was for the decision of her parliament and people. In the present emergency she desired the people to have full time in which to make up their minds regarding the fate of the Irish church. If she accepted Disraeli's resignation she would be compelled to confer office on Gladstone, and her government would be committed to Irish disestablishment. Disraeli pointed out that she could at least defer the evil moment by declining to accept his resignation and by dissolving parliament. An immediate dissolution was undesirable if the appeal were to be made, as all parties wished, to the new constituencies which had been created by the late reform bill. The Scottish and Irish reform bills and the boundary bills which were required to complete that measure had yet to pass through their final stages. Consequently the queen's refusal to accept the existing government's resignation meant its continuance in office during the six months which were needed before all the arrangements for the appeal to the newly enfranchised electors could be accomplished. If the opposition failed to keep the government in power during that period, it ran the risk, in the present temper of the sovereign, of provoking a dissolution before the new electoral reform was consummated. Disraeli, while explaining the situation to the queen, left her to choose between the two possible alternatives, the acceptance of his resignation now and the appeal to the country six months later. After two days' consideration, she elected to take the second course. She was prepared to accept full responsibility for her decision, and when Disraeli announced it to parliament on 5 May he described, with her assent, the general drift of his negotiations with her. Grave doubts were expressed in the House of Commons as to whether his conduct was consistent with that of the ministerial adviser of a constitutional sovereign. In his first conversation with the queen he had acted on his own initiative, and had not consulted his colleagues. This self-reliance somewhat damped enthusiasm for his action in the ranks of his own party. The leaders of the opposition boldly argued that the minister was bound to offer the sovereign definite advice, which it behoved her to adopt, that the constitution recognised no power in the sovereign to exercise personal volition, and that the minister was faithless to his trust in offering her two courses and abiding by her voluntary selection of one. But the argument against the minister was pushed too far. The queen had repeatedly exerted a personal choice between accepting a dissolution and a resignation of a ministry in face of an adverse vote in the House of Commons. The only new feature that the present situation offered was Disraeli's open attribution to the queen of responsibility for the final decision. The net effect of his procedure was to bring into clearer relief than before the practical ascendency, within certain limits, which under the constitution a ministerial crisis assured the crown, if its wearer cared to assert it. The revelation was in the main to the advantage of the prestige of the throne. It conflicted with the constitutional fallacy that the monarch was necessarily and invariably an automaton. But the queen had no intention of exceeding her constitutional power, and when, immediately after the settlement of the ministerial difficulty, the House of Commons, by an irresistible vote of the opposition, petitioned her to suspend new appointments in the Irish church in the crown's control, and to place royal patronage at the parliament's disposal, she did not permit any personal predilections to postpone her assent for a day. On 10 March 1868 the queen, for the first time since her widowhood, held a drawing-room at Buckingham Palace. On 20 June she reviewed twenty-seven thousand volunteers in Windsor Park, and two days later gave a public 'breakfast' or afternoon party in the gardens of Buckingham Palace. She appeared to observers to enjoy the entertainment, but she had no intention of introducing any change into her habitually secluded mode of life. By way of illustrating her desire to escape from court functions, she in August paid a first visit to Switzerland, travelling incognito under the name of the Countess of Kent. She forbade any public demonstration in her honour, but accepted the Emperor Napoleon's courteous offer of his imperial train in which to travel through France. On the outward journey she rested for a day at the English embassy in Paris, where the Empress Eugénie paid her an informal visit (6 Aug.). Next day she reached Lucerne, where she had rented the Villa Pension Wallace near the lake. She stayed there, engaged in the recreations of a private pleasure-seeker, till 9 Sept., when she again passed through France in the emperor's train. She paused at Paris on 10 Sept. to revisit St. Cloud, which revived sad memories of her happy sojourn there thirteen years before. The emperor was absent, but courteous greetings by telegraph passed between him and the queen. Removing, on her arrival in England, to Balmoral, she there gave additional proof of her anxiety to shrink from publicity or court formality. She took up her residence for the first time in a small house, called Glassalt Shiel, which she had built in a wild deserted spot in the hills. She regarded the dwelling as in all ways in keeping with her condition. 'It was,' she wrote, 'the widow's first house, not built by *him*, or hallowed by *his* memory.' On 14 Dec. 1868 a special service was held in her presence at the Frogmore mausoleum, where a permanent sarcophagus had now been placed. It was destined to hold her own remains as well as those of the prince. The whole cost of the completed mausoleum was 200,000*l*. While she was still in Scotland the general election took place, and Disraeli's government suffered a crushing defeat. The liberals came in with a majority of 128, and Disraeli, contrary to precedent, resigned office without waiting for the meeting of parliament. His last official act excited a passing difference of opinion with the queen, and showed how actively she asserted her authority even in her relation to a minister with whose general policy she was in agreement. The archbishopric of Canterbury became vacant on 28 Oct., owing to the death of Archbishop Longley. The queen at her own instance recommended for the post Archibald Campbell Tait, bishop of London, in whom she had long taken a personal interest. Disraeli had another candidate. But the queen persisted; Disraeli yielded, and Tait received the primacy. He was the first archbishop of Canterbury with whom she maintained a personal intimacy. Neither with Archbishop Howley, who held office at her accession, nor his successors, Archbishops Sumner and Longley, had she sought a close association. Disraeli's experience in regard to the appointment of Tait was not uncommon with preceding or succeeding prime ministers. Throughout her reign the queen took a serious view of her personal responsibilities in the distribution of church patronage; and though she always received her ministers' advice with respect, she did not confine herself to criticism of their favoured candidates for church promotion; she often insisted on other arrangements than they suggested. In 1845 she refused to accept Sir Robert Peel's recommendation of Buckland for the deanery of Westminster, and conferred the post on a personal acquaintance, Samuel Wilberforce. Subsequently Dean Stanley owed the same benefice to the queen's personal regard for him. To the choice of bishops she attached an 'immense importance,' and the principles that in her view ought to govern their selection were sound and statesmanlike. She deprecated the display of religious or political partisanship in the matter. 'The men to be chosen,' she wrote to Archbishop Benson, 3 Jan. 1890, 'must not be taken with reference to satisfying one or the other *party* in the *church*, or with reference to any political party, but for their real worth. We want people who can be firm and conciliating, else the church cannot be maintained. We want large broad views, or the difficulties will be insurmountable.' While holding such wise views, she was not uninfluenced by her personal likes or dislikes of individuals, and she would rather fill an ecclesiastical office with one who was already agreeably known to her than with a stranger. She was always an attentive hearer of sermons and a shrewd critic of them. She chiefly admired in them simplicity and brevity. Any failure of a preacher to satisfy her judgment commonly proved a fatal bar to his preferment. She was tolerant of almost all religious opinions, and respected those from which she differed; only the extreme views and practices of ritualists irritated her. She was proud of her connection with the presbyterian establishment of Scotland, and, without bestowing much attention on the theology peculiar to it, enjoyed its unadorned services, and the homely exhortations of its ministers. On Disraeli's resignation the queen at once sent for Gladstone, and he for the first time became her prime minister in December 1868. Although she fully recognised his abilities, and he always treated her personally with deferential courtesy, he did not inspire her with sympathy or confidence. Her political intuitions were not illiberal, but the liberalism to which she clung was confined to the old whig principles of religious toleration and the personal liberty of the subject. She deprecated change in the great institutions of government, especially in the army; the obliteration of class distinctions was for her an idle dream. Radicalism she judged to be a dangerous compromise with the forces of revolution; the theory that England had little or no concern with

European politics, and no title to exert influence on their course, conflicted with her training and the domestic sentiment that came of her foreign family connections. The mutability of Gladstone's political views, and their tendency to move in the direction which the queen regarded as unsafe, tried her nerves. During Gladstone's first ministry he and his colleagues undertook a larger number of legislative reforms than any government had essayed during her reign, and the obligation which she felt to be imposed on her of studying the arguments in their favour often overtaxed her strength. New questions arose with such rapidity that she complained that she had not the time wherein to form a judgment. Gladstone, who was unwearied in his efforts to meet her protests or inquiries, had not the faculty of brevity in exposition. His intellectual energy, his vehemence in argument, the steady flow of his vigorous language, tormented her. With perfectly constitutional correctness she acknowledged herself powerless to enforce her opinion against his; but she made no secret of her private reluctance to approve his proposals. Gladstone's social accomplishments, moreover, were not of a kind calculated to conciliate the queen in intercourse outside official business, or to compensate for the divergences between their political points of view. The topics which absorbed him in his private life were far removed from the queen's sphere of knowledge or interest. Some of Gladstone's colleagues in his first ministry were, however, entirely congenial to her. She was already on friendly terms with Lord Granville, the colonial secretary, and with the Duke of Argyll, the Indian secretary, and she had long placed implicit confidence in Lord Clarendon, who now resumed the post of foreign secretary. The first measure which Gladstone as prime minister introduced was the long-threatened bill for the disestablishment of the Irish church. She avowed vehement dislike of it, and talked openly of her sorrow that Gladstone should have started 'this about the Irish church' (Wilberforce's *Life*, iii. 97). In the correspondence with her daughter Alice she argued that the question would 'be neither solved nor settled in this way. Injustice to protestants might come of it. The settlement was not well considered.' She told Gladstone how deeply she 'deplored the necessity under which he conceived himself to be of raising the question as he had done,' and how unable she was to divest herself of apprehensions as to the possible consequences. But she was under no illusion as to Gladstone's resolve and power to pass the bill through parliament. She frankly admitted that the House of Commons had been 'chosen expressly to speak the feeling of the country on the question,' and she believed that if a second appeal were made to the electorate it would produce the same result. Common sense taught her that the quicker the inevitable pill was swallowed the better for the country's peace. But she saw that a fruitless and perilous resistance was threatened by the House of

Lords. In the previous session they had thrown out the bill suspending further appointments in the Irish church which Gladstone had carried through the House of Commons, and Tait, then bishop of London, had voted with the majority. A collision between the two houses always seemed to the queen to shake the constitution, and she knew that in a case like the present the upper house must invite defeat in the conflict. She therefore, on her own initiative, proposed to mediate between the government and the House of Lords. Gladstone welcomed her intervention, and was conciliatory. Accordingly, the day before parliament opened, 15 Feb. 1869, the queen asked Tait whether the House of Lords could not be persuaded to give way. Gladstone, she said, 'seems really moderate.' The principle of disestablishment must be conceded, but the details might well be the subject of future discussion and negotiation. At her request Tait and Gladstone met in consultation. After the bill had passed through the House of Commons with enormous majorities (31 May), she importuned Tait to secure the second reading in the lords, with the result that it was carried by 33 (18 June). But greater efforts on the queen's part were required before the crisis was at an end. The amendments adopted by the lords were for the most part rejected by Gladstone. On 11 June the queen pressed on both sides the need of concessions, and strongly deprecated a continuance of the struggle. At length the government gave way on certain subsidiary points, and the bill passed safely its last stages (*Life of Tait*, ii. passim). How much of the result was due to the queen's interference, and how much to the stress of events, may be matter for argument; but there is no disputing that throughout this episode she oiled the wheels of the constitutional machinery.

During this anxious period the queen's public activities were mainly limited to a review of troops at Aldershot on 17 April. On 25 May she celebrated quietly her fiftieth birthday, and at the end of June entertained for a second time the khedive of Egypt. On 28 June she gave a 'breakfast' or afternoon party in his honour at Buckingham Palace—the main festivity in which she took part during the season. In the course of her autumn visit to Balmoral she went on a tour through the Trossachs and visited Loch Lomond. Towards the end of the year, 6 Nov., she made one of her rare passages through London, and the first since her widowhood. She opened Blackfriars Bridge and Holborn Viaduct, but she came from Windsor only for the day.

The queen occasionally sought at this period a new form of relaxation in intercourse with some of the men of letters whose fame contributed to the glory of her reign. Her personal interest in literature was not strong, and it diminished in her later years; but she respected its producers and their influence. With Tennyson, whose work her husband had admired, and whose 'In Memoriam' gave her much comfort in her grief, she was already in intimate correspondence, which she maintained till his death; and when he visited her at Windsor and Osborne she treated him with the utmost confidence. Through her friends, Sir Arthur Helps and Dean Stanley, she had come to hear much of other great living writers. Lady Augusta Stanley told her of Carlyle, and she sent him a message of condolence on the sudden death of his wife in 1866. In May 1869 the queen visited the Westminster deanery mainly to make Carlyle's personal acquaintance. The Stanleys' guests also included Mr. and Mrs. Grote, Sir Charles and Lady Lyell, and the poet Browning. The queen was in a most gracious humour. Carlyle deemed it 'impossible to imagine a politer little woman; nothing the least imperious; all gentle, all sincere . . . makes you feel too (if you have any sense in you) that she is queen' (Froude, *Carlyle in London*, ii. 379–80). She told Browning that she admired his wife's poetry (Reid, *Lord Houghton*, ii. 200). Among the novels she had lately read was George Eliot's 'Mill on the Floss,' but Dickens's work was the only fiction of the day that really attracted her. In him, too, she manifested personal interest. She had attended in 1857 a performance by himself and other amateurs of Wilkie Collins's 'The Frozen Deep' at the Gallery of Illustration, and some proposals, which came to nothing, had been made to him to read the 'Christmas Carol' at court in 1858. At the sale of Thackeray's property in 1864 she purchased for 25*l.* 10*s.* the copy of the 'Christmas Carol' which Dickens had presented to Thackeray. In March 1870 Dickens, at Helps's request, lent her some photographs of scenes in the American civil war, and she took the opportunity that she had long sought of making his personal acquaintance. She summoned him to Buckingham Palace in order to thank him for his courtesy. On his departure she asked him to present her with copies of his writings, and handed him a copy of her 'Leaves' with the autograph inscription, 'From the humblest of writers to one of the greatest.' Other writers of whom she thought highly included Dr. Samuel Smiles, whose 'Lives of the Engineers' she presented to her son-in-law of Hesse-Darmstadt in 1865, and whose 'Life of Thomas Edward, the Banff Naturalist,' she examined in 1876 with such effect as to direct the bestowal on Edward of a civil list pension of 50*l.* She was interested, too, in the works of George Macdonald, on whom she induced Lord Beaconsfield to confer a pension in 1877. In 1870 European politics once more formed the most serious topic of the queen's thought, and the death in July of her old friend, Lord Clarendon, the foreign secretary, increased her anxieties. Despite her personal attachment to Lord Granville, who succeeded to Clarendon's post, she had far smaller faith in his political judgment. Although she watched events with attention, the queen was hopeful until the last that the struggle between France and

Germany, which had long threatened, might be averted. In private letters to the rulers of both countries she constantly counselled peace; but her efforts were vain, and in July 1870 Napoleon declared war. She regarded his action as wholly unjustified, and her indignation grew when Bismarck revealed designs that Napoleon was alleged to have formed to destroy the independence of Belgium, a country in whose fortunes she was deeply concerned by reason of the domestic ties that linked her with its ruler. In the opening stages of the conflict that followed her ruling instincts identified her fully with the cause of Germany. Both her sons-in-law, the crown prince and Prince Louis of Hesse-Darmstadt, were in the field, and through official bulletins and the general information that her daughters collected for her, she studied their movements with painful eagerness. She sent hospital stores to her daughter at Darmstadt, and encouraged her in her exertions in behalf of the wounded. When crushing disaster befell the French arms she regarded their defeat as a righteous judgment. She warmly approved a sermon preached before her by her friend, Dr. Norman Macleod, at Balmoral on 2 Oct. 1870, in which he implicitly described France as 'reaping the reward of her wickedness and vanity and sensuality' (*More Leaves*, p. 151). But many of her subjects sympathised with France, and her own tenderness of heart evoked pity for her French neighbours in the completeness of their overthrow. With a view to relieve their sufferings, she entreated her daughter the crown princess, her son-in-law the crown prince, and her friend and his mother the queen of Prussia to avert the calamity of the bombardment of Paris. Bismarck bitterly complained that 'the petticoat sentimentality' which the queen communicated to the Prussian royal family hampered the fulfilment of German designs. The crown prince's unconcealed devotion to her compromised him in the eyes of Bismarck, who deprecated her son-in-law's faith in her genuine attachment to German interests (see the prince's 'Diary,' edited by Professor Geffcken, in *Deutsche Rundschau*, 1888). Nor did the queen refrain from pressing her ministers to offer her mediation with the object not merely of bringing the war to an early close, but of modifying the vindictive terms which Germany sought to impose on France. But her endeavours were of small avail. English influence was declining in the councils of Europe. Russia had made the preoccupation of France and Germany the occasion for breaking the clause in the treaty of Paris which excluded Russian warships from the Black Sea. And this defiant act was acquiesced in by Gladstone's government. Yet the queen's efforts for France were well appreciated there. Some years later (3 Dec. 1874) she accepted, with sympathetic grace, at Windsor an address of thanks, to which she replied in French, from representatives of the French nation, for the charitable services rendered by English men and women during the war; the elaborate volumes of photographs illustrating the campaigns, which accompanied the address, she placed in the British Museum.

Hatred of Napoleon's policy did not estrange her compassion from him in the ruin that overtook him and his family. The Empress Eugénie fled to England in September 1870, and took up her residence at Chislehurst. The queen at once sent her a kindly welcome, and on 30 Nov. paid her a long visit, which the exile returned at Windsor on 5 Dec. Thenceforth their friendship was unchecked. When Napoleon, on his release from a German prison, joined his wife in March 1871, the queen lost no time in visiting him at Chislehurst, and until his death on 9 Jan. 1873 openly showed her fellow-feeling with him in his melancholy fate. The course that domestic affairs were taking during 1870 was hardly more agreeable to her than the course of foreign affairs. In April the attempt by a Fenian to assassinate Prince Alfred while on a visit at Port Jackson, New South Wales, greatly disturbed her, but happily the prince recovered; and she had no reason to doubt the genuineness of public sympathy which was given her in full measure. At home she was mainly troubled by the government's resolve to begin the reorganisation of the army, which had been long contemplated. The first step taken by Cardwell, the secretary of state for war, was to subordinate the office of commander-in-chief to his own. Twice before the queen had successfully resisted or postponed a like proposal. She regarded it as an encroachment on the royal prerogative. Through the commander-in-chief she claimed that the crown directly controlled the army without the intervention of ministers or parliament; but her ministers now proved resolute, and she, on 28 June 1870, signed an order in council which deposed the commander-in-chief from his place of sole and immediate dependence on the crown (*Hansard*, ccii. 10 sq.; *Parl. Papers*, 1870, c. 164). Next session the government scheme for reorganising the army was pushed forward in a bill for the abolition of promotion by purchase which passed through the House of Commons by large majorities. In the House of Lords the Duke of Richmond carried resolutions which meant the ruin of the measure. Characteristically, the queen deprecated a conflict between the houses, but the government extricated her and themselves from that peril by a bold device which embarrassed her. They advised her to accomplish their reform by exercise of her own authority without further endeavour to win the approval of the upper house. The purchase of commissions had been legalised not by statute, but by royal warrant, which could be abrogated by the sovereign on the advice of her ministers without express sanction of parliament. In the special circumstances the procedure violently strained the power of the prerogative against one branch of the legislature, and the queen accepted the ministerial counsel with mixed feelings. She had small sympathy with the proposed reform, and feared to estrange the House of Lords from the crown by procedure which circumvented its authority; but the assertion of the prerogative was never ungrateful to her, and the responsibility for her action was her minister's. Despite her industrious pursuit of public business, the mass of the people continued to deplore the infrequency of her public appearances; of the only two public ceremonies in which she engaged to take part in 1870, she fulfilled no more than one. She opened (11 May 1870) the new buildings of London University at Burlington House; but, to the general disappointment, indisposition led her to delegate to the prince of Wales the opening of so notable a London improvement as the Thames Embankment (13 July 1870). The feeling of discontent was somewhat checked by the announcement in October that she had assented to the engagement of her fourth daughter, Princess Louise, with a subject, and one who was in the eye of the law a commoner. The princess had given her hand at Balmoral to the Marquis of Lorne, eldest son of the Duke of Argyll. It was the first time in English history that the sovereign sanctioned the union of a princess with one who was not a member of a reigning house since Mary, youngest daughter of Henry VII and sister of Henry VIII, married, in 1515, Charles Brandon, duke of Suffolk. James II's marriage to Anne Hyde in 1660 did not receive the same official recognition. The queen regarded the match merely from the point of view of her daughter's happiness. It rendered necessary an appeal to parliament for her daughter's provision; and as her third son Arthur was on the point of coming of age, and also needed an income from public sources, it seemed politic to conciliate popular feeling by opening parliament in person. Accordingly, on 9 Feb. 1871, she occupied her throne in Westminster for the third time since her bereavement. Although Sir Robert Peel, son of the former prime minister, denounced as impolitic the approaching marriage of a princess with 'a son of a member of Her Majesty's government' (the Duke of Argyll, the Marquis of Lorne's father, being secretary for India; *Hansard*, cciv. 359), the dowry of 30,000*l.* with an annuity of 6,000*l.* was granted almost unanimously (350 to 1). Less satisfaction was manifested when the queen requested parliament to provide for Prince Arthur. An annuity of 15,000*l.* was bestowed, but although the minority on the final vote numbered only 11, as many as 51 members voted in favour of an unsuccessful amendment to reduce the sum to 10,000*l.* (*Hansard*, ccviii. 570–90). Meanwhile the court cast off some of its gloom. The marriage of Princess Louise took place at St. George's Chapel, Windsor, with much pomp, on 21 March 1871, in the presence of the queen, who for the occasion lightened her usual mourning attire. With unaccustomed activity in the months that followed she opened the Albert Hall (29 March), inaugurated the new buildings of St. Thomas's Hospital, and reviewed the household troops in Bushey Park, when the young prince imperial joined the royal party (30 June). At Balmoral that year, although the queen suffered severely from rheumatic gout and neuralgia, she entertained a large family party, including the crown prince and princess of Prussia and Princess Alice. The increasing happiness in the royal circle was menaced at the end of the year by a grief almost as great as that which befell it just ten years before. At the end of November the prince of Wales fell ill of typhoid fever, at his house at Sandringham, and as the illness reached its most critical stage, the gravest fears were entertained. The queen went to Sandringham on 29 Nov., and news of a relapse brought her thither again on 8 Dec. with her daughter Alice, who was still her guest. Both remained for eleven days, during which the prince's life hung in the balance. Happily, on the fateful 14 Dec., the tenth anniversary of the prince consort's death, the first indications of recovery appeared, and on the 19th, when the queen returned to Windsor, the danger was passed. A week later the queen issued for the first time a letter to her people, thanking them for the touching sympathy they had displayed during 'those painful terrible days.' As soon as her son's health was fully restored the queen temporarily abandoned her privacy to accompany him in a semi-state procession from Buckingham Palace to St. Paul's Cathedral, there to attend a special service of thanksgiving (27 Feb. 1872). She was dressed in black velvet, trimmed with white ermine. For the last time the sovereign was received by the lord mayor with the traditional ceremonies at Temple Bar, the gates of which were first shut against her and then opened (the Bar was removed in the winter of 1878–9). Next day (28 Feb.) the queen endured renewal of a disagreeable experience of earlier years. A lad, Arthur O'Connor, who pretended to be a Fenian emissary, pointed an unloaded pistol at the queen as she was entering Buckingham Palace. He was at once seized by her attendant, John Brown, to commemorate whose vigilance she instituted a gold medal as a reward for long and faithful domestic service. She conferred the first that was struck on Brown, together with an annuity of 25*l*. On the day following O'Connor's senseless act the queen addressed a second letter to the public, acknowledging the fervent demonstrations of loyalty which welcomed her and her son on the occasion of the public thanksgiving. That celebration, combined with its anxious cause, strengthened immensely the bonds of sentiment that united the crown and the people. There was need of strengthening these bonds. Every year increased the feeling that the queen's reluctance to resume her old place in public life was diminishing the dignity of the crown. The formation of a republic in France at the same time encouraged the tendency to disparage monarchical institutions. Lord Selborne, the lord chancellor, when the queen's guest at Windsor, was bold enough to tell her that if the French republic held its ground it would influence English public opinion in a republican direction (Selborne, *Memorials*, vol. ii.). During the early seventies the cry against the throne threatened to become formidable. Mob-orators prophesied that Queen Victoria would at any rate be the last monarch of England. The main argument of the anti-royalists touched the expenses of the monarchy, which now included large provision for the queen's children. Criticism of her income and expenditure was developed with a pertinacity which deeply wounded her. Pamphlets, some of which were attributed to men of position, compared her income with the modest 10,000*l.* allowed to the president of the United States. A malignant tract, published in 1871, which enjoyed a great vogue, and was entitled 'Tracts for the Times, No. I.: What does she do with it? by Solomon Temple, builder,' professed to make a thoroughgoing examination of her private expenditure. The writer argued that while the queen was constantly asking parliament for money for her children, she was not spending the annuity originally secured to her by the civil list act on the purposes for which it was designed. A comparatively small proportion of it was applied, it was asserted, to the maintenance of the dignity of the crown, the sole object with which it was granted; the larger part of it went to form a gigantic private fortune which was in some quarters estimated to have already reached 5,000,000*l.* To these savings the writer protested she had no right; any portion of the civil list income that at the end of the year remained unexpended ought to return to the public exchequer. Personally, it was said, the queen was well off, apart from her income from the civil list. Besides Neild's bequest she had derived more than half a million from the estate of the prince consort, and the receipts from the duchy of Lancaster were steadily increasing. The assertions in regard to matters of fact were for the most part false. The queen's savings in the civil list were rarely 20,000*l.* a year, and her opportunities of thrift were grossly misrepresented. But in the hands of the advocates of a republican form of government the pecuniary argument was valuable and it was pressed to the uttermost. Sir Charles W. Dilke, M.P. for Chelsea, when speaking in favour of an English republic at Newcastle on 6 Nov. 1871, complained that the queen paid no income tax. Ministers found it needful to refute the damaging allegations. Sir Algernon West, one of the treasury officials, was directed by the prime minister to prepare an answer to the obnoxious pamphlet. Robert Lowe, the chancellor of the exchequer, announced that income tax was paid by the queen. Twice at the end of the session of 1871 Gladstone in the House of Commons insisted that the whole of the queen's income was justly at her personal disposal (*Hansard*, ccvii. 1124, ccviii. 158–9). But the agitators were not readily silenced. Next session, on 19 March 1872, Sir Charles Dilke introduced a motion for a full inquiry into the queen's expenditure with a view to a complete reform of the civil list. His long and elaborate speech abounded in minute details, but he injured his case by avowing himself a republican; and when the same avowal was made by Mr. Auberon Herbert, who seconded his motion, a scene of great disorder followed. Gladstone denied that the queen's savings were on the alleged scale, or that the expenses of the court had appreciably diminished since the prince's death *Hansard*, ccx. 253 sq.). Only two members of the house, Mr. G. Anderson and Sir Wilfrid Lawson, voted with Sir Charles Dilke and Mr. Herbert, and their proposal was rejected by a majority of 274. In the event the wave of republican sentiment was soon spent, but the conviction that the people paid an unduly high price for the advantages of the monarchy remained fully alive in the minds of large sections of the population, especially of the artisan class, until the queen conspicuously modified her habits of seclusion. The main solvent of the popular grievance, however, was the affectionate veneration which was roused in course of time throughout her dominions, by the veteran endurance of her rule, and by the growth of the new and powerful faith that she embodied in her own person the unity of the British empire. From the flood of distasteful criticism in 1872 the queen escaped for a few weeks in the spring (23 March to 8 April) by crossing to Germany in order to visit at Baden-Baden her stepsister, whose health was failing. After her return home the German empress, with whose dislike of war the queen was in thorough sympathy, was a welcome guest (2 May); and in the same month she sought unusual recreation by attending a concert which Gounod conducted at the newly opened Albert Hall. But death was again busy in her circle and revived her grief. She had derived immeasurable comfort from conversation with Dr. Norman Macleod. 'How I love to talk to him,' she said, 'to ask his advice, to speak to him of my sorrows, my anxieties!' (*More Leaves*, pp. 143–161); but on 16 June he passed away. Her first mistress of the robes and lifelong friend, the Duchess of Sutherland, had died in 1868, and she now visited the duchess's son and daughter-in-law at Dunrobin Castle from 6 to 12 Sept. 1872, so that she might be present at the laying of the first stone of a memorial to her late companion. In the same month her stepsister, the Princess Féodore, the last surviving friend of her youth, died at Baden-Baden (23 Sept.), while the death on the following 9 Jan. of Napoleon III, whose amiability to her and her family was never conquered by disaster, imposed on her the mournful task of consoling his widow. She gave the sarcophagus which enclosed his remains in St. Mary's Church, Chislehurst.The year that opened thus sadly witnessed several incidents that stirred in the queen more pleasurable sensations. In March Gladstone's Irish university bill was rejected by the House of Commons, and he at once resigned (11 March). The queen accepted his resignation, and invited Disraeli to take his place, but Disraeli declined in view of the normal balance of parties in the existing House of Commons. Disraeli was vainly persuaded to follow another course. Gladstone pointed out to the queen that the refusal of Disraeli, who had brought about his defeat, to assume office amounted to an unconstitutional shirking of his responsibilities. Disraeli was awaiting with confidence an appeal to the constituencies, which Gladstone was not desirous of inviting at once, although he could not now long delay it. In face of Disraeli's obduracy he was, at the queen's request, compelled, however reluctantly, to return for a season at least to the treasury bench (20 March). His government was greatly shaken in reputation, but they succeeded in holding on till the beginning of next year. When the ministerial crisis ended, the queen paid for the first time an official visit to the east end of London in order to open the new Victoria Park (2 April). The summer saw her occupied in extending hospitality to a political guest, the shah of Persia, who, like the sultan of Turkey, was the first wearer of his crown to visit England. The queen's regal position in India rendered it fitting for her to welcome oriental potentates at her court, and the rivalry in progress in Asia between Russia and England gave especial value to the friendship of Persia. The shah stayed at Buckingham Palace from 19 June to 4 July, and an imposing reception was accorded him. The prince of Wales for the most part did assiduous duty as host in behalf of his mother, but she thrice entertained the shah at Windsor, and he wrote with enthusiasm of the cordiality of her demeanour. At their first meeting, on 20 June, she invested him with the order of the garter; at the second, on 24 June, he accompanied her to a review in Windsor Park; and at the third, on 2 July, he exchanged photographs with her, and he visited the prince consort's mausoleum at Frogmore (*Diary of the Shah*, translated by Redhouse, 1874, pp. 144 sq.). Meanwhile the governments of both Russia and England were endeavouring to diminish the friction and suspicion that habitually impeded friendly negotiations between them. At the opening of the year Count Schouvaloff was sent by the Tsar Alexander II on a secret mission to the queen. He assured her that the Russians had no intention of making further advances in Central Asia. Events proved that assurance to be equivocal; but there was another object of Schouvaloff's embassy, which was of more immediate interest to the queen, and accounted for the extreme cordiality that she extended to him. A matrimonial union between the English and Russian royal houses was suggested. The families were already slightly connected. The sister of the princess of Wales had married the tsarevitch (afterwards Tsar Alexander III). The proposal was regarded by the queen as of great political promise, and at the date of the shah's visit the tsarevitch and his wife were staying at Marlborough House in order to facilitate the project. In July the queen assented to the marriage of Prince Alfred, her second son, with Grand Duchess Marie Alexandrovna, the Tsar Alexander II's only daughter, and the sister-in-law of the tsarevna, the princess of Wales's sister. The queen was elated by the formation of this new tie with the family of England's present rival in Asia, and her old antagonist on the field of the Crimea. Subsequently she chose her friend Dean Stanley to perform at St. Petersburg the wedding ceremony after the Anglican rite (23 Jan. 1874), and she struggled hard to read in the dean's own illegible handwriting the full and vivid accounts he sent her of his experiences. In the following May the coping-stone seemed to be placed on the edifice of an Anglo-Russian peace by her entertainment at Windsor of the Tsar Alexander II, her new daughter-in-law's father. But the march of events did not allow the marriage appreciably to affect the political issues at stake between Russia and England, and within three years they were again on the verge of war. Meanwhile, in January 1874, the queen permitted Gladstone to dissolve parliament. The result was a triumphant victory for the conservatives. To the queen's relief Gladstone's term of office was ended and she did not conceal the gratification with which she recalled Disraeli to power. Her new minister's position was exceptionally strong. He enjoyed the advantage, which no conservative minister since Peel took office in 1841 had enjoyed, of commanding large majorities in both houses of parliament. Despite a few grumblers, he exerted supreme authority over his party, and the queen was prepared to extend to him the fullest confidence. Disraeli's political views strongly commended themselves to her. His elastic conservatism did not run counter to her whiggish sentiment. His theory of the constitution gave to the crown a semblance of strength and dignity with which her recent ministers had been loth to credit it. Moreover his opinion of the crown's relations to foreign affairs precisely coincided with the belief which her husband had taught her, that it was the duty of a sovereign of England to seek to influence the fortunes of Europe. In his social intercourse, too, Disraeli had the advantage of a personal fascination which grew with closer acquaintance, and developed in the queen a genuine affection for him. He conciliated her idiosyncrasies. He affected interest in the topics which he knew to interest her. He showered upon her all his arts and graces of conversation. He did what no other minister in the reign succeeded in doing in private talk with her—he amused her. His social charm lightened the routine of state business. He briefly informed her of the progress of affairs, but did not overwhelm her with details. Nevertheless, he well understood the practical working of the constitution, and, while magnifying the queen's potential force of sovereignty, he did not prejudice the supreme responsibilities of his own office. His general line of policy being congenial to her, argument or explanation was rarely needful; but in developing his policy he was not moved by her suggestions or criticism in a greater degree than his predecessors. Even in the matter of important appointments he did not suffer her influence to go beyond previous limits. But by his exceptional tact and astuteness he reconciled her to almost every decision he took, whether or no it agreed with her inclination. When he failed to comply with her wishes he expressed regret with a felicity which never left a wound. In immaterial matters—the grant of a civil list pension or the bestowal of a subordinate post or title—he not merely acceded to the queen's requests, but saw that effect was given to them with promptness. Comparing his attitude to the queen with Gladstone's, contrasting the harmony of his relations with her and the tension that characterised his rival's, he was in the habit of saying, 'Gladstone treats the queen like a public department; I treat her like a woman.' Disraeli's government began its work quietly. Its main business during its first session was ecclesiastical legislation, with which the queen was in full sympathy. Both the churches of Scotland and England were affected. The public worship regulation bill, which was introduced by Archbishop Tait, was an endeavour to check in England the growth of ritualism, which the queen abhorred, and the Scottish church patronage bill substituted congregational election for lay patronage in the appointment of ministers in the established church of Scotland, whose prosperity the queen made a personal concern. Resistance by the Scottish church leaders to this reform at an earlier date had led to the disruption of the established church of Scotland, and Scottish dissenters, especially those who had left the church, raised stout opposition to a concession which they regarded as too belated to be equitable. To the queen's disgust Gladstone vehemently opposed the measure. His speech against the bill excited her warm displeasure. She denounced it as mere obstruction. 'He might so easily have stopped away,' she remarked to her friend, Principal Tulloch; but the bill was carried in spite of Gladstone's protest. It was the queen's full intention to have opened parliament in person in February 1875, by way of indicating her sympathy with the new ministers; but the serious illness of Prince Leopold from typhoid fever kept her away. On his recovery, in conformity with the views that she and her prime minister held of the obligations of intervention in European politics that lay upon an English monarch, she immersed herself in delicate negotiations with foreign sovereigns. Rumour spread abroad that the Franco-German war was to be at once renewed. Republican France had been pushing forward new armaments, and it was averred that she was bent on avenging the humiliations of 1870–1. The queen's relatives at Berlin and Darmstadt informed her in the spring of 1875 that Bismarck was resolved to avoid a possible surprise on the part of France by suddenly beginning the attack.

Victoria

Her recent friend, Tsar Alexander II, was travelling in Germany, and she wrote appealing to him to use his influence with the German emperor (his nephew) to stay violence. On 20 June 1875 she addressed herself directly to the German emperor. She insisted that her fears were not exaggerated, and declaimed against the iniquity of a new assault on France. Bismarck wrote to his master expressing cynical resentment at the queen's interference, and denied the truth of her information. By Bismarck's advice, the emperor protested to her against the imputation to him of the wickedness of which she accused his policy. That there was a likelihood of an outbreak of hostilities between France and Germany in the early months of 1875 is undoubted, but an accommodation was in progress before the queen intervened, and the scare soon passed away. Although Bismarck affected to scorn her appeals, they clearly helped to incline the political scales of central Europe in the direction of peace (Bismarck, *Recollections*, ii. 191 seq.; Busch, *Conversations with Bismarck; Princess Alice's Letters*, p. 339).

It was agreeable to her to turn from European complications to the plans whereby Disraeli proposed to enhance the prestige of her crown, and to strengthen the chain that, since the legislation of 1858, personally linked her with the great empire of India. Her pride in her relations with India and her interest in the welfare of its inhabitants were always growing. She therefore readily agreed that the prince of Wales should, as her representative, make a state tour through the whole territory, and should visit the native princes. She took an affectionate leave of him at Balmoral on 17 Sept. 1875. The expedition was completely successful, and the prince did not return to England till the following May, when the queen welcomed him in London (11 May 1876). Disraeli's Indian policy also included the bestowal on her of a title which would declare her Indian sovereignty. The royal titles bill, which conferred on her the designation of empress of India, was the chief business of the session of 1876, and she fittingly opened it in person amid much popular enthusiasm (8 Feb.). The opposition warmly criticised Disraeli's proposal, but he assured the House of Commons that the new title of honour would only be employed in India and in Indian affairs. The bill passed through all its stages before 1 May, when the queen was formally proclaimed empress of India in London. After the close of the session she was glad of the opportunity of marking her sense of the devotion that Disraeli had shown her by offering him a peerage (21 Aug. 1876); his health had suffered from his constant attendance in the House of Commons, and he entered the House of Lords next year as Earl of Beaconsfield. On 1 Jan. 1877 at Delhi the governor-general of India, Lord Lytton, formally announced the queen's assumption of her title of empress to an imposing assembly of sixty-three ruling princes. Memory of the great ceremonial was perpetuated by the creation of a new Order of the Indian empire, while a new imperial Order of the Crown of India was established as a decoration for ladies whose male relatives were associated with the Indian government. The queen held the first investiture at Windsor on 29 April 1878. She gloried in her new distinction, and despite Disraeli's assurances soon recognised no restrictions in its use. She at once signed herself 'Victoria R. & I.' in documents relating to India, and early in 1878 she adopted the same form in English documents of state. In 1893 the words 'Ind[iae] Imp[eratrix]' were engraved among her titles on the British coinage. Her cheering relations with Lord Beaconsfield stimulated her to appear somewhat more frequently in public, and she played prominent parts in several military ceremonials in the early days of Disraeli's government. The queen had narrowly watched the progress of the little Ashanti war on the west coast of Africa, and at its successful conclusion she reviewed sailors, marines, and soldiers who had taken part in it in the Royal Clarence Victualling Yard at Gosport on 23 April 1874. At the end of the year, too, she distributed medals to the men. On 2 May 1876 she reviewed troops at Aldershot, and in the following September presented at Balmoral colours to her father's regiment, the royal Scots. She reminded the men of her military ancestry. She suffered a severe shock in the autumn of 1875 when, while crossing to the Isle of Wight, her yacht, the Albert, ran down another yacht, the Mistletoe, and thus caused three of its occupants to be drowned in her presence (18 Aug. 1875); but during the early spring of 1876 she was more active than usual in London. She attended a concert given by her command at the Royal Albert Hall (25 Feb.). She opened in semi-state a new wing of the London Hospital (7 March). Two days later she inspected in Kensington Gardens the gorgeous Albert Memorial, the most elaborate of the many monuments to her husband, a colossal gilded figure of whom fills the central place. Thence, with her three younger daughters, she went to the funeral in Westminster Abbey of her old friend, Lady Augusta Stanley, whose death, after a thirty years' association, deeply moved her; in memory of Lady Augusta she erected a monumental cross in the private grounds at Frogmore. Later in the season of 1876 she left for a three weeks' vacation at Coburg (31 March to 20 April); she travelled from Cherbourg through France, but avoided Paris, and on the return journey had an interview at La Villette station, in the neighbourhood of the capital, with the president of the republic, Marshal MacMahon. The meeting was a graceful recognition on her part of the new form of government. The German empress was once more her guest in May. While going to Balmoral a few months later, she unveiled at Edinburgh yet another Albert memorial (17 Aug.). For the first time since the prince consort's death she kept Christmas at Windsor, owing to illness in the Isle of Wight, and transgressed what seemed to be her settled dislike of court entertainments by giving a concert in St. George's Hall (26 Dec.). During the two years that followed the queen was involved in the intricacies of European politics far more deeply than at any time since the Crimean war. The subject races of the Turkish empire in the Balkans threatened the Porte with revolt in the autumn of 1875. The insurrection spread rapidly, and there was the likelihood that Russia, to serve her own ends, might come to the rescue of the insurgents. Disraeli adopted Palmerston's policy of 1854, and declared that British interests in India and elsewhere required the maintenance of the sultan's authority inviolate. Turkey endeavoured to suppress the insurrection in the Balkans with great barbarity, notably in Bulgaria; and in the autumn of 1876 Gladstone, who had lately announced his retirement from public life, suddenly emerged from his seclusion in order to stir the people of the United Kingdom by the energy of his eloquence to resist the bestowal on Turkey of any English favour or support. One effect of Gladstone's vehemence was to tighten the bond between Beaconsfield and the queen. She accepted unhesitatingly Lord Beaconsfield's view that England was bound to protect Turkey from permanent injury at Russia's hands, and she bitterly resented the embarrassments that Gladstone caused her minister. But she did not readily abandon hope that Russia might be persuaded to abstain from interference in the Balkans. The occupants of the thrones of Russia and Germany were her personal friends, and she believed her private influence with them might keep the peace. Princess Alice met the tsar at Darmstadt in July 1876, and he assured the queen through her daughter that he had no wish for a conflict with England. Thus encouraged, she wrote to him direct, and then appealed to the German emperor to use his influence with him. She even twice addressed herself to Bismarck in the same sense (Busch, *Conversations with Bismarck*, ii. 277). But her efforts failed. Russia declared war on Turkey on 24 April 1877, and before the end of the year had won a decisive victory. All the queen's sympathy with Russia thereupon vanished, and she, no less than Lord Beaconsfield, was resolved that England should regulate the fruits of Russia's success. Twice did she openly indicate her sympathy with her minister in the course of 1877—first by opening parliament in person in February, and secondly by paying him a visit in circumstances of much publicity at his country seat, Hughenden Manor, Buckinghamshire. On 21 Dec. 1877 she, with Princess Beatrice, travelled by rail from Windsor to High Wycombe station, where Beaconsfield and his secretary, Mr. Montagu Corry, met her. The mayor presented an address of welcome. Driving with her host to Hughenden, she stayed there two hours, and on leaving planted a tree on the lawn. A poem in 'Punch' on 29 Dec. 1877, illustrating a sketch by Mr. Linley Sambourne, humorously suggested the powerful impression that the incident created both in England and in Europe. At the beginning of 1878 the sultan made a personal appeal to the queen to induce the tsar to accept lenient terms of peace. She telegraphed to the tsar an entreaty to accelerate negotiations; but when the tsar forced on Turkey conditions which gave him a preponderating influence within the sultan's dominions, she supported Lord Beaconsfield in demanding that the whole settlement should be referred to a congress of the European powers. Through the storms that succeeded no minister received stauncher support from his sovereign than Lord Beaconsfield from the queen. The diplomatic struggle brought the two countries to the brink of war, but the queen deprecated retreat. Before the congress of Berlin met in June 1878, Beaconsfield warned the queen that his determination to prevent Russia from getting a foothold south of the Danube might abruptly end in active hostilities. The queen declared herself ready to face the risk. When, therefore, at an early session of the congress, a deadlock arose between Lord Beaconsfield, who acted as the English envoy, and Prince Gortschakoff, the Russian envoy, and Lord Beaconsfield threatened departure from Berlin so that the dispute might be settled by 'other means,' he made no empty boast, but acted in accord with an understanding which he had previously reached with the queen. Russia yielded the specific point at Bismarck's persuasion; and although both the material and moral advantages that England derived from her intervention were long questioned, the queen welcomed Lord Beaconsfield with unstinted eulogy when he returned from Berlin, bringing, in his own phrase, 'peace with honour.' On 22 July 1878 she invested him at Osborne with the order of the garter. War preparations had meantime been in active progress with the queen's full approval. On 13 May 1878 she had held a review on a great scale at Aldershot in company with the crown prince and princess of Prussia, who were her guests; and on 13 Aug. she reviewed at Spithead in inauspicious weather a strong fleet designed for 'special service.' The situation revived at all stages the queen's memory of the earlier conflict with Russia, the course of which had been largely guided by her husband's resolution. She had lately re-studied closely the incidents of the Crimean war in connection with the 'Life' of the prince consort, on which Sir Theodore Martin was engaged under her supervision. At the end of 1877 there appeared the third volume of the biography, which illustrated the strength of court feeling against Russia when the Crimean war was in progress. The 'Spectator,' a journal supporting Gladstone, censured the volume as 'a party pamphlet' in favour of Lord Beaconsfield, and Gladstone himself reviewed it in self-defence. Domestic incident during 1878 was hardly less abundant than public incident. On 22 Feb. there took place at Berlin the first marriage of a grandchild of the queen, when Charlotte, the eldest daughter of the crown prince and princess, married the hereditary Duke of Saxe-Meiningen. But it was mainly death in the queen's circle that marked her domestic year. Her former ally, Victor Emanuel, had died on 9 Jan. Two attempts at Berlin to assassinate the old German emperor (11 May and 2 June) gave her an alarming impression of the condition of Germany, where she specially feared the advance of socialism and atheism. On 4 June died Lord Russell, and she at once offered his family, through Lord Beaconsfield, a public funeral in Westminster Abbey; but the offer was declined, and he was buried at Chenies. A few days later (12 June) there passed away at Paris her first cousin, the dethroned and blind king of Hanover. She gave directions for his burial in St. George's Chapel, Windsor, and herself attended the funeral (25 June). But the heaviest blow that befell her in the year was the loss of her second daughter, Princess Alice, who had been her companion in her heaviest trials. She died of diphtheria at Darmstadt on 14 Dec., the seventeenth anniversary of the prince consort's death. It was the first loss of a child that the queen had experienced, and no element of sorrow was absent. The people again shared their sovereign's grief, and on the 26th she addressed to them a simple letter of thanks, describing the dead princess as 'a bright example of loving tenderness, courageous devotion, and self-sacrifice to duty.' She erected a granite cross to her memory at Balmoral next year, and showed the tenderest interest in her motherless family.

1879 brought more happiness in its train. Amid greater pomp than had characterised royal weddings since that of the princess royal, the queen attended on 13 March the marriage at St. George's Chapel, Windsor, of her third son, the Duke of Connaught. The bride was daughter of Prince Frederick Charles of Prussia (the red prince), a nephew of the German emperor, and the new connection with the Prussian house was thoroughly congenial to the queen. Twelve days later the queen enjoyed the new experience of a visit to Italy. She stayed for nearly a month, till 23 April, at Baveno on Lago Maggiore. She delighted in the scenery, and was gratified by a visit from the new King Humbert and Queen Margherita of Italy. On her return to England she learned of the birth of her first great-grandchild, the firstborn of the hereditary princess of Saxe-Meiningen. Hardly had the congratulations ceased when she suffered a terrible shock by the death, 19 June 1879, in the Zulu war of the prince imperial, the only child of the ex-empress of the French. He had gone to Africa as a volunteer in the English army, and was slain when riding almost alone in the enemy's country. He was regarded with much affection by the queen and by the Princess Beatrice, and all the queen's wealth of sympathy was bestowed on the young man's mother, the widowed Empress Eugénie. While the prince's remains were being interred at Chislehurst the queen was the empress's sole companion (12 July). At the time the political situation was not promising, and was a source of grave anxiety to the queen. The Zulu war, in which the prince imperial met his death, was only one symptom of the unrest in South Africa which the high-handed policy of the governor of the Cape, Sir Bartle Frere, had brought about. Lord Beaconsfield did not conceal his disapproval of the action of the governor, but his preoccupation with Eastern Europe had not permitted him to control the situation, and he felt bound to defend the positions into which the government had been led by its accredited representative. Equal difficulties were encountered in India, where the rival pretensions of England and Russia to dominate the amir of Afghanistan had involved the Indian government, under Lord Lytton's viceroyalty, in two successive wars with the Afghans (November 1878 and December 1879). The strife of political parties at home greatly complicated the situation, and gave the queen additional cause of distress. Gladstone, during the autumn of 1879, in a series of passionate speeches delivered in Midlothian, charged the government with fomenting disaster by their blustering imperialism. The queen resented his campaign. His persistent attacks on Lord Beaconsfield roused her wrath, and in private letters she invariably described his denunciations of her favourite minister as shameless or disgraceful. Her faith in Beaconsfield was unquenchable. He acknowledged her sympathy in avowals of the strongest personal attachment to her. He was ambitious, he told her, of securing for her office greater glory than it had yet attained. He was anxious to make her the dictatress of Europe. 'Many things,' he wrote, 'are preparing which for the sake of peace and civilisation render it most necessary that her majesty should occupy that position.' But there were ominous signs that Beaconsfield's lease of power was reaching its close, despite all the queen could do to lengthen it. For the fourth time while he was prime minister the queen opened the last session of his parliament on 5 Feb. 1880. The ceremonial was conducted with greater elaboration than at any time since the prince's death. On 24 March parliament was dissolved, and the future of Lord Beaconsfield was put to the hazard of the people's vote. Next day the queen left on a month's visit to Germany. She spent most of her time at her late half-sister's Villa Hohenlohe at Baden-Baden, but went thence to Darmstadt to attend the confirmation of two daughters of the late Princess Alice. In the family circle of her daughter, the crown princess, she found while abroad much to gratify her. Her grandson, Prince William of Prussia (now Emperor William II), was just betrothed to Princess Victoria of [Schleswig-Holstein-Sonderburg] Augustenburg, daughter of Duke Frederick, the claimant to the duchy of Holstein, who had fared so disastrously in the Schleswig-Holstein struggle, and had died in the previous January. She sympathised with the sentiment of the young man's parents that poetic justice was rendered to Duke Frederick, whom Bismarck's Prussian policy had crushed, by the entrance of his daughter into the direct line of succession to the imperial crown of the Prussian ruler's consort. But, in spite of her joy at her grandson's betrothal, her keenest interests were absorbed in the progress of the general election in England. Telegrams passed constantly between her and the prime minister, and her spirits sank when the completeness of the defeat of the conservative party proved to her that he could serve her no longer. Liberals and home rulers had in the new House of Commons no less a majority over the conservatives than 166. On 21 April she was back at Windsor, and next day had two hours' conversation with her vanquished minister. As in 1855 and 1859, when a ministerial crisis brought her in view of the mortifying experience of making prime minister one whom she distrusted, she carefully examined all possible alternatives. As soon as Lord Beaconsfield left her she summoned by his advice Lord Hartington, who was nominal leader of the liberal party; for Gladstone had never formally resumed the post since his retirement in 1875. She invited Lord Hartington to form a ministry (22 April). He told her, to her own and Lord Beaconsfield's disappointment, that Gladstone alone had won the victory and that he alone must reap the rewards. Beaconsfield said that Lord Hartington showed want of courage in hesitating to take office; he 'abandoned a woman in her hour of need.' On returning to London Lord Hartington called on Gladstone. Next morning (23 April) he went back to Windsor with the queen's old friend, Lord Granville, the liberal leader of the House of Lords. Against her will they convinced her that Gladstone alone was entitled to power, and, making the best of the difficult situation, she entrusted them with a message to him requesting an interview. Gladstone hurried to Windsor the same evening, and after a few minutes' conversation he accepted the queen's commission to assume power. Gladstone's second government was soon in being, and, although some of its personnel was little to the queen's taste, she received her new advisers with constitutional correctness of demeanour.

Two acts due to the queen's kindness of heart involved her in some public censure as soon as the new liberal government was installed. She felt lifelong compassion for the family of her exiled cousin, the king of Hanover, and showed great tenderness to his daughter Frederica, whom she called 'the poor lily of Hanover.' She not only countenanced her marriage with Baron von Pawell-Rammingen, who was formerly her father's equerry, but arranged for the wedding to take place in her presence in her private chapel at Windsor (24 April 1880). A few months later she, as visitor of Westminster Abbey, assented to a proposal to place there a monument in memory of the late prince imperial. The House of

Commons in spite of Gladstone's remonstrance, condemned the scheme on the ground of the prince's nationality (16 July 1880). The queen at once appointed a site for the monument in St. George's Chapel, Windsor (21 July).The misgivings with which the queen's new advisers inspired her stimulated her critical activity. She informed Gladstone and his colleagues that she insisted on a full exercise of her right of 'commenting on all proposals before they are matured.' Ministers must take no decision before their completed plans were before her. One of the new government's first domestic measures—the burials bill—at once caused her disquietude. The bill was designed to authorise the conduct of funerals by nonconformist ministers in parish churchyards, and the queen anxiously sought the opinion of Lord Selborne, like herself a devoted adherent of the Anglican establishment, respecting the forms of religious service in churchyards that were to be sanctioned. She was more seriously perturbed by the government's plans for the further reorganisation of the army, the control of which, despite the last liberal government's legislation, she persisted in treating as the crown's peculiar province. In May she stoutly protested against the proposal for the complete abolition of flogging in the army, to which she saw no possible alternative 'in extreme cases of cowardice, treachery, plundering, or neglect of duty on sentry.' She objected to the suspension of the practice of giving honorary colonelcies with incomes as rewards for distinguished officers; any abuse in the method of distribution could be easily remedied. When Childers, the secretary of war, in the winter of 1880 sketched out a scheme for linking battalions and giving regiments territorial designations, she warmly condemned changes which were likely, in her opinion, to weaken the regimental *esprit de corps.* Childers, though he respectfully considered the queen's suggestions, rarely adopted them, and in a speech at Pontefract on 19 Jan. 1882 he felt himself under the necessity of openly contesting the view that the crown still governed the army. During the first months of Gladstone's second administration the queen's main energies were devoted to urging on the ministers the duty of spirited and sustained action in bringing to an end the wars in Afghanistan and South Africa, which their predecessors had left on their hands. The Afghan campaign of 1880 she watched with the closest attention. After the defeat of the English troops at Maiwand (27 July 1880) she wrote to Childers of her dread lest the government should not adequately endeavour to retrieve the disaster. She had heard rumours, she said, of an intended reduction of the army by the government. She thought there was need of increasing it. On 22 Aug. she proved her anxiety by inspecting the troopship Jumna which was taking reinforcements to India. But, to her intense satisfaction and gratitude, Sir Frederick (now Earl) Roberts, by a prompt march on Kandahar, reduced the Afghans to submission. The new amir, Abdur-Rahman, was securely installed on the Afghan throne, and to the queen's relief he maintained to the end of her reign friendly relations with her and her government, frequently speaking to his family and court in praise of her character and rule (Amir Abdur-Rahman, *Autobiography*, 1900). In like manner, after the outbreak of the Boer war in December 1880, and the defeat and death of General Colley on 27 Feb. 1881 at Majuba Hill, the queen was unremitting in her admonitions to the government to bestir themselves. She recommended Sir Frederick Roberts for the vacant chief command in the Transvaal—a recommendation which the government made independently at the same moment. Her ministers however, decided to carry to a conclusion the peace negotiations which had previously been opened with the Boers, and before General Roberts landed in South Africa the war was ended by the apparent capitulation of the queen's advisers to the enemy. The ministerial action conflicted with the queen's views and wishes, and served to increase her distrust of ministerial policy.

But, whatever her opinion of her government's diplomacy, she was not sparing in signs of sympathy with the sufferings of her troops in the recent hostilities. By her desire the colours of the 24th regiment, which had been temporarily lost during the Zulu war at the battle of Isandhlwana, but were afterwards recovered, were brought to Osborne, and while speaking to the officers in charge of the bravery of the regiment and its trials in South Africa, she decorated the colours with a wreath (28 July 1880). During 1882, she once more held a review at Aldershot (16 May), and she presented at Parkhurst, Isle of Wight, new colours to the second battalion of the Berkshire regiment (66th), which had lost their old colours at Maiwand in Afghanistan (17 Aug.). Discontent with her present advisers intensified the grief with which she learned of the death of Lord Beaconsfield—her 'dear great friend' she called him—on 19 April 1881. She and all members of her family treated his loss as a personal bereavement. Two days after his death she wrote from Osborne to Dean Stanley: 'His devotion and kindness to me, his wise counsels, his great gentleness combined with firmness, his one thought of the honour and glory of the country, and his unswerving loyalty to the throne make the death of my dear Lord Beaconsfield a national calamity. My grief is great and lasting.' She knew, she added, that he would wish to be buried beside his wife at Hughenden, but she directed that a public monument should be placed to his memory in Westminster Abbey (Stanley, ii. 565). At the funeral at Hughenden, on the 26th, she was represented by the prince of Wales and Prince Leopold. Of two wreaths which she sent, one, of primroses, bore the inscription, 'His favourite flower. . . . A tribute of affection from Queen Victoria,' and thus inaugurated the permanent association of the primrose with Lord Beaconsfield's memory. But such marks of regard did not exhaust the queen's public acts of mourning. Four days after the burial (30 April) she and the Princess Beatrice visited Lord Beaconsfield's house at Hughenden, and the queen placed with her own hands a wreath of white camellias on the coffin, which lay in the still open vault in the churchyard. Next year, on a site chosen by herself in the church, she set up a memorial tablet—a low-relief profile portrait of the minister—with an inscription from her own pen: 'To the dear and honoured memory of Benjamin, Earl of Beaconsfield, this memorial is placed by his grateful and affectionate sovereign and friend Victoria R.I. ("Kings love him that speaketh right."—Proverbs xvi. 13.) February 27th, 1882.' No sovereign in the course of English history had given equal proofs of attachment to a minister.

The queen's generous sympathies were never wholly absorbed by her own subjects or her friends at home. A few weeks before Lord Beaconsfield's death she was shocked by the assassination of the Tsar Alexander II, father of her daughter-in-law, the Duchess of Edinburgh (13 March), and a few months later the death by a like violence of President Garfield of the United States drew from her an autograph letter of condolence to the widow which the veteran politician Charles Pelham Villiers described as a 'masterpiece' of womanly consideration and political tact. Before the end of 1881 the government was involved in grave difficulties in Egypt. Arabi Pasha, the khedive's war minister, fomented a rebellion against the khedive's authority in the autumn, and by the summer of 1882 he had gained complete control of the Egyptian government. Grave disorders in the administration of Egyptian finance had led England and France in 1878 to form what was known as the dual control of the Egyptian revenue, and this arrangement imposed on them the responsibility of preserving order in the country. France now, however, declined to join England in active defence of the khedive's authority, and the queen's government undertook to repress the insurrection of Arabi single-handed. The queen, quickly convinced of the need of armed intervention, evinced characteristic solicitude for prompt and effectual action. On 10 July, when hostilities were imminent, she inquired of Childers what forces were in readiness, and deprecated the selection of a commander-in-chief until she had had time to consider the government's suggestions. The condition of the transport and the supply of horses demanded, she pointed out, immediate consideration. On the 21st she approved the appointment of Sir Garnet Wolseley as commander-in-chief, with Sir John Adye as chief of the staff. On 28 July she asked for information respecting the press regulations. Her concern for the success of the expedition was increased by the appointment, with her full consent, of her son, the Duke of Connaught, to the command of the guards' brigade in the first division of the army, while the Duke of Teck filled a place on Wolseley's staff. Until the whole of the expeditionary force was embarked she never ceased to advise the war office respecting practical points of equipment, and was peremptory in her warnings in regard to food supplies and hospital equipment. The comfort as well as the health of the troops needed, in her view, attention. In a single day in August she forwarded no less than seventeen notes to the minister of war.

The opening of the campaign sharpened her zeal. On 12 Sept. she wrote from Balmoral, 'My thoughts are entirely fixed on Egypt and the coming battle.' When the news of the decisive victory at Tel-el-Kebir reached her (13 Sept.), she caused a bonfire to be lit on the top of Craig Gowan, thus celebrating the receipt of the news in the same way as that of the fall of Sebastopol in 1855. But her joy at the victory was dashed by the fear that the government would not follow it up with resolution. She was aware of differences of opinion in the cabinet, and she spared no exertion to stiffen the backs of her ministers. On 19 Sept. she protested alike against any present diminution of troops in Egypt, and against the lenient treatment of the rebellious Arabi. On 21 Sept. 1882 she wrote to Childers (*Life*, ii. 33): 'If Arabi and the other principal rebels who are the cause of the deaths of thousands are not severely punished, revolution and rebellion will be greatly encouraged, and we may have to do all over again. The whole state of Egypt and its future are full of grave difficulties, and we must take great care that, short of annexation, our position is firmly established there, and that we shall not have to shed precious blood and expend much money for nothing.' Finally Egypt was pacified, and English predominance was secured, although disorder was suffered to spread in the subsidiary provinces of the Soudan with peril to the future. In the last months of the year the queen turned to the grateful task of meting out rewards to those who had engaged in the recent operations. In October she devised a new decoration of the royal red cross for nurses who rendered efficient service in war; the regulations were finally issued on 7 April 1883. On 18 Nov. she reviewed in St. James's Park eight thousand troops who had just returned from Egypt; and at Windsor, three days later, when she distributed war medals, she delivered to the men a stirring address of thanks.

But it was not only abroad that anxieties confronted the queen and her government during 1882. For the fifth time the queen's life was threatened by assassination. A lunatic, one Roderick Maclean, fired a pistol at her—happily without hitting her—on 2 March at Windsor railway station, as she was returning from London. Soon afterwards disaffection in Ireland reached a climax in the murder of Lord Frederick Cavendish, the chief secretary, and of Thomas Henry Burke, the under-secretary (6 May). Resolution in the suppression of disorder always won the queen's admiration, and she had given every encouragement to W. E. Forster, while Irish secretary, in his strenuous efforts to uphold the law. The more conciliatory policy which ultimately prevailed with Forster's successors awoke no enthusiasm in her. Happily the queen found some compensation for her varied troubles in private life. In the spring she spent a vacation abroad for the first time in the Riviera, staying for a month at Mentone. Once more, too, a marriage in her family gladdened her. Her youngest son, Leopold, duke of Albany, had become engaged to a German princess of the house of Waldeck-Pyrmont, whose sister was second wife of the king of the Netherlands. Parliament was invited on 23 March to increase the prince's income, as in the case of his two next elder brothers, from 15,000*l.* to 25,000*l.* Gladstone pressed the proposal on the House of Commons, but as many as forty-two members—mainly from Ireland—voted against the proposal, which was carried by a majority of 345. The customary corollary that in case of the prince's death 6,000*l.* a year was to be allowed his widow happily passed without dissent. Shortly after the queen's return from Mentone she attended the marriage at St. George's Chapel, Windsor. She purchased in perpetuity the crown property of Claremont, which had been granted her for life by parliament on the death in 1866 of its former holder, King Leopold, and generously presented it to the newly married pair for their residence. Twice during the year she took part in public ceremonies of interest. On 6 May she went to Epping Forest, which the corporation of London had recently secured for a public recreation ground, and she dedicated it formally to public use. At the end of the year, on 4 Dec., at the request of the lord chancellor, she inaugurated the new law courts in the Strand. The prevailing note of the queen's life, owing alike to public and private causes, during the two years that followed was one of gloom. At the close of 1882 she had been deprived by death of another friend in whom she trusted—Archbishop Tait. Fortunately she found Gladstone in agreement with herself as to the fitness of Edward White Benson, the first headmaster of her husband's foundation of Wellington College, and afterwards first bishop of Truro, to succeed to the primacy. Benson's acceptance of the office was, she said, 'a great support to herself,' and with him her relations were uninterruptedly cordial. At the moment that he took the appointment, the queen suffered a new sense of desolation from the death, on 27 March 1883, of her faithful attendant, John Brown. She placed a tombstone to his memory in Crathie churchyard, and invited suggestions from Tennyson for the inscription, which she prepared herself. At Balmoral she caused a statue of Brown to be erected, and at Osborne a granite seat was inscribed with pathetic words to his memory. Subsequently an accidental fall on the staircase at Windsor rendered her unable to walk for many months and increased her depression. Even in January 1884 it was formally announced that she could not stand for more than a few minutes (*Court Circular*, 21 Jan.). In the summer of 1883 she consoled herself in her loneliness by preparing for publication another selection from her journal—'More Leaves from a Journal of Life in the Highlands, 1862–1882,' and she dedicated it 'To my loyal highlanders, and especially to the memory of my devoted personal attendant and faithful friend, John Brown.' She still took a justly modest view of the literary value of her work. When she sent a copy to Tennyson she described herself as 'a very humble and unpretending author, the only merit of whose writing was its simplicity and truth.' Unluckily her reviving spirit was dashed by the second loss of a child. On 28 March 1884, the Duke of Albany, her youngest and her lately married son, died suddenly at Cannes. This trial shook her severely, but she met it with courage. 'Though all happiness is at an end for me in this world,' she wrote to Tennyson, 'I am ready to fight on.' In a letter to her people, dated from Windsor Castle 14 April, she promised 'to labour on for the sake of my children, and for the good of the country I love so well, as long as I can;' and she tactfully expressed thanks to the people of France, in whose territory her son had died, for the respect and kindness that they had shown. Although the pacific temper and condition of the prince's life rendered the ceremony hardly appropriate, the queen directed a military funeral for him in St. George's Chapel, Windsor, on 6 April. The conduct of the government during the year (1883–4) gave her small cause for satisfaction. Egypt, which was now practically administered by England, was the centre of renewed anxiety. Since Arabi's insurrection, the inhabitants of the Soudan had, under a fanatical leader, the Mahdi, been in revolt against Egyptian rule, and they were now menacing the Egyptian frontier. During 1883 the English ministry had to decide whether to suppress by force the rebellion in the Soudan, or by abandoning the territory to the insurgents to cut it off from Egypt altogether. To the queen's dismay the policy of abandonment was adopted, with a single qualification. Some Egyptian garrisons still remained in the Soudan in positions of the gravest peril, and these the English government undertook to rescue. The queen recommended prompt and adequate action, but her words fell on deaf ears (January 1884). In obedience to journalistic clamour the government confined themselves to sending General Gordon, whose influence with the Soudan natives had in the past proved very great, to Khartoum, the capital of the disturbed districts, in order to negotiate with the rebels for the relief of the threatened garrisons. The queen watched Gordon's advance towards his goal with the gravest concern. She constantly reminded the government of the danger he was running. His influence with the natives of the Soudan unluckily proved to be of no avail, and he was soon himself besieged in Khartoum by the Mahdi's forces. Thereupon the queen solemnly and unceasingly warned the government of the obligations they were under of despatching a British expedition to relieve him. The government feared to involve itself further in war in Egypt, but the force of public opinion was with the queen, and in the autumn a British army was sent out, under Lord Wolseley, with a view to Gordon's rescue. The queen reproached the government with the delay, which she treated as a gross neglect of public duty. The worst followed. The expedition failed to effect its purpose; Khartoum was stormed, and Gordon was killed before the relieving force arrived (26 Jan. 1885). No disaster of her reign caused the queen more pain and indignation. She expressed scorn for her advisers with unqualified frankness. In a letter of condolence, written with her own hand, to Gordon's sister she said that she 'keenly felt the stain left upon England' by General Gordon's 'cruel but heroic fate' (17 Feb. 1885). She had a bust of Gordon placed in the corridor at Windsor, and when Miss Gordon presented her with her brother's bible she kept it in a case in the corridor near her private rooms at Windsor, often showing it to her guests as one of her most valued treasures. She greatly interested herself in the further efforts to rescue the Egyptian garrisons in the Soudan. In February 1885 the grenadier guards, who were ordered thither, paraded before her at Windsor, and she was gratified by offers of men from the Australian colonies, which she acknowledged with warm gratitude, although the government declined them. At the end of the year she visited the wounded at Netley, and she distributed medals to non-commissioned officers and men at Windsor. But the operations in the Soudan brought her cold comfort. They lacked the decisive success which she loved to associate with the achievements of British arms, and she regretfully saw the Soudan relapse into barbarism. Home politics had meanwhile kept the queen closely occupied through the autumn of 1884. In the ordinary session of that year the government had passed through the House of Commons a bill for a wide extension of the franchise: this the House of Lords had rejected in the summer, whereupon the government announced their intention of passing it a second time through the House of Commons in an autumn session. A severe struggle between the two houses was thus imminent. The queen had adopted Lord Beaconsfield's theory that the broader the basis of the constitution, the more secure the crown, and she viewed the fuller enfranchisement of the labouring classes with benevolence. At the same time she always regarded a working harmony between the two houses of parliament as essential to the due stability of the monarchy, and in the existing crisis she was filled with a lively desire to settle the dispute between two estates of the realm with the least possible delay. In her private secretary, Sir Henry Ponsonby, she had a tactful counsellor, and she did not hesitate through him to use her personal influence with the leaders of both parties to secure a settlement. Luckily it was soon apparent that the danger of conflict looked greater than it was. Before her intervention had gone far, influential members of the conservative party, including Lord Randolph Churchill and Sir Michael Hicks Beach, had independently reached the conclusion that the House of Lords might safely pass the franchise bill if to it were joined a satisfactory bill for the redistribution of seats. This view rapidly gained favour in the conservative ranks, and was approved by some of Gladstone's colleagues, although he himself at first opposed it. The queen urged on all sides a compromise on these lines, and her influence with leading conservatives of the House of Lords removed what might have proved to be a strong obstacle to its accomplishment. Before the end of the year (1884) the franchise bill and a redistribution of seats bill were concurrently introduced into parliament, and the queen had the satisfaction of seeing averted the kind of warfare that she most dreaded within the borders of the constitution. The queen spent the spring of 1885 at Aix-les-Bains, and on her return journey visited Darmstadt to attend the confirmation of her grandchild, Princess Irene of Hesse-Darmstadt. But there were other reasons for the visit. Her care for the Hesse family had brought her the acquaintance of the grand duke's first cousins, the young princes of Battenberg. They were sons of the grand duke's uncle, Prince Alexander of Hesse, by a morganatic marriage with the Countess von Hauke, who was created countess of Battenberg in 1851. All the brothers were known to the queen, had been her guests, and found favour with her. The eldest, Prince Louis, joined the British navy, became a naturalised British subject, and in 1884 married Princess Alice's eldest daughter and the queen's granddaughter, Princess Victoria of Hesse. Thenceforth the relations of the three brothers with the royal family grew more intimate, with the result that in 1885 the third and youngest of them, Prince Henry of Battenberg, proposed marriage to the queen's youngest daughter, Princess Beatrice. The queen readily assented, and, in letters announcing the engagement to her friends, spoke of Prince Henry's soldierly accomplishment, although, she frankly added, he had not seen active service. The princess had long been the queen's constant companion, and it was agreed that the princess with her husband should still reside with her. Parliament, on Gladstone's motion, voted the princess the usual dowry of 30,000*l.*, with an annuity of 6,000*l.* The minority numbered 38, the majority 337. But the match was not popular in England, where little was known of Prince Henry except his German origin, nor was it well received at the court of Berlin, where the comparatively low rank of the Battenbergs was held to unfit them for close relations with the queen. The marriage took place in a simple fashion, which delighted the queen, at Whippingham church, near Osborne, on 23 July.

All the queen's nine children had thus entered the matrimonial state. The queen's mode of life was in no way affected by the admission of Prince Henry into the royal circle. She always enjoyed the society of the young, and in course of time she was cheered by the presence in her household of the children of Princess Beatrice. Much else happened to brighten the queen's horizon in the summer of 1885. Princess Beatrice's marriage followed hard upon the fall of Gladstone's government. It had been effectually discredited by its incoherent Egyptian policy, and it was defeated on its budget proposals on 8 June 1885. Gladstone at once resigned, and the queen did not permit differences of opinion to restrain her from offering him, in accordance with her practice on the close of a minister's second administration, a reward for long service in the form of an earldom. This honour Gladstone declined. She invited the leader of the conservative party, Lord Salisbury, to form a ministry, and at his request endeavoured to obtain from Gladstone some definite promise of parliamentary support during the few months that remained before the dissolution of parliament in November, in accordance with the provisions of the recent reform bill. Gladstone replied evasively, but the queen persuaded Lord Salisbury to rest content with his assurances, and to take office (24 June). With Lord Salisbury she was at once on good terms. It was therefore disappointing to her that his first tenure of office should be threatened by the result of the general elections in November, when 250 conservative members were returned against 334 liberals and 86 Irish nationalists. The nationalists, by joining the liberals, would leave the government in a hopeless minority. The queen gave public proof of her sympathy with her conservative ministers by opening parliament in person, as it proved, for the last time (21 Jan. 1886). Five days later Lord Salisbury's government was outvoted. The queen accepted their resignation and boldly faced the inevitable invitation to Gladstone to assume power for the third time. The session that followed was the stormiest the queen had watched since Peel abolished the corn laws in 1846. But her attitude to Gladstone through the later session was the antithesis of her attitude to Peel in the earlier. Peel had changed front in 1846, and the queen had encouraged him with all her youthful enthusiasm to persevere in his new path. Gladstone suddenly resolved to grant home rule to Ireland, after having, as it was generally understood, long treated the proposal as a dangerous chimera. To Gladstone's change of front she offered a strenuous resistance. To the bestowal of home rule on Ireland she was uncompromisingly opposed, and she freely spoke her mind to all who came into intercourse with her. The grant of home rule appeared to her to be a concession to the forces of disorder. She felt that it amounted to a practical separation between England and Ireland, and that to sanction the disunion was to break the oath that she had taken at her coronation to maintain the union of the two kingdoms. She complained that Gladstone had sprung the subject on her and on the country without giving either due notice. The voters, whom she believed to be opposed to it, had had no opportunity of expressing their opinion. Gladstone and his friends replied that the establishment of a home rule parliament in Ireland increased rather than diminished the dignity of the crown by making it the strongest link which would henceforth bind the two countries together. But the queen was unconvinced. To her immense relief Gladstone was deserted by a large number of his followers, and his home rule bill was decisively rejected by the House of Commons (7 June). With that result the queen was content; she desired the question to sleep; and, although she did not fear the issue, she deprecated an immediate appeal to the country; she deemed it a needless disturbance of her own and of the country's peace to involve the people in the excitement of a general election twice within nine months. But Gladstone was resolute, and parliament was dissolved. To the queen's satisfaction the ministry was heavily defeated. Gladstone resigned without meeting the new parliament, and in July Lord Salisbury for the second time was entrusted by the queen with the formation of a government. The queen's political anxieties were at once diminished. Although the unexpected resignation on 20 Dec. 1886 of the new leader of the House of Commons, Lord Randolph Churchill, roused in her doubts of the stability of the government, and caused her to scan the chances of yet another dissolution, the crisis passed, and Lord Salisbury's second ministry retained office for a full term of years. Indeed, with an interval of less than three (1892–5), Lord Salisbury now remained her prime minister until her death, fourteen and a half years later, and thus his length of service far exceeded that of any of her previous prime ministers. Her relations with him were uniformly cordial. She knew him of old as the colleague of Lord Beaconsfield. With his general view of policy she was in accord. She especially appreciated his deep interest in, and full knowledge of, foreign affairs. She felt confidence in his judgment and admired his sturdy common sense. Hence there was none of that tension between him and the queen which was inevitable between her and Gladstone. Lord Salisbury's second and third governments gave her a sense of security to which Gladstone had made her a stranger. She soon placed a portrait of Lord Salisbury in the vestibule of her private apartments at Windsor face to face with one of Lord Beaconsfield. Within a few days of the laying of the spectre of home rule, the queen began the fiftieth year of her reign (20 June 1886). The entrance on her year of jubilee, and the coming close of a quarter of a century of widowhood, conquered something of her reluctance to figure in public life, and she resumed much of her earlier public activity. On 26 Feb. 1886 she had listened to Gounod's 'Mors et Vita' at the Albert Hall. On 11 May she visited Liverpool to open an international exhibition of navigation and commerce. But her public appearances were mainly timed so as to indicate her sympathy with that rising tide of imperialist sentiment which was steadily flowing over the whole British empire, and was strengthening the bonds between the colonies and India and the home country. In the early months of 1886 the prince of Wales had actively engaged in organising a colonial and Indian exhibition at South Kensington. In this enterprise the queen manifested great interest, and on 1 May she visited the exhibition, which drew numerous visitors to England from India and the colonies. On 2 July she attended a review at Aldershot held in honour of the Indian and colonial visitors whom, three days later, she entertained at lunch at Windsor. On 8 July she received there Indian and other native workmen who had taken part in the exhibition, and she accepted gifts from them. In August, on her way to Balmoral, she visited another international exhibition at Edinburgh, and later in the year she approved the suggestion made by the prince of Wales to the lord mayor of London to commemorate her fifty years of reign by inviting public subscriptions for the erection of an imperial institute which should be a meeting-place for visitors to England from India and the colonies and should permanently exhibit specimens of the natural products of every corner of her empire. During the next year—her year of jubilee—1887, the queen more conspicuously illustrated her attachment to India by including native Indians among her personal attendants, and from one of them, the munshi Abdul Karim, who served her as groom of the chamber, she began taking lessons in Hindustani. Although she did not make much progress in the study, the munshi remained to instruct her till her death. Since the prince consort's death her visits to London had been few and brief, rarely exceeding two nights. In order suitably to distinguish the jubilee year, 1887, from those that preceded it, she spent in the opening quarter the exceptional period of ten successive days in her capital (19–29 March). The following month she devoted to the continent, where she divided the time between Cannes and Aix-les-Bains. On returning to England she paid another visit to London, and on 14 May opened the People's Palace in the east end. The enthusiastic loyalty which was displayed on her long journey through the metropolis greatly elated her. After her customary sojourn at Balmoral (May–June) she reached London on 20 June to play her part in the celebration of her jubilee. Next day, 21 June, the chief ceremony took place, when she passed in procession to Westminster Abbey to attend a special thanksgiving service. In front of her carriage rode, at her own suggestion, a cortège of princes of her own house, her sons, her sons-in-law, and grandsons, thirty-two in all. In other processions there figured representatives of Europe, India, and the colonies, all of whom brought her rich gifts. From India came a brilliant array of ruling princes. Europe sent among its envoys four kings: those of Saxony, of Belgium, of the Hellenes, and of Denmark, together with the crown princes of Prussia, Greece, Portugal, Sweden, and Austria. The pope sent a representative, the courtesy of whose presence the queen acknowledged next year by presenting the pope at the papal jubilee with a rich golden basin and ewer. The streets through which she and her guests passed were elaborately decorated, and her reception almost overwhelmed her in its warmth. Her route on the outward journey from Buckingham Palace lay through Constitution Hill, Piccadilly, Waterloo Place, and Parliament Street, and on her return she passed down Whitehall and Pall Mall. The first message that she received on reaching Buckingham Palace was an inquiry after her health from her aged aunt, the Duchess of Cambridge. The queen replied at once that she was 'very tired but very happy.' In the evening there were illuminations on a lavish scale in all the chief cities of her dominions, and at a signal given from the Malvern Hills at 10 p.m. beacon fires were lit on the principal promontories and inland heights of Great Britain from Shetland and Orkney to Land's End. Next day the queen accepted a personal gift of 75,000l. subscribed by nearly three million women of England. A small part of this sum she applied to a bronze equestrian statue of the prince consort, by (Sir) Edgar Boehm, after Marochetti, to be erected on Smith's Lawn, Windsor Park, where she laid the foundation-stone on 15 July (she unveiled the statue 12 May 1890). The bulk of the women's gift she devoted to the foundation of a sick nurses' institute on a great scale, which was to provide trained attendants for the sick poor in their own homes. Succeeding incidents in the celebration, in which she took a foremost part, included, apart from court dinners and receptions, a fête in Hyde Park on 22 June to twenty-six thousand poor school children; a visit to Eton on her return to Windsor the same evening; the laying of the foundation-stone of the Imperial Institute on 6 July; a review at Aldershot on 9 July; and a naval review on 29 July. The harmony subsisting between her and her prime minister she illustrated by attending a garden party given by him in honour of her jubilee at his house at Hatfield on 13 July.

The processions, reviews, and receptions proved no transient demonstration. Permanent memorials of the jubilee were erected by public subscription in almost every town and village of the empire, taking the form of public halls, clock towers, fountains, or statues. The celebration had historic significance. The mighty outburst of enthusiasm which greeted the queen, as loudly in the colonies and India as in the United Kingdom, gave new strength to the monarchy. Thenceforth the sovereign was definitely regarded as the living embodiment of the unity not merely of the British nation but of the British empire. But amid the jubilee festivities a new cloud was gathering over the royal house. Since the autumn of 1886 the crown prince, to whose future rule in Germany the queen had for nearly thirty years been looking forward with intense hope, was attacked by a mysterious affection of the throat. Early in June 1887 he and the crown princess came to England and settled at Upper Norwood in the hope of benefiting by change of environment. He was well enough to play a conspicuous part in the jubilee procession, when his handsome figure and his white uniform of the Pomeranian cuirassiers attracted universal admiration. Subsequently he stayed in the Isle of Wight and at Braemar, and he did not return to Germany till 14 Sept. The winter of 1887–8 he spent at San Remo, and it there became apparent that he was suffering from cancer. The queen, who completely identified herself with the happiness of her eldest daughter, was constantly with her and her husband while they remained in England or Scotland, and she suffered greatly from the anxiety. Nor was it lessened when, on 9 March 1888, the queen's old friend, the Emperor William I, died, and the crown which she and her daughter had through earlier days longed to see on the crown prince's head was now at length placed there while he was sinking into the grave. But the queen did not abstain from rejoicings in another of her children's households. On 10 March she dined with the prince and princess of Wales at Marlborough House to celebrate their silver wedding, and at night, on her return to Windsor, she drove through London to witness the illuminations. On 22 March she left England for a month's holiday at Florence. It was her first visit to the city, and it and its surroundings charmed her. King Humbert courteously paid her a visit on 5 April, and the attention pleased her. On 20 April she left for Germany, where she had resolved to visit the dying Emperor Frederick. On the journey—at Innsbruck—she was gratified by meeting the emperor of Austria. It was their second interview; the first was now nearly a quarter of a century old. On 21 April she drove through Berlin to Charlottenburg, her son-in-law's palace. But it was not solely to bid farewell to the stricken prince that she had come. It was to mediate in a quarrel in her daughter's family, which was causing grave embarrassment in political circles in Berlin, and for which she was herself freely held responsible. Her own kindly interest in the young princes of Battenberg was shared by her eldest daughter. Of the three brothers, the eldest had married her granddaughter and the youngest her daughter. The second brother, Alexander, who was still unmarried, and was still no more than thirty-one, had had an adventurous career. For seven years he had been prince of Bulgaria, but he had incurred the distrust of the tsar, and in 1886, having been driven from his throne, retired to private life at Darmstadt. He, like his brothers, was personally known to the queen, whose guest he was at Windsor in 1879; she sympathised with his misfortunes, and she encouraged the notion that he also, like his brothers, might marry into her family. An opportunity was at hand. The second daughter of the Emperor Frederick, Victoria, fell in love with him, and a betrothal was arranged with the full approval of the young princess's mother and grandmother. But violent opposition was manifested at the German court. Prince Bismarck, chancellor of the empire, who had always been on hostile terms with the crown princess, denounced the match as the work of Queen Victoria, who had taken the Battenbergs under her protection. He declared that such a union was injurious to the interest of the German royal family. Not merely did it humiliate the imperial house by allying it with a prince of inferior social standing, but it compromised the good relations of Berlin with St. Petersburg, where Prince Alexander was heartily disliked. Bismarck even credited the queen with a deliberate design of alienating Russia and Germany in the hope of bringing about an Anglo-German alliance against the tsar. When the queen reached Charlottenburg this awkward dispute was at its height. The Empress Frederick stood by her daughter, who was unwilling to abandon Prince Alexander. The dying emperor and his son, the Crown Prince William, in vain endeavoured to move her. Prince Bismarck threatened resignation unless Prince Alexander was summarily dismissed. On 24 April the queen, after much conversation with her daughter, boldly discussed the question in all its bearings with Prince Bismarck. He forced her to realise the complications that resistance to his will would raise, and, yielding to his power, she used her influence with her daughter and granddaughter to induce them to break off the engagement with Prince Alexander. Reluctantly they yielded. The Crown Prince William, who had stoutly opposed his mother, was by the queen's persuasion reconciled to her, and domestic harmony was restored. On the night of her interview with Bismarck, the queen attended a state banquet in the Charlottenburg Palace, and the reconciliation was ratified. None the less the queen always took a kindly interest in Prince Alexander, whose humiliation she deplored; and though she regretted his marriage next year (6 Feb. 1889) to Fräulein Loisinger, a singer at the Dresden and Darmstadt court theatres, she used no harsh language, merely remarking pathetically, 'Perhaps they loved one another.' The prince barely survived his marriage four years; he died on 17 Feb. 1893. On 15 June 1888 the Emperor Frederick died. A week later the queen wrote from Windsor to her friend, Archbishop Benson: 'The contrast between this year and the last jubilee one is most painful and remarkable. Who could have thought that that splendid, noble, knightly prince—as good as he was brave and noble—who was the admiration of all, would *on* the *very* day year—(yesterday) be no longer in *this* world? His loss is indeed a very mysterious dispensation, for it is such a very dreadful public as well as private misfortune' (*Life of Archbishop Benson*, ii. 211). Court mourning prevented any celebration of the fiftieth anniversary of the queen's coronation on 28 June. But on her visit to Balmoral in the autumn she took part in several public ceremonials. She stayed with Sir Archibald Campbell at Blythswood in Renfrewshire in order to open new municipal buildings at Glasgow, and to visit the exhibition there. She also went to Paisley, which was celebrating the fourth centenary of its incorporation as a borough. In November the widowed Empress Frederick was her mother's guest at Windsor for the first of many times in succeeding years; the queen showed her the unusual attention of meeting her on her landing in England at Port Victoria (19 Nov.).

During 1889 the queen's health was good and her activity undiminished. Her spring holiday was spent for the first time at Biarritz, in former days the favoured health resort of the queen's friend, the Empress Eugénie (6 March to 1 April). On 27 March she made an excursion into Spain to visit the queen-regent at San Sebastian. This was another new experience for an English sovereign. None before had set foot on Spanish soil, although Charles I and Charles II went thither as princes. On her return to England she was distressed by the death of her aunt, the Duchess of Cambridge, at the age of ninety-one (6 April). The final link with her childhood was thus severed. The queen wished the duchess to be buried at Windsor, but her aunt had left instructions that she should be buried beside her husband at Kew. The queen was present at her funeral on the 13th, and placed a wreath on the coffin. At the end of the month she paid a visit to her son at Sandringham, and on the 26th she witnessed there a performance by (Sir) Henry Irving and his company of 'The Bells' and the trial scene from 'The Merchant of Venice.' It was the second time that the queen had permitted herself to witness a dramatic performance since the prince consort's death. The first occasion, which was near the end of her twentieth year of widowhood, was also afforded by the prince and princess of Wales, who, when at Abergeldie Castle in 1881, induced the queen to come there and see a London company of actors perform Mr. Burnand's comedy of 'The Colonel' (11 Oct. 1881).

In May 1889 she laid the foundation-stone of new buildings at Eton (on the 18th), and she reviewed troops at Aldershot (on the 31st). On 3 June she presented at Windsor new colours to the regiment with which she had already closely identified herself, Princess Victoria's royal Irish fusiliers; she had presented colours to it in 1833 and 1866. Next day, 4 June, she witnessed at Eton for the first time the annual procession of boats which celebrated George III's birthday. In the summer came difficulties which tried her tact and temper. She turned to consider the pecuniary prospects of her numerous grandchildren. Provision had already been made by parliament for every one of her nine children and for her three first cousins, the Duke of Cambridge and his sisters; and although the deaths of Princess Alice and Prince Leopold had caused a net reduction of 25,000*l.*, the sum annually assigned to members of the royal family, apart from the queen, amounted to 152,000*l.* No responsibility for providing for the German royal family, the offspring of her eldest daughter, the Empress Frederick, or for the family of the Princess Alice of Hesse-Darmstadt, attached to her; but she had twenty-two other grandchildren—domiciled in England—for whom she regarded it as her duty to make provision. In July 1889 events seemed to her to render an appeal to parliament in behalf of the third generation of her family appropriate. The elder son of the prince of Wales was coming of age, while his eldest daughter was about to marry with the queen's assent the Earl (afterwards Duke) of Fife. She therefore sent two messages to the House of Commons requesting due provision for the two elder children of her eldest son. The manner in which her request was approached was not all she could have wished. New life was given to the old cry against the expenses of monarchy. The queen's financial position still from time to time excited jealous comments, not only among her subjects, but in foreign countries. Exaggerated reports of the extent of her fortune were widely current, and small heed was paid to her efforts to correct the false impression. In 1885 it was stated with some show of authority that she had lately invested a million pounds sterling in ground rents in the city of London. Through Sir Henry Ponsonby she denied that she had any such sum at her disposal. At Berlin, Bismarck often joked coarsely over her reputed affluence, to which he attributed the power she exerted over the Crown Prince Frederick and his household. But while the best friends of the crown deprecated such kind of criticism, they deemed it inexpedient for the country to undertake the maintenance indefinitely of the queen's family beyond the second generation. Both the extreme and the moderate opinions found free expression in the House of Commons, and calm observers like Lord Selborne perceived in the discussion ominous signs of a recrudescence of republican sentiment. To the government's proposal to appoint a committee representative of all sections of the house to determine the principles which should govern the reply to the queen's messages, a hostile amendment to refer the whole question of the revenues of the crown to the committee was moved by Mr. Bradlaugh. He argued that the queen's savings on the civil list enabled her unaided to provide for her grandchildren, and that the royal grants were an intolerable burden on the people. The amendment was rejected by a majority of 188, but 125 votes were cast in its favour. On the due appointment of the committee the government recommended, with the queen's approval, the prospective allocation to the prince of Wales's children of annuities amounting on their marriages to 49,000l., besides a sum of 30,000l. by way of dowries. But the grant immediately payable was to be 21,000l. annually and 10,000l. for the dowry of the Princess Louise. Precedent, it was shown, justified public provision for all the children of the sovereign's sons. The daughters of former sovereigns had invariably married foreign reigning princes, and their children, not being British subjects, were outside the purview of the British parliament. The question whether the children of the sovereign's daughters who were not married to foreign reigning princes were entitled to public provision had not previously arisen. The queen and the government perceived that public opinion was not in the mood to permit lavish or unconditional grants, and it was soon apparent that a compromise would be needful. The queen disliked the debate, but showed a wish to be conciliatory. She at once agreed to forego any demand on behalf of her daughters' children; but although she demurred to a formal withdrawal of her claim on behalf of her younger son's children, she stated that she would not press it. Gladstone, whose faith in the monarchy was strong, and who respected the royal family as its symbol, was anxious to ward off agitation, and he induced the government to modify their original proposal by granting to the prince of Wales a fixed annual sum of 36,000l., to be paid quarterly, for his children's support. This proposal was accepted by a majority of the committee; but when it was presented to parliament, although Gladstone induced Parnell and the Irish nationalists to support it, it met with opposition from the radical side of the house. Mr. Labouchere invited the house to refuse peremptorily any grant to the queen's grandchildren. The invitation was rejected by 398 votes against 116. Mr. John Morley then moved an amendment to the effect that the manner of granting the 36,000l. to the prince of Wales left room for future applications from the crown for further grants, and that it was necessary to give finality to the present arrangement. Most of Gladstone's colleagues in the late government supported Mr. Morley, but his amendment was defeated by 355 votes against 134, and the grant of 36,000l. a year was secured (*Hansard*, 3rd ser. cccxxxvii. cols. 1840 sq.). In the course of the debate and inquiry it was officially stated that the queen's total savings from the civil list amounted to 824,025l., but that out of this sum much had been spent on special entertainments to foreign visitors. In all the circumstances of the case the queen accepted the arrangement gratefully, and she was not unmindful of the value of Gladstone's intervention. For a season she displayed unusual cordiality towards him. On 25 July, while the negotiation was proceeding, she sent to him and Mrs. Gladstone warm congratulations on their golden wedding. Meanwhile, on 27 June, she attended the marriage of her granddaughter, Princess Louise of Wales, to the Earl of Fife in the private chapel of Buckingham Palace. After the thorny pecuniary question was settled, hospitalities to foreign sovereigns absorbed the queen's attention. In July 1889 she entertained, for a second time, the shah of Persia, and in August she welcomed her grandson, the German emperor William II, on his first visit to this country since his accession to his throne. The incident greatly interested her, and she arranged every detail of her grandson's reception. The emperor came to Cowes on his way to Osborne in his yacht Hohenzollern, accompanied by twelve warships. The queen held a naval review in his honour at Spithead, 8 Aug., and on 9 Aug. reviewed the seamen and marines of the German fleet at Osborne. All passed off happily, and she congratulated herself on the cordial relations which the visit established between the two countries. The young emperor gave proof of private and public friendship by causing the queen to be gazetted honorary colonel of his first regiment of horseguards, on which he bestowed the title of Queen of England's Own (12 Aug.). The emperor repeated his visit to Osborne next year, when a sham naval fight took place in his presence, and he came back in 1891, when he was officially received in London, in 1893, 1894, and 1895. There was then a three years' interval before he saw the queen again. During the last eleven years (1889–1901) of her long career the queen's mode of life followed in all essentials the fixed routine. Three visits to Osborne, two to Balmoral, a few days in London or in Aldershot, alternated with her spring vacation abroad and her longer sojourns at Windsor. Occasionally, in going to or returning from Balmoral or Osborne, she modified her route to fulfil a public or private engagement. In August 1889, on her way to Scotland, she made a short tour in Wales, which she had been contemplating for some ten years. For four days she stayed at Palé Hall, near Lake Bala. On the 26th, 'the dear prince's birthday,' she paid a visit to Bryntysilio near Llangollen, the residence of Sir Theodore and Lady Martin, both of whom were congenial acquaintances. She was gratified by the loyalty shown by the Welsh people, and thoroughly enjoyed the beauty of the scenery. On 14 May 1890 she paid a visit to Baron Ferdinand de Rothschild's château at Waddesdon Manor. On 26 July following she opened the deep-water dock at Southampton. On 26 Feb. 1891, at Portsmouth, she christened and launched the Royal Sovereign, the largest ironclad in her fleet, and the Royal Arthur, an unarmoured cruiser of new design. On 21 May 1891 she laid the foundation-stone of the new royal infirmary at Derby. On 21 May 1894 she revisited Manchester after an interval of thirty-seven years in order to open officially the great ship canal; on 21 May 1897 she went to Sheffield to open the new town hall; and on 15 Nov. 1899 she performed a last function in the English provinces, when she went to Bristol to open the convalescent home which had been erected to commemorate her length of rule. Only in her foreign tours did she seek change of scene with any ardour. In 1890 her destination was Aix-les-Bains; in 1891, Grasse; and in 1892 Costebelle, near Hyères. In 1893 and again in 1894 she passed the spring at Florence for a second and a third time, and her delight in the city and neighbourhood grew with closer acquaintance. Each of these years King Humbert paid her a visit; and in 1894 Queen Margherita accompanied him. In 1895 she was at Cannes; both in 1896 and 1897 at Nice; and during the two successive years, 1898 and 1899, at Cimiez. On the homeward journey in 1890, 1892, and 1895 she revisited Darmstadt. On her return in 1894 she paid a last visit to Coburg—the city and duchy which were identified with her happiest memories. There she was present, on 19 April 1894, at the intermarriage of two of her grandchildren—the Princess Victoria Melita of Coburg, the second daughter of her second son, Alfred, with the Grand Duke of Hesse, the only surviving son of her second daughter, Alice. On returning from Nice in March 1897, while passing round Paris, she was met at the station of Noisy-le-Sec by M. Faure, the president of the French Republic, who greeted her with every courtesy. On 5 May 1899 she touched foreign soil for the last time when she embarked at Cherbourg on her home-coming from Cimiez. She frequently acknowledged with gratitude the amenities which were extended to her abroad, and sought to reciprocate them. On 19 Aug. 1891 she welcomed the officers of the French squadron which was in the Channel under Admiral Gervais, and on 11 July 1895 she entertained the officers of an Italian squadron which was off Spithead under the Duke of Genoa. The queen's court in her last years regained a part of its pristine gaiety. Music and the drama were again among its recognised recreations. In February 1890 there were private theatricals and tableaux at Osborne, in which the queen's daughters took part, and in their preparation the queen took great personal interest. Next year, for the first time since the prince consort's death, a dramatic performance was commanded at Windsor Castle, 6 March 1891, when Messrs. Gilbert and Sullivan's comic opera of 'The Gondoliers' was performed. In 1894 the Italian actress, Signora Eleanora Duse, performed Goldoni's 'La Locandiera' before the queen at Windsor, and Mr. Tree acted 'The Red Lamp' at Balmoral. Her birthday in 1895 she celebrated by a performance there of Verdi's opera of 'Il Trovatore' in the Waterloo Chamber. On 26 June 1900 Mascagni's 'Cavalleria Rusticana' with a selection from 'Carmen' was given there, and on 16 July 1900 the whole opera of 'Faust.' Domestic incidents continued to bring the queen alternations of joy and grief in abundant measure. In December 1891 she was gratified by the betrothal of Princess Mary (May), daughter of her cousin the Duchess of Teck, to the Duke of Clarence, elder son of the prince of Wales, who was in the direct line of succession to the throne. But death stepped in to forbid the union. On 14 Jan. 1892 the duke died. The tragedy for a time overwhelmed the queen. 'Was there ever a more terrible contrast?' she wrote to Tennyson; 'a wedding with bright hopes turned into a funeral!' In an address to her people she described the occasion as 'one more sad and tragical than any but one that had befallen her.' The nation fully shared her sorrow. Gladstone wrote to Sir William Harcourt: 'The national grief resembles that on the death of Princess Charlotte, and is a remarkable evidence of national attachment to the queen and royal family' (6 Feb. 1892). Lord Selborne foresaw in the good feeling thus evoked a new bond of affection between the queen and the masses of her people. On the Duke of Clarence's death, his brother George, duke of York, became next heir to the crown after his father; and on 3 May 1893 the queen assented to his betrothal to the Princess May of Teck. Sorrow was thus succeeded by gladness. The Duke of York's marriage in the Chapel Royal at St. James's Palace on 6 July 1893, which the queen attended, revived her spirits; and she wrote to her people a letter full of hope, thanking them for their congratulations. Another change in her domestic environment followed. On 22 Aug. 1893 her brother-in-law, Duke Ernest of Saxe-Coburg, died. The cordiality of her early relations with him was not maintained. She had never thought highly of his judgment, and his mode of life in his old age did not commend itself to her. His death gave effect to the arrangement by which the duchy of Saxe-Coburg-Gotha passed to her second son, Alfred, duke of Edinburgh; and he and his family thenceforth made Coburg their chief home. Thus the German principality, which was endeared to her through her mother's and her husband's association with it, was brought permanently under the sway of her descendants. The matrimonial fortunes of her grandchildren occupied much of her attention next year. At the time of the Grand Duke of Hesse's marriage with a daughter of the new Duke of Saxe-Coburg, which she herself attended at Coburg (19 April 1894), she warmly approved the betrothal of the Tsarevitch Nicholas with another granddaughter— Alix, sister of the Grand Duke of Hesse. This was the most imposing match that any of her grandchildren had made, or indeed any of her children save her eldest daughter. Her second son was already the husband of a tsar's daughter. But this union brought the head of the Russian royal family into far closer relations with her own. Before the tsarevitch's marriage, the death of his father, Tsar Alexander III, on 1 Nov. 1894, placed him on the Russian throne. His marriage followed on 23 Nov. The queen gave an appropriately elaborate banquet at Windsor in honour of the event, and made the new Tsar Nicholas II—now the husband of her granddaughter—colonel-in-chief of the second dragoons (Royal Scots Greys). Meanwhile, on 23 June 1894, the birth of a first son (Edward) to the Duke and Duchess of York added a new heir in the fourth generation to the direct succession to her throne. The queen was present at the christening at White Lodge, Richmond, on 16 July. A year later she gave a hearty welcome to a foreign kinsman in the third generation, Carlos, king of Portugal, friendship with whose father and grandparents (Queen Maria II and her consort, Prince Ferdinand of Saxe-Coburg) she had warmly cherished. She celebrated King Carlos's visit by conferring on him the order of the Garter (9 Nov. 1895). Politics at home had once more drifted in the direction which she dreaded. At the end of June 1892 the twelfth parliament of the reign was dissolved after a life of just six years, and a majority of home rulers was returned (355 to 315). Lord Salisbury waited for the meeting of parliament before resigning, but a vote of want of confidence was at once carried against him and he retired (12 Aug.). The queen had no choice but to summon Gladstone for a fourth time to fill the post of prime minister, and with the legislation that his new government prepared the queen found herself in no greater sympathy than on former occasions. Her objections to home rule for Ireland were rooted and permanent; but, though she was depressed by the passage of Gladstone's home rule bill through the House of Commons (27 July 1893), she rejoiced at its rejection by the House of Lords on 8 Sept. by the decisive majority of 378. As far as her reign was concerned the scheme then received its death-blow. She was spared further anxieties in regard to it, and the political horizon brightened for her. On 2 March 1894 Gladstone went to Windsor to resign his office owing to his age and failing health, and the queen accepted his resignation with a coldness that distressed him and friends. She did not meet him again. On 19 May 1898 he died, and though she felt sympathy with his relatives, and was grateful for the proofs he had given of attachment to the monarchy, she honestly refrained from any un-equivocal expression of admiration for his public labours. She was fully alive to the exalted view of his achievements which was shared by a large number of her subjects, and in a telegram to Mrs. Gladstone on the day of his funeral in Westminster Abbey she wrote with much adroitness of the gratification with which his widow must 'see the respect and regret evinced by the nation for the memory of one whose character and in-tellectual abilities marked him as one of the most distinguished statesmen of my reign.' But she did not commit herself to any personal appreciation beyond the concluding remark: 'I shall ever gratefully remember his devotion and zeal in all that concerned my personal welfare and that of my family.' On Gladstone's resignation in 1894, the queen, by her own act and without seeking any advice, chose the Earl of Rosebery to succeed him (3 March). She had long known him and his family (his mother had been one of her bridesmaids), and she admired his abilities. But the government's policy underwent small change. The Welsh disestablishment bill, which was read a second time in the House of Commons on 1 April 1895, ran directly counter to her personal devotion to church establishments. Nor did she welcome the changes at the war office, which relieved her cousin, the Duke of Cambridge, of the commandership-in-chief of the army, and by strictly limiting the future tenure of the post to a period of five years gave the deathblow to the cherished fiction that the commander-in-chief was the sovereign's permanent personal deputy. But Lord Rosebery's government fell in June, and Lord Salisbury, to the queen's satisfaction, resumed power on the understanding that he would be permitted an early appeal to the country. In the new ministry the conservative leaders coalesced with the leaders of liberal unionists. The dissolution of parliament was followed by the return of the unionists in a strong majority, and the unionist party under Lord Salisbury's leadership retained power till her death. With Lord Salisbury and his unionist colleagues her relations were to the last harmonious. Her sympathy with the imperialist sentiments, which Mr. Chamberlain's control of the colonial office conspicuously fostered, was whole-hearted. As in the case of Peel and Disraeli, her first knowledge of him had not prepossessed her in his favour. When he was a leader of a radical section of the liberal party she regarded him with active distrust; but his steady resistance to the policy of home rule, and his secession from the ranks of Gladstone's followers, dissipated her fears, and his imperialist administration of colonial affairs from 1895 till her death was in complete accord with her sentiment. But, despite her confidence in her advisers, her energy in criticising their counsel never slackened. She still required all papers of state to be regularly submitted to her; she was impatient of any sign of carelessness in the conduct of public business, and she pertinaciously demanded full time for the consideration of ministers' proposals. She had lately resumed her early practice of signing commissions in the army, and when in 1895 the work fell into arrears and an appeal was made to her to forgo the labour, she declined the suggestion. Her resolve to identify herself with the army never knew any diminution. Her public appearances came to have almost exclusively military associations. On 10 May 1892 she opened with much formality the Imperial Institute, but participation in civil ceremonial was rare in her closing years. On 4 July 1890 she inspected the military exhibition at Chelsea hospital. On 27 June 1892 she laid the foundation-stone of a new church at Aldershot, and witnessed the march past of ten thousand men. Next year, to her joy, but amid signs of public discontent, her son the Duke of Connaught took the Aldershot command. In July 1894 she spent two days there; on the 11th there was a military tattoo at night in her honour, and a review followed next day. In July 1895, July 1898, and June 1899 she repeated the agreeable experience. In 1898, besides attending a review, she presented colours to the 3rd battalion of the Coldstream guards.

Early in 1896 the military ardour which she encouraged in her immediate circle cost it a sad bereavement. At the end of 1895 Prince Henry of Battenberg, her youngest daughter's husband, who resided under her roof, volunteered for active service in Ashanti, where native races were in revolt against British rule. Invalided home with fever, the prince died on board H.M.S. Blonde on the way to Madeira on 20 Jan. 1896. His body was met on its arrival at Cowes on 5 Feb. by the queen and her widowed daughter, who accompanied it to its last resting-place in the church at Whippingham, where their marriage took place less than eleven years before. In the following autumn (22 Sept.–5 Oct.) she had the gratification of entertaining at Balmoral the Tsar Nicholas II and her granddaughter the tsaritza with their infant daughter. The tsar's father, grandfather, and great-grandfather had all been her guests in earlier days. On 23 Sept. 1896 the queen achieved the distinction of having reigned longer than any other English sovereign. She had worn her crown nearly twice as long as any contemporary monarch in the world, excepting only the emperor of Austria, and he ascended his throne more than eleven years after her accession. Hitherto George III's reign of fifty-nine years and ninety-six days had been the longest known to English history. In 1897 it was resolved to celebrate the completion of her sixtieth year of rule—her 'diamond jubilee'—with appropriate splendour. She readily accepted the suggestion that the celebration should be so framed as to emphasise that extension of her empire which was now recognised to have been one of the most imposing characteristics of her sovereignty. It was accordingly arranged that prime ministers of all the colonies, delegates from India and the dependencies, and representatives of all the armed forces of the British empire should take a prominent part in the public ceremonies. The main feature of the celebration was a state procession through London on 22 June. The queen made almost a circuit of her capital, attended by her family, by envoys from foreign countries, by Indian and colonial officials, and by a great band of imperial troops—Indian native levies, mounted riflemen from Australia, South Africa, and Canada, and coloured soldiers from the West Coast of Africa, Cyprus, Hongkong, and Borneo. From Buckingham Palace the mighty cortège passed to the steps at the west end of St. Paul's, where a short religious service was conducted by the highest dignitaries of the church. Thence the royal progress was continued, over

London Bridge, through the poorer districts of London on the south side of the Thames. Buckingham Palace was finally reached across Westminster Bridge and St. James's Park. Along the six miles route were ranged millions of the queen's subjects, who gave her a rousing welcome which brought tears to her eyes. Her feelings were faithfully reflected in the telegraphic greeting which she sent as she set out from the palace to all parts of the empire: 'From my heart I thank my beloved people. May God bless them!' In the evening, as in 1887, every British city was illuminated, and every headland or high ground in England, Scotland, and Wales, from Cornwall to Caithness, was ablaze with beacons. The festivities lasted a fortnight. There was a garden party at Buckingham Palace on 28 June; a review in Windsor Park of the Indian and colonial troops on 2 July; a reception on 7 July of the colonial prime ministers, when they were all sworn of the privy council; and a reception on 13 July of 180 prelates of English-speaking protestant peoples who were assembled in congress at Lambeth. By an error on the part of officials, members of the House of Commons, when they presented an address of congratulation to the queen at Buckingham Palace on 23 June, were shown some want of courtesy. The queen repaired the neglect by inviting the members and their wives to a garden party at Windsor on 3 July. The only official celebration which the queen's age prevented her from attending in person was a great review of battleships at Spithead (26 June), which in the number of assembled vessels exceeded any preceding display of the kind. Vessels of war to the number of 173 were drawn up in four lines, stretching over a course of thirty miles. The queen was represented by the prince of Wales. Not the least of many gratifying incidents that marked the celebration was the gift to Great Britain of an ironclad from Cape Colony. On 18 July the close of the rejoicings drew from the queen a letter of thanks to her people, simply expressing her boundless gratitude. The passion of loyalty which the jubilee of 1887 had called forth was brought to a degree of intensity which had no historic precedent; and during the few years of life that yet remained to the queen it burned with undiminished force throughout the empire in the breasts of almost every one of her subjects, whatever their race or domicile. The anxieties which are inseparable from the government of a great empire pursued the queen and her country in full measure during the rest of her reign, and her armies were engaged in active hostilities in many parts of the world. Most of her energies were consequently absorbed in giving characteristic proof of her concern for the welfare of her troops. She closely scanned the military expeditions on the frontier of India (1897–1899). The campaign of English and Egyptian troops under Lord Kitchener, which finally crushed the long-drawn-out rebellion in the Soudan at the battle of Omdurman on 2 Sept. 1898, and restored to Egypt the greater part of the territory that had been lost in 1883, was a source of immense gratification to her. In 1898 she indicated the course of her sympathies by thrice visiting at Netley Hospital the wounded men from India and the Soudan (11 Feb., 14 May, and 3 Dec.). When at Balmoral, 29 Oct. 1898, she presented colours to the newly raised 2nd battalion of the Cameron highlanders. On 1 July 1899 she reviewed in Windsor Great Park the Honourable Artillery Company, of which the prince of Wales was captain-general, and a few days later (15 July) she presented in Windsor Castle colours to the Scots guards, afterwards attending a march past in the park. On 10 Aug., while at Osborne, she inspected the Portsmouth volunteers in camp at Ashley, and at Balmoral on 29 Sept. she presented new colours to the 2nd battalion of the Seaforth highlanders. Her chief public appearance during 1899, which was unconnected with the army, was on 17 May 1899, when she laid the foundation-stone of the new buildings of the Victoria and Albert Museum at Kensington. The South Kensington Museum, as the institution had hitherto been named, had been brought into being by the prince consort, and was always identified in the queen's mind with her husband's public services. All other military experiences which had recently confronted the queen sank into insignificance in the autumn of 1899 in the presence of the great Boer war. With her ministers' general policy in South Africa before the war she was in agreement, although she studied the details somewhat less closely than had been her wont. Failing sight disabled her after 1898 from reading all the official papers that were presented to her, but her confidence in the wisdom of Lord Salisbury and her faith in Mr. Chamberlain's devotion to the best interests of the empire, spared her any misgivings while the negotiations with the Transvaal were pending. As in former crises of the same kind, as long as any chance remained of maintaining an honourable peace, she cherished the hope that there would be no war; but when she grew convinced that peace was only to be obtained on conditions that were derogatory to the prestige of her government she focused her energies on entreaties to her ministers to pursue the war with all possible promptitude and effect. From the opening of active operations in October 1899 until consciousness failed her on her deathbed in January 1901, the serious conflict occupied the chief place in her thoughts. The disasters which befell British arms at the beginning of the struggle caused her infinite distress, but her spirit rose with the danger. Defeat merely added fuel to the zeal with which she urged her advisers to retrieve it. It was with her especial approval that in December 1899 reinforcements on an enormous scale, drawn both from the regular army and the volunteers, were hurriedly ordered to South Africa under the command of Lord Roberts, while Lord Kitchener was summoned from the Soudan to serve as chief of the staff. In both generals she had the fullest trust.

Offers of assistance from the colonies stirred her enthusiasm, and she sent many messages of thanks. She was consoled, too, by a visit at Windsor from her grandson, the German emperor, with the empress and two of his sons, on 20 Nov. 1899. Of late there had been less harmony than of old between the courts of London and Berlin. A misunderstanding between the two countries on the subject of English relations with the Boer republics of South Africa had threatened early in 1896. The German emperor had then replied in congratulatory terms to a telegram from President Kruger informing him of the success of the Boers in repelling a filibustering raid which a few Englishmen under Dr. Jameson had made into the Transvaal. The queen, like her subjects, reprobated the emperor's interference, although it had none of the significance which popular feeling in England attributed to it. The emperor's visit to the queen and prince of Wales in November 1899 had been arranged before the Boer war broke out, but the emperor did not permit his display of friendly feeling to be postponed by the opening of hostilities. His meeting with the queen was most cordial, and his relations with the English royal family were thenceforth unclouded. By way of indicating his practical sympathy with the British army, he subscribed 300*l.* to the fund for the relief of the widows and orphans of the men of the 1st royal dragoons who were then fighting in South Africa—a regiment of which he was colonel-in-chief. Throughout 1900 the queen was indefatigable in inspecting troops who were proceeding to the seat of war, in sending to the front encouraging messages, and in writing letters of condolence to the relatives of officers who lost their lives, often requesting a photograph and inquiring into the position of their families. In the affairs of all who died in her service she took a vivid personal interest. Her anxieties at Christmas 1899 kept her at Windsor and precluded her from proceeding to Osborne for the holiday season, as had been her invariable custom, with one exception, for nearly fifty years. On Boxing day she entertained in St. George's Hall, Windsor, the wives and children of the non-commissioned officers and men of the regiments which were stationed in the royal borough. She caused a hundred thousand boxes of chocolate to be sent as her personal gift to every soldier at the front, and on New Year's day (1900) forwarded greetings to all ranks. When the news of British successes reached her in the early months of 1900—the relief of Kimberley (15 Feb.), the capture of General Cronje (27 Feb.), the relief of Ladysmith (28 Feb.), the occupation of Bloemfontein (13 March), the relief of Mafeking (17 May), and the occupation of Pretoria (5 June)—she exchanged congratulations with her generals with abundant enthusiasm. The gallantry displayed by the Irish soldiers was peculiarly gratifying to her, and she acknowledged it in a most emphatic fashion. On 2 March she gave permission to her Irish troops to wear on St. Patrick's day, by way of commemorating their achievements in South Africa, the Irish national emblem, a sprig of shamrock, the display of which had been hitherto forbidden in the army. On 7 March she came to London, and on the afternoons of 8th and 9th she drove publicly through many miles of streets in order to illustrate her watchful care of the public interests and her participation in the public anxiety. Public enthusiasm ran high, and she was greeted everywhere by cheering crowds. On 22 March she went to the Herbert Hospital, at Woolwich, to visit wounded men from South Africa. But the completest sign that she gave of the depth of her sympathy with those who were bearing the brunt of the struggle was her decision to abandon for this spring her customary visit to the South of Europe and to spend her vacation in Ireland, whence the armies in the field had been largely recruited. This plan was wholly of her own devising. Nearly forty years had elapsed since she set foot in Ireland. In that interval political disaffection had been rife, and had unhappily discouraged her from renewing her acquaintance with the country. She now spent in Dublin, at the viceregal lodge in Phœnix Park, nearly the whole of April— from the 4th to the 25th. She came, she said, in reply to an address of welcome from the corporation of Dublin, to seek change and rest, and to revive happy recollections of the warm-hearted welcome given to her, her husband, and children in former days. Her reception was all that could be wished, and it vindicated her confidence in the loyalty, despite political agitation, of the Irish people to the crown. The days were spent busily and passed quickly. She entertained the leaders of Irish society, attended a military review and an assembly of fifty-two thousand school children in Phœnix Park, and frequently drove through Dublin and the neighbouring country. On 5 April she gave orders for the formation of a new regiment of Irish guards. On her departure on 26 April she thanked the Irish people for their greeting in a public letter addressed to the lord lieutenant.

After her return to Windsor on 2 May 1900 she inspected the men of H.M.S. Powerful who had been besieged in Ladysmith, and warmly welcomed their commander, Captain Hedworth Lambton. On the 17th she visited the wounded at Netley. Lord Roberts's successes in South Africa at the time relieved her and her people of pressing anxieties, and ordinary court festivities were suffered to proceed. On 4 May she entertained at Windsor the king of Sweden and Norway, who had often been her guest as Prince Oscar of Sweden. On 10 May she held a drawing-room at Buckingham Palace; it was the only one she attended that season, and proved her last. Next day she was present at the christening of the third son of the Duke of York, when she acted as sponsor. After the usual visit to

Balmoral (22 May to 20 June) she gave several musical entertainments at Windsor. On 11 June there was a garden party at Buckingham Palace, and on 28 June at Windsor a state banquet to the khedive of Egypt, who was visiting the country. Her old friend the Empress Eugénie was her guest at Osborne in September. Apart from the war, she was interested during the session in the passage through the House of Commons of the Australian commonwealth bill, which was to create a federal union among the Australian colonies. She received at Windsor on 27 March the delegates from Australia, who were in England to watch the bill's progress. When in the autumn the bill received the royal assent, she, on 27 Aug., cordially accepted the suggestion that her grandson the Duke of York, with the duchess, should proceed as her representative to Australia in 1901, to open in her name the first session of the new commonwealth parliament. She was especially desirous of showing her appreciation of the part taken by colonial troops in the Boer war, and she directed that the inauguration of the commonwealth at Sydney on 1 Jan. 1901, should be attended by a guard of honour representing every branch of the army, including the volunteers. But the situation in South Africa remained the central topic of her thought, and in the late summer it gave renewed cause for concern. Despite Lord Roberts's occupation of the chief towns of the enemy's territory, fighting was still proceeding in the open country, and deaths from disease or wounds in the British ranks were numerous. The queen was acutely distressed by the reports of suffering that reached her through the summer, but, while she constantly considered and suggested means of alleviating the position of affairs, and sought to convince herself that her ministers were doing all that was possible to hasten the final issue, she never faltered in her conviction that she and her people were under a solemn obligation to fight on till absolute victory was assured. Owing to the prevailing feeling of gloom the queen, when at Balmoral in October and November, allowed no festivities. The usual highland gathering for sports and games at Braemar, which she had attended for many years with the utmost satisfaction, was abandoned. She still watched closely public events in foreign countries, and she found little consolation there. The assassination of her friend Humbert, king of Italy, on 29 July at Monza greatly disturbed her equanimity. In France a wave of strong anti-English feeling involved her name, and the shameless attacks on her by unprincipled journalists were rendered the more offensive by the approval they publicly won from the royalist leader, the Duc d'Orléans, great-grandson of Louis Philippe, to whom and to whose family she had proved the staunchest of friends. Happily the duke afterwards apologised for his misbehaviour, and was magnanimously pardoned by the queen. In October a general election was deemed necessary by the government—the existing parliament was more than five years old—and the queen was gratified by the result. Lord Salisbury's government, which was responsible for the war and its conduct, received from England and Scotland overwhelming support. The election emphatically supported the queen's view that, despite the heavy cost of life and treasure, hostilities must be vigorously pursued until the enemy acknowledged defeat. When the queen's fifteenth and last parliament was opened in December, Lord Salisbury was still prime minister; but he resigned the foreign secretaryship to Lord Lansdowne, formerly minister of war, and he made with the queen's approval some unimpressive changes in the personal constitution of the ministry. Its policy remained unaltered. Death had again been busy among the queen's relatives and associates, and cause for private sorrow abounded in her last years. Her cousin and friend of youth, the Duchess of Teck, had passed away on 27 Oct. 1897. Another blow was the death at Meran of phthisis, on 5 Feb. 1899, of her grandson, Prince Alfred, only son of the Duke of Saxe-Coburg-Gotha. The succession to the duchies of Saxe-Coburg-Gotha, which was thus deprived of an heir, was offered by the diet of the duchies to the queen's third son, the Duke of Connaught; but, although he temporarily accepted it, he, in accordance with the queen's wish, renounced the position in his own behalf and in that of his son a few months later in favour of his nephew, the Duke of Albany, the posthumous son of the queen's youngest son, Leopold. To the queen's satisfaction the little Duke of Albany was adopted on 30 June 1899 as heir presumptive to the beloved principality. The arrangement unhappily took practical effect earlier than she anticipated. A mortal disease soon attacked the reigning duke of Saxe-Coburg, the queen's second son, Alfred, and he died suddenly at Rosenau on 30 July 1900, before a fatal issue was expected. The last bereavement in the royal circle which the queen suffered was the death, on 29 Oct. 1900, of her grandson, Prince Christian Victor of Schleswig-Holstein, eldest son of Princess Helena, the queen's second daughter. The young man had contracted enteric fever on the battlefields of South Africa. But even more distressing was it for the queen to learn, in the summer of 1900, that her eldest child, the Empress Frederick, was herself the victim of a malady that must soon end in death. Although the empress was thenceforth gravely disabled, she survived her mother rather more than six months. On 7 Nov. the queen returned to Windsor from Balmoral in order to console Princess Christian on the death of her son, and twice before the end of the month she took the opportunity of welcoming home a few of the troops from South Africa, including colonial and Canadian detachments. On each occasion she addressed a few words to the men. On 12 Dec. she made her last public appearance by attending a sale of needlework by Irish ladies at the

Windsor town hall. On 14 Dec. she celebrated the thirty-ninth anniversary of the prince consort's death at Frogmore with customary solemnity, and on the 18th she left for Osborne. It was the last journey of her life. Throughout life the queen's physical condition was robust. She always believed in the efficacy of fresh air and abundant ventilation, and those who waited on her had often occasion to lament that the queen never felt cold. She was long extremely careful about her health, and usually consulted her resident physician, Sir James Reid, many times a day. Although she suffered no serious ailments, age told on her during the last five or six years of her life. Since 1895 she suffered from a rheumatic stiffness of the joints, which rendered walking difficult, and from 1898 incipient cataract greatly affected her eyesight. The growth of the disease was steady, but it did not reach the stage which rendered an operation expedient. In her latest year she was scarcely able to read, although she could still sign her name and could write letters with difficulty. It was not till the late summer of 1900 that symptoms menacing to life made themselves apparent. The anxieties and sorrows due to the South African war and to deaths of relatives proved a severe strain on her nervous system. She manifested a tendency to aphasia, but by a strong effort of will she was for a time able to check its growth. She had long justly prided herself on the strength and precision of her memory, and the failure to recollect a familiar name or word irritated her, impelling increased mental exertion. No more specific disease declared itself, but loss of weight and complaints of sleeplessness in the autumn of 1900 pointed to a general physical decay. She hoped that a visit to the Riviera in the spring would restore her powers, but when she reached Windsor in November her physicians feared that a journey abroad might have evil effects. Arrangements for the removal of the court early next year to the Riviera were, however, begun. At Osborne her health showed no signs of improvement, but no immediate danger was apprehended. On Christmas morning her lifelong friend and lady-in-waiting, Jane Lady Churchill, passed away suddenly in her sleep. The queen was greatly distressed, and at once made a wreath for the coffin with her own hands. On 2 Jan. 1901 she nerved herself to welcome Lord Roberts on his return from South Africa, where the command-in-chief had devolved on Lord Kitchener. She managed by an effort of will briefly to congratulate him on his successes, and she conferred on him an earldom and the order of the Garter. On the 10th Mr. Chamberlain had a few minutes' audience with her, so that she might learn the immediate prospect of South African affairs. It was her last interview with a minister. The widowed duchess of Saxe-Coburg-Gotha arrived on a visit, and, accompanied by her, the queen drove out on the 15th for the last time. By that date her medical attendants recognised her condition to be hopeless. The brain was failing, and life was slowly ebbing. On the 19th it was publicly announced that she was suffering from physical prostration. The next two days her weakness grew, and the children who were in England were summoned to her deathbed. On 21 Jan. her grandson, the German emperor, arrived, and in his presence and in the presence of two sons and three daughters she passed away at half-past six in the evening of Tuesday, 22 Jan. She was eighty-one years old and eight months, less two days. Her reign had lasted sixty-three years, seven months, and two days. She had lived three days longer than George III, the longest-lived sovereign of England before her. Her reign exceeded his, the longest yet known to English history, by nearly four years. On the day following her death her eldest son met the privy council at St. James's Palace, took the oaths as her successor to the throne, and was on the 24th proclaimed king under the style of Edward VII. In accordance with a dominant sentiment of her life the queen was accorded a military funeral. On 1 Feb. the yacht Alberta, passing between long lines of warships which fired a last salute, carried the coffin from Cowes to Gosport. Early next day the remains were brought to London, and were borne on a gun carriage from Victoria station to Paddington. In the military procession which accompanied the cortège, every branch of the army was represented, while immediately behind the coffin rode King Edward VII, supported on one side by his brother, the Duke of Connaught, and on the other by his nephew, the German emperor. They were followed by the kings of Portugal and of Greece, most of the queen's grandsons, and members of every royal family in Europe. The funeral service took place in the afternoon, with imposing solemnity, in St. George's Chapel, Windsor. On Monday, 4 Feb., the coffin was removed privately, in the presence only of the royal family, to the Frogmore mausoleum, and was there placed in the sarcophagus which already held the remains of Prince Albert. No British sovereign was more sincerely mourned. As the news of the queen's death spread, impassioned expressions of grief came from every part of the United Kingdom, of the British empire, and of the world. Native chieftains in India, in Africa, in New Zealand, vied with their British-born fellow-subjects in the avowals of a personal sense of loss. The demonstration of her people's sorrow testified to the spirit of loyalty to her person and position which had been evoked by her length of life and reign, her personal sorrows, and her recent manifestations of sympathy with her subjects' welfare. But the strength and popularity which the grief at the queen's death proved the monarchy to enjoy were only in part due to her personal character and the conditions of her personal career. A force of circumstances which was not subject to any individual control largely contributed to the intense respect and affection on the part of the people of the empire which encircled her crown when her rule ended. The passion of loyalty with which she inspired her people during her last years was a comparatively late growth. In the middle period of her reign the popular interest, which her youth, innocence, and simplicity of domestic life had excited at the beginning, was exhausted, and the long seclusion which she maintained after her husband's death developed in its stead a coldness between her people and herself which bred much disrespectful criticism. Neither her partial resumption of her public life nor her venerable age fully accounts for the new sentiment of affectionate enthusiasm which greeted her declining days. It was largely the outcome of the new conception of the British monarchy which sprang from the development of the colonies and dependencies of Great Britain, and the sudden strengthening of the sense of unity between them and the mother country. The crown after 1880 became the living symbol of imperial unity, and every year events deepened the impression that the queen in her own person typified the common interest and the common sympathy which spread a feeling of brotherhood through the continents that formed the British empire. She and her ministers in her last years encouraged the identification of the British sovereignty with the unifying spirit of imperialism, and she thoroughly reciprocated the warmth of feeling for herself and her office which that spirit engendered in her people at home and abroad. But it is doubtful if, in the absence of the imperial idea for the creation of which she was not responsible, she could under the constitution have enjoyed that popular regard and veneration of which she died in unchallenged possession. The practical anomalies incident to the position of a constitutional sovereign who is in theory invested with all the semblance of power, but is denied any of its reality or responsibility, were brought into strong relief by the queen's personal character and the circumstances of her life. Possessed of no commanding strength of intellect but of an imperious will, she laboriously studied every detail of government business, and on every question of policy or administration she formed for herself decided opinions, to which she obstinately adhered, pressing them pertinaciously on the notice of her ministers. No sovereign of England ever applied himself to the work of government with greater ardour or greater industry. None was a more voluminous correspondent with the officers of state. Although the result of her energy could not under the constitution be commensurate with its intensity, her activity was in the main advantageous. The detachment from party interests or prepossessions, which her elevated and isolated position came to foster in her, gave her the opportunity of detecting in ministerial schemes any national peril to which her ministers might at times be blinded by the spirit of faction, and her persistence occasionally led to some modification of policy in the direction that she urged with happy result. Her length of sovereignty, too, rendered in course of years her personal experiences of government far wider and far closer than that of any of her ministers, and she could recall much past procedure of which she was the only surviving witness. Absolutely frank and trustful in the expression of her views to her ministers, she had at the same time the tact to acquiesce with outward grace, however strong her private objections, in any verdict of the popular vote, against which appeal was seen to be hopeless. In the two instances of the Irish church bill of 1869 and the franchise extension bill of 1884 she made personal efforts, in the interest of the general peace of the country, to discourage an agitation which she felt to be doomed to failure. While, therefore, she shrank from no exertion whereby she might influence personally the machinery of the state, she was always conscious of her powerlessness to enforce her opinions or her wishes. With the principle of the constitution which imposed on the sovereign the obligation of giving formal assent to every final decision of his advisers, however privately obnoxious it might be to him, she had the practical wisdom to avoid any manner of conflict. Partly owing to her respect for the constitution in which she was educated, partly owing to her personal idiosyncrasies, and partly owing to the growth of democratic principles among her people, the active force of such prerogatives as the crown possessed at her accession was, in spite of her toil and energy, diminished rather than increased during her reign. Parliament deliberately dissolved almost all the personal authority that the crown had hitherto exercised over the army. The prerogative of mercy was practically abrogated when the home secretary was in effect made by statute absolute controller of its operations. The distribution of titles and honours became in a larger degree than in former days an integral part of the machinery of party politics. The main outward signs of the sovereign's formal supremacy in the state lost, moreover, by her own acts, their old distinctness. Conservative as was her attitude to minor matters of etiquette, she was self-willed enough to break with large precedents if the breach consorted with her private predilections. During the last thirty-nine years of her reign she opened parliament in person only seven times, and did not prorogue it once after 1854. It had been the rule of her predecessors regularly to attend the legislature at the opening and close of each session, unless they were disabled by illness, and her defiance of this practice tended to weaken her semblance of hold on the central force of government. Another innovation in the usages of the monarchy, for which the queen, with a view to increasing her private convenience, was personally responsible, had a like effect. Her three immediate predecessors on the throne never left the country during their reigns. Only three earlier sovereigns of modern times occasionally crossed the seas while wearing the crown, and they were represented at home in their absence by a regent or by lords-justices, to whom were temporarily delegated the symbols of sovereign power, while a responsible minister was the sovereign's constant companion abroad. Queen Victoria ignored nearly the whole of this procedure. She repeatedly visited foreign countries; no regent nor lords-justices were called to office in her absence; she was at times unaccompanied by a responsible minister, and she often travelled privately and informally under an assumed title of inferior rank. The mechanical applications of steam and electricity which were new to her era facilitated communication with her, but the fact that she voluntarily cut herself off from the seat of government for weeks at a time—in some instances at seasons of crisis—seemed to prove that the sovereign's control of government was in effect less constant and essential than of old, or that it might, at any rate, incur interruption without in any way impairing the efficiency of the government's action. Her withdrawal from parliament and her modes of foreign travel alike enfeebled the illusion which is part of the fabric of a perfectly balanced monarchy that the motive power of government resides in the sovereign. In one other regard the queen, by conduct which can only be assigned to care for her personal comfort at the cost of the public advantage, almost sapped the influence which the crown can legitimately exert on the maintenance of a healthy harmony among the component parts of the United Kingdom. Outside England she bestowed markedly steady favour on Scotland. Her sojourns there, if reckoned together, occupied a period of time approaching seven years. She spent in Ireland in the whole of her reign a total period of less than five weeks. During fifty-nine of her sixty-three years of rule she never set foot there at all. Her visit in her latest year was a triumph of robust old age and a proof of undiminished alertness of sympathy. But it brought into broad relief the neglect of Ireland that preceded it, and it emphasised the errors of feeling and of judgment which made her almost a complete stranger to her Irish subjects in their own land during the rest of her long reign. The queen's visits to foreign lands were intimately associated with her devotion to her family which was a ruling principle of her life. The kinsmen and kinswomen with whom her relations were closest were German, and Germany had for her most of the associations of home. She encouraged in her household many German customs, and with her numerous German relatives maintained an enormous and detailed correspondence. Her patriotic attachment to her own country of England and to her British subjects could never be justly questioned, and it was her cherished conviction that England might and should mould the destinies of the world; but she was much influenced in her view of foreign policy by the identification of her family with Germany, and by her natural anxiety to protect the interests of ruling German princes who were lineally related to her. It was 'a sacred duty,' as she said, for her to work for the welfare of Prussia, because her eldest daughter had married the heir to the Prussian crown. As a daughter and a wife she felt bound to endeavour to preserve the independence of the duchy of Saxe-Coburg-Gotha, whence her mother and husband sprang. Her friendship for Belgium was a phase of her affection for her uncle, who sat on its throne. The spirit of patriotic kingship was always strong enough in her to quell hesitation as to the path she should follow when the interest of England was in direct conflict with that of her German kindred, but it was her constant endeavour to harmonise the two. Although the queen disliked war and its inevitable brutalities, she treated it as in certain conditions a dread necessity which no ruler could refuse to face. Thoroughly as she valued peace, she deemed it wrong to purchase it at the expense of national rights or dignity. But she desired that warfare should be practised with all the humanity that was possible, and she was deeply interested in the military hospitals and in the training of nurses. The queen's wealth of domestic affection was allied to a tenderness of feeling and breadth of sympathy with mankind generally, which her personal sorrows accentuated. She spared no exertion personally to console the bereaved, to whatever walk of life they belonged, and she greatly valued a reciprocation of her sympathy. Every instance of unmerited suffering that came to her notice—as in the case of Captain Dreyfus in France—stirred her to indignation. Nor were animals—horses and dogs—excluded from the scope of her compassion. To vivisection she was strenuously opposed, denouncing with heat the cruelty of wounding and torturing dumb creatures. She countenanced no lenity in the punishment of those guilty of cruel acts.

The queen was not altogether free from that morbid tendency of mind which comes of excessive study of incidents of sorrow and suffering. Her habit of accumulating sepulchral memorials of relations and friends was one manifestation of it. But it was held in check by an innate cheerfulness of disposition and by her vivacious curiosity regarding all that passed in the domestic and political circles of which she was the centre. She took a deep interest in her servants. She was an admirable hostess, personally consulting her guests' comfort. The ingenuousness of youth was never wholly extinguished in her. She was easily amused, and was never at a loss for recreation. Round games of cards or whist she abandoned in later years altogether; but she sketched, played the piano, sang, did needlework until old age.

The queen's artistic sense was not strong. In furniture and dress she preferred the fashions of her early married years to any other. She was never a judge of painting, and she bestowed her main patronage on portrait painters like Winterhalter and Von Angeli, and on sculptors like

Boehm, who had little beyond their German nationality to recommend them. 'The only studio of a master that she ever visited was that of Leighton, whose "Procession of Cimabue" the prince consort had bought for her, and whom she thought delightful, though perhaps more as an accomplished and highly agreeable courtier than as a painter.' In music she showed greater taste. Staunch to the heroes of her youth, she always appreciated the operas of Rossini, Bellini, and Donizetti; Handel and Bach bored her, but Mendelssohn also won her early admiration, and Gounod and Sullivan fascinated her later. She never understood or approved Wagner or his school. She was devoted to the theatre from girlhood, and all her enthusiasm revived when in her last years she restored the dramatic performances at court, which her mourning had long interrupted. She was not well read, and although she emulated her husband's respect for literature, it entered little into the business or recreation of her life.

In talk she appreciated homely wit of a quiet kind, and laughed without restraint when a jest or anecdote appealed to her. Subtlety or indelicacy offended her, and sometimes evoked a scornful censure. Although she naturally expected courtesy of address, and resented brusque expression of contradiction or dissent, she was not conciliated by obsequiousness. 'It is useless to ask ———'s opinion,' she would say; 'he only tries to echo mine.' Her own conversation had often the charm of naïveté. When told that a very involved piece of modern German music, to which she was listening with impatience, was a 'drinking song' by Rubinstein, she remarked, 'Why, you could not drink a cup of tea to that.' Her memory was unusually sound, and errors which were made in her hearing on matters familiar to her she corrected with briskness and point.

The queen's religion was simple, sincere, and undogmatic. Theology did not interest her, but in the virtue of religious toleration she was an ardent believer. When Dr. Creighton, the last bishop of London of her reign, declared that she was the best liberal he knew, he had in mind her breadth of religious sentiment. On moral questions her views were strict. She was opposed to the marriage of widows. To the movement for the greater emancipation of women she was thoroughly and almost blindly antipathetic. She never realised that her own position gave the advocates of women's rights their strongest argument. With a like inconsistency she regarded the greatest of her female predecessors, Queen Elizabeth, with aversion, although she resembled Queen Elizabeth in her frankness and tenacity of purpose, and might, had the constitution of the country in the nineteenth century permitted it, have played as decisive a part in history. Queen Victoria's sympathies were with the Stuarts and the jacobites. She declined to identify Prince Charles Edward with his popular designation of 'the Young Pretender,' and gave in his memory the baptismal names of

Charles Edward to her grandson, the Duke of Albany. She was deeply interested in the history of Mary Stuart; she placed a window in Carisbrooke Church in memory of Charles I's daughter Elizabeth (1850), and a marble tomb by Marochetti above her grave in the neighbouring church of St. Thomas at Newport (1856). She restored James II's tomb at St. Germain. Such likes and dislikes reflected purely personal idiosyncrasies. It was not Queen Elizabeth's mode of rule that offended Queen Victoria; it was her lack of feminine modesty. It was not the Stuarts' method of government that appealed to her; it was their fall from high estate to manifold misfortune. Queen Victoria's whole life and action were, indeed, guided by personal sentiment rather than by reasoned principles. But her personal sentiment, if not altogether removed from the commonplace, nor proof against occasional inconsistencies, bore ample trace of courage, truthfulness, and sympathy with suffering. Far from being an embodiment of selfish whim, the queen's personal sentiment blended in its main current sincere love of public justice with staunch fidelity to domestic duty, and ripe experience came in course of years to imbue it with the force of patriarchal wisdom. In her capacity alike of monarch and woman, the queen's personal sentiment proved, on the whole, a safer guide than the best devised system of moral or political philosophy. Of her nine children (four sons—Albert Edward, prince of Wales, Alfred, Arthur, and Leopold—and five daughters—Victoria, Alice, Helena, Louise, and Beatrice), two sons, Leopold and Alfred, and one daughter, Alice, died in the queen's lifetime. She was survived by two sons—the prince of Wales and Arthur duke of Connaught—and by four daughters—Victoria, Empress Frederick, Helena, Princess Christian, Louise, Duchess of Argyll, and Beatrice, Princess Henry of Battenberg. The eldest daughter, Victoria (Empress Frederick), died on 5 Aug. 1901 at her seat, Friedrichshof, near Frankfort. All her children were married, and all except the Princess Louise had issue. The queen's grandchildren numbered thirty-one at the date of her death—nine died in her lifetime— and her great-grandchildren numbered thirty-seven. Seventeen of her grandchildren were married. In two instances there was intermarriage of first cousins—viz. Grand Duke of Hesse (Princess Alice's only surviving son) with Princess Victoria Melita (Prince Alfred's second daughter), and Prince Henry of Prussia (Princess Royal's second son) with Princess Irena Marie (Princess Alice's third daughter). Other marriages of her grandchildren connected her with the chief reigning families of Europe. The third daughter of the Princess Royal (Empress Frederick), Princess Sophie Dorothea, married in 1889 the Duke of Sparta, son of the king of Greece. Princess Alice's youngest daughter (Princess Alix Victoria) married in 1894 Nicholas II, tsar of Russia, while Princess Alice's second daughter

(Elizabeth) married the Grand Duke Serge of Russia, a younger son of Tsar Alexander II and uncle of Tsar Nicholas II. Prince Alfred's eldest daughter (Princess Marie) married in 1893 Ferdinand, crown prince of Roumania. Princess Maud, youngest daughter of the prince of Wales, married in 1896 Prince Charles of Denmark. Only one grandchild married a member of the English nobility, the prince of Wales's eldest daughter, who became the wife of the Duke of Fife. The remaining seven marriages of grandchildren were contracted with members of princely families of Germany. The Emperor William II married Princess Victoria of Augustenburg. The Princess Royal's daughters, the Princesses Charlotte, Frederika Victoria, and Margaretta Beatrice, married respectively the hereditary Prince of Saxe-Meiningen (in 1878), Prince Adolphe of Schaumburg-Lippe (in 1890), and Prince Frederick Charles of Hesse-Cassel (in 1893). Princess Alice's eldest daughter (Victoria) married in 1884 Prince Louis of Battenberg. Prince Alfred's third daughter (Alexandra) married in 1896 the hereditary Prince of Hohenlohe-Langenburg. Princess Helena's elder daughter (Louise Augusta) married in 1891 Prince Aribert of Anhalt.

There was one marriage in the queen's lifetime in the fourth generation of her family. On 24 Sept. 1898 the eldest of her great-grandchildren, Féodora, daughter of the hereditary Princess of Saxe-Meiningen (Princess Royal's eldest daughter), married Prince Henry XXX of Reuss. The queen's portrait was painted, drawn, sculptured, and photographed several hundred times in the course of the reign. None are satisfactory presentments. The queen's features in repose necessarily omit suggestion of the animated and fascinating smile which was the chief attraction of her countenance. Nor is it possible graphically to depict the exceptional grace of bearing which compensated for the smallness of her stature. Among the chief paintings or drawings of her, those of her before her accession are by Sir William Beechey, R.A. (with the Duchess of Kent), 1821; by Richard Westall, R.A., 1830; by Sir George Hayter, 1833; and by R. J. Lane, A.R.A., 1837. Those after her accession are by Alfred Chalon, in state robes (engraved by Cousins), 1838; by Sir George Hayter, 1838; by Sir David Wilkie, 1839 (in Glasgow Gallery); by Sir Edwin Landseer (drawing presented by the queen to Prince Albert), 1839; by F. Winterhalter, 1845 and other years; by Winterhalter (group with Prince Arthur and Duke of Wellington), 1848; by Sir Edwin Landseer, 1866; by Baron H. von Angeli, 1875 (of which many replicas were made for presents, and a copy by Lady Abercromby is in the National Portrait Gallery, London), 1885 and 1897; by Mr. W. Q. Orchardson, R.A. (group with prince of Wales, Duke of York, and Prince Edward of York), 1900; and by M. Benjamin Constant, 1900. There are several miniatures by Sir W. C. Ross, R.A., and one by Robert

Thorburn, A.R.A. (with prince of Wales as a child). There is a clever caricature lithographic portrait, by Mr. William Nicholson, 1897. Every leading episode in the queen's life was commemorated on her commission by a painting in which her portrait appears. Most of these memorial paintings, many of which have been engraved, are at Windsor; a few are at Buckingham Palace or Osborne. They include Sir David Wilkie's 'The Queen's First Council,' 1837; C. R. Leslie's 'The Queen receiving the Sacrament at her Coronation,' 1838, and 'The Christening of the Princess Royal,' 1841; Sir George Hayter's 'Coronation,' 'The Queen's Marriage,' 1840, and 'Christening of the Prince of Wales;' F. Winterhalter's 'The Reception of Louis Philippe,' 1844; E. M. Ward's 'The Queen investing Napoleon III with the Garter' and 'The Queen at the Tomb of Napoleon,' 1855; G. H. Thomas's 'Review in Paris,' 1855; J. Phillip's 'Marriage of Princess Royal,' 1859; G. H. Thomas's 'The Queen at Aldershot,' 1859; W. P. Frith's 'Marriage of the Prince of Wales,' 1863; G. Magnussen's 'Marriage of Princess Helena,' 1866; Sydney P. Hall's 'Marriage of the Duke of Connaught,' 1879; Sir James Linton's 'Marriage of the Duke of Albany,' 1882; R. Caton Woodville's 'Marriage of the Princess Beatrice,' 1885; Laurenz Tuxen's 'The Queen and Royal Family at Jubilee of 1887;' Sydney P. Hall's 'Marriage of the Duchess of Fife,' 1889; Tuxen's 'Marriage of the Duke of York,' 1893. The sculptured presentations of the queen, one or more examples of which is to be found in almost every city of the empire, include a bust by Behnes, 1829 (in possession of Lord Ronald Gower); an equestrian statue by Marochetti at Glasgow; a statue by Boehm at Windsor; a large plaster bust by Sir Edgar Boehm (in National Portrait Gallery, London); a statue at Winchester by Mr. Alfred Gilbert, R.A.; a statue at Manchester by Mr. Onslow Ford, R.A., 1900. A national memorial in sculpture, designed by Mr. Thomas Brock, R.A., has been placed in the Mall opposite the entrance to Buckingham Palace. The portrait head of the queen on the coinage followed three successive types in the course of the reign. Soon after her accession William Wyon designed from life a head which appears in the silver and gold coinage with the hair simply knotted, excepting in the case of the florin, where the head bears a crown for the first time since the coinage of Charles II. In the copper coinage a laurel wreath was intertwined with the hair. In 1887 Sir Edgar Boehm designed a new bust portrait, showing the features in mature age with a small crown and veil most awkwardly placed on the head. This ineffective design was replaced in 1893 by a more artistic crowned presentment from the hand of Mr. Thomas Brock, R.A.

Of medals on which her head appears the majority commemorate military or naval achievements, and are not of great artistic note (cf. John H. Mayo's *Medals and Decorations of the British Army and Navy*, 1897). Many

331

Victoria

medals commemorating events in the queen's reign were also struck by order of the corporation of London (cf. Charles Welch's *Numismata Londinensia*, 1894, with plates). Of strictly official medals of the reign the chief are that struck in honour of the coronation from designs by Pistrucci in 1838; the jubilee medal of 1887, with the reverse designed by Lord Leighton; and the diamond jubilee medal of 1897, with Wyon's design of the queen's head in youth on the reverse, and Mr. Brock's design of the head in old age on the obverse with the noble inscription: 'Longitudo dierum in dextera eius et in sinistra gloria.'

The adhesive postage stamp was an invention of the queen's reign, and was adopted by the government in 1840. A crowned portrait head of the queen was designed for postage stamps in that year, and was not modified in the United Kingdom during her lifetime. In most of the colonies later postage stamps bore a portrait of the queen in old age.

[A life of Queen Victoria based on this article appeared in 1902. There are contemporary biographic sketches by Sir R. R. Holmes, formerly librarian at Windsor (with elaborate portrait illustrations, 1887, and text alone, 1901), by Mrs. Oliphant, by the Rev. Dr. Tulloch, by the Marquis of Lorne (fourth duke of Argyll), by Sarah Tooley, by G. Barnett Smith, and by J. Cordy Jeaffreson (1893, 2 vols.). The outward facts of her reign are best studied in the Annual Register from 1837 to 1900, together with the Times newspaper, Hansard's Parliamentary Debates, and the collected edition of Punch. A vast library of memoirs of contemporaries supplies useful information. For the years before and immediately after the accession, see Mrs. Gerald Gurney's Childhood of Queen Victoria, 1901; Tuer's First Year of a Silken Reign; Memoir of Gabriele von Bülow (Engl. transl.), 1897; Earl of Albemarle's Fifty Years of my Life; Stafford House Letters, 1891, pt. vi.; and Sir Charles Murray's papers in Cornhill Mag. 1897. The portion of the queen's career which has been dealt with most fully is her married life, 1840–61, which is treated in General Grey's Early Years of the Prince Consort, 1868, and in Sir Theodore Martin's Life of the Prince Consort, 5 vols. 1874–80. Both works draw largely on her and her husband's journals and letters. Both General Grey and Sir Theodore Martin write from the queen's point of view; some memoirs published since the appearance of these volumes usefully supplement the information. An important selection from the queen's correspondence between 1837 and 1861 was issued officially in 1907, under the editorship of Viscount Esher and Mr. A. C. Benson. The best authority for the general course of the queen's life and her relations with political history down to 1860 is, apart from this correspondence, to be found in the three series of the Greville Memoirs (1817–60), which are outspoken, and in the main trustworthy. The Duke Ernest of Saxe-Coburg's Memoirs, 4 vols. (English transl. 1888–90), throw side lights on the queen's personal relations with Germany and German politics, and print many of her letters; they carry events from 1840 to 1870. The early years of the same period are covered by the Memoirs of Baron von Bunsen and by Memoirs of Baron von Stockmar, by his son (Engl. transl. 2 vols. 1892).

Other hints from the German side may be gleaned in Th. von Bernhardi Aus dem Leben, pt. v. 1895; Memoirs of Count von Beust; Memoirs of Count Vitzthum von Eckstadt; Moltke's Letters to his Wife and other Relatives, ed. Sidney Whitman (2 vols. 1896); Margaretha von Poschinger's Life of Emperor Frederick (Engl. transl. by Whitman, 1901); Bismarck's Reflections and Reminiscences (2 vols. 1898, Engl. transl.); and Busch's Conversations of Bismarck (3 vols. 1897). For the English relations with Napoleon III (1851–68) see De la Gorce's Histoire du Second Empire (5 vols.). The queen's domestic life from 1838 to 1870 may be traced in Letters from Sarah, Lady Lyttelton, 1797–1870, (privately printed for the family 1873); from 1863 to 1878 in the Letters of Princess Alice, with memoir by Dr. Sell (Engl. transl. 1884); from 1842 to 1882 in the queen's Leaves (1868), and More Leaves (1883) from her Journal in the Highlands; and from 1850 to 1897 in Sir Kinloch Cooke's Life of the Duchess of Teck, 2 vols. 1900. Both court and diplomatic affairs (1837–68) are sketched in Lady Bloomfield's Court and Diplomatic Life (1883, 2 vols.), and diplomatic affairs alone (1837–1879) in Lord Augustus Loftus's Reminiscences, 2 series (4 vols. 1892–4). For home politics see Torrens's Life of Lord Melbourne; the Creevey Papers; the Croker Papers; the Peel Papers (a specially valuable work); Sir Spencer Walpole's Life of Lord John Russell (a most useful biography); Bulwer and Ashley's Life of Lord Palmerston; Lord Malmesbury's Memoirs of an Ex-Minister; Benham and Davidson's Life of Archbishop Tait (1891); Lord Selborne's Memorials; Gladstone's Gleanings, vol. i.; Childers's Life of Hugh C. E. Childers (1901); Morley's Life of Gladstone, 1903; Fitzmaurice's Life of Lord Granville, 1905; Sir Algernon West's Recollections. Personal reminiscences of the queen in private life abound in Donald Macleod's Life of Norman Macleod (2 vols. 1876), Mrs. Oliphant's Life of Principal Tulloch (1888), Prothero's Life of Dean Stanley, Lord Tennyson's Memoir of Lord Tennyson, Benson's Memoirs of Archbishop Benson, and Sir Theodore Martin's Queen Victoria as I Knew Her (1906), all print some letters of hers. A character sketch is in Quarterly Rev., April 1901. Slighter particulars are in Trevelyan's Life of Macaulay; Ashwell and Wilberforce's Life of Bishop Wilberforce (3 vols. 1879); Reid's Lord Houghton and W. E. Forster; Fanny Kemble's Records; Lang's Lord Iddesleigh; Maxwell's Life of W. H. Smith; Sir Theodore Martin's Life of Helena Faucit, Lady Martin (1900); Sir John Mowbray's Seventy Years at Westminster; Laughton's Life of Henry Reeve (1899); W. A. Lindsay's The Royal Household (1897); Lord Ronald Gower's Reminiscences; and Wilkinson's Reminiscences of King Ernest of Hanover. In the preparation of this article the writer has utilised private information derived from various sources.]

SIDNEY LEE

published 1901

GEORGE William Frederick Charles

(1819–1904)

Second Duke of Cambridge, Earl of
Tipperary and Baron Culloden

Field-marshal and commander-in-chief of the army, was only son of
Adolphus Frederick, first duke, the youngest son of George III. His mother
was Augusta Wilhelmina Louisa, daughter of Frederick, landgrave of
Hesse Cassel. He was born at Cambridge House, Hanover, on 26 March
1819, and being at that time the only grandchild of George III, his birth was
formally attested by three witnesses—the duke of Clarence (later William
IV), the earl of Mayo, and George Henry Rose, P.C. His father was
governor-general of Hanover, and Prince George lived there till 1830, when
he was sent to England to be under the care of William IV and Queen
Adelaide. His tutor was John Ryle Wood, afterwards canon of Worcester,
who had great influence over him and won his lasting attachment. At
Wood's instance he began a diary, as a boy of fourteen, a singularly naive
confession of his shortcomings, and he kept it up to within a few months
of his death. In 1825 he was made G.C.H., and in Aug. 1835 K.G. In 1836 he
rejoined his parents in Hanover, his tutor being replaced by a military
governor, lieutenant-colonel William Henry Cornwall of the Coldstream
guards. He had been colonel in the Jäger battalion of the Hanoverian
guards since he was nine years old; he now began to learn regimental duty
both as a private and an officer.

On the accession of his first cousin, Queen Victoria, in June 1837,
Hanover passed to the duke of Cumberland, and the duke of Cambridge
returned with his family to England. On 3 Nov. Prince George was made
brevet colonel in the British army, and in Sept. 1838 he went to Gibraltar to
learn garrison duties. He was attached to the 33rd foot for drill. After
spending six months there and six months in travel in the south of Europe,
he came home, and was attached to the 12th lancers, with which he served
for two years in England and Ireland. On 15 April 1842 he was gazetted to
the 8th light dragoons as lieutenant-colonel, but ten days afterwards he
was transferred to the 17th lancers as colonel. He commanded this
regiment at Leeds, and helped the magistrates to preserve the peace of the
town during the industrial disturbances in August.

On 20 April 1843 he was appointed colonel on the staff, to command the
troops in Corfu. He spent two years there, and on Lord Seaton's recommendation he received the G.C.M.G. He was promoted major-general on 7
May 1845. After commanding the troops at Limerick for six months, he was

appointed to the Dublin district on 1 April 1847, and held that command five years. He had a large force under him, and worked hard at the training of the troops. In 1848 political disturbances made his post no sinecure. By the death of his father on 8 July 1850 Prince George became duke of Cambridge, and an income of 12,000l. a year was voted him by Parliament. He was made K.P. on 18 Nov. 1851. For nearly two years from 1 April 1852 he was inspecting general of cavalry at headquarters, and the memoranda on the state of the army which he then drew up (Verner, i. 39–59) show how much he concerned himself with questions of organisation. He was in command of the troops at the funeral of the duke of Wellington. On 28 Sept. 1852 he was transferred as colonel from the 17th lancers to the Scots fusilier guards.

In February 1854 the duke was chosen to command a division in the army to be sent to the Crimea. He accompanied Lord Raglan to Paris on 10 April, and went thence to Vienna, bearing a letter from the Queen to the Emperor Francis Joseph. Leaving Vienna on 1 May, he reached Constantinople on the 10th. He was promoted lieutenant-general on 19 June, went with his division (guards and highlanders) to Varna, and thence to the Crimea. At the Alma (20 Sept.) he and his men were in second line, behind the light division; but when the latter fell back before the Russian counter attack, the guards and highlanders came to the front and won the battle. At Inkerman (5 Nov.) the duke with the brigade of guards (the highlanders were at Balaclava) came to the help of the 2nd division very early in the day, and retook the Sandbag battery. His horse was shot under him, and he found himself left with about 100 men, while the rest pushed on down the slope. Kinglake describes him 'with an immense energy of voice and gesture . . . commanding, entreating, adjuring' the men to keep on the high ground. By the advance of another Russian column he was nearly cut off from the main position, and he and his aide-de-camp 'had regularly to ride for it in order to get back' (Verner, i. 79). The guards lost 622 officers and men out of 1361 engaged.

The duke's courage was high, but he had not the imperturbability needed for war, and his health had suffered at Varna. Of the Alma he notes, 'When all was over I could not help crying like a child' (Verner, i. 73). Three days before Inkerman he had written to Queen Victoria gloomily about the situation of the army. He was 'dreadfully knocked up and quite worn out' by the battle, and was persuaded to go to Balaclava for rest. He was on board the frigate Retribution, when it narrowly escaped wreck in the great storm of 14 November. On the 25th he left the Crimea for Constantinople, and on 27 Dec. a medical board invalided him to England. He was mentioned in despatches (*Lond. Gaz.* 8 Oct., 12 and 22 Nov. 1854) and received the thanks of parliament, the medal with 4 clasps, the Turkish medal, and the G.C.B. (5 July 1855). He declined the governorship of

Gibraltar, and was anxious to return to the Crimea. When general Sir James Simpson resigned command of the army there in November, the duke tried in vain to succeed him. In January 1856 he was sent to Paris, to take part in the conference on the further conduct of the war, but the conclusion of peace in March made its plans of no effect.

On 15 July Lord Hardinge resigned, and the duke succeeded him as general commanding in chief. He was promoted general, and on 28 July was sworn of the privy council. The breakdown in the Crimea had led to great changes in army administration. The secretary of state for war (separated in 1854 from the colonies) took over the powers of the secretary at war, and of the board of ordnance, which was abolished. He also took over the militia and yeomanry from the home office and the commissariat from the treasury. He became responsible to parliament for the whole military administration; but the general commanding in chief, as representing the crown, enjoyed some independence in matters of discipline and command, appointments and promotions. The abolition of the board of ordnance brought the artillery and engineers under his authority, and the duke was made colonel of these two corps on 10 May 1861. The amalgamation (of which he was a strong advocate) of the European troops of the East India Company with the army of the crown in 1862 gave him general control of troops serving in India.

The volunteer movement of 1859 brought a new force into existence. He was not unfriendly to it, but had no great faith in it, and was opposed to a capitation grant. He became colonel of the 1st City of London brigade on 24 Feb. 1860. He was president of the National Rifle Association, which was founded in 1859 and had till 1887 its ranges at Wimbledon, on land of which he was principal owner; then he found it necessary to call upon it to go elsewhere, and the ranges were transferred to Bisley. He took an active part in military education, and helped to found the Staff College. He had been appointed a commissioner for Sandhurst and for the Duke of York's school in 1850, and was made governor of the Military Academy at Woolwich in 1862. On the death of the Prince Consort he exchanged the colonelcy of the Scots fusilier guards for that of the Grenadier guards. On 9 Nov. 1862 he was made field-marshal.

During the first thirteen years of his command the duke was in accord with successive war ministers, though he was continually remonstrating against reductions or urging increase of the army. But in December 1868 Edward (afterwards Viscount) Cardwell became secretary of state, with Gladstone as premier, and they took in hand a series of reforms which were most distasteful to him. First of all, the so-called dual government of the army, which divided responsibility and was a hindrance to reform, was abolished. By the War Office Act of 1870 the commander-in-chief was definitely subordinated to the war minister, and became one of three departmental chiefs charged respectively with combatant personnel, supply, and finance. To mark the change, the duke was required in Sept. 1871 to remove from the Horse Guards to Pall Mall. He regarded this as a blow not only to his own dignity but to the rights of the crown, and the Queen intervened on his behalf; but he had to give way.

The reconstruction of the war office was followed by the adoption of short service, the formation of an army reserve, the linking of battalions, and their localisation. The purchase of commissions was abolished, and seniority tempered by selection became the principle of promotion. The duke was opposed to all these innovations. His watchwords were discipline, *esprit de corps*, and the regimental system, all of which seemed to him to be threatened. But holding it to be for the interest of the crown and the army that he should remain at his post, he accepted a system of which he disapproved. The system held its ground notwithstanding party changes, and in 1881 it was carried a stage further by H. C. E. Childers, the linked battalions being welded into territorial regiments in spite of the duke's efforts to unlink them.

On 24 Nov. 1882 he was made personal aide-de-camp to Queen Victoria, to commemorate the campaign in Egypt; and on 26 Nov. 1887, when he had completed fifty years' service in the army, he was made commander-in-chief by patent. At the end of that year his functions were much enlarged, the whole business of supply being handed over to him. Cardwell had assigned it to a surveyor-general of the ordnance, who was meant to be an experienced soldier; but the office had become political, and the complaints about stores during the Nile campaign led to its abolition. Everything except finance now came under the control of the commander-in-chief, with the adjutant-general as his deputy. During the next few years much was done to fit the army for war: supply and transport were organised and barracks improved; but the secretary of state found that the military hierarchy hindered his personal consultation of experts.

In June 1888 a very strong commission was appointed, with Lord Hartington (afterwards duke of Devonshire) as chairman, to inquire into naval and military administration; and in May 1890 they recommended that the office of commander-in-chief should be abolished when the duke ceased to hold it, and that there should be a chief of the staff. Sir Henry Campbell-Bannerman, who became war minister in 1892, dissented from this recommendation; but he thought the powers of the commander-in-chief ought to be diminished, and the duke's retirement was a necessary preliminary. The call for this step grew louder, and in the spring of 1895 the duke consulted the Queen. Though 76 years of age, he felt himself physically and mentally fit for his office. The Queen replied, reluctantly, that he had better resign (Verner, ii. 395), and on 31 October he issued his farewell order, handing over the command of the army to Lord Wolseley. To soften the blow, the Queen appointed him her chief personal aide-de-camp and colonel-in-chief to the forces, with the right of holding the parade on her birthday.

In announcing to the House of Commons the duke's approaching retirement, on the eve of his own fall (21 June) Campbell-Bannerman touched on his attractive personality, his industry and activity, his devotion to the interests of the army, and his familiarity with its traditions and requirements; but dwelt especially on his common sense and knowledge of the world, his respect for constitutional proprieties and for public opinion. The army was attached to him because of his fairness. He bore no ill-will to officers who differed from him, but could discuss points of difference with good temper (Verner, ii. 272, seq.). Though in the training of the troops, as in other things, he was conservative, his thorough knowledge of close-order drill, and his outspoken, not to say emphatic, comments made him a formidable inspecting officer and kept up a high standard.

Devoted as the duke was to the army, it by no means absorbed all his energies. He undertook with alacrity the duties that fell to him as a member of the royal family, which were especially heavy after the death of the Prince Consort. For instance, in 1862 he was called upon to open the international exhibition, to entertain the foreign commissioners, and distribute the prizes. He was connected with a large number of charitable institutions, and took real interest in them; but two were pre-eminent— the London Hospital and Christ's Hospital—over both of which he presided for fifty years. He was elected president of Christ's Hospital on 23 March 1854, and was the first president who was not an alderman of the City. From that time onward he worked unsparingly for it, though latterly his efforts were mainly in opposition to the removal of the school to Horsham, 'the most wanton thing that ever was undertaken' (Sheppard, ii. 322). He was in great request as a chairman at dinners and meetings for benevolent purposes, for though not eloquent he was fluent, and had the art of getting on good terms with his audience.

In private life he was the most affectionate of men. His mother lived long enough to send her blessing to 'the best son that ever lived,' while he was being entertained at the United Service Club to celebrate his military jubilee. She died on 6 April 1889, and within a year he had another heavy blow in the death of his wife. Disregarding the Royal Marriage Act, he had married morganatically on 8 Jan. 1840 Miss Louisa Fairbrother, an actress, then 24 years of age. She lived in Queen Street, Mayfair, as Mrs. Fitzgeorge till her death on 12 Jan. 1890. She was buried at Kensal Green, the duke being chief mourner.

The duke had rooms at St. James's Palace from 1840 to 1859, when he removed to Gloucester House, Park Lane, left to him by his aunt, the duchess of Gloucester. On the death of the duchess of Cambridge the Queen granted him Kew Cottage for his life. He had been made ranger of Hyde Park and St. James's Park in 1852, and of Richmond Park in 1857. In addition to the orders already mentioned, he was made K.T. on 17 Sept. 1881, grandmaster and principal grand cross of St. Michael and St. George on 23 May 1869, G.C.S.I. in 1877, G.C.I.E. in 1887, and G.C.V.O. in 1897. Of foreign orders he received the black eagle of Prussia in 1852, the grand cordon of the legion of honour in 1855, St. Andrew of Russia in 1874, and the order of merit of Savoy in 1895. He was made colonel-in-chief of the king's royal rifle corps on 6 March 1869, of the 17th lancers on 21 June 1876, and of the Middlesex regiment on 9 Aug. 1898. He was also colonel of two Indian regiments—the 10th Bengal lancers, and the 20th Punjabis; of the Malta artillery, the Middlesex yeomanry, and the 4th battalion Suffolk regiment; of the Cambridge dragoons in the Hanoverian army (1852–66), and of the 28th foot in the Prussian army (Aug. 1889). He received the honorary degree of D.C.L. Oxford on 1 June 1853; of LL.D. Cambridge on 3 June 1864; and of LL.D. Dublin on 21 April 1868; and became one of the elder brethren of the Trinity house on 11 March 1885. He received the freedom of the City of London, with a sword, on 4 Nov. 1857, and on 19 Oct. 1896 he was presented with an address from the corporation and his bust (by Francis Williamson) was unveiled at the Guildhall. He was made a freeman of York in 1897, of Bath and of Kingston in 1898.

A series of banquets at the military clubs and messes marked the duke's retirement, but he continued for several years to preside at regimental dinners and to keep in close touch with the army. He was very vigorous for his age, rode in Queen Victoria's diamond jubilee procession of 1897, and at her funeral in 1901. He paid his last visit to Germany in August 1903, but his strength was then giving way. He died at Gloucester House on 17 March 1904 of hæmorrhage of the stomach, having outlived by a few weeks the commandership-in-chief which he held so long. On the 22nd he was buried, in accordance with his wish, beside his wife at Kensal Green. The first part of the service was at Westminster Abbey with King Edward VII as chief mourner. Five field-marshals and thirteen generals were pall-bearers. Tributes were paid to his memory in both houses of parliament. He had three sons: Colonel George William Adolphus Fitzgeorge; Rear-admiral Sir Adolphus Augustus Frederick Fitzgeorge, K.C.V.O., who became equerry to his father in 1897; and Colonel Sir Augustus Charles Frederick Fitzgeorge, K.C.V.O., C.B., who was his father's private secretary and equerry from 1886 to 1895.

In June 1907 a bronze equestrian statue of him by Captain Adrian Jones was placed in front of the new war office in Whitehall, and there is also a statue at Christ's Hospital, Horsham. There is a memorial window in the chapel of St. Michael and St. George in St. Paul's Cathedral. Of the many portraits of him the chief are one, at the age of 18, by John Lucas (at Windsor), and three as a field-marshal, by Frank Holl (at Buckingham Palace), Arthur S. Cope (at the United Service Club), and Sir Hubert von Herkomer (at the R.E. mess, Chatham). A caricature portrait appeared in 'Vanity Fair' in 1870.

[Willoughby C. Verner, Military Life of the Duke of Cambridge, 1905; J. E. Sheppard, George, Duke of Cambridge, a memoir of his private life, 2 vols. 1906; The Times, 18 March 1904; Letters of Queen Victoria, 1907; Kinglake, Invasion of the Crimea, 1863, &c.; The Panmure Papers, 1908; Sir Robert Biddulph, Lord Cardwell at the War Office, 1904; E. S. C. Childers, Life of Hugh C. E. Childers, 1901; Pearce, Annals of Christ's Hospital, 1908; Third Report of Lord Northbrook's committee on army administration, 12 Feb. 1870 (c. 54); Report of Royal Commission (Penzance) on Army Promotion, 5 Aug. 1876 (c. 1569); Report of Royal Commission (Hartington) on Naval and Military Administration, 11 Feb. 1890 (c. 5979); Catalogues of the Duke's collection of plate, pictures, porcelain, books, &c., sold at Christie's in 1904.]

ERNEST MARSH LLOYD

published 1912

BROWN John

(1826–1883)

Queen Victoria's Highland servant, was born 8 December 1826 in Crathienaird, Aberdeenshire, on the Balmoral estate, the second of the nine sons of John Brown, crofter, and his wife Margaret Leys, daughter of the local blacksmith. His story is the apotheosis of the Victorian servant. He began as stable-lad to Sir Robert Gordon. He embarked on his career of gillie in 1849 as Prince Albert's gillie, and was mentioned in the queen's journal on 11 September 1849 as 'young J. Brown' who looked after her on an outing. In 1858 he became the queen's personal servant in Scotland. In 1864, three years after the prince consort's death, Brown was brought south to Osborne as her groom to give the secluded widow more riding exercise. His responsibilities and favours escalated and he was soon her personal attendant and constant companion. Like all Scots he seemed to her intelligent and well-bred, but uniquely devoted after he saved her from two carriage accidents and two assailants.

His loyalty was spiced with coarseness. 'Wumman, can ye no hold yerr head up?' a tourist heard him shout as he pinned her cape, pricking her chin. Not only was he rude to the queen, but he also behaved badly with visitors at Osborne and Balmoral. The queen always forgave his disrespectful behaviour, and became increasingly dependent upon him. Her children denounced 'the brute'; her household reacted to his familiarities with jealous rows, though her private secretary, Sir Henry Ponsonby, called him 'a child of nature', arguing that in view of the queen's loneliness, they might have done worse. The scandal-mongering press represented the unmarried Brown as indeed worse: Victoria's lover, husband, or handsome, kilted medium putting her in touch with Albert. These fictions had ceased before a whisky-sodden Brown died of erysipelas at Windsor Castle, 27 March 1883. The queen was grief-stricken at his death. Mourned with wreaths from statesmen and verses by Alfred, Lord Tennyson, he was remembered on his gravestone as Victoria's 'Beloved Friend'. In 1884 Queen Victoria published *More Leaves from a Journal of our Life in the Highlands*, dedicated to John Brown, and planned to publish a memoir, a 'Life of John Brown', but the household managed to prevent it. In her coffin she wore his photograph on her wrist, above Prince Albert's dressing-gown and other treasured souvenirs. Queen Victoria always needed the support of a dedicated man and for nineteen years she found it in Brown. A photograph of Brown's bust by (Sir) Edgar Boehm is at Windsor.

[Elizabeth Longford, *Victoria R.I.*, 1964; Michael Reid, *Ask Sir James*, 1987; unpublished letters of Sir Henry Ponsonby.]

ELIZABETH LONGFORD

published 1993

KNOLLYS Francis

(1837–1924)

First Viscount Knollys, of Caversham

Private secretary to King Edward VII, was born in London 16 July 1837, the second son of General Sir William Thomas Knollys, by his wife, Elizabeth, daughter of Sir John St. Aubyn, fifth baronet. He was educated in Guernsey, and proceeded in 1851 to the Royal Military College at

Sandhurst. Although he received a commission as ensign in the 23rd regiment of Foot in 1854, Knollys decided to abandon a military career and to enter the civil service. He became junior examiner in the department of the Commissioners of Audit in 1855. When his father was appointed treasurer and comptroller of the household to Albert Edward, Prince of Wales, in 1862, Knollys helped him with his work, and in 1870 was appointed private secretary to the prince.

The Prince of Wales's interests were very varied, and although he relied on experts to advise him in many matters, it was to his private secretary that he usually turned for information and counsel. He soon found that he could rely on Knollys's sound judgement and carefully considered advice. In cases like the Mordaunt divorce suit (1870), when the Prince of Wales was brought in quite unnecessarily, and the baccarat scandal (1891), which was grossly mishandled at the start, the advantage of having some one with whom he could talk freely, some one who would tell him the whole truth, however unpalatable, was incalculable. Knollys's tact and discretion could always be relied upon, and his knowledge of men, and of the motives which actuated them when they put forward requests, enabled the Prince of Wales to deal successfully with many difficult problems. In 1868 Queen Victoria, in order to show her appreciation of Knollys's services, appointed him gentleman usher in her household. In 1875 he accompanied the Prince of Wales on his Indian tour as private secretary, and was the pivot of a large staff which had been chosen to go with the prince.

When the Prince of Wales ascended the throne as King Edward VII in 1901, Knollys naturally continued to be his private secretary, and was raised to the peerage as Baron Knollys, of Caversham, in 1902. In accordance with tradition, the Prince of Wales had become more and more liberal as Queen Victoria became more and more conservative, but this suited Knollys, as his instincts were wholly liberal. During the reign of King Edward, however, the fact that Knollys was so strong an adherent of the liberal party was the subject of much criticism among conservatives, who considered that the private secretary to the sovereign should be as unbiased as a civil servant. None the less, his absolute impartiality was recognized by Mr. Balfour, who was prime minister at the beginning of the reign, and by the other ministers of the conservative government.

Knollys was a past master at letter writing, and had the gift of expressing himself concisely without omitting anything of importance. He usually wrote his letters standing up at a high desk and considered a stenographer unnecessary and tiresome, but after King Edward's accession the number of letters and telegrams increased so much that Knollys was forced to dictate most of his answers, although he continued to write all political letters with his own hand up to the end. He was an omnivorous reader, and his grasp of political questions combined with a quaint sense of humour made him a delightful companion. He had a certain contempt for orders and decorations, both British and foreign—a trait in his character which was quite unintelligible to King Edward. He was created K.C.M.G. in 1886, K.C.B. in 1897, G.C.V.O. in 1901, I.S.O. in 1903, G.C.B. in 1908, and received many foreign orders. He was made a privy councillor in 1910, and was advanced to a viscounty in 1911.

On the death of King Edward in 1910 Knollys was pressed by King George V to remain as joint private secretary with Lord Stamfordham. This he did for three years, but in 1913 he asked to be allowed to retire. In 1910 he became lord-in-waiting to Queen Alexandra, a purely honorary post which he accepted in order that he might be of some assistance to the queen in her retirement. He died at Rickmansworth 15 August 1924.

Knollys married in 1887 the Hon. Ardyn Mary, daughter of Sir Henry Thomas 'Tyrwhitt, third baronet, and had one son, Edward George William Tyrwhitt (born 1895), who succeeded his father as second viscount, and one daughter.

[Private information; personal knowledge.]

F. E. G. PONSONBY

published 1937

VICTORIA Adelaide Mary Louise

(1840–1901)

Princess Royal of Great Britain and German Empress

Born at Buckingham Palace at 1.50 p.m. on 21 Nov. 1840, was eldest child of Queen Victoria and Prince Albert. The princess was baptised at Buckingham Palace on 10 Feb. 1841. Lord Melbourne, the prime minister, remarked 'how she looked about her, conscious that the stir was all about herself' (Martin, *Life of Prince Consort*, i. 100). Her English sponsors were Adelaide, the queen dowager, the duchess of Gloucester, the duchess of Kent, and the duke of Sussex. Leopold I, king of the Belgians, who was also a godfather, attended the ceremony in person, while the duke of Wellington represented the duke of Saxe-Coburg-Gotha.

Queen Victoria and Prince Albert bestowed unremitting care on the education of the princess. From infancy she was placed in the charge of a French governess, Mme. Charlier, and she early showed signs of intellectual alertness. At the age of three she spoke both English and French with fluency (*Letters of Queen Victoria*, ii. 3), while she habitually talked German with her parents. By Baron Stockmar she was considered 'extraordinarily gifted, even to the point of genius' (Stockmar, *Denkwürdigkeiten*, p. 43), and both in music and painting she soon acquired a proficiency beyond her years. Yet she remained perfectly natural and justified her father's judgment: 'she has a man's head and a child's heart.' (Cf. Lady Lyttelton's Letters, 1912, *passim*.).

Childhood and girlhood were passed at Windsor and Buckingham Palace, with occasional sojourns at Osborne House, which was acquired in 1845, and at Balmoral, to which the royal family paid an annual visit from 1848. In August 1849 the princess accompanied her parents on their visit to Ireland, and on 30 Oct. following she was present with her father and eldest brother at the opening of the new Coal Exchange in London. Strong ties of affection bound her closely to her brothers and sisters, and to her eldest brother, the Prince of Wales, afterwards King Edward VII, she was devotedly attached. She shared his taste for the drama, and in the theatricals which the royal children organised for their parents' entertainment (Jan. 1853) she played the title rôle in Racine's 'Athalie' to the Prince of Wales's Abner. She joined her brothers in many of their studies, and impressed their tutors with her superior quickness of wit.

At the age of eleven the princess royal first met her future husband, Prince Frederick William, who came to London with his father, Prince William of Prussia, for the Great Exhibition of 1851. On Prince Frederick William she made an impression which proved lasting. In 1853, when the prince's father again visited England, a matrimonial alliance with the princess was suggested. But the prince's uncle, Frederick William IV, king of Prussia, whose assent was needful and who was mainly influenced by Russophil advisers, was at first disinclined to entertain the proposal, and the outbreak of the Crimean war in 1854 quickened his Russian sympathies.

The Crimean war was responsible, too, for the princess's first trip abroad. In Aug. 1855 she accompanied her parents and the Prince of Wales on a visit at the Tuileries to Napoleon III, England's ally in the Russian war. She was delighted with her reception and completely enchanted by the Empress Eugénie. Paris had throughout life the same fascination for her as for her brother King Edward VII. In later life, however, national animosities debarred her from visiting the French capital save under the strictest incognito.

At length in 1855 King Frederick William IV yielded to sentimental rather than to political argument and sanctioned his nephew's offer of marriage. On 14 Sept. of the same year the young prince arrived at Balmoral. A few days later Queen Victoria and Prince Albert accepted his proposal for the hand of the princess. She was fifteen and he was twenty-four, although young for his age. The parents at first desired that the child princess should know nothing of the plan until after her confirmation (*Letters of Queen Victoria*, iii. 186). But an excursion with the princess on 29 Sept. to Craig-na-Ben gave the prince his opportunity. 'He picked a white piece of heather (the emblem of good luck), which he gave to the princess, and this enabled him to make an allusion to his hopes and wishes' (*Journal of our Life in the Highlands*, p. 154). On 1 Oct. the prince left Balmoral; it was understood that the marriage should take place after the girl's seventeenth birthday. Henceforth her education was pursued with a special eye to her future position. The prince consort himself devoted an hour a day to her instruction. He discussed with her current social and political questions and fostered liberal and enlightened sympathies. At his suggestion she translated into English Johann Gustav Droysen's 'Karl August und die Deutsche Politik' (Weimar, 1857), a plea for a liberal national policy in Germany. The princess now first took part in social functions. On 8 May 1856 she made her début at a court ball at Buckingham Palace. On 20 March the same year she was confirmed by John Bird Sumner, archbishop of Canterbury, in the private chapel of Windsor Castle.

The betrothal was not publicly announced until 29 April 1856, on the conclusion of the Crimean war by the treaty of Paris. But the secret had leaked out already, and the news was received coolly in both countries. 'The Times' (3 Oct. 1855) poured contempt on Prussia and its king. On 19 May 1857 Parliament voted a dowry of 40,000l., with an annuity of 4000l. In June Prince Frederick, accompanied by Count Moltke, came to England, and made his first public appearance with the princess at the Manchester Art Exhibition (29 June). The marriage negotiations were not concluded with the Prussian court without a hitch. Queen Victoria refused the Prussian proposal that the marriage should take place at Berlin. 'Whatever may be the practice of Prussian princes,' she wrote to Lord Clarendon, secretary for foreign affairs, 'it is not every day that one marries the daughter of the Queen of England' (*Letters of Queen Victoria*, iii. 321). Accordingly the marriage was fixed to take place in London early in 1858. The bridegroom arrived in London on 23 Jan. and the marriage was celebrated in the chapel royal, St. James's Palace, on the 25th. The honeymoon was spent at Windsor. The public was at length moved to enthusiasm. Richard Cobden hailed the bride as 'England's daughter' (*ib.* iii. 334). On 2 Feb. she and her husband embarked at Gravesend for Germany.

In Germany the princess was well received. Her childish beauty and charm of manner won the sympathy of all classes on her formal entry into Berlin (8 Feb. 1858). After her reception by King Frederick William IV her husband telegraphed to Prince Albert 'The whole royal family is enchanted with my wife.' Princess Hohenlohe gave Queen Victoria an equally glowing account of the favourable impression which the princess created at Berlin (Martin, *Life of the Prince Consort*, iv. 172). 'I feel very happy,' she told a guest at a court reception on 27 March, 'and am proud to belong to this country' (Bernhardi, *Aus meinem Leben*, iii. 17).

During the early years of her married life the princess made a tour of the smaller German courts, but she lived much in retirement in Berlin, at first in the gloomy old Schloss. Her first summer in Germany was spent at the castle of Babelsberg, where her father visited her in June 1858, and both he and her mother in August. On 20 Nov. following she and her husband moved into the Neue Palais on the Unter den Linden, which was henceforth her residence in Berlin. There on 27 Jan. 1859 she gave birth to her eldest son, William, afterwards German Emperor.

From the first, many of the conditions of the princess's new life proved irksome. The tone of the Prussian court in matters of religion and politics was narrower than that in England. The etiquette was more constrained and the standard of comfort was lower. The princess chafed somewhat under her mother-in-law's strict surveillance, and few sympathised with her unshakeable faith in the beneficence of constitutional government as it was practised in England. She could not conceal her liberal convictions or hold aloof from political discussion. She steadily continued the historical and literary studies to which her father had accustomed her, and she wrote to him a weekly letter, asking his advice on political questions, and enclosing essays on historical subjects. His influence over her was unimpaired till his death. In Oct. 1858 her father-in-law, Prince William, assumed the regency, and his summons of a moderate liberal ministry evoked an expression of her satisfaction which irritated the conservative party at court. In December 1860 she delighted her father with an exhaustive memorandum, whereby she thought to allay the apprehensions of the Prussian court, on the advantages of ministerial responsibility (Martin, *Life of the Prince Consort*, v. 259). She was outspoken in all her criticism of her environment, and her active interests in art and philanthropy as well as in politics ran counter to Prussian ideas and traditions. She was constantly comparing her life in Germany with the amenities of her English home (Bernhardi, *Aus meinem Leben*, vi. 116), and she wounded Prussian susceptibilities by pointing out England's social advantages. Over her husband she rapidly acquired a strong influence which increased distrust of her in court circles. Her energy and independence undoubtedly conquered any defect of resolution in him, but his liberal sentiments were deeply rooted. Meanwhile the English press was constantly denouncing the illiberality of Prussian rule, and the unpopularity of the princess, who was freely identified with such attacks, increased. 'This attitude of the English newspapers,' wrote Lord Clarendon in 1861, 'preys upon the princess royal's spirits, and materially affects her position in Prussia' (*Memoirs and Letters of Sir Robert Morier*, i. 295).

In Jan. 1861, when King William I succeeded his brother Frederick William IV on the throne of Prussia, the princess and her husband became crown princess and crown prince. On 18 Oct. she attended the coronation of her father-in-law at Königsberg. Before the close of the year she suffered the shock of her father's premature death (14 Dec. 1861). Her husband represented her at the funeral, which her delicate health prevented her from attending. In her father the princess lost a valued friend and counsellor, while the Prussian king was deprived of an adviser, whose circumspect advice had helped him to reconcile opposing forces in Prussian politics.

In March 1862 a breach between the king of Prussia and both the moderate and advanced liberals led him to summon to his aid Bismarck and the conservative (Junker) party. To the new minister constitutional principles had no meaning, and the crown prince and princess made open declaration of hostility. The crown prince absented himself from cabinet meetings, which he had attended since the king's accession, and he and his wife withdrew from court (Bernhardi, *Aus meinem Leben*, v. 8). In October 1862 they left Berlin, and subsequently joined the Prince of Wales, a frequent visitor at his sister's German home, on a cruise in the Mediterranean. Early in 1863 the crown princess with her son and consort was in England, where she filled the place of her widowed mother, Queen Victoria, at a drawing-room at Buckingham Palace (28 Feb.). On 10 March she was present at the Prince of Wales's wedding at Windsor.

The steady growth under Bismarck's ascendancy of absolutist principles of government in Prussia intensified the resentment of the crown princess and her husband. In June 1863 the crown prince made an open protest in a speech at Dantzig. The princess, with characteristic want of discretion, frankly told President Eichmann that her opinions were those of the liberal press (Whitman, *Emperor Frederick*, p. 162). Bismarck imputed to her a resolve 'to bring her consort more into prominence and to acquaint public opinion with the crown prince's way of thinking' (Busch's *Bismarck*, iii. 238). The king demanded of the crown prince a recantation of the Dantzig speech. The request was refused, but the prince offered to retire with his family to some place where he could not meddle with politics. In the result Bismarck imposed vexatious restrictions on the heir-apparent's freedom of action. Spies in the guise of aides-de-camp and chamberlains were set over him and his wife at Berlin, and by 1864 the whole of their retinue consisted of Bismarck's followers (*Memoirs of Sir Robert Morier*,

i. 343, 410). The vituperative conservative press assigned the heir-apparent's obduracy to his wife's influence.

The princess met Queen Victoria at Rosenau near Coburg in August 1863, and in her mother she had a firm sympathiser. The queen contemplated active intervention at Berlin on her daughter's behalf, and was only dissuaded by (Sir) Robert Morier. From September to December following the crown prince and his wife made a prolonged visit to the English court, and on their return to Berlin held aloof for a season from political discussion (Bismarck, *Neue Tischgespräche und Interviews*, ii. 33).

The reopening of the Schleswig-Holstein question by the death of King Frederick VIII of Denmark (15 Nov. 1863) widened the breach with Bismarck. The crown princess and her husband warmly espoused the claims to the duchies of Duke Frederick of Augustenburg. The controversy divided the English royal family. The rival claim of Denmark had strong adherents there. While staying at Osborne the princess engaged in warm discussion with her sister-in-law, the Princess of Wales, the king of Denmark's daughter (Bernhardi, *Aus meinem Leben*, v. 282). Bismarck's cynical resolve to annex the duchies to Germany thoroughly roused the anger of the crown princess. Bismarck complained that she was involving herself, with her husband, her uncle (the duke of Coburg), and her mother, in a conspiracy against Prussian interests. When she and the minister met, bitter words passed, and she ironically asked Bismarck whether his ambition was to become king or president of a republic (Horst Kohl, *Bismarck: Anhang*, i. 150).

The Austro-Prussian conflict of 1866 was abhorrent to the princess, and it accentuated the strife between her and the minister. On the outbreak of war (18 June) the crown prince took command of the second division of the Silesian army operating in Bohemia. Dislike of the conflict and its causes did not affect the princess's anxiety to relieve its suffering, and she now showed conspicuously for the first time that philanthropic energy and organising capacity which chiefly rendered her career memorable. She organised hospitals and raised money for the care of the wounded. It was mainly due to her efforts that the national fund for disabled soldiers (Nationalinvalidenstiftung) was inaugurated at the close of the war. The Prussian victory involved, to the princess's sorrow, the deposition of Austria's allies among the princely families of Germany. With George V, the dispossessed king of Hanover, the princess avowed very lively sympathy.

The crown prince's exclusion from business of state continued, to his wife's unconcealed irritation. Bismarck declared that her devotion to English as opposed to Prussian interests rendered the situation inevitable.

On occasion, however, the crown prince was suffered to represent his father on visits to foreign sovereigns. Delicate health and the cares of a growing family did not always allow the crown princess to accompany him. But in May 1867 she went with him to Paris for the opening of the International Exhibition, and there she made the acquaintance of Renan. Subsequently in April 1873 she was the guest of the Emperor Francis Joseph at Schönbrunn on the occasion of the International Exhibition at Vienna. In Jan. 1874 she attended at St. Petersburg the wedding of her brother Alfred, duke of Edinburgh, with the grand duchess Maria Alexandrovna. But foreign travel in less formal conditions was more congenial to her, and she lost no opportunity of journeying incognito through the chief countries of Europe.

The Franco-German war of 1870–1 plunged the crown princess in fresh controversy. The impression generally prevailed in Germany that England was on the side of France. She sought to convince Bismarck of the genuineness of England's professions of neutrality, but only provoked an incredulous smile. 'The English,' she wrote to Queen Victoria on 9 Aug. 1870, 'are more hated at this moment than the French. Of course *cela a rejailli* on my poor innocent head. I have fought many a battle about Lord Granville, indignant at hearing my old friend so attacked, but all parties make him out French' (Fitzmaurice, *Life of Lord Granville*, ii. 38). At the same time the crown princess bestirred herself in the interest of the German armies in the field. She appealed for funds on behalf of the soldiers' families (19 July 1870). In September she joined her sister, Princess Alice of Hesse-Darmstadt, at Homburg, and was indefatigable in organising hospitals for the wounded, in recruiting volunteer corps of lady nurses, and in distributing comforts to the troops on the way to the front. Yet compassionate kindness to French prisoners exposed her to suspicion. The threatened bombardment of Paris after the investment horrified her, and she appealed to her father-in-law to forbid it. The step was ineffectual, and excited the bitter sarcasm of Bismarck. Undeterred by failure, she started a scheme to collect supplies in Belgium for the rapid provisioning of Paris after the capitulation. The British government and other neutral powers were approached, but Bismarck stepped in to foil the plan (*Memoirs and Letters of Sir Robert Morier*, ii. 211).

The crown princess welcomed the proclamation of the German Emperor at Versailles on 18 Jan. 1871, and took part in the festivities at Berlin on the return of the victorious German army. In Sept. 1871 she and her husband visited London, and were received with cordiality by Queen Victoria and the Prince of Wales. Their reception did much to dissipate the atmosphere of tension which had prejudiced the relations of England and Germany during the war.

The princess's public interests extended far beyond politics, and embraced philanthropy, education, art, and literature. Indeed enlightened progress in all branches of effort powerfully appealed to her. She cultivated the society of leaders of thought, art, and science. As a hostess she ignored the conventions of etiquette which restricted her guests to members of the aristocracy. Her receptions were invariably attended by the historians Mommsen and Dove, by Zeller the philosopher, by the scientist Virchow, and by Gustav Freytag the writer, who dedicated to her 'Die Ahnen' (six parts, 1872–80). With especial eagerness the princess encouraged intercourse with German painters and sculptors. Art was one of her main recreations. Elected a member of the Berlin Academy in 1860, she studied in her leisure hours sculpture under Begas and painting under Prof. Hagen. She drew correctly, but showed little power of imagination (for examples of her work cf. *Magazine of Art*, May and Sept. 1886). Her favourite artists were Werner and von Angeli, and with the latter she was long on intimate terms.

Prussia was almost the last state in Germany to assimilate the artistic development of the nineteenth century, and it was the crown princess who gave a first impulse towards the improvement of applied art. She carefully followed the progress of industrial art in England, and in 1865 she commissioned Dr. Schwabe to draw up a report, entitled 'Die Forderung der Kunst-Industrie in England and der Stand dieser Frage in Deutschland.' Her efforts to stimulate the interest of the Prussian government bore fruit. Schools of applied art were established in Prussia, and on 15 Sept. 1872 she had the satisfaction of witnessing the opening of an industrial art exhibition at Berlin. Subsequently she and her husband set to work to form a permanent public collection of 'objets d'art,' and the Berlin Industrial Art Museum (Kunst-Gewerbe Museum); which was opened on 20 Nov. 1881, was mainly due to her personal initiative. In the structural evolution of the modern city of Berlin the princess's interest was always keen and her active influence consistently supported the civic effort to give the new city artistic dignity.

Her early endeavours in philanthropy were mainly confined to hospitals. The experiences of the wars of 1866 and 1870 had shown the inadequacy of existing hospital organisations in Germany. A more scientific training for nurses was a first necessity. The crown princess was well acquainted with the reforms effected in England by Florence Nightingale, and in 1872 she drafted an exhaustive report on hospital organisation. At her instigation the Victoria House and Nursing School (Viktoria-Haus für Krankenpflege), which was named after her, was established at Berlin in 1881, and soon the Victoria sisters, mainly women of education, undertook the nursing in the municipal hospital at Friedrichshain. Out of the public gift to her and her husband on their silver wedding in 1883 she applied 118,000 marks to the endowment of the Victoria House. The success of the school led to the establishment of similar institutions throughout Germany. The value of her work for hospitals was recognised beyond Germany. In 1876 she received a gold medal at the Brussels exhibition for her designs for a barrack hospital, and on 26 May 1883 she was awarded the Royal Red Cross by Queen Victoria on the institution of that order.

From hospitals the crown princess soon passed to schemes for ameliorating the social conditions of the working classes. On her initiative the society for the promotion of health in the home (Gesellschaft für häusliche Gesundheit) was started in 1875; it undertook regular house to house visits for the purposes of sanitary inspection. Both at Bornstedt, her husband's country seat, and later at Cronberg, whither she retired after his death, she founded hospitals, workhouses, schools, and libraries.

The cause of popular education, especially for women, was meanwhile one of her chief concerns. In the development in Germany of women's higher education, the crown princess was a pioneer whose labour had far-reaching results. Her untiring work for her own sex brought about a general improvement in the social position of German women. In 1868 at her instance Miss Georgina Archer was invited to Berlin and started the Victoria Lyceum, the first institution in Germany for the higher education of women. Two educational institutions, the Lette Verein (1871), a school for the technical training of soldiers' orphans; and the Heimathaus für Töchter hoherer Stände, or home for girls of the higher middle classes, were mainly set on foot by her exertions, while her interest in modern educational methods was apparent in her patronage of the Pestalozzi-Fröbel Haus (1881). No less than forty-two educational and philanthropic institutions flourished under her auspices, and the impulse she gave to women's education throughout Germany swept away most of the old reactionary prejudices against opening to women the intellectual opportunities which men enjoyed.

Despite the public services of the princess, the value of which the German people acknowledged, the humiliating political position of her husband and herself underwent no change. Knowledge of political business was still denied them (Gontaut-Biron, *Dernières Années de l'ambassade*, p. 298). In June 1878 the Emperor William was wounded by an assassin (Nobiling), and the crown prince was appointed regent. But Bismarck contrived that his office should not carry with it any genuine authority. The prompt recovery of his father fully restored the old situation. At the end of 1879 the crown princess withdrew from Berlin on the ground of ill-health, and she spent several months with her husband and family at Pegli near Genoa. During the following years her appearances in public were few. In May 1883 she visited Paris incognito, and on 24 May 1884 she laid the foundation stone of St. George's (English) church at Berlin. The health of the old emperor was now declining, and the crown prince's accession to the throne was clearly approaching. Bismarck showed some signs of readiness to cultivate better relations with the heir apparent and his family. On 21 Nov. 1884 he attended a soirée given by the crown princess in honour of her birthday (Bismarck, *Neue Tischgespräche und Interviews*, ii. 127).

But the crown princess's long-deferred hopes of a happy change of estate were doomed to a cruel disappointment. In the autumn of 1886 the crown prince contracted on the Italian Riviera an affection of the throat, which gradually sapped his strength. For nearly two years her husband's illness was the princess's main preoccupation, and she undertook with great efficiency the chief responsibilities of nursing. In May 1887, when the Berlin physicians diagnosed cancerous symptoms, an English physician, (Sir) Morell Mackenzie, was called into consultation with the princess's assent, and his optimism initiated an unedifying controversy with his German colleagues, which involved the princess's name. She treated the English specialist with a confidence which the German specialists thought that she withheld from them. Both prince and princess took part in the celebration of Queen Victoria's jubilee (21 June 1887). After a visit to Toblach in Tyrol they moved in November to the Villa Zirio, San Remo, where the fatal progress of the malady no longer admitted of doubt. On 9 March 1888 the old emperor William died at Berlin, and the crown prince, a dying man, succeeded to the throne as Frederick III.

The Emperor Frederick and his consort immediately left San Remo for Charlottenburg, and in a rescript addressed to the chancellor, Prince Bismarck, the new sovereign announced his intention of devoting the remainder of his life to the moral and economic elevation of the nation. He was no longer able to speak, and all communications had to be made to him in writing. The empress undertook to prepare her husband for necessary business (H. Blum, *Lebenserinnerungen*, ii. 220), and Bismarck's jealousy of her influence was aroused. A family quarrel embittered the difficult situation. Already in 1885 the princess had encouraged a plan for the marriage of her second daughter, Princess Victoria, to Alexander of Battenberg, Prince of Bulgaria. But the scheme had then been rejected. It was now revived, and the old quarrel between the empress and Bismarck found in the proposed match new fuel. The chancellor threatened to resign. He declared the marriage to be not only a breach of caste etiquette owing to Prince Alexander's inferior social rank, but to be an insult to Russia, which had declared its hostility to the Bulgarian ruler. The empress, who regarded her daughter's happiness as the highest consideration, ignored Bismarck's arguments. The chancellor prompted an unscrupulous press campaign which brought public opinion to his side. The dying emperor yielded to the combined pressure of Bismarck and public opinion, and on 4 April 1888 he agreed to a postponement of the announcement of the marriage. The empress remained obdurate. But Queen Victoria visited Berlin (24 April) and was convinced by Bismarck of the fatal consequences of further resistance. The empress out of deference to her mother's wishes acquiesced in the situation. Crown Prince William sided with Bismarck throughout the dispute, but Queen Victoria reconciled him to his mother.

On 1 June 1888 the court moved from Charlottenburg to the new palace (Friedrichskron) at Potsdam, and there on 15 June the emperor died in the presence of his wife and family.

One of the last acts of the dying monarch was to place Bismarck's hand in that of the empress as a symbol of reconciliation. But the chancellor did not spare her humiliation in the first days of her widowhood. After her husband's death a cordon of soldiers was drawn round the palace at Potsdam to prevent the removal of any compromising documents; when the empress requested Bismarck to visit her, he replied that he had no time and must go to her son the emperor, his master (Hohenlohe, ii. 419). Bismarck had taken timely precautions against the adoption by the new emperor of the liberal views of his parents; he had instilled into the young man his own political principles. Mother and son were as a consequence for a time estranged. Even the memory of the Emperor Frederick became involved in acute controversy. Extracts from the late emperor's diary were published by Dr. Friedrich Heinrich Geffcken in the 'Deutsche Rundschau' (Sept. 1888). They were intended as a reply to his traducers and as proof of the part that he had played while crown prince in the achievement of German unity. The suppression of the offending review by Bismarck's orders and the imprisonment of Dr. Geffcken (who was not convicted) on the charge of high treason excited the empress's deepest indignation. Bismarck's triumph, however, was short-lived. The new emperor dismissed him from office in March 1890. With curious inconsistency the fallen minister invited the empress's sympathy (Hohenlohe, ii. 419), and in the presence of a witness she reminded him that his own past treatment of her had deprived her of any power of helping him now.

In 1891 a political rôle was assigned to her by the emperor. He was anxious to test the attitude of the French people towards his family. Under strict incognito she accordingly made a week's stay (19–27 Feb.) at the German embassy in Paris. Queen Victoria was anxious that the English ambassador should arrange a meeting between her and the French president. The empress met in Paris French artists and visited the studios of Bonnat, Détaille, and Carolus Duran. But an indiscreet excursion to Versailles and St. Cloud, where memories of the German occupation of 1870 were still well alive, brought the experiment to an unhappy end. The French nationalist party protested against her presence, threatened a hostile demonstration, and cut short her sojourn (Gaston Routier, *Voyage de l'impératrice Frédéric à Paris en 1891*).

After the death of her husband the Empress Frederick settled at Cronberg, where she purchased an estate on the slopes of the Taunus hills. With a legacy left her by the duchess of Galliera she built there a palatial country seat, which she named Friedrichshof. There she still followed the current course of politics, literature, and art, and entertained her relatives. During the last few months of her life she initiated the Empress Frederick Institute for the higher scientific education of members of the medical profession; this was opened at Berlin on 1 March 1906 after her death. Her relations with her son improved on the removal of Bismarck, and she was touched by the many tributes he paid to his father's memory. During her last years she repeatedly visited England, and on 22 June 1897 she took part in Queen Victoria's Diamond Jubilee procession. In the autumn of 1898 a fall from her horse, while out riding at Cronberg, brought on the first symptoms of cancer. She bore her sufferings with the same heroic patience as her husband had borne his. She outlived her mother six months, and died at Friedrichshof on 5 Aug. 1901. She was buried beside her husband in the Friedenskirche at Potsdam.

The empress's interests and accomplishments were of exceptional versatility and variety, and if there was a touch of dilettantism about her discursive intellectual aptitudes, her devotion to intellectual and artistic pursuits was genuine. She was a clever artist, and an experienced connoisseur in music, though her skill as a performer was inferior to that of Queen Victoria. To philosophy and science she cherished a lifelong devotion, and followed their notable developments in her own time with eagerness. Although she retained her attachment to the Church of England, her religion was undogmatic, and she sympathised with the broad views of Strauss, Renan, Schopenhauer, and Huxley. An ardent champion of religious toleration, she severely condemned anti-semitism. In politics she was steadfast to the creed of civil liberty in which her father had trained her, and she declined to reconcile herself to the despotic traditions of the Prussian court. She made little effort to adapt herself to her German environment, which was uncongenial to her. She often acted unwisely on the impulse of the moment; she was no good judge of character and was outspoken in her dislikes of persons, which she frequently conceived at first sight. Her unflinching resistance to Bismarck proves her courage, and her persistent support of social, artistic, and philanthropic reform in Prussia bears permanent testimony to the practical quality of her enlightenment. Her wise benevolence earned the gratitude of the German people, but she failed to win their affection.

Of her eight children she was survived by her two eldest sons (the Emperor William II and Prince Henry) and four daughters. Her third son, Sigismund, died as an infant on 19 June 1866, and she lost her youngest son, Waldemar, on 27 March 1879, at the age of eleven. She lived to see the marriages of all her remaining children. The Emperor William married, on 27 Feb. 1881, Princess Augusta Victoria of Schleswig-Holstein, and Prince Henry married on 24 May 1888 Princess Irene of Hesse-Alt. Her four daughters, Princesses Charlotte, Victoria, Sophie, and Margarete, wedded respectively Prince Bernard of Saxe-Meiningen (on 18 Feb. 1878), Prince Adolph of Schaumburg-Lippe (on 19 Nov. 1890), Constantine, Duke of Sparta (on 27 Oct. 1889), and Prince Frederick Charles of Hesse (on 25 Jan. 1893). All her children, except Princess Victoria of Schaumburg-Lippe, had issue, and her grandchildren numbered seventeen at the time of her death. Her grandchild Féodora (b 1879), daughter of Princess Charlotte of Saxe-Meiningen, married on 24 Sept. 1898 Prince Henry XXX of Reuss.

As princess royal of England from her infancy and then as crown princess of Germany the Empress Frederick was frequently drawn, painted, and sculptured. The earliest portrait, perhaps, is that in 'The Christening of the Princess Royal,' painted by Charles Robert Leslie, R.A., now at Buckingham Palace. As a child the princess was painted more than once by Sir William Ross, R.A., in miniature, and by Sir Edwin Landseer, R.A., with a pony, and again with Eos, her father's favourite greyhound. In the series of small statuettes in marble, by Mary Thornycroft, now at Osborne House, the princess royal appears as 'Summer.' Another bust was made by Emil Wolff in 1851. The princess appears in the large family group of Queen Victoria and Prince Albert, by Winterhalter in 1846, and she was painted by the same artist at different stages of her life—as a girl, on her first début in society, at her marriage, and as princess of Prussia. 'The Marriage of the Princess Royal and Prince Frederick William of Prussia' (1858), painted by John Phillip, R.A., is now at Buckingham Palace. Among other English artists who drew portraits of the princess were Thomas Musgrave Joy and Edward Matthew Ward, R.A. After her marriage portraits were painted by A. Graefle, F. Hartmann, Ernst Hildebrand, and other leading German artists. Most of these remain in the private possession of her family in England and Germany. Many of them became well known in England in engravings. The picture by Hildebrand is in the Hohenzollern Museum at Berlin. In 1874 an important drawing was made by von Lenbach, as well as a portrait in oils in the costume of the Italian

Victoria

Renaissance by Heinrich von Angeli of Vienna, who then succeeded Winterhalter as favourite painter of Queen Victoria and her family. A half-length by the same artist (1882) is in the Wallace Collection in London, and another (1885) is in the Museum at Breslau. In 1894 Angeli painted a noble and pathetic portrait of the widowed empress, seated, at full-length, one version of which is at Buckingham Palace; it has been mezzotinted by Borner. The crown princess is conspicuous in the large painting by Anton von Werner of 'The Emperor William I receiving the Congratulations of his Family on his Birthday,' which was presented to Queen Victoria at the Jubilee of 1887 by the British colony at Berlin (information kindly supplied by Mr. Lionel Cust). Among other German artists who portrayed her, Begas executed a very life-like bust (1883) and also the sarcophagus over her tomb in the Friedenskirche, Potsdam. A cartoon by 'Nemo' appeared in 'Vanity Fair' in 1884. Memorial tablets were placed in the English church at Homburg (1903) and in the St. Johanniskirche, Cronberg (1906). A bust by Uphues was erected in 1902 on the Kaiser Friedrich promenade at Homburg. A striking statue of the empress in coronation robes, executed by Fritz Gerth, was unveiled by the Emperor William II on 18 Oct. 1903, opposite the statue of her husband in the open space outside the Brandenburg gate at Berlin.

[No complete biography has been published. A summary of her life appeared in The Times, and Daily Telegraph, 6 Aug. 1901, and in a memoir by Karl Schrader in the Biographisches Jahrbuch und Deutscher Nekrolog (Berlin, 1905, vii. 451). Her early years may be followed in Sir Theodore Martin's Life of the Prince Consort (1874–80); Letters of Sarah Lady Lyttelton, 1912; in Sir Sidney Lee's Queen Victoria (1904), and Edward VII, Suppl. II; Queen Victoria's Letters, 1837–61 (1907). For her career in Germany see especially Martin Philippson's Friedrich III als Kronprinz und Kaiser (Wiesbaden, 2nd edit. 1908) and Margarete von Poschinger's Life of the Emperor Frederick (trans. by Sidney Whitman, 1901). Other biographies of her husband by H. Hengst (Berlin, 1883), V. Böhmert (Leipzig, 1888), E. Simon (Paris, 1888), Sir Rennell Rod (London, 1888), and H. Müller-Bohn (Berlin, 2nd edit. 1904) are also useful. Hints as to the princess's relations with German politicians may be gleaned from the Memoirs of Duke Ernest of Saxe-Coburg-Gotha (trans. 4 vols. 1888–70); T. von Bernhardi's Aus meinem Leben, vols. ii., v., and vi. (Berlin, 1893–1901); R. Haym's Das Leben Max Dunckers (Berlin, 1891); Memoirs of Prince Chlodwig of Hohenlohe-Schillings-fürst (trans. 2 vols. 1906); Moritz Busch's Bismarck, some secret Pages of his History (trans. 3 vols. 1898); Bismarck, His Reflections and Reminiscences (trans. 2 vols. 1898); untranslated supplement ('Anhang') to latter work edited by H. Kohl in 2 vols. entitled respectively Kaiser Wilhelm und Bismarck and Aus Bismarck's Briefwechsel (Stuttgart, 1901); Gustav zu Putlitz, Ein Lebensbild (Berlin, 1894); H. Abeken's Ein Schlichtes Leben in bewegter Zeit, 1898, and H. Oncken's Rudolf von Bennigsen (2 vols. Stuttgart, 1910). The empress's artistic and philanthropic work are mainly described in L. Morgenstern's Viktoria,

Kronprinzessin des Deutschen Reichs (Berlin, 1883); D. Roberts's The Crown Prince and Princess of Germany (1887); B. von der Lage's Kaiserin Friedrich (Berlin, 1888); and J. Jessen's Die Kaiserin Friedrich (1907). References of varying interest may be found in Lady Bloomfield's Reminiscences of Court and Diplomatic Life (2 vols. 1883); Princess Alice's Letters to Queen Victoria, 1885; Sir C. Kinloch-Cooke's Mary Adelaide, Duchess of Teck (1900); le Vicomte de Gontaut-Biron's Mon Ambassade en Allemagne, 1872–3 (Paris, 1906), and Dernières Années de l'ambassade en Allemagne (Paris, 1907); Memoirs and Letters of Sir Robert Morier, 1826–76 (2 vols. 1911); G. W. Smalley's Anglo-American Memoirs, 1911; W. Boyd Carpenter's Some Pages of my Life, 1911; T. Teignmouth Shore's Some Recollections, 1911; and Walburga Lady Paget's Scenes and Memories, 1912. Lady Blennerhassett has kindly supplied some unpublished notes. A character sketch by Max Harden in Köpfe (pt. ii. Berlin, 1910) represents the extreme German point of view. Some account of her latter years may be gathered from H. Delbrück's Kaiser Friedrich und sein Haus (Berlin, 1888); E. Lavisse's Trois Empereurs d'Allemagne (Paris, 1888; Sir Morell Mackenzie's Frederick the Noble, 1888; and G. A. Leinhaas, Erinnerungen an Kaiserin Friedrich (Mainz, 1902); see also Fortnightly Review and Deutsche Revue, September 1901; Quarterly Review and Deutsche Rundschau, October 1901 for general appreciations.]

GABRIEL S. WOODS

published 1912

EDWARD VII (1841–1910)

King of Great Britain and Ireland and of the British Dominions beyond the Seas, Emperor of India, was eldest son and second child of Queen Victoria and her husband Prince Albert. Their first-born child, Victoria, Princess Royal, was born on 21 Nov. 1840.

The prince was born at Buckingham Palace at 10.48 a.m. on Tuesday 9 Nov. 1841, and the birth was duly recorded in the parish register of St. George's, Hanover Square. The conservative prime minister, Sir Robert Peel, who had just come into office, with the duke of Wellington, the archbishop of Canterbury (William Howley), and other high officers of state, attended the palace to attest the birth. No heir had been born to the reigning sovereign since the birth of George IV in 1762, and the event was the signal for immense national rejoicings. The annual feast of the lord mayor of London took place the same evening, and the infant's health was drunk with abundant enthusiasm. A special thanksgiving service was arranged for the churches by the archbishop of Canterbury, and the birth was set as the theme of the English poem at Cambridge University for the next year, when the successful competitor was Sir Henry Maine. The child was named Albert Edward—Albert after his father, and Edward after his mother's father, the duke of Kent. In the family circle he was always called 'Bertie,' and until his accession his signature was invariably 'Albert Edward.' He inherited according to precedent the titles of Duke of Cornwall and Rothsay, Earl of Carrick, Baron of Renfrew, Lord of the Isles, and Great Steward of Scotland, but by his parents' wish he was gazetted in addition as Duke of Saxony, his father's German title. The innovation was adversely criticised by Lord Palmerston and his friends, who disliked the German leanings of the court. On 4 Dec. 1841 he was further created, in accordance with precedent, by patent under the great seal, Prince of Wales and Earl of Chester.

From the outset it was his mother's earnest hope that in career and character her son should be a copy of his father. On 29 Nov. 1841 she wrote to her uncle, King Leopold of Belgium, 'Our little boy is a wonderfully strong and large child. I hope and pray he may be like his dearest papa' (*Letters*, i. 456). A week later she repeated her aspirations to her kinsman: 'You will understand how fervent are my prayers, and I am sure everybody's must be, to see him resemble his father in *every, every* respect both in body and mind' (Martin, *Life of Prince Consort*). From the boy's infancy to his manhood Queen Victoria clung tenaciously to this wifely wish.

The prince was baptised by the archbishop of Canterbury on 25 Jan. 1842 at St. George's Chapel, Windsor. The boy's grand-uncle, the duke of Cambridge, seventh son of George III, and his great-aunt, Princess Sophia, daughter of George III, were the English sponsors. The princess's place was filled through her illness by the duke of Cambridge's daughter Augusta, afterwards grand duchess of Mecklenburg-Strelitz. The other sponsors were members of German reigning families. At their head came Frederick William IV, king of Prussia, who was present in person with Baron Alexander von Humboldt, the naturalist, in attendance upon him. The king much appreciated the office of godfather. He was chosen instead of the queen's beloved counsellor and maternal uncle, King Leopold of Belgium, for fear of giving offence to her difficult-tempered uncle, King Ernest of Hanover, but the plan hardly produced the desired effect of conciliation. The other German sponsors were absent. They were Prince Albert's stepmother, the duchess of Saxe-Coburg, who was represented by Queen Victoria's mother, the duchess of Kent; Prince Albert's widowed kinswoman, the duchess of Saxe-Gotha, who was represented by the duchess of Cambridge; and Prince Albert's uncle, Duke Ferdinand of Saxe-Coburg, who was represented by Princess Augusta of Cambridge.

The Queen specially asked the duke of Wellington to bear at the ceremony the sword of state.

Gifts and orders, which were always congenial to the prince, were showered on his cradle by foreign royalty. The king of Prussia, whose baptismal offering was an elaborate gold shield adorned with figures cut in onyx, conferred on him the Order of the Black Eagle. The Emperor Ferdinand I of Austria, Emperor Francis Joseph's uncle, made the infant 'quite proud' with his present of the Grand Cross of St. Andrew on 18 June 1844. Louis Philippe sent him a little gun on his third birthday.

The lines which the education of the heir-apparent should follow became his parents' anxious concern very soon after he was born. Baron Stockmar, Prince Albert's mentor, whose somewhat pedantic counsel carried great weight in the royal circle, was from the first persistent in advice. Before the boy was six months old, the baron in detailed memoranda defined his parents' heavy responsibilities. He warned them of the need of imbuing the child with a 'truly moral and truly English sentiment,' and of entrusting him to the care of 'persons morally good, intelligent, well-informed, and experienced, who fully enjoyed the parental confidence' (6 March 1842). After due consultation and deliberation Lady Lyttelton was installed as head of Queen Victoria's nursery establishment in April 1842. Her responsibilities grew with the rapid increase of the queen's family. She held the post till 1851, and inspired the prince with the warmest affection.

In 1843 an anonymous pamphlet—'Who shall educate the Prince of Wales?'—which was dedicated to Queen Victoria, bore witness to the importance generally attached to the character of the prince's training. The anonymous counsellor restated Stockmar's unexceptionable principles, and Prince Albert sent a copy to the sententious baron. An opinion was also invited from Lord Melbourne, the late prime minister, in whom the queen placed the fullest confidence (19 Feb. 1843). He laid stress on the 'real position' and 'duties' which attached to the rank of heir-apparent and on 'the political temptations and seductions' to which previous heirs-apparent, notably George III's eldest son, the prince regent (afterwards George IV), had succumbed. Melbourne recalled the tendency of English heirs-apparent to incur the jealousy of the reigning sovereign and to favour the party in opposition to the sovereign's ministers. Without Lord Melbourne's reminder Queen Victoria was well aware that her uncle George IV was a signal object-lesson of the evil propensities to which heirs-apparent were liable. Nor did she forget that she herself, while heir-presumptive to the crown, had suffered from the jealous ill-will of King William IV (*Queen's Letters*, i. 580).

In the result Lord Melbourne's hints and Stockmar's admonitions decided Queen Victoria and her consort's educational policy. Stockmar,
tackling the question afresh, on 28 July 1846 deduced from the spirit of
revolution abroad the imperative need of endowing the child with a sense
of the sacred character of all existing institutions, a sound faith in the
Church of England, a capacity to hold the balance true between conservative and progressive forces, and a sympathy with healthful social
movements. With the utmost earnestness the boy's parents thereupon
addressed themselves in Stockmar's spirit to the task of making their son a
model of morality, of piety, of deportment, and of intellectual accomplishment, at the same time as they secluded him from any active political
interest. Their effort was not wholly beneficial to his development. Yet,
whether or no the result were due to his parents' precautions, the country
was spared in his case, despite occasional private threatenings, any
scandalous manifestation of the traditional rivalry between the sovereign
and the next heir to the throne.

English, French, and German governesses soon joined the royal
household. German the prince spoke from infancy with his father and
mother, and he habitually conversed in it with his brothers and sisters
(Bunsen's *Memoirs*, ii. 120). He always retained through life a full mastery of all the complexities of the language. To his many German
relations he spoke in no other tongue, and to his grand-uncle, King
Leopold I of Belgium, and to that monarch's son and successor, King
Leopold II, with both of whom he was through youth and manhood in
constant intercourse, he talked in German preferably to French. Yet
French, too, he learned easily, and acquired in due time an excellence of
accent and a width of vocabulary which very few Englishmen have
equalled.

Childhood and boyhood were wholly passed with his parents, sisters,
and brothers in an atmosphere of strong family affection. His eldest sister,
Victoria, whose intellectual alertness was in childhood greatly in excess of
his own, was his inseparable companion, and his devotion to her was
lifelong. His next sister, Alice (*b* 25 April 1843), and next brother, Alfred (*b* 6
Aug. 1844), soon joined in the pursuits of the two elder children, but the tie
between the prince and Princess Victoria was closer than that between
him and any of his juniors. The children's time was chiefly spent at
Buckingham Palace or Windsor Castle, but there were frequent sojourns
at Claremont, Esher, the residence of King Leopold, and at seaside resorts.
The prince stayed as a baby with the duke of Wellington at Walmer Castle
(Nov. 1842), and several times in infancy at the Brighton Pavilion, the royal
residence which was abandoned by the queen in 1845, owing to the
pertinacity of sight-seers. In the same year Osborne House in the Isle of

Wight became the regular seaside home of the royal family, and was thenceforth constantly visited by the prince.

In 1846 he and the rest of the family made a first yachting excursion from Osborne, paying a first visit to Cornwall, which was his own appanage. Next year he made a tour through Wales, the principality which gave him his chief title. In the autumn of 1848 he paid his first visit to Scotland, staying at Balmoral House, then a hired shooting lodge. The Scottish visit was thenceforth an annual experience. The future Archbishop Benson saw the royal party at their first Braemar gathering (15 Sept. 1848), and described the little prince as 'a fair little lad of rather a slender make with an intelligent expression.' A like impression was made on all observers. 'Pretty but delicate looking' was Macaulay's description of him when the child caught the historian's eye as he stood shyly holding the middle finger of his father's hand at the christening of his third sister, Princess Helena, at Windsor on 26 July 1846 (Lord Broughton's *Recollections*, vi. 181).

In 1849 he made his first acquaintance with another part of his future dominions. He accompanied his parents on their first visit to Ireland. Queen Victoria on her return commemorated the Irish people's friendly reception of her and her family by creating her eldest son by letters patent under the great seal, Earl of Dublin (10 Sept. 1849). Her father had borne the same title, and its revival in the person of the heir-apparent was a politic compliment to the Irish capital. The visit to Ireland was repeated four years later, when the royal family went to Dublin to inspect an exhibition of Irish industries (Aug. 1853). In later life no member of the royal family crossed the Irish Channel more frequently than the prince.

Meanwhile his education was progressing on strict lines. In the spring of 1849 Henry Birch, an undermaster of Eton, 'a young, good-looking, amiable man,' according to Prince Albert, was after careful inquiry appointed his first tutor. Birch held office for two years, and was succeeded by Frederick W. Gibbs, a barrister, who was recommended to Prince Albert by Sir James Stephen, then professor of history at Cambridge. Gibbs filled his post till 1858. Other instructors taught special subjects, and with M. Brasseur, his French teacher, the prince long maintained a cordial intimacy.

Endowed with an affectionate disposition, which was readily moved by those about him, he formed with most of his associates in youth of whatever age or position attachments which lasted for life. Very typical of his fidelity to his earliest acquaintances in all ranks was his lifelong relation with (Sir) David Welch (1820–1912), captain of the Fairy and Alberta, Queen Victoria's earliest royal yachts. The prince made his first sea voyage

Edward VII

in Welch's charge when little more than seven, and thenceforth until the prince's death Welch belonged to his inner circle of friends. They constantly exchanged hospitalities until the last year of the prince's life, nearly sixty years after their first meeting.

The prince's chief tutors performed their functions under the close surveillance of Prince Albert, who not only drafted elaborate regulations for their guidance and made almost daily comments on their action, but in the name of the queen and himself directly addressed to his son long written exhortations on minutest matters of conduct. To his religious training especial care was attached, and a sense of religion, if of a rather formal strain, soon developed in permanence. But to his father's disappointment, it was early apparent that the prince was not studious, that books bored him, and that, apart from progress in speaking French and German, he was slow to learn. It was difficult to interest him in his lessons. The narrow range of books at his disposal may partly explain the defect. History, the chief subject of study, was carefully confined to bare facts and dates. Fiction was withheld as demoralising, and even Sir Walter Scott came under the parental ban. In the result the prince never acquired a habit of reading. Apart from the newspapers he practically read nothing in mature years. He wrote with facility and soon corresponded voluminously in a simple style. By his parents' orders he kept a diary from an early age, and maintained the habit till his death, but the entries were invariably brief and bald. At the same time he was as a boy observant, was quick at gathering information from talk, and developed a retentive memory for facts outside school study.

His parents meanwhile regarded the drama, art, and music as legitimate amusements for their children. The prince showed some liking for drawing, elocution, and music, and was soon introduced to the theatre, visiting Astley's pantomime as early as 24 March 1846. From 1848 to 1858 he attended all the annual winter performances at Windsor, where Charles Kean and his company provided the chief items of the performance. As a boy he saw at Windsor, too, the younger Charles Mathews in 'Used up' and the farce of 'Box and Cox' (4 Jan. 1849). To the London theatres he paid frequent visits. In 1852 he heard Meyerbeer's 'Huguenots' at the Opera House in Covent Garden. In the spring of 1853 he witnessed more than once Charles Kean's revival of 'Macbeth' at the Princess's Theatre. In 1855 he witnessed at Drury Lane a pantomime acted by amateurs for the benefit of Wellington College, in which his father was deeply interested, and he showed the utmost appreciation of the fun. In 1856 he saw Mme. Celeste in pantomime at the Adelphi, and was a delighted spectator of some old farces at the same house. The early taste for drama and opera never left him.

362

The royal children were encouraged by their father to act and recite, and George Bartley the actor was engaged to give the prince lessons in elocution. He made sufficient progress to take part in dramatic entertainments for his parents' amusement. In Jan. 1853 he played the part of Abner to the Princess Royal's Athalie in some scenes from Racine's tragedy. Next month he played Max in a German piece, 'Die Tafelbirnen,' his sisters and brother supporting him, and on 10 Feb. 1854 he in the costume of 'Winter' recited lines from Thomson's 'Seasons.'

As a draughtsman he showed for a time some skill. Edward Henry Corbould gave him instruction. For an art exhibition in the spring of 1855 in aid of the Patriotic Fund for the benefit of soldiers' families during the Crimean war, he prepared a drawing called 'The Knight,' which sold for fifty-five guineas. Opportunities for experiment in other mechanical arts were provided at Osborne. There a Swiss cottage was erected in 1854 as a workshop for the prince and his brothers. The prince and his brother Alfred during the Crimean war were busy over miniature fortifications in the grounds.

The gravest defect in Prince Albert's deliberate scheme of education was the practical isolation which it imposed on the prince from boys of his own age. Prince Albert to a greater extent than the queen held that members of the royal family and especially the heir-apparent should keep aloof from their subjects, and deprecated intercourse save in ceremonial fashion. He had a nervous fear of the contaminating influence of boys less carefully trained than his own sons. There were always advisers who questioned the wisdom of the royal policy of exclusiveness, and Prince Albert so far relented, when his eldest son was a child of six or seven, as to invite a few boys whose parents were of high character and good position to play with the prince in the gardens of Buckingham Palace. Among these child associates were Charles Carington (afterwards first Earl Carrington and Marquis of Lincolnshire) and Charles Lindley Wood (afterwards second Viscount Halifax). Some seven years later the practice was continued at Windsor, whither a few carefully chosen Eton boys were summoned to spend an occasional afternoon. Besides Charles Wood, there now came among others George Cadogan (afterwards fifth Earl Cadogan) and Lord Hinchingbrooke (afterwards eighth earl of Sandwich); but the opportunities of intercourse were restricted. Prince Albert, who was often present, inspired the boy-visitors with a feeling of dread. The young prince's good-humour and charm of manner endeared him to them and made most of them his friends for life, but owing to his seclusion from boys' society he was ignorant of ordinary outdoor games, and showed small anxiety to attempt them. This want was never supplied. Subsequently he showed some interest in croquet, but ordinary games made no appeal to him, and he betrayed no aptitude for them. The only outdoor recreation which his parents urged on him was riding. He was taught to ride as a boy, and as a young man rode well and hard, possessing 'good hands' and an admirable nerve, while at the same time he developed a genuine love of horses and dogs.

Meanwhile the prince's presence at public ceremonies brought him into prominent notice. On 30 Oct. 1849 he attended for the first time a public function. He then accompanied Prince Albert to the City to open the Coal Exchange. His sister, princess royal, accompanied him, but the queen was absent through illness. The royal party travelled in the royal barge from Westminster to London Bridge. On 1 May 1851 he was at the opening of the Great Exhibition, and was much impressed by the stateliness of the scene. With his tutor and his brother Alfred he frequently visited the place in the next few months, and in June 1854 he attended the inauguration at Sydenham of the Crystal Palace, into which the exhibition building was converted. He accompanied his parents to the art treasures exhibition at Manchester, staying at Worsley Hall with Lord Ellesmere (29 June–2 July 1857). He was twice at Eton (4 June 1853 and 1855) and once at Harrow (29 June 1854) for the speech days, but solely as an onlooker. More important was his first visit to the opening, on 12 Dec. 1854, of a new session of parliament, which was called in view of public anxiety over the Crimean war. That anxiety was fully alive in the royal circle. With his parents the prince visited the wounded soldiers in Brompton Hospital, and was at his mother's side when she first presented the V.C. decoration in Hyde Park (July 1857).

To the Crimean war, which brought his mother into alliance with Napoleon III, emperor of the French, the youth owed a new and more interesting experience than any that had yet befallen him. In August 1855 he and his eldest sister accompanied their parents on their glorious visit to Napoleon III and the Empress Eugénie at the Tuileries. It was the boy's first arrival on foreign soil. At once he won the hearts of the French people. His amiability and his delight in the attentions paid him captivated everybody. Prince Albert wrote to Stockmar with unusual lightness of heart how his son, 'qui est si gentil,' had made himself a general favourite. The impression proved imperishable. Frenchmen of every class and political creed acknowledged his boyish fascination. 'Le petit bonhomme est vraiment charmant,' wrote Louis Blanc, a French exile in England, who as he wandered about London caught frequent sight of the boy; 'il a je ne sais quoi qui plaît et, aux côtés de ses parents, il apparaît comme un vrai personnage de féerie.' This early friendship between the prince and France lasted through his life, and defied all vicissitudes of his own or of French fortunes.

While the prince's general demeanour gratified his parents, they were not well satisfied with his progress. He was reported to be wanting in enthusiasm and imagination, and to be subject to fits of ill-temper, which although brief were easily provoked. Prince Albert earnestly sought new means of quickening his intelligence. The curriculum was widened. In January 1856 the prince and his brother Alfred attended Faraday's lectures on metals at the Royal Institution; and William Ellis was summoned to the palace to teach the prince and his eldest sister political economy. Ellis, like all the royal tutors, noted the superior quickness of the girl, and failed to move much interest in the boy. At the end of August 1856, a fortnight's walking tour was made with his tutor Gibbs and Col. William Henry Cavendish, groom-in-waiting to Queen Victoria and a first cousin of the duke of Devonshire. Starting from Osborne, the party slowly travelled incognito through Dorset, for the most part on foot, putting up at inns without ceremony. But the secret of the prince's identity leaked out, and the experiment was spoilt by public curiosity.

Prince Albert did not conceal his anxiety over his son's backwardness. He invited the counsel of Lord Granville (22 Jan. 1857). Granville frankly advised 'his being mixed up with others of his own age away from home.' He ridiculed as futile 'the visits of Eton boys to the Castle for a couple of hours.' Never out of the sight of tutors or elderly attendants, he was not likely to develop the best boyish characteristics. A foreign tour with boys of his own age was suggested, and at some future date a voyage through the colonies and even to India.

In a modified fashion the advice was at once taken. In the spring of 1857 a second tour was made to the English lakes in the company of certain of the Eton boys who had been already occasional visitors to Windsor. Among them were Charles Wood, Mr. Gladstone's son, W. H. Gladstone, and Frederick Stanley, afterwards earl of Derby. Dr. Alexander Armstrong went as medical attendant and Col. Cavendish and Gibbs were in general charge. Lancaster, Bowness, Grasmere, and Helvellyn were all visited. But on the prince's return Prince Albert examined his son's diary and was distressed by its scantiness. A foreign tour followed in the summer. It was designed to combine study, especially of German, with the pleasures of sightseeing. On 26 July 1857 the prince left England to spend a month at Königswinter near Bonn on the Rhine. The same company of boys went with him and the suite was joined by Prince Albert's equerries, Col. Grey and Col. Ponsonby, as well as Charles Tarver, afterwards canon of Chester, who was appointed to act as classical tutor. No very serious study was pursued, but the experiences were varied. On the journey down the Rhine, the party met the ill-fated Archduke and Archduchess Maximilian of Austria, who were on their honeymoon. From Germany the prince and his companions went on to Switzerland. At Chamonix Albert Smith acted as guide. The prince walked over the Great Scheidegg, and Roundell Palmer (afterwards Earl Selborne), who was traversing the same pass, wrote with enthusiasm in his diary of 'the slender fair boy' and of his 'frank open countenance,' judging him to be 'everything which we could have wished the heir to the British throne at that age to be' (Selborne, *Memorials*, ii. 327). The prince also visited at the castle of Johannisburg the old statesman Prince Metternich, who reported to Guizot that 'le jeune prince plaisait à tout le monde, mais avait l'air embarrassé et très triste' (Reid, *Life of Lord Houghton*).

Home again at the end of October, he enjoyed in the winter his first experience of hunting, going out with the royal buckhounds near Windsor. He found the sport exhilarating, and soon afterwards tried his hand at deer-stalking in Scotland. In January 1858 the festivities in honour of his elder sister's marriage with Prince Frederick of Prussia absorbed the attention of his family. The prince attended the ceremony at St. James's Palace dressed in highland costume (25 Jan.). He felt the parting with the chief companion of his childhood, but corresponded incessantly with his sister and paid her repeated visits in her new home. The close relations with the Prussian royal family which had begun with his baptism were thus greatly strengthened. On 1 April 1858 he was confirmed at Windsor by the archbishop of Canterbury, John Bird Sumner. 'Bertie,' wrote his father, 'acquitted himself extremely well,' in the preliminary examination by Gerald Wellesley, dean of Windsor. His mother described 'his whole manner' as 'gentle, good and proper,' epithets which well expressed his attitude towards religion through life. A few days later he made a short pleasure tour with his tutor to Ireland. It was his third visit to that country. He now extended his knowledge of it by going south to Killarney and leaving by way of Cork.

A further trial of the effect of absence from home was made in May. It was decided that he should join the army, and on 5 May 1858, with a view to preparing him for military service, he was sent to stay at White Lodge in Richmond Park, the unoccupied residence of the ranger, the duke of Cambridge. A sort of independent household was there first provided for him. In view of the approach of manhood, his parents redoubled their precautions against undesirable acquaintances, but after careful investigation three young officers, Lord Valletort (the earl of Mount Edgcumbe's son), Major Christopher Teesdale, and Major Lindsay, afterwards Lord Wantage, were appointed to be the prince's first equerries. For their confidential instruction, Prince Albert elaborated rules whereby they might encourage in the prince minute care of his 'appearance, deportment, and dress,' and foster in him good 'manners and conduct towards others' and the 'power to acquit himself creditably in conversation or whatever may be the occupation of society.'

Already at fifteen he had been given a small allowance for the purchase of hats and ties, for which he carefully accounted to his mother. Now he was advanced to the privilege of choosing his own dress, and the queen sent him a formal minute on the sober principles which should govern his choice of material. To neatness of dress he always attached importance, and he insisted on a reasonable adherence to laws of fashion on the part of those about him. To the formalities of official costume he paid through life an almost exaggerated attention. This quality was partly inherited from his grandfather, the duke of Kent, but was greatly stimulated by his parents' counsel. Gibbs was in chief charge at White Lodge, and intellectual society was encouraged. Richard Owen the naturalist was several times invited to dine, and Lord John Russell, who was residing at Pembroke Lodge, was an occasional guest. The talk ranged over many topics, but was hardly calculated to interest very deeply a boy under seventeen (*Life of R. Owen*). He spent some time rowing on the river, and attended his first dinner-party at Cambridge Cottage, Kew, the residence of his great-aunt, the duchess of Cambridge, but all was too strictly regulated to give a youth much satisfaction. His sojourn at White Lodge was interrupted in August, when he went with his parents to Cherbourg, and renewed his acquaintance with the emperor and empress of the French. On 9 Nov. 1858, his seventeenth birthday, one purpose of his retirement to Richmond was fulfilled. He was made a colonel in the army unattached and at the same time was nominated K.G., though the installation was postponed. The date was regarded by his parents as marking his entry on manhood. Among their gifts was a memorandum signed by themselves solemnly warning him of his duties as a Christian gentleman. Gibbs, too, retired from the prince's service, and his precise post was allowed to lapse.

But there was no real change in the situation. His parents relaxed none of their vigilance, and a more complete control of the prince's affairs and conduct than Gibbs had exercised was now entrusted to a governor, Colonel Robert Bruce. The colonel fully enjoyed Prince Albert's confidence; his sister, Lady Augusta, was a close friend of the queen and was lady-in-waiting of his grandmother, the duchess of Kent. At the same time Charles Tarver was formally installed as instructor in classics.

For the next four years the prince and Col. Bruce were rarely parted, and Col. Bruce's wife, Catherine Mary, daughter of Sir Michael Shaw Stewart, usually assisted her husband in the strict discharge of his tutorial functions. The first incident in the new régime was a second foreign expedition of more imposing extent than the first. Travel was proving attractive, and his parents wisely encouraged his taste for it. During

December a short visit, the first of many, was paid to his married sister at Potsdam (December 1858). Next month he with Colonel and Mrs. Bruce started from Dover on an Italian tour. Stringent injunctions were laid on Bruce by his parents to protect the prince from any chance intercourse with strangers and to anticipate any unprincipled attempt of journalists to get into conversation with him. The prince was to encounter much that was new. He travelled for the first time under a formal incognito, and took the title of Baron of Renfrew. On leaving England he presented colours to the Prince of Wales's royal (100th) Canadian regiment, which was in camp at Shorncliffe (10 Jan. 1859), and delivered to the soldiers his first speech in public. The duke of Cambridge was present and pronounced it excellent. From Dover he crossed to Ostend to pay at the palace of Laeken, near Brussels, a first visit to his grand-uncle, King Leopold I. The king's influence over him was hardly less than that which he exerted on the boy's mother and father. Passing through Germany, the party made a short stay at Berlin, where Lord Bloomfield gave a ball in his honour. It was the first entertainment of the kind he had attended, and he was 'very much amused' with his first cotillon. He reached Rome near the end of January and settled down for a long stay. King Victor Emanuel was anxious to offer him hospitality at Turin. But Queen Victoria deemed King Victor's rough habit of speech, of which she had some experience at Windsor in 1855, an example to be avoided, and the invitation, somewhat to Cavour's embarrassment, was declined. At Rome the prince was soon busily engaged in seeing places and persons of interest. Attended by Bruce, he called on the Pope, Pius IX, and talked with him in French. The interview 'went off extremely well,' Queen Victoria wrote to King Leopold (15 Feb. 1859), and the pope interested himself in the endeavour to make the visit to Rome 'useful and pleasant' (*Queen's Letters*, iii. 411). Of duly approved English sojourners the prince saw many. He impressed Robert Browning as 'a gentle, refined boy'; he was often in the studio of the sculptor John Gibson, and an introduction there to Frederic Leighton led to a lifelong intimacy.

The outbreak of war between Italy and Austria in April hastened the prince's departure at the end of three months. H.M.S. Scourge carried him from Civita Vecchia to Gibraltar, where he was met by the royal yacht Osborne. From Gibraltar he passed to Lisbon, where he was entertained by Pedro V, king of Portugal. Queen Victoria and Prince Albert were attached to the Portuguese royal house by lineal ties and sentiments of affection. King Pedro's mother, Queen Maria, had been a playmate of Queen Victoria, and his father, Prince Ferdinand of Saxe-Coburg, was a first cousin of both Queen Victoria and her consort. With Portugal's successive monarchs the Prince of Wales was always on friendliest terms.

The prince only reached home in June, after six months' absence, and was then formally invested K.G. with full ceremony. On 26 June Prince Hohenlohe, the future chancellor of Germany, dined at Buckingham Palace, and learned from the prince's lips something of his travels. The young man gave the German visitor an impression of good breeding, short stature, and nervous awe of his father.

Prince Albert was not willing to allow his son's educational course to end prematurely. An academic training was at once devised on comprehensive lines, which included attendance at three universities in succession. A beginning was made at Edinburgh in the summer of 1859. Holyrood Palace was prepared for his residence. His chief instruction was in science under the guidance of Lyon Playfair, whose lectures at the university on the composition and working of iron-ore the prince attended regularly. He showed interest in Playfair's teaching, visiting with him many factories to inspect chemical processes, and proved his courage and obedient temper by dipping at Playfair's bidding in one of the workshops his bare arm into a hissing cauldron of molten iron by way of illustrating that the experiment could be made with impunity (Grant Duff, *Notes from a Diary*, 1877–86, ii. 27). At the same time Leonhard Schmitz taught him Roman history, Italian, German, and French. For exercise he paraded with the 16th lancers, who were stationed in the city, and made excursions to the Trossachs and the Scottish lakes. But the stay in Edinburgh was brief.

On 3 Sept. the prince consort held a conference there with the youth's professors and tutors to decide on his future curriculum. The Edinburgh experience was proving tedious and cheerless. The prince mixed with none but serious men advanced in years. The public at large was inclined to protest that now when it seemed time to terminate the state of pupilage, there were visible signs of an almost indefinite extension. 'Punch' voiced the general sentiment in a poem entitled 'A Prince at High Pressure' (24 Sept. 1859). But Prince Albert was relentless, and in October the prince migrated to Oxford on conditions as restrictive as any that went before. The prince matriculated as a nobleman from Christ Church, of which Dr. Liddell was dean, on 17 Oct.

It was the first recorded occasion on which a Prince of Wales had become an undergraduate of the University of Oxford. Tradition alone vouches for the story of the matriculation in 1398 of Prince Henry, afterwards Henry V—Prince Hal, with whom the new undergraduate was occasionally to be linked in satire hereafter. No other preceding Prince of Wales was in any way associated with Oxford. But Prince Albert's son was not to enjoy any of an undergraduate's liberty. A special residence, Frewen Hall, a house in the town, was taken for him. Col. Bruce accompanied him and rarely left him. Prince Albert impressed on Bruce the boy's need of close application to study, and of resistance to social calls, as well as the undesirability of any free mingling with undergraduates. Herbert Fisher, a student of Christ Church, was on the recommendation of Dean Liddell appointed his tutor in law and constitutional history. He did not attend the college lectures, but Goldwin Smith, professor of modern history, with three or four chosen undergraduates, waited on him at his residence and gave him a private course in history. The text-book was the 'Annals of England,' by W. E. Flaherty (1855), and the professor only partially compensated by epigram for the dryness of the work. By Prince Albert's wish, Arthur Penrhyn Stanley, then professor of ecclesiastical history, gave him some religious instruction, while Dr. Henry Acland, his medical attendant, occasionally invited him to social gatherings at his house. With both Stanley and Acland the prince formed very friendly relations. He saw comparatively little of the undergraduates. He confirmed his acquaintance with Mr. Charles Wood. At the same time fox-hunting was one of his permitted indulgences, and the recreation brought him into touch with some young men of sporting tastes, to a few of whom, like Mr. Henry Chaplin and Sir Frederick Johnstone, he formed a lifelong attachment. He hunted with the South Oxfordshire hounds, of which Lord Macclesfield was master, and he saw his first fox killed near Garsington on 27 Feb. 1860, when he was presented with the brush. Hunting was his favourite sport till middle age. The discipline which Col. Bruce enforced prohibited smoking. But the prince made surreptitious experiments with tobacco, which soon induced a fixed habit.

The prince remained in residence at Oxford with few interruptions during term time until the end of the summer term 1860. He was summoned to Windsor on 9 Nov. 1859 for the celebration of his eighteenth birthday, which was reckoned in royal circles a virtual coming of age. His parents again presented him with a carefully penned exhortation in which they warned him that he would henceforth be exempted from parental authority, but that they would always be ready with their counsel at his request. As he read the document the sense of his parents' solicitude for his welfare and his new responsibilities moved him to tears. But the assurance of personal independence lacked genuine significance. In the Easter vacation of 1860 he paid a first visit to his father's home at Coburg, and made 'a very good impression.' He pleased his parents by the good account he brought them of 'dear' Stockmar's state of health (*Letters of Queen Victoria*, iii. 5; 25 April 1860). On his return home he found (Sir) Richard Owen lecturing his brothers and sisters on natural history, and he attended once (23 April 1860). In London at the opening of the long vacation he enjoyed the first of his many experiences of laying foundation stones. He performed the ceremony for the School of Art at Lambeth.

A formidable journey was to interrupt his Oxford undergraduate career. In July 1860 he carried out a scheme long in his parents' minds, which exerted on his development a far more beneficial effect than any likely to come of his academic training. During the Crimean war the Canadian government, which had equipped a regiment of infantry for active service, had requested the queen to visit Canada. She declined the invitation, but promised that the Prince of Wales should go there as soon as he was old enough. When that decision was announced, the president of the United States, James Buchanan, and the corporation of New York, both sent the queen requests that he should visit America. The queen very gradually overcame maternal misgivings of the safety of an English prince among American republicans. The American invitations were at length accepted, with the proviso that the American visit was to be treated as a private one. In any case the projected tour acquired something more than a merely colonial interest. An impressive introduction to public life was thus designed for the heir to the English throne. A large and dignified suite was collected. The prince was accompanied by the duke of Newcastle, secretary of state for the colonies, by the earl of St. Germans, lord steward of the royal household, and by Col. Bruce, his governor. Major Teesdale and Capt. Grey (d. 1874), son of Sir George Grey, went as equerries, and Dr. Acland as physician. Young Lord Hinchingbrooke, one of the Eton associates, was to join the party in America.

Leaving Southampton on 9 July 1860 in H.M.S. Hero, with H.M.S. Ariadne in attendance, the prince reached Newfoundland on the 23rd. The colonial progress opened at St. John's with processions, presentations of addresses, reviews of volunteers, levees, and banquets, which were constant features of the tour. Thence they passed to Halifax and Nova Scotia (30 July). On 9 Aug. he landed on Prince Edward Island, and on the 12th, near the mouth of the St. Lawrence, the governor-general of the Canadas, Sir Edmund Head, boarded the royal vessel. On the 20th the prince made a state entry into Quebec, the capital of French Canada. He stayed at Parliament House, which had been elaborately fitted up for his residence, and a guard of honour of 100 men was appointed to form his escort through the colony. At Montreal on 1 Sept. he opened the great railway bridge across the St. Lawrence; and passing thence to Ottawa, he there laid the foundation stone of the Parliament building. On the way to Toronto, the capital of upper Canada, the only untoward incident took place. Strong protestant feeling in the upper colony resented the enthusiasm with which the French Roman catholics of lower Canada had welcomed the prince, and the Orange lodges resolved to emphasise their principles by forcing on the prince's notice in their street decorations the emblems of their faith. At Kingston on Lake Ontario the townsfolk refused to obey the duke of

Newcastle's direction to remove the orange colours and portraits of William III from the triumphal arches before the royal party entered the town. Consequently the royal party struck the place out of their itinerary and proceeded to Toronto, where a like difficulty threatened. Happily the Orangemen there yielded to persuasion, and the reception at Toronto proved as hearty as could be wished.

Leaving Canada for the United States, the prince made an excursion to Niagara Falls (17 Sept.), where, somewhat to his alarm, he saw Blondin perform on the tight rope, and at the neighbouring village of Queenstown (18 Sept.) he laid the crowning stone on the great monument erected to the memory of Major-general Sir Isaac Brock, who was slain in the American war of 1812. Crossing Detroit river, he touched United States soil at Detroit on 19 Sept.; there he was met by Lord Lyons, minister at Washington. At once scenes of extravagant enthusiasm belied all fears of a cool reception. Short stays in Chicago, St. Louis, Cincinnati, and Pittsburg preceded his arrival at Washington (3 Oct.), where President Buchanan (an old man of seventy-seven) received him at the White House with friendliest cordiality. A crowded levee at White House was given in his honour. With the president he visited on 5 Oct. Mount Vernon, Washington's home and burial place, and planted a chestnut by the side of the tomb. Such a tribute from the great-grandson of George III was greeted by the American people with loud acclamations of joy, and England was hardly less impressed. 'The Prince of Wales at the Tomb of Washington' was the subject set for the English poem at Cambridge University in 1861, and the prize was won by Frederic W. H. Myers. Going northwards, the prince stayed at Philadelphia (7 Oct.), where he heard Madame Patti sing for the first time. At New York (11 Oct.) he remained three days. A visit was paid later to the military school at West Point, and proceeding to Boston he went over to Cambridge to inspect Harvard University. At Boston he met Longfellow, Emerson, and Oliver Wendell Holmes. He embarked for home in H.M.S. Hero from Portland in Maine on 20 Oct. and arrived after a bad passage at Plymouth on 15 Nov., six days after completing his nineteenth year.

Everywhere the prince's good-humour, courteous bearing, and simple delight in novel experiences won the hearts of his hosts. 'Dignified, frank, and affable,' wrote the president to Queen Victoria (6 Oct. 1860), 'he has conciliated, wherever he has been, the kindness and respect of a sensitive and discriminating people.' The tour differed in every regard from his previous trips abroad. It was originally planned as a ceremonial compliment to the oldest and most important of English colonies on the part of the heir to the throne travelling as the reigning sovereign's official representative. No British colony had previously received a like attention.

Canada accorded the prince all the honours due to his royal station. In the United States, too, where it was stipulated by Queen Victoria that he should travel as a private person under his incognito of Baron of Renfrew, the fiction went for nothing, and he was greeted as England's heir-apparent no less emphatically than in British North America. The result satisfied every sanguine hope. It tightened the bond of affection between Canada and the mother country at the moment when a tide of public sentiment seemed setting in another direction, and it reinforced the sense of unity among the British American colonies, which found expression in their internal union of 1867. On the relations of the United States and England the effect was of the happiest. On 29 Nov. 1860 Sir Charles Phipps, who was high in the confidence of Queen Victoria and Prince Albert, gave expression to the general verdict in a letter to Dr. Acland. 'The success of the expedition has been beyond all expectation; it may be reckoned as one of the most important and valuable state measures of the present age, and whether we look to the excitement and encouragement of loyalty and affection to the mother country in Canada, or to the soothing of prejudice and the increase of good feeling between the United States and Great Britain, it seems to me impossible to overrate the importance of the good results which the visit promises for the future.'

On the youth himself the tour exerted a wholly beneficial influence. The duke of Newcastle noticed in the prince a perceptible intellectual development. The journey left a lasting impression on his mind. If at times in later reminiscence he associated Canadian life with some want of material comfort, he always cherished gratitude for the colonial hospitality, and never lost a sense of attachment to the American people. His parents felt pride in the American welcome, and a year later, when Motley, then American minister at Vienna, was passing through England, he was invited to Balmoral, to receive from Queen Victoria and Prince Albert expressions of their satisfaction. Some American publicists were inclined to attribute to the heartiness of the prince's reception Prince Albert's momentous diplomatic intervention in behalf of the north over the affair of the Trent. When the American civil war broke out next year, Prince Albert on the eve of his death powerfully discouraged English sympathy with the revolt against the authority of the government at Washington, which had given his son an ovation.

The prince's career in England pursued its normal course. He returned to Oxford in November for the rest of the Michaelmas term, and in December the queen paid him a visit there. At the end of the year he left Oxford for good. Next month his protracted education was continued at Cambridge. As at Oxford, a private residence, Madingley Hall, was hired for him. The Cambridge house was of more inspiring character than

Frewen Hall; it was an old and spacious country mansion, four miles from the town, 'with large grounds and capital stables.' Col. Bruce and his wife took domestic control, and under their eyes the prince was free to entertain his friends. He entered Trinity College, while Dr. Whewell was Master, on 18 Jan. 1861. A set of rooms in the college was placed at his disposal, but he did not regularly occupy them. Joseph Barber Lightfoot was his college tutor, and when in 1897 the prince visited Durham, of which Lightfoot was then bishop, he recalled the admiration and regard with which Lightfoot inspired him. History remained his main study and was directed by the professor of history, Charles Kingsley. The prince attended Kingsley's lectures at the professor's own house, together with some half-dozen carefully selected undergraduates, who included the present Viscount Cobham, and George Howard, ninth earl of Carlisle. The prince rode over thrice a week to the professor's house and each Saturday Kingsley recapitulated the week's work with the prince alone. He was examined at the end of each term; the course finally brought English history up to the reign of George IV. Kingsley was impressed by his pupil's attention and courtesy, and like all who came into contact with him, bore him thenceforth deep affection.

In 1861 there began for the court a period of gloom, which long oppressed it. On 16 March the prince's grandmother, the duchess of Kent, died; and he met his first experience of death at close quarters. He first attended a drawing-room on 24 June 1861 in the sombre conditions of official mourning. But more joyful experience intervened, before there fell on him the great blow of his father's premature death. In the summer vacation he went for a fourth time to Ireland, at first as the guest of the lord-lieutenant, the eighth Earl of Carlisle; but his chief purpose was to join in camp at the Curragh the second battalion, grenadier guards. For the first time in his life he was freed from the strict and punctilious supervision of his veteran guardians and mentors. The pleasures of liberty which he tasted were new to him. A breach of discipline exposed him to punishment, and he grew impatient of the severe restrictions of his previous career. His mother and father came over in August to a review of the troops in which he took part. 'Bertie,' she wrote, 'marched past with his company, and did not look at all so very small' (*Letters*, 26 Aug. 1861). With his parents he spent a short holiday in Killarney, and then for a second time he crossed the Channel to visit his sister, the Princess Royal, at Berlin (Sept. 1861). After accompanying her and her husband on a tour through the Rhenish provinces, he witnessed at Coblenz the military manœuvres of the German army of the Rhine.

This German tour had been designed with an object of greater importance than mere pleasure or change. The prince was reaching a marriageable age, and the choice of a wife was in the eyes of King Leopold, of Stockmar, and of the youth's parents a matter of momentous concern. It was inevitable that selection should be made from among princely families of Germany. Seven young German princesses were reported to be under the English court's consideration as early as the summer of 1858 (*The Times*, 5 July 1858). Fifth on this list was Princess Alexandra, eldest daughter of Prince Christian of Schleswig-Holstein-Sonderburg-Glucksburg, next heir to the throne of Denmark, which he ascended on 15 Nov. 1863 as Christian IX. She was barely seventeen, nearly three years the prince's junior. Her mother, Louise of Hesse-Cassel, was sole heiress of the old Danish royal family, and the princess was born and brought up at Copenhagen. Though her kinship was with Germany, her life was identified with Denmark. King Leopold, who discussed the choice of a bride with Queen Victoria, reported favourably of her beauty and character. But the prince's parents acknowledged his right of selection, and a meeting between him and Princess Alexandra was arranged, while he was in Germany in the summer of 1861. The princess was staying near at hand with her mother's father, the Landgrave of Hesse-Cassel, at the castle of Rumpenheim. The prince saw her for the first time in the cathedral at Speier (24 Sept. 1861). Next day they met again at Heidelberg. Each made a favourable impression on the other. On 4 Oct. Prince Albert writes: 'We hear nothing but excellent accounts of the Princess Alexandra; the young people seem to have taken a warm liking to one another.' Again, when the Prince of Wales returned to England a few days later, his father writes to Stockmar: 'He has come back greatly pleased with his interview with the princess at Speier.'

For the present nothing further followed. The prince resumed his residence at Cambridge. He was in London on 31 Oct., when he was called to the bar at the Middle Temple, was elected a bencher, and opened the new library at the Inn. But his studies at Cambridge went forward during the Michaelmas term. The stringent discipline was proving irksome, and he was involuntarily coming to the conclusion, which future experience confirmed, that his sojourns at the two English universities were mistakes. On 25 Nov. Prince Albert arrived to offer him good counsel. He stayed the night at Madingley Hall. A chill caught on the journey developed into what unhappily proved to be a fatal illness. On 13 Dec. the prince was summoned from Cambridge to Windsor to attend his father's deathbed. Prince Albert died next day.

At his father's funeral in St. George's Chapel on 23 Dec. the prince was chief mourner, in his mother's absence. He joined her the same day at Osborne. At the queen's request he wrote a day or two later a letter publicly identifying himself with her overwhelming anxiety to pay her husband's memory all public honour. On the 28th he offered to place, at his own expense, in the gardens of the Royal Horticultural Society, a statue of the prince instead of one of the queen which had already been cast for erection there, by way of memorial of the Great Exhibition of 1851.

The sudden death of his father, when the prince was just turned twenty years of age, was a momentous incident in his career. The strict discipline, to which his father had subjected him, had restrained in him every sense of independence and had fostered a sentiment of filial awe. He wholly shared his mother's faith in the character and attainments of the dead prince. In her husband's lifetime the queen had acknowledged his superior right to control her sons. But after his death she regarded herself to be under a solemn obligation to fill his place in the family circle and to regulate all her household precisely on the lines which he had followed. To all arrangements which the prince consort had made for her sons and daughters she resolved loyally to give effect and to devise others in the like spirit. The notion of consulting their views or wishes was foreign to her conception of duty. Abounding in maternal solicitude, she never ceased to think of the Prince of Wales as a boy to whom she owed parental guidance, the more so because he was fatherless. A main effect of his father's death was consequently to place him, in his mother's view, almost in permanence 'in statu pupillari.' She claimed to regulate his actions in almost all relations of life.

Earlier signs were apparent, even in Prince Albert's lifetime, of an uneasy fear on the queen's part that her eldest son might, on reaching manhood, check the predominance which it was her wish that her husband should enjoy as her chief counsellor. In 1857 she had urged on ministers a parliamentary enactment for securing Prince Albert's formal precedence in the state next to herself. Stockmar was asked to press upon her the imprudence of her proposal, and it was with reluctance dropped (Fitzmaurice, *Lord Granville*). But the episode suggests the limitations which threatened the Prince of Wales's adult public activity. In his mother's sight he was disqualified by his filial relation from filling the place which her husband had held in affairs of state or from relieving her of any political duties. His mother accurately described her lasting attitude alike to her husband's memory and to her children in a letter to King Leopold (24 Dec. 1861): 'And *no human power* will make me swerve from *what he* decided and wished. I apply this particularly as regards our children—Bertie, &c.—for whose future he had traced everything *so* carefully. I am *also determined* that *no one* person, may *he* be ever so good, ever so devoted among my servants—is to lead or guide or dictate to *me*' (*Letters*, iii. 606).

The Prince of Wales always treated his mother with affectionate deference and considerate courtesy. Naturally docile, he in his frequent letters to her addressed her up to her death in simple filial style, beginning 'Dear Mama' and ending 'Your affectionate and dutiful son.' To the queen the formula had a literal significance. But on reaching man's estate the prince's views of life broadened. He travelled far from the rigid traditions in which he had been brought up. Difference of view regarding his official privileges became with the prolongation of his mother's reign inevitable. The queen was very ready to delegate to him formal and ceremonial labours which were distasteful to her, but she never ceased to ignore his title to any function of government. His place in the royal succession soon seemed to him inconsistent with that perpetual tutelage, from which Queen Victoria deemed it wrong for him to escape in her lifetime. Open conflict was averted mainly by the prince's placable temper, which made ebullitions of anger of brief duration; but it was a serious disadvantage for him to be denied by the queen any acknowledged responsibility in public affairs for the long period of nearly forty years, which intervened between his father's death and his own accession to the throne.

As soon as the first shock of bereavement passed, Queen Victoria set herself to carry out with scrupulous fidelity two plans which her husband devised for his eldest son's welfare, another foreign tour and his marriage.

The tour to the Holy Land which was to conclude his educational travel had been arranged by Prince Albert in consultation with Arthur Penrhyn Stanley. The suite included Gen. Bruce, Major Teesdale, Col. Keppel, Robert Meade, who had been associated with Lord Dufferin on his mission to Syria in 1860, and Dr. Minter as physician. The queen's confidence in Stanley was a legacy from her husband, and at her persuasion he somewhat reluctantly agreed to join the party. The prince travelled incognito, and owing to the family mourning it was the queen's wish that ceremonial receptions should as far as possible be dispensed with. Leaving Osborne on 6 Feb. 1862, the prince and his companions journeyed through Germany and Austria. At Darmstadt he was welcomed by the Grand Duke, whose son was to marry his second sister, Alice; thence he passed to Munich, where he inspected the museums and the galleries and saw the king of Bavaria. At Vienna he met for the first time the Emperor Francis Joseph, who formed a favourable impression of him, and thenceforth cherished a genuine affection for him. At Vienna he was introduced to Laurence Oliphant, who was well acquainted with the Adriatic coast of the Mediterranean. Oliphant readily agreed to act as guide for that part of the expedition. From Trieste, where Stanley joined the party, the royal yacht Osborne brought the prince to Venice, to Corfu, and other places of interest on the passage to Egypt. Oliphant, who served as cicerone for ten days, wrote that the prince 'was not studious nor highly intellectual, but up to the average and beyond it in so far as quickness of observation and general intelligence go.' He recognised the charm of his 'temper and disposition' and deemed travelling the best sort of education for him. His defects he ascribed to a 'position which never allows him responsibility or forces him into action' (Mrs. Oliphant's *Life of L. Oliphant*, i. 269). The prince was on his side attracted by Oliphant, and many years later not only entertained him at Abergeldie but took him to dine at Balmoral with Queen Victoria, who shared her son's appreciation of his exhilarating talk.

The prince disembarked at Alexandria on 24 Feb. Passing to Cairo, he lodged in the palace of Kasr-en-nil, and every attention was paid him by the viceroy Said. A three weeks' tour was made through upper Egypt. He climbed the summit of the Great Pyramid without assistance and with exceptional alacrity; he voyaged up the Nile to Assouan (12 March), and explored the temple of Carnac at Luxor. At length on 31 March he arrived in the Holy Land, where no English prince had set foot since Edward I, more than six hundred years before.

Jerusalem was thoroughly explored, and the diplomacy of General Bruce gained admission to the mosque of Hebron, into which no European was known to have penetrated since 1187. 'High station,' remarked the prince, 'has after all some merits, some advantages.' Easter Sunday (20 April 1862) was spent on the shores of Lake Tiberias and at Galilee. Through Damascus the party reached Beyrout and thence went by sea to Tyre, Sidon, and Tripoli (in Syria). During the tour Stanley succeeded in interesting the prince in the historic traditions of Palestine. While he was easily amused, he was amenable to good advice, and readily agreed that sporting should be suspended on Sundays. 'It is impossible not to like him,' Stanley wrote. 'His astonishing memory of names and persons' and his 'amiable and endearing qualities' impressed all the party.

On 15 May the Osborne anchored at the isle of Rhodes. Thence the prince passed to Constantinople, where he stayed at the embassy with Sir Henry Bulwer, ambassador, and was formally entertained in his rank of Prince of Wales by the sultan. He saw the sights of the city. His host reported favourably of his tact and manner, and while he did not anticipate that he would learn much from books, he discerned powers of observation which would well supply the place of study. But he detected a certain danger in an ease of demeanour which at times challenged his dignity and in the desire for amusement. A first sojourn in Athens, where he was to be a frequent visitor, and a landing at Cephallonia brought him to Marseilles. At Fontainebleau he was welcomed hospitably by the Emperor Napoleon III and the Empress Eugénie, and on 13 June he rejoined his mother at

Windsor. One unhappy incident of the highly interesting journey was the serious illness contracted by General Bruce in the marshes of the upper Jordan. He managed with difficulty to reach London, but there he died on 27 June 1862. The prince was thus deprived finally of the close surveillance which his father had deemed needful to his welfare.

While the court was still in deep mourning the marriage of his second sister, Princess Alice, to Prince Louis of Hesse-Darmstadt took place at Windsor on 1 July 1862.

The International Exhibition of 1862, which the prince consort had designed, had been duly opened in May by the duke of Cambridge, to whom much court ceremonial was for the time delegated by Queen Victoria. The prince inspected the exhibition in the summer and received with charming grace the foreign visitors—to one of whom, General de Galliffet, he formed a lifelong attachment. But the queen's chief preoccupation was the scheme for the prince's marriage which King Leopold and the prince consort had inaugurated the previous year. In the summer the queen wrote to Prince Christian, formally soliciting the hand of his daughter, Princess Alexandra, for her eldest son. Assent was readily given. At the end of August Queen Victoria left England to revisit Coburg, her late husband's home. On the journey she stayed with her uncle Leopold at his palace of Laeken, near Brussels. Her future daughter-in-law was with her father on a visit to Ostend, and Princess Alexandra came over to Laeken to meet Queen Victoria for the first time. The queen left for Coburg on 4 Sept. On the same date the prince set out to meet his mother and to begin what proved another long continental tour. On the 7th he arrived at Brussels, and paid his respects to Princess Alexandra at Ostend. Both were summoned by King Leopold to the palace of Laeken, and there on 9 Sept. 1862 they were formally betrothed. Next day they went over the battlefield of Waterloo together, and in the evening they attended a court banquet which King Leopold gave in their honour. They travelled together to Cologne, where they parted, and the prince joined his mother at Coburg.

The engagement was made public on 16 Sept. in a communication to the press drafted by Queen Victoria. It was stated that the marriage 'privately settled at Brussels' was 'based entirely upon mutual affection and the personal merits of the princess,' and was 'in no way connected with political considerations.' 'The revered Prince Consort, whose sole object was the education and welfare of his children, had,' the message continued, 'been long convinced that this was a most desirable marriage.' On 1 Nov. 1862 the queen gave her formal assent to the union at a meeting of the privy council. The announcement was received in England with enthusiasm. The youth and beauty of the princess and her association with

Denmark appealed to popular sympathies. 'I like the idea of the Danish connection; we have had too much of Germany and Berlin and Coburgs,' wrote Lady Palmerston (Reid, *Lord Houghton*, ii. 83). In spite of the queen's warning, a political colour was given to the match in diplomatic circles. Prussia and Austria were steadily pushing forward their designs on the Schleswig-Holstein provinces which Denmark claimed. Public feeling in England, which favoured the Danish pretensions, was stimulated. In Germany it was openly argued that the queen and prince consort had betrayed the German cause.

Although the match was wholly arranged by their kindred, it roused a mutual affection in the prince and princess. But they saw little of each other before their marriage. On 8 Nov. Princess Alexandra paid her first visit to England, coming with her father to Osborne as the guest of the queen. There and at Windsor she remained three weeks, spending much of her time alone with the queen.

By Queen Victoria's wish the prince was out of the country during his bride's stay. On leaving Coburg he had invited his sister and her husband, the crown prince and princess of Prussia, to accompany him on a Mediterranean tour on the yacht Osborne. They embarked at Marseilles on 22 Oct. 1862. A most interesting itinerary was followed. A first experience of the Riviera was obtained by a landing at Hyères. Palermo, the capital of Sicily, was visited, and thence a passage was made to Tunis, where the ruins of Carthage were explored. Owing to an accident to the paddle-wheel of the royal yacht, the vessel was towed by the frigate Doris from the African coast to Malta. On 5 Nov. the party reached Naples, and there the prince's twenty-first birthday was passed without ceremony. There was some incongruity in celebrating so interesting an anniversary in a foreign country. Yet the experience was not out of harmony with the zest for travel and for foreign society which was born of the extended and varied wanderings of his youth. Before leaving southern Italy he ascended Vesuvius, and on the return journey to England he revisited Rome. From Florence he made his way through Germany by slow stages. At Lille on 3 Dec. he met Princess Alexandra on her way from England. He reached home on 13 Dec. By far the greater part of the year had been spent abroad on three continents—America, Asia, and Europe. Although he was barely turned one and twenty, the prince was probably the best travelled man in the world. There was small chance that he should cultivate in adult life any narrow insularity.

A separate establishment was already in course of formation at home. On reaching his majority he had come into a substantial fortune. The duchy of Cornwall was his appanage, and provided a large revenue. Owing to the careful administration of the prince consort the income of the duchy had risen from 16,000l. a year at the time of his son's birth to 60,000l. in 1862. The receipts had been allowed to accumulate during his minority, and these were now reckoned to amount to 700,000l. Out of these savings, the sum of 220,000l. was bestowed with the prince consort's approval on the purchase for his son from Spencer Cowper of the country residence and estate of Sandringham in Norfolk. The transaction was carried out in 1861. The estate covered 7000 acres, which the prince subsequently extended to 11,000; and the rental was estimated at 7000l. a year. The existing house proved unsuitable and was soon rebuilt. A London house was provided officially. Marlborough House had reverted to the crown in 1817 on the lapse of the great duke of Marlborough's long lease. It had since been lent to the Dowager Queen Adelaide, widow of William IV, on whose death in 1849 it was employed as a government art school and picture gallery. In 1859 it was decided to fit it up as a residence for the Prince of Wales. During 1861 it was thoroughly remodelled, and in 1862 was ready for his occupation.

For the next three months preparations for his marriage absorbed his own and the country's attention. Simultaneously with his return to England the 'London Gazette' published an official list of his first household. General Sir William Knollys, the prince consort's close friend, became comptroller and treasurer and practically chief of the establishment; Earl Spencer was made groom of the stole; the Earl of Mount Edgcumbe and Lord Alfred Hervey lords of the bedchamber; Robert Henry Meade and Charles Wood, afterwards Lord Halifax, grooms of the bedchamber; and Major Teesdale, Captain G. H. Grey, and Lieut.-colonel Keppel equerries. Herbert Fisher, his Oxford tutor, who had resumed his work at the bar, was recalled to act as private secretary, and he held the office till 1870. Mr. Wood was a very early companion, and all save Earl Spencer, General Knollys, and Lord Alfred Hervey had been closely associated with the prince already.

On 14 Dec. 1862 the prince was at Windsor, celebrating with his mother the first anniversary of his father's death. The queen refused to relax her habit of seclusion, and on 25 Feb. 1863 the prince took her place for the first time at a ceremonial function. He held a levee in her behalf at St. James's Palace. The presentations exceeded 1000, and severely tested his capacity for the fatigue of court routine. At a drawing-room which followed at Buckingham Palace (28 Feb.) the prince was again present; but his sister, the crown princess of Prussia, represented the sovereign.

Parliament opened on 5 Feb. 1863, and the prince took his seat for the first time in the House of Lords with due formality as a peer of the realm. He was introduced by the dukes of Cambridge and Newcastle. He showed his interest in the proceedings by staying till half-past nine at night to listen to the debate, which chiefly dealt with the cession of the Ionian islands to Greece.

The queen was absent. Her speech from the throne, which had been read by the lord chancellor at the opening of the session, announced the conclusion of her son's marriage treaty, which had been signed at Copenhagen on 10 Jan. 1863, and ratified in London the day before. The prime minister, Lord Palmerston, informed the House of Commons that the marriage might 'in the fullest sense of the word be called a love match' and was free of any political intention (Hansard, *Commons Report*, 5 Feb. 1863). A few days later a message from the queen invited the House of Commons to make pecuniary provision for the bridegroom. Parliament on the motion of Palmerston granted him an annuity of 40,000*l*., which with the revenues of the duchy of Cornwall brought his annual income up to 100,000*l*. At the same time an annuity of 10,000*l*. was bestowed on Princess Alexandra, with a prospective annuity of 30,000*l*. in case of widowhood. Advanced liberals raised the issue that the revenues of the duchy of Cornwall supplied the prince with an adequate income, and that parliament was under no obligation to make addition to it. It was complained, too, that public money had been voted to the prince on his creation as K.G. and for the expenses of his American tour. But Gladstone defended the government's proposal, and the resolutions giving it effect were carried *nem. con.* The grant finally passed the House of Commons without a division. No other of Queen Victoria's appeals to parliament for pecuniary grants to her children enjoyed the same good fortune.

The marriage was fixed for 10 March. The princess left Copenhagen on 26 Feb. and spent three days (2–5 March) on the journey in Brussels as the guest of King Leopold, who was a chief sponsor of the union. On 7 March the prince met his bride on her arrival at Gravesend. Travelling by railway to the Bricklayers' Arms, Southwark, they made a triumphal progress through the City of London to Paddington. The six carriages, headed by a detachment of life-guards, seemed to many onlookers a mean pageant, but a surging mass of people greeted the couple with boundless delight (cf. Louis Blanc's *Lettres sur l'Angleterre*, 2nd ser. i. 13 seq.). At times the pressure of the enthusiastic mob caused the princess alarm. From Paddington they went by railway to Slough, and drove thence to Windsor. The poet laureate, Tennyson, summed up the national exultation in a Danish alliance when in his poetic 'Welcome,' 7 March 1863, he greeted the princess, with some poetic licence, as

> 'Sea-kings' daughter as happy as fair,
> Blissful bride of a blissful heir,
> Bride of the heir of the kings of the sea.'

The wedding took place on 10 March in St. George's Chapel, Windsor. The prince was in the uniform of a general and wore the robes of the Garter. Queen Victoria in widow's weeds overlooked the proceedings from a gallery. 'A fine affair, a thing to remember,' wrote Disraeli of the ceremony. Kingsley, who attended as royal chaplain, admired 'the serious, reverent dignity of my dear young master, whose manner was perfect.' The crown princess brought her little son, Prince William (afterwards the German Emperor William II), who wore highland dress. The short honeymoon was spent at Osborne.

On 17 March the prince and princess were back at Windsor, and on the 20th they held a court at St. James's Palace in honour of the event. At Marlborough House they received an almost endless series of congratulatory addresses. Numerous festivities and entertainments followed, and the prince's social experience widened. On 2 May he attended for the first time the banquet of the Royal Academy. He had hardly spoken in public before, and he had learnt by heart a short speech. His memory momentarily failed him and he nearly broke down. The accident led him to rely henceforth in his public utterances on the inspiration of the moment. He mastered the general idea beforehand but not the words. His tact and native kindliness stood him in good stead, and he soon showed as an occasional speaker a readiness of delivery and a grace of compliment which few of his contemporaries excelled. Lord Houghton, who was a pastmaster in the same art, judged the prince to be only second to himself.

The corporation of the City of London presented the prince with the freedom on 7 June, and gave a ball in honour of himself and his bride on the same evening at the Guildhall. He had already identified himself with civic life by accepting the freedom of the Fishmongers' Company on 12 Feb., which his father had enjoyed. A second City company, the Merchant Taylors', paid him a like compliment on 11 June. In this busy month of June the prince and princess went, too, to Oxford to take part in the pleasures of Commemoration. They stayed with Dean Liddell at the prince's college, Christ Church (16–18 June), and at the encænia he received from the chancellor, Lord Derby, the honorary degree of D.C.L. A year later similar experiences awaited the prince and princess at Cambridge during May week. They stayed in the royal apartments at Trinity College, and the prince received the honorary degree of LL.D. Meanwhile a sumptuous ball given by the guards regiment in the exhibition building at South Kensington on 26 June 1863 brought the gaieties of their first season to an end.

The prince's married life was mainly spent at Marlborough House. But Sandringham constantly drew him from London; he visited friends in all parts of the country for sport or society, and was in Scotland every autumn. Nor was his habit of foreign travel long interrupted. Part of the early spring was soon regularly devoted to Cannes or Nice in the Riviera, and part of the early autumn to Homburg, while tours on a larger scale were not infrequent.

Outside London his career for the most part resembled that of any man of wealth and high station. At Sandringham the prince until his death spent seven or eight weeks each year, living the life of a private country gentleman. The first Easter after his marriage was spent at Sandringham, but the old house was then condemned as inadequate, and a new mansion was completed in 1870. The hospitality at Sandringham was easy and unconstrained; and the prince's guests were drawn from all ranks and professions. He interested himself in his tenants, and maintained his cottages in admirable repair. On every detail in the management of the estate he kept a watchful eye. The furniture and decorations of the house, the gardens, the farm, the stables, the kennels, were all under his personal care. For his horses and dogs he always cherished affection. The stables were always well filled. In the kennels at Sandringham were representatives of almost every breed. He was an exhibitor of dogs at shows from 27 May 1864, and was patron of the Kennel Club from its formation in April 1873. He actively identified himself with the sport of the county. For some twelve years he hunted with the West Norfolk hounds, at times with the princess for his companion, but after 1880 he abandoned hunting, both at home and on visits to friends. Shooting at Sandringham gradually took its place as the prince's main sport. To his shooting parties were invited his Norfolk neighbours as well as his intimate circle of associates. He reared pheasants and partridges assiduously, profiting by useful advice from his neighbour, Thomas William Coke, earl of Leicester, of Holkham. Partridge-driving grew to be his favourite sporting recreation. He was a variable and no first-rate shot, but was successful with high pheasants.

For his autumnal vacation at Scotland during September and October Queen Victoria lent him Abergeldie Castle, on Deeside near Balmoral, which she had leased in 1862 for sixty years. He varied his sojourn there by visits to Scottish noblemen, with one of whom, the duke of Sutherland, he formed an intimate friendship. The duke's mother was a beloved associate of Queen Victoria, and at the ducal seat, Dunrobin Castle, the prince was a frequent guest. In Scotland the prince's chief sports were grouse-shooting and deerstalking. He had killed his first stag on 21 Sept. 1858; on 30 Aug. 1866 he killed as many as seven, and for years he was no less successful. Fishing never attracted him. But he was always fond of the sea, and his early life on the Isle of Wight made him an eager yachtsman. Succeeding his father as patron of the Royal Yacht Squadron at Cowes, he became a member on 8 July 1865, commodore in 1882, and finally admiral in 1901. He was soon a regular witness of the Cowes regatta in August, and as early as 1866 was owner of a small yacht, the Dagmar. But neither horse-racing nor yacht-racing occupied much of his interest till he reached middle life.

But while country life had no lack of attraction for the prince, London, which Queen Victoria had practically abandoned for Osborne, Balmoral, or Windsor, was the chief centre of his mature activities. In the capital city he rapidly became the leader of fashionable life. The queen's withdrawal left him without a rival as ruler and lawgiver of the world of fashion, and his countenance was sedulously sought by all aspirants to social eminence. With manhood he developed increasingly an accessibility and charm of manner, a curiosity about persons, a quickness of observation, and a love of hearing promptly the current news. He took genuine pleasure in the lighter social amusements, and gave them every encouragement. Consequently society in almost all its phases appealed to him, and the conventions of royal exclusiveness, to which he had been trained, gave way to his versatile human interests. There was a democratic and a cosmopolitan breadth about his circle of companions. He did not suffer his rank to exclude him from gatherings to which royalty rarely sought admission. He attended the reunions of the Cosmopolitan Club as a private member, or dined with friends at the Garrick Club, or attended the more bohemian entertainments of the Savage Club. In 1869 there was formed under his immediate auspices and guidance a new club called the Marlborough Club, with a house in Pall Mall almost overlooking Marlborough House. The members were drawn from the wide range of his personal acquaintances, and he joined them at the Marlborough Club without ceremony. A chance meeting at the Cosmopolitan Club in 1867 with the Hungarian traveller, Arminius Vambéry, made the stranger thenceforth a favoured associate. The experience was typical of his easy catholicity of intercourse.

His mother, while denying his title to political responsibility, was well content that the prince should carry on in her behalf her husband's works of charity and public utility. He readily obeyed her wish in this regard. No public institution or social movement, which his father had favoured, sought his countenance in vain. Of the Society of Arts he was soon elected president (22 Oct. 1863) in succession to the prince consort. He always took an active part in the choice of the recipient of the Albert medal, which was founded by the society in 1862 in his father's memory to reward conspicuous service in the arts, manufactures, and commerce. When on his accession to the throne he exchanged the post of president for that of patron, he accepted with much satisfaction the award of the Albert medal to himself. But he went far beyond his father in his personal association with great public institutions. He created a new precedent by accepting the presidency of St. Bartholomew's Hospital on 20 March 1867, an office which he also held till his accession. His public energy in any genuine cause of social improvement, education, or philanthropy knew indeed no slackening till his death. In every part of the country he was busy pronouncing benedictions on good works. Among his early engagements of this kind were the opening of the British Orphan Asylum at Slough (24 June 1863); the opening of the new town hall at Halifax (August 1863); the laying of foundation stones of the new west wing of the London Hospital (June 1864), of the British and Foreign Bible Society (11 June 1866), and of new buildings at Glasgow University (8 Oct. 1868); and the unveiling of the statue of Peabody, the American philanthropist, in the City of London (23 July 1869). He presided at innumerable charity festivals, beginning on 18 May 1864 with the Royal Literary Fund dinner, and he repeated that experience at the centenary celebration of the Fund in 1890. Like his father, too, he was especially active, when the opportunity offered, in organising exhibitions at home and abroad.

Early visits to Ireland had brought that country well within the scope of his interest, and although political agitation came to limit his Irish sojourns, he lost few opportunities in manhood of manifesting sympathy with efforts for the country's industrial progress. As guest of the viceroy, Lord Kimberley, on 8 May 1865, he opened the Grand International Exhibition at Dublin. It was thus in Ireland that he first identified himself in an authoritative way with the system of exhibitions. He returned to Dublin in the spring of 1868 on a visit of greater ceremony, and the princess came with him to pay her first visit to the country. The lord-lieutenant was the marquis (afterwards first duke) of Abercorn, whose eldest son, Lord Hamilton, had joined the prince's household in 1866 and was a very intimate associate. The prince was now invested on 18 April with the order of St. Patrick; he was made honorary LL.D. of Trinity College, Dublin, witnessed the unveiling of Burke's statue outside the college, attended Punchestown races, and reviewed the troops in Phœnix Park. It was the period of the Fenian outbreak, and there were threats of disturbance, but they came to little, and the prince and princess were received with enthusiasm. The lord mayor of Dublin in an address of welcome expressed a hope that the prince would acquire a royal residence in Ireland. Before and since the recommendation was pressed on the English government and it was assumed that it had the prince's acquiescence. A third visit was paid to Ireland during the prince's adult career, in August 1871, when he opened the Royal Agricultural Exhibition at Dublin. Earl Spencer, the lord-lieutenant, and Lord Hartington, the chief secretary, were his personal friends, and under their auspices he enjoyed a week of brilliant festivity. Unluckily at its close (Sunday, 7 Aug.), while he was staying at the Viceregal Lodge in Phœnix Park, a proposed meeting in the park of sympathisers with Fenian prisoners in England was prohibited. A riot broke out by way of demonstrating that 'patriots are dearer to [Irish] hearts than princes.' The political disaffection, although it did not prejudice the prince's relations with the Irish masses, was not easily silenced, and fourteen years passed before the prince sought a new experience of Irish hospitality.

His mother's desire to exclude the prince from all political counsels was not altogether fulfilled. Her ministers at the outset of his adult career questioned her prudence in keeping him in complete ignorance of political affairs. From 1864 onwards the prince, stirred in part by the princess's anxiety for the fortunes of her family, was deeply interested in the wars which disturbed central Europe. Prussia and Austria continued their endeavours to deprive Denmark of all hold on Schleswig-Holstein. The prince's Danish sentiment was in accord with popular English feeling. But it caused embarrassment to Queen Victoria, who in spite of her private German leanings was resolved on the maintenance of England's neutrality. Her relations with her son were often strained by his warm support of the Danes.

In 1865 Lord Russell, the prime minister, avowed sympathy with the prince's request for access to those foreign despatches which were regularly placed at the disposal of all cabinet ministers. The queen reluctantly so far gave way as to sanction the communication to the prince of carefully selected specimens of the confidential foreign correspondence. The restrictions which guarded the privilege dissatisfied the prince, and his endeavours to secure their diminution or removal formed a constant theme of debate with the sovereign and ministers till near the end of his mother's reign. The queen's oft-repeated justification for her restraints was the prince's alleged lack of discretion and his inability to keep a secret from his intimates. Resigning himself with some impatience to the maternal interdict, the prince sought other than official means of information and influence in foreign matters. To foreign ambassadors he offered abundant hospitality, and with them he always cherished frank and cordial intercourse.

The prince's relations with the French ambassador in London, Prince de la Tour d'Auvergne, during the Danish crisis of 1864 show him in a characteristic light. On 8 Jan. 1864 a first child, a boy, had been born to the prince and princess at Frogmore. There were many festive celebrations, and the prince's guests were influential. But the rejoicings over the new experience of fatherhood did not lessen the prince's excitement regarding the foreign situation. On 10 March the christening took place at Buckingham Palace. At a concert in the evening the French ambassador was present.

Napoleon III was making proposals for arbitration between Denmark and the German powers. The prince at once questioned his French guest on the subject with what the latter described to his government as the prince's customary indifference to rules of etiquette. The prince warned the ambassador with heat that the Danes were a brave people, who were ready to meet death rather than any kind of humiliation (10 March 1864). King Leopold, who was staying with Queen Victoria, sought to moderate the prince's energy. Twelve days later the ambassador dined at Marlborough House, and was surprised by signs of greater prudence and moderation in the prince's talk, which he attributed to the influence of King Leopold. The prince now agreed that Denmark would be wise in assenting to a pacification. He also spoke in favour of the idea of Scandinavian unity. The ambassador in reporting fully to his government the prince's deliverances, pointed out that the views of the heir to the English throne needed consideration, and that it would be wise for France, in view of the prince's opinion, to do what was practicable in support of Danish interests (*Les origines diplomatiques de la guerre de 1870–1*, Paris 1910, tom. ii. pp. 109 seq.). Thus while Queen Victoria and her ministers held that the prince's opinions counted for nothing, he contrived privately to give foreign ambassadors quite a different impression. The discrepancy between the home and foreign verdicts on his relations with foreign policy grew steadily.

The prince's tact always more or less controlled his personal feelings. Gladstone detected only 'a little Danism' in the prince's conversation. If the prince was careful to prevent Count von Beust, the Austrian ambassador, whose hostility to Denmark was admitted, from even approaching the princess, he succeeded in establishing the best social relations between himself and the count. A passion for direct personal intercourse with all who dominated great events tended to override personal sentiment and prejudice. In April 1864 he drew on himself a severe rebuke in the royal circle by visiting Garibaldi, who was staying with the prince's friend, the duke of Sutherland, at Stafford House. He sought out first-hand intelligence of all that was passing abroad. In July of the same year, when he dined with Lord Palmerston, Sir Horace Rumbold, who was then secretary of legation at Athens, was of the company. The prince at once sent for him to learn the exact position of affairs in Greece, where his wife's brother, Prince William of Denmark, had just been elected king as George I.

It was, too, never his practice to depend for his knowledge of foreign complications on those whom he met at home. Scarcely a year passed without a foreign tour which combined amusement with political discussions. In September 1864 the prince paid a visit to his wife's family in Denmark, crossing from Dundee to Copenhagen. He extended his tour to

Stockholm, where he was entertained by King Charles XV and had a first experience of elk-shooting. He freely discussed the political situation from various points of view. The expedition extended his intimacy among the royal families of Europe. Not only did he make a lasting acquaintance with the cultured Swedish ruler, King Charles XV, who as the grandson of General Bernadotte had a warm affection for France and a keen suspicion of Prussia, but he then inaugurated a long and cordial intimacy with the Russian dynasty. During his visit to Copenhagen the Princess of Wales's sister Dagmar was betrothed to the Grand Duke Nicholas of Russia, the heir of the Tsar Alexander II. The grand duke's death next year annulled the match, but the princess transferred her hand to the grand duke's next brother, Alexander, afterwards Tsar Alexander III, and a first link between the royal families of England and Russia was thereby forged.

From Denmark the prince proceeded to Hanover and thence visited his sister Alice in Darmstadt. On the return journey he was the guest at Brussels of his grand-uncle King Leopold, who was fertile in political counsel. The prince was home again on 6 Nov. The visit to Germany was repeated in 1865, when Queen Victoria unveiled a statue of the prince consort at Coburg. The prince there saw much of his German and Prussian relatives, with some of whom he stalked and shot bustards.

His foreign engagements in 1866 brought him for the first time to Russia. On the journey he stayed for a few days at Berlin, where his sister and her husband gave in his honour a banquet which the king of Prussia attended. On 9 Nov., his twenty-fifth birthday, he reached St. Petersburg to attend the wedding of his wife's sister Dagmar with the tsarevitch Alexander. The ceremony took place at the Winter palace. A visit to Moscow preceded his return to Berlin on the way home. On the Russian court he exerted all his habitual charm. Indeed throughout Europe his personal fascination was already acknowledged. Lord Augustus Loftus, the English ambassador in Berlin, noted on his leaving Berlin that the golden opinions he was winning in every country and every court of Europe had an 'intrinsic value' in England's international relations. On the affection of Parisians he had long since established a hold. France welcomed him with marked cordiality when, as the guest of Napoleon III, he visited the International Exhibition in Paris in June 1867. He served on the royal commission for the British section—a first taste of a common later experience. A fellow guest in Paris was Abdul Aziz, the sultan of Turkey, whose acquaintance he had made at Constantinople in 1862. The sultan reached England next month, and the prince was active in hospitalities on the queen's behalf.

The prince's family was growing. A second son, George, who ultimately succeeded him on the throne as George V, was born to him at

Marlborough House on 3 June 1865. Their first daughter, Princess Louise (afterwards Princess Royal), was born at Marlborough House on 20 Feb. 1867. A second daughter, Princess Victoria, was born on 6 July 1868, and a third daughter, Princess Maud, on 26 Nov. 1869. Visitors at Sandringham or Marlborough House were invariably introduced to the children without ceremony and with parental pride. After the birth of Prince George in 1865, the princess accompanied the prince on a yachting cruise off Devonshire and Cornwall, in the course of which they visited the Scilly Islands and descended the Botallack tin mine near St. Just. For the greater part of 1867, after the birth of Princess Louise, the Princess of Wales was disabled by severe rheumatism, and in the autumn her husband accompanied her to Wiesbaden for a six weeks' cure.

A year later a foreign trip of the comprehensive type, to which the prince was well accustomed, was accomplished for the first time with his wife. In November 1868 they left England for seven months' travel. At Paris they stayed at the Hotel Bristol, which was the prince's favourite stopping place in Paris through life. They visited the emperor at Compiègne, and the prince took part in a stag hunt in the park. Thence they passed to Copenhagen. The prince paid another visit to the king of Sweden at Stockholm, and there his host initiated him into the Masonic order, in which he subsequently found a new interest. Christmas was celebrated at the Danish court. Another sojourn at Berlin with the crown prince and princess (15–20 Jan. 1869) was attended by elaborate festivities. The king of Prussia formally invested the prince with the collar and mantle of the order of the Black Eagle. He had been knight of the order since his birth, but the full investiture could be performed only in the Prussian capital. The collar was the one which the prince consort had worn. In the evening there was a state banquet in the prince's honour, and then he had his first opportunity of conversing with Prince Bismarck, who with rare amiability wore, by command of his master, the Danish order of the Dannebrog in compliment to the guests. From Berlin the prince and princess passed to the Hofburg palace at Vienna, where the Emperor Francis Joseph was their host, and renewed an earlier acquaintance with the prince. They offered their consolation to the exiled king and queen of Hanover before leaving for Trieste.

There they embarked on H.M.S. Ariadne, which was fitted up as a yacht, and travel began in earnest. The duke of Sutherland was chief organiser of the expedition, and he enlisted in the company Sir Samuel Baker the African explorer, Richard Owen the naturalist, (Sir) William Howard Russell the war correspondent, and (Sir) John Fowler the engineer, who were all capable of instructive guidance. The ultimate aim was to inspect the great enterprise of the Suez Canal, which was nearing completion, but by way of prelude a voyage was made up the Nile. The itinerary followed the same route as the prince had taken eight years before. At Cairo the party saw much of the viceroy Ismail Pasha. On the Nile, Baker arranged for the prince's sport, Owen gave lectures on geology, and Fowler described the wonders of the Suez venture. The prince was in the gayest spirits, playing on his guests harmless practical jokes, and putting all at their ease.

On 25 March the prince and his party reached Ismailia to visit the Suez Canal works. The Khedive was awaiting them, but a more interesting figure, M. de Lesseps, conducted them over the newly excavated waterway. The prince opened the sluice of a completed dam, allowing the Mediterranean to flow into an empty basin connecting with the Bitter Lakes. Before the Khedive parted with his English friends at Ismailia he invited Baker to take command of an expedition against the slavers on the White Nile. The prince took an active part in the negotiation and suggested the terms of service, which Baker finally accepted with good result (W. H. Russell's *Diary*).

The prince was deeply impressed by the proofs he witnessed of M. de Lesseps' engineering skill. The Suez Canal was opened on 16 Nov. following, and next summer Lesseps paid a visit to London. On 4 July 1870 the prince, as president of the Society of Arts, formally presented to him the Albert gold medal founded in his father's memory for conspicuous service. In an admirable French speech he greeted Lesseps as his personal friend, whose attendance on him at Suez he reckoned an inestimable advantage.

On the return journey from Alexandria on 1 April 1869, the royal party paused at Constantinople, where the Sultan Abdul Aziz was their host. But the prince interrupted his stay there to make a tour of the Crimean battlefields and cemeteries. Subsequently they went to Athens, to stay with the Princess of Wales's brother, King George of Greece, and to visit the country's historic monuments. Paris was reached by way of Corfu, Brindisi, and Turin. For a week Napoleon III offered them splendid entertainment at the Tuileries. Not until 12 May 1869 were they home again at Marlborough House.

A year later France was exposed to external and internal perils, and the prince's generous host fell from his high estate. The whole tragedy moved the prince; it stimulated his political interests and thirst for political news. It was at a dinner-party at Marlborough House that Delane, the editor of 'The Times,' who was one of the guests, received the first intelligence in England of the outbreak of the Franco-German war on 15 July 1870 (Morier, *Memoirs*). Throughout the conflict the prince's sympathies inclined to France. His mother's hopes lay with the other side. But the queen was no less anxious than her son to alleviate the sufferings of the emperor and empress of the French, when they sought an asylum in England from their own country. The empress arrived at Chislehurst in September 1870, and the emperor on release from his German prison in March 1871. The prince and princess were assiduous in their attention to the exiles. To the young Prince Imperial especially he extended a fatherly kindness, and when in 1879 the French youth met his death in the Zulu war in South Africa, the prince personally made arrangements for the funeral at Chislehurst, and was himself a pall-bearer. He was a moving spirit of the committee which was formed for erecting a monument to the French prince's memory in Westminster Abbey in 1880, and when the House of Commons refused to sanction that project, he urged the transfer of the memorial to St. George's Chapel, Windsor. He was present, too, when a statue of the French prince was unveiled at Woolwich (13 Jan. 1883). But the downfall of the French empire and the misfortunes of the French imperial family in no wise diminished the cordiality of the prince's relations with France under her new rulers. No sooner was the republican form of government recognised than he sought the acquaintance of the republican leaders, and he left no stone unturned to maintain friendly relations with them as well as with his older friends in the French capital. The perfect quality of his social charm enabled him to keep on good terms with all political parties in France without forfeiting the esteem of any. The prince showed his lively curiosity about the incidents of the Franco-German war by exploring in August 1871 the battle-fields round Sedan and Metz in the company of Prince de Ligne and of his equerry, Major Teesdale. He travelled incognito as Baron of Renfrew. From Alsace he passed on to join the princess once again at Kissingen. His strong French leanings were kept well under control in German company. A certain coolness towards the Prussian royal family was popularly imputed to him during the course of the recent war. But when the crown prince of Prussia visited London in Sept. 1871 the prince greeted him with a geniality which caused surprise in Germany. His courtesies led Bismarck's circle to imagine some diminution of his affection for France. But his conduct merely testified to his natural complacency of manner in social life.

While performing with admirable grace the ceremonial and social functions attaching to his station, and while keenly studying current political events from a detached and irresponsible point of view, the prince somewhat suffered in moral robustness through the denial to him of genuine political responsibility, and his exclusion from settled and solid occupation. The love of pleasure in his nature which had been carefully repressed in boyhood sought in adult life free scope amid the ambiguities of his public position. The gloom of his mother's court helped to provoke reaction against conventional strictness. From the early years of his married life reports spread abroad that he was a centre of fashionable frivolity, favouring company of low rank, and involving himself in heavy debt. There was gross exaggeration in the rumours. But they seemed in many eyes to receive unwelcome confirmation, when a member of fashionable London society, Sir Charles Mordaunt, brought an action for divorce against his wife, and made in his petition, solely on his wife's confession, a serious allegation against the Prince of Wales. The prince was not made a party to the suit, but the co-respondents, Viscount Cole, afterwards earl of Enniskillen, and Sir Frederick Johnstone, were among his social allies. The case opened before Lord Penzance on 16 Feb. 1870, and the prince volunteered evidence. Amid great public excitement he denied the charge in the witness-box (23 Feb.), and the court held him guiltless. Apart from the prince's intervention, the case presented legal difficulties which riveted on it public attention. Lady Mordaunt was proved to have become hopelessly insane before the hearing, and on that ground the court in the first instance refused the petitioner relief, but after five years' litigation the divorce was granted (11 March 1875).

Public feeling was roused by the proceedings, and the prince's popularity was for a time in peril with the austere classes of the nation. The sensational press abounded in offensive scandal, and during the spring of 1870 the prince's presence at the theatre, and even on Derby racecourse, occasioned more or less inimical demonstrations. He faced the situation with characteristic courage and coolness. The public censure was reinforced by a wave of hostility to the principle of monarchy which, partly owing to the republican triumph in France, was temporarily sweeping over the country. Enterprising writers sought to drive the moral home. At the end of 1870 there was published a clever parody of Tennyson's 'Idylls of the King' called 'The Coming K——,' which with much insolence purported to draw the veil from the prince's private life. The assault was pursued next year by the same authors in 'The Siliad,' and the series was continued in 'The Fijiad' (1873), 'Faust and 'Phisto' (1874), 'Jon Duan' (1875), and finally in a prophetically named brochure, 'Edward VII; a play on the past and present times with a view to the future' (1876). All current politics and society came under the satirists' lash. But the burden of the indictment, phrased in various keys of scurrility, was that the prince's conduct was unfitting him for succession to the throne. The recrudescence of Queen Victoria's popularity and the manifest good-nature and public spirit of the prince soon dissipated for the most part the satiric censure. Yet an undercurrent of resentment against reputed indulgences of the prince's private life never wholly disappeared.

There was never any serious ground for doubting the prince's desire to serve the public interest. On 13 July 1870 the queen's dread of public ceremonies imposed on him the important task of opening the Thames Embankment. The queen had promised to perform the ceremony, and her absence exposed her to adverse criticism. Three days later the prince illustrated his fixed resolve to conciliate democratic feeling and to encourage industrial progress by inaugurating the Workmen's International Exhibition at the Agricultural Hall. His attendance proved his native tolerance and broad-minded indifference to social prejudice. The trades-union leaders who were the organisers existed on sufferance in the eye of the capitalist public, and Auberon Herbert, who received the prince on behalf of the promoters, was a leading advocate of republicanism. But it was the sturdy faith in the virtue of exhibitions which he had inherited from his father that chiefly brought him to the Agricultural Hall. Already on 4 April 1870 he had placed himself at the head of a movement for the organisation of annual international exhibitions at South Kensington in modest imitation of former efforts. He played an active part in preliminary arrangements, and he opened the first of the series on 1 May 1870. The experiment was not a success, but it was continued for four years. The prince was undaunted by the failure, and a few years later revived the scheme on a different plan.

The year 1871 was one of sadness in the prince's household. On 6 April his last child, a son, was born to the princess and died next day. In the autumn he went into camp with his regiment, the 10th hussars, at Bramshill, and commanded the cavalry division in manœuvres in Hampshire. A private visit which he paid from the camp to his Cambridge lecturer Kingsley at Eversley illustrates his kindly memory for his early associates. Subsequently in October he stayed with the earl and countess of Londesborough at Londesborough Lodge near Scarborough. On returning to Sandringham early in November typhoid fever developed (19 Nov.), and a critical illness followed. Two of his companions at Londesborough Lodge, the eighth earl of Chesterfield and his own groom, Blegge, were also attacked, and both died, the earl on 1 Dec. and Blegge on 14 Dec. (cf. *The Times* 22 Jan. 1872). The gravest fears were entertained for the prince. His second sister, Alice, was staying at Sandringham, and she and the Princess of Wales were indefatigable in their attendance in the sick chamber. On 29 Nov. Queen Victoria arrived for a few days, and a serious relapse on 6 Dec. brought her back on an eleven days' visit (8–19 Dec.). Sunday 10 Dec. was appointed as a day of intercession in the churches with a special form of prayer. Four days later, on the tenth anniversary of the prince consort's death, there were signs of recovery which proved true. The date was long thankfully remembered. Princess Alexandra presented to Sandringham church a brass eagle lectern inscribed 'A thanksgiving for His mercy, 14 Dec. 1871.'

By Christmas the danger was past, and rejoicing succeeded to sorrow. There was an elaborate national thanksgiving at St. Paul's Cathedral on 27 Feb. 1872, when the prince accompanied the queen and the princess in public procession. The queen privately demurred to 'this public show' on the ground of 'the dreadful fatigue' for the prince, and of the incongruity of making religion 'a vehicle' for a display of popular feeling. But the whole nation had shared the anxiety of the royal family, and claimed a share in their elation.

A visit to the Riviera completed the prince's convalescence. He left on a yachting expedition to Nice on 11 March, and afterwards voyaged down the coast to Italy. Before coming home he repeated an early experience which always interested him. In full state he paid a third visit to Pope Pius IX. He was home again on 1 June ready for his public work. In the interests of health he made his headquarters at Chiswick House, which the duke of Devonshire lent him. There he gave garden parties, which surprised many by the number and range of invited guests. His chief public engagement in London was a rare visit to the East End in behalf of the queen. On 24 June he opened the Bethnal Green Museum, to which Sir Richard Wallace had lent a portion of his great collection. The prince's appearance at Ascot in the same month was the occasion of a highly popular greeting.

The prince's illness evoked a new enthusiasm for the monarchy. The duke of Cambridge voiced the general sentiment, when he wrote to his mother that it had 'routed' the recent republican agitation. 'The republicans say their chances are up—thank God for this! Heaven has sent this dispensation to save us' (Sheppard's *Duke of Cambridge*, i. 310). Yet the mighty outbreak of popular sympathy, though it discredited and discouraged criticism of the prince, had not wholly silenced it, nor was the anti-monarchical agitation altogether extinguished. On 19 March 1872 Sir Charles Dilke, then a rising liberal politician, who had lately preached through the country republican doctrine, moved in the House of Commons for a full inquiry into Queen Victoria's expenditure, and the motion was seconded by Auberon Herbert, who shared Dilke's republican views. Gladstone, the prime minister, who strenuously resisted the motion, impressively confessed his firm faith in the monarchy, amid the applause of the whole house. But at the same time Gladstone in private admitted the moment to be opportune to improve the prince's public position. With the prince Gladstone's relations were uninterruptedly happy. He often spoke with him on politics, thought well of his intelligence and pleasant manners, and treated him with punctilious courtesy. On 25 Jan. 1870 Gladstone spent an hour explaining to the prince the Irish land bill, and was gratified by the prince's patience. The prince was no party politician, and he cherished no rigid political principles. His interest lay in men rather than in measures, and his native tact enabled him to maintain the best personal terms with statesmen whose policy he viewed with indifference or disapproval. Gladstone's considerate treatment of him conciliated his self-esteem without affecting materially his political opinions. The personal tie between the political leader and the heir-apparent was involuntarily strengthened, too, by the comprehensive differences which separated Queen Victoria from the liberal statesman.

In the summer of 1872, to Queen Victoria's barely concealed chagrin, Gladstone invited her attention to the delicate question of the prince's official status. The welfare of the prince and the strength and dignity of the crown required, Gladstone urged, that he should be regularly employed. At great length and with pertinacity Gladstone pressed his views in writing on the sovereign. He offered various suggestions. The prince might be associated with the rule of India and join the Indian council. With somewhat greater emphasis Ireland was recommended as a fit field for the prince's energies. Some of the duties of the lord-lieutenant might be delegated to him, and a royal residence might be purchased for his occupation for several weeks each year. The Irish secretary, Lord Hartington, the prince's intimate friend, favoured the proposed Irish palace. But the queen was unconvinced. She doubted whether the duties of the Indian council were onerous enough to keep the prince employed. In Ireland the prince's intimacy with the family of the duke of Abercorn imbued him with Orangeism. She evasively allowed that increased occupation would be advantageous to the prince, and she gave vague assurances of assent to Gladstone's general proposition. But her unwillingness to pursue the matter in detail brought the negotiation to an end.

The prince's career underwent no essential change, although there was a steady widening of experience on the accepted lines. New titular honours were from time to time bestowed on him. On 29 June 1875 he was, much to his satisfaction, made a field-marshal. The distinction stimulated his interest in the army, which was in name at least his profession. Foreign tours abroad became more frequent, alike in France, Germany, and Austria. The great International Exhibition at Vienna in 1873 gave him opportunity of assiduous work. He was president of the royal commission for the British section, and took an active share in its organisation. At the opening ceremonies in Vienna in May he was the guest of the Emperor Francis Joseph, and played his part with his accustomed grace. At the beginning of 1874 he went for a second time to St. Petersburg, again as a wedding guest, now to attend the marriage of his next brother, Alfred, the duke of Edinburgh, to the Duchess Marie. The bride was Tsar Alexander II's daughter, and her sister-in-law, the tsarevna, was the Princess of Wales's sister. The prince's amiability won him fresh laurels at the Russian court. On his way home he stayed once more in Berlin with the old German Emperor William I, and then with the crown prince and princess at Potsdam, joining his brother-in-law in a boar-hunt. In July 1874 the prince and princess gave evidence of their earnest wish to play with brilliance their part at home at the head of London society. They then gave at Marlborough House a fancy dress ball on a more splendid scale of entertainment than any they had yet attempted. The prince wore a Van Dyck costume, with doublet cloak of light maroon satin embroidered in gold. The only guests who were excused fancy dress were the duke of Cambridge and Disraeli. Two days later the duke of Wellington acknowledged the force of the example by offering the prince a similar festivity at Apsley House, where the prince appeared in the same dress.

An experience a few months later illustrated the good-humour and cool conciliatory temper in which the prince faced public affairs. The prince and princess decided to pay a first visit to the city of Birmingham. The mayor, Mr. Joseph Chamberlain, a friend of Sir Charles Dilke, was acquiring a general reputation as an advocate of extreme radicalism, and had in articles in the 'Fortnightly Review' shown republican leanings. The programme included a procession of the royal party through the streets of the city, the reception of an address in the town hall, an entertainment at lunch by the mayor, and visits to leading manufactories. All anticipations of constraint or unpleasantness between the prince and the mayor were belied. With a tact which the prince himself could not excel, Mr. Chamberlain proposed his guest's health in the words: 'Here in England the throne is recognised and respected as the symbol of all constituted authority and settled government.' The prince was as discreet in reply (3 Nov.). (Sir) John Tenniel's cartoon in 'Punch' (14 Nov. 1874), entitled 'A Brummagem Lion,' showed Mr. Chamberlain as a lion gently kneeling before the prince and princess, and the accompanying verses congratulated him on concealing his 'red republican claws and teeth,' and on comporting himself as 'a gentleman' in the glare of the princely sun. The episode merely served to illustrate the natural felicity with which both the chief actors in it could adapt themselves to circumstance.

In spite of the queen's qualms a more important public duty was laid on the prince than had yet been assigned him. Even in his father's lifetime a tour in India had been suggested, and Gladstone had considered a plan for associating the prince with the government of India at home. Early in 1875 Disraeli's government decided that the prince should make a tour through India, with a view to proving the sovereign's interest in her Indian subjects' welfare (20 March). The unrest from which native India was never wholly free seemed to involve the project in some peril, and at the outset controversial issues were raised by politicians at home. The expenses were estimated at a sum approaching 200,000l., although in the result they did not exceed 112,000l. The government decided to debit the amount to the Indian exchequer, and radical members of parliament raised a cry of injustice. The prince's status in India also raised a perplexing problem of a more academic kind. The unofficial position of the prince in England seemed to the queen and her advisers a just ground for denying him in India the formal rank of her official representative. That position was already held by the viceroy, and his temporary suspension was deemed impolitic. Consequently the prince went nominally as the guest of the viceroy. The distinction was a fine one, and made little practical difference to the character of his reception. But the precedence of the viceroy was left in form unquestioned, and the queen's exclusive title to supremacy was freed of any apparent risk of qualification for the time being. The prince's suite was large. It included the chief officers of his household, Lord Suffield, Colonel (Sir) Arthur Ellis, and Mr. Francis (now Lord) Knollys, who had become private secretary on Herbert Fisher's retirement in 1870, and held that office till his master's death. Other members of the company were Sir Bartle Frere and General (Sir) Dighton Probyn, both of whom had seen much service in India; Frere took with him Albert Grey (now Earl Grey) as his private secretary. Colonel (later General) Owen Williams and Lieutenant (now Admiral) Lord Charles Beresford acted as aides-de-camp; Canon Duckworth went as chaplain; (Sir) Joseph Fayrer as physician; (Sir) W. H. Russell as honorary private secretary (to write an account of the tour), and Sydney P. Hall as artist to sketch the chief incidents. Lord Alfred Paget, clerk marshal to Queen Victoria, was commissioned to go as her representative. Private friends invited by the Prince of Wales to be his guests were the duke of Sutherland, the earl of Aylesford, and Lord Carrington. The tour was so planned as to combine a political demonstration of amity on the part of the English crown with opportunity of sport and recreation for the prince. In both regards the result was thoroughly successful. The prince showed keenness and courage as a big game sportsman, bearing easily and cheerfully the fatigue, while he performed all the ceremonial functions with unvarying bonhomie.

The prince started from London on 11 Oct. 1875, and embarked at Brindisi on H.M.S. Serapis, an Indian troopship, which had been converted into a royal convoy. He stayed at Athens with King George of Greece, visited the khedive and Cairo, and after passing through the Suez Canal landed for a few hours at Aden. He arrived off Bombay on 8 Nov., was received by the viceroy, Lord Northbrook, and was welcomed by the reigning princes. At Bombay he stayed with the governor, Sir Philip

Wodehouse, at Government House, where his birthday was celebrated next day. Having laid the foundation stone of the Elphinstone dock on 11 Nov. he picnicked at the caves of Elephanta (12 Nov.), and left on the 18th on a visit to the Gaekwar of Baroda. The Gaekwar provided him with his first opportunity of big game hunting. By his own special wish he came back to Bombay before the end of the month in order to proceed to Ceylon, where he engaged in some venturesome elephant shooting. Returning to the mainland, he reached Madras on 13 Dec., laid the first stone of a new harbour, and attended many festivities. Sailing for Calcutta on 18 Dec., he arrived on the 23rd. There the viceroy became his host, and he spent Christmas at the viceroy's suburban residence at Barakpore. On New Year's Day 1876 he held a chapter of the order of the Star of India, and unveiled a statue of Lord Mayo, the viceroy who had been assassinated in 1872. After receiving the honorary degree of D.C.L. from Calcutta University, he proceeded to North India, where he inspected scenes of the mutiny, and laid at Lucknow the first stone of a memorial to Sir Henry Lawrence and to those who fell in the defence of the city. On 11 Jan. he entered Delhi in formal procession. Passing thence to Lahore, he later in the month went into camp in Cashmere as the guest of the Maharajah of the state. At Agra on 25 Jan. he visited the Taj Mahal. February was mainly devoted to big game shooting, chiefly tigers, at Moradabad and in Nepal. A visit to Allahabad early in March and to Jabalpur as a guest of the Maharajah preceded his embarkation at Bombay on the Serapis (13 March). Smallpox was raging in the town and his departure was hurried. In a farewell letter to the viceroy he bore testimony to the satisfaction with which he had realised a long cherished hope of seeing India and its historic monuments, and of becoming more intimately acquainted with the queen's Indian subjects.

On the return journey he showed many tactful attentions. At Suez he received Lord Lytton, who was on his way out to succeed Lord Northbrook as viceroy. At Cairo he was again the guest of the khedive at the Ghezireh Palace. After leaving Alexandria he paused at two English possessions—Malta, where he met his brother, the duke of Connaught, and at Gibraltar. Subsequently he landed at Cadiz for the purpose of visiting Alfonso XII, the new king of Spain, at Madrid. Thence he passed by rail to Lisbon to enjoy the hospitality of Luis I, king of Portugal.

On 5 May the Serapis reached Portsmouth, and the prince was met there by the princess and their children. The English people welcomed him with enthusiasm, and at the public luncheon at the Guildhall on 19 May he expressed anew his delight with the great experience. The Indian tour conspicuously broadened the precedent which the prince had set in boyhood by his visit to Canada. The personal tie between the princes of

India and English royalty was greatly strengthened by his presence among them in their own country. In future years the prince's two sons successively followed his Indian example. His elder son, the duke of Clarence, in 1889–90, and his younger son and successor, George (when Prince of Wales), in 1905–6, both made tours through India in their father's footsteps. When King George visited India for the second time in the winter of 1911–12 after his coronation he went over much of the same ground and observed many of the same ceremonies as his father had done thirty-six years before.

The prince at once resumed his usual activities at home and on the European continent. The fascination which France exerted on him from boyhood had fully ripened, and in 1878 the popularity, which came of his repeated presence in Paris, acquired a signal strength. His position there was based on ever broadening foundations. Even when he was a favoured guest of the imperial court, he had not limited his French acquaintance to imperial circles. Louis Philippe and most of his large family, into whom the prince consort's kindred had married, had been exiles in England since 1848, and the prince from boyhood shared his parents' intimacy with them and their partisans. Thoroughly at home in Paris, he always succeeded in the difficult task of maintaining the friendliest intercourse with persons who were wholly alienated from one another by political sentiment or social rank. He enjoyed visits to the duc and duchesse de la Rochefoucauld-Bisaccia (15 Oct. 1874) and to the duc d'Aumale at Chantilly (22 Oct. 1874). La comtesse Edouard de Pourtalès, le comte La Grange, le marquis de Breteuil, and all the royalist members of the French Jockey Club who stood outside the political sphere, were among the most intimate of his French associates, and with them he exchanged frequent hospitalities. The marquis de Galliffet, one of Napoleon's generals, who afterwards served the republic, was many times a guest at Sandringham. At the same time the prince was on equally good terms with republican politicians of all views and antecedents. On private visits to Paris the prince gained, too, admission to theatrical and artistic society. Freeing himself of all official etiquette, he indeed so thoroughly explored Parisian life that he was in person as familiar to the public of Paris as to that of London. To the French journalists and caricaturists he was a 'bon garçon,' an arbiter of fashions in dress, 'le plus parisien des anglais,' even 'plus parisien que les parisiens.' If the press made somewhat insolent comment on his supposed debts, his patronage of fashionable restaurants, his pupilage to his mother, and his alleged intimacies with popular favourites of the stage, the journalistic portrayal of him as a jovial Prince Hal was rarely ungenial (cf. Jean Grand Carteret, *L'Oncle de l'Europe*, 1906, passim).

The International Exhibition in Paris of 1878 gave the prince an opportunity of publicly proving his identity with French interests in all their variety. The prince presided over the royal commission which was formed to organise the British section, and he impressed its members, among whom were the leaders of British commerce, with his business capacity as well as his courtesy. He spared no effort in promoting the success of the movement, which was intended to give the world assurance of France's recovery from the late war, and of the permanence of the new republican form of government. The prince entertained the members of the English commission at the Café de la Paix on 29 April before the exhibition opened. In the days that followed he together with the princess took part in Paris in an imposing series of public celebrations, and his presence deeply impressed the French people. On 13 May he attended in state the opening ceremony, which was performed by Marshal MacMahon, the French president. With the marshal and his ministers he was at once on the friendliest terms and lost no opportunity of avowing his affection for their country, and his strong desire for a good understanding between her and England. He was the president's guest at the Elysée, and Lord Lyons, the English ambassador, whose acquaintance he had made at Washington, gave in his honour a brilliant ball, which was attended by the president and the chieftains of political and diplomatic society. At an entertainment provided by M. Waddington, minister for foreign affairs, the prince met for the first time Gambetta, whose career had interested him and whose oratory he had admired as a chance visitor to the Chambre des Députés. Lord Lyons undertook the introduction. Gambetta thanked the prince for his frank expression of sympathy with France, and the prince assured the republican statesman that he had never at any time been other than France's warm friend. The interview lasted three quarters of an hour. Before they parted the prince expressed the hope of seeing Gambetta in England. Though that hope was not fulfilled, the prince sought further intercourse with Gambetta in Paris. Later in the year (22 Oct.) the prince met the English exhibitors at the British embassy, and gracefully spoke of his wish to unite France and England permanently in bonds of amity. Nearly a quarter of a century later he was to repeat as king in the same place almost the identical words, with the effect of arresting the attention of the world.

The prince was less curious about domestic than about foreign policy, but his lively interest in every influential personality led him to cultivate the acquaintance of all who controlled either. It was still the queen's wish that her ministers should treat him with official aloofness, and habits of reticence were easy to Lord Beaconsfield, her favourite prime minister. Assiduously courting his royal mistress's favour, he tacitly accepted her modest estimate of her son's political discretion. Yet Lord Beaconsfield's forward foreign policy in opposition to Russia was quite as congenial to the prince as to his mother, and he made many professions of his agreement. In all companies he announced his anti-Russian sentiment, and he talked of applying for a command in the field, if war broke out between Russia and England (cf. Rumbold, *Further Recollections*, 1903, p. 126). He sedulously cultivated the conservative leader's society. In January 1880, when Lord Beaconsfield's political position speciously looked as strong as ever, the prince went by his own invitation on a visit to Hughenden, the prime minister's country residence (12 Jan.). The old statesman was somewhat embarrassed by the compliment. After his fall from power, the prince's attentions continued, and Lord Beaconsfield dined with the prince at Marlborough House on 19 March 1881. It was the last time Lord Beaconsfield dined from home. Exactly a month later he died. The prince represented Queen Victoria at the funeral, and laid on the coffin a wreath with a card on which he wrote 'A tribute of friendship and affection.'

With a complete freedom from party prepossessions, the prince was at the same time seeking to extend his personal knowledge of the liberal leaders. The advanced radical wing of the liberal party won before the dissolution of 1880, both in parliament and the country, a prominent place which roused high expectations. Sir Charles Dilke was the radical chief, and Mr. Chamberlain, whom the prince met at Birmingham in 1874, was Dilke's first lieutenant. An invitation to Mr. Chamberlain to dine at Marlborough House in 1879 caused the group surprise, and when on 12 March 1880 Lord Fife, a member of the prince's inner circle, invited Dilke to dinner to meet the Prince of Wales, 'who would be very happy to make your acquaintance,' the situation looked to the radical protagonist a little puzzling. But the prince's only purpose was to keep in personal touch with the promoters of every rising cause. To Dilke the prince 'laid himself out to be pleasant.' They talked nearly all the evening, chiefly on French politics and the Greek question.

From an early period the prince had occasionally attended debates in both houses of parliament, seated in the upper chamber on the cross benches and in the House of Commons in the peers' gallery in the place over the clock. He rarely missed the introduction of the budget or a great political measure. On 6 May 1879 he personally engaged in the parliamentary conflict. He voted for the second reading of the deceased wife's sister bill, which, in spite of his support, was rejected by 101 to 81. Lord Houghton seems to have persuaded him to take the step, which challenged the constitutional tradition of the heir-apparent's insensibility in public to controversial issues. With the accession of Gladstone and the liberals to power in the spring of 1880 he set himself to follow the course of politics with a keener zest. He took the oath in the House of Lords at the opening of the new parliament with a view to regular attendance. The prime minister was willing to gratify his request for the regular communication to him of the confidential despatches, but Queen Victoria was still unwilling to assent, save on terms of rigorous selection by herself, which the prince deemed humiliating. He let it be known that he asked for all the confidential papers or none. But Gladstone encouraged his thirst for political knowledge, although it could only be partially and informally satisfied.

With Dilke, who became under-secretary for foreign affairs in Gladstone's administration in May 1880, the prince rapidly developed a close intimacy, and through him apparently hoped to play a part on the political stage. The prince anxiously appealed to the under-secretary 'to be kept informed of foreign affairs.' Dilke perceived that the prince's views of modern history were somewhat vitiated by the habitual refusal to him of official knowledge. But in Feb. 1881 Dilke willingly assented to the prince's proposal that while in Paris next month he should see M. Jules Ferry, the premier, and endeavour to overcome his unreadiness to negotiate promptly a new Anglo-French treaty of commerce. Dilke prepared a note of what the prince should say. In March he satisfactorily performed his mission, which was a new and pleasing experience. Gambetta, who was Dilke's personal friend, wrote that the prince 'had made some impression.' But the general negotiation moved forward slowly. In the autumn Dilke arrived in Paris. The prince was there again at the time, and once more offered to use his influence, both with M. Ferry and with M. Tirard, minister of commerce. The prince showed himself anxious to become better acquainted with Gambetta, and Dilke invited the two to meet at 'déjeuner' (24 Oct. 1881). A day or two later (on a suggestion from the prince made through Dilke) Gambetta sent him his photograph, which he signed thus: 'Au plus aimable des princes. L. Gambetta, un ami de l'Angleterre.'

The cordiality of the relations between Gambetta and the prince forms an interesting episode in the career of both men. Gambetta was clearly impressed by the width of the prince's interest in European affairs. The prince in the Frenchman's eyes was far more than 'un festoyeur'; he loved France 'à la fois gaîment et sérieusement,' and his dream was of an Anglo-French entente. According to Madame Adam, Gambetta's confidante, the prince, by disclosing to the statesman at an early meeting secret negotiations between Bismarck and Lord Beaconsfield, led Gambetta to qualify the encouragement which he was proposing to offer Greek ambitions for territorial expansion. But Madame Adam seems here to exaggerate the influence of the prince (Adam, *Mes Souvenirs*, vii. 15 seq.).

In March 1881 the royal family was greatly shocked by the assassination of the Tsar Alexander II in St. Petersburg. Lord Dufferin, the English ambassador, promptly advised, on grounds of humanity and policy, that the prince and princess, whose sister was the tsarevitch's wife, should come to Russia for the funeral of the murdered sovereign. Queen Victoria deemed the risk almost prohibitive, and warned Lord Dufferin that the responsibility for any untoward result would rest on him (Lyall's *Life of Lord Dufferin*). But neither prince nor princess hesitated for a moment. They attended the funeral, and the prince invested the new tsar with the order of the Garter. Their presence proved an immense consolation to the Russian royal family and lightened the heavy gloom of the Russian court and capital. Courage was never lacking in the prince. In the summer of 1882 the outbreak of rebellion in Egypt, and the resolve of the English government to suppress it by force of arms, deeply stirred his patriotic feeling. He at once offered to serve in the campaign. The duke of Cambridge, the commander-in-chief, to whom he addressed his proposal, forwarded it to the government, and Lord Granville, the foreign minister, replied to the duke on 30 July 1882, 'It is highly creditable to the pluck and spirit of the prince to wish to run the risks, both to health and to life, which the campaign offers, but it is clearly undesirable H.R.H. should go' (Verner, *Duke of Cambridge*, 1901, ii. 234–5). Precedents for the appearance of the heir-apparent on the field of battle abounded in English and foreign history, but they were held to be inapplicable.

A desire to be useful to the state, in spite of his lack of official position, repeatedly found expression during Gladstone's second administration. In the struggle between the two houses over the franchise bill (November 1884), the prince offered his services in negotiating a settlement. He asked Lord Rowton to let it be known that he was willing to act as intermediary between Gladstone and Lord Salisbury, the leader of the opposition. But the friendly suggestion was not seriously entertained. The prince shared the queen's habitual anxiety concerning warfare between lords and commons, but his proffered intervention probably reflected nothing beyond a wish to figure in political affairs.

Friendliness with members of the liberal government did not always imply acquiescence in their policy. Of the liberal government's attitude to many of the problems which South Africa and Egypt presented, the prince openly disapproved. He was frank in private expression of dissatisfaction alike with the recall from the Cape in 1880 of Sir Bartle Frere, his companion in India, and with the treaty of peace made with the Boers after the defeat of Majuba in 1881. He was president of the committee for erecting a statue of Frere on his death, and unveiled it on the Thames Embankment on 5 June 1888, when he called Frere 'a highly esteemed and dear friend of myself.' Next year (1 Aug. 1889), when he presided at the Guildhall over a memorable meeting to celebrate the jubilee of the abolition of slavery in the British colonies, he paid in a stirring speech a further tribute to the services of his friend Sir Bartle Frere. Of the pusillanimity which seemed to him to characterise the liberal party's treatment of the Soudan in 1884 he spoke with impatience, and he earnestly deplored the sacrifice of General Gordon. When Lord Salisbury moved a vote of censure on the government for their vacillating policy he was in his place in the House of Lords on 25 Feb. 1885. He was present at the memorial service in St. Paul's Cathedral on the day of mourning for Gordon's death (13 March 1885). He actively interested himself in the movement for commemorating Gordon's heroism. He attended the first meeting for the purpose at the Mansion House on 30 May 1885, and moved the first resolution. He summoned another meeting at Marlborough House on 12 Jan. 1886, when the scheme of the Gordon boys' memorial home (now at Chobham) was inaugurated. On 19 May 1890 he unveiled Gordon's statue at Chatham.

On 8 Feb. 1884 the government decided to appoint a commission on the housing of the working classes. The prince's friend Dilke, now president of the local government board, was made chairman, and the prince expressed a desire to serve. Gladstone at once acceded to his request. The matter was referred to the queen, who raised no objection (13 Feb.). The subject interested him deeply. As duke of Cornwall he was owner of many small houses in south London, and as the leases fell in he was proposing to retain the buildings in his own hands, with a view to converting them into better habitations. The change in tenure improved the profits of the estate as well as the character of the dwellings. On 22 Feb. 1884 Lord Salisbury moved an address to the crown for the appointment of the commission. The prince supported the motion, making on the occasion his first and only speech as a peer in the House of Lords. 'I take the keenest and liveliest interest in this great question,' he said. He was flattered at having been appointed a member of the commission. He had greatly improved the dwellings on his Sandringham estate; he had 'visited a few days ago two of the poorest courts in the district of St. Pancras and Holborn, and had found the conditions perfectly disgraceful.' He hoped measures of a drastic kind would follow the inquiry.

The commissioners formed an interesting but hardly homogeneous assembly. Cardinal Manning had accepted a seat, and difficulties arose as to his precedence. The prince's opinion was invited. He thought that Manning, being a cardinal, ranked as a foreign prince next to himself. Among the other members of the commission, the marquis of Salisbury held highest rank. The queen with certain qualifications took the prince's view, which was finally adopted, but not without some heart-burnings.

The commissioners included, too, Henry Broadhurst, a labour member of parliament, and Mr. Joseph Arch, a leader of agricultural labourers. The prince attended the meetings with regularity, and abridged his holiday at Royat in May 1884 in order to be present at one of the early sittings. On 16 Nov. he entertained many of the members at Sandringham. With all his colleagues he established very cordial relations. With Mr. Arch, who lived in Warwickshire, at Barford Cottage, he was especially friendly, and the liking for him never waned. When Mr. Arch sat in the House of Commons (1885–6, 1892–1900) for the division of North West Norfolk in which Sandringham stands, the prince greeted him as his own representative and visited him at his home in the summer of 1898.

The commission decided to take evidence at both Edinburgh and Dublin (January 1885). It was deemed politic for the prince, if he travelled with the commission at all, to go to Dublin if he went to Edinburgh. The final decision was that he should go to Dublin independently of the commission and study the housing question there privately. In spite of the political agitation that was raging in the country, both the queen and Lord Spencer, the lord-lieutenant, saw some advantage in such an expedition. The prince had not been to Ireland for fourteen years. It was now settled that he and the princess should revisit the country in April. The conditions admitted of his inspecting the crowded slums of Dublin and at the same time of his testing anew the loyalty of the Irish people.

The experiment was not without its dangers, but the threats of opposition came to little. The nationalist leaders issued a manifesto urging on their followers an attitude of reserve. The lord mayor and corporation of Dublin refused to present an address of welcome, but a city reception committee well filled their place (9 April). The prince visited without protection the poor districts of the city and was heartily received. On 10 April he laid the foundation stone of the New Museum of Science and of the national library; at the Royal University he received the hon. degree of LL.D. and the princess that of Mus.Doc. Next day he opened the new dock at the extremity of North Wall, and named it the Alexandra basin. He paid a visit to Trinity College, Dublin, and presented in the gardens of Dublin Castle new colours to the duke of Cornwall's light infantry.

On 13 April the royal party started for Cork. The home rulers of the south urged the people to resent the visit as a degradation. On the road hostile demonstrations were made. But the prince was undisturbed. From Cork he passed to Limerick, where no jarring notes were struck, and thence went by way of Dublin to Belfast, where there was abundant enthusiasm (23 April). After a day at Londonderry (26 April), he left Larne for Holyhead (27 April). The nationalists' endeavour to prove the disloyalty of Ireland met with no genuine success.

One of the interests which grew upon the prince in middle life was freemasonry, which powerfully appealed to his fraternal and philanthropic instincts. He lent his patronage to the craft in all parts of the British empire. Initiated into the order in Sweden in December 1868, he received the rank of Past Grand Master of England at a meeting of Grand Lodge on 1 Sept. 1869. In Sept. 1875, after the resignation of the marquis of Ripon, he was installed in great splendour at the Albert Hall as Grand Master of the order.

During the twenty-six years that the Prince of Wales filled the office he performed with full masonic rites the many ceremonies of laying foundation stones in which he took part. He did what he could to promote the welfare of the three great charitable institutions of freemasons, the Boys' School, the Girls' School, and the Benevolent Institution. He presided at festival dinners of all the charities, twice at the first (1870 and 1898) and the second (1871 and 1888), and once at the third (1873). On his accession to the throne he relinquished the grand mastership and assumed the title of protector of the craft in England. His interest in freemasonry never slackened.

Meanwhile Gladstone remained faithful to his resolve to provide the prince with useful and agreeable employment. One office which Lord Beaconsfield's death rendered vacant was filled on the prime minister's recommendation by the prince, with the result that he entered on a new if minor sphere of interest which proved very congenial. On 6 May 1881 he was appointed a trustee of the British Museum, and eight days later joined the standing committee, again in succession to Lord Beaconsfield. Until the prince's accession to the throne he constantly attended the committee's meetings, kept himself well informed of all matters of importance in the administration of the museum, and warmly supported the action of the director whenever it was called in question. It was with reluctance that he retired from the management of the museum at his accession, on learning that a sovereign could not be member of a body which was liable to be sued in a court of law. One of the prince's services to the museum was the election, through his influence, of his friend Baron Ferdinand de Rothschild as fellow trustee; the baron's Waddesdon bequest was an important addition to the museum's treasures. In the capacity of trustee the prince received on 9 June 1885 the statue of Darwin, which was erected at the entrance of the Natural History Museum, South Kensington, and was unveiled by Professor Huxley.

Association with the British Museum stimulated his earlier interest in new educational institutions, especially those which developed technical or artistic instruction. In music he delighted from childhood, and to efforts for the expansion of musical teaching he long lent his influence. As early as 15 June 1875 he had presided at a conference at Marlborough House to consider the establishment of a National Training School for Music. Three years later he accepted a proposal to institute a National College of Music. On 28 Feb. 1882 he presided at a representative meeting at St. James's Palace, and in an elaborate speech practically called into being the Royal College of Music. He formally inaugurated the college on 7 May 1883 in temporary premises, with Sir George Grove as director. Six years later he personally accepted from Samson Fox a sum of 30,000*l.* (increased to 40,000*l.*) for the provision of a special building, the foundation stone of which he laid on 8 July 1890. He opened the edifice in May 1894 and never lost his enthusiasm for the venture.

In no part of the country did he fail to encourage cognate enterprises with a readiness altogether exceeding that of his father, in whose steps in these regards he was proud to follow. In every town of England he became a familiar figure, opening colleges, libraries, art galleries, hospitals, parks, municipal halls, and docks. On 2 May 1883 he was at Oxford laying the foundation stone of the Indian Institute. On 28 April 1886 he visited Liverpool to inaugurate the working of the great Mersey tunnel. Very readily he went on like errands to places which no member of the royal family had hitherto visited. The centres of industry of every magnitude, Sheffield, Leeds, Wigan, Bolton, Hull, Newcastle, Portsmouth, Blackburn, Middlesbrough, Great Grimsby, and Swansea, as well as Birmingham, Liverpool, and Manchester, all possess public buildings which were first dedicated to public uses by the prince. One of the most memorable of his provincial engagements was his laying the foundation stone of the new cathedral at Truro on 20 May 1880. It was the first cathedral erected in England since St. Paul's was rebuilt in 1697. The bishop, Edward White Benson, was well known to the prince in his earlier capacity of headmaster of Wellington College. By the prince's wish the ceremony was performed, despite clerical misgivings, with full masonic rites. Some seven years later (3 Nov. 1887) the prince returned to attend the consecration of the eastern portion of the building, the first portion to be used for divine worship. Dr. Benson, then archbishop of Canterbury, was his companion.

The development of his property at Sandringham stirred in him an active interest in agriculture, and his provincial visits were often associated with the shows of the Royal Agricultural Society, of which he was elected a life governor on 3 Feb. 1864, and subsequently became an active member. He was four times president, for the first time in 1869, when the show was held at Manchester, afterwards in 1878 at Kilburn, in 1885 at Preston, and in 1900 at York. He rarely failed to attend the shows in other years, being present at Gloucester in the year before his death; he subsequently accepted the presidency for the meeting at Norwich in 1911, which he did not live to see. In 1889, the jubilee year of the society, he acted at Windsor for the queen, who was president, and presided the same year at the state banquet given in St. James's Palace to the council and chief officers of the society. He showed minute interest in the details of the society's work.

At the same time, there was no district of London to which he was a stranger. He not only laid the foundation stone of the Tower Bridge on 21 June 1886 but opened the complete structure on 30 June 1894. He showed interest in the East End by opening a recreation ground in Whitechapel on 24 June 1880. He laid the foundation stone of the People's Palace on 28 June 1886, and on 21 June 1887 he opened for a second time new buildings at the London Hospital. His educational engagements in the metropolis were always varied. They included during this period the formal installation of the Merchant Taylors' School in the old buildings of Charterhouse on 6 April 1878, the opening of the new buildings of the City of London School on 12 Dec. 1882, and of the City of London College in Moorfields on 8 July 1883, together with the new foundation of the City and Guilds of London Institute on 25 June 1884. On 21 Dec. 1885 he went to Sir Henry Doulton's works at Lambeth in order to present Doulton with the Albert gold medal of the Society of Arts in recognition of his services to the manufacture of pottery.

His faith in the advantage of exhibitions was not shaken by the inauspicious experiments of 1871–4, and he actively aided in 1883 a revival on a more limited scale of the old scheme. His neighbour in Norfolk, Sir Edward Birkbeck, had interested him in his attempts to improve the fishing industry of the country, and under the prince's direct auspices a National Fisheries Exhibition at Norwich in April 1881 developed in 1883 into an International Fisheries Exhibition at South Kensington, which the prince ceremonially opened and closed (14 May–31 Oct.). The success of the undertaking justified sequels at the same place, in the International Health Exhibition next year, and in the International Inventions and Music Exhibition in 1885. There followed a far more ambitious enterprise in 1886, when the prince with exceptional vigour helped to organise an exhibition of the manufactures and arts of India and the colonies. It was the only one of these ventures which was controlled by a royal commission, and the prince was president of the commissioners. Queen Victoria, on her son's representations, showed an unwanted activity by opening this exhibition in person (4 May 1886). Great popular interest was shown in the enterprise, and a handsome profit was realised.

The prince was anxious to set on a permanent basis the scheme which had made so powerful an appeal to the public not only of Great Britain but of India and the colonies. Queen Victoria's jubilee was approaching, and many suggestions for a national celebration were under consideration. In the autumn of 1886 the prince proposed to the lord mayor of London that a permanent institute in London, to form a meeting-place for colonial and Indian visitors, and a building for the exhibition of colonial and Indian products, should be erected as a memorial of the queen's long reign. The prince professed anxiety to pursue his efforts to strengthen the good feeling between the mother country, India, and the colonies. At a meeting which he called at St. James's Palace on 12 Jan. 1887, the project of an Imperial Institute at South Kensington was adopted and a fund was started with 25,000*l.* out of the profits of the recent Indian and colonial Exhibition. Large donations were received from India and the colonies. All promised well. Queen Victoria laid the foundation stone on 4 July 1887, and on 28 April 1891 the prince was formally constituted president of the corporation. The completed building was opened by Queen Victoria on 10 May 1893. A week later the Prince of Wales gave a great reception to all who had shown interest in the movement. Some interesting functions took place there under his guidance. On 28 July 1895 he presided when Dr. Jameson lectured on Rhodesia, and he attended a banquet to the colonial premiers on the occasion of the queen's diamond jubilee on 18 June 1897. But in spite of his active support the Institute failed to enjoy public favour. It satisfied no public need, and evoked no general enthusiasm. The prince reluctantly recognised the failure, and in 1899 assented to the transfer of the greater part of the building to the newly constituted London University. The operations of the Institute were thenceforth confined to very modest dimensions. Despite its chequered career, the venture gave the prince a valuable opportunity of identifying himself with the growing pride in the colonial empire, with that newborn imperialism which was a chief feature of the national sentiment during the close of his mother's reign.

Punctuality and a methodical distribution of his time enabled the prince to combine with his many public engagements due attention to domestic affairs, and at the same time he enjoyed ample leisure wherein to indulge his love of recreation at home and abroad. The education of his two sons, Albert Victor and George, called for consideration. In 1877 they were respectively thirteen and twelve years old. The prince had little wish to subject them to a repetition of his own strict and elaborate discipline. Nor had he much faith in a literary education for boys in their station. A suggestion that they should go to a public school, to Wellington College, met with Queen Victoria's approval; but the prince finally decided to send them as naval cadets to the Britannia training-ship at Dartmouth. He met his mother's criticism by assuring her that the step was experimental. But the prince was satisfied with the result, and in 1879 he pursued his plan of a naval training by sending the boys on a three years' cruise in H.M.S. Bacchante to the Mediterranean and the British colonies. The plan had the recommendation of novelty. In providing for the youths' further instruction, the prince followed less original lines. The younger boy, George, like his uncle Alfred, Queen Victoria's second son, made the navy his profession, and he passed through all the stages of nautical preparation. The elder son, Albert Victor, who was in the direct line of succession, spent some time at Trinity College, Cambridge, in 1883, according to precedent. He then proceeded to Aldershot to join the army. In all important episodes in his elder son's career his father's presence testified his parental concern. When Albert Victor, on coming of age, received the freedom of the City of London (29 June 1885), his father was the chief guest at the luncheon in the Guildhall which the corporation gave in honour of the occasion. The prince was with his son at Cambridge not only when he matriculated at Trinity in 1883 but when he received the honorary degree of LL.D. in 1888. A few years later the young man, pursuing most of his father's experiences, set out for an Indian tour, and his father accompanied him as far as Ismailia (October 1891).

Family rejoicings attended the celebration of the prince and princess's silver wedding on 10 March 1888, when Queen Victoria dined with them at Marlborough House for the first time. The old German emperor, William I, died the day before. With him the prince was always on affectionate terms and he had repeatedly accepted the emperor's hospitality in Berlin. He had visited him on 18 March 1885 to congratulate him on his eighty-eighth birthday. Queen Victoria was especially anxious to show his memory due respect, but she assented to the suspension of court mourning for the prince's silver wedding. The number of congratulations and presents bore striking witness to the prince's popularity.

The royal family was bound to experience many episodes of sorrow as well as joy. The prince was pained by the death in 1878 of his second sister, Alice, princess of Hesse-Darmstadt, who had helped to nurse him through his illness of 1871. To his acute distress, too, his youngest brother, Leopold, duke of Albany, died suddenly while on holiday at Cannes (24 March 1884), and the prince at once went thither on the melancholy errand of bringing the remains home. Subsequently he unveiled with much public ceremony a statue of the duke at Cannes. But the prince and all his domestic circle were perhaps more deeply affected by the tragic death of his brother-in-law, the crown prince of Prussia, who after a three months' reign as Frederick III had succumbed to the painful disease of cancer of the throat (15 June 1888). The tragedy gave the prince many grounds for anxiety. His lifelong affection for the Empress Frederick, his eldest sister, was quickened by her misfortune. He showed her every brotherly attention. On her first visit to England during her widowhood the prince crossed over to

Flushing to escort her to her native country (19 March 1889). In Germany her position was difficult. Her English predilections and her masterful disposition often roused hostility. Bismarck and his son Herbert had treated her and her husband with scant respect. The prince's sympathies lay with his sister in her struggles abroad, and not unfrequently was he moved to anger by what seemed to him the cruel indifference of the Bismarcks to her feelings. The complexity of the situation was increased by the conduct of her eldest son, the prince's nephew, who now became, as William II, German emperor in succession to his father. His uncompliant attitude to his mother often wounded his uncle and threatened alienation. Yet the native amiability of the prince did not suffer any lasting breach between himself and those whose conduct roused his disapproval. In his family circle there were some whose dislike of the young ruler was far more firmly rooted than his own. But the prince sought paths of peace and conciliation. The new emperor was his mother's favourite grandson and had at command a social charm which equalled his uncle's. When in 1890 the emperor dismissed Bismarck from his service and he became politically his own master, the outer world came to attribute to uncle and nephew a personal and political rivalry which hampered the good relations of the two peoples. This allegation was without foundation in fact. On occasion the kinsmen caused each other irritation, but there was no real estrangement. The mutual resentments which at times ruffled their tempers were harboured solely when they were absent from one another. The ill-feeling disappeared when they met. The prince's unconcealed leanings to France barely touched the personal relation with his nephew. The prince's good-nature was comprehensive. The younger Bismarck's manner was even less complacent than that of his rough-spoken father, but the prince's social tact enabled him to meet the older man with a perfect grace and to extend a courteous greeting to Count Herbert Bismarck on his private visits to England.

No lack of cordiality marked the first meetings of uncle and nephew after the emperor's accession. The emperor arrived at Spithead on 2 Aug. 1889 in order to present himself to his grandmother in his new dignity; the prince met him on landing and welcomed him with warmth. Next year the prince and his second son, George, were the emperor's guests at Berlin (April 1890), just after Bismarck's dismissal. The emperor attested his friendly inclinations by investing Prince George with the distinguished order of the Black Eagle.

In 1889 a new factor was introduced into the prince's domestic history. The first marriage in his family took place. On 27 July 1889 his eldest daughter, Princess Louise, married the sixth earl of Fife, then created first duke. The prince's son-in-law, who was eighteen years senior to his wife, belonged to his most intimate circle of friends. Objection was raised in some quarters on the ground of the bridegroom's age and of his place in the prince's social coterie, and in other quarters owing to his lack of royal status. But the union proved thoroughly happy, and it made opportune a review of the financial provision for the prince's children. The prince's family was growing up, and his domestic expenses caused him some anxiety. His income had undergone no change since his marriage, and he deemed it fitting to raise the question of parliamentary grants to his children. The prince's income was not exorbitant in view of the position that he had long been called on to fill, now that Queen Victoria had ceased to play her part in society.

Early in 1885, when his elder son came of age, the prince discussed the matter with the queen with the knowledge of the liberal ministry. There was no unwillingness on any side to treat his wishes considerately, but neither the queen nor her ministers showed undue haste in coming to close quarters with the delicate issue.

Lord Salisbury was now prime minister, but the conservative government was as reluctant as any liberal government to lay a large fresh burden on the revenues of the state in the interests of the royal family. The queen sent a message to the House of Commons, asking provision for the prince's two eldest children (July 1889). A committee of inquiry representative of all parties in the House of Commons was thereupon appointed. Mr. Bradlaugh opposed the appointment on the ground that the queen should make the necessary provision out of her savings. The government proposed, with the approval of the queen, that the eldest son of the Prince of Wales should receive an annuity of 10,000l., to be increased to 15,000l. on his marriage. The second son was to receive, on coming of age, an annuity of 8000l., to be increased on his marriage to 15,000l. Each of the three daughters was to receive on coming of age an annuity of 3000l., with a dowry of 10,000l. on marriage. There would thus fall due immediately 21,000l. a year, with 10,000l. for Princess Louise. But signs of discontent were apparent in the committee, and Gladstone, who deprecated any weakening of the monarchy by a prolonged controversy over its cost, recommended the compromise that the prince should receive a fixed additional annual sum of 36,000l. for his children's support, and that the new provision should terminate six months after Queen Victoria's death. The proposal was adopted by the committee, but was severely criticised in the House of Commons. Henry Labouchere bluntly moved a peremptory refusal of any grant to the queen's grandchildren. His motion was rejected by 398 votes to 116. Mr. John Morley moved an amendment complaining that room was left for future applications from the crown for further grants to the queen's grandchildren, and that the proposed arrangement ought to be made final. Most of Gladstone's colleagues supported Mr. Morley; but his amendment was defeated by 355 votes to 134 and the grant of 36,000l. a year was secured.

On 17 May 1891 the prince enjoyed the new experience of becoming a grandfather on the birth of the duchess of Fife's first daughter. But a severe blow was to befall his domestic circle within a year. In December his second son, George, fell ill of enteric fever, from which he recovered; but early in the next year Albert Victor, his elder son, who had been created duke of Clarence (24 May 1890), was seized by influenza, which turned to pneumonia and proved fatal (14 Jan. 1892). The calamity was for the moment crushing to both parents. But the sympathy of the nation was abundant, and in a published letter of thanks the prince and princess gratefully acknowledged the national condolence. The duke's death was the more distressing owing to his approaching marriage to Princess Mary (May) of Teck. Next year, after the shock of mourning had passed away, Princess May was betrothed to the second son, Prince George, who filled his brother's place in the succession to the throne and was created duke of York on 24 May 1892. The marriage took place on 6 July 1893, and the succession to the throne was safely provided for when a first child, Prince Edward of Wales, was born on 23 June 1894.

Amid all his domestic responsibilities and his other engagements the prince always found ample leisure for sport and amusement. Of the theatre and the opera he was from boyhood an ardent admirer, and both in London and Paris he enjoyed the society of the dramatic and musical professions. The lighter forms of dramatic and musical entertainment chiefly attracted him. But his patronage was comprehensive. Wagner's operas he attended with regularity, and Irving's Shakespearean productions at the Lyceum Theatre from 1872 onwards stirred his enthusiasm. With Irving, the leader of the dramatic profession through a great part of the prince's career, his social relations were of the friendliest. He supped on the stage of the Lyceum with Irving and a few of his friends after the performance of 'Much Ado about Nothing' (8 May 1883), and when Queen Victoria was on a visit to Sandringham (26 April 1889), he invited Irving to perform in her presence 'The Bells' and the trial scene from 'The Merchant of Venice.' With the comic actor J. L. Toole he was on like cordial terms, and thrice at the prince's request Toole appeared in characteristic parts on visits to Sandringham. Toole was there at the celebration of Prince Albert Victor's coming of age on 8 Jan. 1885. (Sir) Charles Wyndham, (Sir) Squire Bancroft, (Sir) John Hare, and many other actors in addition to Irving and Toole were the prince's guests on occasion at Marlborough House. The dramatic profession generally acknowledged his sympathetic patronage by combining to present him on his fiftieth birthday (9 Nov. 1891) with a gold cigar box. To the prince's influence is attributable the bestowal of official honours on leading actors, a practice which was inaugurated by the grant of a knighthood to Henry Irving in 1895.

But the recreation to which the prince mainly devoted himself from middle life onwards with unremitting delight was horse-racing. He joined the Jockey Club on 13 April 1864. But it was not for at least ten years that he played any part on the turf. His colours were first seen at the July meeting at Newmarket in 1877. In 1883 he leased a few horses at John Porter's Kingsclere stable, and two years later he inaugurated a breeding stud at Sandringham. In 1893 he left John Porter's stable at Kingsclere, and thenceforward trained horses at Newmarket under Richard Marsh, usually having at least eleven horses in training. By that date he was a regular visitor at Newmarket, occupying a set of rooms at the Jockey Club. That practice he continued to the end of his life. He was a fair judge of horses, though hardly an expert. His luck as an owner was variable, and signal successes came late in his racing career. His main triumphs were due to the merits of the three horses Florizel II, Persimmon, and Diamond Jubilee, which he bred in 1891, 1893 and 1897 respectively out of the dam Perdita II by the sire St. Simon. With Persimmon, the best thoroughbred of his era, the prince won for the first time the classic races of the Derby and the St. Leger in 1896, and the Eclipse Stakes and the Gold Cup at Ascot in 1897. In 1900, when his winning stakes reached a total of 29,585*l.*, he first headed the list of winning owners. In that year his racing triumphs reached their zenith, when Persimmon's brother, Diamond Jubilee, won five great races, the Two Thousand Guineas, the Derby, Newmarket Stakes, Eclipse, and St. Leger. He had played a modest part in steeplechasing since 1878. But his only conspicuous success in that sport was also achieved in 1900, when his Ambush II won the Grand National at Liverpool. So imposing a series of victories for an owner in one year was without precedent. No conspicuous prosperity attended his racing during the early years of his reign. But in 1909 he was for a third time winner of the Derby with the horse Minoru, and was in the same year third in the list of winning owners. At the time of his death he had twenty-two horses in training, and his winning stakes since 1886 then amounted to 146,344*l.* 10*s.* 1*d.* The pastime proved profitable. He sold Diamond Jubilee to an Argentine breeder for 31,500*l.* The skeleton of Persimmon he presented to the South Kensington Museum (5 Feb. 1910).

With fellow patrons of the turf the prince always maintained cordial intimacy. The members of the Jockey Club included his closest friends. For twenty years he entertained to dinner all the members at Marlborough House and afterwards at Buckingham Palace on Derby night. Rarely missing an important race meeting, he was regularly the guest of Lord

Sefton at Sefton Park or of Lord Derby at Knowsley for the Grand National, of Lord Savile at Rufford Abbey for the St. Leger at Doncaster, and of the duke of Richmond at Goodwood for the meeting in the park there.

In yacht racing also for a brief period he was only a little less prominent than on the turf. In 1876 he first purchased a racing schooner yacht, Hildegarde, which won the first queen's cup at Cowes in 1877. In 1879 he acquired the well-known cutter Formosa, and in 1881 the schooner Aline, both of which enjoyed racing reputations. But it was not till 1892 that the prince had a racing yacht built for him. The vessel known as the Britannia was designed by George Lennox Watson, and was constantly seen not only in the Solent, on the Thames, and on the Clyde, but also at Cannes. For five years the yacht enjoyed a prosperous career, winning many races in strong competitions, often with the prince on board. In 1893 prizes were won on the Thames (25–26 May), and the Victoria gold challenge cup at Ryde (11 Sept.). Twice at Cannes the Britannia won international matches (13 March 1894 and 23 Feb. 1895); and on 5 July 1894 it defeated on the Clyde the American yacht Vigilant; but that result was reversed in a race between the two on the Solent on 4 Aug. 1895. In 1895 the German emperor first sent out his yacht Meteor to meet his uncle's Britannia, and for three years interesting contests were waged between the two vessels. Thrice in English waters during 1896 was the German yacht successful—at Gravesend (4 June), at Cowes (11 June), and at Ryde (13 Aug.). But after several victories over other competitors the Britannia won the race for the queen's cup against the Meteor at Cowes (3 Aug. 1897), and three days later the emperor's Meteor shield was awarded his uncle's vessel.

The prince's open indulgence in sport, especially in horse-racing, attracted much public attention, and contributed to the general growth of his popularity. But in 1891 there was some recrudescence of public impatience with his avowed devotion to amusement. An imputation of cheating against a guest at a country house when the prince was of the company led to a libel action, at the hearing of which the prince for a second time appeared as a witness in a court of law (5 June 1891). The host was Mr. Arthur Wilson, a rich shipowner of Hull, and the scene of the occurrence was his residence at Tranby Croft. The evidence showed that the prince had played baccarat for high stakes. A wave of somewhat reckless gambling had lately enveloped English society, and the prince had occasionally yielded to the perilous fascination. Cards had always formed some part of his recreation. From early youth he had played whist for moderate stakes, and he impressed Gladstone in a homely rubber at Sandringham with his 'whist memory.' On his tours abroad at Cannes and Homburg he had at times indulged in high play, usually with fortunate results. The revelations in the Tranby Croft case shocked middle-class opinion in England, and there was a loud outburst of censure. In a private letter (13 Aug. 1891) to Dr. Benson, archbishop of Canterbury, long on intimate terms with the royal family, the prince expressed 'deep pain and annoyance' at the 'most bitter and unjust attacks' made on him not only 'by the press' but 'by the low church and especially the noncon-formists.' 'I am not sure,' he wrote, 'that politics were not mixed up in it.' His genuine attitude he expressed in the following sentences: 'I have a horror of gambling, and should always do my utmost to discourage others who have an inclination for it, as I consider that gambling, like intemperance, is one of the greatest curses which a country could be afflicted with.' The scandal opened the prince's eyes to the perils of the recent gambling vogue, and he set himself to discourage its continuance. He gradually abandoned other games of cards for bridge, in which, though he played regularly and successfully, he developed only a moderate skill.

During Lord Salisbury's ministry (1886–1892) the prince's relations to home and foreign politics remained as they had been. Queen Victoria's veto on the submission of official intelligence was in no way relaxed. The prince was socially on pleasant terms with Lord Salisbury, who was foreign secretary as well as prime minister. The prince visited him at Hatfield, but they exchanged no confidences. Independently however of ministerial authority and quite irresponsibly, the prince with increasing freedom discussed foreign affairs with friends at home and abroad. At Biarritz, where he stayed in 1879, at Cannes, or at Paris he emphatically declared in all circles his love of France, his hope of a perpetual peace between her and England, and his dread of another Franco-German war. Nor did he qualify such sentiments when he travelled in Germany. He showed his open-mindedness as to the Channel tunnel scheme by inspecting the works at Dover (March 1882). In the spring of 1887 he was at Cannes during an alarming earthquake, and his cool and courageous behaviour during the peril enhanced his reputation in southern France. In the same year M. Taine, the historian, attached value to a rumour which credited the prince with meddling in internal French politics in order to keep the peace between France and Germany. The French prime minister, M. Rouvier, was threatened with defeat in the chamber of deputies at the hands of M. Floquet and M. Boulanger, who were reputed to be pledged to an immediate breach with Germany. The prince was reported to have persuaded the Comte de Paris to detach his supporters in the chamber from the war-faction and to protect with their votes the ministry of peace. M. Taine's rumour doubtless misinterpreted the prince's cordial relations with the Orleanist princes, but it bears witness to the sort of political influence which was fancifully assigned to the prince in France. It was rare, however, that his good-will to France incurred suspicion of undue interference. The monarchs of Europe looked askance on the French International Exhibition of 1889, which was designed to commemorate the revolution of 1789, and the prince abstained from joining the British commission, of which he had been a member in 1867 and president in 1878. But he had no scruples in visiting the exhibition together with the princess and his sons. They ascended under M. Eiffel's guidance to the top of the Eiffel Tower, which was a chief feature of the exhibition buildings. Before leaving the French capital, the prince exchanged visits with President Carnot, went over the new Pasteur Institute, took part in a meet of the French Four-in-Hand Club, and attended the races at Auteuil. A few years later (March 1894), when diplomatic friction was arising between France and England over events in northern Africa, Lord Dufferin, the English ambassador in France, addressed the British Chamber of Commerce, and denounced popular exaggeration of the disagreement. The prince, who was at Cannes, at once wrote to the ambassador, eagerly congratulating him on his prudent handling of his theme and reporting to him the commendations of German and Russian royal personages whom he was meeting on the Riviera. In Germany he was less suave in pronouncing his opinions. He complained to Prince von Hohenlohe at Berlin in May 1888 of the folly of the new and irritating system of passports which had lately been devised to discourage Frenchmen from travelling in Germany. But Bismarck ridiculed the notion that any importance attached to his political views. In Germany he was rarely regarded by publicists as other than a votary of Parisian gaiety.

A few months later, in Oct. 1888, he illustrated his love of adventure and his real detachment from current diplomatic controversy by extending his travels further east, where political conflict was rife among most of the great powers. He spent a week with the king of Roumania at his country palace of Sinaïa, engaging in a bear hunt in the neighbourhood, and attending military manœuvres. Thence he proceeded to Hungary to join the ill-starred crown prince Rudolph (d. 30 Jan. 1889) in bear-hunting at Görgény and elsewhere, finally accompanying him to Vienna (16 Oct.). No political significance attached to the tour. Subsequently he more than once boldly challenged the patrician prejudices of the German and Austrian courts by passing through Germany and Austria in order to shoot in Hungary as the guest of his friend Baron Hirsch, a Jewish millionaire, who was excluded from the highest Austrian social circles. In the autumn of 1894 he spent no less than four weeks with the baron at his seat of St. Johann. The sport was on a princely scale. The head of game shot during the visit numbered 37,654, of which 22,996 were partridges. According to German and Austrian strict social codes, the prince's public avowal of friendship with Baron Hirsch was a breach of royal etiquette. But he allowed neither social nor diplomatic punctilio to qualify the pleasures of foreign travel. His cosmopolitan sympathies ignored fine distinctions of caste.

Russia throughout this period was the diplomatic foe of England, and the prince vaguely harboured the common English suspicion of Russian intrigues. But he lost no opportunity of confirming his knowledge of the country. Substantially Russia meant to him the home of close connections of his wife and of the wife of his brother Alfred. He signally proved how closely he was drawn to the land by ties of kindred in 1894, when he twice within a few months visited it at the call of family duty. In July 1894 he went to St. Petersburg to attend the wedding at Peterhof of the Grand Duchess Xenia, the daughter of Tsar Alexander III (the Princess of Wales's niece), to the Grand Duke Alexander Michaïlovitch. At the end of October 1894 he hurried to Livadia to the deathbed of his wife's brother-in-law, Tsar Alexander III. He arrived when all was over, but he attended the funeral ceremonies and greeted the accession of his wife's nephew, Tsar Nicholas II, who soon married a niece of his own. The old link between the prince and the Russian throne was thereby strengthened, but its strength owed nothing to diplomatic influences or to considerations of policy.

When Gladstone became prime minister in 1892, the problem of the prince's access to state business received a more promising solution than before. Gladstone sought to gratify the prince's wish that information of the cabinet's proceedings should be placed at his disposal. The queen's assent was not given very readily. She suggested that she herself should decide what official news should be passed on to her son. She deprecated the discussion of national secrets over country-house dinner-tables. But she finally yielded, and thenceforth the prince was regularly supplied by the prime minister's confidential secretary, Sir Algernon West, with much private intelligence. The privilege which the prince had long sought was thus granted on somewhat exceptional terms. The prince freely commented in writing on what was communicated to him. His interest was chiefly in persons, and he frankly criticised appointments or honours, and made recommendations of his own. He avoided intricate matters of general policy, but on minor issues he offered constant remark. Of the common prejudice of rank he gave no sign. Royal commissions of inquiry into social reforms continued to appeal to him. In 1891 he had sought Lord Salisbury's permission to serve on the labour commission, but his presence was deemed impolitic. When the agricultural commission was in process of formation in 1893, he urged the nomination of Mr. Joseph Arch, his colleague on the housing commission. The queen protested, but Arch owed to the prince an invitation to sit. In the same year another royal commission was constituted to inquire into the question of old age pensions, under the chairmanship of Lord Aberdare. Of this body the prince was a member; he attended regularly, put pertinent questions to witnesses, and showed sympathy with the principle at stake. Gladstone informed the prince of his impending resignation in February 1894, and thanked him for unbounded kindness. The prince replied that he valued their long friendship. When Lord Rosebery formed a government in succession to Gladstone, the prince had for the only time in his life a close personal ally in the prime minister. But his influence on public business saw no increase. Lord Rosebery's administration chiefly impressed him by the internal dissensions which made its life precarious.

Gladstone and the prince continued to the last to exchange marks of mutual deference. When on 26 June 1896 the prince opened at Aberystwyth the new University of Wales, of which he had become chancellor, Gladstone in spite of his infirmities came over from Hawarden to attend the ceremony, and at the lunch which followed it the old statesman proposed the prince's health. They met again at Cimiez next year, when Gladstone took his last farewell of Queen Victoria. On 25 May 1898 the prince and his son George acted as pall-bearers at the funeral of Gladstone in Westminster Abbey. So emphatic an attention caused among conservatives some resentment, which was hardly dissipated by the prince's acceptance of the place of president of the committee formed to erect a national memorial to Gladstone (1 July 1898). But it was not in a spirit of political partisanship that the prince publicly avowed his admiration of Gladstone. The prince acknowledged Gladstone's abilities, but he was chiefly grateful for the cordial confidence which had distinguished Gladstone's relations with him. Gladstone, who respected his royal station and deemed him the superior in tact and charm of any other royal personage within his range of knowledge, saw imprudence in Queen Victoria's denial to him of all political responsibility.

On the fall of Lord Rosebery's ministry and the accession to office of Lord Salisbury, the prince illustrated his attitude to the party strife by inviting the out-going and the in-coming ministers to meet at dinner at Marlborough House. Other men of distinction were there, including the shahzada, second son of the amir of Afghanistan, who was visiting this country. The entertainment proved thoroughly harmonious under the cheerful influence of the prince. A little later, when Lord Salisbury's administration was firmly installed, the prince's right to receive as matter of course all foreign despatches was at length formally conceded. Like the members of the cabinet he was now invested with a 'cabinet' key to the official pouches in which private information is daily circulated among ministers by the foreign office. The privilege came too tardily to have much educational effect, but it gave the prince a better opportunity than he had yet enjoyed of observing the inner routine of government, and it diminished a veteran grievance. Yet his main energies were, even more conspicuously than of old, distributed over society, sport, and philanthropy, and in spite of his new privileges he remained an unofficial onlooker in the political arena.

In some directions his philanthropic interest seemed to widen. The ardour and energy with which at the end of the nineteenth century the problems of disease were pursued caught his alert attention, and he gave many proofs of his care for medical research. He regularly performed the duties of president of St. Bartholomew's Hospital, and learned much of hospital management there and elsewhere. He did what he could to encourage the study of consumption, and the investigation of cancer interested him. When he laid the foundation stone of the new wing of Brompton Consumption Hospital in 1881, he asked, if the disease were preventable, why it was not prevented. On 21 Dec. 1888 he called a meeting at Marlborough House to found the National Society for the Prevention of Consumption. It was, too, under his personal auspices that the fund was formed on 18 June 1889 to commemorate the heroism of Father Damien, the Belgian missionary who heroically sacrificed his life to the lepers of the Sandwich Islands. A statue of Father Damien which was set up at Kalawayo was one result of the movement. Another was the National Leprosy Fund for the treatment and study of the disease, especially in India. On 13 Jan. 1890 the prince presided at a subscription dinner in London in support of this fund, and to his activity was in part attributable the foundation of the Albert Victor Hospital for leprosy at Calcutta. He was always on good terms with doctors. Through his friendship with Sir Joseph Fayrer, who had accompanied him to India, he was offered and accepted the unusual compliment of being made honorary fellow of the Royal College of Physicians on 19 July 1897. He received not only the diploma but a model of the goldheaded cane in possession of the college, whose line of successive owners included Radcliffe and the chief physicians of the eighteenth century.

In the summer of 1897 the prince took an active part in the celebration of Queen Victoria's diamond jubilee. The queen gave public expression of her maternal regard, which no differences on political or private matters effectually diminished, by creating in his behalf a new dignity—that of Grand Master and Principal Grand Cross of the Order of the Bath. In all the public festivities the prince filled a chief part. Among the most elaborate private entertainments which he attended was a fancy dress ball given by his friends the duke and duchess of Devonshire at Devonshire

House, where the splendours recalled the prince's own effort of the same kind at Marlborough House in 1874.

But the prince was responsible for a lasting memorial of Queen Victoria's diamond jubilee in the form of a scheme for permanently helping the London hospitals to lessen their burden of debt. On 5 Feb. 1897 the prince in honour of the jubilee inaugurated a fund for the support of London hospitals to which would be received subscriptions from a shilling upwards. The prince became president of the general council, and a meeting at Marlborough House christened the fund 'The Prince of Wales's Hospital Fund for London.' Success was at once achieved. Within a year the donations amounted to 187,000*l.*, and the annual subscriptions to 22,050*l.* The fund continued to flourish under the prince's and his friends' guidance until his accession to the throne, when it was renamed 'King Edward VII Hospital Fund,' and his son took his place as president. The effort has conspicuously relieved the pecuniary strain on the chief London hospitals.

Three years and a half were to pass between the celebration of Queen Victoria's sixty years of rule and the end of her prolonged reign. French caricaturists insolently depicted the extreme senility which would distinguish the prince when his time for kingship would arrive. But the prince as yet showed no loss of activity and no narrowing of interest. As soon as the diamond jubilee festivities ended the prince and princess proved their liking for modern music by attending the Wagner festival at Bayreuth (Aug. 1897). Thence the prince went on his customary holiday to Homburg, and on his way home visited his sister the Empress Frederick at Cronberg. One of those recurring seasons of coolness was dividing his nephew the German emperor and himself. Private and public events alike contributed to the disagreement. There was a renewal of differences between the emperor and his mother, and the emperor had imprudently expressed by telegram his sympathy with President Kruger of the Transvaal Republic, who was resisting the demands of the British government in South Africa. The emperor disclaimed any intention of wounding English susceptibilities. He deemed himself misunderstood. The prince, however, for the time absented himself from Berlin on his foreign travels, and did not recommend himself to German public favour by an emphatic declaration of unalterable personal devotion to France, at the moment that a period of estrangement menaced that country and England. In the spring of 1898, when the two governments were about to engage in a sharp diplomatic duel over their relations in north Africa, the prince laid the foundation stone of a new jetty at Cannes and pleaded in public the cause of peace.

Varied anxieties and annoyances were accumulating. The ambiguity of his position at home was brought home to him in April, when he was requested to preside, for the first and only time in his career of heir-apparent, over the privy council. Since 1880, when Queen Victoria had made it her practice to spend the spring in the Riviera, a commission had been privately drafted empowering the prince and some of the ministers to act, in cases of extreme urgency, on her behalf in her absence from the council. Hitherto the commission had lain dormant, and the prince merely learnt by accident that such a commission existed and that his name was included in it. The concealment caused him annoyance. Now in April 1898, on the outbreak of the Spanish-American war, it was necessary to issue a proclamation of neutrality, and he was called upon to fill the queen's place in the transaction.

In the summer an accidental fall while staying at Waddesdon with his friend Baron Ferdinand de Rothschild caused a fracture of his kneecap (18 July 1898), and disabled him for two months. The illness of his next brother, Alfred, now become duke of Saxe-Coburg, was a serious grief. His relations with the duke, who died on 30 July 1900, had been close from boyhood, and the wrench with the past was severe. At the end of 1899 the gloom had been lightened by the arrival, after a four years' absence, of the German emperor on a friendly visit to Queen Victoria and the prince. The episode was an eloquent proof that there was no enduring enmity between the emperor and either his uncle or his uncle's country, whatever were the passing ebullitions of irritation. The emperor arrived just after the outbreak of the South African war, in the course of which the prince was to learn that even in France there were limits to the effective exercise of his personal charm.

During 1899 and 1900 misrepresentations of England's aim in the war excited throughout Europe popular rancour which involved the prince, equally with his mother and the English ministers, in scurrilous attack. The war was denounced as a gross oppression on England's part of a weak and innocent people. The emperor's presence in England when the storm was breaking was a welcome disclaimer of approval of the abusive campaign. But in the spring of 1900 the prince suffered practical experience of the danger which lurked in the continental outcry. On his way to Denmark, while he and the princess were seated in their train at the Gare du Nord, Brussels, a youth, Sipido, aged fifteen, fired two shots at them (4 April). They were unhurt, and the prince showed the utmost coolness. The act was an outcome of the attacks on England which were prompted by the Boer war. It was the only occasion on which any nefarious attempt was made on the prince's life. The sequel was not reassuring to British feeling. Sipido and three alleged accomplices were put on their trial at Brussels on 1 July. The three associates were acquitted, and Sipido was held irresponsible for his conduct. Ordered to be kept under government supervision till he reached the age of twenty-one, he soon escaped to France, whence he was only extradited by the Belgian government after a protest by British ministers. There was much cause for friction at the time between England and Belgium. Not only had the Boer war alienated the Belgian populace like the other peoples of Europe, but the old cordiality between the royal houses had declined. The close intimacy which had bound Queen Victoria to her uncle the late king, Leopold I, had been echoed in the relations between his successor King Leopold II and the prince. But the queen's sense of propriety was offended by reports of her royal cousin's private life, and the charges of cynical cruelty to which his policy in the Congo gave rise in England stimulated the impatience of the English royal family. After the outrage at Brussels, the prince and King Leopold II maintained only the formalities of social intercourse. The hostile sentiment which prevailed in Europe deterred the prince from attending the Paris International Exhibition of 1900. This was the only French venture of the kind in the long series of the century which he failed to grace with his presence. As in the case of 1878 he was president of the royal commission for the British section, and he was active in the preliminary organisation. During 1899 he watched in Paris the beginnings of the exhibition buildings. But the temper of France denied him the opportunity of seeing them in their final shape.

Early in 1901 the prince's destiny was at length realised. For some months Queen Victoria's strength had been slowly failing. In the middle of January 1901 physical prostration rapidly grew, and on 20 Jan. her state was critical. The Prince of Wales arrived at Osborne on that day, and was with his mother as life ebbed away. Her last articulate words were an affectionate mention of his name. Whatever had occasioned passing friction between them, her maternal love never knew any diminution. The presence of his nephew, the German emperor, at the death-bed was grateful to the prince and to all members of his family. Queen Victoria died at Osborne at half-past six on the evening of Tuesday, 22 Jan. 1901.

Next morning the new king travelled to London, and at a meeting of the privy council at St. James's Palace took the oaths of sovereignty under the style of Edward VII. 'I am fully determined,' he said, 'to be a constitutional sovereign in the strictest sense of the word, and as long as there is breath in my body to work for the good and amelioration of my people.' He explained that he had resolved to be known by the name of Edward, which had been borne by six of his ancestors, not that he undervalued the name of Albert, but that he desired his father's name to stand alone.

King Edward's first speech as sovereign, deliberately and impressively spoken, was made without any notes and without consultation with any minister. According to his habit, he had thought it over during his journey, and when he had delivered it he embarrassed the officials by his inability to supply them with a written copy. He had expected a report to be taken, he explained. The published words were put together from memory by some of the councillors and their draft was endorsed by the king. The episode, while it suggested a certain unfamiliarity on his part with the formal procedure of the council, showed an independent sense of his new responsibilities. A few days later (29 Jan. 1901) the king issued appropriate addresses to the army and the navy, to his people of the United Kingdom, to the colonies, and to India.

In the ceremonies of Queen Victoria's funeral (2–4 Feb.) the king acted as chief mourner, riding through London behind the bier from Victoria station to Paddington, and walking through the streets of Windsor to St. George's Chapel, where the coffin was first laid. On Monday he again walked in procession from the Albert Memorial Chapel at Windsor to the burial place at the Royal Mausoleum at Frogmore. His nephew, the German emperor, was at his side throughout the funeral ceremonies. The emperor's brother, Prince Henry of Prussia, and his son the crown prince were also in the mourning company. Almost the first act of the king's reign was to give public proof of his good relations with his royal kinsmen of Germany. It had been Queen Victoria's intention to invest the crown prince her great-grandson with the order of the Garter. This intention the king now carried out; at the same time he made the emperor a field-marshal and Prince Henry a vice-admiral of the fleet. By way of marking his chivalric resolve to associate his wife with all the honour of his new status, he devised at the same time a new distinction in her behalf, appointing her Lady of the Garter (12 Feb. 1901).

His first public function as sovereign was to open in state the new session of parliament on 14 Feb. 1901. This royal duty, which the queen had only performed seven times in the concluding forty years of her reign and for the last time in 1886, chiefly brought the sovereign into public relation with the government of the country. The king during his nine years of rule never omitted the annual ceremony, and he read for himself the speech from the throne. That practice had been dropped by the queen in 1861, and had not been resumed by her.

Queen Victoria had been created Empress of India in 1876, and King Edward was the first British sovereign to succeed to the dignity of Emperor of India. By Act of Parliament (1 Edw. VII, cap. 15) another addition was now made to the royal titles with a view to associating the crown for the first time directly with the colonial empire. He was declared by statute to be King not only of Great Britain and Ireland but of 'the British dominions beyond the seas.' On the new coinage he was styled 'Britt. Omn. Rex,' in addition to the old designations.

Queen Victoria left the new king her private residences of Osborne and Balmoral, but her pecuniary fortune was distributed among the younger members of her family. The king was stated on his accession to have no debts and no capital. Gossip which erroneously credited him with an immense indebtedness ignored his business instincts and the good financial advice which he invariably had at his disposal in the inner circle of his friends. Like Queen Victoria he relinquished on his accession the chief hereditary revenues of the crown, which had grown in value during her reign from 245,000*l.* to 425,000*l.* As in 1837, the duchies of Lancaster and Cornwall were held, despite radical misgivings, to stand on another footing and to be royal appanages in the personal control of the royal family. The duchy of Lancaster, which produced 60,000*l.* a year, was reckoned to be the sovereign's private property, and the duchy of Cornwall, which was of like value, that of the heir-apparent. On his ceasing to be Prince of Wales the parliamentary grant to him of 40,000*l.* lapsed, while the duchy of Cornwall passed to his son. The king's income, in the absence of a new parliamentary grant, was thus solely the 60,000*l.* from the duchy of Lancaster. The Act of 1889, which provided 36,000*l.* a year for his children, became void six months after the late sovereign's death.

On 5 March a royal message invited the House of Commons to make pecuniary provision for the king and his family. A select committee of twenty-one was appointed on 11 March 1901 to consider the king's financial position. The Irish nationalists declined to serve, but Henry Labouchere represented the radical and labour sections, to whom the cost of the monarchy was a standing grievance. The committee was chiefly constituted of the leaders of the two chief parties in the state. It was finally decided to recommend an annual grant of 470,000*l.*, a sum which was 85,000*l.* in excess of the income allowed to the late queen. The increase was justified on the ground that a larger sum would be needed for the hospitalities of the court. No special grant was made to Queen Alexandra, but it was understood that 33,000*l.* would be paid her out of that portion (110,000*l.*) of the total grant allotted to the privy purse; 70,000*l.* was secured to her in case of widowhood. The king's son and heir, George, duke of York, who now became duke of Cornwall and York, received an annuity of 20,000*l.*, and his wife, the duchess, received one of 10,000*l.*, with an additional 20,000*l.* in case of widowhood; the three daughters of the king were given a joint annual income of 18,000*l.* Some other expenses, like the repair of the royal palaces (18,000*l.*) and the maintenance of royal yachts (23,000*l.*), were provided for independently from the Consolidated Fund. The resolutions to these effects were adopted by 250 to 62. They were resisted by the Irish nationalists and by a few advanced radicals, including

Henry Labouchere, Mr. Keir Hardie, and Mr. John Burns. Mr. Burns warmly deprecated a royal income which should be comparable with the annual revenues of Barney Barnato, Alfred Beit, or Mr. Andrew Carnegie. The civil list bill which embodied the resolutions was finally read a third time on 11 June 1901 by 370 against 60, and it became law on 2 July (1 Edw. VII, cap. 4). The generous terms were accepted by the nation with an enthusiasm which proved the sureness of the crown's popularity and augured well for the new reign. The Irish opposition was mainly due to a feeling of resentment at the refusal of the government to alter the old terms of the sovereign's accession oath, in which while declaring himself a protestant he cast, in the view of Roman catholics, insult on their faith. Nowhere was there any sign of personal hostility to the new ruler.

The king came to the throne in his sixtieth year endowed with a personality of singular charm and geniality, large worldly experience, wide acquaintance with men and women, versatile interests in society and philanthropy, enthusiasm for sport, business habits, and a resolve to serve his people to the best of his ability. Among the king's friends there were fears that he would prove himself unequal to his new station, but the anticipations were signally belied. His mother's deliberate exclusion of him from political work placed him under some disadvantages. He was a stranger to the administrative details of his great office and he was too old to repair the neglect of a political training. Nor was he of an age at which it was easy to alter his general mode of life. He cherished a high regard for his mother's statesmanship and political acumen, but he had no full knowledge of the precise manner in which they had been exercised. At the outset there were slight indications that he over-estimated the sovereign's power. In consultation over a king's speech he seemed in some peril of misinterpreting the royal function. But his action was due to inexperience and to no impatience of ministerial advice. Despite his share in two royal commissions he had never studied deeply domestic legislation, and about it he held no well-defined views. He had watched more closely the course of foreign politics. His constant habit of travel, his careful maintenance of good relations with his large foreign kindred, his passion for making the personal acquaintance of interesting men and women on the continent, gave him much knowledge of foreign affairs both political and social. Yet the diplomatic details of foreign policy lay outside his range of study. While he was desirous of full information from his ministers, he soon came to view them as responsible experts whose procedure was rarely matter for much personal comment. The minutes of each cabinet meeting, with which the prime minister supplied the sovereign, usually provoked from Queen Victoria's pen voluminous criticism. King Edward VII usually accepted the prime minister's notes without remark, or if he was moved to avowal of acquiescence or remonstrance, he resorted to a short personal interview. The immense correspondence between the sovereign and the prime minister which continued during Queen Victoria's reign almost ceased, and its place, so far as it was filled at all, was taken by verbal intercourse, of which the king took no note. To appointments and the bestowal of honours he paid closer attention than to legislative measures or details of policy, and he was never neglectful of the interests of his personal friends, but even there he easily and as a rule gracefully yielded his wishes to ministerial counsel. His punctual habits enabled him to do all the formal business that was required of him with despatch. In signing papers and in dealing with urgent correspondence he was a model of promptitude. No arrears accumulated, and although the routine tried his patience, he performed it with exemplary regularity. He encouraged more modern technical methods than his mother had approved. He accepted type-written memoranda from ministers, instead of obliging them as in the late reign to write out everything in their own hands. He communicated with ministers through his chief secretary more frequently than had been customary before. Although he was for most of his life a voluminous letter writer, his penmanship greatly deteriorated in his last years and grew difficult to decipher. When the situation did not admit of an oral communication, he preferred to use a secretary's pen.

It was inevitable that his place in the sphere of government should differ from that of his mother. Queen Victoria for the greater part of her reign was a widow and a recluse, who divided all her thought with unremitting application between politics and family affairs. The new king had wider interests. Without his mother's power of concentration or her tenacity of purpose, he distributed his energies over a more extended field. On acceding to his new dignity there was no lessening of his earlier devotion to sport, society, and other forms of amusement. He was faithful to his old circle of intimate friends and neither reduced nor extended it. His new official duties failed to absorb his whole attention. But it was in the revived splendours and developments of royal ceremonial that to the public eye the new reign chiefly differed from the old. Though Queen Victoria had modified her seclusion in her latest years, her age and her dislike of ceremonial functions had combined to maintain the court in much of the gloom in which the prince consort's death had involved it. The new king had a natural gift for the exercise of brilliant hospitality, and he sought to indulge his taste with liberality. London became the headquarters of the court for the first time for forty years. No effort was spared to make it a prominent feature of the nation's social life. Over the ceremonial and hospitable duties of sovereignty the king exercised a full personal control, and there he suffered no invasion of his authority.

The first year of the new reign was a year of mourning for the old. In its course it dealt the royal family another sorrowful blow. The king's eldest sister, the Empress Frederick, was suffering from cancer. On 23 Feb., within a month of his accession, the king left England for the first time during the reign to pay her a visit at Friedrichshof, her residence near Cronberg. They did not meet again. She died on 5 Aug. following. The king with the queen now crossed the Channel again to attend the funeral at Potsdam. Then the king went, according to his custom of thirty years' standing, to a German watering place, Homburg. No change was apparent there in his old habits which ignored strict rules of royal etiquette. Subsequently he joined the queen at Copenhagen, where he met his wife's nephew, the Tsar Nicholas of Russia, and the tsar's mother, the dowager empress, sister of Queen Alexandra. It was a family gathering of the kind which the king had long since been accustomed to attend periodically. As of old, it was wholly innocent of diplomatic intention. But the increased publicity attaching to the king's movements in his exalted station misled some domestic and many foreign observers into the error of scenting a subtle diplomatic purpose in his established practice of exchanging at intervals visits of courtesy with his royal kindred on the European continent. With his insatiable curiosity about men and things, he always liked frank discussion of European politics with foreign statesmen, and he continued the practice till his death. But such debate was scarcely to any greater degree than in earlier years the primary aim of his foreign tours.

Meanwhile the king accepted without change the arrangements already made for a colonial tour of his son and his daughter-in-law. On 17 March he took leave of the duke and duchess of Cornwall and York on their setting out for Australia in the Ophir in order to open the new commonwealth parliament at Melbourne. On their return journey they visited Natal and Cape Colony, and thence traversed the whole of Canada. The king after a first visit as sovereign to Scotland met them on their arrival at Portsmouth on 1 Nov., and declared the tour to be a new link in the chain which bound the colonial empire to the throne. A few days later he created by letters patent the duke of Cornwall Prince of Wales. It was not easy, suddenly, to break the long association of that title with himself.

On 22 Jan. 1902 the year of mourning for the late queen ended, and court festivities began on a brilliant scale. Buckingham Palace and Windsor Castle had been thoroughly overhauled and newly decorated, the former becoming the chief residence of the court. Windsor saw comparatively little of the new king. Sandringham remained his country residence, and he spent a few weeks each autumn at Balmoral, but Osborne he abandoned, giving it over to the nation as a convalescent home for army and navy officers (9 Aug. 1902). Although little of his time was spent at Windsor or Balmoral, he greatly improved the facilities of sport in both places in the interests of his guests.

The first levee of the new reign was held on 11 Feb. at St. James's Palace, and the first evening court on 14 March at Buckingham Palace. The court initiated a new form of royal entertainment; it was held at night amid great magnificence, and replaced the afternoon drawing-rooms of Queen Victoria's reign. A tour in the west of England during March gave the king and queen an opportunity of showing their interest in the navy. At Dartmouth the foundation stone of the new Britannia Naval College was laid, while the queen launched the new battleship Queen at Devonport and the king laid the first plate of the new battleship Edward VII. A few weeks later he made a yachting tour off the west coast, paying a visit to the Scilly Isles on 7 April. The expedition followed a course with which he had familiarised himself in early youth.

Throughout the early period of the reign the nation's political horizon was clouded. Not only was the war in South Africa still in progress, but the alienation of foreign public opinion, which was a fruit of the conflict, continued to embarrass England's foreign relations. Neither in France nor Germany had scurrilous caricature of the king ceased. The king had always shown the liveliest sympathy with the British army in the field, and he did not conceal his resentment at the attacks made in England by members of the liberal party during 1901 on the methods of the military operations. On 12 June he presented medals to South African soldiers, and then conferred the same distinction on both Lord Roberts and Lord Milner, who was on leave in England discussing the situation. The king, though he did not interfere with the negotiations, was frank in his expressions of anxiety for peace. It was therefore with immense relief that he received the news that the pacification was signed in South Africa on 31 May 1902. He at once sent messages of thanks to the English plenipotentiaries, Lord Milner, high commissioner for South Africa, and Lord Kitchener, who had lately been in chief military command, and to all the forces who had been actively engaged in the war. On 8 June the king and queen attended a thanksgiving service in St. Paul's.

The peace seemed an auspicious prelude to the solemn function of the coronation, which had been appointed for 26 June 1902. The king warmly approved proposals to give the formality exceptional magnificence. Since the last coronation sixty-four years ago the conception of the monarchy had broadened with the growth of the colonial empire. The strength of the crown now lay in its symbolic representation of the idea of imperial unity. There were anachronisms in the ritual, but the central purpose well served the present and the future. Representatives were invited not only from all the colonies but, for the first time, from all manner of administrative institutions—county councils, borough councils, learned societies, friendly societies, and railway companies. The king desired to render the event memorable for the poor no less than for the well-to-do. He gave the sum of 30,000*l.* for a commemorative dinner to 500,000 poor persons of London, while the queen undertook to entertain the humble class of general servants in the metropolis. Two other episodes lent fresh grace to the ceremony. The king announced his gift of Osborne House to the nation, and he instituted a new order of merit to be bestowed on men of high distinction in the army, navy, science, literature, and art. The order was fashioned on the lines of the Prussian 'pour le mérite' and was a more comprehensive recognition of ability than was known officially in England before. The total official cost of the coronation amounted to the large sum of 359,289*l.* 5*s.*, a sum greatly in excess of the 200,000*l.* voted by parliament for Queen Victoria's coronation (cf. *Blue Book* (382), 1909).

A few days before the date appointed for the great ceremony rumours of the king's ill-health gained currency and were denied. But on 24 June, two days before Coronation Day, it was announced, to the public consternation, that the king was suffering from perityphlitis. An operation was performed the same morning with happy results, and during the next few weeks the king made a steady recovery.

While still convalescent he had his first experience of a change of ministry. Lord Salisbury, whose failing health counselled retirement from the office of prime minister, had long since decided to resign as soon as peace in South Africa was proclaimed. But when that happy incident arrived, he looked forward to retaining his post for the six weeks which intervened before the coronation. The somewhat indefinite postponement of the ceremony led him to carry out his original purpose on 11 July 1902. On his recommendation his place was taken by Lord Salisbury's nephew, Mr. Balfour, who was already leader of the House of Commons. There was no immediate change in the complexion or the policy of the government, and no call for the sovereign's exertion. Although there was little in common between the temperament and training of the king and his first prime minister, the king was sensible of the value of Lord Salisbury's experience and wisdom, and the minister, whose faith in the monarchical principle was strong, showed him on his part a personal deference which he appreciated. The intellectual brilliance of Lord Salisbury's successor often dazzled the king, but a thoroughly constitutional conception on each side of their respective responsibilities kept a good understanding alive between them.

On 9 August the postponed coronation took place in Westminster Abbey. The ritual was somewhat abbreviated, but the splendour scarcely diminished. Although many of the foreign guests had left London, the scene lost little of its impressiveness. The crown was placed on the king's head by Frederick Temple, archbishop of Canterbury. Queen Alexandra was crowned at the same time by W. D. Maclagan, archbishop of York. There followed a series of public functions which aimed at associating with the ceremony various sources of imperial strength. An investiture and parade of colonial troops took place on 12 Aug., a review of Indian troops on 13 Aug., and a naval review at Spithead on 16 Aug. Next day at Cowes the king received visits from the Boer generals Delarey, De Wet, and Botha, who had greatly distinguished themselves in the late war and had come to England to plead on behalf of their conquered country for considerate treatment. The shah of Persia arrived to pay the king his respects three days later. On 22 Aug. the king and queen started for Scotland in the royal yacht Victoria and Albert; they went by the west coast, and visited on the passage the Isle of Man. On the return of the court to the metropolis, the king made a royal progress through south London (24 Oct.), and lunched with the lord mayor and corporation at the Guildhall. Two days later he attended at St. Paul's Cathedral a service of thanksgiving for his complete restoration to health.

With the close of the South African war England began to emerge from the cloud of animosity in which the popular sentiment of a great part of Europe had enveloped her. There was therefore every reason why the king should now gratify his cosmopolitan sympathies and his lively interest in his large circle of kinsmen and friends abroad by renewing his habit of foreign travel. Save during the pro-Boer outbreak of ill-will, he had always been a familiar and welcome figure among all classes on the continent. His cheering presence invariably encouraged sentiments of good-will, and it was congenial to him to make show of a personal contribution to an improvement of England's relations with her neighbours, and to a strengthening of the general concord. He acknowledged the obligation that lay on rulers and statesmen of preserving European peace; and he wished England, subject to a fit recognition of her rights, to stand well with the world. At the same time his constitutional position and his personal training disqualified him from exerting substantive influence on the foreign policy which his ministers alone could control. He repeatedly gave abroad graceful expression of general approval of his ministers' aims, and his benevolent assurances fostered a friendly atmosphere, but always without prejudice to his ministers' responsibilities. He cannot be credited with broad diplomatic views, or aptitude for technical negotiation. While he loved conversation with foreign statesmen, his interest in foreign lands ranged far beyond politics. In the intimacies of private intercourse he may have at times advanced a personal opinion on a diplomatic theme which lacked official sanction. But to his unguarded utterances no real weight attached in official circles either at home or abroad. His embodiment in foreign eyes of English aspirations inevitably exaggerated the popular importance of his public activities abroad. The foreign press and public often made during his reign the error of assuming that in his frequent interviews with foreign rulers and statesmen he was personally working out a diplomatic policy of his own devising. Foreign statesmen and rulers knew that no subtler aim really underlay his movements than a wish for friendly social intercourse with them and the enjoyment of life under foreign skies, quite unencumbered by the burden of diplomatic anxieties.

In his eyes all rulers of state were bound together by ties of affinity, and these ties were strengthened for him by many bonds of actual kinship. At his accession the rulers of Germany, Russia, Greece, and Portugal were related to him in one or other degree, and two additions were made to his large circle of royal relatives while he was king. In October 1905 his son-in-law, Prince Charles of Denmark, who had married his youngest daughter, Maud, in 1896, was elected king of Norway (as Haakon VII) when that country severed its union with Sweden; while on 31 May 1906 Alfonso XIII, king of Spain, married Princess Ena of Battenberg, daughter of the king's youngest sister, Princess Beatrice. There was good justification for the title which the wits of Paris bestowed on him of 'l'oncle de l'Europe.' Most of the European courts were the homes of his kinsfolk, whose domestic hospitality was always in readiness for him. In return it gratified his hospitable instinct to welcome his royal relatives beneath his own roof.

To no country of Europe did his attitude as king differ from that which he had adopted while he was prince. To France his devotion was always pronounced. He had delighted in visiting Italy, Russia, Austria, and Portugal. His relations with Germany had always stood on a somewhat peculiar footing, and they, too, underwent small change. They had been coloured to a larger extent than his other foreign connections by the personal conditions of family kinship. Since the Danish war, owing to the influence of his wife and her kindred, he had never professed in private much sympathy with German political ambitions. The brusque speech and manner, too, with which Bismarck invariably treated the English royal family had made German policy uncongenial to them. Despite the king's affection for his nephew, the German emperor, short seasons of domestic variance between the two were bound to recur, and the private differences encouraged the oldstanding coolness in political sentiment. But the king was never long estranged from his nephew. He was thoroughly at home with Germans and when he went among them evoked their friendly regard. No deliberate and systematic hostility to the German people could be truthfully put to the king's credit. His personal feeling was very superficially affected by the mutual jealousy which, from causes far beyond his control, grew during his reign between the two nations.

While ambitious to confirm as king the old footing which he had enjoyed on the European continent as prince, his conservative instinct generated involuntary misgivings of England's friendship with peoples outside the scope of his earlier experience. He was startled by so novel a diplomatic step as the alliance with Japan, which was concluded during the first year of his reign (12 Feb. 1902) and was expanded later (27 Sept. 1905). But he was reassured on learning of the age and dignity of the reigning Japanese dynasty. When the Anglo-Japanese arrangement was once effected he lent it all the advantage of his loyal personal support. He entertained the Japanese Prince and Princess Arisugawa on their visit to London, and conferred on the prince the distinction of G.C.B. (27 June 1905). In 1906, too, after the Russo-Japanese war, he admitted to the Order of Merit the Japanese heroes of the conflict, Field-marshals Yamagata and Oyama, and Admiral Togo.

Family feeling solely guided the king's first steps in the foreign arena. After his eldest sister's death the king and emperor made open avowal of mutual affection. On 26 Jan. 1902 the Prince of Wales was the emperor's guest at Berlin for his birthday, and on the king's coronation the emperor made him an admiral of the German fleet. At the end of the year, on 8 Nov. 1902, the emperor arrived at Sandringham to attend the celebration of his uncle's sixty-first birthday. He remained in England twelve days, and had interviews with the prime minister and the foreign secretary. Details of diplomacy were not the theme of the uncle and nephew's confidences. Rumours to a contrary effect were current early next year, when the two countries made a combined naval demonstration in order to coerce the recalcitrant president of the Venezuelan republic, who had defied the just claims of both England and Germany. It was imagined in some quarters that the king on his own initiative had committed his ministers to the joint movement in an informal conversation with the emperor at Sandringham. Much wrangling had passed between the statesmen and the press of the two countries. But the apparently sudden exchange of a campaign of altercation for concerted action to meet a special emergency was no exceptional diplomatic incident.

The spring of 1903 saw the first foreign tour of the king's reign and his personal introduction to the continent in his new rôle. On 31 March 1903 he left Portsmouth harbour on board the royal yacht the Victoria and Albert, on a five weeks' cruise, in the course of which he visited among other places Lisbon, Rome, and Paris. The expedition was a vacation exercise, which gave him the opportunity of showing friendly courtesy to foreign rulers and peoples. He went on his own initiative. His travelling companions were members of his own household, who were personal friends. There was also in his retinue a member of the permanent staff of the foreign office, the Hon. Charles Hardinge, assistant under-secretary there. Mr. Hardinge, who was made K.C.V.O. and K.C.M.G. in 1904, and Baron Hardinge of Penshurst in 1910, served as British ambassador at St. Petersburg from 1904 to 1906 and was permanent under-secretary at the foreign office from 1906 till the king's death. While he was attached to the foreign office, he usually accompanied the king on his foreign tours, and the precise capacity in which he travelled with the sovereign occasionally raised a constitutional controversy, which the true facts deprived of genuine substance. The presence of the foreign minister or at any rate of a cabinet minister was necessary to bring any effective diplomatic negotiation within the range of the king's intercourse with his foreign hosts. Mr. Hardinge was personally agreeable to the king. He was well fitted to offer advice or information which might be of service in those talks with foreign rulers or statesmen on political themes in which the sovereign occasionally indulged. He could also record suggestions if the need arose for the perusal of the foreign minister. In debates in the House of Commons some ambiguity and constitutional irregularity were imputed to Mr. Hardinge's status in the king's suite, but it was made clear that no ministerial responsibilities devolved either on the king or on him during the foreign tours, and that the foreign policy of the country was unaffected by the royal progresses (*Hansard*, 23 July 1903 and 4 June 1908).

The king's route of 1903 was one with which he was familiar. His first landing-place was Lisbon, where he was the guest of King Carlos. The two monarchs complimented each other on their lineal ties and on the ancient alliance between their two countries. After short visits to Gibraltar and Malta, the king disembarked at Naples on 23 April, and four days later reached Rome. The good relations which had always subsisted between England and Italy had been little disturbed by pro-Boer prejudice. The Roman populace received King Edward with enthusiasm, and he exchanged with King Victor Emanuel professions of warm friendship. With characteristic tact the king visited Pope Leo XIII at the Vatican, where he had thrice before greeted Pope Pius IX. From Rome the king passed with no small gratification to his favourite city of Paris for the first time after more than three years. He came at an opportune moment. The French foreign minister, M. Delcassé, had for some time been seeking a diplomatic understanding with England, which should remove the numerous points of friction between the two countries in Egypt, Morocco, and elsewhere. The king's ministers were responsive, and his visit to Paris, although it was paid independently of the diplomatic issue, was well calculated to conciliate French public opinion, which was slow in shedding its pro-Boer venom. On the king's arrival the temper of the Parisian populace looked doubtful (1 May), but the king's demeanour had the best effect, and in his reply to an address from the British chamber of commerce on his first morning in Paris he spoke so aptly of the importance of developing good relations between the two countries that there was an immediate renewal of the traditional friendliness which had linked him to the Parisians for near half a century. The president, M. Loubet, and M. Delcassé did everything to enhance the cordiality of the welcome. The president entertained the king at a state banquet at the Elysée and the speeches of both host and guest gave voice to every harmonious sentiment. The king accompanied the president to the Théâtre Français, to a military review at Vincennes, and to the races at Longchamps. He did not neglect friends of the old régime, and everywhere he declared his happiness in strengthening old ties. His words and actions closely resembled those which marked his visit to Paris under Marshal MacMahon's auspices in 1878. But, in view of his new rank and the recent political discord, the episode was generally regarded as the propitious heralding of a new departure. On 5 May he returned to London and was warmly received.

The king lost no time in returning the hospitalities of his foreign hosts. On 6 July President Loubet came to London to stay at St. James's Palace as the king's guest, and M. Delcassé was his companion. Friendly negotiations between the two governments took a step forward. On 17 Nov. the king and queen of Italy were royal guests at Windsor, and were followed just a year later by the king and queen of Portugal. There was nothing in the visits of the foreign sovereigns to distinguish them from the ordinary routine of courtesy. The visit of the president of the French republic was unprecedented. It was proof of the desire of France to make friends with England and of the king's sympathy with the aspiration. M. Delcassé's policy soon bore practical fruit; on 14 Oct. 1903 an arbitration treaty was signed by the two governments. Its provisions did not go far, but it indicated a new spirit in the international relation. The Anglo-French agreement, which was concluded on 8 April 1904 between M. Delcassé and Lord Lansdowne, the English foreign secretary, was an instrument of genuine consequence. It formally terminated the long series of difficulties which had divided England and France in many parts of the world, and was a guarantee against their recurrence. The king's grace of manner both as guest and host of President Loubet helped to create a temper favourable to the 'entente cordiale.' But no direct responsibility for its initiation or conclusion belonged to him. Some French journalists who were oblivious of his aloofness from the detail of state business placed the understanding to his credit, and bestowed on him the title of 'le roi pacificateur.' The title is symbolically just but is misleading if it be taken to imply any personal control of diplomacy.

It was not the king's wish to withhold from Germany and the German emperor, whatever the difficulties between the two governments, those attentions which it had been his habit to exchange with his nephew from the opening of the emperor's reign. On 29 June 1904 the king sailed for Kiel in his yacht Victoria and Albert, attended by an escort of naval vessels. He was received by the emperor with much cordiality, visited under his nephew's guidance the German dockyards, attended a regatta off Kiel, and lunched at Hamburg with the burgomaster. In his intercourse with the German emperor it flattered the king's pride to give to their meetings every show of dignity, and contrary to his usual practice a cabinet minister now joined his suite. The presence of Lord Selborne, first lord of the admiralty, gave the expedition something of the formal character of a friendly naval demonstration, but no political significance attached to the interchange of civilities. An arbitration treaty with Germany of the same tenour as that with France was signed on 12 July 1904, but such a negotiation was outside the king's sphere of action. The failure of the Kiel visit to excite any ill-feeling in France indicated the purely external part which his charm of manner and speech was known to play in international affairs.

The king's habitual appetite for foreign tours was whetted by his experience in the spring of 1903. While constant movement characterised his life at home, and a business-like distribution of his time enabled him to engage in an unending round of work and pleasure through the greater part of his reign, he spent on an average some three months of each year out of his dominions. His comprehensive travels did not embrace the colonies or dependencies outside Europe, but his son and heir, who had visited the colonies in 1901, made a tour through India (Nov. 1905–May 1906), and the king thus kept vicariously in touch with his Indian as well as with his colonial subjects. His travelling energy was freely lavished on countries nearer at hand. Five or six weeks each spring were spent at Biarritz, and a similar period each autumn at Marienbad. These sojourns were mainly designed in the interests of health. But with them were combined four cruises in the Mediterranean (1905, 6, 7, and 1909) and one cruise in the North Sea (1908), all of which afforded opportunities of pleasurable recreation, and of meetings with foreign rulers. In addition, he paid in the winter of 1907 a visit to Prussia and in the summer of 1908 one to Russia. Such frequent wanderings from home greatly increased the king's foreign reputation. It was only occasionally that he paid visits to foreign courts in the panoply of state. He travelled for the most part incognito. Few episodes, however, of his migrations escaped the notice of the journalists, who sought persistently to confirm the erroneous impression that he was invariably engaged on a diplomatic mission.

In Paris he resumed his old career. Each year, on his way to or from the south, he revisited the city, seeing old friends and indulging in old amusements. In meetings with the president of the French republic and his ministers he repeated his former assurances of amity. When M. Loubet retired in January 1906, he showed equal warmth of feeling for his successor, M. Fallières, to whom he paid the courtesy of a state visit (3 May). In the summer of 1908 he had the satisfaction of entertaining the new president in London with the same ceremony as was accorded to his predecessor in 1904. He was loyal to all his French acquaintances new and old. On M. Delcassé's fall from power in June 1905 he continued to exchange friendly visits with him during his later sojourns in the French capital. M. Clemenceau, who became prime minister in October 1906, and held office for nearly three years, was reared in Gambetta's political school, members of which had always interested the king since his pleasant meetings with their chief. M. Clemenceau was the king's guest at Marienbad on 15 Aug. 1909. Political principles counted for little in his social intercourse. He was still welcomed with the same cordiality by representatives of the fashionable royalist noblesse as by republican statesmen. A modest estimate was set on his political acumen when in informal talk he travelled beyond safe generalities. An irresponsible suggestion at a private party in Paris that the entente ought to be converted into a military alliance met with no response. Nor was much heed paid to some vague comment which fell from his lips on the intricate problem of the relations of the European powers on the north coast of Africa. But everyone in France appreciated his French sympathies and acknowledged his personal fascination.

His cruises to the Mediterranean during these years took him to Algiers in 1905, and to Athens and the Greek archipelago in April 1906; at Athens, where he was the guest of his brother-in-law, King George I, he witnessed the Olympic games. In 1907 he landed from his yacht at Cartagena to meet the young king of Spain, who had married his niece the year before. Twice in the course of the same journey he also met the king of Italy, first at Gaeta (18 April), and secondly on the return journey by rail outside Rome (30 April). Two years later (1909) he enjoyed similar experiences, meeting the king of Spain at San Sebastian and Biarritz, and the king of Italy at Baiae; then he also visited Malta and Sicily, besides Pompeii and other environs of Naples. In April 1908 he cruised in the North Sea, and he visited in state the three northern courts of Denmark, Sweden, and Norway. In Denmark he was a familiar figure. To the new kingdom of Norway, where his son-in-law reigned, he went for the first time. At

Stockholm he had been the frequent guest of earlier Swedish kings while he was Prince of Wales.

During a single year, 1905, the German emperor and the king failed to exchange hospitalities. Germany lay outside the ubiquitous route of his pleasure cruises, and circumstances deterred the king from deliberately seeking personal intercourse with his nephew. For the continued friction between Germany and England the king had no sort of responsibility. But the emperor was for the moment inclined to credit his uncle with want of sympathy, and there followed one of those short seasons of estrangement to which their intimacy was always liable. Reports of unguarded remarks from the royal lips in the course of 1905 which reached the emperor from Paris had for him an unfriendly sound. Meanwhile the German press lost no opportunity of treating the king as a declared enemy of Germany. The king's voyages were held to be shrewd moves in a diplomatic game which sought German humiliation. The meetings of the king with the king of Italy were misconstrued into a personal attempt on the king's part to detach Italy from the triple alliance. The interview at Gaeta in April 1907 was especially denounced as part of the king's Machiavellian design of an elaborate coalition from which Germany was to be excluded. Adverse comment was passed on his apparent desire to avoid a meeting with the emperor. He was represented as drawing a cordon round Germany in the wake of his foreign journeys, and there were even German politicians who professed to regard him as a sort of Bismarck who used the velvet glove instead of the iron hand. He was deemed capable of acts of conciliation to suit his dark purposes. It was pretended that, with a view to soothing German irritation for his own objects, he by his own hand excised from the official instructions to the English delegates at the Hague conference (June 1907) his ministers' orders to raise the question of a general reduction of armaments. Serious French publicists well knew the king to be innocent of any such wiles. French caricaturists, who made merry over his 'fièvre voyageuse,' only echoed the German note in a satiric key. They pictured the king as a 'polype Européen' which was clutching in its tentacles all the sovereigns of Europe save the German emperor, without prejudice to the international situation.

The German fancies were complete delusions. The king had no conception of any readjustment of the balance of European power. There was no serious quarrel between emperor and king. The passing cloud dispersed. On 15 Aug. 1906 the king visited the emperor at Friedrichshof near Cronberg on his journey to Marienbad, and a general conversation which only dealt in part with politics put matters on a right footing. Sir Frank Lascelles, the English ambassador at Berlin, who had accompanied the king from Frankfort, was present at the interview. Just a year later (14 Aug.

1907) a like meeting at Wilhelmshöhe renewed the friendly intercourse, and in the same year the German emperor and empress paid a state visit to Windsor (11–18 Nov.). The emperor exerted all his charm on his host and his fellow guests. The formal speeches of both emperor and king abounded in felicitous assurances of good-will. During the emperor's stay at Windsor the king gathered about him as imposing an array of royal personages as ever assembled there. On 17 November he entertained at luncheon twenty-four men and women of royal rank, including the king and queen of Spain, Queen Amélie of Portugal, and many members of the Orleans and Bourbon families, who had met in England to celebrate the marriage of Prince Charles of Bourbon to Princess Louise of Orleans. The entertainment showed the king at the head of the royal caste of Europe, and attested his social power of reconciling discordant elements. The emperor remained in England till 11 December, sojourning privately at Highcliffe near Bournemouth on leaving Windsor. Again on his way to Marienbad the king spent another pleasant day with the emperor at Friedrichshof (11 August 1908). King Edward returned the German emperor's formal visit to Windsor in February 1909, when he and the queen stayed in Berlin. For the second time during his reign a cabinet minister bore him company on a foreign expedition. At Kiel some four years earlier the first lord of the admiralty, Lord Selborne, had been in the king's suite when he met his nephew. The king was now attended by the earl of Crewe, secretary for the colonies. On neither of the only two occasions when a cabinet minister attended the king abroad did the foreign minister go. In both instances the minister's presence was of complimentary rather than of diplomatic significance, and was a royal concession to the German emperor's love of ceremonial observance. The king's Berlin expedition did not differ from his visits of courtesy to other foreign capitals.

With the aged emperor of Austria, whom he had known and liked from boyhood, and in whose dominions he had often sojourned, the king was equally desirous of repeating friendly greetings in person. He paid the emperor a visit at Gmünden on his way out to Marienbad in August 1905, and on each of the two meetings with the German emperor at Cronberg, in August 1907 and August 1908, he went the next day to Ischl to offer salutations to Emperor Francis Joseph. All these meetings fell within the period of the king's usual autumn holiday. But on his second visit to Ischl the emperor of Austria entertained him to a state banquet, and Baron von Aerenthal, who was in attendance on his master, had some political conversation on affairs in Turkey and the Balkan provinces with Sir Charles Hardinge, who was in King Edward's retinue. But the king's concern with the diplomatic problem was remote. He was once more illustrating his zeal for ratifying by personal intercourse the wide bounds of his friendships with European sovereigns.

On the same footing stood the only visit which the king paid to the tsar of Russia during his reign. He made with the queen a special journey (9 June 1908) to Reval. It was the first visit ever paid to Russia by a British sovereign. It followed his cruise round the other northern capitals, and the king regarded as overdue the personal civility to the tsar, who was nephew of his wife, and to whom he was deeply attached. The tsar had been driven from his capital by revolutionary agitation and was in his yacht off Reval. The interview proved thoroughly cordial. French journalists hailed it with satisfaction; Germans scented in it a new menace, but the journey was innocent of diplomatic purpose. Objection was raised in the House of Commons that the king's visit showed sympathy with the tsar's alleged oppression of his revolutionary subjects. The suggestion moved the king's resentment. He acknowledged no connection between a visit to a royal kinsman and any phase of current political agitation. The unrest in Russia was no concern of his, and only awoke in him sympathy with the ruler whose life it oppressed. Unwisely the king took notice of the parliamentary criticism of his action, and cancelled the invitation to a royal garden party (20 June) of three members of parliament, who had questioned his prudence. His irritation soon passed away, but his mode of avowing annoyance was denounced by the labour party 'as an attempt by the court to influence members of parliament.' It was the only occasion during the reign on which the king invited any public suspicion of misinterpreting his constitutional position. The criticism to which he was subjected was due to a misunderstanding of the character of his foreign tours, but the interpellation was no infringement of public right.

He was hardly conscious of the deep-seated feeling which the alleged tyranny of the Russian government had excited in many quarters in England. When in the customary course of etiquette the king received the tsar as his guest at Cowes in August 1909 a fresh protest against his friendly attitude took the form of an influentially signed letter to the foreign secretary. But politics did not influence the king's relations with the tsar. The tsar was accompanied at Cowes by his foreign minister, M. Isvolsky; but as far as the king was concerned, the visit was solely a confirmation of old personal ties with the Russian sovereign, and lengthened impressively the roll of European rulers whom he sought to embrace in his comprehensive hospitality.

With the perilous vicissitudes of royalty the king naturally had a lively sympathy, and he suffered a severe shock on learning of the assassination of his friend and cousin and recent guest, King Carlos of Portugal, and of his son the crown prince in Lisbon on 2 Feb. 1908. Queen Amélie of

Portugal had been a prominent figure in the great assembly of royal personages at Windsor less than three months before. By way of emphasising their intense sorrow the king and queen and other members of the royal family defied precedent by attending a requiem mass at St. James's church, Spanish Place, near Manchester Square, on 8 Feb. in memory of the murdered monarch. It was the first time that an English sovereign had attended a Roman catholic service in Great Britain since the Reformation. By the king's wish, too, a memorial service was held next day in St. Paul's cathedral, which he and his family also attended. Both houses of parliament presented an address to the crown expressing indignation and deep concern at the outrages. The king's heartfelt sympathy went out to the new king of Portugal, the late king's younger son, Manoel, and in November next year he entertained the young monarch at Windsor, investing him with the order of the Garter, and greeting him at a state banquet on 16 Nov. as 'the heir of our oldest ally in history.' King Manoel was King Edward's last royal guest. There was some irony in the circumstance. King Manoel's royal career was destined to be brief, and within five months of King Edward's death his subjects established a republic and drove him from his throne to seek an asylum in England.

Although so substantial a part of his reign was passed abroad, the king manifested activity in numberless directions when he was at home. From London, which was his headquarters, he made repeated expeditions into the country. As of old he was regular in attendance at Newmarket and other race meetings. Although he did not repeat during the reign his early triumphs on the turf, the successes of his horse Minoru, who won the Derby in 1909, greatly delighted the sporting public. He encouraged the opera and the theatres by frequent attendance. He was lavish in entertainment at Buckingham Palace and freely accepted hospitalities at the London houses of his friends. He was indefatigable in paying attention to foreign visitors to the capital, especially those of royal rank. When the duke of Abruzzi came at the end of 1906 to lecture to the Royal Geographical Society on his explorations of the Ruwenzori mountains in east Africa, the king was present and with impromptu grace and manifest desire to prove his interest in foreign policy moved a vote of thanks to the lecturer, whom he hailed as a kinsman of his ally the king of Italy (2 Jan. 1907). At stated seasons he was the guest for shooting or merely social recreation at many country houses, where he met at ease his unchanging social circle. From 1904 to 1907 he spent a week each January with the duke of Devonshire at Chatsworth. In the autumn he went a round of Scottish mansions.

While unremitting in his devotion to social pleasures, he neglected few of the philanthropic or other public movements with which he had already identified himself. Occasionally his foreign tours withdrew him from functions which could only be performed effectively at home. During the colonial conference of 1907 he was away from England, but he returned in time to entertain the colonial premiers at dinner on 8 May. On his birthday later in the year (9 Nov.) he received as a gift from the Transvaal people the Cullinan diamond, the largest diamond known, which was a notable tribute to the efficiency of the new settlement of south Africa. Two sections of the magnificent stone were set in the royal crown.

Every summer the king was at work both in London and the provinces, laying foundation stones and opening new public institutions. In London and the neighbourhood his varied engagements included the inaugurations of St. Saviour's cathedral, Southwark (3 July 1905); of the new streets Kingsway and Aldwych (18 Oct. 1905); of the new Victoria and Albert Museum, South Kensington (22 June 1909), and the laying of the first stone of the new buildings of the Imperial College of Science and Technology, South Kensington (8 July 1909).

To his earlier interests in medicine and therapeutics he was always faithful. On 3 Nov. 1903 he laid the foundation stone of the King Edward Sanatorium for Consumption at Midhurst, and he opened the building on 13 June 1906. He gave abundant proofs of his care for general hospitals; he opened a new wing of the London Hospital (11 June 1903) and laid foundation stones of the new King's College Hospital, Denmark Hill (20 July 1909), and of the new King Edward Hospital at Windsor (22 June 1908). His broad sympathies with philanthropic agencies he illustrated by receiving at Buckingham Palace 'General' Booth of the Salvation Army (22 June 1904) and Prebendary Carlile, head of the Church Army (13 Jan. 1905). His veteran interest in the housing of the poor led him to pay a visit (18 Feb. 1903) to the L.C.C. model dwellings at Millbank, and he showed a characteristic anxiety to relieve the sufferings of poverty by giving 2000 guineas to Queen Alexandra's Unemployment Fund (17 Nov. 1905).

In the country his public labours were year by year even more conspicuous. On 19 July 1904 he laid the foundation stone of the new Liverpool cathedral; and inaugurated the new King's Dock at Swansea (20 July) and the new water supply for Birmingham at Rhayader (21 July). A year later he visited Sheffield to instal the new university, and he went to Manchester to open a new dock of the Manchester Ship Canal and to unveil the war memorial at Salford. On 10 July 1906 he opened the high-level bridge at Newcastle, and later new buildings at Marischal College, Aberdeen (28 Sept.). In 1907 he laid the foundation stones of new buildings of University College of Wales at Bangor (9 July) and opened Alexandra Dock at Cardiff (13 July). In 1908 he opened the new university buildings at Leeds (7 July) and the new dock at Avonmouth, Bristol (9 July). In 1909 he returned to Manchester to open the new infirmary (6 July), and then passed on to Birmingham to inaugurate the new university buildings. His last public philanthropic function was to lay the corner stone of a new wing of the Norfolk and Norwich Hospital at Norwich (25 Oct. 1909).

To the public schools he showed as before many marks of favour. He twice visited Eton, on 13 June 1904, and again on 18 Nov. 1908, when he opened the hall and library, which formed the South African war memorial there. He was at Harrow School on 30 June 1905, and he opened the new buildings of University College School, Hampstead, on 26 July 1907, and a new speech room at Rugby on 3 July 1909. To Wellington College, founded by his father, he remained a frequent visitor, and on 21 June 1909 he attended the celebration of the college's jubilee. He proved his friendly intimacy with the headmaster, Dr. Bertram Pollock, by nominating him, as his personal choice, just before his death in 1910, to the bishopric of Norwich. It was the diocese in which lay his country seat.

To Ireland, where, in spite of political disaffection, the prince's personal charm had always won for him a popular welcome, he gave as king evidence of the kindliest feeling. In July 1903 he and the queen paid their first visit in their capacity of sovereigns soon after his first foreign tour. They landed at Kingstown on 31 July. Although the Dublin corporation refused by forty votes to thirty-seven to present an address, the people showed no lack of cordiality. The king with customary tact spoke of the very recent death of Pope Leo XIII whom he had lately visited, and he bestowed his favours impartially on protestant and Roman catholic. The catholic archbishop of Dublin, Dr. Walsh, attended a levee, and the king visited Maynooth College. He subsequently went north to stay with Lord Londonderry at Mount Stewart, and after a visit to Belfast made a yachting tour round the west coast, making inland excursions by motor. Coming south, he inspected the exhibition at Cork, and on leaving Queenstown on 1 August issued an address of thanks to the Irish people for his reception. He expressed a sanguine belief that a brighter day was dawning upon Ireland. There was good ground for the anticipation, for the Land Purchase Act which was passed during the year gave promise of increased prosperity.

A second visit to Ireland of a more private character followed in the spring of 1904 and confirmed the good impression of the first visit. Two visits of the sovereign in such rapid succession were unknown to recent Irish history. The king was now the guest of the duke of Devonshire at Lismore Castle, and of the marquis of Ormonde at Kilkenny Castle, and he attended both the Punchestown and Leopardstown races. His chief public engagement was the laying of the foundation stone of the new buildings of the Royal College of Science at Dublin (25 April–4 May). A third and last visit to Ireland took place in July 1907, when the king and queen opened at

Dublin the International Exhibition (10 July). The popular reception was as enthusiastic as before.

In his relations with the army and the navy he did all that was required of their titular head. Like his mother he was prouder of his association with the army than with the navy, but he acknowledged the need of efficiency in both services, and attached vast importance to details of etiquette and costume. He was an annual visitor at Aldershot, and was indefatigable in the distribution of war medals and new regimental colours. He did not study closely the principles or practice of army or navy organisation and he deprecated breaches with tradition. But he put no real obstacles in the way of the effective application of expert advice. He received daily reports of the army commission inquiry at the close of the South African war (1902–3), which led to extensive changes. The chief military reform of his reign was the formation in 1907 by Mr. (afterwards Viscount) Haldane of a territorial army. The king shared Queen Victoria's dislike of any plan that recalled Cromwell's régime, and he mildly demurred to the employment of Cromwell's term, 'County Association,' in the territorial scheme. But he was flattered by the request to inaugurate personally the new system. On 26 Oct. 1907 he summoned the lord-lieutenants of the United Kingdom to Buckingham Palace, and addressed them on the new duties that had been imposed on them as officers of the new territorial army. Twice in 1909—on 19 June at Windsor and on 5 July at Knowsley—he presented colours to territorial regiments. His attitude to measures was always conditioned to a large extent by his interest in the men who framed them, and his liking for Mr. Haldane, the war minister who created the territorial army, mainly inspired his personal patronage of the movement. In the navy the same sentiment was at work. His faith in Lord Fisher, who played a leading part in the re-organisation of the navy during the reign, reconciled him to alterations which often conflicted with his conservative predilections. A large increase in the navy took place while he was king, and one of his last public acts was to review in the Solent on 31 July 1909 an imposing assembly of naval vessels by way of a royal benediction on recent naval policy.

In home politics the king was for the most part content with the rôle of onlooker. He realised early that the constitution afforded him mere formalities of supervision which required no close application. He failed to persuade his ministers to deal with the housing question. Few other problems of domestic legislation interested him deeply, and he accepted without searching comment his ministers' proposals. To complicated legislative details he paid small heed, and although he could offer shrewd criticism on a subsidiary point which casually caught his eye or ear, he did not invite elaborate explanation. His conservative instinct enabled him to detect intuitively the dangers underlying political innovations, but he viewed detachedly the programmes of all parties.

When the tariff reform controversy arose in 1903 he read in the press the chief pleas of the tariff reformers, and remarked that it would be difficult to obtain popular assent to a tax on bread. He deprecated licensing reform which pressed unduly on the brewer and he was displeased with political oratory which appealed to class prejudice and excited in the poor unwarranted hopes. He was unmoved by the outcry against Chinese labour in south Africa. He was not in favour of woman's suffrage.

Disapproval of political action usually took the shape of a general warning addressed to the prime minister. In filling all offices he claimed to be consulted, and freely placed his knowledge and judgment of persons at his minister's disposal. But, save occasionally where he wished to serve a friend in a military, naval, colonial, diplomatic, or ecclesiastical promotion, the minister's choice was practically unfettered. The personal machinery of government interested him, however, more than its legislative work or policy, but he effected little of importance even in that direction. When in 1904 resignations rent asunder Mr. Balfour's ministry and reconstruction became necessary, the king made some endeavour to repair the breaches. He sought to overcome in a powerful quarter hesitation to co-operate with Mr. Balfour. But to the king's disappointment nothing came of his effort. It was one of many illustrations of his virtual powerlessness to influence political events.

On 5 Dec. 1905 the king accepted Mr. Balfour's resignation, and admitted to office his third prime minister, Sir Henry Campbell-Bannerman, the leader of the liberal party. The change of ministry was emphatically ratified by the general election of January 1906, and the liberals remained in power till the king's death. The fall of the conservatives caused the king little disquiet. The return of the liberals to office after a ten years' exclusion seemed to him to be quite fair, and to maintain a just equilibrium between opposing forces in the state. His relations with Gladstone had shown that a distrust of the trend of liberal policy need be no bar to friendly intimacy with liberal leaders. He had slightly known Campbell-Bannerman as minister of war in the last liberal administration of 1892–5. But the politician's severe strictures on military operations in south Africa during 1901 had displeased the king. Early in the reign he had hesitated to meet him at a private dinner party, but he suppressed his scruples and the meeting convinced him of Campbell-Bannerman's sincere anxiety to preserve the peace of Europe, while his Scottish humour attracted him.

With constitutional correctness the king abstained from interference in the construction of the new cabinet, and he received the new ministers with open-minded serenity. The innovation of including among them a labour member, Mr. John Burns, was not uncongenial to him. His earlier relations with Mr. Broadhurst and Mr. Arch taught him the prudence of bestowing responsible positions on representatives of labour. Mr. Burns personally interested him, and he was soon on cordial terms with him. With another of the liberal ministers, Lord Carrington, afterwards marquis of Lincolnshire, minister for agriculture, he had been intimate since boyhood. Mr. Herbert Gladstone, home secretary, was a son of his old friend. Mr. Haldane, secretary for war, whose genial temper and grasp of German life and learning appealed to him, quickly became a *persona grata*. With the ministers in other posts he found less in common, and he came into little contact with them, save in ceremonial functions.

The grant by the new ministry of self-government to the newly conquered provinces of south Africa excited the king's serious misgivings, and he feared a surrender of the fruits of the late war. But he contented himself with a remonstrance, and there was no diminution of his good relations with the liberal prime minister. After little more than two years of power Campbell-Bannerman fell ill, and from February 1908 his strength slowly failed. Just before setting out on his annual visit to Biarritz the king took farewell of the statesman at his official residence in Downing Street (4 March 1908). The king manifested the kindliest sympathy with his dying servant. A month later the prime minister forwarded his resignation, and recommended as his successor Mr. Asquith, the chancellor of the exchequer. The king was still at Biarritz, and thither Mr. Asquith travelled to surrender his old place and to be admitted to the headship of the government. There was a murmur of dissatisfaction that so important a function of state as the installation of a new prime minister should be performed by the king in a foreign hotel. Nothing of the kind had happened before in English history. The king's health was held to justify the breach of etiquette. But the episode brought into strong relief the king's aloofness from the working of politics and a certain disinclination hastily to adapt his private plans to political emergencies.

Mr. Asquith's administration was rapidly formed without the king's assistance. It mainly differed from that of his predecessor by the elevation of Mr. Lloyd George to the chancellorship of the exchequer and the admission of Mr. Winston Churchill to the cabinet. Neither appointment evoked royal enthusiasm. Mr. Lloyd George's speeches in the country often seemed to the king reckless and irresponsible. Mr. Churchill's father, Lord Randolph, had long been a close friend. Knowing the son from his cradle, the king found it difficult to reconcile himself to the fact that he was a grown man fitted for high office. With his new prime minister he was at once in easy intercourse, frankly and briefly expressing to him his views on current business, and suggesting or criticising appointments.

While he abstained from examining closely legislative details, and while he continued to regard his ministers' actions as matters for their own discretion, he found little in the ministerial proposals to command his personal approval. Especially did Mr. Lloyd George's budget of 1909, which imposed new burdens on landed and other property, cause him searchings of heart. But his tact did not permit him to forgo social courtesies to ministers whose policy seemed to him dangerous. In society he often gave those of them whose political conduct he least approved the fullest benefit of his charm of manner.

Domestic politics in the last part of his reign brought the king face to face with a constitutional problem for which he had an involuntary distaste. All disturbance of the existing constitution was repugnant to him. In view of the active hostility of the upper chamber to liberal legislation, the liberal government was long committed to a revision of the powers of the House of Lords. The king demurred to any alteration in the status or composition of the upper house, which in his view, as in that of his mother, was a bulwark of the hereditary principle of monarchy. A proposal on the part of conservative peers to meet the outcry against the House of Lords by converting it partly or wholly into an elective body conflicted as directly with the king's predilection as the scheme for restricting its veto. The king deprecated the raising of the question in any form.

In the autumn of 1909 a very practical turn was given to the controversy by the lords' threats to carry their antagonism to the year's budget to the length of rejecting it. Despite his dislike of the budget, the king believed the lords were herein meditating a tactical error. He resolved for the first time to exert his personal influence to prevent what he judged to be a political disaster. He hoped to exert the reconciling power which his mother employed in 1869 and again in 1884, when the two houses of parliament were in collision: in the first year over the Irish church disestablishment bill, in the second year over the extension of the franchise. The circumstances differed. In neither of the earlier crises was the commons' control of finance in question. Nor was the king's habit of mind as well fitted as his mother's for the persuasive patience essential to success in a difficult arbitration. The conservative peers felt that the king was in no position, whatever happened, to give their house protection from attack, and that he was prone by temperament to unquestioning assent to ministerial advice, which was the path of least resistance. Early in October 1909 he invited to Balmoral Lord Cawdor, one of the most strenuous champions of the uncompromising policy of the peers. The interview produced no result. A like fate attended the king's conversation, on his arrival at Buckingham Palace later in the month (12 Oct.), with the leaders of the conservative opposition in the two houses, Lord Lansdowne and

Mr. Balfour. Although these negotiations could only be strictly justified by the emergency, there was no overstepping of the limits of the royal power. Mr. Asquith was willing that the interviews should take place. The conversations were in each case immediately communicated by the king to the prime minister in personal audience.

The king's proved inability to qualify the course of events was a disappointment. The finance bill, which finally passed the House of Commons on 5 November by a majority of 379 to 149, was rejected by the lords on 30 November by 350 to 75. War to the knife was thereupon inevitable between the liberal party and the House of Lords, and the king at once acquiesced in the first steps of his government's plan of campaign. On 15 Dec. by the prime minister's advice he dissolved parliament, for the second time in his reign. The general election gave the government a majority which was quite adequate for their purpose. They lost on the balance seventy-five seats, and their former numerical superiority to any combination of other parties disappeared. But with nationalists and labour members they still were 124 in excess of their unionist opponents, and their efficient power to challenge the House of Lords' veto was unmodified. Mr. Asquith continued in office. The king was in no way involved in Mr. Asquith's declaration at the Albert Hall on the eve of the general election (10 Dec. 1909) that he would not again assume or hold office without the safeguards necessary to give legislative effect to the decisions of the majority in the House of Commons. Before the new parliament opened Mr. Asquith saw the king when he was staying privately at Brighton on 13 Feb. 1910. The king offered no impediment to the government's immediate procedure, which was publicly proclaimed eight days later when the king opened parliament and read his ministers' words: 'Proposals will be laid before you, with all convenient speed, to define the relations between the houses of parliament, so as to secure the undivided authority of the House of Commons over finance and its predominance in legislation. These measures, in the opinion of my advisers, should provide that this House [of Lords] should be so constituted and empowered as to exercise impartially, in regard to proposed legislation, the functions of initiation, revision, and, subject to proper safeguards, of delay.'

The presence in the second sentence of the phrase 'in the opinion of my advisers' gave rise to the misconception that the words were the king's interpolation, and were intended to express his personal unwillingness to identify himself with his ministers' policy. As a matter of fact the phrase was, like the rest of the paragraph, from the prime minister's pen, and the king made no comment on it when the draft was submitted to him. A similar formula had appeared previously in the speeches of sovereigns to parliament when they were under the formal obligation of announcing a warmly controverted policy of their ministers' devising. The king's personal misgivings of the constitutional change were well known, and it was courteous to absolve him of any possible implication of a personal responsibility.

In March the cabinet drafted resolutions (with a view to a future bill) which should disable the lords from rejecting or amending a money bill, and which should provide that a bill being passed by the commons in three successive sessions and being thrice rejected by the lords should become law in spite of the lords' dissent. The terms of the resolutions were laid before the king, and he abstained from remonstrance. The resolutions were duly carried on 12 April, and the bill which embodied them was formally introduced into the commons. Meanwhile Lord Rosebery on 14 March moved that the House of Lords resolve itself into committee to consider the best means of reforming its constitution so as to make it strong and efficient, and on 16 March the lords agreed to Lord Rosebery's motion. For such a solution of the difficulty the king had no more zest than for the commons' scheme. On 25 April parliament adjourned for Easter, and next day the text of the commons' veto bill was circulated. The controversy went no further in the king's lifetime.

The ministers were resolved in case of the peers' continued obduracy to advise the king to employ his prerogative so as to give their policy statutory effect. Should the majority of peers decline to pass the bill for the limitation of their veto, the ministers determined on a resort to Lord Grey's proposed plan of 1832, whereby a sufficient number of peers favourable to the government's purpose would be formally created in the king's name to outvote the dissentients. But the time had not arrived when it was necessary directly to invite the king's approval or disapproval of such a course of action. The king for his part did not believe that the matter would be pressed to the last extremity, and was content to watch the passage of events without looking beyond the need of the moment.

The political difficulty caused the king an anxiety and irritation which domestic policy had not previously occasioned him. He found no comfort in the action of any of the parties to the strife. The blank refusal of the conservative leaders to entertain his warnings was unwelcome to his *amour propre*. The prospect of straining his prerogative by creating peers solely for voting purposes could not be other than uncongenial. But while he tacitly recognised his inability to decline the advice of his responsible ministers, he had before him no plan for the creation of peers to call for an expression of opinion. To the last he privately cherished the conviction that peace would be reached by some less violent means. His natural buoyancy of disposition and his numerous social pleasures and interests outside the political sphere effectually counteracted the depressing influence of public affairs. While the last battle of his reign was waging in the houses of parliament he was spending his annual spring holiday at Biarritz, where his time was mainly devoted to cheerful recreation. He returned to England on 27 April, just when the Easter vacation called a parliamentary armistice. Within nine days he was dead.

On the political situation the effect of his death was a prolongation of the truce. A conference of representatives of the two parties met in the endeavour to adjust amicably the differences between the two houses. The effort failed (15 Nov. 1910), and after another dissolution of parliament (28 Nov.) the liberal government's plan, in which King Edward had tacitly acquiesced, was carried into law, with the consent of a majority of the upper chamber and without the threatened special creation of peers (10 Aug. 1911).

Since his severe illness of 1902 the king's physical condition, though not robust, had borne satisfactorily the strain of a busy life. He benefited greatly by his annual visits to Biarritz and Marienbad and by his yachting cruises, and he usually bore the appearance of good health. A somewhat corpulent habit of body rendered exercise increasingly difficult. He walked little and ate and smoked much. On the shooting expeditions in which he still took part he was invariably mounted, and his movements were slow. There were occasionally disquieting symptoms, and the king was not very ready in obeying medical directions when they interfered with his ordinary habits. But his general health was normal for his age.

For the past few years he was subject to sudden paroxysms of coughing, which indicated bronchial trouble. A seizure of the kind took place at the banquet at the British Embassy in Berlin on 8 Feb. 1909. On the outward journey to Biarritz early in March 1910 he stayed two days in Paris. A cold caught in the Théâtre Porte St. Martin, where he witnessed the performance of M. Rostand's 'Chantecler,' developed rapidly on the way south. A severe attack of bronchitis followed and caused his physician in attendance (Sir James Reid) much anxiety. The news of the illness was not divulged, and at the end of ten days recovery was rapid. A motor tour through the Pyrenees as far as Pau preceded his return home.

The king arrived in London from the continent on 27 April in good spirits. The same evening he went to the opera at Covent Garden. Queen Alexandra was absent on a Mediterranean cruise, sojourning for the time at Corfu. Next day the king paid his customary visit to the Royal Academy exhibition. On 29 April he entertained at lunch Viscount Gladstone on his departure for south Africa, where he had been appointed governor-general. Sunday, 1 May, was spent at Sandringham, where the king inspected some planting operations. There he contracted a chill. He reached Buckingham Palace next afternoon, and imprudently dined out in private the same evening. On reaching Buckingham Palace late that night his breathing became difficult, and a severe bronchial malady set in. Next morning his physicians regarded his condition as somewhat serious, but no early crisis was anticipated. The king rose as usual and transacted business, making arrangements for his reception the following week of Mr. Theodore Roosevelt, the late president of the United States of America, who had announced a visit to England. He spoke regretfully of the superiority of the climate of Biarritz to that of London. During the two following days the symptoms underwent little change. The king continued to transact business, receiving each morning in formal audience one or more representatives of the colonies. On Thursday, 5 May, he received Sir John Dickson-Poynder, Lord Islington, who had been appointed governor of New Zealand, and he considered details of the welcome to be accorded to a royal visitor from Japan, Prince Fushimi. He sat up and was dressed with his customary spruceness, but he was counselled against conversation. The breathing difficulty fluctuated and did not yield to treatment. Meanwhile Queen Alexandra had been informed of the king's illness and was returning from Corfu. The king was reluctant for any public announcement of his condition to be made. But on the Thursday evening (5 May) he was persuaded to assent to the issue of a bulletin on the ground that his enforced inability to meet the queen, according to custom on her arrival at the railway station, called for explanation. He modified the draft with his own hand. Queen Alexandra reached the palace that night, and next morning (6 May) the news of the king's condition appeared in the press. That day proved his last. He rose as usual, and in the morning saw his friend, Sir Ernest Cassel. As the day advanced, signs of coma developed. In the evening his state was seen to be hopeless. About ten o'clock at night he was put to bed. He died just before midnight.

The shock of grief was great at home and abroad. The public sorrow exceeded that mighty outburst which his mother's death awoke in 1901. Yet the king may fairly be judged to be 'felix opportunitate mortis.' To the last he was able to conduct his life much as he pleased. In the course of the illness he had faced without repining the thought of death. He was spared any long seclusion from society or that enforced inactivity of slowly dwindling strength of which he cherished a dread. His popularity had steadily grown through his reign of nine years and three and a half months. There had been no conflicts with public opinion. Practically all his actions, as far as they were known, had evoked the enthusiasm of the mass of his subjects. There was a bare possibility of his injuring, there was no possibility of his improving, his position, in which he had successfully reconciled pursuit of private pleasure with the due performance of public duty.

On 7 May the king's only surviving son met the privy council at St. James's Palace, and was proclaimed as King George V on 9 May. On 11 May the new monarch formally announced his bereavement in messages to both houses of parliament, which had been in recess and were hastily summoned to meet. Addresses of condolence were impressively moved by the leaders of the two great parties in both houses of parliament—in the House of Lords by the earl of Crewe and Lord Lansdowne, and by Mr. Asquith and Mr. Balfour in the House of Commons. Mr. Enoch Edwards, on behalf of the labouring population, also gave voice in the lower house to the general sentiment of admiration and grief.

Fitting funeral ceremonies followed. For two days (14–15 May) the coffin lay in state in the throne room at Buckingham Palace, and there it was visited privately by relatives, friends, and acquaintances. On 16 May the coffin was removed in ceremonial procession to Westminster Hall, and there it lay publicly in state for four days. Some 350,000 persons attended. The interment took place on 20 May. The procession passed from Westminster Hall to Paddington station, and thence by train to Windsor. After the funeral service in St. George's Chapel, the coffin was lowered to the vault below. Besides the members of the king's family the chief mourners included the German emperor (the king's nephew), the king of Norway (his son-in-law), and the kings of Denmark and Greece (his brothers-in-law). Four other kings were present, those of Spain, Bulgaria, Portugal, and Belgium, together with the heirs to the thrones of Austria, Turkey, Roumania, Servia, and Montenegro. There were also kinsmen of other rulers, the prince consort of the Netherlands, Grand Duke Michael of Russia, and the duke of Aosta. The American republic had a special envoy in Mr. Roosevelt, lately president, and the French republic in M. Pichon, minister for foreign affairs. No more representative assembly of the sovereignty of Europe had yet gathered in one place. The exclusively military character of the ceremonial excited some adverse comment, but all classes took part in memorial services and demonstrations of mourning, not only in London and the provinces but throughout the empire and the world. In India, Hindus and Mohammedans formally celebrated funeral rites.

Edward VII eminently satisfied contemporary conditions of kingship. He inherited the immense popularity which belonged to the crown at the close of his mother's reign, and his personality greatly strengthened the hold of royalty on public affection. The cosmopolitan temperament, the charm of manner, the social tact, fitted him admirably for the representative or symbolic function of his great station. A perfect command of the three languages, English, French, and German, in all of which he could speak in public on the inspiration of the moment with no less grace than facility, gave him the ear of Europe. Probably no king won so effectually the good-will at once of foreign peoples and of his own subjects. He was a citizen of the world, gifted with abounding humanity which evoked a universal sympathy and regard.

The outward forms of rule were congenial to him. He deemed public ceremony essential to the royal state, and attached high value to formal dignity. Spacious splendour appealed to him. By all the minutiæ of etiquette he set great store, and he exerted his authority in securing their observance. For any defect in costume or uniform he had an eagle eye and was plainspoken in rebuke.

King Edward cannot be credited with the greatness that comes of statesmanship and makes for the moulding of history. Neither the constitutional checks on his power nor his discursive tastes and training left him much opportunity of influencing effectually political affairs. No originating political faculty can be assigned him. For the most part he stood with constitutional correctness aloof from the political arena at home. On questions involving large principles he held no very definite views. He preferred things to remain as they were. But he regarded all party programmes with a cheerful optimism, sanguinely believing that sweeping proposals for reform would not go very far. From youth he followed with close attention the course of foreign politics, and it was not only during his reign that he sought in tours abroad and in hospitalities at home to keep in personal touch with foreign rulers and statesmen. His main aim as a traveller was pleasurable recreation and the exchange of social courtesies. But he rarely missed an occasion of attesting his love of peace among the nations. Not that he was averse from strong measures, if he thought them necessary to the due assertion of his country's rights. But in his later years he grew keenly alive to the sinfulness of provoking war lightly, and to the obligation that lay on rulers of only appealing to its arbitrament in the last resort. He was a peacemaker, not through the exercise of any diplomatic initiative or ingenuity, but by force of his faith in the blessing of peace and by virtue of the influence which passively attached to his high station and to his temperament. His frequent absences from his dominions remotely involved his position in a certain element of danger. There was a specious ground for the suggestion that in home affairs he did too little and in foreign affairs too much. The external show of personal control which belongs to the crown at home seemed at times to be obscured by his long sojourns in foreign countries. The impression was at times encouraged, too, that the king was exerting abroad diplomatic powers which under the constitution belonged to his ministers alone. He grew conscious of the exaggerated importance which the foreign public attached to his foreign movements, and he confessed at times to some embarrassment. But he fully realised the futility of encroaching on ministerial responsibilities, and in his intercourse with foreign rulers and diplomatists, so far as politics came within the range of the conversation, he confined himself to general avowals of loyal support of ministerial policy.

His sociability, his love of pleasure, and the breadth of his human interests stood him in good stead in all relations of life. He had an unaffected desire for others' happiness, and the sport and amusements in which he openly indulged were such as the mass of his subjects could appreciate and share. The austere looked askance on his recreations or deemed that the attention he paid them was excessive. But his readiness to support actively causes of philanthropy and social beneficence almost silenced articulate criticism. His compassion for suffering was never in question. He valued his people's approbation, and welcomed suggestions for giving every class opportunities of greeting him in person. Many times he cheerfully responded to a schoolmaster's request that in passing a schoolhouse on a private or public journey he should pause and exchange salutations with the schoolchildren. With the promptitude of an expert man of business, he was able to distribute his energies over a very wide field with small detriment to any of the individual calls on his time. He had a passion for punctuality. The clocks at Sandringham were always kept half an hour fast. He gave every encouragement to the progress of mechanical invention for the economising of time which distinguished his reign. He became an ardent devotee of motoring, in which he first experimented in 1899, and which during his last years formed his ordinary mode of locomotion at home and abroad. In the development of wireless telegraphy he also showed much interest, exchanging some of the earliest wireless messages across the Atlantic with Lord Minto, governor-general of Canada (21 Dec. 1902), and with President Roosevelt (19 Jan. 1903).

He had a strong sense of ownership and was proud of his possessions. Though his attitude to art was largely that of a rich owner of a great collection, he had a keen eye for the fit arrangement of his treasures, and knew much of their history. He disliked wasteful expenditure, but personally made careful provision for his own and his friends' comfort. No pride of rank limited his acquaintance, and he always practised hospitality on a generous scale. If he had a predilection for men of wealth, his catholic favour embraced every kind of faculty and fortune. He rejoiced to escape from the constraints of public life into the unconventional ease of privacy. At times he enjoyed practical joking at the expense of close friends. But while encouraging unembarrassed social intercourse, he tacitly made plain the limits of familiarity which might not be overstepped with impunity. He loved the old fashions of domesticity. His own and his relatives' birthdays he kept religiously, and he set high value on birthday congratulations and gifts.

While he derived ample amusement from music and the drama, chiefly from the theatre's more frivolous phases, he showed small capacity for dramatic criticism. A man of the world, he lacked the intellectual equipment of a thinker, and showed on occasion an unwillingness to exert his mental powers. He was no reader of books. He could not concentrate his mind on them. Yet he was always eager for information, and he gathered orally very varied stores of knowledge. A rare aptitude for rapidly assimilating the outlines of a topic enabled him to hold his own in brief talk with experts in every subject. He did not sustain a conversation with much power or brilliance; but his grace and charm of manner atoned for any deficiency of matter. If his interest lay more in persons than in things, he remembered personal details with singular accuracy. He illustrated his curiosity about persons by subjecting all his guests at Sandringham to the test of a weighing machine, and by keeping the record himself. At the same time he deprecated malicious gossip, and his highest praise of anyone was that he spoke no ill-natured word. He was never happy save with a companion who could talk freely and cheerfully. Solitude and silence were abhorrent to him.

A loyal friend, he was never unmindful of a friendly service, and he was always faithful to the associates of his early days. He was fond of offering his friends good advice, and was annoyed by its neglect. He could be at times hasty and irritable; but his anger was short-lived, and he bore no lasting ill-will against those who excited it. His alert memory enabled him from boyhood to death to recognise persons with sureness, and many stories are told how instantaneously he greeted those to whom he had been once casually introduced when meeting them years afterwards in a wholly unexpected environment. His circle of acquaintants at home and abroad was probably wider than that of any man of his time. But he never seems to have forgotten a face.

Physical courage was an enduring characteristic. By bodily peril or adverse criticism he was wholly unmoved. If his native shrewdness stimulated an instinct of self-preservation, he never showed any sign of flinching in the face of danger. He admired every manifestation of heroism, and in 1907 he instituted the Edward medal to reward heroic acts performed by miners and quarrymen. Two years later a like recognition was designed for brave service on the part of policemen and firemen. While religion played no dominant part in his life, he was strict in religious observances, and required those in his employment at Sandringham to attend church regularly. He had a perfect tolerance for all creeds, and treated with punctilious courtesy ministers of every religious persuasion.

He was greatly attached to dumb animals, and his love for dogs excelled even that for horses. A favoured dog was always his companion at home and abroad. On tombstones in the canine graveyard at Sandringham there are many inscriptions bearing witness to the king's affection for his dog companions. The latest of these favourites, his terrier, 'Caesar,' was led behind his coffin in the funeral procession.

As the heir to the crown, the eldest son of Queen Victoria and Prince Albert was the subject of portraiture from his infancy. The earliest portrait apparently is the large chalk drawing by Sir George Hayter in 1842. As a child the Prince of Wales was painted several times by Winterhalter, the court painter, and was also drawn and painted in miniature by Sir William C. Ross. Most of these early portraits, some of which are familiar from engravings or lithographs, remain in the royal collection at Buckingham Palace or Windsor Castle. The prince was painted in groups with his parents and brothers and sisters by Sir Edwin Landseer and Robert Thorburn, as well as by Winterhalter. A portrait by W. Hensel was painted in 1844 for King Frederick William of Prussia, one of the prince's godfathers. Other portraits were also drawn by R. J. Lane and artists who enjoyed the queen's confidence. As the youth of the Prince of Wales happened to synchronise with the invention and great development of portrait photography, his portraits during boyhood up to the time of his marriage were for the most part based on photography, several excellent engravings being made from them. When about sixteen the prince was drawn and painted by George Richmond, R.A., and in 1862 a portrait in academical robes was painted by command for the University of Oxford by Sir J. Watson Gordon. Portraits of the prince in plain clothes were painted by S. Walton (1863) and Henry Weigall (1865). After the prince entered the army and joined the 10th hussars, he was painted in uniform several times by Winterhalter (1858), by Lowes C. Dickinson (1868), by H. Weigall (1870), and by H. von Angeli (1876). At the time of his marriage to Princess Alexandra of Denmark in 1863 a pair of portraits of the bridal couple were painted by Winterhalter. Among foreign artists who painted the Prince of Wales were Karl Sohn and Theodor Jentzen, but perhaps the most interesting was J. Bastien-Lepage, to whom the prince sat in Paris in 1880. During his later years as Prince of Wales the prince was not very frequently painted, except for official purposes, such as the portraits by Frank Holl, painted in 1884 for the Middle Temple and in 1888 for the Trinity House. A full-length portrait, painted by G. F. Watts, R.A., for Lincoln's Inn, was not considered successful, and was therefore withdrawn by the painter; it is now in the Watts Gallery at Compton in Surrey. The most successful of official pictures was the full-length standing portrait by A. Stuart-Wortley, painted in 1893 for the United Service Club. W. W. Ouless's painting of the prince as commodore of the Royal Yacht Squadron was executed in 1900. After the accession of King Edward VII to the throne in 1901, portraits of his majesty became more in demand. The official state portrait was entrusted to Mr. (afterwards Sir) Luke Fildes, R.A., and was exhibited at the Royal Academy in 1902. The design for the portrait of the king on the coinage, postage-stamps, and certain medals was entrusted to Mr. Emil Fuchs. Subsequent portraits of the king were painted by H. Weigall (for Wellington College), Harold Speed (for Belfast), Colin Forbes (for the Canadian Houses of Parliament at Ottawa), A. S. Cope, A.R.A. (in Garter robes; for Sir Ernest Cassel), P. Tennyson-Cole (for the Liverpool Chamber of Commerce, by whom it was presented to the king; a replica is in the possession of the Grocers' Company), James Mordecai (now in St. James's Palace), and Sir E. J. Poynter P.R.A. (for the Royal Academy). During the reign and after the king's death the number of pictorial presentments of every description increased to an indefinite extent. The king sat to more than one foreign painter. The greater number of the portraits mentioned here were exhibited at the Royal Academy.

Portraits in sculpture of King Edward VII as Prince of Wales or as king are also very numerous, whether busts or statues, from his childhood to his death, while posthumous busts continue in demand. He sat to both English and foreign sculptors, including Canonica, the Italian. A colossal bronze equestrian statue of the Prince of Wales as colonel of the 10th hussars, by Sir J. Edgar Boehm, was presented to the city of Bombay by Sir Albert Sassoon in 1878.

The pictures of public events in which the king played the chief part are very many, including his baptism in 1842, painted by Sir George Hayter, Louis Haghe, George Baxter, and others; his marriage in 1863, painted by W. P. Frith, R.A., and G. H. Thomas; the paintings of the jubilee ceremonies in 1887 and 1897; the marriages of his brothers, sisters, and children; ceremonies at Windsor Castle, such as 'The Visit of Louis Philippe' and 'The Emperor of the French receiving the Order of the Garter'; leading up to the events of his own reign, 'The King opening his First Parliament' by Max Cowper; 'The King receiving the Moorish Embassy in St. James's Palace' by J. Seymour Lucas, R.A.; 'The Coronation of King Edward VII' by E. A. Abbey, R.A., and like events. During the Indian tour of 1875 a number of incidents were recorded in drawings by Sydney P. Hall, W. Simpson, and other artists. Most of these remain in the royal collection. A valuable collection of original drawings for illustrated periodicals, depicting scenes in his majesty's reign, is in possession of Queen Alexandra.

King Edward was a good and willing sitter, but a difficult subject. Hardly any portrait gives a satisfactory idea of a personality in which so much depended upon the vivacity of the likeness. One of the best likenesses is considered to be that in the group of the Prince of Wales and the duke of Connaught at Aldershot, painted by Edouard Détaille, and presented to Queen Victoria by the royal family at the Diamond Jubilee in 1897. Another good portrait is that in the group of Queen Victoria with her son, grandson, and great-grandson, painted by (Sir) W. Q. Orchardson, R.A., in 1900 for the Royal Agricultural Society.

Memorials of the king were planned after his death in all parts of the world. In England it was decided that there should be independent local memorials rather than a single national memorial. In London it is proposed to erect a statue in the Green Park, and to create a park at Shadwell, a poor and crowded district of east London. In many other cities a statue is to be combined with some benevolent purpose, such as a hospital or a fund for fighting disease. Statues have been designed for Montreal, Calcutta, and Rangoon, and hospitals are also in course of erection at Lahore, Calcutta, Bombay, Madras, Secunderabad, Cashmere, Bornu, Bassein, and Poona. Memorial tablets have been placed in the English churches at Homburg, Marienbad, and Copenhagen. A statue by M. Denys Puech was unveiled at Cannes on 13 April 1912 by M. Poincaré, prime minister of France, amid an imposing naval and military demonstration. A new street and a 'place' in the heart of Paris are to be named after 'Edouard VII.' At Lisbon a public park was named after him in memory of the visit of 1903. At Cambridge University Sir Harold Harmsworth endowed in 1911 'The King Edward VII chair of English literature.'

[No attempt at a full biography has yet been made. The outward facts are summarised somewhat hastily and imperfectly in the obituary notices of the press (7 May 1910), but they are satisfactorily recorded, with increasing detail as the years progressed, in The Times, to which the indexes are a more or less useful guide. The fullest account of the external course of his life from his birth to his accession is given in W. H. Wilkins's Our King and Queen (1903), republished in 1910 with slight additions as Edward the Peacemaker. Various periods and episodes of his career have been treated either independently or in the biographies of persons who were for the time associated with him. A good account of the king's education from private documents at Windsor by Lord Esher appeared anonymously in the Quarterly Review, July 1910. The main facts of his youth are detailed in A. M. Broadley's The Boyhood of a Great King (1906); Queen Victoria's Letters 1837–61 (ed. Esher and Benson, 1907); Sir Theodore Martin's Life of Prince Consort (1874–80). The Greville Memoirs and the memoirs of Baron Stockmar are also useful. For his early manhood and middle age Sidney Whitman's Life of the Emperor Frederick (1901) is of value. For the Canadian and American tour of 1860 see N. A. Woods, The Prince of Wales in Canada and the United States (1861), Bunbury Gooch's The King's visit to Canada, 1860 (1910), and J. B. Atlay's Life of Sir Henry Acland (1903). For the tour in the Holy Land of 1862 see Prothero and Bradley's Life of Dean Stanley (1883), who published Sermons before the Prince during the Tour (1863). For the tour of 1869 see Mrs. William Grey's Journal of a Visit to Egypt, Constantinople, the Crimea, Greece, &c., in the Suite of the Prince and Princess of Wales (1869), and (Sir) W. H. Russell, A Diary in the East during the Tour of the Prince and Princess of Wales (1869). The chief account of the Indian tour is W. H. Russell's Diary (1877). Sir Joseph Fayrer, who privately printed Notes of the Indian Tour, gives very many particulars in Recollections of my Life (1900). The prince's philanthropic work can be followed in Sir H. C. Burdett's An Account of the Social Progress and Development of our own Times, as illustrated by the Public Life and Work of the Prince and Princess of Wales (1889), with The Speeches and Addresses of the Prince of Wales, 1863–1888, ed. by James Macaulay (1889), and The Golden Book of King Edward VII (1910), which collects many of his public utterances. References of varying interest appear in Lady Bloomfield's Reminiscences of Diplomatic Life (1883); Lord Augustus Loftus's Reminiscences (1892–4); Lord Malmesbury's Memoirs (1884); Sir Henry Keppel's A Sailor's Life under Four Sovereigns (1899); Col. R. S. Liddell's Memoirs of the 10th Royal (Prince of Wales's own) Hussars (1891); Arminius Vambéry's Memoirs (1904); Morley's Life of Gladstone; Sir Alfred Lyall's Life of Lord Dufferin (1905); Sir Horace Rumbold's Recollections of a Diplomatist (2 vols. 1902), Further Recollections (1903), and Final Recollections (1909); Edgar Sheppard's George, Duke of Cambridge, a Memoir of his Private Life (chiefly extracts from his diary), 2 vols. 1906; Sir C. Kinloch-Cooke's Mary Adelaide, Duchess of Teck (1900); as well as in Lives of Charles Kingsley, (Sir) Richard Owen, Laurence Oliphant, Sir Richard Burton, Lord Houghton, and Sir Samuel Baker. Some hints on the social side of his career are given in The Private Life of King Edward VII (1903); Society in the New Reign, by a foreign resident (i.e. T. H. S. Escott) (1904); Paoli's My Royal Clients (1911), gossip of a detective courier, and more authentically in Lady Dorothy Nevill's Reminiscences (1906) and Mme. Waddington's Letters of a Diplomat's Wife (1903). His chief residences are described in Mrs. Herbert Jones's Sandringham (1873) and A. H. Beavan's Marlborough House and its Occupants (1896); A full account of The Coronation of King Edward VII, by J. E. C. Bodley, appeared in 1903. Edward VII as a Sportsman (1911), by Alfred E. T. Watson, with introd. by Capt. Sir Seymour Fortescue, and contributions by various friends, gives an adequate account of the king's sporting life. Of foreign estimates of the king, which are for the most part misleading, the most interesting are Louis Blanc's Lettres sur l'Angleterre (1867); J. H. Aubry's Edward VII Intime (Paris, 1902), a favourable but outspoken estimate; Jean Grand-Carteret's L'oncle de l'Europe (1906), a study of the king in French and other caricature; M. Henri Daragon's Voyage à Paris de S.M. Édouard VII (1903), a detailed journal of the visit; Émile Flourens' La France Conquise: Édouard VII et Clemenceau (1906), an indictment of the policy of the 'entente cordiale,' and an allegation that King Edward was personally moved by a Machiavellian design of holding France in subjection to English interests; and Jacques Bardoux, Victoria I; Édouard VII; Georges V (Paris, 2nd ed. 1911, pp. 149 seq.). The German view may be gleaned from Austin Harrison's England and Germany (1909) and Max Harden's Köpfe (part ii., Berlin, 1912). Some hints of the king's relations with the successive rulers

of Germany are given in: Memoirs of Prince Chlodwig of Hohenlohe-Schillings-
fürst (trans., 2 vols. 1906); Moritz Busch's Bismarck, Some Secret Pages from his
History (trans., 3 vols. 1898); Bismarck, His Reflections and Reminiscences
(trans., 1898); untranslated Supplement ('Anhang') to latter work, in 2 vols. respectively entitled Kaiser Wilhelm und Bismarck and Aus Bismarcks Briefwechsel, ed. Horst Kohl (Stuttgart, 1901). The account of the portraits has been
supplied by Mr. Lionel Cust. In preparing this article the writer has had the
benefit of much private information, but he is solely responsible for the use
to which the material has been put.]

SIDNEY LEE

published 1912

Maud Mary

(1843–1878)

Princess of Great Britain and Ireland, duchess of Saxony, and grand
duchess of Hesse-Darmstadt, the third child and second daughter of
Queen Victoria and the Prince Consort, was born at Buckingham Palace
on 25 April 1843. Her third name was given in honour of the queen's
aunt, the Duchess of Gloucester, who had been born on St. Mark's day
sixty-seven years before. 'Bright, joyous, and singularly attractive' (Earl
Granville) almost from her cradle, she was early described by her father as
'the beauty of the family, and an extraordinary good and merry child.'

The Princess Alice became one of the most accomplished young ladies
in England. She was sympathetic and affectionate. In a characteristic letter
of condolence, 24 May 1861, to one of her instructors, she describes herself
as having 'so lately for the first time seen death,' the allusion being to the
Duchess of Kent, whose decease had taken place in the month of March
previous. In December of the same year she became more widely known
as the assiduous nurse of her father during his last illness, when she was, in
the queen's own words, 'the great comfort and support' of her mother.

On 1 July 1862 she became the wife of Prince Frederick William Louis of
Hesse, nephew of Louis III, grand duke of Hesse-Darmstadt, to whose
throne he succeeded, as Louis IV, on 13 June 1877. 'The principal
characteristics of her married life appear to have been—first, absolute
devotion to her husband and children; next, a course not merely of benevolence, but of unceasing, thoughtful benevolence to all depending
upon her; and, lastly, a remarkable talent for acquiring the sympathy and

461

attracting the regard of some of the most gifted of the intellectual country which she had adopted, and to whose interests she was devoted, without ever breaking a link in the chain of memories and associations which bound her to the country of her birth' (Earl Granville, 17 Dec. 1878). Brilliant but solid in her accomplishments, she took an increasing interest in German art and literature, and was an accomplished sculptor and painter. At her death it was said of her by a German authority that 'Art mourned in her her noblest patroness.' D. F. Strauss, whose acquaintance she made in 1868, read his 'Voltaire' to her in manuscript in 1870, and dedicated it to her when published by her express desire.

The Franco-German war called forth her philanthropy, and she set the example of nursing the sick and wounded, French as well as German, as they crowded the hospital at Darmstadt, in the midst of anxieties for the safety of her husband, then in the field. She became the foundress of the Women's Union for nursing the Sick and Wounded in War, which was called after her name. In December 1871 she contributed by her devoted nursing to the recovery of her brother the Prince of Wales.

The family of the Princess Alice and her husband consisted of five daughters and two sons, one of whom, Prince Frederick William, a child of less than three years of age, fell, almost under her eyes, from a window of the palace, 29 May 1873, and received injuries from which he died. On 16 Nov. 1878 her youngest child, the Princess Mary, died in her fifth year from diphtheria, an epidemic which had within eight days, 6–14 Nov., prostrated nearly every member of the grand-ducal family. The mother, already worn out by her ministrations to her husband and children, caught the infection. 'My lords,' said the Earl of Beaconsfield, in addressing the House of Peers upon the occasion, 'there is something wonderfully piteous in the immediate cause of her death. The physicians who permitted her to watch over her suffering family enjoined her under no circumstances whatever to be tempted into an embrace. Her admirable self-restraint guarded her through the crisis of this terrible complaint in safety. She remembered and observed the injunctions of her physicians. But it became her lot to break to her son, quite a youth, the death of his youngest sister, to whom he was devotedly attached. The boy was so overcome with misery that the agitated mother clasped him in her arms, and thus she received the kiss of death.' She died on 14 Dec. 1878, being the seventeenth anniversary of the decease of her father. She was buried, 18 Dec., in the mausoleum at Rosenhohe. The English flag was laid upon her coffin, in accordance with a desire she had fondly expressed.

The beneficence of the grand duchess was varied and discriminating. She took pains to instruct herself in the methods of philanthropy, attending meetings and visiting institutions without parade, and 'as a woman among women.' She translated into German some of Miss Octavia Hill's essays 'On the Homes of the London Poor,' and published them with a little preface of her own (to which only her initial A. was affixed), in the hope that the principles which had been successfully applied in London by Miss Hill and her coadjutors might be put into action in some of the German cities.

[A memoir by Dr. Sell of Darmstadt, with a translation of the princess's letters to her mother, was published in German in 1883; and the letters in the original, with a translation of the memoir, were published in London, 1884. See also Martin's Life of the Prince Consort; The Princess Alice in Social Notes, 4 Jan. 1879; Speeches of the Earl of Beaconsfield and Earl Granville, 17 Dec. 1878; the Queen's letter to the Home Secretary, 26 Dec. 1878; Times, December 1878.]

ARTHUR HENRY GRANT

published 1885

ALFRED Ernest Albert

(1844–1900)

Duke of Saxe-Coburg and Gotha

Second son of Queen Victoria and Prince Albert, was born at Windsor Castle on 6 Aug. 1844. In 1856 Lieutenant (afterwards Sir John) Cowell of the royal engineers was appointed his governor, and in October 1857 he was established at Alverbank, a cottage near Gosport, where he was prepared for the navy by the Rev. William Rowe Jolley, a chaplain and naval instructor. It was the wish of the prince consort that the boy should pass the usual entry examination, which he did in August 1858, when he was appointed to the Euryalus, a 50-gun screw frigate, specially commissioned by Captain John Walter Tarleton, well known as a good and careful officer. The Euryalus went in the first instance to the Mediterranean, and afterwards to the Cape of Good Hope and Natal, giving the young prince the opportunity for an excursion into the Orange Free State. On his return to Cape Town he tilted (on 17 Sept. 1860) the first load of stones into the sea for the breakwater in Table Bay. From the Cape the Euryalus went to the West Indies, and returned to England in August 1861. The prince was then appointed to the St. George with Captain the Hon. Francis Egerton for service in the Channel, North America, West Indies, and the Mediterranean, being, by the special desire of his father, treated on board as the other midshipmen; on shore he occasionally took his place as the son of the queen. It was not, however, considered necessary, or indeed advisable, to subject him to the prescribed limits of age and service.

In the winter of 1862–3 a prospect of securing a foreign throne was suddenly presented to Prince Alfred, and as suddenly withdrawn. The citizens of the kingdom of Greece, having deprived their despotic king, Otho, of the crown, marked their confidence in England by bestowing the dignity on the queen of England's second son by an overwhelming majority of votes, cast on an appeal to universal suffrage (6–15 Dec. 1862). The total number of votes given was 241,202; of these Prince Alfred received 230,016. His election, which was hailed throughout Greece with unqualified enthusiasm, was ratified by the National Assembly (3 Feb. 1863). The queen was not averse to Prince Alfred's acceptance of the honour, but Lord Palmerston, the prime minister, with Earl Russell, the foreign secretary, knew that the proposal contravened an arrangement already entered into with Russia and France, whereby no prince of any of these countries could ascend the throne of Greece. Accordingly, the crown was refused. At Lord Russell's suggestion, however, negotiations were opened with Prince Alfred's uncle, Duke Ernest of Saxe-Coburg-Gotha, with a view to his filling the vacant office, but it was deemed essential that Duke Ernest, who was childless, should, if he assented, renounce at once his duchy of Saxe-Coburg in favour of his nephew, Prince Alfred. This condition Duke Ernest and his council declined to entertain, and the Greek throne was finally accepted (30 March 1863) by (William) George, second son of Prince Christian of Schleswig-Holstein-Glücksburg, who, in accordance with an earlier treaty, soon became king of Denmark (15 Nov. 1863). Meanwhile Alexandra, the sister of the newly chosen king of Greece and daughter of Prince Christian, married, on 10 March 1863, Prince Alfred's brother, the Prince of Wales. One result of these transactions was the formal execution by the Prince of Wales, who was the next heir to his uncle Ernest of Saxe-Coburg-Gotha in the succession to the throne of that duchy, of a deed of renunciation, which transferred his title in the duchy to Alfred, his next brother (19 April 1863). After more than thirty years the deed took effect (Malmesbury, *Memoirs*, p. 567; Duke Ernest of Saxe-Coburg, *Memoirs*, iv. 85–90; Finlay, *History of Greece*, vii. 289 seq.).

Meanwhile, Prince Alfred steadily pursued his career in the British navy. On 24 Feb. 1863 he was promoted to be lieutenant of the Racoon with Captain Count Gleichen. In her he continued for three years, and on 23 Feb. 1866 he was promoted to be captain (passing over the intermediate rank of commander). At the same time he was granted by parliament an income of 15,000l. a year, dating back to the day of his majority (6 Aug. 1865), and on the queen's birthday (24 May 1866) he was created Duke of

Edinburgh and Earl of Ulster and Kent. The orders of the Garter, Thistle, and St. Patrick, Grand Cross of the Bath, St. Michael and St. George, Star of India, Indian Empire, and all the principal foreign orders were conferred on him. In March 1866 he was elected master of the Trinity House; in June he received the freedom of the city of London.

In January 1867 he commissioned the Galatea, and in her visited Rio Janeiro, the Cape, Adelaide, Melbourne, Tasmania, and Sydney. At this last place he was shot in the back by an Irishman named O'Farrell (12 March 1868). The wound was fortunately trifling, but the indignation excited was very great, and O'Farrell was tried, convicted, and executed in the course of a few weeks. The Galatea returned to England in the summer of 1868. After a short stay she again sailed for the far East, visiting India, China, and Japan, where the duke was honourably received by the Mikado. The Galatea returned to England and was paid off in the summer of 1871. In February 1876 the duke was appointed to the ironclad Sultan, one of the fleet in the Mediterranean under Sir Geoffrey Thomas Phipps Hornby. With Hornby he proved himself an apt pupil. He attained a particular reputation for his skill in manœuvring a fleet, and that not as a prince, but as a naval officer.

On 30 Dec. 1878 he was promoted, by order in council, to the rank of rear-admiral, and in November 1879 was appointed to the command of the naval reserve, which he held for three years. During that period he mustered the coastguard ships each summer, and organised them as a fleet in the North Sea or the Baltic. On 30 Nov. 1882 he was promoted to be vice-admiral, and from December 1883 to December 1884 commanded the Channel squadron. From 1886 to 1889 he was commander-in-chief in the Mediterranean, and it was specially at this time that his skill in handling a fleet was most talked of. It was commonly said that, with the exception of Hornby, no one in modern times could be compared with him. On 18 Oct. 1887 he was made an admiral, and from 1890 to 1893 he was commander-in-chief at Devonport. On 3 June 1893 he was promoted to the rank of admiral of the fleet.

A little more than two months afterwards, 22 Aug. 1893, on the death of his father's brother, he succeeded him as reigning duke of Saxe-Coburg and Gotha, in virtue of the renunciation in 1863 by his brother, the Prince of Wales, of the title to that duchy. The question was then raised whether as a German sovereign prince he could retain his privileges as an English peer or his rank as an English admiral of the fleet. This last he was permitted to hold by an order in council of 23 Nov. 1893, but it was understood that he had no longer a voice or seat in the House of Lords. He relinquished, too, the income of 15,000l. which had been settled on him on attaining his majority, but kept the further 10,000l. which was granted on his marriage in 1874, as an allowance to keep up Clarence House, London, where he resided for a part of each year. In Germany there were many who affected to resent the intrusion of a foreigner among the princes of the empire; but among his own subjects he speedily overcame hostile prejudices, adapting himself to his new duties and new surroundings, and taking an especial interest in all that concerned the agricultural and industrial prosperity of the duchies. A keen sportsman, a man of refined tastes, passionately fond of music, and a good performer on the violin, he was yet of a somewhat reserved disposition which prevented him from being so popular as his brothers; but by those who were in a position to know him best he was admired and esteemed. He died suddenly at Rosenau, near Coburg, on 30 July 1900 of paralysis of the heart, which, it was understood, saved him from the torture of a slow death by an internal disease of a malignant nature. He was buried on 4 Aug. in the mausoleum erected by his uncle Duke Ernest II in the cemetery at Coburg.

Duke Alfred married, at St. Petersburg on 23 Jan. 1874, the Grand Duchess Marie Alexandrovna, only daughter of the Tsar of Russia, Alexander II, and left by her four daughters, three of whom married in their father's lifetime, in each case before completing their eighteenth year. The eldest daughter, Princess Marie Alexandra Victoria (*b* 29 Oct. 1875), married, 10 Jan. 1893, Ferdinand, crown prince of Roumania; the second daughter, Princess Victoria Melita (*b* 25 Nov. 1876), married, on 19 April 1894, her first cousin Louis, grand duke of Hesse; the third daughter, Princess Alexandra Louise Olga Victoria (*b* 1 Sept. 1878), married the Hereditary Prince of Hohenlohe-Langenburg on 20 April 1896; the fourth daughter, Princess Beatrice Leopoldine Victoria, was born on 20 April 1884.

Duke Alfred's only son, Alfred Alexander William Ernest Albert, born on 15 Oct. 1874, died of phthisis at Meran on 6 Feb. 1899. The succession to the duchy of Saxe-Coburg-Gotha thus passed, on the renunciation both of Duke Alfred's next brother, the Duke of Connaught, and of his son, to Duke Alfred's nephew, the Duke of Albany, posthumous son of his youngest brother, Leopold, duke of Albany, Queen Victoria's youngest son.

A portrait of the duke by Von Angeli, dated 1875, is at Windsor, together with a picture of the ceremony of his marriage at St. Petersburg, which was painted by N. Chevalier.

[Times, 1 Aug. 1900; Army and Navy Gazette, 4 Aug.; Milner and Briarley's Cruise of Her Majesty's ship Galatea, 1867–8; Sir Theodore Martin's Life of the Prince Consort; Prothero's Life and Letters of Dean Stanley; Navy Lists; Foster's Peerage.]

JOHN KNOX LAUGHTON

published 1901

ALEXANDRA Caroline Mary Charlotte
Louise Julia

(1844–1925)

of Denmark

Queen-consort of King Edward VII, was born at the Gule Palace, Copenhagen, 1 December 1844, the eldest daughter and second of the six children of Prince Christian of Schleswig-Holstein-Sonderburg-Glücksburg, by his wife, Louise, daughter of the Landgrave William of Hesse-Cassel. Her parents lived in modest circumstances at Copenhagen, but her mother, as niece to King Christian VIII (1839–1848), was the natural heiress, after her childless cousin King Frederick VII (1848–1863), and subject to the renunciations of her mother and brother, to the throne of Denmark. In the duchies of Schleswig-Holstein, however, the Salic law had not been repealed, and, with the Duke of Sonderburg-Augustenberg ready to reassert his claim, trouble was already brewing over them. At the instigation of the Tsar Nicholas I of Russia, a correspondence was circulated through the courts of Europe, as the result of which a protocol was signed in London in 1852 which set out that, failing male issue to the reigning king, the crown of Denmark, together with the duchies—under a nominal German supervision—should revert to Prince and Princess Christian.

Princess Alexandra was brought up very simply with her brothers and sisters at Copenhagen and at the château of Bernstorff, ten miles from the capital. She was taught foreign languages, including English, and showed a marked aptitude for music. Hans Andersen was a friend of her parents and on intimate terms with the children. She was only thirteen years old when negotiations were set on foot which ultimately issued in her coming to England. In 1858 the question of a bride for Albert Edward, Prince of Wales, was under discussion, and Leopold, King of the Belgians, on whose advice Queen Victoria and Prince Albert largely relied, sent to Windsor a list of seven eligible young princesses with the name of Prince Christian's daughter heavily underlined. The project was, however, allowed to simmer until, on 24 September 1861, a meeting between the two young people in the cathedral town of Speier was ingeniously arranged by the crown princess of Prussia, the eldest sister of the Prince of Wales. 'We hear nothing but good of Princess Alexandra; the young people seem to have taken a warm liking to one another', Prince Albert wrote to the crown princess on 4 October. The untimely death of her husband on 14 December only sharpened Queen Victoria's determination to carry out what he had clearly wished. The formal betrothal took place on 9 September 1862 at the palace of Laeken, near Brussels. The princess landed at Gravesend on 7 March 1863, and on 10 March the marriage was solemnized in St. George's chapel, Windsor. Queen Victoria, clad in deepest mourning, witnessed the ceremony from the royal closet above the chancel.

The self-enforced seclusion of the queen quickly gave to her son and daughter-in-law a virtual sovereignty over the social world, and under their kindly sway English society soon assumed a gayer complexion, while the English aristocracy, on which the Prince Consort had looked with scant favour, resumed its former importance in royal circles. The princess was no less desirous than her husband that Marlborough House, their London home, and Sandringham—the Norfolk estate bought in 1861 with the savings from the duchy of Cornwall revenues which had accumulated during the prince's minority—should be open to any one who could claim real and honourable distinction; they both delighted in entertaining and were quite willing, in certain well-recognized circumstances, to be entertained themselves. Their hospitality was large, and at one time a malicious rumour spread that the Prince and Princess of Wales had outrun their income and that the prince was rather heavily in debt. *The Times* was inspired to give an explicit contradiction to a report which was without foundation, but the public was reminded that the prince and princess were carrying out official and social duties which had scarcely been contemplated when their marriage settlement was drawn up.

Meanwhile the Princess of Wales had secured, seemingly without an effort, the affections, not only of those with whom she came in contact, but of the British people at large. Her perfect simplicity played no small part in her perfect correctness. Her presence at any gathering involved no 'stiffness', but she carried to it a peculiar dignity, not easy to define but impossible to deny. Unlike some of her predecessors in the same position, she never allowed herself to be caught in the labyrinth of politics—though she numbered Mr. Gladstone among her closest friends—but certainly no foreign princess ever did half so much to mould the social life of the country of her adoption or strove more eagerly to better and brighten the lot of the poorer classes.

In the first year of her marriage two events occurred to dignify further Alexandra's position. The death in November of King Frederick VII placed the princess's father on the throne of Denmark as Christian IX, and her second brother, William, was chosen by the European powers to be king of the Hellenes, and crowned under the name of George, the patron saint of Greece. The crown proved no easy one to wear; from his accession to his assassination fifty years later, King George's chequered fortunes were a source of constant anxiety to his sister, whose sober advice and substantial help were frequently invoked.

The close of the year 1863 was to be embittered for the princess by the outbreak of the struggle in which three parties were engaged and which issued in the triumph of Prussian might over Danish claims. By signing the new Danish constitution which his predecessor had proclaimed shortly before his death, King Christian had asserted his claim to the duchies of Schleswig-Holstein, which was promptly disputed both by Frederick, Duke of Augustenberg, who repudiated the renunciation made by his father in 1852, and by King William I of Prussia, who induced the Emperor Francis Joseph of Austria to join him in expelling the Danes from the coveted territories, with the understanding that after the struggle they should be the joint possessors. Queen Victoria, though bent on peace, remembered the Prince Consort's desire for a powerful Prussia; her eldest daughter, the crown princess of Prussia, favoured the pretensions of Duke Frederick; while the Princess of Wales, whose anxiety for her country was painful to witness, imposed silence on herself, except when at Windsor she reminded her English relations that the duchies belonged to her father by right and could only be wrested from him by force, a remark which caused the queen to forbid the subject to be mentioned again in her presence.

The reticence of the princess was the more laudable—and cost her no less effort—because she was aware that the Cabinet seriously contemplated armed interference on behalf of Denmark, and that a word spoken by her would have roused the sympathy of many. Her hold over the affections of the English people was further strengthened when on 8 January 1864 she gave birth to a son, Albert Victor, afterwards Duke of Clarence, who stood as successor to the throne in the second generation.

The humiliations which her parents and her country were to suffer at the hands of Prussia were bitterly resented by the princess, but she found much solace in the whole-hearted support of her husband, who shedding for the moment political restraints, openly proclaimed his sympathy with his wife. The war over (August 1864), Alexandra was anxious to go to Denmark to see her parents, but Queen Victoria, who had forbidden her son to visit Copenhagen at the time of his betrothal, again imposed the same veto on him, and it required the intervention of Lord Palmerston—the princess's constant champion—for the queen to withdraw it. The prince and princess left England in September, but the prince had to give his written undertaking that he would say nothing and do nothing which would savour of Danish leanings; and it was further stipulated that the visits to Copenhagen and to Stockholm—to which the tour was to be extended—should be regarded as strictly private. This proviso King Charles XV of Sweden, to Queen Victoria's annoyance, brushed aside when he organized a public reception for the royal travellers and insisted on their being state guests at his palace.

Alexandra

For Bismarck the seizure by Prussia of the duchies of Schleswig-Holstein was but a stepping-stone, and in 1866, after the battle of Sadowa (3 July) had closed the contest between Austria and Prussia, the princess was to see her family further despoiled. By the terms of the Treaty of Prague (23 August), not only did Hesse-Darmstadt, of which her favourite sister-in-law, Princess Alice, was grand duchess, and Hanover pass into Prussian hands, but Hesse-Cassel, where she had found a second home, ceased to be the domain of her uncle and became an incorporated Prussian province. Once more the princess suffered in silence, but through the ensuing decades indignation smouldered in her breast and the very word Prussia would cause her to tighten her lips lest some injudicious expression should escape them. She clung tenaciously to the clause in the Treaty of Prague which gave Denmark the hope of recovering some portion of her lost provinces—viz. the northern district of Schleswig. In vain the people of this area pleaded for a referendum, and for forty years their grievance rankled in Alexandra's mind. Her joy was manifest when she learned that the Treaty of Versailles (1919) provided for an immediate transference of territory to Denmark, while a year later, under the plebiscite for which she had constantly pleaded, Northern Schleswig was handed over to the country of her birth.

'Le Prussianisme, voilà l'ennemi', was Gambetta's dictum, and while the Princess of Wales would entirely have endorsed it, she would not allow her subsequent mistrust of Germany or her dislike of Kaiser Wilhelm II to deter her from taking a cheerful part in any occasion which, by improving Anglo-German relations, might promote the peace of Europe. She visited Berlin whenever circumstances demanded it of her, and in later life formed a close friendship with her sister-in-law, the Empress Frederick. At Windsor, Sandringham, and Cowes she would play to perfection the part of hostess, and offer to her imperial nephew a welcome with which he could find no fault.

On 3 June 1865 Alexandra gave birth to her second son who, forty-five years later, was to succeed his father on the throne of England as King George V. Four other children were born to the Prince and Princess of Wales: Louise (20 February 1867) afterwards Duchess of Fife and princess royal; Victoria (6 July 1868); Maud (26 November 1869) afterwards Queen of Norway; and John (born 6, died 7, April 1871). In 1867, immediately after the birth of Princess Louise, Alexandra was severely attacked by an acute form of rheumatism which lodged in the knee-joint, causing her intense pain and for some time baffling the skill of her doctors. So long as there existed any public anxiety Marlborough House was besieged by anxious inquirers. Recovery was slow, and the illness, of which the patient herself was disposed to make light, left a permanent, though almost imperceptible, mark. The princess was a bold and skilful horsewoman, and for more than a quarter of a century afterwards was still a forward figure in the hunting field, but she had to ride on the 'reverse' side.

Mr. Disraeli, on assuming office in February 1868, pressed the queen to allow the Prince and Princess of Wales to be the guests of the newly appointed viceroy of Ireland, the Marquess of Abercorn, who was about to be advanced to a dukedom. The queen showed some hesitation, partly because the prince and princess had been indirectly approached on the subject before her own wishes had been consulted, and partly because she feared lest the presence of the heir to the throne across the Irish channel might be used for political purposes. There was also the element of risk to be considered, since Fenianism was rife, nor was the queen sure whether her daughter-in-law had sufficiently recovered from her illness to undergo the fatigue of the visit. But the princess discounted both the fatigue and the risk in her desire to see Ireland and to let the Irish see her. Accordingly, on 15 April the prince and princess landed at Kingstown and carried out, with evident enjoyment, a nine-days' programme, which included the installation of the prince as a knight of St. Patrick, the unveiling of Edmund Burke's statue in College Green, a review in Phoenix Park, and races at Punchestown; the princess struck a happy note by insisting that her husband should wear a green tie whenever possible, and by herself appearing on every appropriate occasion in Irish poplin with a mantilla of Irish lace. The whole visit, unpunctuated by any manifestation of ill will, proved such a success that before leaving Dublin a message was sent to the queen urging her to come over to Ireland and 'satisfy yourself on the force of affectionate feeling'. The princess was to cross again to Ireland in 1885, and to pay three visits there as queen consort; on each occasion she received the same enthusiastic welcome, which was no less emphatic because of a rumour that she had not been altogether averse from Mr. Gladstone's more moderate schemes of Home Rule.

At Balmoral in the autumn of 1868 the prince and princess informed the queen of their wish to spend the winter abroad and travel to the Near East. The princess had not altogether shaken off the effects of her illness, and change of scene and climate was strongly recommended; they were both anxious to see the Suez Canal, then approaching completion, and thought that it would be polite, and politic, to return the recent visit to London of the Sultan of Turkey. The princess, too, had been annoyed by foolish stories about the high play in which the prince was, quite erroneously, supposed to have indulged, and by ill-founded rumours as to the 'fastness' of some of those who composed the, so-called, Marlborough House set; for these and other reasons both Edward and Alexandra were anxious to leave England for a time, and they cheerfully accepted the terms with which the queen qualified her consent. They set out in November and were absent from England until the following May. The tour of Egypt (February–March 1869)—the only occasion on which the princess quitted Europe—was extended to Wadi Halfa, and as, in the meanwhile, threatened hostilities between Turkey and Greece had been averted, Queen Victoria, rather grudgingly, permitted the travellers on their way back in April to accept a very cordial invitation from the sultan and to pay a visit—the first of many—to the newly married king and queen of the Hellenes.

The princess was on a visit to Denmark when, in July 1870, war between France and Germany was declared. Queen Victoria, knowing that France looked to Denmark as a possible ally, and deprecating as usual her daughter-in-law's 'Danish partisanship', insisted on Alexandra returning to England at once. The misfortunes of France provoked the liveliest sympathy in the Princess of Wales, the more so, perhaps, because, with the victories of the German army, the letters of the crown princess of Prussia to her mother assumed an increasingly provocative tone. As often happened, the princess's outlook differed sharply from that of the queen whose expressed view that 'a powerful Germany can never be dangerous to England' she found it difficult to comprehend; the proclamation of the King of Prussia as German Emperor filled her with forebodings.

Except where the country of her birth, or Greece, were concerned, the Princess of Wales made no intrusion into foreign politics, although in 1877, when Russia declared war on Turkey, the report ran that the royal family was as sharply divided in its sympathies as the Cabinet. The queen, leaning wholly on Lord Beaconsfield, and the Prince of Wales, irritated by the trend of events in Russia, were admittedly Turcophil, while the princess was said to take her cue from Lord Salisbury and Lord Derby and to affirm Russia's right to save Christian states from the clutches of the infidel. While the suggestion of any attempt to exercise political influence was wholly unfounded, the princess certainly regarded herself as bound to Russia by family ties; her visits to Russia were frequent and often protracted, and with characteristic disregard of danger, she insisted in March 1881 on travelling to St. Petersburg to be beside her sister, the Empress Marie, after the assassination of the Emperor Alexander II, although at that moment even the police force was known to have Nihilist conspirators in its ranks. Throughout the Empress Marie's troubled life Alexandra was wholeheartedly in sympathy with her, and after the revolution of 1917 her Russian relations became her constant care and proved to be no small strain on her resources.

In 1889 the princess's eldest daughter, Louise, was married to Alexander, Earl of Fife, whom the queen promptly advanced to a dukedom. Five years elapsed before her surviving son, George, was united to Princess Victoria

Mary of Teck, the daughter of Francis, Duke of Teck and her favourite cousin, Princess Mary Adelaide, of Cambridge. Meanwhile she had suffered a blow from which she never wholly recovered. On 14 January 1892 her elder son, who had been created Duke of Clarence two years previously and was betrothed to the princess who was yet to become her daughter-in-law, died at Sandringham of an especially vicious form of influenza then prevalent. While the second daughter, Princess Victoria, remained her mother's constant companion, the youngest, Princess Maud, was in 1896 married to her cousin, Prince Charles, the second son of the crown prince of Denmark, an alliance which later proved to have some political significance. When, in 1905, the kingdoms of Norway and Sweden were separated, the Norwegian vote for a new king was accorded by general count to Prince Charles of Denmark, who, largely under Queen Alexandra's advice, declined to leave Copenhagen until summoned to Christiania in virtue of a referendum.

On 19 January 1901 the Princess of Wales, with other members of the royal family, was hurriedly summoned to Osborne, and, three days later, she was close to Queen Victoria's bedside when she died. Through forty years comment had not been infrequent as to the points of contact between a sovereign whose authority brooked neither criticism nor contradiction and a princess whose gentleness of manner concealed much strength of character. The contrast between them, both in outlook and method, was acute. Their divergence of views suffered little change in the passage of time, but in both of them loyalty of purpose was so deeply ingrained that mutual trust and wholehearted affection for one another grew stronger every year; the death of Queen Victoria was felt by the princess, on her own admission, as the loss of a second mother.

The accession to the position of queen consort could not do much to enhance the status of a princess whose popularity with society—in the widest sense of the word—had been supreme for forty years. But King Edward VII was determined to give his queen the most exalted rank it was in his power to bestow, and one of his first acts was to convene a special chapter of the Order of the Garter and to revive in favour of Queen Alexandra a custom instituted by Richard II but which had fallen into disuse since Henry VII 'Gartered' his mother. Both before and after her accession, Queen Alexandra's energies and a substantial slice of her income were spent in the relief of suffering and poverty. Her charities were perhaps dictated by her heart rather than by her head, and so far as she herself was concerned were wholly unostentatious, but her example unquestionably gave a great stimulus to beneficent work on the part of wealthy and influential people and went some way to solve certain social problems. The dinners which she gave to celebrate Queen Victoria's

473

diamond jubilee in 1897, when 400,000 poor people were her guests; the hospital ship which she equipped for the sick and wounded soldiers in the South African War; the tea given at her coronation to 10,000 maids-of-all-work; the fund—amounting to over a quarter of a million sterling—raised, on her initiative, in 1906 in aid of unemployed workmen; the institution of the Queen Alexandra Imperial Military Nursing Service in 1902; the introduction of the Finsen lamp into the London Hospital in 1899—all these go to testify no less to her fertility in suggestion than to her insistence on the execution of her sometimes rather daring plans.

The death of King Edward occurred 6 May 1910; Queen Alexandra was in Italy and no news calculated to give her special anxiety had reached her, but she had a sudden premonition that the king's hours were numbered, and travelling rapidly from Venice, reached his bedside some thirty hours before he died. After his death the queen withdrew into comparative retirement. There remained plenty to occupy her, and her interest in the London Hospital and in many schemes to alleviate suffering only seemed to grow with her declining years; but she preferred now to help rather than to head any movement. In 1913, in order to mark what she described as 'the fiftieth anniversary of my coming to this beloved country', 'Alexandra Day' (in June) was instituted, with roses for its outward and visible sign; and ever since on every 'rose day' myriads of flowers have been sold, and British hospitals have benefited thereby to the extent of hundreds of thousands of pounds.

The European War fired again Queen Alexandra's desire to help, and now especially to help the wounded; her time and her purse were constantly available for any calls made upon them. Her influence was incessantly invoked for this or that concession, but she declined to interfere at any point except to put in a plea for the mothers who had been doubly bereaved; and to her pleading was largely due a ruling that when two sons in a family had been killed, the others should, if possible, be kept behind the firing-line. Her friendship with Lord Kitchener was of long standing, and she greatly appreciated, and never divulged to any one, the daily bulletin of war news which he caused to be sent to her. Careless of danger for herself, her sense of danger for others was acute, and on learning of the proposed mission of the secretary of state for war to Russia in 1916, she was persuaded that disaster would attend it and begged, but of course in vain, that it might be cancelled. When, after the tragedy of the *Hampshire*, a memorial to Lord Kitchener was inaugurated, the queen mother at once placed herself at the head of the appeal, which quickly produced a sum never before approached by any memorial fund.

The last two years of Queen Alexandra's life were spent quietly at Sandringham, the home which she loved and which King Edward had bequeathed to her. There, without struggle or suffering, she died 20 November 1925. Prior to the burial at Windsor, the queen lay in state for twelve hours in Westminster Abbey, and a long line of 50,000 men, women, and children filed past the bier, headed by a band of 'Queen Alexandra' nurses.

The key to Queen Alexandra's life was her essential goodness, which showed itself not merely in her family relations and private life, but in the use which she made of her public position, alike as princess and as queen consort. All who gave their services to the sick or the sorrowful, who tried to help children, who cared for birds or animals, could rely on her practical sympathy and eager—sometimes perhaps too eager—readiness to help. Simplicity, charm of manner, and a keen sense of humour combined with her attractive character to make Queen Alexandra one of the best loved of British royal personages. Alone of all the royal consorts who have come to Great Britain from abroad she was never regarded as a foreigner.

Queen Alexandra's beauty often provoked the despair of the painter, the sculptor, and the photographer; the deep blue eyes, the swift play of expression, the smile, irresistible because it was absolutely genuine, seemed incapable of reproduction on canvas or in clay. 'Alix looked lovely in grey and white and more like a bride just married than a silver one of twenty-five years' is an entry in Queen Victoria's diary for 10 March 1888, and certainly for a quarter of a century successive years had only seemed to enhance her daughter-in-law's physical attractions. Perhaps the happiest picture of her is by Richard Lauchert, who painted the Princess of Wales at the age of eighteen; Luke Fildes executed the state portrait (1901) and another, painted some eight years earlier; while other, more or less successful, portraits were painted by F. Winterhalter, Sir W. B. Richmond, H. von Angeli, Benjamin Constant, and Edward Hughes. A drawing appeared in *Vanity Fair* 7 June 1911.

[*The Letters of Queen Victoria*, first series edited by A. C. Benson, 3 vols., 1908, second and third series edited by G. E. Buckle, 6 vols., 1926–1928 and 1930–1932; Sir Sidney Lee, *King Edward VII, a biography*, 2 vols., 1925; Sir George Arthur, *Queen Alexandra*, 1934; private information.]

G. Arthur

published 1937

LOUISE Caroline Alberta

(1848–1939)

Princess of Great Britain and Ireland, Duchess of Argyll, was born at Buckingham Palace 18 March 1848, the sixth child and fourth daughter of Queen Victoria. She was the most beautiful and not the least gifted of the Queen's daughters, and her intelligence and wit made her a favourite with her father and attracted the notice of Carlyle. In 1871 the Princess married John Douglas Sutherland Campbell, Marquess of Lorne, who in 1900 succeeded his father as ninth Duke of Argyll. She was the first member of the royal family for more than fifty years to contract matrimony with a subject of the sovereign, and the innovation (especially as the bridegroom was a Scotsman) had the strong approval of the Queen. There were no children of the marriage.

Princess Louise spent five years (1878–1883) in Canada as the consort of the governor-general, and a memorial of her stay is the name given to Lake Louise near Laffan in the Rocky Mountains. After their return to this country, the princess and Lord Lorne were able to promote the causes which they had at heart with singular unanimity, as both were endowed with the same literary and artistic tastes. Leading an extremely quiet and retired life, giving only small parties, eschewing royal functions as far as possible, and not showing over-much attention to the conventions of her station, the princess wrote articles for magazines under the nom de plume of 'Myra Fontenoy', and made her home at Kensington Palace a rendezvous for artists and sculptors, of whom the chief was Sir J. E. Boehm, and who also numbered among them (Sir) Alfred Gilbert, J. Seymour Lucas, and Sir Lawrence Alma-Tadema. Of the causes to which the princess gave her support the Ladies' Work Society, which enabled poor ladies to gain a living from needlework, was perhaps nearest to her heart, but far more important was the impetus which she gave to the education of women, for under her strong encouragement the National Union for the Higher Education of Women was founded in 1872. She was its first president, and the growth and spread of high schools for girls all over the country will probably be her most lasting and influential work. She was not content to be a mere figurehead, but followed the work closely, and took an active share in it by means of speeches, letters to the press, and an especial interest in the teaching of art.

As a working artist, the princess early exhibited gifts as a sculptress, and she was instructed by Mary Thornycroft. Of the princess's works the best known is the marble statue of Queen Victoria at Kensington Palace overlooking the Round Pond. The monument to Prince Henry of Battenberg in Whippingham church, near Cowes, is also highly esteemed, and she designed the memorial in St. Paul's Cathedral to the Canadian soldiers who fell in the South African war.

After the Duke of Argyll's death in 1914, the princess lived a life yet more retired, and divided her time between London and Roseneath House in Dumbartonshire. In 1919 she was given the colonelcy-in-chief of the Argyll and Sutherland Highlanders. After long enjoyment of good health she died at Kensington Palace in her ninety-second year 3 December 1939.

[*The Times*, 4 and 8 December 1939; personal knowledge.]

DOROTHY CANTELUPE

published 1949

BIGGE Arthur John

(1849–1931)

Baron Stamfordham

Private secretary to King George V, was born at Linden Hall, near Morpeth, Northumberland, 18 June 1849, the fourth of the five sons of John Frederick Bigge, vicar of Stamfordham in the same county, by his wife, Caroline Mary, only daughter of Nathaniel Ellison, barrister and commissioner in bankruptcy, of Newcastle-upon-Tyne. He was educated at Rossall School and at the Royal Military Academy, where he was a fellow cadet with Prince Arthur, later Duke of Connaught. In 1869 he obtained a commission in the Royal Artillery, from which he retired as lieutenant-colonel (1892) in 1898. A few years after he entered the army there was attached to his battery the Prince Imperial, the only son of Napoleon III, and the close friendship which sprang up between the two young men determined Bigge's career.

Serving in the Kaffir and Zulu wars of 1878–1879, Bigge was mentioned in dispatches after the battle of Kambula on 29 March 1879: the part played by the Horse Artillery battery in which he was serving is thus commended by Sir (Henry) Evelyn Wood (*From Midshipman to Field-Marshal*, vol. ii, p. 59): 'I have never known a battery so exceptionally fortunate in its sub-alterns. ... Both Bigge and Slade were unsurpassable; they with their gunners stood up in the open from 1.30 p.m. till the Zulus retreated at 5.30 p.m.' Later in that year the Prince Imperial was killed in South Africa and Bigge had the melancholy task of escorting the body of his friend back to

England. He went to Abergeldie to tell the Empress Eugénie of the circumstances in which the Prince had been killed, and while staying there he had several interviews at Balmoral with Queen Victoria, who wrote of him to her eldest daughter (24 October): 'He is a charming person, of the very highest character, clever, amiable and agreeable, as well as good looking.' Three days later the Queen recorded in her diary: 'After tea saw Lieut. Bigge, with whom I had a long talk. He was at Inhlobane and Kambula, his horse being killed under him at the latter. . . . After Kambula Lieut. Bigge became very ill indeed and the Prince Imperial came to see him in hospital, when he said he hoped they would meet again soon. This was only a week before the Prince was killed, and humanly speaking it seemed more likely that Lieut. Bigge should die than that the other should happen. He cautioned and begged the Prince to be very careful, which he promised he would. . . . We spoke of the Empress' wish, indeed determination, to go to South Africa to visit the spot where her dear son fell, which will be difficult to carry out, but not impossible.'

On 1 January 1880 the Queen appointed Bigge a groom-in-waiting to herself, giving him leave first to accompany Wood, to whom he was at that time aide-de-camp, and who had undertaken to conduct the Empress to the scene of the tragedy. Bigge went ahead, on 11 March, to make arrangements. On their return from South Africa at the end of July he went for two nights to Osborne to report to the Queen, who immediately appointed him assistant private secretary and assistant privy purse, 'as both Sir Henry Ponsonby and I think no-one better fitted than him' (Diary, 2 August). This association with Sir Henry Ponsonby proved most happy on both sides, and Bigge carried with him to the grave an unstinted admiration for his former chief. He resigned as groom in May 1881, having been appointed equerry in the previous month. He was made C.B. in 1885 and C.M.G. in 1887. In May 1895 he was advanced to K.C.B. upon succeeding Ponsonby as private secretary to the Queen, a post which he held until the close of her reign.

King Edward VII came to the throne already provided with a private secretary in the person of Sir Francis (later Viscount) Knollys. But when the heir to the throne, Prince George, Duke of Cornwall and York, made his famous tour through the British Dominions in 1901, Bigge accompanied him as private secretary. At the close of the tour Bigge was appointed G.C.V.O. and K.C.M.G. He retained the post of private secretary to the Prince of Wales throughout King Edward's reign and accompanied him to India in 1905. He was appointed K.C.S.I. in 1906.

On his accession in 1910 King George V at first made use of the services and experience of both Knollys and Bigge as joint private secretaries. Knollys retired in 1913, and Bigge, who had been raised to the peerage as

Baron Stamfordham in 1911, remained until his death eighteen years later principal private secretary. He was sworn of the Privy Council in 1910, attended the King to India in 1911, and was appointed G.C.I.E. in 1911 and G.C.B. in 1916. He also received several foreign decorations, including the Legion of Honour, and in 1906 the university of Durham conferred upon him the honorary degree of D.C.L.

Among Stamfordham's few but distinguished predecessors in his office his place is deservedly high. As private secretary to two sovereigns he revealed qualities of tact and wisdom, a sure grasp of affairs, and an unswerving rectitude. Politically he was at once less eager and less radical than either of his immediate forerunners. The affinity between Ponsonby and Gladstone, or that between Knollys and Asquith, found its natural parallel in the intimacy which for nearly fifty years linked Stamfordham with Randall Davidson. His impartiality was never questioned. Upon vacating office in December 1916 Asquith wrote to him: 'Our intercourse, official and personal, during all these years, is one of the pleasantest memories of my public life. The times have not been easy, and of late more than difficult, but our task has been lightened by complete mutual confidence and ever-growing friendship.'

Stamfordham was a man of persistent industry, making it his practice to finish the day's work within the day, whatever the cost in leisure or the physical burden. This towards the close of Queen Victoria's life became heavy, for her eyes began to fail, and by 1895 the task of writing to her legibly had become so exacting that the prime minister permitted himself to communicate with her through Bigge, dictating his letters to an amanuensis with a clear handwriting (Lord Crewe, *Lord Rosebery*, vol. i, p. 508). For his part, Bigge used to dry his submissions in a stove of ingenious design instead of blotting them; and he taught himself afresh to write. It was thus that he acquired the bold script which remained to the end the joy and envy of his correspondents. His letters were largely handwritten; if they lack the astringency and sparkle of Ponsonby's they are marked by a like economy of phrase.

Against the wiles of the importunate he knew well how to guard himself, and fashionable company he resolutely eschewed. A certain austerity which he had imbibed in the north-country vicarage mellowed in later years to a gentler tolerance, and he came to be regarded by his colleagues with a love which perhaps never wholly cast out fear. But the young, the shy, and the inexperienced were drawn towards him by the candour and the simplicity of his bearing. 'I shall never forget', wrote Ramsay MacDonald after his death, 'the kindness he shewed to my colleagues and myself when we were but prentices in 1924. The country has lost a devoted servant who for many years bore delicate responsibilities with a sagacity and resourcefulness which smoothed many a difficult road and enabled change to come gently and be accepted without misgiving as a thing belonging to the natural flow of time.'

Stamfordham had learnt his trade in the service of an aged queen, of towering personal ascendancy, unrivalled experience, and marked political capacity. It was to a different scene that he returned a decade later, at a period of strong civil ferment, the intermediary this time between a reticent and untried sovereign and a resourceful prime minister. It was Stamfordham's solicitude which brought confidence to the new king at the same time as his experience brought counsel in statecraft. There was in him an absence of self-esteem which responded to a like quality in his master, establishing between them more than a merely professional relationship throughout the thirty years of their association. On the day of his death at St. James's Palace 31 March 1931, the King wrote in his diary: 'Dear Bigge passed peacefully away at 4.30 to-day. I shall miss him terribly. His loss is irreparable.'

Stamfordham married in 1881 Constance (died 1922), second daughter of William Frederick Neville, vicar of Butleigh, Somerset, and had one son, who was killed in action in 1915, and two daughters. He had but one grandchild, Major Michael Adeane.

A portrait of Stamfordham, by H. A. Olivier (1927), is in the possession of the family, and a charcoal drawing, by Francis Dodd (1931), is in the Royal Library, Windsor Castle. A poor cartoon of him, by 'Spy', appeared in *Vanity Fair* 6 September 1900.

[*The Times*, 1 April 1931; published *Letters*, and unpublished diary, of Queen Victoria; P. H. Emden, *Behind the Throne*, 1934; private information; personal knowledge.]

OWEN MORSHEAD

published 1949

ARTHUR William Patrick Albert

(1850–1942)

Duke of Connaught and Strathearn

The third son and seventh child of Queen Victoria, was born at Buckingham Palace 1 May 1850, the eighty-first birthday of his godfather the Duke of Wellington, after whom he received his first name; his second name was after the Prince of Prussia, later German Emperor, his third in remembrance of Queen Victoria's visit to Ireland in 1849; Albert was after his father. He became the favourite son of the Queen who 'adored our little Arthur from the day of his birth. He has never given us a day's sorrow or trouble, she may truly say, but ever been like a ray of sunshine in the house.' Even in early days he was attracted to things military, and in the gardens at Osborne there still stand miniature earthworks of military formations about which he used to play. When the Prince was not yet nine years old, (Sir) Howard Crawfurd Elphinstone was appointed his governor, and so began a companionship and friendship which was to last for more than thirty years.

Until 1862 Prince Arthur's life had been spent at home, but in that year he took up residence at Ranger's House, Greenwich Park. His life, he said, was a lonely one, 'called at 6.45 a.m., my studies began about 7.15 and I worked till about 9 a.m., when I breakfasted, work being resumed at 10 a.m. until 1 p.m. Then I had a short walk and lunched at 2 p.m. In the afternoon I walked and twice a week boys came from various schools to play with me. We played football, hockey, etc. Lessons were again resumed at 5 p.m. until 7.30 p.m. Supper at 8 p.m. and afterwards I prepared lessons until about 10 p.m. for the following day.' In 1864 he began to see more of the world for himself: he stayed at the Rosenau for two months perfecting his German, went on a walking tour in Switzerland and did some climbing; then to improve his French he went to Ouchy near Lausanne, and returned to England after a further short visit to Germany with his great friend Prince Adolphus of Mecklenburg-Strelitz. Next year he made a tour of the Mediterranean in the *Enchantress*, visiting Italy, Greece, Asia Minor, and Palestine. His first public function was performed in 1865, when he unveiled a statue of his father at Tenby; in the next year he 'passed very well' into the Royal Military Academy, Woolwich, where, still living at Ranger's House, he underwent the military training common to all cadets. A visit to the Emperor Napoleon in 1867 and a severe attack of smallpox interrupted his studies, but he passed out in 1868, and at the final inspection he was called out to receive his commission in the Royal Engineers at the hands of the Duke of Cambridge, the commander-in-chief, feeling 'very proud at having at last become an officer'.

After a short period at the School of Military Engineering, the Prince visited Switzerland and was then transferred to the Royal Artillery at Woolwich, where he had charge of men, horses, and guns, and acquired 'an idea of responsibility'. In 1869 he was transferred to the 1st battalion of the Rifle Brigade, then stationed at Montreal. His company commander, finding the Prince a keen soldier, went on leave and left him in command. From the political point of view, the posting was opportune. Canada was restless, loyal to the Queen, but exasperated with the home Government. 'The more I visit Canada', wrote Prince Arthur to the Queen, 'the more I like and admire the people. They are a set of fine honest free thinking but loyal Englishmen.' Among the various visits paid was one to the head-quarters of the Fenians at Buffalo in the United States: reports were rife that the Prince would be held as a hostage, but the visit was a complete success. After a brief visit to Washington, New York, and Boston, where he thoroughly enjoyed himself, he saw action in 1870 against a body of Fenians who had invaded Canada. At the end of a 'very happy and interesting year', he rejoined his battalion at Woolwich.

On coming of age in 1871 Prince Arthur, who had been invested as K.G. on the Queen's birthday in 1867, was promoted captain and given the command of 'B' company. He also received the freedom of the City of London and was introduced into the Privy Council. On a visit to his eldest sister Victoria, then the German Crown Princess, in 1872 he was admitted to the Order of the Black Eagle, 'a tremendous function'. In 1873 at a visit to his second sister Alice, afterwards Grand Duchess of Hesse-Darmstadt, the Prince was introduced to the sport of wild-boar hunting, and next visited Rome where he was received by Pope Pius IX. Later in the year, after a visit to Vienna for the opening of the International Exhibition, Elphinstone was able to allay the anxieties of the Queen about this visit to this gayest of capitals by reporting that it had done a great deal of good, as the Prince became wearied with the constant life of pleasure and the late hours. In January 1874 he was best man at St. Petersburg to his brother Alfred, Duke of Edinburgh, at his wedding to the Grand Duchess Marie, daughter of the Emperor Alexander II. When the Emperor and Empress of Russia visited Queen Victoria in May the Prince's troop ('A') of the 7th Hussars (to which he had been transferred in April) was sent as an escort and he was in attendance on various occasions and inspections, during one of which the Duke of Cambridge, the commander-in-chief, ordered the Prince to 'charge the crowd', which he said he did with great reluctance.

In spite of all these special duties, the chief interest and occupation of the Prince, who in 1874 was created Duke of Connaught and Strathearn and Earl of Sussex, were his military duties. In 1873 he had been attached to the staff of an infantry brigade at Aldershot, and during the manœuvres later he was brigade-major. His room in one of the lower huts of his battalion was 'so small that I could lie in bed and open the window and poke the fire', while of his work, his colonel wrote: 'Prince Arthur works like a slave and his General told me that no poor man in the Army working for his advancement could work harder than he does or do his duty better.' In 1875 he attended the German army manœuvres, a sig-nificant event for him personally, for he met the 'Red Prince', Prince

Frederick Charles Nicholas of Prussia, and in October he took up the duties of assistant adjutant-general at Gibraltar. By nature a good linguist, he took the opportunity of learning Spanish, and in company with the Prince of Wales he visited King Alfonso XII at Madrid in the spring of 1876, rejoining at Gibraltar after visiting Toledo and Seville for the Easter ceremonies. Later he went to Liverpool to take command of a detached squadron, and he was present in August when the Queen unveiled the statue of the Prince Consort at Edinburgh. A change came in September when he went from the 7th Hussars to the command of the 1st battalion of his old regiment, the Rifle Brigade, as lieutenant-colonel, stationed in Dublin. Throughout the next year and until 1878 the Duke was at the Curragh, but in February he went to Berlin to attend the weddings of the Crown Princess's daughter Charlotte to Prince Bernhard of Saxe-Meiningen and of a daughter of the Red Prince to the Grand Duke of Oldenburg. The Duke then fell in love with the Red Prince's third daughter Louise Margaret Alexandra Victoria Agnes and, though the Queen was anxious about the match at first, the visit of the Princess to her in May was the beginning of a deep and lasting affection between mother and daughter-in-law. The marriage took place at St. George's Chapel, Windsor, 13 March 1879 and until the Duchess died thirty-eight years later the union was an ideally happy one. The honeymoon was mainly spent on board the royal yacht *Osborne* in a trip to Lisbon, Gibraltar, Spain, Malta, Sicily, the Aegean, Greece, and the Adriatic to Venice, whence the Duke returned home and resumed the command of his battalion at Aldershot. It was not until after Christmas 1880 that the Duke and Duchess were able to take up residence at Bagshot Park, where the Duke found real joy in the beautiful grounds on which he spent time and care and in the glorious trees of which he had expert knowledge and which he was never tired of inspecting and showing to his friends. For London residence, until the death of Queen Victoria, they lived at Buckingham Palace, but thereafter their London home was Clarence House.

The importance which the Duke attached to thoroughness in his military career is illustrated by a letter which he wrote to the Queen before his marriage. The question of promotion having arisen, he wrote: 'up to now I have worked my way up through every grade, from Lieutenant to Lieutenant-Colonel, and I should not wish to skip the rank of Colonel' (Royal Archives). In 1880 he was promoted colonel-in-chief of the Rifle Brigade: the Prince of Wales relinquished the post reluctantly, but took up that of colonel-in-chief of the Household Cavalry; the Duke was also promoted major-general in 1880, and appointed to command the 3rd Infantry brigade at Aldershot, but in 1882 he was put in command of the 1st Guards brigade, then serving in the Egyptian war, under (Sir) G. H. S.

Willis. From reading his notes it is easy to realize the constant care which the Duke had for his men in conditions in which comfort was very deficient. He had a narrow escape from death in action when a shell burst between himself and another officer. He was thrice mentioned in dispatches, and Sir Garnet (later Viscount) Wolseley writing to the Queen in September 1882 says that he 'takes great interest in his work and is indefatigable in his duties as Brigadier'; and again, after the battle of Tel-el-Kebir, 'On all sides I hear loud praises of the cool courage displayed yesterday, when under an extremely heavy fire, by H.R.H. the Duke of Connaught. . . . He is a first-rate Brigadier-General, and takes more care of his men and is more active in the discharge of his duties than any of the Generals now with me.' The Duke of Cambridge wrote: 'He has won golden opinions from everyone.' On his own share in the action, the Duke characteristically entreated the Queen not to give him any honour greater than an officer commanding a brigade would naturally receive. 'I covet', he wrote, 'a C.B., and if I get that I shall be so proud.' He was appointed C.B. and received the thanks of both Houses of Parliament. Wolseley appointed him commandant of Cairo, and he subsequently went for an extended trip up the Nile, after which he returned home in November and was invested by the German Crown Prince with the Prussian Order *pour le mérite*. In 1883 he was appointed colonel of the Scots Guards.

The Duke next served in Bengal until 1886 when, after some discussion, Lord Salisbury's Cabinet approved his appointment to the Bombay Command. This post he held for four years, managing, in spite of difficulties, to attend the Queen's jubilee in 1887. He was promoted lieutenant-general in 1889. During these years both he and the Duchess devoted their time and their services to India and its peoples of whom he ever after spoke with understanding and affection. They learnt to speak Hindustani fluently. One friendship, which left a permanent mark on the decoration of the billiard-room at Bagshot, was with Rudyard Kipling's father, then curator of the museum at Lahore. On problems even then arising in India, the Duke deprecated 'a tendency . . . to bring forward Indian questions for party purposes at home' lest it should lead to 'serious trouble in India'.

On his return to England in 1890 the Duke was appointed to command the Southern district at Portsmouth, and it was the first of a series of disappointments to him when his desire to be commander-in-chief in India was not realized; nor did he ever become commander-in-chief at home. This project came up repeatedly in the last years of Queen Victoria, who was anxious that the office should be retained and that her son should hold it. Neither of Lord Salisbury's Cabinets, however, nor Lord Rosebery's could meet her wishes. Wolseley indeed urged the Duke's claims to be made adjutant-general as a preparation for succeeding the Duke of Cambridge. In 1895, when the Duke, hitherto in ignorance of what was going on between the Queen and her ministers, was told that he was not to be commander-in-chief, he was greatly vexed, and he had to undergo the same disappointment when Lord Roberts succeeded Lord Wolseley in 1901.

In 1893 the Duke, who had found Portsmouth uncongenial, was promoted general and appointed to the Aldershot Command. The five years' tenure of this office was punctuated by missions abroad: to the coronation of the Emperor Nicholas II, at Moscow, in 1896, to the centenary of the birth of the Emperor William I, at Berlin, in 1897, and, more professionally, to the autumn manœuvres of the French Army in 1898 when he received the grand cordon of the Legion of Honour. In spite of his desire to go on active service in South Africa, consent was not forthcoming and he made no secret of his disappointment. Instead he was appointed commander-in-chief in Ireland (1900), and he was there when his mother made her historic visit to Dublin.

In 1899 the Duke was called to make an important decision about his future life. The hereditary prince of Saxe-Coburg-Gotha died early in the year, leaving the Duke in the direct succession to the duchy, then held by his second brother Alfred, Duke of Edinburgh. After discussions between the Queen, the Duke, and Lord Salisbury, the Duke and his son Prince Arthur renounced their right to the ducal throne, which consequently devolved on the Duke's nephew, Charles Edward, Duke of Albany.

With the death of the Queen, the Duke reached the summit of his military career. In 1902 his brother King Edward VII appointed him a field-marshal and his representative at the coronation durbar held at Delhi in 1903. In 1904 he was appointed inspector-general of the forces, visiting South Africa in 1906 and making an extended tour in the Far East in 1907. In that year he became high commissioner and commander-in-chief in the Mediterranean, a post which he held until 1909. In 1910 he opened the newly formed Union Parliament of South Africa on behalf of his nephew King George V. The press hailed the visit as 'a great personal triumph' for the Duke who had been 'accessible to British, Dutch, and native alike. What can be done to improve the relations between the white races has been done.'

The visit to South Africa was the prelude to a greater mission. In October 1911 the Duke took up one of the posts in which his personality found vivid expression. As governor-general of Canada, he renewed the affection he had felt for the Canadians ever since he had been quartered among them as a subaltern. Without exacting great deference to himself, he won popularity with all classes of people by his friendliness and affability. No programme of public engagements was too heavy for him. If he kept greater state at Rideau Hall than his predecessors, the presence there of a royal prince was a valuable stimulant to Canadian patriotism during the war of 1914–18. The only unfortunate episode of his term of office which lasted until 1916 was a quarrel with the extremely eccentric Sir Sam Hughes, then minister of militia, which arose from the intelligible desire of an experienced professional soldier of the highest rank to play in military affairs a role incompatible with his constitutional position as governor-general. In 1918 the Duke visited Greece, Egypt, and Palestine, going up to Khartoum and returning after three months of travelling, which covered 20,000 miles. In December 1920 he left for an extensive visit to India. In February 1921 at Delhi he opened the new Chamber of Princes, the Imperial Legislative Assembly and the Council of State. In 1928 he received the congratulations of the Army Council on completing sixty years of service in the army.

The Duke had suffered cruel losses in the previous ten years. The Duchess had died in 1917 and the sorrow cast a shadow over the remainder of his life; in 1920 his elder daughter, the Crown Princess of Sweden, died rather suddenly. In 1928 he ceased, although still physically and mentally active, to take an active part in public life, dividing his time between Bagshot Park and Clarence House and, until his later years, spending a part of every year in the south of France, first at Beaulieu and later at his own villa, 'Les Bruyères', at Cap Ferrat; here his love of horticulture found full scope, and many officers and men of the Royal Navy remembered his garden which he threw open to all ranks when units of the fleet came to Villefranche. He often spoke of his pleasure at the French acknowledgement of his position in the military world in making him honorary 'caporal' in a battalion of the Chasseurs Alpins. When visits to France became inadvisable, winters were spent at Sidmouth or at Bath. The Duke died at Bagshot Park 16 January 1942. He had issue a son, Prince Arthur, who died in 1938, and two daughters, Princess Margaret Victoria Augusta Charlotte Norah, who married in 1905 Prince Gustavus Adolphus, Duke of Scania, later King Gustavus VI of Sweden, and Princess Victoria Patricia Helena Elizabeth, who married in 1919 Captain (subsequently Rear-Admiral Sir) Alexander Robert Maule Ramsay, son of the thirteenth Earl of Dalhousie, taking rank, as Lady Patricia Ramsay, next below duchesses. The Duke was succeeded by his grandson, the Earl of Macduff, and on the latter's death in 1943 the dukedom of Connaught and Strathearn and the earldom of Sussex became extinct.

It was a natural consequence of his birth that the Duke held many of the highest honorary posts in civil life. One of his greatest interests was in freemasonry; he became grand master of the United Grand Lodge in 1901 and kept in close touch with it down to his death. He succeeded King

George V as master of Trinity House, presiding regularly at the Trinity Monday courts; he was grand prior and bailiff of the Order of St. John of Jerusalem and on one occasion his intervention during the war of 1914–18 brought the activities of the order into better relation with those of the British Red Cross Society. But the Duke's overriding interest was in the army, and the constant care which he showed for the welfare of the men under his command, entirely consistent with his personal character, won him a degree of affectionate respect which has been accorded to few. He fully carried out his mother's advice given to him in 1871: 'Continue to be kind and considerate to those below you, and treat those who faithfully serve you as friends'; and again: 'It is by those below us that we are most judged and it is of great value to be beloved' (Royal Archives). Beloved the Duke certainly was both by the army in particular and the people generally, but more particularly by those who knew him personally, and especially by his mother.

The Duke has often, and justly, been spoken of as a great gentleman. Endowed with a great measure of administrative ability, he was naturally impatient of official obstruction. He was invariably courteous and considerate, and if he was quick to notice irregularities, however trivial, in uniform or etiquette, his correction did not hurt. The absolute straightforwardness of his character found no room for pettiness or insincerity in others; he gave his friendship unstintingly, but expected a high standard of loyalty in return.

The Duke received from his mother all the honours which it was in her power to give. After her death he became great master of the Order of the Bath in 1901, and received the Royal Victorian Chain in 1902; in 1917 his nephew appointed him G.B.E. He received honorary degrees from many universities.

Of existing portraits of the Duke, the following may be mentioned. In the royal collections there are three by F. X. Winterhalter: 'The First of May, 1851' in which the Duke of Wellington is presenting a casket to the infant Prince in the presence of the Queen and the Prince Consort; a small portrait at the age of about three years; and another in Scots Guards uniform, at the age of about five; one by (Sir) Hubert von Herkomer (*c.* 1900) in the full-dress uniform of a general; one by J. S. Sargent (1910) in blue frogged frock-coat of the Grenadier Guards (with a replica at Government House, Ottawa); a large equestrian portrait by Edouard Detaille in the blue frock-coat of a general, with King Edward VII (as Prince of Wales) at an Aldershot review (*c.* 1898). A small sketch of the Duke's figure in this picture, by Edouard Detaille himself, belongs to Lady Patricia Ramsay, who also possesses an unfinished head and shoulders, in field-marshal's uniform, by Sir A. S. Cope (1923). A portrait (1878) by H. von

Angeli, in Rifle Brigade uniform, belongs to the officers of the Rifle Brigade. Cartoons by 'Spy' appeared in *Vanity Fair* 17 June 1876 and 2 August 1890. A bronze statue of the Duke in uniform (before 1907) by George Wade was erected on the waterfront at Hong Kong.

[Royal Archives, Windsor Castle, *passim*; M. H. McClintock, *The Queen Thanks Sir Howard*, 1945; *Letters of Queen Victoria*, second and third series, 1926–32; private information; personal knowledge.]

BADELEY

published 1959

BRETT **Reginald Baliol**

(1852–1930)

Second Viscount Esher

Government official, was born in London 30 June 1852, the elder son of William Baliol Brett, afterwards first Viscount Esher, master of the Rolls, by his wife, Eugénie, daughter of Louis Mayer, an Alsatian. His mother, a stepdaughter of Colonel John Gurwood, the editor of Wellington's dispatches, belonged to the D'Orsay-Blessington circle and also had influential friends in Paris. Reginald Brett was educated at Eton, where A. C. Ainger was his tutor, and where he came under the influence of William Johnson Cory, and at Trinity College, Cambridge. At both he made important friendships and developed social as well as political and literary interests. In 1879 he married Eleanor, third daughter of Sylvain Van de Weyer, the Belgian minister in London, who was a close friend of Queen Victoria.

As private secretary to the Marquess of Hartington for seven years (1878–1885), the last three of them spent at the War Office, Brett lived in a society which still retained something of the Disraeli atmosphere; knowing 'everybody', handling confidential affairs touching great men, freely suggesting ideas and actions to ministers, generals, viceroys, and in touch also with literature and the stage. In 1880 he was elected to parliament in the liberal interest as one of the members for Penryn and Falmouth, but at the general election of 1885 he unsuccessfully contested Plymouth and never stood again. Maintaining his friendships, Brett withdrew to Orchard Lea near Windsor Forest, where he was admitted to the queen's private circle; entertained, wrote some minor books, mainly biographical, kept for a time a small racing stable and breeding stud, shot, and fished. But sport was never his passion, and after ten rather aimless years the civil service attracted him. In 1895 his school friend Lord Rosebery, then prime minister, after Brett had refused to enter diplomacy, made him secretary of the Office of Works. He showed such practical talents in improving the domestic arrangements of the royal residences and in superintending the diamond jubilee of 1897 (in which year he was made C.B.) that the queen held him to his post when he succeeded his father as second viscount in 1899, and again, when, in 1900, he was offered the permanent under-secretaryship at the War Office. Esher had already (1899) refused the same post at the Colonial Office under Mr. Chamberlain, and the governorship of Cape Colony, declining to work in leading-strings. The queen created him K.C.V.O. in December 1900 just before her death. After so long a reign, memories of a sovereign's funeral and coronation were dim; he mastered the precedents, and took charge of both ceremonies with complete success.

Queen Victoria had made Esher one of her intimate friends, and she often visited Orchard Lea informally. King Edward VII gave him close friendship and wider scope, in connexion with the new civil list, as secretary of the committee of the Queen Victoria Memorial fund, as deputy constable and lieutenant-governor of Windsor Castle (1901), and as editor, in collaboration with Arthur Christopher Benson, of *Selections from the Correspondence of Queen Victoria* (1907). Esher also published *The Girlhood of Queen Victoria* in 1912. Whatever he touched succeeded, and the king's confidence seemed boundless.

In the universal anxiety about the state of the army, its reform became with Esher an obsession. He saw that the key to it lay in the rejected proposals of the Hartington commission of 1890: viz. no commander-in-chief, a War-Office council on the Admiralty model, and an inspector-general; and he at once sought the ear of the king. He retired from the Office of Works and was created K.C.B. in 1902. In the same year he was made a member of the royal commission appointed, under the chairmanship of the ninth Earl of Elgin, to inquire into the military preparations for and conduct of the South African War. Esher commented on the commission's proceedings in daily letters to the king, who by the end of the year had accepted his views. Although general War Office reform was outside the commission's reference, Esher appended to its report (July 1903) a note formulating his proposals. The prime minister, Mr. Balfour, Esher's lifelong friend, assured of the king's support, definitely approved the policy without further debate, and asked Esher to become secretary of state for war in order to carry it through. Esher would not re-enter politics, but proposed to do the work as chairman of a prime minister's committee, independent of the secretary of state about to be appointed, Mr. Arnold-Forster. The War Office Reconstruction Committee, generally known as the Esher Committee, was set up accordingly, with Admiral Sir John (afterwards Baron) Fisher and Colonel Sir George Clarke (formerly secretary of the Hartington commission, and afterwards Baron Sydenham) as members and Lieutenant-Colonel (afterwards Lieutenant-General Sir) Gerald Ellison as secretary. On 11 January 1904, a fortnight after Clarke's return from the governorship of Victoria, Part I of the Report proposed in outline the creation of an Army Council on Admiralty lines, and an inspector-general of the forces. The Committee would go no further until this had been accepted. That done, and the Council formally constituted (6 February), it produced in quick succession Parts II (26 February) and III (9 March), containing detailed proposals, claiming that they followed logically from the action already taken, and insisting that the Report should be accepted as an organic whole, without any alteration. It was, in fact, approved as it stood. It made two important improvements on Esher's note, namely, the provision of a permanent naval and military secretariat for Mr. Balfour's Committee of Imperial Defence, on which political and service chiefs sat together under the prime minister, and the creation of a General Staff for the army. With the internal working of the War Office (of which Esher's experience was out of date and the other members had none) the Committee dealt less successfully, and many of its recommendations, designed to remove financial control, were founded on errors of fact, and after due trial abandoned within five years. Esher's note had put the adjutant-general first of the military members of the newly-formed Army Council, and the director-general of military intelligence, head of an incomplete thinking department, last. The Committee created a chief of the general staff, ranking first, charged with everything pertaining to operations of war and to training, and furnishing to commanders, in war and peace, staffs trained in such duties. This all-important change was a complete reversal of recent War Office evolution, in which peace and personal considerations had destroyed system. Under the Duke of Cambridge (who commanded in chief 1856–1895) the adjutant-general, as his chief staff officer, had been allowed to swallow whole the surveyor-general (Lord Cardwell's business head) and to eat the quartermaster-general (Wellington's right-hand man) leaf by leaf, that empty title being transferred to a soldier purveyor of transport and supplies. Operations had dropped out of sight. In the field, similarly, there had been a factotum chief staff officer; no clear line had been drawn between command and the business of supply; and no organized operations staff had existed. Accustomed in India to a quartermaster-general, in Wellington's sense of the term, at the head of the operations staff, and to an adjutant-general dealing with personnel and discipline, Lord Roberts had been shocked to find this state of things prevailing in South Africa. At the War Office, therefore, on becoming commander-in-chief (1901), he had overruled opposition and ordered the preparation of a staff manual on Wellingtonian lines. Colonel Ellison, who had worked out the ground-plan of this under Roberts's orders before being appointed secretary to the Esher Committee, produced it to the Committee, which adopted it entire and distributed War Office duties accordingly, only changing the title of Roberts's quartermaster-general to that of chief of the general staff. Thus Esher's uncompromising dictatorship combined with Roberts's initiative to produce a true General Staff which, expanded later by Lord Haldane into the Imperial General Staff, embracing India and the Dominions, built up the armies of the British Empire during the European War of 1914–1918.

His committee dissolved, Esher joined the Committee of Imperial Defence in its search for an improved army system, becoming a permanent member of it in 1905, just before political changes transferred the secretaryship of state for war to Lord Haldane. His support of Lord Fisher's case for a stronger navy brought upon him a personal attack by Kaiser Wilhelm II. A conscriptionist, Esher yet saw that the voluntary system must have full trial, and he gave Haldane invaluable support in his army reforms, commending them to the king as the best work accomplished since Cardwell's secretaryship (1868–1874); and he became the very active chairman (1909–1913) and later (1912–1921) president of the London County Territorial Force Association. His position at this period is perhaps best described as *liaison* between king and ministers. He gave advice freely, but all action was taken constitutionally by the responsible minister. Neither Sir Henry Campbell-Bannerman's succession as prime minister in December 1905 nor the accession of King George V in May 1910 caused any interruption of this relation.

An admirable committee man, Esher was in great demand for boards such as those of the British Museum (of which he was a king's trustee), the Imperial College of Science (of which he was governor), and the Wallace Collection; but after two years' trial of *haute finance* in the City he abandoned it as uncongenial (1904). He was created G.C.V.O. (1905) and G.C.B. (1908), sworn a privy councillor (1922), and appointed keeper of the king's archives (1910) and governor and constable of Windsor Castle (1928); but he refused the viceroyship of India in 1908 and an earldom at some date not known to his family. From September 1914 onwards he was in France on a confidential mission, at the request of Lord Kitchener, subsequently renewed by Mr. Asquith and by Mr. Lloyd George. The documents relating to it remain under seal in the British Museum until

1981 together with Esher's diaries for the first half of the War and other papers, but it is known that in 1917–1918 he was present at conferences with French ministers on military matters.

After the return of peace in 1919, Esher devoted much time to literature and published some more biographical books, including *Ionicus* (1923), an informal biography of William Johnson Cory. He died suddenly 22 January 1930 at his London house, leaving a widow, two sons, and two daughters. His family life was peculiarly happy, and, in particular, his relations with his younger son, Maurice, even while at Eton, as revealed in Esher's published *Journals and Letters*, were rather those of a brother than a father. He was succeeded as third viscount by his elder son, Oliver Sylvain Baliol (born 1881).

Inheriting marked ability, great social gifts, and influential connexions, Esher possessed all the qualifications for success in public life except the conviction that it was worth while. The first Viscount Esher had been spurred, by love and by lack of independent means, to set his foot on the path that led him to professional eminence; the second, whose dislike of the dust of the arena outweighed his liking for power, might have returned to the earlier Brett tradition of enjoying life as it came, without effort, had not his association with the royal family pointed a way to the power without the dust, and justified him in recording, when refusing the viceroyalty, that, with his opportunity of influencing vital decisions at the centre, India for him 'would be (it sounds vain, but it isn't) parochial'. This influence he exercised behind a curtain, seeking neither personal advancement nor the interests of a political party, but only the public good as he saw it—and his vision was acute. His work on the committee which goes by his name and his effective backing of Lord Haldane's army reforms at a critical juncture made no mean contribution to the Allied victory of 1918.

There are three portraits of Lord Esher at Watlington Park, Oxfordshire, painted by Julian Storey, Edmund Brock, and Glyn Philpot in or about 1885, 1905, and 1925 respectively.

[Maurice V. Brett, *Journals and Letters of Reginald Viscount Esher* (to 1910), 2 vols., 1934; C. H. Dudley Ward, *A Romance of the Nineteenth Century*, 1923; Sir Gerald Ellison, *Lord Roberts and the General Staff*, in the *Nineteenth Century*, December 1932; private information; personal knowledge.]

C. HARRIS

published 1937

LEOPOLD George Duncan Albert

(1853–1884)

Duke of Albany

Fourth and youngest son of Queen Victoria and the prince consort, was born at Buckingham Palace on 7 April 1853. So delicate was his health that his baptism was deferred until the ensuing 28 June (Coronation day), when the rite was performed at Buckingham Palace, his sponsors being George V, king of Hanover (after whom he was named George), Prince Ernest of Hohenlohe-Langenburg, Augusta, princess of Prussia (afterwards German Empress), and Princess Mary of Cambridge, afterwards Duchess of Teck. The prince was named Leopold after his great-uncle, Leopold II, king of the Belgians, Albert after his father, and Duncan in compliment to Scotland. His ill-health debarred him from the ordinary sports of boyhood, and even precluded a systematic course of education. His mind, however, was active, he early evinced a love of books—Shakespeare and Sir Walter Scott were his favourite authors—and he showed remarkable aptitude for music and modern languages. He was instructed in the rudiments of religion and science by Canon Duckworth, Dean Stanley, and Professor Tyndall. Later on his principal tutor was Mr. (later Sir) Robert Hawthorn Collins, afterwards comptroller of his household, with whom he went into residence at Oxford in 1872, matriculating at Christ Church (27 Nov.). He lived at Wykeham House, St. Giles's, near the parks; attended, in the garb of a gentleman-commoner, the lectures of the professors of history, poetry, music, fine art, and political economy, and studied science at the museum and modern languages at the Taylorian Institution.

On coming of age in 1874 the prince was sworn of the privy council, and granted an annuity of 15,000*l*. In the winter of 1874–5 his life was threatened by a severe attack of typhus fever. In 1876 he left the university with the honorary degree of D.C.L., and established himself at Boyton House, Wiltshire, whence he removed in 1879 to Claremont. Part of the intervening years he spent in travel in France, Germany, Switzerland, and Italy, and in 1880 he made a tour in Canada and the United States. In 1878 he was elected president of the Royal Society of Literature, and in 1879 vice-president of the Society of Arts. He was a graceful and effective public speaker, and took a lively interest in social questions. In 1879 he spoke in favour of the movement for university extension (Mansion House, 19 Feb.), advocated the cause of technical education in presiding at the prize distribution at the Birkbeck Institute, Chancery Lane (25 Feb.), took the chair and spoke at a meeting at Grosvenor House in support of the Royal

Institution in aid of the Deaf and Dumb (16 May), and opened Firth College, Sheffield (20 Oct.). In 1880 he laid the foundation-stone of the Oxford High School (14 April). In 1881 he presided at the first meeting of the Kyrle Society (27 Jan.), opened University College, Nottingham (30 June), advocated the establishment of a national conservatoire of music at a soirée at Manchester (12 Dec.), and laid the foundation-stone of the Princess Helena College at Ealing (17 Dec.).

Meanwhile the prince had been created (24 May 1881) Duke of Albany, Earl of Clarence, and Baron Arklow, and had taken his seat in the House of Lords (24 June). He spent the following autumn at Frankfort, where he made the acquaintance of Princess Helen Frederica Augusta, daughter of H.S.H. George Victor, prince of Waldeck-Pyrmont, to whom (the queen having given her consent, 29 Nov.) he was married in St. George's Chapel, Windsor, on 27 April 1882. His allowance was now raised to 25,000l., provision being also made for a jointure for the princess of 6,000l. in the event of her widowhood. The prince and princess resided at Claremont, the prince, so far as his health permitted, continuing his exertions in the cause of education, though his public appearances were fewer than formerly. One of the latest of them was the laying of the foundation-stone of the new buildings of the Birkbeck Institute (23 April 1883). In the spring of 1884 his health compelled a visit to the south of France. At first he seemed to be benefited by the change, but a fall in a clubhouse at Cannes led to an attack of epilepsy, of which he died at the Villa Nevada on 28 March. The funeral took place in St. George's Chapel, Windsor, on 6 April. He left a daughter (Princess Alexander of Teck); a posthumous son, born 19 July, became Duke of Saxe-Coburg in 1900.

The prince was K.G., K.T., G.C.S.I., G.C.M.G., D.C.L. of the university of Durham, a bencher of Lincoln's Inn, an elder brother of Trinity House, a freeman of the city of London, and a freemason. He was also honorary colonel of the third battalion Seaforth Highlanders, and a member of various foreign orders.

A portrait by Carl Sohn, jun., belongs to the Duchess of Albany. Sir James Linton painted a picture of the duke's marriage, which is now at Windsor.

[Obituary and other notices in the Times, Morning Post, Ann. Register; Academy, xxv. 242; Transactions of the Royal Society of Literature, 2nd ser.; Journal of the Society of Arts, 1879 et seq.; Hansard Parl. Deb. 3rd ser. ccxxi. 268, 645, 978; Warre's Life and Speeches of H.R.H. Prince Leopold (1884); Martin's Life of the Prince Consort; Foster's Alumni Oxonienses, and Burke's Peerage.]

JAMES McMULLEN RIGG

published 1892

LANGTRY Emilie Charlotte ('Lillie')
(1853-1929)

Actress, was born 13 October 1853 at St Saviour's rectory, Jersey, the only daughter and sixth of the seven children of William Corbet Le Breton, dean of Jersey, and his wife Emilie Davis Martin. Educated at home, she developed into a socially ambitious and remarkably beautiful young woman. In 1874 she married Edward Langtry, son of a Belfast shipowner. Within three years the couple were established in London where Lillie became celebrated, not only as a 'professional beauty'—a society woman whose photographic likenesses were on sale to the public—but as the mistress of Albert Edward, Prince of Wales. For the following three years she enjoyed a period of heady social success. Her portrait was painted by most leading artists of the day; the best known being 'A Jersey Lily' by (Sir) John Everett Millais, which is in the possession of the Société Jersiaise in Jersey.

Towards the end of her three-year liaison with the Prince of Wales, Lillie met Prince Louis of Battenberg. In Paris, in March 1881, she bore him a daughter, who was christened Jeanne-Marie, with the surname of Langtry. The birth of this child coincided with the bankruptcy of Edward Langtry and the break-up of Lillie's marriage.

Exceptionally resilient, Lillie embarked on a new career—as an actress. Her appearance in a charity performance led to an offer to join the Bancrofts' company at the Haymarket Theatre. Appreciating that it was her notoriety, as the ex-mistress of the Prince of Wales, that was attracting audiences, Lillie soon founded her own company. Between 1882 and 1889 she divided her time between tours of the United States and appearances on various London stages. Although never more than a competent actress, she was an extremely decorative and popular one, at her best in plays about upper-class society. In 1889 she returned permanently to England. To her career as an actress, the always practical Lillie now added another: that of a highly successful racehorse owner.

In 1899, two years after the death of the by then destitute Edward Langtry, Lillie married Hugo, the son of Sir Henry de Bathe, baronet. Her new husband was eighteen years her junior. On the death of her father-in-law in 1907, Lillie became Lady de Bathe.

With her attempt to establish a company at the Imperial Theatre, Westminster, having failed, Lillie resumed touring. After World War I, she bought a villa in the south of France and in 1925 published a highly selective book of memoirs. She died in Monte Carlo 12 February 1929 and was buried in St Saviour's churchyard, Jersey.

Mountbatten

[*The Times*, 13 February 1929; Emilie Charlotte Langtry, *The Days I Knew*, 1925; Philip Magnus, *King Edward the Seventh*, 1964; private information.]

THEO ARONSON

published 1993

MOUNTBATTEN Louis Alexander, formerly styled Prince

(1854–1921)

First Marquess of Milford Haven

Admiral of the fleet, the eldest son of Prince Alexander of Hesse (a younger son of Louis II, Grand Duke of Hesse-Darmstadt) by his wife, Countess Julia Theresa von Haucke, was born at Gratz, Austria, 24 May 1854. The friendship between his mother and Princess Alice, daughter of Queen Victoria and consort of Prince Frederick of Hesse (afterwards Grand Duke Louis IV), led to Prince Louis settling in this country as a boy; and, having become naturalized as a British subject, he entered the royal navy as a cadet in 1868. In 1869 he was rated midshipman, and joined the *Royal Alfred*, flagship of Vice-Admiral (Sir) Edward Fanshawe on the North America and West Indies station. When the Admiralty took over the *Serapis* in 1874 for the visit of the Prince of Wales to India, Prince Louis, then sub-lieutenant, was selected to serve as one of the complement of officers. He already gave promise of distinction. His sympathies were entirely British, and Queen Victoria watched his career with almost motherly interest. His abilities as a linguist proved of no slight advantage to him in later life. At the conclusion of the Indian tour he was promoted to lieutenant, and served in the *Inconstant* during the Egyptian War, taking part in the bombardment of Alexandria (11 July 1882). He subsequently landed with the naval brigade, in command of a Gatling gun battery, for the occupation of Alexandria. After a period of service in the royal yacht, he was promoted to commander in 1885.

At this period the defence policy of this country was undergoing a gradual readjustment in accordance with the theories of what became known as 'the blue-water school', and Prince Louis was selected by the Admiralty to act as naval adviser to the inspector-general of fortifications, with a view to co-ordinating naval and military ideas. He took up this appointment in 1892, having been promoted captain in the preceding year, and held it until October 1894. In February 1894 he was chosen to act as joint secretary of the naval and military committee on defence, which afterwards was developed into the committee of imperial defence. During these years he applied himself seriously to the study of the defence problem in its naval and military aspects and was peculiarly well qualified when, in 1900, he was made assistant-director of naval intelligence. After a short period of service in the Mediterranean, he returned to the Admiralty in 1902 as director of naval intelligence, and retained that position until 1905, having been promoted to rear-admiral in 1904.

By this time Prince Louis, who in 1884 had married his cousin, Princess Victoria, daughter of Louis IV of Hesse-Darmstadt and Princess Alice, was regarded throughout the service as an officer who had established his fitness for high command at sea. On leaving the Admiralty in 1905 he hoisted his flag in the *Drake* as rear-admiral commanding the second cruiser squadron. In these circumstances he began his career as an admiral at sea, and that he was to exercise no slight influence upon the training of the British navy soon became apparent. After two years in the second cruiser squadron, his selection as second in command of the fleet in the Mediterranean met with general approval in the navy. In the meantime Lord Fisher had become the dominating figure at the Admiralty, and it was no matter of surprise when in 1908 Prince Louis was directed to move his flag into the Atlantic fleet as commander-in-chief. After two years in that command he was appointed vice-admiral commanding the third and fourth divisions of the newly constituted home fleets, and from thence in December 1911 he returned to the Admiralty as second sea lord. Mr. Winston Churchill had become first lord in that year, and he selected Prince Louis as first sea lord a year later on the retirement of Sir Francis Bridgeman. This selection was probably unwise on grounds of political expediency, in view of the circumstances of Prince Louis's birth, and of the threatening situation which was developing abroad.

In July 1914 a test mobilization of the naval reserves was carried out, and the ships were due to disperse, after carrying out exercises in the English Channel, at the moment when relations between this country and Germany had become strained. Owing to the illness of his wife, Mr. Churchill was absent from the Admiralty during the critical week-end (25–27 July) when it had to be decided whether the fleet should be dispersed and the reserve ships demobilized, in accordance with the plans already made, or whether preliminary steps should be taken to place the squadrons at their various war stations. This decision rested with the first sea lord. After a telephone conversation with the first lord at Cromer, Prince Louis, as he subsequently explained in a published letter, 'directed the secretary, as a first step, to send an Admiralty order by telegraph to the commander-in-chief of the home fleets at Portland to the effect that no ship was to leave that anchorage until further orders'. War had not then been declared, but the prevision of the first sea lord ensured that when it became inevitable the navy should be in a state of readiness. Political events moved rapidly. At four o'clock on the morning of 3 August the mobilization of the navy had been completed. The prompt initiative which Prince Louis had exhibited in this emergency did not shield him from attack in subsequent months on account of his 'German origin'. On 29 October, as the final act of patriotism in his long and distinguished naval career, he resigned his position as first sea lord. He lived to see the complete triumph of the naval weapon which he had helped to forge, dying on 11 September 1921 in his chambers at Half Moon Street, Piccadilly, at the age of sixty-seven.

With the coming of peace, tribute was paid to the services which he had rendered the country, by his promotion to the rank of admiral of the fleet. In July 1917, by the request of the King, Prince Louis relinquished the style and title of serene highness and prince, assumed for himself and his descendants the surname of Mountbatten, and was raised to the peerage of the United Kingdom as Marquess of Milford Haven, Earl of Medina, and Viscount Alderney. He left two sons and two daughters, and was succeeded in the marquessate by his elder son, George Louis, Earl of Medina.

Prince Louis, who was of a commanding presence and possessed great charm of manner, looked the beau-ideal of the British naval officer, and took throughout his life a keen interest in British naval history. He was particularly interested in the Navy Records Society and was the first president of the Society of Nautical Research. He was also associated with Admiral Sir Percy Scott in the invention of the cone signalling apparatus, and introduced into the service an instrument to enable the complicated calculations, which are necessary before certain tactical manœuvres can be carried out, to be resolved mechanically.

A portrait of Prince Louis is included in Sir A. S. Cope's picture 'Some Sea Officers of the Great War', painted in 1921, which is in the National Portrait Gallery.

[Private information; personal knowledge.]

ARCHIBALD HURD

published 1927

Princess of Great Britain and Ireland, the fifth daughter and youngest child of Queen Victoria, was born at Buckingham Palace, 14 April 1857. From her earliest days she gave promise of unusual personality and charm, and when two years old was described by a contemporary diarist as 'a delicious child ... full of wit and fun'. To her, the much-loved 'Baby' of the Prince Consort, the Queen turned for solace at the time of her husband's death, and the young Princess was never long out of her sight. When her elder sisters married she was the daughter who always stayed at home, and she was soon filling, with great discretion and tact, the difficult role of the Queen's constant companion and close confidante. Great pains were taken over her education, and her marked artistic talents were fostered in every possible way. She was a first-rate pianist and a talented musician, several of whose compositions were published. In her younger days she knew most of the great musicians, and was a friend of many of them. For some years she had no thought of marriage, but at the age of twenty-eight she fell in love with Prince Henry Maurice of Battenberg and the Queen consented to their union on the strict understanding that, so long as she lived, they should remain under her roof and make their home with her. The marriage took place in Whippingham church, near Osborne, 23 July 1885. Four children were born of the marriage. The only daughter, Princess Victoria Eugénie Julia Ena, married King Alfonso XIII of Spain. The three sons were Prince Alexander Albert (subsequently the Marquess of Carisbrooke), Prince Leopold Arthur Louis (later Lord Leopold Mountbatten) who died in 1922, and Prince Maurice Victor Donald, who as a lieutenant in the 60th Rifles was killed in the first battle of Ypres in 1914. Prince Henry of Battenberg volunteered for active service in 1895 and died on the way home from the Ashanti expedition 20 January 1896. After his marriage the Queen had appointed him governor of the Isle of Wight, an ancient office analogous to that of lord lieutenant. Princess Henry was now given this appointment, and continued her close attendance on the Queen, so that it was not until the Queen's death in 1901 that she and her children were to know a home of their own at Osborne Cottage. Later, in 1914, the Princess made the governor's house at Carisbrooke Castle her summer residence, the winters being spent abroad or at Kensington Palace.

Queen Victoria bequeathed to the Princess all her private journals, consisting of many manuscript volumes dating back to before 1837, with the injunction that she was to modify or destroy any portions which appeared to her unsuitable for permanent preservation. This work she carried out with devoted care, every page being transcribed in her own hand, and the original manuscript thereupon destroyed. The task was so vast that it was not completed until 1942, and the transcribed journal is now preserved among the royal archives at Windsor. From an historical point of view it is perhaps to be regretted that Queen Victoria's private opinion of various contemporary personages and events may thus have been lost to posterity, but the Princess acted in accordance with her instructions, and nothing was allowed to remain which, in her opinion, might hurt the feelings of the persons concerned, or even of their relations. Her other literary work included the translation of extracts from the diary of Queen Victoria's maternal grandmother Augusta, Duchess of Saxe-Coburg-Saalfeld, which were published in 1941 under the title of *In Napoleonic Days*.

In 1917 the family name of Battenberg was changed at the request of King George V to Mountbatten, and the Princess resumed her former title of Princess Beatrice. During her long tenure of the governorship of the Isle of Wight, despite an inherited shyness which she was never able to eradicate, the Princess was zealous in the performance of her public duties, and particularly in the support of every movement for the relief of sickness and distress. Her understanding sympathy undoubtedly derived from her own long experience of sorrow. Her whole youth had been darkened by the pall of perpetual mourning which shrouded her life for so many years after her father's death; she herself had been widowed at the age of thirty-eight and had subsequently mourned the loss of two sons. She was ever guided by a deep sense of duty and an unfailing kindness of heart, while those admitted to her friendship could never forget her great loyalty, her sense of humour, and her devoutly religious convictions. She died at Brantridge Park, Balcombe, Sussex, 26 October 1944, and after the war was buried beside her husband in the chapel which she had prepared at Whippingham.

The best portrait of Princess Beatrice was painted by P. A. de László in 1912. There are two others by H. von Angeli (at the ages of eighteen and thirty-five), one by J. Sorolla (1904), and a small head by F. X. Winterhalter. All are in the possession of the Marquess of Carisbrooke.

[Private information; personal knowledge.]

C. F. ASPINALL-OGLANDER

published 1959

HENRY Maurice of Battenberg

(1858–1896)

Prince

Born at Milan on 5 Oct. 1858, was third son of Prince Alexander of Hesse (1823–1888) and his morganatic wife, the countess Julie von Haucke, daughter of an ex-minister of war for Poland, to whom was granted, in 1858, the title of Princess of Battenberg. His elder brother Alexander was on 29 April 1879 elected first prince of Bulgaria; he abdicated on 6 Sept. 1886 and died on 17 Nov. 1893. His brother, Prince Louis of Battenberg, married, on 30 April 1884, Victoria, eldest daughter of the Princess Alice of Hesse, third daughter of Queen Victoria, and this connection brought Prince Henry, who had received a military education and become lieutenant in the 10th regiment of Rhenish hussars, into contact with the English court. On 23 July 1885 he was married at Whippingham church by the archbishop of Canterbury to the Princess Beatrice, youngest daughter of Queen Victoria. He was naturalised by an act of parliament which passed the House of Lords on 31 July in the same year, was elected K.G. on 22 July, and was granted the title of royal highness; he was also made colonel in the army and captain-general and governor of the Isle of Wight. He took great interest in the Isle of Wight volunteer corps. In November 1895 he volunteered for service with the Ashanti expeditionary force. He sailed on 8 Dec., at first as merely an auxiliary, but he was afterwards made military secretary to the commander-in-chief, Sir Francis Scott. He marched with the force to within thirty miles of Kumasi, when he was attacked by fever; he returned to Cape Coast Castle and embarked on the Blonde cruiser on 17 Jan. 1896. He died at sea on the 20th; his remains were brought to England and interred at Whippingham on 5 Feb. He left issue three sons, Princes Alexander, Leopold, and Maurice, and one daughter, the Princess Victoria of Battenburg, afterwards Queen of Spain.

[Almanach de Gotha, 1895; Times, 23 Jan. to 6 Feb. 1896, passim; Burke's Peerage, 1895; Men of the Time, 14th edit.]

ALBERT FREDERICK POLLARD

published 1901

GREVILLE Frances Evelyn

(1861–1938)

Countess of Warwick

Was born in London 10 December 1861, the elder daughter and co-heiress of Colonel Charles Henry Maynard (only son of the last Viscount Maynard), by his second wife, Blanche Adeliza, second daughter of Henry FitzRoy, of Salcey Lawn, Northamptonshire. She was educated at home. In 1881 she married Francis Richard Charles Guy Greville, Lord Brooke, who succeeded his father as fifth Earl of Warwick in 1893 and died in 1924. They had three sons, of whom the eldest became sixth Earl of Warwick and died in 1928, and the second died in infancy, and two daughters.

Lady Warwick was a celebrated late Victorian and Edwardian beauty and a member of the 'Marlborough House set' which grew up about the Prince of Wales (afterwards King Edward VII) as a reaction from the inflexible and limited social life of Queen Victoria's court. She inherited Easton Lodge, Dunmow, Essex, from her grandfather and at first made it a country retreat for fashionable Edwardians. After her husband had inherited Warwick Castle, Lady Warwick gave a ball there in 1895, the extravagance of which was criticized in *The Clarion*. As a result of this she met the editor, Robert Blatchford, and under his influence she was converted to socialism. She recalled at the time that the motto of her husband's family was *Vix ea nostra voco*. Her devotion to the cause of labour and its champions was as complete as her early conquests in society. She established a school at Dunmow to encourage rural occupations, and the first college for training women in horticulture and agriculture at Studley Castle, Warwickshire. At the general election of 1923 she stood as labour candidate for Warwick and Leamington, but was defeated by the conservative, Mr. Anthony Eden, brother-in-law of her eldest son. In 1925 Lady Warwick wished the labour party to accept Easton Lodge as an international labour university, but the plan was considered impracticable and her offer was refused. Easton, however, became an unofficial meeting-place for labour reformers, and Lady Warwick's interest in the improvement of conditions among the working class continued to the end of her life. She was also solicitous for the preservation of birds and animals, and she formed a sanctuary at Easton where she collected a multitude of birds, domestic animals, and horses about her. She used her social position, her fortune, and her continuous vitality for all her charitable and social interests and achieved results equal to those of any woman of her class in her time.

Lady Warwick wrote with ease and an amiable interest in both the past and the present. Of her numerous books *Warwick Castle and its Earls* (1903) records the historical background of her married life: *A Woman and the War* (1916), *Life's Ebb and Flow* (1929), and *Afterthoughts* (1931) revealed her conversion from the luxurious standards of Edwardian society to care for the working classes. Her intelligent comprehension of problems made her a valuable advocate of the labour cause, and her kindness of heart no less than her opinions won for her regard from those ranks of society which she sought to help.

Lady Warwick died at Easton Lodge 26 July 1938. A portrait by Carolus-Duran is at Warwick Castle; another, by J. S. Sargent, is in America.

[*The Times*, 27 July 1938; private information; personal knowledge.]

HECTOR BOLITHO

published 1949

ALBERT VICTOR Christian Edward

(1864–1892)

Duke of Clarence and Avondale and *Earl of Athlone*

Born at Frogmore, Buckinghamshire, on 8 Jan. 1864, was the eldest son of Albert Edward, prince of Wales (now Edward VII), and (Queen) Alexandra, eldest daughter of Christian IX, king of Denmark. Queen Victoria was his grandmother, and Prince Albert Victor stood next to his father in the direct line of succession to the throne. He was baptised in Buckingham Palace chapel on 10 March following his birth, and was privately educated until 1877, when he was sent to join the training ship Britannia at Dartmouth. In 1879 he went with his younger brother Prince George (now Prince of Wales) on a three years' cruise in H.M.S. Bacchante, which sailed round the world and visited most of the British colonies. An account of the cruise, 'compiled from the private journals, letters, and note-books' of the young princes, was published in 1886 in two stout volumes by their tutor, the Rev. John N. (afterwards Canon) Dalton. After some tuition in 1882–3 from James Kenneth Stephen, Prince Albert Victor was in October 1883 entered at Trinity College, Cambridge; during the long vacations he studied at Heidelberg, and in 1888 he was created hon. LL.D. of Cambridge. He was then sent to Aldershot, became lieutenant in the 10th hussars in 1886, major in 1889, and in 1889 captain in the 9th lancers, captain in the 3rd king's royal rifles, and aide-de-camp to the queen. In 1887 he visited Ireland, and in 1889–90 India (see J. D. Rees, *The Duke of Clarence in Southern India*, London, 1891). On 24 May 1890 he was created Earl of Athlone and Duke of Clarence and Avondale. On 7 Dec. 1891 his betrothal was announced with his cousin, the Princess Victoria Mary ('May') of Teck (now the Princess of Wales). The wedding was fixed for 27 Feb. 1892, but on 14 Jan. 1892 the duke died of pneumonia following influenza at Sandringham. He was buried in St. George's Chapel, Windsor, on 20 Jan. His place in the direct line of succession to the throne was taken by his brother George, then Duke of York. A portrait painted by J. Sant, R.A., in 1872, and another of him and Prince George as midshipmen, painted by C. Sohn, were exhibited in the Victorian Exhibition; other portraits are reproduced in Vincent's 'Memoir.' His death was the occasion of many laments in prose and verse, of which Tennyson's elegy, published in the 'Nineteenth Century,' February 1892, is the most notable. Lord Selborne wrote at the time, 'I do not think there has been a more tragic event in our time, or one which is more likely to touch the hearts of the people generally' (*Memorials*, ii. 373). On 18 Dec. 1892 King Edward VII, then Prince of Wales, laid the foundation-stone of the 'Clarence Memorial Wing' of St. Mary's Hospital, Paddington, which was designed to commemorate the duke's name.

[Memoir by J. G. Vincent, 1893; G. E. C[okayne]'s Complete Peerage, viii. 237–8; Dalton's Cruise of the Bacchante, 1886; Men of the Time, ed. 1891; Times, 15–21 Jan. 1892; Brit. Mus. Cat.]

ALBERT FREDERICK POLLARD

published 1901

GEORGE V (1865–1936)

King of Great Britain, Ireland, and the British Dominions beyond the seas, Emperor of India, was born at Marlborough House, London, 3 June 1865, the second child of the Prince and Princess of Wales, later King Edward VII and Queen Alexandra. He was baptized at Windsor Castle on 7 July following by the names of George Frederick Ernest Albert. Like Richard I, Henry VIII, Charles I, and other notable sovereigns he was not born to the expectation of kingship: his elder brother, Prince Albert Victor Christian Edward, Duke of Clarence, (known as Prince Eddy), was his senior by seventeen months, and Prince George remained a younger son for the first twenty-six years of his life. Nor at that moment in the history of the monarchy could it have been asserted with confidence that he would have attained to the throne even had he been the elder. There were many still living who remembered the peculiar contribution to the history of their times made by the sons of George III; and although twenty-one years of ideal married life had done much to endear Queen Victoria to her subjects, the period of muffled seclusion which had elapsed since the death of the Prince Consort was already beginning to be the subject of murmuring, and the reported manner of life of the Prince of Wales lent support to the nascent republican sentiment.

But of disquieting possibilities such as these the young princes and their three sisters were unaware as their childhood pursued its course in an atmosphere of sustained happiness and affection. In his attachment to his children the Prince of Wales was only surpassed by their mother; her happiest hours were spent in the nursery, and Prince George's mind was formed from earliest infancy under the spell of her charm and merriment. To her, as also to the memory of his father, he remained devoted throughout life.

An intellectual circle it was not, neither did the arts find place within the sphere of its interests, beyond a certain proficiency at the piano on the part of the mother. But all the ingredients for happiness were there, the family was sufficiently numerous to mitigate the disadvantages of isolation, and with the simple pleasures of childhood the early years passed in uneventful contentment. No undue stress was laid upon book-learning, of which in his youth the Prince of Wales had received a surfeit. They lived while in London at Marlborough House; their seaside visits were based upon Osborne in the Isle of Wight; August and September would find them at Abergeldie adjoining the Balmoral estate in Scotland. But for the most part it was Sandringham House in Norfolk that they regarded as home, the house which his father had built and for which King George himself all his life retained a particular affection. Here in an extensive domain of heath and pine in the bracing east coast air they roamed and played and rode, leading the normal country life of the days before motors, sharing the pride of other Norfolk families in their county and their home.

Within the family circle Prince George was distinguished by an irrepressible fund of spirits: 'so affectionate, though sometimes rather naughty', as Queen Victoria noted in her diary. In later years he would credit his youthful self with a hot temper, the germ perhaps of that occasional irascibility which marked his nature without disguising the essential kindliness beneath. He showed from the first more character than his elder brother. His open manner and twinkling eye brought him in boyhood friendships that endured through life. With the same loyalty he retained an abiding affection for the Rev. John Neale Dalton, his tutor between the ages of six and eighteen. Dalton left to become a canon of Windsor; his death in 1931 terminated an unbroken intimacy of sixty years.

At the age of twelve (1877) Prince George, together with his brother, joined the old wooden training ship *Britannia* at Dartmouth as a naval cadet. Younger than his fellows (indeed the youngest cadet ever admitted) and small even for his age, he underwent the full curriculum, in addition to further instruction in the humanities from Dalton who continued in attendance as tutor. The brothers were allowed to share a special cabin, but their only other distinction, as the King was wont to recall in later years, was that their services were at the command of all who desired a princely fag. Thus with the theory of navigation the future Prince of Wales acquired the practice of *Ich Dien*. To the seamanship he took kindly from the first, enjoying in particular the handling of a boat, in which sphere later on his proficiency was to become marked.

After the prescribed course of two years the brothers passed out in the summer of 1879. Prince George, whose nature always responded to the call of the sea, had already set his heart upon a naval career, and this aspiration found favour both with his father and the Queen. Both brothers were posted in August to the *Bacchante*, a fully-rigged cruiser-corvette with auxiliary engines and a complement of four hundred and fifty. This proved to be their home for the next three years. In it they first made an eight months' cruise to the West Indies by way of Gibraltar and a preliminary excursion into the Mediterranean. Prince Eddy's sixteenth birthday was celebrated when they were at Port of Spain, Trinidad (8 January 1880); the occasion was marked by their being both rated as midshipmen. This brought them level with two of King George's lifelong friends among their shipmates, John Scott (later seventh Duke of Buccleuch) and Rosslyn Wemyss (later Lord Wester Wemyss) who was destined to rise to the top of his profession.

From this short cruise the princes returned in May 1880. After two months' leave they set off again in the *Bacchante*, which was now to form part of a flying squadron of five ships of the line detached for an extended training cruise round the Horn to Vancouver and thence to China and Japan, the passages being made largely under sail. Dalton accompanied them as governor, being entered on the ship's books as acting chaplain; and he it was who subsequently edited from the princes' diaries and letters two ponderous volumes, published in 1886, entitled *The Cruise of H.M.S. 'Bacchante' 1879–1882*. In the course of some 1,500 pages every detail of both cruises is recorded, together with a mass of interesting information about the topography and development of the places visited; but the work is conceived in so improving a style as to iron out all traces of individuality in the two princes.

The squadron assembled off Vigo, whence on 31 October (1880) course was set for the River Plate; Monte Video was reached on 22 December. Resuming the cruise on 19 January (1881) they reached the Falkland Islands on the 24th. Here they were intercepted by a signal from home bidding them abandon the projected passage to the Pacific and sail instead to the Cape of Good Hope, there to show the flag at a moment when British prestige in South Africa was at a low ebb. They accomplished this 4,000-mile voyage in three weeks, arriving at the Cape on 16 February, eleven days before the third successive humiliation inflicted by the Boers upon the British, at Majuba Hill.

The squadron was not in the event called upon to land a force. On 9 April it sailed once more, this time on a 5,000-mile trip across the Indian Ocean to Australia. Visits were paid to Albany (15 May), Adelaide, Melbourne, Ballarat (where the brothers descended a gold mine), Sydney, and Brisbane. They left the shores of Australia on 20 August with regret after enjoying the hospitality of its inhabitants for three months. They now set off for Fiji, where they passed a week (3–9 September) before embarking on another voyage of 4,000 miles to Japan. Yokohama was reached on 21 October, and after a month in the country they crossed to Shanghai (22 November) and thence passed down the coast to Hong-Kong (20 December), and so to Singapore (9 January 1882). Returning by Colombo to Suez (1 March), they were able to enjoy a month's sightseeing in Egypt, after which they crossed to Jaffa (28 March) and made their way on horseback through the Holy Land, covering thus close on 600 miles in the course of six weeks. On 6 May they rejoined the *Bacchante* at Beirut and crossed to Athens, where for ten days the brothers were the guests of their maternal uncle, King George of the Hellenes, before returning home through the Mediterranean.

Immediately upon their return to Portsmouth both princes were confirmed by Archbishop Tait in Whippingham church (8 August) in the presence of Queen Victoria. Exactly three years had passed since she had taken leave of Prince George, then a child of fourteen. Now at seventeen he was on the threshold of manhood, more travelled by far than his father at forty; incomparably more so than herself at sixty-three or than any of her predecessors on the throne. Throughout 45,000 miles of voyaging he had shared cheerfully and unselfishly in the hard fare and arduous duties of a young officer at sea, in standards of comfort which would now be regarded as primitive. He had measured himself against the responsibility of every junior officer for the lives of the men in his cutter. When the journey had first been mooted the Queen had noted (Diary, 15 May 1879): 'Mr. Smith and others are afraid lest something might happen if both boys went': her will had prevailed, but something very nearly had happened when the *Bacchante* narrowly escaped shipwreck in a storm off Southern Australia. From the first the understanding had been (Diary, 7 February 1877) that 'Georgie should only enter the Navy if he liked it'. Now he had tasted the salty life of the sea and found it good.

For the next year Prince George remained ashore. After a holiday, of which the most enjoyable part was the shooting at Abergeldie, the two brothers were taken to Lausanne in order to improve their French. Upon their return in the following June (1883) their ways parted: the elder entered the army; the younger, bereft of Dalton's affectionate tutelage, joined the corvette *Canada* for service on the North America station. Her captain, Francis Durrant, became his governor and remained his friend. He stayed with his aunt Princess Louise, whose husband (the Marquess of Lorne) was governor-general of Canada; and a visit to Niagara just warranted the modest claim made in later years that he had set foot on the soil of the United States of America. Before his return to England in July 1884 he had visited his future dominions in the West Indies for the second time. On his nineteenth birthday (3 June 1884) he had been promoted sub-lieutenant, and on 4 August he was invested with the Order of the Garter by Queen Victoria at Osborne.

In September Prince George joined the Royal Naval College at Greenwich, 'where the work is very hard; nine hours a day' (Queen's diary, 7 December). After six months he secured a first class in seamanship, gunnery, and torpedo work, and he next proceeded to Portsmouth for his course in pilotage. Here, as in the *Britannia*, his advancement owed little to his august station, for Captain (afterwards Admiral of the Fleet Lord) Fisher wrote: 'Prince George only lost his first class at Pilotage by 20 marks. The yarn is that one of his examiners, an old salt-horse sailor, didn't think it would do to let him fancy he knew all about it.' These obstacles negotiated, he was promoted lieutenant.

To his satisfaction Prince George was now appointed as fifth lieutenant to the *Thunderer*, under Captain (Sir) Henry Stephenson, whom he had known all his life, as equerry to his father, as captain of the royal yacht, and as captain of a ship accompanying the *Bacchante* on her long cruise. To him the Prince gave unstinted loyalty and devoted service, and from him he received in return disinterested counsel in the spirit of the father's dictum, 'you can do him no greater service than being very strict with him'.

Prince George remained until November 1888 on the Mediterranean station, where his uncle Prince Alfred, Duke of Edinburgh, was commander-in-chief. At the jubilee Queen Victoria appointed him her personal naval aide-de-camp on 21 June 1887. He was in London for this occasion, and again on 1 June 1889 when he received the freedom of the City at Guildhall. A month later he attained his first independent command on commissioning torpedo boat No. 79. In May 1890 he was advanced to the command of a gunboat of the first class, the *Thrush*, which he at once took across the Atlantic to Montreal after towing a torpedo boat out to Gibraltar on the way. Still a lieutenant, he brought his ship home in the following year and was promoted commander in August 1891 on paying her off.

Although he commanded the cruiser *Melampus* in the autumn manœuvres of 1892, the curtain had now fallen on Prince George's cherished naval career, save for a brief reappearance in 1898 when he took the first-class cruiser *Crescent* for a three months' cruise. A stroke of fate, as calamitous at the time as it proved fortunate in the event, substituted for the career of his choice the prospect of a lifelong burden which few would choose. On 14 January 1892 the Duke of Clarence died of pneumonia. Overnight Prince George found himself second in succession to the throne.

The death of his brother fell like a hammer-blow upon Prince George. For the first eighteen years of his life he had hardly been separated for a day from Prince Eddy, with whom he had shared a community of interest both within the circle of a singularly united family and in the turbulent days of their first introduction to naval life. He was himself only just recuperating from typhoid fever. While he had still been confined to bed the betrothal had been announced between the Duke of Clarence and their cousin, Princess Victoria Mary (May) of Teck. Six weeks later the Duke had in turn fallen ill, and within six days had died.

In the Queen's birthday honours list (1892) Prince George was created Duke of York, with the subsidiary titles of Earl of Inverness and Baron Killarney. He was introduced into the House of Lords on 17 June by his father and his uncle the Duke of Connaught. A suite of apartments was arranged for him in St. James's Palace, together with an unpretentious cottage in the grounds of Sandringham; to these the appellations York House and York Cottage were respectively assigned.

The next year (1893) brought him to another important milestone, his betrothal (3 May) to the Princess who was to have been his sister-in-law. She was the daughter of Prince Francis Paul Charles Louis Alexander, Duke of Teck, a member of the royal house of Württemberg long resident in England, and of Princess Mary Adelaide Wilhelmina Elizabeth of Cambridge, granddaughter of King George III and thus first cousin to Queen Victoria. The marriage took place in the Chapel Royal, St. James's

Palace, on 6 July. 'I cannot say how pleased I am', wrote the Queen to her daughter, the Empress Frederick. 'The more I see of her the more I like her. . . . She is really a very dear good sensible girl, and very wise, and so *distinguée*. I feel *very* happy about them.' This union, which the Queen with characteristic discernment had commended, brought to the future King the greatest blessing of his life. Their close companionship, which was to last to the end of his reign, exemplified a lofty standard of family life in an age of loosening domestic ties; and his Consort, by her gentle tact and wisdom, her studied detachment from politics, her informed interest in the royal collections, and her supreme dignity and presence, was destined to reveal herself to the realm and empire as a queen of stature rarely equalled, never surpassed.

The seven years which followed were to prove the quietest period that the Duke was to know. In November 1894 he visited St. Petersburg for the funeral of his uncle the Emperor Alexander III (who had married the Princess of Wales's sister) and the wedding of his ill-fated successor Nicholas II. Between the latter and himself there was a startling physical resemblance and a brotherly affection; the bride, moreover, being a granddaughter of Queen Victoria, was also his first cousin. In August 1897 and again in April 1899 the Duke and Duchess paid visits to Ireland, where they were received with enthusiasm. For the rest, there were continual engagements and claims, all of which were met with cheerfulness. Now, as ever, the Duke delighted to devote his leisure to various forms of outdoor sport, chief among them being yachting and shooting. During these years too were born his first four children: Prince Edward, later King Edward VIII and Duke of Windsor (23 June 1894); Prince Albert, later Duke of York and King George VI (14 December 1895); Princess Mary, later Princess Royal and Countess of Harewood (25 April 1897); and Prince Henry, later Duke of Gloucester (31 March 1900); to these were subsequently added a further two sons: Prince George, later Duke of Kent (20 December 1902), who was killed on active service 25 August 1942; and Prince John (12 July 1905) who died 18 January 1919.

On 22 January 1901 the death of Queen Victoria brought to a close an epoch both in time and in social outlook. The Duke now became Duke of Cornwall as of right, and eligible for the Principality of Wales when it should please his father to confer it upon him. His new position necessarily involved an increase in his public duties as the only son of a sexagenarian king. Tension between sovereign and heir neither began nor ended in the Victorian age; and a comparison between the dispositions of King Edward VII and his son can have afforded little hope of an amelioration in this traditionally uneasy relationship. But it had been given to Queen Alexandra to forge throughout her family a powerful bond of mutual love, and she was now to witness its happy fulfilment. Unlike though they were in disposition, between King Edward VII and his son there existed on both sides a degree of trust and affection rare in their respective stations, and not a passing cloud disturbed the harmony of their intercourse throughout the reign. Every day the Prince of Wales would discuss current topics with the King; nor, after his own accession, did a day pass without its recollection of a father to whose memory he remained jealously devoted to the end.

The outset of a new reign involves changes and adjustments in the royal household. From the ensuing redistribution the Duke of Cornwall and York (as he now for a short while became) drew the services of Sir Arthur Bigge (later Lord Stamfordham), and an association thus began which was to end only with the latter's death thirty years later. Bigge had served a fifteen years' apprenticeship under Sir Henry Ponsonby, whom in 1895 he had succeeded as private secretary to Queen Victoria. He thus brought to his work for the new heir to the throne an intimate acquaintance with the politics and personalities of the preceding twenty years; and this knowledge of affairs, coupled with a selfless devotion and an immense capacity for work, proved an asset to his master of which it is impossible to overestimate the importance. King George's household was at all times a happy and efficient structure, reflecting his perspicacity in the right choice of men: but the acquisition of Bigge was an uncovenanted stroke of fortune which the King and the ministers of a whole generation were destined to bless.

As early as 1893, a few months after his marriage, the Duke had received an invitation from the various colonies in Australia to make a tour in those parts, and the New Zealand government had raised the question afresh after the diamond jubilee of 1897. For his part he would willingly have acceded, but various circumstances had operated to postpone the plan. In August 1900, however, Queen Victoria had signified her consent, urged thereto by an important development in the structure of the empire which called for a demonstration of her imperial interest. On 18 September a proclamation was issued in London announcing that from New Year's Day 1901 the constituent colonies in Australia, together with Tasmania, would be federated into a single unit: it was the first session of this new Commonwealth parliament that was to provide the occasion for the royal tour. Early in December the Queen sanctioned the extension of the itinerary to include a visit to Canada. Preparations were well advanced when the Queen died. It was decided that the tour should take place as planned, but that mourning should be worn and festivities correspondingly curtailed.

Leaving Portsmouth in the *Ophir* on 16 March 1901 the Duke and Duchess followed the route through the Mediterranean. At Gibraltar they inspected the embryo harbour works then under construction and the subject of controversy at home. At Malta they found a comfortable assurance of security in the fact that no land-battery could be constructed within a range of sixty miles: nevertheless a vigilant Admiralty was experimenting with the new Brennan torpedo, of which a demonstration was witnessed. In the words of Sir Donald Mackenzie Wallace: 'Whether this ingenious instrument would prove a formidable weapon in real warfare the experts alone can decide, but it is certainly a very pretty toy to play with in time of peace.' The inconveniences of distance were already being mitigated by wireless telegraphy, which enabled a message to be received from as far as 180 miles away with the aid of a ship stationed midway; it was evident that it might presently 'in certain circumstances be of enormous assistance to the navy'.

After calling at Suez and Aden the royal party reached Colombo on 12 April, and here in the course of an address the Duke first alluded to the need for increased trade with the mother country which was to prove the keynote of his observations throughout the tour. Thence they proceeded via Singapore to call for the second time in his life at Albany, Western Australia, before passing along the southern coast to Melbourne. Here on 9 May, amid scenes of the greatest enthusiasm, he opened parliament in the Exhibition Building in the presence of 15,000 spectators. After paying tribute to the spontaneous participation of the land and sea forces of Australia in the South African war, he expressed the King's heartfelt satisfaction and thankfulness for the achievement of political union among the Australian colonies. Here, as also at Brisbane and Sydney which they next visited, an enthusiastic ovation was accorded them, and the Duchess won all hearts by her simple dignity and practical interest in all that they were shown. From Sydney they crossed to New Zealand, where particular attention was devoted to the welfare of the Maori population. On the return journey calls were made at Hobart and Adelaide; and so across the Indian Ocean to Mauritius and Durban. At Pietermaritzburg the Duke held a military investiture in the presence of Lord Kitchener, then conducting the final stages of the South African war.

After calling at Cape Town course was set across the Atlantic for Quebec, where the Duke and Duchess landed on 16 September. In the course of the ensuing five weeks they crossed and recrossed Canada in a train specially built by the Canadian Pacific Railway, making many stops on the way. In a series of felicitous speeches the Duke thanked the Canadian people for the timely help accorded to the home country in her hour of need, and was once more impressed by the fervent loyalty to the throne which he had observed on his first visit eighteen years earlier.

Leaving Newfoundland on 25 October, the Duke was received at Portsmouth by the King on 1 November and experienced the joy of seeing his children once more. It had not been easy for the King to spare his services for so long a period at a time when only the Duke of Connaught was available to assist in the functions inseparable from the opening of a new reign. In a letter written on his sixtieth birthday (9 November) King Edward wrote to his son: 'In creating you to-day Prince of Wales and Earl of Chester I am not only conferring on you ancient titles which I bore for upwards of 59 years, but I wish to mark my appreciation of the admirable manner in which you carried out the arduous duties to the Colonies which I entrusted you with. I have but little doubt that they will bear good fruit in the future and knit the Colonies more than ever to the Mother Country. God bless you, my dear boy, and I know I can always count on your support and assistance in the heavy duties and responsible position I now occupy.'

On 5 December, in the course of a memorable speech at Guildhall, the Prince of Wales paid tribute to the intense loyalty which animated the inhabitants of the territories which he had visited; and with this loyalty, he said, were evidences of their readiness to share the burden and responsibility of membership of the Empire. In a passage which attained world-wide attention he then spoke of 'the impression that seems generally to prevail among our brethren across the seas, that the old country must wake up if she intends to maintain her old position of pre-eminence in her colonial trade against foreign competitors'.

During the nine years of his father's reign the Prince of Wales devoted himself to the public duties incumbent upon the heir to the throne. He was now the only son, and the Duke of Connaught was still pursuing a distinguished military career, largely overseas. Active and intelligent though King Edward VII was, he was no longer young; moreover, he was in the habit of passing a quarter of the year on the continent. In political affairs the Prince had much to learn. The King, his own experience fresh in his mind, saw to it that state papers were at his son's disposal: ministers would come to see him, and he formed the habit of listening to debates in both Houses. How great was his debt during these formative years to the sage and experienced Bigge he acknowledged at Christmas 1907 in a letter which does credit to both: 'I was much touched by your kind letter received this morning. You have nothing to thank us for, it is all the other way. I fear sometimes I have lost my temper with you, and often been very rude, but I am sure you know me well enough by now to know that I did not mean it. . . . For all these past services I offer you my thanks from the bottom of my heart. I am a bad hand at saying what I feel, but I thank God I have a friend like you.'

The Prince lived during these years at Marlborough House when in London. For country retreats he had Frogmore House in the Home Park at Windsor, Abergeldie Castle near Balmoral, and York Cottage at Sandringham—always his favourite home. Here through many a winter day he perfected his shooting, the sport at which he early reached and long retained pre-eminence. In these middle years too he sometimes fished, occasionally rode to hounds, and often played golf and lawn tennis. Cricket and football he always enjoyed as a spectator. But above all he delighted in sailing his famous yacht *Britannia*, the closely contested supremacy of which he noted with statistical pride in his diary. Long experience, coupled with an Englishman's love of the sea, had wrought in him the ideal yachtsman, and he revelled in a sport in which he did not need the advice of any man. For indoor recreation he relied upon his lifelong interest in the postage stamps of the British Empire. Here, as with shooting and yachting, he was an expert in his own right, his knowledge in this specialized field being scientific and detailed. It remained his hobby until the end of his life and served as a relief from the cares of state, particularly during the years of war. Thus, whether indoors or out, he was as amply furnished with internal resources as most men, and this boon contributed not a little to his buoyancy of spirits in a position necessarily lonely.

As Prince of Wales he paid several visits to the courts of Europe, spent twelve days in Ireland in January 1905, and enjoyed yet another visit to Canada in July 1908. But his most important overseas undertaking was the tour which he and the Princess carried out in India under the guidance of Sir Walter Lawrence in the winter of 1905–1906. Reaching Bombay in the *Renown* on 9 November they were immediately involved in a series of visits which took them from the Khyber Pass to Rangoon and Mandalay, across by sea to Madras and up to the Afghan frontier again before re-embarking at Karachi on 19 March. As the guest of Lord Kitchener the Prince had followed the course of the manœuvres in the Frontier country: 'Lord Kitchener is a perfect host', he wrote in his diary; 'I have the greatest admiration for him as a strong man and a good soldier.' He enjoyed the four and a half months of this visit, in the course of which he formed lasting friendships and laid the foundation of that pride and affection which always marked his references to India and its inhabitants.

The death of King Edward VII on 6 May 1910 was an overwhelming sorrow which the pressure of immediate events was powerless to alleviate. The funeral on the 20th was attended by the rulers of Norway, Denmark, Belgium, Germany, Spain, Portugal, Greece, and Bulgaria. As they dispersed to their countries (from which all but the first three were destined to be evicted) it was in no cheerful spirit that the new King turned to face responsibilities which he had never sought. The political climate was such as to tax even his experienced and popular father: he felt himself alone, ill-equipped to handle a complex situation, and little known to his four hundred million subjects. He was, moreover, vexed by the circulation of a story concerning his alleged marriage in 1890 to a lady in Malta, a criminal libel which brought the maximum term of imprisonment to its utterer on 1 February 1911. It was a strange charge to bring against a sovereign of unimpeachable virtue, whose crowning benediction was a happy domestic life.

For the first twelve months of his reign the King was sufficiently occupied in acquiring the habit of sovereignty. There were political problems to master, acquaintances to be made, rulings to be given upon domestic rearrangements. For these purposes he welcomed the respite from public and social functions which the long term of public mourning afforded. But the midsummer pomps of 1911 were the prelude to a period of activity. The coronation ceremony in Westminster Abbey on 22 June was a triumph of careful preparation. Its pageantry and ritual made a profound impression upon all, and not least upon the central figure, who was touched to deep emotion by the solemnity of the occasion and heartened by the bewildering ovations of his crowded capital. In the following week Their Majesties carried out two public drives through London, attended a thanksgiving service at St. Paul's Cathedral, gave a party at the Crystal Palace to 100,000 London schoolchildren, and reviewed at Spithead the largest naval fleet ever assembled. A fortnight after the coronation the King and Queen set out for Dublin, where they were accorded an enthusiastic reception during a five-day visit. Recrossing to Wales, they spent a similar period in the Principality, their most memorable function being the investiture of the Prince of Wales at Carnarvon Castle on 13 July: 'the dear boy did it all remarkably well and looked so nice', the King recorded in his diary. From Wales they passed on to Holyrood, there to be greeted by the plaudits of loyal Scottish subjects.

Back in London, at a time of strong political ferment, the King's thoughts were engaged upon the state visit to his Indian Empire upon which he had set his heart. On 11 November 1911 he set out from Portsmouth with the Queen in the *Medina*, escorted by four cruisers, and with this flotilla (containing little short of 4,000 officers and men) arrived at Bombay on 2 December. At the ancient capital of Delhi he was accommodated in an enormous camp of 40,000 tents, and here as King Emperor he held on the 12th a state Durbar of matchless magnificence. With his coronation robes he wore a crown of diamonds provided by the Indian government in order to obviate the necessity of transporting the traditional regalia overseas. Enthroned upon a platform set in a spacious amphitheatre, His Majesty received the homage of the ruling princes and British governors, and announced the substantial boons customary upon such occasions. He then made a dramatic announcement, the secret of which had been well kept. Speaking in a clear voice he declared that the seat of government was to be transferred from Calcutta to Delhi and that there was to be established a governorship of Bengal similar to those of Madras and Bombay.

These ceremonies concluded, the King turned to the enjoyment of ten days' tiger shooting in Nepal, after which he 'took leave of the kind Maharajah, his sons and all his people, with much regret. They have spoilt us with kindness and given us the best sport in the world.' Their Majesties spent nine days in Calcutta before re-embarking at Bombay on 10 January 1912. How much this visit had meant to the King is clear from his diary: 'To-day I regret to say is our last day in India. The Legislative Council presented an address of farewell. I quite broke down in reading my answer. . . . Our second visit to India is now over and we can thank God that it has been an unqualified success from first to last. It was entirely my own idea to hold the Coronation Durbar at Delhi in person, and at first I met with much opposition. But the result has I hope been more than satisfactory and has surpassed all expectations. I am vain enough to think that our visit will have done good in India. We have been fully repaid for our long journey.'

The King, in assuming the troubled inheritance bequeathed to him by his father, had found himself immediately confronted with a constitutional crisis of the gravest character. In order to meet the cost of the old age pensions and the increased estimates necessitated by the threat of German naval competition, the liberal government had been faced with the task of levying additional taxation. The budget of 1909 had consequently raised the income-tax from 1s. to 1s. 2d. and imposed a novel supertax of 6d., together with certain land taxes. The House of Lords, which had not endeared itself to the Commons by rejecting several of their proposed measures of reform, on 30 November had taken the unprecedented step of throwing out the budget *in toto*, thus setting the stage for a trial of strength between the two chambers. The issue was barely joined before the throne was deprived of a sovereign of exceptional political acumen, and a crucial responsibility devolved upon his untried and inexperienced successor.

The new King was unaware that within a month of his father's death important meetings and conversations had taken place between the King's private secretary, Lord Knollys, Archbishop Davidson, Balfour, and Esher, concerning the possibility of King Edward being pressed by Asquith to give a contingent guarantee for the creation of peers: he only learned this in December 1913 [Royal Archives, *sub* Home Rule iii. 63]. But it was known that King Edward had caused an intimation to be conveyed by Knollys (15 December 1909) that in no event would he consent to an *ad hoc* creation until after a second general election, in which the issue should have been placed squarely before the people. It is a reasonable inference, but no more, that had the condition been fulfilled and the need arisen, King Edward would not have withheld the use of his prerogative. The first election took place immediately upon the Lords' rejection of the budget, upon the text that the Commons alone were to control finance and that any non-financial bill sent up to the Lords in three successive sessions should receive the royal assent. With this mandate the liberals were again returned to power (28 January 1910) with a majority reduced from 335 to the still effective figure of 123. The Lords now (28 April) accepted the budget. But they had been playing for high stakes and were faced with the parliament bill, which limited their powers for the future. It was at this juncture (6 May) that King Edward died.

In the political truce which followed it was at Asquith's suggestion that the question at issue was referred to a constitutional conference consisting of four liberals and four conservatives. The conference met from June until November without achieving agreement, and the prime minister proceeded to fulfil the condition which the late King had postulated. In December 1910, for the second time within a twelvemonth, the country was once more consulted, and again returned the liberals, with a majority of 125. To anticipate the course of events it may here be added that on 10 August 1911, in an atmosphere of political excitement unsurpassed in modern times, the Lords accepted the parliament bill by the narrow majority of seventeen votes.

But before the December election the new King had been placed in an unenviable position. Asquith was unexcelled in the use of language at once precise and enigmatic. On 14 April 1910 he had told the House of Commons: 'In no case would we recommend dissolution except under such conditions as will ensure that in the new parliament the judgement of the people as expressed in the election will be carried into law.' On 11 November he explained the political situation to the King, pointing out that should the Lords remain obdurate a final settlement could only be brought about by the willingness of the Crown to exercise its prerogative. He told the King that he would not ask for any guarantees before the election [Royal Archives, K. 2552 (2). 72]: for the moment he contented himself with stating the case, and left it for consideration [Spender and Asquith, vol. i, p. 296].

None the less, five days later Asquith and Crewe felt constrained to seek from the King at Buckingham Palace (16 November) a secret and 'hypothetical understanding' that sufficient peers would be created should need arise in the parliament that was yet to be elected. 'His Majesty said that his only wish was to do what was right and constitutional and best for the country in the present circumstances. The King then felt with reluctance that it would be impossible not to act upon their advice and therefore agreed to the understanding' [Royal Archives, *ut sup.*]. In the carefully chosen words of Crewe (House of Lords, 8 August 1911), 'We ascertained His Majesty's view that, if the opinion of the country were clearly ascertained upon the parliament bill, in the last resort a creation of peers might be the only remedy, and might be the only way of concluding the dispute. His Majesty faced the contingency and entertained the suggestion as a possible one with natural, and if I may be permitted to use the phrase, in my opinion with legitimate reluctance. But it is altogether inaccurate, and I might use a stronger phrase, to say that at that time we asked His Majesty for guarantees. The whole position was obviously hypothetical.'

Shades of meaning were here involved to which the King's mind was a stranger. It can hardly be matter for surprise that he should feel that he was being expected to underwrite the words uttered in April by the prime minister, and to implement in advance the construction which plain men would place upon them in the constituencies. He felt for the rest of his life that he might have been trusted to take the right step should the occasion have arisen. Asquith, for his part, held the Crown in high veneration: as the case presented itself to him it was not a matter of trusting the King, but of coercing the conservative peers, who were in no mood to be persuaded though one rose from the dead. Even when at a later date (18 July) the secret was by agreement divulged, there were those who declined to believe that the sovereign would indeed subject the constitution to so severe a strain.

The King harboured no resentment either against Crewe, who remained to the end one of his closest personal friends, or against Asquith, for whom he reserved a high, if watchful, esteem. When, in the hour of Asquith's political adversity, the King, of his own mere motion, created his former prime minister one of the now less powerful peers (February 1925) he interpreted with characteristic insight the corporate feeling of the nation, and took a personal pleasure in doing so.

The Parliament Act, in drawing the teeth of the House of Lords, created for the King a difficulty unforeseen, by him at any rate, at the time. Its preamble announced the intention to set up a new second chamber; but since this could not be done at once the Act made provision for restricting the powers of the House of Lords in the meanwhile. Although not intended to affect the position of the sovereign, it nevertheless removed the first check upon the operations of the Commons; and this elimination of one branch of the legislature necessarily increased the responsibility of the King when a bill, thrice rejected by the upper House, came up for the royal assent. No longer could the Lords force a dissolution, even in the few cases where they had that power before the passing of the Act; henceforth the sovereign alone must decide whether a bill which comes from a single chamber is of such gravity that, with all the attendant risks of bringing the Crown into party politics, an appeal to the country against the advice of his ministers would be justified.

This dilemma was not long in making itself felt. Already by the spring of 1912 preparations of a military nature in the province of Ulster were affording grounds for misgiving, and the debates which followed the introduction of the home rule bill on 11 April were carried on in an atmosphere of passion. The same autumn (27 September) Bonar Law, staying at Balmoral, took occasion to indicate the thankless position in which it appeared that the King would find himself. The government, he argued, admitted its responsibility for carrying out the preamble of the Parliament Act, and in the meanwhile the constitution was in suspense: it was doubtful whether the government still had the support of the country: it would once more rely upon the exercise of the royal prerogative to overcome the opposition of the peers. It was the identical quandary expressed in different terms, and it seemed that the King would again find himself compromised.

The home rule bill, forced through the Commons by the aid of the closure and the support of the Irish and labour members, was first rejected by the Lords on 13 January 1913. Re-submitted, it was thrown out afresh on 15 July. Then followed ten months during which the King observed with dismay a worsening situation in which, to the disorders attendant upon the suffragette menace, it seemed certain that an uprising in Ireland was to be added. To imagine that in a time of crisis it is the ministers alone who tender advice to the sovereign would be to overlook the operations of the Post Office and the press. From all sides he was urged to take this course or that: to dismiss his ministers, to impose a dissolution, to demand a referendum, to issue a state paper defining his position and intentions, to grant (or alternatively to withhold) the royal assent. Whatever the nature of the advice there was evident in all quarters a recognition of his impartiality, a desire to safeguard his constitutional position, a disposition to seek a possible solution, and a loyal sympathy in the dilemma in which he was placed.

His course was not made easier by the rosy optimism with which the prime minister appeared to confront the rising storm. The King listened with inward sympathy to those who counselled strong action, but schooled himself in the exercise of a stronger forbearance. An anxious winter gave way to the yet more vexed summer of 1914, and still his voice was heard, now by one leader and now by another, urging patience and restraint in public utterance, suggesting fresh lines of accommodation, a renewal of private negotiation, concession here, conciliation there. Whether Ireland was to have home rule or not, he had told Asquith on 13 December, was for the politicians to settle. But as king he held that it was his duty by every means in his power to prevent the outbreak of civil strife in any part of his kingdom; that was his responsibility and he should do his best to fulfil it.

Space forbids a detailed examination of the part played by the King throughout the long-drawn-out crisis, but a month, that of February 1914, may be chosen as a sample. On the 2nd Stamfordham wrote a letter of reassurance on the King's behalf to Bonar Law, saying that His Majesty was not so pessimistic as he, and that as to any special communication to his ministers the King's action would be guided by time and circumstance. On the 5th the King saw Asquith at Windsor and had a serious conversation about possible trouble in the army, such as eventually occurred at the Curragh, and repeated that he could not allow bloodshed among his loyal subjects without exerting every means in his power to avert it. On the 11th he wrote personally congratulating Asquith upon his moderate and conciliatory speech in the House. On the 12th Stamfordham was sent to ask Asquith whether he thought that it would be helpful for the King to urge moderation upon Bonar Law and Sir Edward Carson in entertaining the government proposals. On the 20th he had members of the opposition to dinner. On the 25th Stamfordham wrote on his behalf to Bonar Law regretting the rasping tone of his speech the night before; and on the following day to Asquith deploring the acrimonious nature of the debates. On the 27th the King had the members of the government to dinner and held long conversations with the prime minister. Next morning he sent Stamfordham to tell Carson that His Majesty had delivered to Asquith the kindly personal messages with which Carson had entrusted him; that Asquith had been touched and would like to reopen negotiations with him; and to express the King's hope that Carson would refrain from making a bitter speech on the following Tuesday. And so it went on for month after month, the King, with a degree of patience formerly to seek in his natural habit of mind, propounding every means that ingenuity could devise for effecting a reconciliation.

On 21 March, after a number of officers at the Curragh had resigned rather than take part in the coercion of Ulster, the King addressed to the prime minister a letter of sharp protest that he had been left to learn of the incident from the public press next day. It was not, as it happened, Asquith's fault; and it proved fortunate in the event since it subsequently cleared the King from the imputation of complicity which in the heat of the moment had been directed against him in certain quarters.

On 1 May the King, on his own initiative, invited Mr. James Lowther (later Viscount Ullswater) to Buckingham Palace and there prevailed upon him to address to the prime minister an offer to invite the various leaders to meet under his presidency, as Speaker, with a view to arriving at a solution. On 22 June (Coronation Day) the King wrote a personal letter to Asquith recalling to his memory a sentence in the message which he had addressed to his subjects on that occasion three years previously. 'Whatever perplexities or difficulties may lie before me and my people', he had then written, 'we shall all unite in facing them resolutely, calmly and with public spirit, confident that under Divine guidance the ultimate outcome may be to the common good.' 'The perplexities and difficulties', he now wrote, 'have not grown less with time, and there is greater need than ever that they should be met and dealt with in that spirit upon which I then felt I could confidently depend. I know that I can count upon your support in the fulfilment of my hopes and prayers of three years ago.'

The prospect of a conference was discussed on 16 July between Stamfordham and Asquith, with the result that on the following day the latter submitted to the King a request that he might be allowed to announce that His Majesty would invite representatives of all parties to Buckingham Palace for a full and free discussion of the outstanding issues. On the 18th invitations were sent by Stamfordham to Lansdowne and Bonar Law, Carson and Craig, Redmond and Dillon; Asquith and Crewe represented the government, and the Speaker presided. The speech with which His Majesty welcomed the members on the 21st was a model of simple eloquence. 'For months', the King said, 'we have watched with deep misgivings the course of events in Ireland. The trend has been surely and steadily towards an appeal to force, and to-day the cry of civil war is on the lips of the most responsible and sober minded of my people. We have in the past endeavoured to act as a civilising example to the world, and to me it is unthinkable, as it must be to you, that we should be brought to the brink of a fratricidal war upon issues apparently so capable of adjustment as those you are now asked to consider, if handled in a spirit of generous compromise. My apprehension in contemplating such a dire calamity is intensified by my feelings of attachment to Ireland and of sympathy for her people who have always welcomed me with warmhearted affection. Gentlemen, you represent in one form or another the vast majority of my subjects at home. You also have a deep interest in my Dominions overseas, who are scarcely less concerned in a prompt and friendly settlement of this question. I regard you then in this matter as trustees for the honour and peace of all. Your responsibilities are indeed great. The time is short. You will I know employ it to the fullest advantage and be patient, earnest and conciliatory in view of the magnitude of the issues at stake. I pray that God in His infinite wisdom may guide your deliberations so that they may result in the joy of peace and settlement.'

These hopes were not to be fulfilled. After four meetings the conference broke down upon a point insignificant in comparison with the issues involved. But the King had done his best; and if during the lapse of valuable time the forces unleashed in Ireland had become too strong for their leaders, it was due to no inactivity on his part. Events of yet greater moment supervened to avert the immediate consequences, and the controversy was laid aside, as it was hoped, for the duration of the European war. In a letter to the King dated 17 September Asquith wrote: 'He hopes he may be allowed to express his respectful sympathy with, and admiration of, the patience and the strict observance of constitutional practice, together with the tact and judgment, which in a time of exceptional difficulty and anxiety, Your Majesty has never for a moment failed to exercise.'

War on the cosmic scale of that which was now about to break out involves every citizen in strain and distress from which the sovereign is not immune. The rhythm of his work is intensified; the inspection of hospitals brings the horror of the conflict continually before his eyes; he is apprised of perils without, and doubts and dissensions within, of which his subjects are unaware. But from the constitutional point of view war provides few occasions for the intervention of a king who finds himself at the head of a united and harmonious nation, intent upon the pursuit of a common purpose. For months King George had nursed the hope that agreement upon the Irish question would have been reached. Patiently he had studied the timing of his final attempt to produce a settlement. Now, when his conference had failed, it could hardly be otherwise than with a sense of momentary relief that he observed the dramatic unfolding of events. Overnight the nation which had been sliding rapidly into disruption and civil war had braced itself to meet a sterner issue, standing united once more before the threat from without.

Of its implications the King was in no doubt. As early as 8 December 1912 he had written from Sandringham to the foreign secretary: 'My dear Grey, Prince Henry of Prussia paid me a short visit here two days ago. In the course of a long conversation with regard to the present European situation, he asked me point blank, whether in the event of Austria and Germany going to war with Russia and France, England would come to the assistance of the two latter powers. I answered undoubtedly yes under certain circumstances. He professed surprise and regret but did not ask what the circumstances were. He said he would tell the Emperor what I told him. Of course Germany must know that we could not allow either of our friends to be crippled. I think it is only right that you should know what passed between me and the Emperor's brother on this point.'

Now, on 26 July 1914, the day on which the Admiralty cancelled leave and bade the fleet stand by at Portland, it happened that the King received another visit from Prince Henry, then on a holiday in England. At that moment Belgium had not been invaded and the Cabinet was working against wind and tide to avert a European conflict. The King told the prince that England still hoped not to be drawn in, and the Emperor, to whom his brother reported the conversation, interpreted it as an assurance of British neutrality, come what might. The incident is dealt with in a letter from Lord Wigram to *The Times* of 2 June 1938. The German claim subsequently based upon the interview was demolished by the archivist of the House of Hohenzollern, Dr. Kurt Jagow, in the *Berliner Monatshefte* for July–August 1938 [see *The Times*, 30 June 1938, under 'The Word of a King', with leading article].

Most of the war the King spent at Buckingham Palace, visiting Windsor for a month at Easter and six weeks in the late summer; Balmoral was too remote, but at times he enjoyed a few days at Sandringham, occasionally taking out his gun to shoot game which he sent to the hospitals. Early in 1915 he made a gift to the Exchequer of £100,000, an example which was later followed by others. On 6 April 1915 he gave orders that no wine, spirits, or beer should be consumed in the royal household, observing a like abstinence himself; and from February 1917 strict adherence to the new rationing regulations was imposed throughout the palace, from the royal table downwards. The war had not long started when, within the space of little more than a week, there fell in action three members of his personal suite to whom he was especially devoted, Lord Charles Petty-Fitzmaurice, Lord Crichton, and Lord John Hamilton, together with his first cousin Prince Maurice of Battenberg. His own two eldest sons were hostages to fortune, the Prince of Wales in the army from the outset, Prince Albert in the battle of Jutland in May 1916. The removal in deference to an unreasoning popular outcry in October 1914 of his brilliant cousin by marriage, Prince Louis of Battenberg (afterwards Marquess of Milford Haven), from his office of first sea lord, involved the King in a conflict of loyalties. The dramatic loss of Lord Kitchener in June 1916 he felt as something more than a national calamity, for he had long held him in personal affection as well as the highest professional esteem.

The formation of Asquith's coalition government in May 1915 brought the first labour minister into the King's service in the person of Arthur

Henderson at the Board of Education. The next change of government, in December 1916, involved the extrusion of Asquith by Lloyd George, to whose talents the King frequently paid generous and encouraging tribute, although on personal grounds he missed the sturdy and unruffled presence of his first prime minister. The fissures and stresses which gave birth to the new administration have been recorded in the leading political biographies, and in great detail in Lord Beaverbrook's *Politicians and the War* (1928). Asquith resigned on 5 December and Bonar Law was invited to form a government. At the instance of the latter the King on the following day held a conference attended by Asquith, Balfour, Bonar Law, Lloyd George, and Henderson; but since Asquith felt unable to serve under his leadership, Bonar Law abandoned the attempt and the King accordingly entrusted the task to Lloyd George. In reply to the King's letter offering him the Garter Asquith wrote: 'I trust that Your Majesty will permit me, in all gratitude and humility, to decline. I have had the honour of serving Your Majesty as Prime Minister continuously from the first day of your reign. Through times of much difficulty and peril Your Majesty has honoured me with unstinted confidence and unwavering support. I desire no higher distinction.'

On 20 June 1917 the following announcement appeared in the press: 'The King has deemed it desirable, in the conditions brought about by the present war, that those princes of his family who are his subjects and bear German names and titles should relinquish these titles, and henceforth adopt British surnames.' In consequence of this decision four new peerages were created. The Duke of Teck and his brother, Prince Alexander, became Marquess of Cambridge and Earl of Athlone; Princes Louis and Alexander of Battenberg became Marquesses of Milford Haven and Carisbrooke; members of the Teck and Battenberg families adopted the surnames Cambridge and Mountbatten respectively. At a meeting of the Privy Council held on 17 July His Majesty announced his intention, embodied in a royal proclamation of the same date, of adopting on his own behalf and that of all his subjects descended from Queen Victoria the name of Windsor for the Royal House and Family. The 'sublime inspiration', as Lord Rosebery called it, came to Lord Stamfordham, who was unaware at the time that King Edward III had been styled 'Sir Edward de Windsor, King of England' in a deed dated 1375 [Record Office, C. 2121]. Finally, by letters patent dated 11 December 1917, the Princely title and its attendant appellation Royal Highness were confined to the children of a sovereign and of the sons of a sovereign (with the addition of the special case of the eldest living son of the eldest son of the Prince of Wales). To the grandchildren of the sons of a sovereign in the direct male line was assigned the style and title of the children of dukes.

The extent of the burden shouldered by the King during the war years was not apparent to the public owing to the secrecy which necessarily cloaked his movements. The record of his activities reveals that he paid 300 visits to military hospitals, each a taxing ordeal for a sensitive nature; nor was the personal distribution of 58,000 decorations accomplished without fatigue. He inspected 300 naval and military formations and a like number of factories engaged upon war work. He paid five visits to the Grand Fleet and seven to his armies in France and Belgium. In October 1915, after the abortive battles of Neuve Chapelle and Loos, murmurs demanding a change in the high command made themselves heard (prime minister's secretary to Stamfordham, 7 October), and the King was able during his tour later in the month to ascertain the views of the leading generals in the field. It was early in December that Sir John French was replaced by Sir Douglas Haig, a change effected by Asquith upon his sole responsibility [Spender and Asquith, vol. i, p. 191]. This same tour in France came to an untimely end when a restive mount, frightened by the cheering of the troops, reared and fell backwards on the King fracturing his pelvis. Such visits to his armies in the field had a stimulating effect upon the troops, none more so than that undertaken at his own instance at the end of March 1918, a week after the opening of the final German onslaught.

The labours of the King during the war had been pursued with an absence of publicity congenial to him, but the conclusion of hostilities brought him to the front once more. The agony and triumph of the past four years were over and with the sudden release of tension the relief of millions found expression in widespread demonstrations of affection and loyalty to the throne. Alike on Armistice Day and in the later celebrations of Peace Day in 1919 it was to the palace that all steps were turned in the exuberance of a common emotion. In a series of public appearances the King and Queen were greeted with a demonstrativeness of affection to which the past afforded no parallel, and the scenes witnessed in the course of six drives through the capital in the days immediately succeeding the armistice were re-enacted at the close of the month both in Edinburgh and in Paris. Particularly notable was the address delivered to both Houses of Parliament on 19 November in which the King dwelt on the dedication of the whole British race to the demands of war and called for a heightened sense of individual and national duty in the years ahead. 'For centuries past', he declared, 'Britain has led the world along the path of ordered freedom. Leadership may still be hers among the peoples who are seeking to follow that path.'

If hostilities had ceased on the continent the case was otherwise in Ireland, where the best that the government could claim was that it had murder by the throat. The Home Rule Act of December 1920, although repudiated by the South, had been accepted by Northern Ireland, and the Ulster parliament was to be opened in June 1921. Despite the untoward aspect of Irish affairs the Cabinet felt that an occasion of such high imperial significance should be marked by the presence of the sovereign in person. The King would have been other than himself had he not readily acceded. 'As is naturally to be expected', Stamfordham wrote to the prime minister of Northern Ireland on 9 June, 'there is a very strong difference of opinion about the King going to Belfast, and many Irishmen, including those residing in that country, tell me that His Majesty is running considerable risk in going. Once the Government had expressed the wish that His Majesty should go, you may be quite certain that the King would not look back for one instant: and as to personal risk, I can frankly say that this has not entered into His Majesty's calculations—it would be entirely contrary to his nature for it to do so.' At the last minute the Ulster government expressed the desire that the Queen should go too, and the invitation was accepted with equal alacrity. Their Majesties crossed to Belfast on 22 June and there, in the City Hall, the King delivered a speech striking in its dramatic timing and sincerity of utterance. 'I am emboldened', His Majesty declared, 'to look beyond the sorrow and the anxiety which have clouded of late my vision of Irish affairs. I appeal to all Irishmen to pause, to stretch out the hand of forbearance and conciliation. It is my earnest desire that in Southern Ireland too there may ere long take place a parallel to what is now passing in this hall. The future lies in the hands of my Irish people themselves. May this historic gathering be the prelude of a day in which the Irish people, under one parliament or two, as those parliaments may themselves decide, shall work together in common love for Ireland upon the sure foundation of mutual justice and respect.'

'None but the King', wrote Lloyd George, 'could have made that personal appeal.' It was the more unfortunate that, on the evening before it was uttered, the lord chancellor (Birkenhead) should have held threatening language in the House of Lords, and that on the same day the secretary of state for war should have announced in the Commons that more troops and every soldier available would be sent to Ireland.

Three days later the King sent Stamfordham to urge the prime minister to make fresh overtures to Southern Ireland while the iron was hot. General Smuts, then providentially in London for the Imperial Conference, crossed to Dublin on 5 July; and assuredly there was no one who, from personal experience and elevation of character, was better qualified to act as intermediary. The subsequent interviews in London between Lloyd George and Mr. de Valera were followed by a series of communications which continued into the autumn, the Cabinet insisting that allegiance to the throne and membership of the Commonwealth should be postulates to any conversations.

A critical point had been reached when Lloyd George, then in Scotland, summoned a Cabinet meeting at Inverness on 7 September to approve the dispatch of a note couched in aggressive language and possibly naming a time limit for the truce which had been in operation since 11 July. It happened that the King was then staying at Moy, twelve miles from Inverness. His Majesty received the prime minister at breakfast on the morning of the Cabinet meeting, and the proposed draft was discussed between them. The King suggested numerous alterations in the text, the elimination of all threats and contentious phrases, and the inclusion of an invitation to the Sinn Fein representatives to meet the prime minister at once. The latter then drew up a fresh draft in the conciliatory tone which the King had advocated, and this was accepted by the Cabinet later in the morning. The Irish delegates came to London in mid-November, and the articles of agreement inaugurating the Irish Free State were signed on 6 December. 'I humbly congratulate Your Majesty', wrote the prime minister, 'on the triumph of the famous Ulster speech from the throne.'

It is the characteristic of King George's reign that his constitutional troubles came early. High seas had been running when the sailor King had put out: the Irish strife, the parliament bill, the embittered struggle over Welsh disestablishment, the bizarre war conducted by the suffragettes against the community, these all had been overwhelmed in the crowning convulsion of the European conflict, with the passing of which it seemed that the storm had spent its force. Difficulties remained, both in the national and international spheres, but with one or two exceptions they were such as called for no personal intervention on the part of the King. To the ceaseless round of duty which is the inescapable lot of the sovereign, he addressed himself with a devotion which bore fruit in the increasing regard and affection of all ranks of his subjects. In a period of disillusionment and moral disintegration the King and Queen were observed by all men to set a course of public service and to uphold the traditional standards of family life. The marriage of Princess Mary in 1922 proved an occasion of rejoicing to the entire nation, and the later marriages of his younger sons brought the King three daughters each of whom in turn greatly endeared herself to him. Always at his easiest with children, he reserved the tenderest affection for Princess Elizabeth, whose infant presence never failed to ensure his happiness during the closing decade of his life.

The 'coupon' election of December 1918 had given to Lloyd George's coalition a further lease of life until November 1922, when the conservative party was returned and the King sent for Bonar Law. An ailing man at the time, he sank beneath the load in the following May, giving it to be understood that he would prefer not to tender advice as to his successor. The King decided to summon Stanley (later Earl) Baldwin, then little known, in preference to the brilliant and experienced Lord Curzon. To mitigate the disappointment he caused Curzon to be invited to return from the country in order to learn from Stamfordham the reason for the choice. (It is not the case that the King summoned Curzon with the intention of offering him the premiership but was persuaded to the contrary.). Curzon was mortified upon his arrival to find the purpose of the interview to be other than that which his eagerness had led him to expect; but he bore the intimation with nobility and the King spoke words of healing and gratitude to him at their meeting on 29 May. That the blow should have been so bitter reveals the fallibility of human memory and judgement where self-interest is most strongly engaged; for on 24 May 1919 Curzon himself, in a letter to the King concerning his precedence as lord president, had written: 'The Prime Minister, who is commonly a member of the House of Commons, and will in all likelihood almost invariably be so in the future, has already been placed before the Lord President.' If ever there would recur circumstances in which the prime minister might reasonably be a peer it was not now, when labour was the official opposition, and being unrepresented in the Lords would be unable to hear policy expounded by the head of the government.

Five months after taking office Baldwin sought a dissolution in order to obtain a mandate for protection, which Bonar Law had pledged himself not to introduce. The King deprecated a second election within the twelvemonth, but the prime minister 'said that he had committed himself' (King's diary, 12 November 1923) and the King yielded. After the election in December, for the first time a House of Commons was returned in which there were three parties, each prepared to form a government, yet none commanding a majority. Parliament met on 15 January; a week later the government was defeated and Baldwin resigned. The King sent for Ramsay MacDonald.

At this first attainment of labour to office there were many croakers. The King was not among them. 'Thank God', he once wrote to a friend, 'I am an optimist, and I believe in the commonsense of the people of this country.' It was by the twin landmarks of character and principle that he had been in the habit of judging men, and in the mirror of working-class opinion he had always found the reflection of his own unassuming dignity and friendliness. 'To-day', recorded Stamfordham on 22 January 1924, 'the King saw Mr. Ramsay MacDonald and entrusted to him the formation of a new Government, which he undertook. He assured the King that, though he and his friends were inexperienced in governing and fully realised the great responsibilities which they would now assume, nevertheless they were honest and sincere, and his earnest desire was to serve his King and country. They may fail in their endeavours, but it will not be for want of trying to do their best. The King told Mr. Ramsay MacDonald that he might count upon his assistance in every way. His Majesty asked only for frankness between them. His Majesty went on to say that, little expecting to occupy his present position, he served in the Navy for fourteen years and thus had opportunities of seeing more of the world and mixing with his fellow creatures than would otherwise have been the case; while during the past fourteen years he had naturally gained much political knowledge and experience of the working of the machine of government under four different Prime Ministers. Mr. Ramsay MacDonald spoke very openly and said he was sure the King would be generous to him and understand the very difficult position he was in.'

With the members of the new administration the King was at once at home. That they might get to know each other's outlook on the world he gave it to be understood that he would like to see them in turn, at their convenience, for a quiet talk, and his diary records twenty such interviews in the month of February. 'He is an extreme socialist', he noted of the minister of health, 'and comes from Glasgow. I had a very interesting conversation with him.' The household arrangements worked smoothly because both parties intended that they should. The King made it known informally that the question of court dress was one for the ministers to settle as might seem best to them; and judging that it would conduce to the greater convenience of their guests, Their Majesties initiated a series of afternoon parties at the Palace. In his turn the prime minister, unlike Peel in 1839, himself desired the King to take the political appointments in the royal household and deal with them as His Majesty thought fit. It was agreed that after placing the customary whips at the disposal of the government the King should nominate the lord chamberlain, lord steward, master of the horse, the captains of the bodyguard and yeomen, and three of the lords in waiting: but in order to safeguard the constitutional position the submissions continued to be made by the prime minister, and the officials concerned undertook not to speak or vote against the government or participate in political activities outside.

'Some day', declared an eminent scientist as late as 1920, 'we may have the Prime Minister, or even the Monarch himself, addressing by word of mouth, and at one and the same time, all the different parts of the entire British Empire.' This daring forecast came true on St. George's Day 1924, when the King opened the British Empire Exhibition at Wembley; and, thus established, the precedent was followed on several occasions towards the close of the reign. Over a long period of time he had stood for peace and goodwill among the family of nations under his care, and it was natural that he should be in their thoughts at Christmas time. In a series of admirably turned broadcasts each Christmas Day from 1932 onwards his voice found a welcome in British homes throughout the world, establishing a new intimacy between sovereign and subject and kindling in all hearts the proud sense of kinship one with another. He essayed no flights of oratory, being content to greet each family with a personal message of kindliness and to assert a simple faith in the continued guidance of a divine Providence. Recordings of these homely addresses will enable posterity to judge the nature of the man, and go far to explain the singular hold which he established upon the affections of a quarter of the population of the world.

Under a three-party system the lot of a minority government is unenviable, for a nod exchanged between the opposition leaders can terminate its life at any moment: nor for the sovereign is the position free from ambiguity, for the dissolution and re-election of parliament may only prolong the position of stalemate. To a conservative vote of censure on the Campbell case the liberals moved, on 8 October 1924, an amendment calling for the milder step of a committee of inquiry into the withdrawal of the prosecution. But MacDonald chose to stand at bay on the first issue. He had only held office for nine months, but he had shown that labour was capable of bearing rule, proved himself an acceptable minister to the King, done well in the vexed sphere of foreign affairs, and equipped his Cabinet with political experience. His numerical strength was insufficient to effect the introduction of socialism in the present parliament, and he was not ill content to declare his innings closed. The King accordingly returned from Balmoral on the morning after the government's defeat (9 October) and received the prime minister, who sought a dissolution. That the Campbell case was in itself insufficient justification for a third general election within two years was manifest, but the circumstances were unusual. To decline the first request of a young and inexperienced party might have exposed the King's impartiality to question; and moreover it was clear that any extension of the government's lease could only be for a term of weeks. The King therefore granted the dissolution, but took the step of recording his reasons in a memorandum addressed to the prime minister. After the election on 29 October he sent for Baldwin, whose government was destined to last for more than four years.

As early as June 1916 Asquith had announced that an Imperial Conference would be held after the war to consider the recasting of the government of the Empire. When the Dominions were enrolled as separate members of the League of Nations the time had come to define that elusive constitution which was the casual offering of the British race to the science of politics. It was Lord Balfour who, with a courageous sweep of onward vision, devised the formula adopted as the Nicene Creed of the Commonwealth in 1926 and embodied in the Statute of Westminster in 1931. No longer was parliament in the home country to control the overseas Dominions: henceforward the King alone was to constitute the bond in a voluntary association of free peoples, whose co-operation would be effective only in so far as it was willingly accorded. The abdication of the sovereign in 1936 still further loosened the attachment of the Irish Free State: the furnace of a second war served but to anneal the links with the remainder of the British Empire. If Great Britain was fortunate in 1926 in having at hand a statesman of the stature of Balfour, she was no less fortunate in the possession of a King fitted alike by character and by experience to retain the allegiance of her sister nations.

The General Strike in May 1926 was a challenge to constitutional government which the Cabinet met with firmness and the nation with good humour. To an informal suggestion that recourse might be had to the precedent of the Buckingham Palace conference of 1914 the King replied that he would take no such action except upon the advice of his prime minister. He grasped the significance of a football match at Plymouth between the police and the strikers; and when the Cabinet was considering 'freezing' trade union funds he observed with dry common sense that men denied the use of their own money were apt to turn to other people's. He took exception to the announcement in the official *British Gazette* that all ranks of the armed forces of the Crown would receive the full support of the government in any action taken in the honest endeavour to aid the civil power. When after nine days the strike collapsed, 'Let us forget', he wrote in a message to his people, 'whatever elements of bitterness the events of the past few days may have created, and forthwith address ourselves to the task of bringing into being a peace which will be lasting because, forgetting the past, it looks only to the future with the hopefulness of a united people.'

Hitherto King George had been blessed with good health. He was no stranger to a passing attack of rheumatism, was a little careful about his food, and was not immune from the common cold: indeed an intractable bout of influenza in the spring of 1925 had even induced him to commission the royal yacht for a month's cruise in the Mediterranean, averse though he was from foreign travel. But apart from his typhoid fever in 1891 he had escaped lightly until, at the age of sixty-three, he contracted an illness of the gravest character. On 21 November 1928 he took to his bed at Buckingham Palace with a streptococcal infection which necessitated a severe operation for the drainage of the chest on 12 December.

A week earlier the King had been able to execute a warrant appointing six counsellors of state: the Queen, his two eldest sons, the archbishop of Canterbury, lord chancellor, and prime minister. 'Whereas We have been stricken by illness and are unable for the time being to give due attention to the affairs of Our Realm', the preamble stated, any three of the counsellors were empowered to discharge the royal office: but they were not to dissolve parliament, nor confer titles, 'nor act in any manner or thing in which it is signified by Us or appears to them that Our special approval should be previously obtained.' The council was held in a manner identical with that adopted when Queen Victoria was *en retraite* after the death of the Prince Consort (*Letters*, series ii, vol. i, p. 6): the council assembled in the audience chamber adjoining the bedroom, the home secretary read the order paper standing in the communicating doorway, the King assented and signed the document with his own hand.

Throughout the sombre December days crowds kept vigil outside the palace railings; thousands upon thousands read the bulletins and turned silently away. For several weeks death hovered about the sick chamber and kept in doubt the issue upon which the hopes of millions turned. At length patience and courage had their reward, and on 9 February 1929 the patient was taken by ambulance to Craigweil House, near Bognor. Here he remained until 15 May, when he made the journey to Windsor.

The wound, however, was not yet healed and the King was in considerable discomfort when, during the first week in June, he had to deal with a change of ministry. Baldwin's government had reached the end of its course while he had been ill: the labour party had been returned (again in a minority) at the general election on 30 May, and on 8 June the new ministers journeyed to Windsor to receive their seals of office. If it was a strange complexion of political parties, it was a singular council that assembled once more outside the bedroom in which the King was seated in his dressing-gown. On the previous afternoon he had braced himself to receive separately each member of the outgoing ministry, and had accepted the custody not only of their seals of office but also of the great seal of the realm. Sidney Webb (later Lord Passfield) received two separate seals, for the Dominions and for the Colonies, notwithstanding that he was at the time a member of neither House. The King himself broke the customary silence with a kindly comment, observing that Miss Bondfield became *ipso facto* a privy councillor as minister of labour, and was the first woman to attain either status.

On 1 July the King returned to London, and on the 7th drove with the Queen to St. Paul's Cathedral for a service of national thanksgiving upon his nominal recovery. But he was not yet out of the wood. Eight days later he was subjected to a further small operation which delayed until the end of August his departure to Sandringham for recuperation in the health-giving and familiar surroundings of home. In the new year (21 January 1930) his voice was once more heard on the wireless when he opened the London Naval Conference, and he broadcast again in the following November at the inauguration of the Indian Round Table Conference. During the years that remained to him he passed for a fit man, although he was induced to take things more easily and to spare himself undue exertion.

It was largely on account of the unemployment position that the labour party had come into power, but it found itself in the grip of forces far transcending the strength of one party in one country. When it took office there were just over a million unemployed in Great Britain; despite all the government's efforts the figure had doubled in the next twelve months, and risen afresh to 2,800,000 by September 1931, when the cost of un-employment benefits exceeded contributions by more than a million pounds a week. As early as October 1930 the grave financial prospect had been engaging the attention of the Cabinet, and early in June 1931 a royal commission had recommended the unpalatable step of saving £24,000,000, partly by increasing workmen's contributions. A crisis was precipitated by the publication on 31 July of the report of the Economy Committee under the chairmanship of Sir George (later Lord) May, calling for the raising of an extra £120,000,000 if the next year's budget was to be balanced; and events proved that even this was an under-estimate by fifty millions. The situation thus revealed spread alarm among foreign nations which had deposited their gold reserves for safety in London, and a rapid series of withdrawals brought the Bank of England to the edge of bankruptcy.

The position was already threatening when on 20 August the King went north to Balmoral: his own inclination was to have postponed his de-parture, but in order not to disturb public confidence the prime minister advised his adhering to his programme. He arrived there on the Friday morning, but on the Saturday the reports from London were so grave that he decided to return that evening, and he was back at Buckingham Palace by breakfast time on Sunday (23 August). At 10.30 he saw MacDonald, who reported that while he and some of his colleagues favoured a ruthless policy of retrenchment, Henderson and a substantial proportion of the Cabinet were unyielding in their opposition. He accordingly felt that he would have no option but to resign, but the King urged him to remain in office and cheered him with words of encouragement and support. At 12.30 the King saw Sir Herbert (later Viscount) Samuel, acting leader of the liberal party, and was impressed by his clear arguments in favour of an all-party government under MacDonald's leadership. At 3 the King saw Baldwin, who patriotically undertook to sink party differences and serve under MacDonald; or, failing that, to carry on the government with the aid of the liberals, having previously obtained the King's consent to a dissolution as soon as the financial situation had been restored.

At 10.15 the same evening the prime minister returned to the palace to tender the resignation of the Cabinet in view of its continued internal dissension. The King urged him to reconsider his own position in view of the support which the other parties were willing to lend him and the confidence which a united front would inspire among foreign creditors at a moment when the banking resources of the country were to be measured rather in hours than in days. The prime minister asked the King to hold a conference of the three party leaders next morning. At 10 o'clock on the 24th the King accordingly received MacDonald, Baldwin, and Sir Herbert Samuel and requested them to come to some arrangement for carrying on the government; after half an hour His Majesty withdrew, and an hour later was gratified to learn that they had come to a provisional agreement. At 4 MacDonald returned and accepted the commission to form an all-party administration. 'If you will permit me to say so', he wrote on the 29th in answer to a generous letter from the King, 'Your Majesty's own conduct has been a great inspiration and guidance to my colleagues and myself, not only during these recent days of great trouble and heart-searching, but throughout the years when we have had the honour of being your special servants.'

Interpreting the mood of the nation, the King spontaneously gave up £50,000 of his civil list and the other members of the Royal Family made corresponding sacrifices, thus identifying themselves with those of all classes upon whose incomes drastic cuts were now imposed. The flight of capital had been checked, but not wholly stemmed. The economic blizzard was beginning to strike other countries, which were calling home their capital in order to strengthen their own position; moreover, the fundamental issue of a protective tariff could only be solved by a general election, the result of which continued to disturb foreign confidence. It was, however, the mutiny in the Atlantic Fleet at Invergordon in the middle of September, consequent upon the reduction in naval rates of pay, which immediately started a fresh run on the Bank, causing the government to abandon on 20 September the gold standard to which Great Britain had returned in May 1925. The general election on 27 October resulted in an overwhelming endorsement by the nation of the King's action in promoting an all-party government.

In considering advice from Lord Rosebery as prime minister it would have been open to Queen Victoria to observe that she had been on the throne before he was born. In like manner Time, the sovereign's friend, had dealt kindly with King George, whose shadow had lengthened as his day drew in. Those who had moved in public affairs throughout the preceding quarter of a century had learned to repose trust in his disinterested judgement: deprived though he had been of Stamfordham in March 1931, few among his advisers could claim a greater store of political experience, and his later ministers were apt not only to tender but to seek advice. The extent to which he had become the father of his people was disclosed during the silver jubilee celebrations in 1935, on the eve of his seventieth birthday. He had observed the preparations with a detached, even a deprecatory eye, and he was frankly taken aback by the welcome which awaited himself and the Queen on their return to London after the customary Easter residence at Windsor. On 6 May Their Majesties drove to St. Paul's Cathedral through sunlit streets gay with flags and packed with cheering crowds. Although advancing years had taken their toll and he was no longer the man he had been, none discerned in the happy joy-bells the knell of a passing reign. The numerous jubilee functions were hardly concluded when, on 7 June, MacDonald resigned the leadership of the all-party government and the King took leave with regret of one who had been his valued prime minister for over a quarter of his reign. He replaced the conduct of affairs with confidence in the hands of Baldwin and withdrew to Sandringham for a rest. Here, six months later, after an illness short and peaceful in its close, he died 20 January 1936.

Happy alike in the manner and the moment of his passing, King George was well spared the events of the ensuing years. Many and moving were the tributes paid to his memory throughout the world while the life of the Empire was stilled in the silence of a deep and intimate sorrow. For four days and nights his coffin lay in a sublime setting beneath the ancient rafters of Westminster Hall and 800,000 of his subjects waited in the wintry weather to witness a scene breath-taking in its august majesty. On 28 January the funeral took place at Windsor, where in due course a tomb of rare beauty and symbolic simplicity was erected in the nave of St. George's Chapel.

In person King George was slightly below the middle height, neatly made, and impeccably dressed in the style before last. His voice was strong and resonant, his prominent eyes arrestingly blue. Moderate in diet, he drank hardly at all but smoked heavily. His mode of life was of an extreme regularity, his occupations being predictable to the day, almost indeed to the hour, given the precedent of the previous years. His naval training had implanted habits of discipline. Punctual himself, he discountenanced unpunctuality in others. Rules were made to be obeyed, and he was not slow to check infractions of traditional observances and duties, by whomsoever they were committed. His disapproval of the High Court of Parliament assuming the appearance of a dormitory during the course of an all-night sitting was marked by a letter which, but for the vigilance of a subordinate official, would have raised the hoary spectre of the rights of his faithful Commons. So valued a counsellor as Balfour, when betrayed by pressure and inadvertence into undertaking a foreign mission without previously notifying the sovereign, incurred a brisk reminder that the throne was not unoccupied. He did not lack moral courage, as when he bluntly told Lloyd George that he knew nothing of the army, or reminded Birkenhead on one occasion, and Joynson-Hicks on another, that Cabinet ministers were expected to conform to a dignified standard of dress when appearing on a public platform. Such occasions, however, were rare, and he never suffered them to impair the ease and cordiality of his personal intercourse. Towards his labour ministers in particular he revealed a generous consideration.

Although not pietistically inclined, the King was all his life a sound churchman and early formed the habit of daily Bible reading. He attended Sunday morning service wherever he might be; when travelling in India his train used to be stopped for the purpose. Both archbishops of Canterbury (Davidson and Lang) were among his closest personal friends; he secured promising men as preachers and week-end guests, and took pains to inform himself independently about candidates recommended for higher preferment. Among the fighting services the navy never lost the hold which it had early established upon his affections. He loved the ships and their men; he knew the leading officers, read the leading books. If the army ranked second it was by the narrowest of margins. Nearly every summer with the Queen he would enjoy a week at the Royal Pavilion at Aldershot and be among the soldiers from early morning until nightfall. He would ride out to watch the training, visit barracks in the afternoon, and give dinner parties every evening in order to get to know the younger officers and their wives. The occasion (12 June 1922) when the Irish regiments, disbanded after the formation of the Free State, handed to him their colours to be laid up in Windsor Castle was one of the most affecting experiences of his life. It was with pride and admiration that he observed the rise of the Royal Air Force, and he manfully opposed its suggested abolition, during the disarmament phase in the early 'thirties. At the notion of entering an aeroplane himself he would shake his head.

It was with humility that King George recognized his shortcomings in the field of the humanities. He would deplore the technical nature of his education, ruefully wishing that he had been taught Latin instead of trigonometry. In French he was reasonably proficient, in German less so. To the perusal of state documents he applied himself with diligence tempered with distaste; he was concerned on one occasion to find that Baldwin himself had not studied certain papers issued by the Cabinet, and his secretaries had to read the newspaper carefully if they were to escape being similarly ensnared. His private reading amounted to some forty books a year, largely contemporary biographies. Writing he found uncongenial. 'Naturally my language does not approach yours in style or finish', he wrote, in sending to Stamfordham a clear account of a certain interview. It is true that his letters and the diary which he kept throughout his life owed little to the graces of composition or calligraphy; but no one could write a more generous message of encouragement to an overdriven prime minister or an exiled governor-general, and his letters gained in sincerity what they lacked in stylistic virtuosity. One of the most unrewarding fruits of human toil is the weekly letter home of a schoolboy son: he had four such, and to each he would return a hand-wrought reply even at moments of greatest pressure.

In London the King was commonly to be seen in the summer riding in Rotten Row with a friend before breakfast. He often went to the theatre and he enjoyed a musical play and the more familiar operas. He did not like to miss a good Rugby match at Twickenham, a cup-tie final at Wembley, a test match at Lord's, or the lawn tennis championship at Wimbledon: at such spectacles and many others throughout the season no figure was more familiar or more welcome. His nature also responded to such revelations of human endurance as the various attempts upon Mount Everest or the polar regions, and he was apt to send for individual members of the expeditions upon their return in order to ply them with questions.

In private life the King's interests lay in the pursuits associated with the English country gentleman. Apart from those already alluded to, his love of racing far outstripped the meagre successes of his own stable, and he was as faithful to Newmarket, Epsom, and Aintree as to Ascot itself. Farming he both encouraged and practised, although it was never numbered among his more personal hobbies. It is noteworthy, however, that his experimental plot of flax at Sandringham was in 1931 the only example of its cultivation in England, and it was to a large extent due to the King's persistence in this field in the period between the wars that home-grown flax was enabled to contribute towards the needs of the war of 1939–1945. When in the country he was attentive to his social duties and every year would pay a round of calls on his neighbours, tenants, and village friends, many of whom he had known all his life. He almost always had guests in the house and was a gifted host. He had a remarkable memory and was a good raconteur. His recollections of past events were interesting and often of an unreserved frankness; concerning current affairs he observed a more guarded discretion. Beneath a bluff and bantering manner he was a man of marked kindness and geniality, of the type

537

that likes to see others happy. Although he was modest about his own accomplishments, he possessed in fact the range of qualities best calculated to appeal to Englishmen of all classes, not least in his mistrust of cleverness, his homespun common sense, his dislike of pretension, his ready sense of the ludicrous, and his devotion to sport.

King George was served by a household knit together in the fellowship of a common loyalty. Some had been chosen from among the friends of his childhood, not a few from his associates in the navy; others, recruited with care as his establishment increased, were assimilated into a circle from which retirement was rare. The daily round was governed by protocol and precedent. This unwritten code was respected at every level, with the result that contentment reigned, and unhastening order prevailed alike on occasions of ceremonial pageantry and in the well-regulated routine of domestic life. In former times it was the custom to speak of the prince and his 'family': of King George it may truly be said that he had two families, and that he was hardly less devoted to his household than to his children. Affection was thus harnessed to the service of duty in a court remarkable alike for the precision of its arrangements and the harmony of its personal relationships.

King George sat for the following artists in the years shown. Sir Luke Fildes (1912, for the state portrait, Windsor). (Sir) Arthur Cope (1912, for H.M. Queen Mary, the United Service Club, and the Royal Naval College, Dartmouth [destroyed by enemy action in 1942]; 1926, for Windsor; 1928, for the Royal Academy): his portrait for the Royal Yacht Squadron, Cowes, was lost by fire in 1929. (Sir) John Lavery (1913, for the conversation piece, with the Queen, the Prince of Wales, and Princess Mary, National Portrait Gallery). A. T. Nowell (1920, for the Leys School, Cambridge). Charles Sims (1924, for a portrait which proved unsuccessful). Richard Jack (1926, for Fulham Town Hall and the Junior Constitutional Club). Oswald Birley (1928, for the National Museum of Wales, Cardiff; 1930, for the Royal Yacht Squadron, Cowes; 1932, for the Royal Welch Fusiliers, Wrexham; 1933, for Lincoln's Inn and the Royal Artillery Mess, Chatham; 1934, for Windsor). John Berrie (1931, for the King's Liverpool Regiment; 1935, for the Canberra War Memorial, Australia). Harrington Mann (1932, for the Junior United Service Club). F. W. Elwell (1932, for the throne room at Holyrood).

His Majesty also gave sittings to the following sculptors. Sir George Frampton (1913, for the marble bust in Guildhall, London). (Sir) Bertram Mackennal (1913, for two marble statues for India, presumably Delhi and Madras): he also designed the head on the coinage, the reverse of which was the work of G. Kruger Gray. (Sir) W. Reid Dick (1933, for the bust in marble at Buckingham Palace and in bronze at the Mansion House, London): he also executed the memorials in Sandringham and

Crathie churches, the recumbent effigy in St. George's Chapel, Windsor, and the statue outside the east end of Westminster Abbey. Kathleen Scott (Lady Kennet) (1935, for the bronze bust for the Hearts of Oak, Euston Road).

[John Gore's *King George V: a Personal Memoir*, 1941, will remain the standard authority on the life of the King, especially in its more intimate aspect. This truthful and revealing book was promoted by King George VI and Queen Mary while the memory of its subject was fresh in the minds of those who had known him: no information was withheld from its author, who received assistance from many of the King's friends. The political background may be conveniently followed in D. C. Somervell's *The Reign of King George the Fifth*, 1935, and John Buchan's *The King's Grace*, 1935. Much further information is contained in the memoirs and biographies of the leading figures of the reign. John Stephenson, *A Royal Correspondence*, 1938; Sir Donald Mackenzie Wallace, *The Web of Empire*, 1902; H. F. Burke, *The Historical Record of the Coronation of King George V and Queen Mary*, 1911; John Fortescue, *Narrative of the Visit to India of King George V and Queen Mary*, 1912; Stanley Reed, *The King and Queen in India*, 1912; J. A. Spender and C. Asquith, *Life of Lord Oxford and Asquith*, 2 vols., 1932; Harold Nicolson, *Curzon, the Last Phase, 1919–1925* (1934), pp. 353 ff.; L. S. Amery, *Thoughts on the Constitution*, 1947, pp. 21, 22; *Journal* of the Royal Society of Arts, December 1920 and October 1944; Royal Archives; personal knowledge.]

OWEN MORSHEAD

published 1949

LOUISE Victoria Alexandra Dagmar

(1867–1931)

Princess Royal of Great Britain and Ireland, Duchess of Fife, was born at Marlborough House 20 February 1867, the third child and eldest daughter of the Prince and Princess of Wales. She was educated at home and developed a strong taste for outdoor life. In 1889 the princess married Alexander William George Duff, sixth Earl of Fife, who was eighteen years her senior and was created a duke on his marriage: by a special remainder of 1900, the dukedom of Fife passed to the princess's daughters and their male issue. This union enabled the princess to live in entire privacy, and, in the stretches of the Dee at Mar Lodge, near Braemar, and in the Deveron at Duff House, near Banff, to indulge freely in her favourite sport of salmon-fishing, in which she developed exceptional skill. In 1905 the princess was declared princess royal and her two daughters, Lady

Mary

Alexandra Duff (later Princess Arthur of Connaught) and Lady Maud Duff (later Countess of Southesk), were created princesses with the title of 'highness'. On 13 December 1911, as the princess and her family were travelling to Egypt for the sake of her health, which was never robust, their ship was wrecked in a gale near Cape Spartel. The princess refused to leave until all the women and children on board had been taken off, and the hardships endured by the party were severe as the boat which was taking them to land was swamped. The death of the duke at Assuan 29 January 1912 was hastened by this misadventure. After continuing to live in retirement, the princess died at her house in Portman Square 4 January 1931.

[*The Times*, 5 January 1931; private information.]

published 1949

MARY (1867–1953)

Queen consort of King George V, was born 26 May 1867 at Kensington Palace in the room in which Queen Victoria was born. She was the eldest child and only daughter of Francis, Prince (after 1871 Duke of) Teck and his wife, Princess Mary Adelaide. The Prince was the only son of Duke Alexander of Wurtemberg by his morganatic marriage with Claudine, Countess Rhédey, of an illustrious Protestant Hungarian house. Her ancestor, Samu Aba, married a sister of St. Stephen and was King of Hungary (1041–5). The Prince was brought up in Vienna and in due course served the Emperor with considerable military promise in the 7th Imperial Hussars. At the invitation of the Prince of Wales he first paid a visit to England in 1864, but it was not until 1866 that he met Princess Mary Adelaide. His wooing was of the briefest. Queen Mary's mother was the younger daughter of Adolphus, Duke of Cambridge (seventh son of George III), and therefore a first cousin of Queen Victoria. Three sons in due course followed the Princess: Princes Adolphus (afterwards created Marquess of Cambridge, died 1927), Francis (died 1910), and Alexander (afterwards the Earl of Athlone, died 1957) for whom his sister always felt a special devotion, perhaps tinged with envy for his successes in public life in fields open only to men. The Princess was popularly known as Princess May until her marriage although she used the official 'Victoria Mary' as her signature.

Early influences in the formation of Princess May's character are not to be lightly dismissed. The Tecks were a devoted if tempestuous couple and remarkably different in character. He was tall and good-looking, orderly and neat in dress and habits, often quick-tempered, extremely conservative especially on the question of women's spheres of usefulness, and a stickler for etiquette. He had some artistic tastes and hobbies, but outside his family his life perhaps was not made as happy as his modest ambitions may have expected. He may have suffered some of the handicaps which early faced the Prince Consort. The Duchess was liberal-minded, expansive, cheerful, warm-hearted, a garrulous but very intelligent conversationalist, a good mixer, catholic in her choice of friends—her devoted admirers came from every class—typically English if rather bohemian, a bad manager, and incurably unpunctual; indeed her unpunctuality was heinous in a royalty; but she delighted in and deserved her popularity. The Duke had no private fortune. The Duchess's parliamentary grant, eked out by graces and favours from the Queen, was insufficient to meet the costs of moderate 'State' in the rooms allotted at Kensington Palace and at the large and graceful White Lodge in Richmond Park, and generous gifts to charity.

Princess May in her childhood was constantly with her popular mother and learned from her to understand and sympathize in the lives and aspirations of all classes, and to comprehend the relative values of money in the income groups. For the Duchess had an understanding far ahead of her times of what 'the poor' really needed, as her Village Homes at Addlestone and her Holiday Homes proved. Princess May was clearly often overshadowed by her mother's popularity and no doubt by reaction she acquired the virtue of punctuality; she had few opportunities of practising small talk in her mother's company. Her parents had no ambition for her education beyond the normal drawing-room accomplishments of her kind in her day. It was her own determination, later reinforced by her Alsatian governess, Hélène Bricka, a very strong-minded, well-educated, politically liberal companion, to pursue it beyond that range. Accordingly when in 1883–5 the family spent eighteen months in Italy by the need for retrenchment, although the Princess was at first intensely homesick, her interest in art and history, later to be enlarged among the royal collections, quickly expanded. When she returned to England, to enter the social round of London society, she continued for several hours a day to improve her own education without parental encouragement, and she became proficient in French and German and in European history. By the time she became Queen, she had gained a wide knowledge of political and social life in the German principalities.

Mary

She had from childhood seen something of the children of the Prince of Wales, the first cousins being all too young to share their interests, and she and her brothers had sometimes found the rough manners and boisterous fun of their second cousins rather trying. In 1887 she began to know them well. From the first Queen Victoria, who was fond of the Duchess, had taken an interest in the daughter and henceforth watched her closely and began to see in her a worthy choice for the Prince of Wales's eldest son, the Duke of Clarence. She had all the qualifications, lacking only the self-confidence which is required of a social leader. In later life Queen Mary sometimes questioned the verdict that she was very shy. She certainly never shared Queen Alexandra's taste for ragging nor perhaps Queen Victoria's liking for an occasional robust laugh, although among her intimates she could reveal her own sense of fun. She argued that a love of serious conversation and of relevance could be described as shyness and suggested that people who were themselves natural and truth-loving had no need to be shy in her presence. Yet the attribution that she was shy and shy-making survived and it cannot be said that in her twenties the Prince of Wales's family helped her to cure it. Nevertheless, Princess May enjoyed her dancing years in London with her brothers, now coming to man's estate and all destined for the army, and amid the rural charms of White Lodge and in the pre-Edwardian circle of the Prince.

There was a certain inevitability in the announcement of her engagement to the Duke of Clarence at the end of 1891 when Princess May was approaching twenty-five. She was the only available English Princess not descended from the Queen. In that sense, it was an 'alliance'. The test of whether it would prove a love match was eliminated by the Duke's sudden death in January 1892. Prince George, becoming heir to the throne next after his father, was created Duke of York and the public's anxiety for the succession was transferred to him. In May 1893 his engagement to Princess May was announced to the intense satisfaction of the Queen. The Prince of Wales approved it, if the Princess's enthusiasm was modified by the recent memory of her elder son's death. The marriage was solemnized 6 July 1893 in the chapel of St. James's Palace. Once more no doubt it was argued that this was a 'marriage of convenience'. The Duke of York's private diary and contemporary letters to his friends make it quite clear that it was soon very much a love match, and in the first years of marriage, largely spent at York Cottage at Sandringham, his home for much of his life, his happiness grew and broadened into a placid contentment with his lot. They were quiet years. Children were born—the eldest (subsequently the Duke of Windsor) at White Lodge, 23 June 1894, the second (subsequently King George VI) at York Cottage 14 December 1895; on 25 April 1897 a daughter (subsequently the Princess Royal); and on 31 March 1900 a third son (subsequently the Duke of Gloucester). The Duke's diary is proof positive that for him life was an idyll whether at York House, St. James's, or at the ugly, inconvenient cottage at beloved Sandringham.

For the Duchess, as her family increased, the idyll was sometimes marred by the benevolent tyranny exercised from the Big House. The Duke himself was aware of it. To his mother he remained to the last the second son. She always addressed her letters to him as 'King George', never 'The King'. In a letter to the writer (25 July 1939) Queen Mary commented that for King George V his reign was the most interesting part of his life 'but a good deal of the early times helped him to understand the human point of view. The rough and tumble of former days was very good for us both.' Those early years had an influence on the Duchess's character. She was living on an estate which drew its inspiration wholly from the Prince and Princess of Wales and she had married into a family which was certainly a closely guarded clique and was not far short of a mutual-admiration society. It was a family little given to intellectual pursuits, not easily to be converted to any other manner of life than that which they had found all-sufficing. The Duchess was intellectually on a higher plane, and constantly seeking to increase her store of knowledge in many fields beyond the range of the Princess of Wales and Princess Victoria. Their recreations were not hers. She needed outlets and wider horizons; sometimes her intellectual life may have been starved and her energies atrophied.

It was for her no training in self-confidence. Her husband was very conservative, not easy to convert or remould. Sandringham ways were perfect in his eyes. His admiration for his father was boundless and tinged with awe. Yet soon enough the Duchess began to improve his taste and education. Late in her life, in conversation with an intimate and in her valiance for the truth, Queen Mary remarked: 'It is always supposed that my mother-in-law had no influence whatever over my father-in-law and that I have strong influence over my husband. The truth happens to be the exact opposite in each case.' Some influence over the Duke must, however, be conceded her in those early times. But all her life she was afraid of taking too much upon herself, in her reverence for 'The Sovereign'. Indeed, in many ways she was timid.

Shortly after the diamond jubilee the Duke and Duchess paid a most successful visit to Ireland. With the death of Queen Victoria and the coronation of Edward VII they began to assume (but modestly) some of the duties of the heir to the throne. Before mourning for the Queen was over the *Ophir* tour gave them an opportunity to test their own qualities and to find their feet in an Empire which knew little of them and in a society which regarded them as too little go-ahead for Edwardian brilliance and initiative. They travelled as Duke and Duchess of Cornwall (to which title the Duke succeeded) and York. The prime purpose was to open the first federal Parliament of the new Commonwealth of Australia, but the tour embraced the greater part of the Empire and lasted more than seven months. Of the two, the Duchess was better equipped to meet the tests. Once or twice, when the Duke was overstrained, she stepped into the breach and did his part. Her own embraced the interests of the women of the Empire and for both of them it was a successful education and graduation under the careful coaching of Sir Arthur Bigge (afterwards Lord Stamfordham). The bitter parting from their young family was forgotten in the happy reunion and the warm approval of the people and of the King who now created the Duke Prince of Wales. In a speech in the City the Prince jolted the public out of its complacent views on the Empire and revealed that he had gained a good deal of self-confidence during his tour.

The new Prince and Princess of Wales began to take a larger share of ceremonial and of the responsibilities of the heir to the throne. They resisted, with mild criticism from some quarters, going with the Edwardian stream. Nevertheless, they entertained constantly and carried out a number of engagements during and after the coronation, a few months after which on 20 December 1902 the Princess gave birth to her fourth son, Prince George (subsequently the Duke of Kent). In the next year they moved into Marlborough House. On 12 July 1905 the youngest child, Prince John, was born; he died 18 January 1919. Never robust, he was very dear to his family who treasured his quaint sayings.

In the winter of 1905–6 the Prince and Princess of Wales had another opportunity to extend their knowledge of the Empire and increase their self-confidence when they made a highly successful tour of India. Their coach and guide on this occasion was Sir Walter Lawrence and before and during the arduous tour they both went through the most complete and detailed preparation. The Princess's interest, assiduity, and energy in mastering and executing her special functions among the women of India were highly praised. The tour covered India from end to end, and all her life Queen Mary's love of India was graven on her heart. She would sometimes compare her sense of loss, when the Indian Empire ceased, to another Queen Mary's feelings over the loss of Calais.

In May 1906 they went to Madrid for the marriage of Princess Ena of Battenberg to the King of Spain and were unhurt when a bomb was thrown at the wedding procession. In June they were in Norway for the coronation of the King and Queen. Thenceforward to the end of the reign of King Edward their lives continued on a fixed and not too arduous pattern. No shadow of jealousy marred the relations between the King and his heir. King Edward died 6 May 1910 and the new Queen became known as Queen Mary. She and the King faced some early criticism of a pin-pricking sort. There were lampoons ('The King is duller than the Queen' and vice versa, ran a refrain) whispered among the old set which feared (with reason) that the 'great days' and the brilliance were gone from court and society, and some scandalous imputations against the King were soon exploded. In the face of these small discouragements (not unfamiliar at the accession of British sovereigns), the King and Queen soon began to strike out a line of their own and once again proved that the changing times had found appropriate leadership from the throne. After the exhausting funeral ceremonies, followed in 1911 by the unveiling of Queen Victoria's memorial in the Kaiser's presence and by the coronation, made specially remarkable by the grace and dignity of the new Queen, they paid their second visit to India for the durbar. Neither ever forgot the splendours and the strain of this tour (1911–12) throughout which the energy and sustained interest of the Queen were universally remarked and praised.

State visits to Berlin (1913) and Paris (1914) further impressed on the nation the worth and the dignity of the new sovereigns. There were also tours of industrial areas. There Queen Mary was in her element. Margaret Bondfield once remarked that Queen Mary would have made a good factory inspector. She could comprehend poverty, her sympathy was genuine, her clear mind, her curiosity and skill in detail enabled her to enter with remarkable understanding into the problems of the small house and the family budget. Not for her the dazzling smile, the apt and gracious word in a non-stop progress. Her visits were exhaustively and exhaustingly carried out, and they created a new model of a sovereign's functions. She was genuinely interested and never taken in by surface appearances.

In their private life the King and Queen continued to live very simply and sought to accord to their children a sensible and, as far as possible, democratic upbringing. From the earliest years, and even as her official and self-imposed functions increased, Queen Mary usually found time for 'the children's hour'. She superintended their religious grounding, and gave them practical rather than sentimental attention. The maternal instincts were never strong in her, although she had an understanding of children, a sympathy too, unless they were spoilt and tiresome. She always backed up the justified discipline meted out by tutors, governesses, and servants, but was always ready to contest any over-harsh discipline by their father. She would reason her eldest son out of his natural revolts, insisting on the obligations of his unique position. For already with her and her husband loyalty to the monarchy transcended all other loyalties. Soon enough it was to her the children turned for sympathy and advice, for their father's methods inspired in them an awe and unease which in time (until their marriages, and always with the eldest) grew into a major and almost national tragedy. Her influence over them grew. It was a pity that her influence over her husband on such matters did not keep pace. With her children she was not austere. No doubt Prince George was her favourite son because he most keenly shared her intellectual tastes. She joined occasionally in their jokes, even practical jokes, and taught them hobbies; and since she disliked yachting, although she usually attended Cowes week, and was bored by grouse shooting, she would have the children to herself in August and September at Frogmore or Abergeldie, when she did not go abroad. Gradually life consolidated into an unchanging routine, as the boys moved on from Osborne, Dartmouth, or private schools to Oxford or into the Services. The King and Queen set a new pattern in the face of criticism which soon enough turned to approval and admiration. And so they came to the test of world war.

Queen Mary's part between 1914 and 1918 was arduous and invaluable. She turned her Needlework Guild into a world-wide collecting and distributing organization. There was at first some fear, which Mary Macarthur did not hesitate to express to the Queen, that this voluntary work might increase the already serious problem of unemployment among women. The Queen at once insisted that the problem should be tackled. The Central Committee on Women's Employment was set up with Mary Macarthur as honorary secretary and The Queen's Work for Women Fund was administered by the committee. This brought Queen Mary into close touch with the leading women in the Labour movement such as Gertrude Tuckwell. Queen Mary was indefatigable in visiting hospitals and largely responsible for founding the workshops at Roehampton and a number of hospitals for troops in and round London. When the reputation of the Women's Army Auxiliary Corps stood low Queen Mary gave it her patronage. She directed the austerity of the royal household and her example and unwearying energy were everywhere acknowledged. The King's duties were heavy at home and in his visits to the troops and navy. In the summer of 1917 the Queen accompanied him to France where her visits to the hospitals established a legend of her tirelessness and practical sympathy. And through it all, a very personal anxiety for their sons and other relations and friends played a heavy part in the strain and stress of war. When it ended, both had triumphantly passed their supreme tests.

The war had marked them both, and the King, who was never the same man after an accident in France, showed it clearly. The armistice and the celebrations of their silver wedding in 1918 gave them further proofs of public respect and affection and led the way to an abnormal amount of state ceremonial in the years which followed. There were state visits from allied sovereigns and leaders, the great Wembley Exhibition, and more personal and private events to occupy them in the marriages of Princess Mary (1922) and the Duke of York (1923). The post-war years passed in a social revolution which affected all classes and called for the highest examples of restraint, dignity, and tact, and to these duties the King and Queen gave constant attention. Their concern for the convenience of the first Labour Government did much to remove socialist misconception about the monarchy. For the King they were years of almost ceaseless difficulty and anxiety which he was physically ill-fitted to endure. When in 1928 he became desperately ill, Queen Mary proved, first to the doctors and to her family, and gradually to the whole nation, the strength of her character. The King's doctors acknowledged her great share in the miracle of his recovery. The Duke of York, meeting the Prince of Wales on his arrival from East Africa, remarked: 'Through all the anxiety she has never once revealed her feelings to any of us. She is really far too reserved . . . I fear a breakdown if anything awful happens. She has been wonderful.' There was no breakdown. In the period of convalescence, in the years which remained to the King, she knew the truth: she carried the anxiety and maintained before the world a serenity and calm and dignity, half comprehended and wholly admired. Henceforward, the King was physically unfit for half the duties of his office and he was not an easy man to deflect from duty or habituated routine. She was constantly at his side in his public engagements. In the celebrations of their jubilee in 1935 the full realization of the nation's respect and affection for them came to both, and King George's personal reference to her, spoken in deep emotion in Westminster Hall, acknowledged his own debt to her lifelong service to himself and the nation. Eight months later the King died at Sandringham on 20 January 1936, in the presence of his family, soon after the last council at his bedside. At once the Queen kissed the hand of her eldest son. Her self-command in those anxious hours was noted by all who saw her. She completed the last entry in King George's diary with a touching note and spoke in a message to the nation her heartfelt gratitude for the affection shown to them.

After the King's death, Queen Mary moved into Marlborough House which had stood empty since the death of Queen Alexandra. It had been to some extent renovated and, when Queen Mary's taste had had full play in the arrangement of her own collections, gradually assumed a dignity and even charm which it had never known. But the normal period of mourning held for her the tremendous stress and strain of the abdication crisis. She met it with the calmness, sympathy, tact, restraint, and dignity of which she was a mistress and was guided in her course by the chief loyalty of her life—to the monarchy—in the best interest of the nation. But that crisis might well have marked and aged a woman less physically and mentally strong. It was not in her character to accept retirement or the hitherto conventional lifelong privacy of Queen Mothers. She began to resume her public engagements and created a precedent in attending the coronation of her son King George VI. Her interest in works of art continued to develop and she made her own a large variety of cultural and industrial projects. She was already famous for her interest (and endurance) at the British Industries Fair (it was calculated that from first to last she walked a hundred miles round the Fairs); and she became a regular visitor to the Wimbledon tennis championships.

In May 1939 Queen Mary had a car accident which severely shook her and permanently injured her eyesight. With the outbreak of war she reluctantly accepted the necessity for her removal from London and she established herself at Badminton, the home of her nephew-by-marriage, the Duke of Beaufort. Her activities varied but did not lessen: she worked and planned in the woods, visited the neighbouring towns, would stop to give lifts to servicemen, and got through a great deal of tapestry work at which she was an acknowledged expert. Some of it—a great carpet in particular—was exhibited and sold overseas and earned praise and dollars for worthy objects. She was at Badminton when she received the news of the death of the Duke of Kent in a Service flying accident 25 August 1942. She went at once to her daughter-in-law and attended the funeral at Windsor. She refused to surrender to the shock and bitter grief. She returned to London when the war with Germany was over and resumed her public engagements right up to and indeed beyond the death of King George VI in 1952. She never failed to receive important visitors such as J. C. Smuts and General Eisenhower and many social workers from the dominions. In 1947 she celebrated her eightieth birthday, an occasion saddened by the death of her son-in-law the Earl of Harewood. Her own death took place after a short illness, 24 March 1953, at Marlborough House, in her eighty-sixth year, and she was buried beside King George V in St. George's chapel, Windsor. Her effigy, later set over the tomb beside that of King George, had been made simultaneously by Sir William Reid Dick. Her death and funeral evoked remarkable tributes of public respect and affection. (Sir) Winston Churchill in a broadcast spoke of the long range of her experience; but Queen Mary, he said, did not cling to the past. She moved easily in the swiftly changing scenes. New ideas had no terrors for her. Dispassionate in judgement, practical in all things, she was far too much interested in the present to be unduly prejudiced by the past. Above all, she died in the knowledge that the Crown was far more broadly based on the people's love and on the nation's will than in the sedate days of her youth.

She was a great queen-consort. It was her destiny during many troubled years of war and social revolution to serve as an example at the head of the State, through times of bitterness and disillusion when ethical standards and conventions were being questioned or abandoned and a looser morality gained ground in society; and the chief quality with which she performed her function was perhaps a golden sense of what was fitting, not alone for a queen, a court, or a monarchy, but for men and women in every rank of life. She was elastic for change, rigid for conduct, resolute for the dignity of the Crown and of human life. She possessed few of the graces and the dazzling charms of her mother-in-law. Indeed, she was formidable and could appear austere. But she had the charm of incisive judgement tempered by great kindness. Nothing could hide her practical human sympathy or chill the warmth of her heart. Simple, straightforward, forthright, blazingly truthful, she could feel sympathy for the delinquent when she visited the juvenile courts in East London, but none for the liar, while to the end her spirit scorned the laggard and the fainthearted. Only her remarkable physical strength and extraordinary self-discipline and mental vigour could have enabled her to do the public work she did in anxiety, sorrow, and old age.

'Genius' in the usual sense cannot justly be applied in any field to Queen Mary. Her genius lay in her intense loyalty and selfless service to the monarchy, in her tact and most particularly in her political tact, for she never discussed politics (taking a lesson from Queen Adelaide's failing), in her safety as a recipient of confidences, in her rigid upholding of all that was of good report, in her self-discipline in controlling inherent timidity and shyness.

But genius in the accepted sense of rare intellectual powers she would not have claimed. Her mind, essentially urban, was factual rather than analytical. Of country matters she knew little. Life at Balmoral was not to her taste; she preferred Sandringham which was less remote. Diligent always, she absorbed information and stored it in a strong and orderly memory. Thus, her collection of art treasures was guided less by intuition and taste than by accepted doctrine. The monarchy being her first interest, her preference in paintings spread outward from the basic subject of English royal portraiture and, although this led her into wider fields, she never acquired a taste for gallery pictures outside the historical. This did not prevent her lending continuous encouragement to museums and galleries, and often she impressed the staffs by her memory. The latter years of her life were chiefly devoted to adding to her collection of bibelots, and perhaps the quality of the whole would have profited had she paid more for less. Her reading she pursued steadily to the end, usually in the field of serious memoirs, historical and contemporary, English and foreign. She read some current fiction, but when in her last years her ladies read to her, she usually chose classic novels. Her brief and factual diary throws little light on her private thoughts and inner life, and is devoid of criticism of political events or of personalities. She cared intensely, to the minutest detail, for any subject great or small which she set out to master, or for any object to achieve, however trivial, even to the choice of a birthday present (she was the first Queen to visit the shops) or some practically thoughtful action to a humble dependant who had served her well.

It was this capacity, allied to that refusal to be prejudiced by the past, which enabled her with her husband King George V to create a new conception of constitutional monarchy and its responsibilities. It was durable and remained a pattern for succeeding reigns because it was based on the human virtues of duty and integrity, simplicity and sympathy, loyalty and love.

In appearance Queen Mary was above the average height of women. Her intimates among women considered that she looked her best in black, a colour she detested. Her own favourites were pale pastel shades, preferably blue. She always wore a toque, except occasionally in the garden when she would wear a hat, and on suitable occasions she carried a long umbrella or parasol. She appeared often, owing to her dress and carriage, to tower over King George, although she was exactly the same height. This gave her in the public view the appearance of moral ascendancy also. It was an illusion. The King was very much master in his house and she, even to the subduing of an innate gaiety of heart, known only to her intimates, was a submissive partner in her loyalty to the monarchy.

Queen Mary sat to many artists during her life. (Sir) William Llewellyn painted the state portrait (1911–12), remarkable for its dignity, which is now at Buckingham Palace. (Sir) John Lavery's group (1913) of the King and Queen with the Prince of Wales and Princess Mary is in the National Portrait Gallery where there is also a bronze by Sir William Reid Dick. There are several more portraits at Windsor Castle or the Palace. A. T. Nowell produced the best likeness. Tyrell, von Angeli, G. Koberwein, and E. Hughes painted her before 1900; (Sir) Oswald Birley, David Jagger, and Simon Elwes painted her in the thirties or later. She was a good and constant subject for photographers.

[H.R.H. The Duke of Windsor, *A King's Story*, 1951; John Gore, *King George V*, 1941; James Pope-Hennessy, *Queen Mary*, 1959; Queen Mary's private diaries; private information.]

JOHN GORE

published 1971

VICTORIA Alexandra Olga Mary

(1868–1935)

Princess of Great Britain and Ireland, was born at Marlborough House 6 July 1868, the fourth child and second daughter of the Prince and Princess of Wales. Living constantly at home as the only unmarried daughter, the princess was never much in the public eye except as the companion of her father and mother, but both at Marlborough House and at Buckingham Palace she made herself their indispensable helpmeet. During Queen Alexandra's widowhood she was her mother's inseparable companion, and it was not until her death that at the age of fifty-seven the princess gained independence in a household of her own at Coppins, Iver, in Buckinghamshire. There during the last ten years of her life she found rest in her favourite recreations of music and gardening, and gave full rein to her kindly feelings towards animals. She inherited to the full her mother's endless generosity and sympathy for those in need. If this benevolence seemed to others misplaced, such a consideration was never allowed to stand in the way of a benefaction, once she had decided to make it. She was a true and lovable friend, and no common bond of affection united her to her brother King George V, with whom scarcely a day passed without communication, and whose precarious health was further impaired by the shock of her death at Coppins 3 December 1935.

[*The Times*, 4 December 1935; personal knowledge.]

EDWARD SEYMOUR

published 1949

KEPPEL Alice Frederica

(1868–1947)

Mistress of King Edward VII, was born in Woolwich 29 April 1868, the youngest in the family of eight daughters and one son of William Edmonstone, later fourth baronet, of Duntreath Castle, Stirlingshire, and his wife Mary Elizabeth Parsons. Educated at home, Alice early on showed evidence of the beauty, tact, and vivacity for which she was to become renowned. In 1891 she married George Keppel, third son of William Coutts Keppel, seventh Earl of Albemarle. There were two children: Violet, born in 1894, who was later to win notoriety for her turbulent love affair with Victoria ('Vita') Sackville-West, and Sonia, born in 1900.

In 1898 the twenty-nine-year-old Alice met and soon became the mistress of the fifty-six-year-old Albert Edward, Prince of Wales. His accession to the throne in 1901, as King Edward VII, in no way diminished her role. For not only did Mrs Keppel maintain her position as *maîtresse en titre* but she became one of the leading personalities of the Edwardian court. Throughout the ten years of Edward VII's reign, Alice was an accepted, respected, and highly visible member of the royal entourage. She remained, in the widely used phrase, 'La Favorita'. Her ability to keep the notoriously impatient monarch amused was greatly appreciated in royal circles. Financially astute, Alice cultivated people like the financier, Sir Ernest Cassel, and is said to have realized a considerable sum by the sale of certain rubber shares presented to her by her royal lover.

The widely believed story that as King Edward VII lay dying, his wife Queen Alexandra magnanimously sent for Mrs Keppel to take leave of him, is inaccurate. Much against the queen's will, Alice Keppel insisted on seeing the dying king; on being asked to leave the death chamber, she made an embarrassing scene and had to be escorted out. Alice afterwards—in an effort to safeguard her position—claimed that it was the queen who had summoned her and who had promised to look after her in the future.

During World War I Alice divided her time between entertaining in her home in Grosvenor Street and helping her friend, Lady Sarah Wilson, run a hospital for wounded soldiers in Boulogne. In 1927 the Keppels sold their London house and bought the Villa dell'Ombrellino, above Florence. Celebrated as the ex-mistress of Edward VII, as an international *grande dame*, and as a matchless hostess, Alice Keppel reigned like a queen over Florentine society. During World War II the Keppels established themselves at the Ritz Hotel in London. At the end of the war they returned to the Villa dell'Ombrellino where, 11 September 1947, at the age of seventy-nine, Alice died.

[Wilfrid Scawen Blunt's unpublished diary, Fitzwilliam Museum, Cambridge; Sonia Keppel, *Edwardian Daughter*, 1958; James Lees-Milne, *The Enigmatic Edwardian*, 1986; Philip Magnus, *King Edward VII*, 1964; Violet Trefusis, *Don't Look Round*, 1952.]

THEO ARONSON

published 1993

MAUD Charlotte Mary Victoria

(1869–1938)

Princess of Great Britain and Ireland, Queen of Norway, was born at Marlborough House 26 November 1869, the fifth child and third and youngest daughter of the Prince and Princess of Wales. Her versatile and vivacious character took full advantage of the education of the time and the many distinguished visitors to Marlborough House and Sandringham gave her numerous friends and a very wide knowledge of world affairs, while she fully appreciated her mother's love of music and art.

Princess Maud's love of country life, her horses, and her dogs was fully gratified when in 1896 she married Prince Christian Frederick Charles George Valdemar Axel, second son of the Crown Prince (afterwards King Frederick VIII) of Denmark, and made her home at Appleton House, Sandringham, where her only child Alexander Edward Christian Frederick (Crown Prince Olav) was born in 1903. When Prince Charles (as he was known) was elected to the throne of Norway in 1905, taking the name of King Haakon VII, Queen Maud entered into her duties and learnt the ways of her new country, which could not be better exemplified than in her upbringing of her son in the sports of the country, yachting and ski-ing, at which he excelled at a very early age. Very soon the Queen had laid out an English garden at Bygdo Kongsgaard, which she loved to show to all her friends, and whenever it was possible for her, she was to be seen riding and, when the snow came, running on skis.

Queen Maud's great love of children and animals led her to support any good cause, but quietly and almost shyly, according to her nature; many a musician and artist will remember her personal encouragement. Except during the war of 1914–1918 the Queen was able to visit Appleton every year: her last public appearance in this country was at the coronation of her nephew King George VI in 1937. She died in London 20 November 1938, and was buried in Oslo.

[*The Times*, 21 November 1938; personal knowledge.]

published 1949

HELENA VICTORIA (1870–1948)

Princess

Was born at Frogmore, Windsor Park, 3 May 1870, the third child and elder daughter of Prince Christian of Schleswig-Holstein and Princess Christian, Queen Victoria's third daughter, Princess Helena Augusta Victoria. Her early life was spent at Windsor where her parents had a house in the Park of which her father was Ranger. She naturally saw a great deal of her grandmother who in her letters always referred to her as 'Thora', a childhood contraction of her first name.

As a public figure Princess Helena Victoria grew up to follow the example of her mother and supported many and various philanthropic and benevolent causes, among them the Princess Christian Nursing Home at Windsor of which she succeeded her mother as president. She particularly identified herself with the Young Men's Christian Association and took the closest interest in every branch of its work, visiting France on its behalf during the war of 1914–18. It was she who obtained from Lord Kitchener permission to send musical and theatrical entertainments to the troops at the front. In 1917 King George V accorded her the style of Highness and the territorial name of Schleswig-Holstein was dropped.

In contemporary social life the Princess made for herself a definite place: she played lawn tennis, and also golf at a time when few women had become its votaries; and she maintained a lifelong zest for ballroom dancing. She had inherited the musical tastes of both her maternal grandparents and in the period between the two wars she and her sister, Princess Marie Louise, made their home, the last house in Pall Mall to be used as a private residence, into a musical centre. She died in London 13 March 1948 after some years of failing health.

A portrait by Harrington Mann was in the possession of Princess Marie Louise.

[Contemporary newsprints; private information.]

H. E. Wortham

[H. H. Princess Marie Louise, *My Memories of Six Reigns*, 1956.]

published 1959

Princess

Was born at Cumberland Lodge, Windsor, 12 August 1872, the youngest child of Prince Christian of Schleswig-Holstein and his wife, Princess Helena Augusta Victoria, Queen Victoria's third daughter. Her conventional education at home was relieved by holidays with relations in Germany, during one of which visits she met Prince Aribert of Anhalt. With the encouragement of her cousin the Emperor William II she married him in St. George's chapel, Windsor, 6 July 1891. He proved an unsatisfactory husband. After nine distressing years the childless marriage was annulled by Prince Aribert's father, exercising his medieval right as a sovereign prince. The Princess, a devout churchwoman, believed her wedding vows to be binding and never remarried.

Returning to her family in England, she devoted more than half a century of her life to furthering charitable causes and social services. Nursing, the care of lepers, youth clubs, the relief of poverty, and organizations for international understanding particularly touched her imagination. She became a familiar figure at balls and bazaars, committees and receptions, commemorative services and picture exhibitions. Standing above average height and with imposing features, she brought to all formal occasions an air of dignity softened by kindliness. Her neat and pointed speeches always refreshed and sometimes surprised her audience. There was charm, too, in her conversation. She was a tireless traveller, and few corners of the world had escaped her curiosity or failed to stimulate her talents for humour and mimicry.

Princess Marie Louise's patronage of the arts enabled her to acquire a wider circle of friends than usually surrounds royal personages. She moved at ease in the society of writers, actors, and musicians, and at one time in her life lived contentedly in a bedsitting-room at a ladies' club. Her happiest years were spent between the wars at Schomberg House, Pall Mall, which she shared with her sister Princess Helena Victoria. Together they gave memorable parties which became a valued institution among London music lovers. From her mother Princess Marie Louise had inherited a passion for Bach, to which was added a later appreciation of Wagner. She visited Bayreuth more than once, attended Covent Garden regularly, and was the friend of Lauritz Melchior, the tenor.

Among the Princess's recreations was the delicate art of enamelling in precious metals. Her work in this medium included the clasp on the cope worn by the prelate of the Order of St. Michael and St. George. She was also an assiduous collector of Napoleonic relics, though free from the megalomania which often accompanies such a pursuit. A self-imposed task which gave her pleasure was the planning of an elaborate doll's house, now at Windsor Castle, for presentation to Queen Mary. To secure contributions to this record of twentieth-century craftsmanship she wrote two thousand letters in her own masterful but barely legible hand.

Throughout her long life the Princess was a voracious reader, particularly of history, biography, and detective fiction. In November 1956 she published a volume of her own reminiscences. *My Memories of Six Reigns*, of which 40,000 copies were sold within a few months, is a penetrating portrait of a vanished age. In a style of confiding intimacy, the Princess mingled a playful disrespect for the etiquette of German courts with a loving reverence for her grandmother Queen Victoria. Although in visibly failing health she insisted on attending a luncheon to mark the publication of the book, but was unable personally to deliver the message of greeting she had composed for all who shared her delight in writing.

She died a few days later, 8 December 1956, at her grace-and-favour residence in Fitzmaurice Place. The funeral was at Windsor on 14 December, that most melancholy of dates in Victorian memory, exactly ninety-five years after the death of her grandfather the Prince Consort. The congregation in St. George's chapel included three 'pearly queens' and a 'pearly king' who, in the gay colours of their calling, had come from Finsbury to pay a farewell tribute to their friend and patron. The remains of the Princess were later transferred to the private cemetery at Frogmore.

Princess Marie Louise, the last British princess to bear the style of Highness, was also one of the last surviving members of the Royal Order of Victoria and Albert. She was appointed a lady of the Imperial Order of the Crown of India by Queen Victoria (1893), G.B.E. by King George V (1919), and G.C.V.O. by Queen Elizabeth II (1953). There is a portrait by Harrington Mann in the Forum Club, Belgrave Square.

[H. H. Princess Marie Louise, *My Memories of Six Reigns*, 1956; private information; personal knowledge.]

Kenneth Rose

published 1971

(1873–1960)

First Baron Wigram

Private secretary to King George V (1931–6), was born 5 July 1873 at Madras, the eldest son of Herbert Wigram, Madras Civil Service (of the family of Wigram, baronets of that name since 1805). His mother, Amy Augusta, was a daughter of Lieutenant-General John Wood Rideout, of the Indian Army. His two younger brothers had distinguished careers in the senior fighting Services, both dying unmarried before him. He was educated at Winchester where his prowess at ball games, notably cricket and rackets, became a legend. Later on, in India, he became a fine polo player and shone at cricket as an all-rounder. In due course, he was to inspire King George V with some of his enthusiasm for sporting events. In 1893 he was commissioned in the Royal Artillery and two years later was appointed aide-de-camp to Lord Elgin, viceroy of India. In 1897 he exchanged into the 18th Bengal Lancers, serving in the Tirah and other campaigns on the North-West Frontier, and he was in South Africa with Kitchener's Horse in 1900. Lord Curzon on succeeding Elgin retained him as aide-de-camp until 1904. When Sir Walter Lawrence was invited in 1905 to act as chief of staff to the Prince of Wales on his first visit to India, he 'made it a condition' that Wigram should be his assistant. After the tour Wigram was appointed equerry to the Prince. In 1906 he received his brevet majority and in 1908 became military secretary to the commander-in-chief at Aldershot. He relinquished this post in 1910 when the Prince succeeded to the throne as King George V to become his assistant private secretary. In the view of his military contemporaries he thereby sacrificed an army career of great promise.

Four-fifths of Wigram's long service in the secretariat was spent as assistant to Arthur Bigge, Lord Stamfordham, during which time he profited by the wisdom and experience of a great private secretary who steered the King through the major shoals of his reign. He learned to appreciate the ever-growing importance of the office, as a result of the gradual acceptance that a constitutional sovereign's prerogative is strictly limited to the right 'to be consulted, to encourage, and to warn' and in consequence of the far-reaching changes in dominion status. From Bigge's example he learned too, to be selfless and tireless, to be completely trusted by his sovereign, yet hardly less so by politicians of all parties from whom, as 'eyes and ears' of the King, he must seek the best sources of information. Above all, he learned that in matters trenching on the sovereign's prerogative, one false step in intervention might precipitate a constitutional crisis.

Wigram

When Stamfordham died in 1931 the King expressed himself as 'utterly lost' at the death of the man who 'taught me how to be a King'. But he wrote in his diary: 'His loss is irreparable. I shall now make Wigram my Private Secretary.' Wigram, appointed K.C.V.O. in 1928, had long enjoyed the close friendship and trust of the King and Queen. If in the five years of his tenure of the office he never attained Bigge's mastery as a draftsman and précis writer, he proved that he had acquired many of the essentials. He was more approachable than Bigge, for his nature was genial and he was a man with many friends and possessed of a fund of practical sympathy for all sorts and conditions of men, young and old. Shrewd, but far from subtle, his success was due to the virtues of constant loyalty and honesty rather than to intellectual gifts. Indeed, he was very like the King he served, in his geniality, in his simple and direct nature and his hatred of shams and deceit. He knew the King's mind.

Within a few months of his appointment, he, too, was faced with a major problem when the 'national' Government was set up to meet the financial crisis of that year. In the subsequent five years several matters arose on which the King felt deeply, as trenching on his own 'prerogative' or threatening the integrity of the Commonwealth of which he was now the sole unifying symbol. They included the questions of the appointment of governors-general, of the royal title and of the removal of vestiges of subordination in dominion status, and the question of honours. Not less anxiously did the King follow the emergence of Indian nationalism and the Government of India Act.

Before these matters were all decided, the King's health rapidly declined and Wigram's responsibilities increased, while he added to his other duties the post of keeper of the privy purse. As the end approached, with Queen Mary's co-operation, he added the role of nurse and played his full part as trusted friend and counsellor to his dying master.

Six months after the King's death, he handed over to Alexander Hardinge (later Lord Hardinge of Penshurst) and was appointed deputy constable and lieutenant-governor of Windsor Castle, living in the Norman Tower where he applied his mind to horticulture and gradually converted the moat garden into a botanical showplace. After the abdication he was briefly recalled by King George VI and appointed permanent lord-in-waiting. He finally left the secretariat in the latter half of 1937. In 1945, having reached the age limit, he resigned his remaining court appointments and went to live in London.

Wigram received a variety of honours. He had the rare distinction of gaining three brevets. He was appointed C.S.I. in 1911; between 1918 and 1933 he was advanced from C.B. to G.C.B.; and between 1903 and 1932 rose step by step in the grades of the Victorian Order to G.C.V.O., receiving the

Victorian Chain in 1937. He was sworn of the Privy Council in 1932 and raised to the peerage in 1935. He held a number of foreign orders and was a fellow of the Royal Geographical, Horticultural, and Zoological societies. From 1932 to 1945 he was colonel of the 19th (K.G.O.) Lancers, Indian Army.

During and long after his tenure of the office of private secretary, Wigram was constantly active in the welfare and promotion of many educational and hospital institutions. He was at various times a fellow of Winchester and a governor of Wellington and of Haileybury. For a quarter of a century he worked inspiringly on behalf of the Westminster Hospital; he was a very active vice-president of King Edward VII's Sanatorium, on the council of Queen Mary's Hospital, Roehampton, vice-president of the National Association of Boys Clubs, and on the board of the Jubilee Trust and other youth organizations. He was for many years a director of the Midland Bank and of the L.M.S. Railway.

In appearance Wigram was good looking, nearly six feet tall, of athletic build and soldierly bearing, retaining his youthful appearance and vigour of speech to a remarkable degree until near the end of his long life.

Wigram married in 1912 Nora Mary, only daughter of Colonel Sir Neville Chamberlain, K.C.B. They had two sons, the younger of whom was killed in action in 1943, and a daughter. They were a devoted family. Lady Wigram died in 1956 and his daughter two years later. Thereafter Wigram's health declined and his mental powers began to fail. He died in London 3 September 1960 and was succeeded by his elder son, George Neville Clive (born 1915).

A not very successful picture by L. Calkin, painted in 1925, is in the possession of the family. There is a tablet to Wigram's memory in the north quire aisle of St. George's Chapel, Windsor.

[John Gore, *King George V*, 1941; Harold Nicolson, *King George V*, 1952; John W. Wheeler-Bennett, *King George VI*, 1958; *The Times*, 5 September 1960; private information; personal knowledge.]

JOHN GORE

published 1971

Alexander Augustus Frederick
William Alfred George

(1874–1957)

Earl of Athlone

Was born at Kensington Palace 14 April 1874, the third son of Princess Mary Adelaide and the Duke of Teck, and brother of the future Queen Mary. Originally styled His Serene Highness, Prince Alexander of Teck, he was known to his family as 'Alge'. In 1917 in accordance with policy he relinquished his titles and the name of Teck and took the family name of Cambridge and the title of Earl of Athlone. Although his new name and titles had hereditary associations he and many others regarded these changes as unnecessary and even undignified.

The Prince was educated at Eton and Sandhurst, was commissioned second lieutenant in the 7th Hussars in 1894, joined his regiment in India, and thereafter received his promotion in the normal way. He served in the Matabele war of 1896–7 and was mentioned in dispatches. He transferred to the Inniskilling Dragoons in order to be able to serve in the South African war during which he was mentioned again in dispatches and appointed to the D.S.O. He was spoken of as a capable and enterprising officer and a cheerful comrade, ever willing to endure and to share with his troopers the discomforts of a nomad campaign.

In 1904 the Prince married Princess Alice Mary Victoria Augusta Pauline, daughter of Queen Victoria's fourth son, the Duke of Albany. On this occasion he was appointed G.C.V.O. Their first child, May Helen Emma, was born in 1906; in the following year they had a son, Rupert Alexander George Augustus, later Viscount Trematon. A second son, Maurice Francis George, died in 1910 before he was six months old.

The Prince joined the Royal Horse Guards in 1904. In 1911, at the request of King George V, he transferred to the 2nd Life Guards with the rank of major. At the coronation he was appointed G.C.B. In 1914 he was nominated governor-general of Canada but did not take up the appointment owing to the outbreak of war in which he served as lieutenant-colonel in the Life Guards. Later he joined the staff as G.S.O. 2 and was attached to the British military mission to the Belgian Army. He was promoted G.S.O. 1 with the rank of brigadier-general in 1915 and received Belgian, French, and Russian decorations. He was twice mentioned in dispatches and in 1918 he joined the general headquarters staff.

After the war Athlone retired from the army and took an active interest in national and social work. A man of compassion, he was especially attracted to the work of institutions connected with the relief of human suffering. He had been chairman of the Middlesex Hospital since 1910 and in 1921 the minister of health appointed him chairman of a committee composed of the foremost doctors and surgeons of the day to investigate the needs of medical practitioners. Under his enthusiastic guidance the 'Athlone committee' produced a comprehensive report which recommended the appropriation of substantial sums from public funds to finance the establishment of a postgraduate medical school (to be associated with the university of London and existing medical institutions) to promote postgraduate instruction and medical research. The work thus initiated by the Athlone committee was carried on by committees presided over by Neville Chamberlain and Arthur Greenwood. The Postgraduate School, subsequently attached to the Hammersmith Hospital, became one of the most famous institutions of its kind. Athlone took a special interest and pride in the school which he frequently visited in later years.

Athlone was closely identified also with the promotion of education. He was chancellor of the university of London (1932–55), taking office at a difficult time in the development of the university under its new statutes. He was an honorary bencher of the Middle Temple, a fellow of the Royal Society, vice-president of the Royal Academy of Music, an honorary fellow of the Royal College of Surgeons, and a knight grand cross of the Order of St. John of Jerusalem.

In 1923 Athlone was appointed governor-general of the Union and high commissioner for South Africa, being appointed G.C.M.G. and promoted to the rank of major-general. He arrived in South Africa in time to open Parliament in January 1924. Shortly afterwards J. B. M. Hertzog succeeded J. C. Smuts as prime minister. A difficult period followed. Racial feeling between British and Afrikaners was inflamed by a Nationalist proposal to adopt a new flag for the Union omitting anything symbolic of the British connection. Athlone worked quietly behind the scenes to secure the inclusion of a Union Jack in the white central panel. His speech at the unveiling of this compromise flag in Cape Town did much to soothe and reconcile animosities. His frequent tours in the provinces enhanced his prestige and popularity among all sections of the community and did much to bring the two white races closer together. His patience, courtesy, and tact won the trust and esteem of the political leaders of all parties. He was appointed K.G. in 1928 in recognition of his services and his term of office was extended at the request of the Government. The death of their son, Viscount Trematon, as the result of a motor accident in France in

April 1928 was a cruel and shattering blow to the Athlones. The expressions of sympathy they received from all over Southern Africa revealed a depth of affectionate sympathy and personal regard which must have robbed their sorrow of some of its bitterness.

At the conclusion of his very successful term of office, Athlone was sworn of the Privy Council in 1931 and appointed governor and constable of Windsor Castle. He and Princess Alice took up residence at Brantridge Park and afterwards transferred to Kensington Palace which they decorated with trophies of their big-game hunting expeditions and paintings of African landscapes by local artists whom they had patronized and encouraged during their tour of duty. They continued their interest in South African affairs and personalities and resumed their social activities in England. Queen Mary and her brother had always been close companions and regular correspondents. After the King recovered from his serious illness he expressed the wish that Lord Athlone should, for family reasons, remain in England.

In 1940, King George VI showed his uncle a telegram from W. L. Mackenzie King asking if he might submit Athlone's name for the governor-generalship of Canada. Greatly as he appreciated the compliment, Athlone thought a younger man should be appointed, but the King persuaded him to accept for a period of two years. In the event he served the full term of five years. He entered upon his new duties with his usual enthusiasm and took a keen interest in efforts to establish in the dominion various military training schemes and factories for the production of war materials. He travelled extensively at all seasons of the year to attend troop reviews and encourage munition workers. In addition he and Princess Alice were always ready to entertain members of official missions, including those of President Roosevelt and (Sir) Winston Churchill, and they offered open hospitality to royalties and other distinguished exiles from allied countries under German occupation. Although Athlone had occasional differences with Mackenzie King, he had a natural gift for getting on with people and their personal relations always remained very friendly. His unsuccessful efforts to reconcile differences between the prime minister and his defence minister, J. L. Ralston, were a disappointment to him.

In August 1944, on the twenty-fifth anniversary of his leadership of his party, Mackenzie King wrote to the governor-general that he was 'particularly happy that the last four years, the most eventful of all, should have been shared with Your Excellency in the administration of Canada's war effort, and that throughout every day of that time I should have had the constant and helpful co-operation of Your Excellency and Princess Alice.' Later the prime minister wrote: 'Your years here, as Representative of the King, have strengthened the country's attachment to the Crown. I doubt if that attachment were ever stronger than it is today.'

Those who knew Athlone intimately and worked with him would agree that kindness was his outstanding characteristic. Yet, like many kind people, he had a quick temper which subsided as rapidly as it flared up. His military training had endowed him with an eye for detail and a keen perception of the manners and peculiarities of others upon which he liked to exercise his quizzical sense of humour. He gave the impression that he modelled his conduct on the precepts of Polonius—especially those relating to manners and deportment. His dress was meticulous but never 'expressed in fancy'. He had an exact sense of symmetry and tidiness and would often adjust ornaments and pictures. His memory for names and faces was quite extraordinary and he was a good judge of character. In public affairs he was tolerant and strove to induce others to modify fixed or extreme opinions before giving expression to his own. His natural tact and intellectual modesty enabled him to impress his counsel upon ministers without provoking opposition or appearing to intrude upon their constitutional prerogatives. His command over the loyalty and affection of his staff was exceptional and he delighted in renewing friendships with them in after years. At the conclusion of his term of office in Canada in 1946 he and Princess Alice made time to stay in Trinidad with their former secretary in South Africa. On his return to England Athlone resumed his interest in national affairs. In 1936 he had been appointed grand master of the Order of St. Michael and St. George, an order associated especially with the dominions, colonial, and foreign services. In that office he presided over the last tributes paid to many of Britain's most distinguished sons. On his death at Kensington Palace, 16 January 1957, he received in his turn the homage of members of the order who, like himself, had faithfully and diligently served their country. The peerage became extinct.

At Kensington Palace there is a portrait of Athlone by H. de T. Glazebrook and a conversation piece with Princess Alice by Norman Hepple. At Government House, Ottawa, there is a portrait by Henry Carr; the university of London has a portrait by Augustus John and the Middlesex Hospital (at Athlone House, Kenwood, Hampstead Lane) one by Francis Hodge. At the Vintners' Hall there is a portrait by (Sir) James Gunn.

[Private information; personal knowledge; *For My Grandchildren*, Some reminiscences of Her Royal Highness Princess Alice, Countess of Athlone, 1966.]

BEDE CLIFFORD

published 1971

(1883–1981)

Princess of Great Britain and Ireland and Countess of Athlone, was born at Windsor Castle 25 February 1883, the elder child and only daughter of Prince Leopold George Duncan Albert, first Duke of Albany, Queen Victoria's fourth and youngest son, and his wife, Princess Helene Friederike Auguste of Waldeck-Pyrmont. Her father died of haemophilia little more than a year after her birth and she was brought up by her mother at Claremont House, near Esher.

In 1904 Princess Alice was married to the younger brother of the future Queen Mary, Prince Alexander of Teck, whose full names were Alexander Augustus Frederick William Alfred George. A serving officer in the British Army, he abandoned his German title in 1917, adopted the family name of Cambridge, and was created Earl of Athlone.

Princess Alice's lifelong vivacity concealed anxiety and sorrow. Her brother Prince Charles Edward, second Duke of Albany, had at the age of fifteen been taken away from Eton to be brought up in Germany as heir to his uncle, the reigning Duke of Coburg. He entered on his unfortunate inheritance in 1900, became a general in the German Army, fought for his adopted country during World War I, and was deposed in 1918. In the following year he was stripped of his British dukedom of Albany and later became a fervent supporter of the Nazi regime. These events naturally distressed Princess Alice, whose heart was torn between patriotism and affection for an only brother.

As wife of the governor-general of South Africa in 1923–31 and of Canada in 1940–6, Princess Alice proved a memorable proconsul in her own right: graceful, sympathetic, and perpetually amused. But tragedy struck again in 1928. Her son, Rupert Alexander George Augustus, Viscount Trematon (born 1907), had inherited the haemophilia of his grandfather, Prince Leopold. He died of injuries in a motoring accident from which others might have recovered. A younger son, Maurice Francis George, had died in 1910 before he was six months old. There was also one daughter of the marriage, Lady May Helen Emma Cambridge (born 1906), who married a soldier, (Sir) Henry Abel Smith, governor of Queensland 1958–66.

From marriage until 1923, the Princess and her husband lived in Henry III tower, Windsor Castle. Later they had an apartment in Kensington Palace with a country place at Brantridge Park, Sussex. Lord Athlone's death in 1957 dissolved a partnership of more than half a century but did not deflect his widow from a way of life both industrious and convivial.

Well into her tenth decade, she remained an active patron of many institutions; the Royal School of Needlework and the Women's Transport Service (FANY) earned her particular interest. Princess Alice's leisure hours were no less productive, and she would continue to knit even while walking up a mountain at Balmoral.

A sense of adventure as well as of thrift led Princess Alice to travel about London by bus. For many years she similarly crossed the Atlantic each winter in a banana boat, combining her duties as chancellor (1950–71) of the University of the West Indies with a holiday in Jamaica. Several times she revisited South Africa and made the long journey to stay with her son-in-law and daughter in Australia.

Although below middle height, Princess Alice had a patrician presence, with aquiline features, observant eyes, and a stylish sense of fashion. She was an engaging talker and needed little prompting to recall life at Windsor under Queen Victoria, whose unsuspected laughter still rang in the ears of her last surviving granddaughter almost a century later. Not all her memories were benign. She never forgave W. E. Gladstone for having cheated her family of a whole year's civil list when her father died a few days before the start of the fiscal year; or Sir Winston Churchill for filling her drawing-room with pungent cigar smoke during the Quebec conference of 1943. Some of these recollections she confided to an entertaining volume of memoirs, *For My Grandchildren* (1966). Her views on public affairs were emphatic and not always predictable. When a colonial governor of radical bent expressed his belief in universal suffrage, she replied: 'Foot, I have never heard such balderdash in my life.' Yet she was the first member of the royal family publicly to advocate birth control; and like her cousin King George V, did not harbour a trace of colour prejudice.

Princess Alice, the last surviving member of the Royal Order of Victoria and Albert, was also appointed GBE in 1937 and GCVO in 1948. She had many honorary degrees. She died 3 January 1981 at Kensington Palace in her ninety-eighth year. After a funeral service in St George's chapel, Windsor, her remains were buried at Frogmore.

[Princess Alice, *For My Grandchildren*, 1966; Theo Aronson, *Princess Alice*, 1981; personal knowledge.]

Kenneth Rose

published 1990

RAMSAY (Victoria) Patricia
(Helena Elizabeth)

(1886–1974)

Lady

Princess of Great Britain and Ireland, was born in London at Buckingham Palace on St. Patrick's Day, 17 March 1886. She was the third and youngest child and younger daughter of Prince Arthur William Patrick Albert, Duke of Connaught and Strathearn, the third son of Queen Victoria, and his wife, Princess Louise Margaret Alexandra Victoria Agnes, third daughter of Prince Frederick Charles Nicholas of Prussia. The Duchess of Connaught, the dominant partner in the marriage, who had herself spent an unhappy childhood, was an undemonstrative and sometimes neglectful parent. The young princess, 'Patsy', as she was called in the family, had to wear her elder sister's cast-off clothing, and to the end of her life suffered from painful feet, the result of her mother's refusal to buy her well-fitting shoes.

Although Princess Patricia of Connaught grew up to be tall, handsome, and intelligent, she was handicapped by an inculcated lack of self-confidence that made her feel unwanted and helped delay her acceptance of a suitor in marriage until she was thirty-three. King Alfonso XIII of Spain, who in 1906 married her cousin Princess Victoria Eugénie, was among those who sought her hand in vain.

Meanwhile, she travelled the world in the wake of her father, who held a succession of military appointments in India, the Mediterranean, Canada, and Ireland. During the Duke's years as governor-general of Canada, 1911–16, his wife was in declining health (she died in 1917) and Princess Patricia acted as his hostess. The Canadians appreciated her beauty, her charm, and her devotion to war work. She was persuaded to sign innumerable miniature portraits of herself to be sold in aid of the Red Cross, and embroidered the original colour of Princess Patricia's Canadian Light Infantry which was carried into battle on the western front. Immensely proud at being appointed their colonel-in-chief, she visited her regiment many times over the years, even after her retirement from public duties. Canada also paid the princess the compliment of naming after her an extension to Ontario's boundaries and a bay in British Columbia.

On 27 February 1919 she was married in Westminster Abbey to Captain the Honourable (Sir) Alexander Robert Maule Ramsay, a younger son of John William Ramsay, the thirteenth Earl of Dalhousie and a serving naval officer. It was a love match born of a friendship that had begun even before Ramsay's attachment to the Duke of Connaught's staff in Canada; impossible during her mother's lifetime, it also marked the more relaxed post-war attitude of the royal family towards marriage with a commoner, and was to bring the princess the first real happiness she knew. There was one child of the marriage, Alexander Arthur Alfonso David, born 21 December 1919, who fought in the Grenadier Guards during World War II and was severely wounded. Admiral Ramsay died in 1972. Two days before the wedding King George V gave his permission for the bride to relinquish, at her own wish, her royal title, style, and rank and to assume the style of Lady Patricia Ramsay, with precedence immediately before the marchionesses of England.

Thereafter Lady Patricia scarcely ever emerged from the seclusion of her private life except to attend an exhibition of her own paintings; even then she would not submit her work to the Royal Academy, although willing to become patron of the less publicized Royal West of England Academy. She found much fulfilment in her art, insisting always that it be judged only by exacting professional standards. The earliest of her 600 paintings were of flowers. During travels abroad, her imagination was caught by marine life and tropical vegetation, and in later years she turned to abstracts. Lady Patricia experimented boldly with bright colours and bold contrasts that owed something to the influence of Gauguin and Van Gogh. She was equally deft in oils, water-colours, pen-and-ink, and gouache. Most of her works are in the possession of her son.

As the wife of a naval officer, Lady Patricia had no house of her own until 1942, when she took possession of Ribsden Holt, Windlesham, bequeathed to her by her aunt Princess Louise, Duchess of Argyll. It was there that she died 12 January 1974 in her eighty-eighth year. The funeral took place in St. George's chapel, Windsor, and the burial at Frogmore.

The most striking portraits of Lady Patricia Ramsay are by Ambrose McEvoy (1926), in the possession of her son, and A. S. Hartrick (c. 1920), of whom she was a pupil, in the possession of the artist's niece. There are more formal portraits by Charles Sims at Bagshot Park, Surrey, on loan to the Royal Army chaplains department; and by Charles Shannon in Currie Barracks, Edmonton, Alberta.

[*The Times*, 14 January 1974; private information.]

KENNETH ROSE

published 1986

(1887–1969)

Queen consort of King Alfonso XIII of Spain, was born at Balmoral 24 October 1887, the second of the four children and only daughter of Prince and Princess Henry of Battenberg. Her mother, Princess Beatrice, was the fifth and youngest daughter of Queen Victoria. She was christened Eugénie after her godmother, the Empress Eugénie, but the name Ena, by which she was known before her marriage, was due to the minister misreading her mother's writing of the name Eva. Her childhood was spent partly at Balmoral and partly in the Isle of Wight, where her father was governor. His death in 1896 deeply affected the Princess, but she concentrated her energies in helping her mother in her philanthropic work and in developing her music in which she showed early and unusual talent.

On 31 May 1906, in Madrid, the Princess married King Alfonso XIII of Spain. In April King Edward VII had conferred on her the style of 'royal highness' and shortly before the announcement of her engagement in March she had been received into the Roman Catholic Church. The change of denomination was not popular in Britain although King Alfonso himself was well liked, partly on account of the courage he had shown at the attempt on his life in Paris in 1905. The wedding was marred by another such attempt: a bomb was thrown at the carriage in which the King and Queen were returning after the ceremony and landed just in front of the carriage, behind the rear pair of horses. Although a number of people were killed and many wounded the King and Queen escaped unharmed and remained composed, albeit greatly shaken. That evening they rode in a carriage unescorted around the streets to assure the people that they were unharmed.

The tragic occurrence had one happier effect in bringing admiration and sympathy to the Queen; there had been suggestions that a British consort might not prove popular with the Spanish people. While respecting the traditions of the country, Queen Victoria Eugénie's ease of manner broke down to a considerable extent the extreme rigidity of the Spanish court. Her friendly manner, her avoidance of involvement in politics, and her help and hard work for the poor, all contributed to the respect and affection in which she came to be held. She particularly encouraged the provision of better hospitals and health facilities, giving much time to the reorganization of the Spanish Red Cross which during the war of 1914–18 became responsible for a scheme of international aid.

She also founded a needlework guild, the Ropero de Santa Victoria, and did much to encourage education in a country which had a high rate of illiteracy. Apart from a still-born son (1910), the King and Queen had four sons and two daughters. The Queen gave much care to the upbringing of her family and faced with fortitude the unfortunate maladies from which three of the sons suffered. The eldest, Alfonso (1907–38), and the youngest, Gonzalo (1914–34), were both afflicted with haemophilia, a disease which ultimately caused their deaths when they were involved in motor-car accidents. The second son, Jaime (1908–75), was born a deaf mute, although with patient and sympathetic training he managed later to learn to speak. The third son, Juan Carlos (born 1913), served as a midshipman in the British navy (1933–5), becoming in 1936 an honorary lieutenant. Both the daughters, the Infantas Beatriz (born 1909) and Maria Christina (born 1911), married and had issue.

In 1931 the municipal elections in Spain showed that republicanism was sweeping the country and to avoid civil war the King, while refusing to renounce his throne, left the country from Cartagena, 15 April, too suddenly to be accompanied by his family. They afterwards joined him in France and lived in exile in Italy. Later the King and Queen decided to separate, but on the King's illness the Queen went to him and was with him when he died in Rome 28 February 1941. She subsequently left Italy for Switzerland. After 1945 she made frequent visits to England, staying often with her only surviving brother, the Marquess of Carisbrooke, until his death in 1960. In 1968 she visited Spain for the first time since her exile to attend the christening of Felipe Juan, first son of Juan Carlos, the elder son of her third son, Don Juan. On this occasion she was received by General Franco and his wife. She died in Lausanne 15 April 1969. In that year her grandson, Juan Carlos, was selected by General Franco as his successor designate as head of state in preference to his father, Don Juan, and on Franco's death Juan Carlos became King of Spain 23 November 1975.

Queen Victoria Eugénie was tall and slender and possessed a gracious ease in her manner and movement. She dressed fashionably and in good taste, many of her clothes being made in Paris. Her favourite colours were grey and blue which set off her English complexion and clear gold hair, features well exemplified in her portrait by P. A. de László which is reproduced in Graham's biography. Another portrait, showing her wearing a mantilla, by the same artist, painted in the King's silver jubilee year, was later placed in the Madrid Modern Art Gallery. She was a Dame Grand Cross of the Sovereign Order of Malta and held the Grand Cross of Maria Louisa and of Public Beneficence of Spain.

Lascelles

[Evelyn Graham (Netley Lucas), *The Queen of Spain*, 1929; David Skene Duff, *The Shy Princess: the life of H. R. H. Princess Beatrice*, 1958; *Daily Telegraph*, 17 April 1969.]

G. K. S. HAMILTON-EDWARDS

published 1981

LASCELLES A l a n F r e d e r i c k

(1887–1981)

Sir

Royal secretary, was the sixth and youngest child and only surviving son (the other died in infancy) of Commander Frederick Canning Lascelles, second son of the fourth Earl of Harewood and godson of the viceroy of India, Earl Canning. His mother, Frederica Maria, daughter of Sir Adolphus Frederic Octavius Liddell, son of the first Baron Ravensworth, died in March 1891. 'Tommy', as he was known from childhood, was born 11 April 1887, the birthday of his ancestor George Canning, prime minister, at Sutton Waldron House, Dorset, where his father had retired after naval service. Lascelles was brought up by a not very competent governess and his older sisters until he went to preparatory school and on to Marlborough (1900–5) where he was not very happy.

In 1905 he went to Trinity College, Oxford, and at once found himself at home. For him Oxford became 'the Beloved City'. Lascelles was one of a brilliant generation, centred on Balliol, including Julian Grenfell, Charles Lister, Edward Horner, and others. Most of this glittering circle were killed in World War I. In the vacations he was able to move from country house to country house and pursue his favourite sports of hunting and fishing; he rode well in the field and point-to-point. In 1909 he was placed in the second class in *literae humaniores*, though hopes had been entertained of a first. During his time at Oxford he had read widely and cultivated a growing taste in music, particularly that of Wagner and Brahms (he eventually became an honorary fellow of the Royal Academy of Music). He could hardly write a dull letter.

For some years Lascelles had difficulty in finding his vocation. He sat in vain twice for the Foreign Office, jettisoned the idea of the Indian Civil Service, and tried a brief spell in the City. In 1913 he joined the Bedfordshire Yeomanry, and with them he was mobilized on the outbreak of war. During its course he was wounded, won the MC (1919), and was mentioned in dispatches. At its close he noted: 'Even when you win a war, you cannot forget that you have lost your generation.'

Early in 1919 he sailed for India as aide-de-camp to his brother-in-law Sir George Ambrose (later Lord) Lloyd, the designated governor of Bombay. During his stay he met and married the daughter of the viceroy; his cousin H. G. C. Lascelles (later the Earl of Harewood) generously made the wedding possible from his own inheritance. On his return to England in 1920 he was appointed assistant private secretary to the Prince of Wales (later Edward VIII) and with one interval the rest of his active life was passed in royal service. In 1929 he left the Prince of Wales and from 1931 to 1935 he was private secretary to the governor-general of Canada (V. B. Ponsonby, Earl of Bessborough); in 1933 he was appointed CMG for his work at the Ottawa conference. However in 1935 he returned to the palace as assistant private secretary to George V, and in succession to Edward VIII and George VI, to whom he became private secretary in 1943, retaining the post for the first year of Queen Elizabeth II's reign. By the time of Edward VIII's abdication he was out of sympathy with his master. He was keeper of the royal archives from 1943 to 1953. He was admitted to the Privy Council in 1943.

Lascelles was every inch a courtier, tall, slim, good-looking, and quick-moving. His discretion was impeccable, though he committed much to journals which have yet to be published. He instituted a press office at Buckingham Palace and encouraged a newer style of royal biography such as the life of George V by his old friend, John Gore. His memory was remarkable and his reading extensive, with a late devotion to Horace Walpole. He was promoted GCVO in 1947 (his KCVO was given in a royal train in America in 1939 and his MVO in 1926) and GCB in 1953. He was offered a peerage but refused it. He became a director of the Midland Bank; he was chairman of the Pilgrim Trust (1954–60) and chairman of the Historic Buildings Council for England (1953–63). His old college made him an honorary fellow in 1948, and Oxford University gave him a DCL in 1963. He also had honorary LLDs from Bristol and Durham.

In retirement he occupied a grace and favour house in Kensington Palace: in widowhood he grew a beard and remained the best of company. He married in 1920 Joan Frances Vere (1895–1971), eldest daughter of Frederic John Napier Thesiger, first Viscount Chelmsford, viceroy of India. They had a son, who became ill and tragically died in 1951, just when the health of George VI was beginning to give anxiety, and two daughters, one of whom was married to the second Viscount Chandos. Lascelles died in Kensington Palace 10 August 1981. There is a drawing of 1922 by Oswald Birley.

Alexandra

[*The Times*, 11 August 1981; Duff Hart-Davis (ed.), *End of an Era, Letters and Journals of Sir Alan Lascelles from 1887 to 1920*, 1986, and *Letters and Journals ... from 1920 to 1936*, 1989; private information; personal knowledge.]

MICHAEL MACLAGAN

published 1990

ALEXANDRA Victoria Alberta Edwina Louise Duff

(1891–1959)

Princess Arthur of Connaught, Duchess of Fife

Elder daughter of the first Duke of Fife and of Princess Louise, eldest daughter of the then Prince of Wales, was born at Mar Lodge, Braemar, 17 May 1891. Her father, the sixth Earl of Fife, who bore titles in the peerages of both the United Kingdom and Ireland, had been created a duke by Queen Victoria on the occasion of his marriage with the Queen's granddaughter in 1889; but a new creation was made in 1900 whereby the succession might pass to his daughters, the second of whom, the Lady Maud, was born in 1893. In 1905 King Edward VII created his eldest daughter Princess Royal and granted her two children the style and title of Princess and Highness, with precedence after members of the royal family styled Royal Highness.

In December 1911, Princess Alexandra set out with her parents and sister for their fourth winter in Egypt. In the early hours of 13 December, their ship, the P. & O. liner *Delhi*, ran ashore off Cape Spartel, on the coast of Spanish Morocco. Boats from the *Duke of Edinburgh* put off to the rescue, but many passengers, including the Duke of Fife's party, were completely submerged and greatly buffeted by the waves before reaching shore. Wet through and in piercing cold, they struggled through a gale of wind and rain to Cape Spartel lighthouse, where they were revived; but they did not reach the British legation at Tangier until six o'clock in the evening, after a ten-mile ride on muleback. After a few days' rest the party returned to Gibraltar and thence proceeded to Egypt and the Sudan. On 19 January the Duke of Fife contracted a chill which developed into pleurisy and pneumonia; he died at Aswan, 29 January 1912, aged sixty-two. His titles, other than those of the creation of 1900, became either extinct or dormant, but Princess Alexandra succeeded him as Duchess of Fife and Countess of Macduff.

In July of the following year came the announcement of the engagement of the Duchess of Fife to her cousin Prince Arthur, the only son of the Duke of Connaught and Princess Louise of Prussia. They were married in the Chapel Royal, St. James's, 15 October 1913, and on 9 August 1914 was born their only child, Alastair Arthur, who bore the title of Earl of Macduff.

The war of 1914–18 gave to Princess Arthur of Connaught the opportunity to embrace a vocation of nursing in which she subsequently made a highly successful career. In 1915 she joined the staff of St. Mary's Hospital, Paddington, as a full-time nurse and worked untiringly in this capacity until the armistice. After the war she continued her training at St. Mary's, becoming a state registered nurse in 1919 and being awarded a first prize for a paper on eclampsia (convulsions in late pregnancy). She also served in Queen Charlotte's Hospital where she specialized in gynaecology, receiving a certificate of merit. Throughout these years Princess Arthur increasingly impressed her superiors by her technical skill and practical efficiency.

When in 1920 Prince Arthur of Connaught was appointed governor-general of the Union of South Africa, Princess Arthur ably seconded him and shared his popularity. Her tact and friendliness made her many friends among the South Africans, who also greatly admired the interest which she displayed in hospitals, child welfare, and maternity work throughout the Union. To these subjects she brought her exceptional personal knowledge and experience, which enabled her to make many effective and valuable suggestions.

On her return to London (1923) Princess Arthur resumed her nursing career at the University College Hospital, where she was known as 'Nurse Marjorie', and at Charing Cross Hospital. At this time she was specializing in surgery, proving herself a competent, dependable, and imperturbable theatre sister, who was capable of performing minor operations herself and of instructing juniors in their duties. Her services to the nursing profession were recognized in July 1925, when she was awarded the badge of the Royal Red Cross.

The outbreak of war in 1939 afforded Princess Arthur further scope for her nursing abilities. She refused the offer of a post as matron of a hospital in the country, preferring to become sister-in-charge of the casualty clearing station of the 2nd London General Hospital. Shortly thereafter, however, she opened the Fife Nursing Home in Bentinck Street which she personally equipped, financed, and administered as matron for ten years with great competence.

The death of her husband in 1938 was followed by that of her father-in-law, the Duke of Connaught, in 1942. He was succeeded by his grandson,

Alastair, but little more than a year later the young Duke, who had seen service in Egypt as a subaltern in the Scots Greys, died of pneumonia in Ottawa, 26 April 1943.

Princess Arthur served as a counsellor of state during King George VI's absences abroad in 1939, 1943, and 1944. She was appointed colonel-in-chief of the Royal Army Pay Corps in 1939 and was also president and later patron of the Royal British Nurses' Association (of which she held the honorary diploma) and patron of the Plaistow Maternity Hospital.

In 1949 the multiple-rheumatoid-arthritis, from which Princess Arthur had suffered for many years, rendered her completely crippled and necessitated the closing of her nursing-home. She retired to her house in Regent's Park where she wrote for private circulation two autobiographical fragments in a vivid and entertaining style: *A Nurse's Story* (1955) and *Egypt and Khartum* (1956), in which she gave a graphic account of the wreck of the *Delhi*; she was engaged on a further volume on big-game hunting in South Africa when she died at her London home, 26 February 1959. At her special request she was cremated, her ashes being laid in the chapel of Mar Lodge. The dukedom of Fife devolved upon her nephew, Lord Carnegie, the son of her sister, who had married the eleventh Earl of Southesk in 1923 and died in 1945.

[Private information; personal knowledge.]

JOHN WHEELER-BENNETT

published 1971

HARDINGE Alexander Henry Louis

(1894–1960)

Second Baron Hardinge of Penshurst

Private secretary to King Edward VIII and King George VI, was born in Paris 17 May 1894, the younger son of Charles Hardinge, later first Baron Hardinge of Penshurst. He was educated at Harrow and Trinity College, Cambridge, and in 1915–16 was aide-de-camp to his father, then viceroy of India, who had recently sustained the loss of both his wife and his elder son. He served in France and Belgium in 1916–18 with the Grenadier Guards, was wounded and awarded the M.C., and in 1919–20 was adjutant of his regiment.

In 1920 Hardinge became assistant private secretary to King George V, being trained in his duties by Lord Stamfordham and Clive (later Lord)

Wigram. In 1935 he became in addition assistant keeper of the privy purse. In May 1936 King Edward VIII appointed him principal private secretary. At no time did the new King take him into his confidence over his personal dilemma arising from his wish to marry Mrs. Simpson, but as early as August Hardinge began to warn him, as was his duty, of the constitutional difficulties he was likely to encounter. When Mrs. Simpson's divorce proceedings became imminent in October, Hardinge urged Stanley Baldwin, the prime minister, to see the King; and later himself saw to it that the King was aware of the open expression of opinion coming in from overseas whilst the press in this country still kept silent.

Finally, on 13 November 1936, after Baldwin had informed Hardinge that he had arranged a meeting of senior ministers to discuss the matter, Hardinge warned the King by letter that the silence might break at any moment; informed him of the meeting which was to take place; and advised him that in the event of the Government's resigning it was 'hardly within the bounds of possibility' that anyone else would be found capable of forming a government; the alternative would be a general election 'in which Your Majesty's personal affairs would be the chief issue—and I cannot help feeling that even those who would sympathize with Your Majesty as an individual would deeply resent the damage which would inevitably be done to the Crown . . .'. He ended by begging the King to consider the desirability of Mrs. Simpson's leaving the country without delay.

To a man of Hardinge's courage and integrity and with his wide knowledge and balanced judgement of men and affairs there could be no doubt where his duty lay in warning the King of the gravity of the situation. Nor did the King deny this (although he later claimed to having been 'shocked and angry'); but while continuing to conduct normal business with Hardinge, thereafter he made no reference to the subject and no use of him in the negotiations which culminated in the abdication.

On 29 November 1955 Hardinge included the text of his letter to the King in an article in *The Times* in which he refuted allegations that there had been a conspiracy to bring about the abdication and recalled that 'the one thing that everybody was trying to do was to keep the King on the throne'. Before dispatching his letter, he recorded, he had shown it to Geoffrey Dawson, feeling that he 'desperately needed an outside opinion as to the general wisdom and propriety' of his letter; and he had shown it to a member of Baldwin's staff so that the prime minister might be aware of its contents. But 'both in conception and execution the idea was entirely my own'.

Exhausted by the strain, Hardinge went on three months' sick leave from which he returned to serve King George VI with unassuming devotion and efficiency through the difficult early years of his reign, then of the war, until in 1943 ill health compelled his resignation. In the following year he succeeded his father as second baron. He had been appointed M.V.O. (1925), C.V.O. (1931), C.B. (1934), G.C.V.O. and K.C.B. (1937), and G.C.B. (1943), and was sworn of the Privy Council in 1936. He was a governor of St. Bartholomew's Hospital and of the King's School, Canterbury, where his genuine and lively interest in the boys made him many friends.

In 1921 Hardinge married Helen Mary, only daughter of the late Lord Edward Cecil and his wife, who in that year became the Viscountess Milner. They had two daughters and one son, George Edward Charles (born 1921), who succeeded as third baron when Hardinge died at Penshurst 29 May 1960.

[John W. Wheeler-Bennett, *King George VI*, 1958; Helen Hardinge, *Loyal to Three Kings*, 1967; *The Times*, 29 November 1955 and 30 May 1960; private information.]

HELEN M. PALMER

published 1971

EDWARD VIII (1894–1972)

King of Great Britain, Ireland, and the British Dominions beyond the seas, Emperor of India—the only British sovereign to relinquish the crown voluntarily—was born at White Lodge, Richmond Park, 23 June 1894, the eldest of the family of five sons and one daughter of the then Duke and Duchess of York. With the death of Queen Victoria in 1901 his parents became Prince and Princess of Wales, and in 1910, when Edward VII died, King George V and Queen Mary. As their eldest son Prince Edward was from birth in the direct line of succession, and of the seven names (Edward Albert Christian George Andrew Patrick David) given to him at his baptism four were those of British patron saints. In the family he was always known as David.

Though in most respects pampered by Fate, he was unlucky in the inability of his parents to communicate easily with their children, who consequently suffered from a lack of human warmth and encouragement in early life. Their father, though kind-hearted, was a martinet in his treatment of them, and their mother was deficient in the normal maternal instincts. Nor did the man chosen to be their principal tutor, Henry Peter

Hansell, make up for what their parents failed to give, since he too was a rather aloof and limited character.

Edward was an intelligent child, endowed with curiosity and a powerful memory. Though it is unlikely that he would ever have developed as a scholar, his mental gifts deserved imaginative teaching. As it was, he grew up with a poor grounding of knowledge, no taste at all for any books worth the name, and unable even to spell properly. Only as a linguist were his attainments equal to his position, since he learnt French and German in childhood, and later acquired a fluent command of Spanish.

Other valuable qualities belonged to him naturally. Despite his small stature he had exceptional good looks, which never lost their boyish appeal. He had boundless energy and zest, and was full of courage. Above all, he had a spontaneous charm of manner which drew people to him and put them at their ease. His personality would have been re-markable even if he had not been royal; allied to his princely status it was irresistible.

In 1907 he was sent to Osborne, and two years later to Dartmouth. While he was there his father became King, and he himself heir apparent to the throne. On his sixteenth birthday he was created Prince of Wales, and on 13 July 1911 became the first English holder of the title to be formally invested at Caernarvon castle. The ceremony was stage-managed by the constable of the castle, David Lloyd George (later Earl Lloyd-George of Dwyfor) who personally taught him a few words of Welsh to utter when he was presented to the crowd at Queen Eleanor's gate.

The following year he went into residence at Magdalen College, Ox-ford, but there was little to show for his brief university career. During vacations he paid two visits to Germany and one to Scandinavia. In 1914 he was anyway due to leave Oxford at the end of the academic year, to begin a period of service in the army; but in the event he did so as Britain was entering the most terrible war in her history.

Commissioned in the Grenadier Guards, he asked only to be allowed to fight alongside his contemporaries, but was told that this would not be possible, because of the danger that he might be captured and used as a hostage. Soon, however, he managed to get himself posted to the staff of the British Expeditionary Force's commander in France, and thereafter spent most of the war abroad, attached to various headquarters but es-sentially serving as a visitor of troops and general morale-raiser. He lived frugally and, though provided with a Daimler, preferred to travel around on a green army bicycle, covering hundreds of miles. His desire always was to be at the scene of action, and he had a narrow escape when visiting front-line positions before the battle of Loos.

Given his enforced role as a non-combatant he could hardly have done more to share the ordeal of other young men of his generation. Yet he was mortified that he could not share it more fully, and genuinely embarrassed when he was awarded the MC. The humility of his attitude enhanced the value of the work he did, which was never forgotten by the countless ordinary soldiers to whom he brought understanding and cheer.

His war service was a crucially formative episode in his own life, vastly broadening his range of human experience and showing how good he was at establishing contact with his fellow-men, whatever their backgrounds. As well as meeting people of all classes from the United Kingdom, he also got to know Allied troops, including Americans, and a variety of British subjects from overseas. While visiting the Middle East in the spring of 1916 he met Australians and New Zealanders evacuated from Gallipoli. At the time of the armistice in 1918 he was with the Canadian Corps in France, and after the armistice was attached to the Australian Corps in Belgium.

Thus he was unconsciously introduced to the next and most fruitful phase of his career, which began with his visits to Newfoundland, Canada, and the United States in the summer and autumn of 1919. Lloyd George, now prime minister, was convinced that 'the appearance of the popular Prince of Wales in far corners of the Empire might do more . . . than half a dozen solemn Imperial Conferences'. So it proved. The Canadian tour was a triumphal success, in Quebec no less than in the English-speaking provinces. Wherever he went the response was overwhelming. In Alberta he bought a ranch for himself—an admirable gesture, though a source of trouble to him later.

His first visit to the United States was equally successful, though briefer and far less extensive. In Washington, he called on the stricken President Wilson, and in New York was given a ticker-tape welcome as he drove to the City Hall to receive the freedom. Yet it was not such important occasions that lingered most persistently in his mind after his return to England, but rather the song 'A Pretty Girl is like a Melody', which he had heard at the Ziegfeld Follies. His endless whistling of this 'damned tune' caused annoyance to his father, and shows that American culture had made an immediate conquest.

In 1920 he visited New Zealand and Australia, travelling there in the battleship *Renown*, by way of the Panama canal, Hawaii, and Fiji. Again, he carried all before him. In 1921-2 he toured India, where nationalists had been disappointed by the modest scope of the Montagu–Chelmsford reforms, and where the Amritsar massacre was still a recent memory. Despite the unfavourable circumstances, he made an excellent impression on such Indians as he was allowed to meet, many of whom were quoted by a British observer as saying: 'If only all you Europeans were like him!' In many places large and friendly crowds turned out to greet him, defying the Congress boycott of his visit.

The same voyage took him to Nepal, Burma, Malaya, Hong Kong, Japan, the Philippines, Borneo, Ceylon, and Egypt. On his return to London after eight months' absence there was a banquet in his honour at Guildhall, at which his health was eloquently proposed by Lloyd George—the last official act of his premiership.

This intensive travelling during the early post-war years was not a flash in the pan, but set the pattern for his subsequent way of life as Prince of Wales. In all but three years until his accession he spent long periods outside Britain. Hardly any part of the Empire, however small or remote, failed to receive at least one visit from him, and he was also welcomed in many foreign countries. Particularly noteworthy were his South American tours in 1925 and 1931, which inspired the greatest enthusiasm in a region traditionally important to Britain, though much neglected by British public figures. (A by-product of the second tour was the Ibero–American Institute of Great Britain, founded under his auspices, which led in turn to the creation of the British Council in 1935.)

At home, too, he was very busy and mobile, giving special attention to ex-servicemen and young people. In a period of mass unemployment and widespread social deprivation there might be little he could do to help the victims, but at least he went out of his way to talk to them, and it was obvious that they had his sympathy.

For all his exertions in the public interest, his life was by no means all work. While touring overseas, no less than in Britain, he would always devote a lot of his time to games and sport, and at the end of the most arduous day he was usually eager to dance into the small hours. His daylight recreations could be dangerous—after repeated spills and fractures he was prevailed upon to give up steeplechasing, only to take to flying instead—but in the long run his late nights were more harmful to him. A tendency to unpunctuality and moodiness was certainly made worse by lack of sleep.

As he moved from youth to middle age the strain of his life began to tell upon a nature that was nervous as well as physically robust; and at the same time, inevitably, he was becoming rather spoilt by the universal adulation to which he was exposed. Above all he seemed increasingly solitary, and without any firm base to his existence.

From 1919 he had his own London establishment at York House, St. James's Palace, and in 1929 he obtained from his father the 'grace and favour' use of Fort Belvedere, a small architectural folly near Windsor (originally built for the Duke of Cumberland in the 1750s, but improved by Sir Jeffry Wyatville, in the reign of George IV). 'The Fort' became his favourite residence, where he could entertain a few friends at weekends, and in whose garden he invested much of his own—and his guests'—hard labour. But something vital was missing, as no one knew better than himself.

While his brothers were acquiring wives, the world's most eligible bachelor remained single. His natural craving for domesticity was satisfied only by a succession of affairs with married women. For many years he was very closely attached to Mrs (Freda) Dudley Ward, and his love for her was not fundamentally affected by passing affairs with Lady (Thelma) Furness and others. But through Lady Furness he became acquainted with her friend and fellow-American, Mrs Simpson (died 1986), and within a few years acquaintance had turned into the supreme passion of his life.

Wallis Simpson, daughter of Teakle Wallis Warfield who died when she was a few months old, came from Baltimore, Maryland, where she was brought up as a rather impoverished member of a family with pride of ancestry on both sides. When her first marriage (to Lieutenant Earl Winfield Spencer, of the US Navy, who became an alcoholic) ended in divorce, she married an Anglo-American, Ernest Simpson (who had a shipping business in England), with whom she lived comfortably in London. For a time they were together friends of the Prince, but when it became apparent that he wanted nothing less than to make Wallis his wife, Simpson resigned himself to divorce.

Her attraction, so far as it can be defined, owed much to her vivacity and wit, her sophisticated taste, and her ability to make a house feel like a home. She and the Prince shared a mid-Atlantic outlook—he being a child of Old-World privilege excited by American informality, she an east coast American with a hankering for the Old World and its gracious living. They met, as it were, half-way.

When George V died, on 20 January 1936, Edward came to the throne in the strong hope that he would be able to make Wallis Queen. This may, indeed, have been his principal motive for accepting a charge which he had often said, privately, he would rather be spared. Impatient of ritual and routine, he knew that his temperament would be less well suited to the role of King than to that of Prince of Wales.

There was, indeed, much that needed changing in the royal set-up, and it is possible that Edward VIII might have had some success as a reforming monarch if he had reigned for a fair number of years, with his mind on the job. No judgement can confidently be made either way on the strength of his brief reign, during which he was largely distracted by his anxiety about Wallis and their future. As it was, he merely gave offence to old courtiers and retainers by relatively trifling changes, and caused misgivings in official quarters by his casual attitude to state papers.

The public, however, neither knew nor cared about such matters, and he was a popular King. There was a shock when, in July, a loaded revolver was thrown in front of his horse on Constitution Hill, and relief that he had come to no harm. Later in the year he was cheered lustily in the Mall by the Jarrow hunger marchers at the end of their pilgrimage.

Meanwhile the so-called 'King's matter' was unfolding in a way destined to bring his reign to a swift close. It was only in Britain that his intimacy with Mrs Simpson was a secret. When, during the summer, she accompanied him on a cruise in the Adriatic and eastern Mediterranean, in the private yacht *Nahlin*, full reports appeared in the foreign press, more especially in the United States, with the correct conclusions either stated or implied. The British press remained silent from a sense of loyalty, but it could not be long before the story would break at home. At the end of October the Simpsons' divorce suit was due to come up, and this might well arouse speculation even though it was to be heard in a provincial court.

On 20 October, therefore, the prime minister, Stanley Baldwin (later Earl Baldwin of Bewdley), saw the King by request and raised with him for the first time the question of his relations with Mrs Simpson. At this meeting Baldwin tried to enlist the King's co-operation in persuading her to withdraw her divorce petition, but to no avail. The King would not co-operate, and at the end of the month a decree *nisi* was duly granted.

An interlude followed during which (on 3 November) the King opened Parliament—driving there in a closed car rather than in the traditional open carriage—and inspected the fleet at Portsmouth. But on 16 November there was another meeting with Baldwin, at which the King stated his determination to marry Mrs Simpson, despite the prime minister's advice that the marriage would not receive the country's approval. On 18–19 November he visited the distressed areas of south Wales, where he made the much-quoted remark about the unemployed: 'Something must be done to find them work.' His hearers little knew how soon he would be unemployed himself.

On 25 November he saw Baldwin again, having meanwhile been persuaded by Esmond Harmsworth (later Viscount Rothermere) to suggest that he might marry Mrs Simpson morganatically. This was a disastrous error, since it could be said to carry the admission that she was unfit to be Queen.

It is probable, though unprovable, that majority opinion in Britain and throughout the Empire would have been against the idea of Mrs Simpson as Queen, though whether most people would have maintained their opposition, knowing that the price would be to lose Edward as King, is more doubtful. Ecclesiastical anathemas counted for much less, even then, than those who pronounced them liked to believe, and objections to Mrs Simpson on social grounds were likely to be much stronger in privileged circles than among the people at large. But the idea of a morganatic marriage would almost certainly have been less generally acceptable.

In any case it would have required legislation, and this the government was not prepared to introduce. Moreover, the leader of the opposition, Clement (later Earl) Attlee, told Baldwin that Labour would not approve of Mrs Simpson as Queen, or of a morganatic marriage; and similar, though rather less clear-cut, views were expressed by the dominion prime ministers. When, therefore, the facts were at last given to the British public on 3 December, the crisis was virtually over. If the King had no option but to renounce either Mrs Simpson or the throne, the only possible outcome—granted the man he was—was abdication.

He would have liked to make a broadcast, taking his subjects into his confidence, before reaching a final decision; but when Baldwin told him that this would be unconstitutional and divisive, he at once abandoned the idea. Even (Sir) Winston Churchill's plea that he should stand and fight went unheeded. On 10 December he signed an instrument of abdication, and the following day ceased to be King when he gave his assent to the necessary Bill. That evening he delivered his farewell broadcast from Windsor Castle, containing the celebrated words: 'I have found it impossible to carry the heavy burden of responsibility, and to discharge my duties as King as I would wish to do, without the help and support of the woman I love.'

Later the same night he crossed to France, and the rest of his life was spent in almost permanent exile. It was some months before Mrs Simpson's divorce became absolute, but in June 1937 she and Edward were married, at a chateau in Touraine, by a Church of England parson acting without authority from his bishop. No member of the royal family came to the wedding, which was attended only by a few old friends, including Walter Monckton (later Viscount Monckton of Brenchley), the attorney-general to the Duchy of Cornwall, and a busy go-between during the abdication crisis, and Major E. D. ('Fruity') Metcalfe, who was best man. There were no children of the marriage.

The new King, George VI (formerly Duke of York), had some of the qualities of his father, George V, but hardly any of his elder brother's—a fact of which he was painfully conscious. From the moment of his accession he seems to have been haunted by the fear that the ex-King would overshadow him, and this fear was undoubtedly shared by his wife and other members of his entourage. It was felt to be essential that the ex-King should be kept out of England, out of the limelight, out of popular favour;

and self-righteousness came to the aid of self-interest, in the form of a myth that the Prince's abdication and marriage had brought disgrace upon the British monarchy.

Though it is unlikely that George VI was familiar with *The Apple Cart* by G. B. Shaw, he was nevertheless immediately alive to the theoretical danger that his brother might, unless made a royal duke, be tempted to stand for the House of Commons, in the manner of Shaw's King Magnus. The first act of his reign was, therefore, to confer upon Edward the title of Duke of Windsor. But under letters patent issued the following year the title Royal Highness was restricted to him, and expressly denied to his wife and descendants, if any. This studied insult to the Duchess cannot have been solely due to uncertainty about the duration of the marriage, since it was maintained by George VI and his successor throughout the thirty-five years that the Windsors were man and wife (and into the Duchess's widowhood).

As a result relations between the Duke and his family were poisoned, and further bitterness was caused by an indecent wrangle over money. No provision was made for the Duke in the Civil List, but the King eventually agreed that he should receive a net £21,000 a year, which was mainly interest of the sale of Sandringham and Balmoral to royal trustees, at a valuation which favoured the King rather than the Duke. An attempt to make the agreement conditional upon the Duke's willingness to stay abroad at the King's pleasure was only with difficulty resisted. (In addition to the income thus assured, the Duke had capital deriving from Duchy of Cornwall revenue unspent while he was Prince of Wales.)

Between their marriage and World War II the Windsors lived in France, but in October 1937 they paid an ill-advised visit to Germany as guests of the Nazi government. The Duke's declared reason for going was to see how unemployment had been tackled and to study labour relations, but of course the Nazis made the most of the visit for propaganda purposes, as he should have foreseen. At a meeting with Hitler the Duke gave no indication (according to the interpreter) of any sympathy with Nazi ideology, and there is, indeed, virtually no evidence that he had any such sympathy. But he had considerable affection for the German people, with whom he had many links, and above all he had the feeling—overwhelmingly prevalent at the time—that another war would be an unimaginable calamity.

When war came, however, he at once offered to return to Britain without conditions, and at first was offered a choice of two jobs, one of which, that of assistant regional commissioner in Wales, would have enabled him to stay in Britain. But when he accepted it, no doubt unexpectedly, it was promptly withdrawn, and he was then obliged to take the other job, that of liaison officer with the French army (which involved a drop in rank from field-marshal to major-general). He did it well, among other things sending home a remarkably prescient report of French weakness on the Ardennes front. But when France fell in the summer of 1940 he and the Duchess had to escape as best they might.

They made their own way to Madrid, whence the Duke was able to communicate with the British government, now headed by his old friend Winston Churchill. His requests for suitable employment at home, and the barest recognition for the Duchess (not that she should have royal status, but merely that his family should receive her) were turned down, even Churchill having in the circumstances neither time nor inclination to champion the Duke's cause against Buckingham Palace. He then reluctantly accepted the governorship of the Bahamas, and on 1 August sailed from Lisbon, as agreed, despite an elaborate plot engineered by Ribbentrop to keep him in Europe. Though at this time he undoubtedly believed that there would have to be a negotiated peace, he did not despair of his country and had no desire to be a German puppet.

In the Bahamas the Windsors were on the whole a conspicuous success, in a post which was both difficult and unpleasant. The Duke stood up to the 'Bay Street boys' (as the local white oligarchy was called), achieved some economic improvement in the neglected outer islands, and dealt effectively with a serious outbreak of rioting for which he was in no way to blame. In December 1940 he had the first of about a dozen wartime meetings with Franklin D. Roosevelt, at the president's invitation, and the two men got on particularly well. The authorities in London tried very hard to prevent the meeting, and in general did not at all favour visits by the Windsors to the United States, though a few were grudgingly permitted. The Duke's immense popularity there was regarded at home as invidious and embarrassing, rather than as a major potential asset to Britain.

In May 1945 the Windsors left the Bahamas and returned to Europe, no better alternative having been offered to the Duke than the governorship of Bermuda. The rest of his life was spent chiefly in France, where he was treated as an honoured guest. Partly to repair his finances—which had suffered from mismanagement, and more especially from a costly and futile attempt to strike oil on his Canadian ranch—he turned to authorship. With the help of 'ghosts' he wrote his memoirs, which were serialized in *Life* magazine and then published in book form as *A King's Story* (1951). This became a world bestseller, and was later turned into a film. He also published two much slighter books—*Family Album* (1960) and *The Crown and the People 1902–1953* (1953)—and two more were written, though unpublished at the time of his death.

Because of the continued ostracism of the Duchess, his post-war visits to Britain were brief and rare. On 28 May 1972 he died at his house in the Bois de Boulogne, from throat cancer. His body was then flown back to England and lay in state for three days in St. George's chapel, Windsor, while 57,000 people came—many over long distances—to pay their respects. On 5 June there was a funeral service in the chapel, and afterwards the Duke was buried in the royal mausoleum at Frogmore. The Duchess was present as the Queen's guest.

Though King for less than a year, Edward VIII will rank as an important figure in the history of the British monarchy. During the dangerous and volatile period which followed World War I, when republicanism was sweeping the world, he and his father succeeded, in their very different ways, in giving new strength to an old tradition. Neither could have succeeded so well without the other, and the contrast between them was of great value to the monarchy.

Edward will also be remembered as a character out of the ordinary. His faults were substantial, and aggravated by the circumstances of his life. His mind, inadequately trained, was incapable of deep reflection and prone to erratic judgement. He could on occasion be selfish, mean, inconsiderate, ungrateful, or even callous. Yet his virtues more than compensated for his faults. He was a brave man, morally as well as physically, and his nature was basically affectionate. He had a marvellous gift for conversing easily with people, and for making charming, unpompous speeches off the cuff. There was about him the indefinable aura known as star quality.

In a sense he was a harbinger of the Americanization of Europe. Superficially, his values were more those of the New World than of the Old. Playing the bagpipes wearing a white kilt or golfing in plus-eights, he seemed more like a Hollywood representation of a Scottish laird or English gentleman than like the genuine article. His anyway slightly Cockney accent became overlaid with American intonations (in his farewell broadcast he referred to the *Dook* of York), and he also acquired a number of American habits long before he was married to an American.

Yet at heart he was more a creature of the Old World than he appeared to be, or probably realized himself. What a Labour MP, Josiah (later Lord) Wedgwood, said at the time of the abdication—that he had given up his royalty to remain a man—was only a half-truth. Though he had, indeed, given up his kingship, he never ceased to be royal. Had it been otherwise, there would have been no problem about the duchess's status. All the same, he surely deserves honour for the chivalrousness of his decision to abdicate, no less than for the perfect constitutional propriety with which it was carried out; and above all for his pioneering work as Prince of Wales.

There are many portraits of Edward, representing almost every phase of his life. Only a selection can be mentioned here. A caricature appeared in *Vanity Fair* on 21 June 1911 (the original is in the National Portrait Gallery). The first full-length portrait in oil was painted by Sir A. S. Cope in 1912, the year after Edward's investiture as Prince of Wales. It is in the Royal Collection, which also contains, from the same period, a sketch (head only) by Sir John Lavery. A charcoal drawing by J. S. Sargent (*c.* 1918) belonged to the Duchess of Windsor. In 1919 H. L. Oakley painted a full-length profile, and in *c.* 1920 R. G. Eves a half-length portrait in uniform. Both of these are in the National Portrait Gallery. A full-length portrait in golfing dress (1928), by Sir William Orpen, hangs in the Royal and Ancient Golf Club, St. Andrews; and a full-length portrait in Welsh Guards uniform (1936) done by W. R. Sickert from photographs, in the Beaverbrook Art Gallery, Fredericton, NB, Canada. A full-length portrait in Garter robes by Sir James Gunn (*c.* 1954) was in the Duchess of Windsor's possession, as were a number of portraits by the French artist A. Drian. Apart from paintings and drawings, there is a bronze statuette by Charles S. Jagger (1922) in the National Museum of Wales at Cardiff, and a marble bust by Charles Hartwell (*c.* 1920–4) belonging to the Corporation of London.

[Hector Bolitho, *Edward VIII*, 1937; Compton Mackenzie, *The Windsor Tapestry*, 1938; Duke of Windsor, *A King's Story*, 1951; Duchess of Windsor, *The Heart Has Its Reasons*, 1956; John W. Wheeler-Bennett, *King George VI*, 1958; Frances Donaldson, *Edward VIII*, 1974; Michael Bloch, *The Duke of Windsor's War*, 1982, and *Operation Willi*, 1984; private information.]

JOHN GRIGG

published 1986

GEORGE VI (1895–1952)

King of Great Britain, Ireland, and the British Dominions beyond the seas, was born at York Cottage, Sandringham, 14 December 1895, the second of the five sons of the Duke and Duchess of York, afterwards King George V and Queen Mary. His birth on the anniversary of the deaths of the Prince Consort (1861) and Princess Alice (1878) was an occasion for apprehensive apology, but Queen Victoria was gratified to become the child's godmother and presented him with a bust of the Prince Consort as a christening present. He was baptized at Sandringham 17 February 1896, receiving the names Albert Frederick Arthur George, and was known thereafter to the family as Bertie.

A shy and sensitive child, Prince Albert tended to be overshadowed by his elder brother, Prince Edward, and his younger sister Princess Mary. A stammer, developed in his seventh or eighth year, inhibited him still further, and of all the children it was probably he who found it least easy to withstand his father's bluff chaffing or irascibility. The boy withdrew into himself, compensating with outbursts of high spirits or weeping.

Nevertheless life passed evenly enough in the 'glum little villa' of York Cottage and in the other residences to which the migrations of the court took them, interrupted by such events as the funeral of Queen Victoria or the coronation of King Edward VII. By 1902 Prince Albert and his elder brother had graduated to the schoolroom under the care of Henry Peter Hansell, an Oxford graduate, formerly tutor to Prince Arthur of Connaught. Although he gained the affection of his pupils, Hansell was not the man to inspire small boys with a desire for learning. He himself thought they should have been at school; but his earnest attempt to create the illusion that they were was not convincing. In the spring of 1907 Prince Edward departed for Osborne and Prince Albert, now 'head boy' with Prince Henry in second place, was left to struggle with the mathematics which seemed likely to prevent him from following suit. But here he showed that ability to face up to and overcome difficulties which was to be the marked characteristic of his career. When he passed into Osborne his oral French, despite his stammer, was almost perfect, and his mathematics 'very fair indeed'.

At Osborne and Dartmouth (1909–12), years which saw his father's accession to the throne, Prince Albert was never very far from the bottom of the class; but he was popular as a 'trier' and a good comrade, and there was a steady development of both character and ability. He was confirmed at Sandringham on 18 April 1912, a day he remembered as one on which he 'took a great step in life'.

After a training cruise in the *Cumberland*, during which he visited the West Indies and Canada, Prince Albert was posted in September 1913 as a midshipman to the *Collingwood* in the Home Fleet. To his great satisfaction he was able to see active service in her as a sub-lieutenant at the battle of Jutland, 31 May 1916. But the war years were in the main frustrating. Always a poor sailor, he was now suffering almost continuously from gastric trouble. An operation for appendicitis, performed in Aberdeen 9 September 1914, brought only temporary relief and there followed three years of misery before on 29 November 1917 an operation for duodenal ulcer proved more successful. The subsequent great improvement in the Prince's health was marked in 1920 by his winning the Royal Air Force tennis doubles with his comptroller, who had long been his mentor and friend, (Sir) Louis Greig. That he lost to Greig in the semi-finals of the singles did not surprise him.

Meantime the Prince had been forced to admit that life at sea was too much for him and in November 1917 he transferred to the Royal Naval Air Service and on 1 April 1918 was gazetted flight lieutenant in the new Royal Air Force. It was now that his interest in physical fitness was aroused through his work in the training of boys and cadets. He was in France when the war ended and was asked by his father to represent him when the King of the Belgians made his official entry into Brussels on 22 November: the first state occasion on which he acted for the King.

Returning to England in the following February, Prince Albert, disregarding his dislike of flying, became a fully qualified pilot, 31 July 1919, and received his commission as a squadron leader on the following day. But the time had come for him to leave Service life and take his share of the burden of public duties which falls to a royal family. As further preparation, in company with Prince Henry, he spent a year at Trinity College, Cambridge, which might have been more fruitful had they lived in college. He studied history, economics, and civics, and in particular the development of the Constitution; and tackled an increasing number of public engagements, each one an ordeal by reason of the stammer for which he had so far found no cure. He became president of the Industrial Welfare Society and thereafter until he came to the throne made it his special interest to visit industrial areas and seek to make contact with the people as informally as possible. His own personal contribution towards better relations between management and workers took the form of what became the famous Duke of York's camps for boys from public schools and industry which were held annually, with one exception, from 1921 until 1939. He remained keenly interested in them to the end and delighted in the informality of his visits to the camps when he always joined vigorously in singing the camp song 'Under the Spreading Chestnut Tree'.

In the birthday honours of June 1920 the King created his second son Baron Killarney, Earl of Inverness, and Duke of York. He had already conferred the Garter upon him in 1916 on the occasion of his twenty-first birthday and was to confer the Order of the Thistle on him on his wedding day. The Duke went on his father's behalf to Brussels in 1921 and twice in 1922 to the Balkans where his bearing during elaborate state occasions earned the highest praise.

On 26 April 1923 in Westminster Abbey the Duke married Lady Elizabeth Angela Marguerite Bowes-Lyon, youngest daughter of the fourteenth Earl of Strathmore and Kinghorne, and together they entered upon that path of domestic happiness and devotion to public duty which was to earn them the nation's gratitude. They made their home first at White Lodge in Richmond Park which had been Queen Mary's childhood home; then from 1927 at 145 Piccadilly, with, later, the Royal Lodge, Windsor Great Park, as their country residence. Two daughters were born to them: Princess Elizabeth Alexandra Mary (21 April 1926) and Princess Margaret Rose (21 August 1930).

Official visits to the Balkans (1923) and Northern Ireland (1924) and many public engagements at home were followed by a tour of East Africa and the Sudan in the winter of 1924-5 which gave the Duke and Duchess a welcome holiday and the opportunity for big-game hunting. On his return the Duke presided over the second year of the British Empire exhibition at Wembley. Public speaking was still an ordeal for him but in 1926 he first consulted the speech therapist, Lionel Logue, who over the years was able to help him to overcome his stammer so that speech came much more easily to him and the listener was aware of little more than an occasional hesitation. It was therefore with a lighter heart that he left with the Duchess in 1927 for a strenuous tour of New Zealand and Australia, the highlight of which was the opening on 9 May of the first meeting of Parliament at the new capital city of Canberra. The natural sincerity of the Duke and the radiance of the Duchess evoked an enthusiastic response throughout the tour. On their return to London they were met at Victoria Station by the King and Queen, the Duke having been forewarned by his father: 'We will not embrace at the station before so many people. When you kiss Mama take yr. hat off': attention to detail inherited by the Duke who was in many ways his father's son.

During the King's illness of 1928-9 the Duke, who had been introduced into the Privy Council in 1925, was one of the counsellors of State. In May 1929 he was lord high commissioner to the General Assembly of the Church of Scotland, and, as his father was not sufficiently recovered to visit Scotland, he returned to Edinburgh in October to represent the King as lord high commissioner of the historic first Assembly of the two re-united Scottish Churches.

These were quiet years of home-making and of public duties faithfully performed, overshadowed perhaps by the King's failing health but with no realization of what was to come. With the death of King George V on 20 January 1936 and the abdication of his successor in the following December all this was changed. The Duke and his elder brother had always been on good terms, but after the latter's accession the Duke found himself increasingly excluded from the new King's confidence. It was with the utmost reluctance that he finally brought himself to accept the fact that the King was determined to marry Mrs. Simpson even at the cost of the throne. Of this resolve the King informed him on 17 November. The days which followed were filled with 'the awful & ghastly suspense of waiting' until on 7 December the King told the Duke of his decision to abdicate. Two days later the Duke had a long talk with his brother but could do nothing to alter his decision and so informing his mother later in the day 'broke down & sobbed like a child'. On 12 December 1936 he was proclaimed King, choosing George VI as his style and title. His brother he created H.R.H. the Duke of Windsor.

Thus there came to the throne a man who had 'never even seen a State Paper', at a time when the monarchy had suffered the successive blows of death and abdication. 'I am new to the job', the King wrote to Stanley Baldwin at the end of the year, 'but I hope that time will be allowed to me to make amends for what has happened.' To this task he brought his own innate good sense and courage in adversity, disciplined by his naval training and sustained by the strength which he drew from his marriage, the sterling qualities of his mother, and the goodwill of the nation. The King had the same simple religious faith as his father and the coronation which took place in Westminster Abbey on 12 May 1937 was a genuine act of dedication on the part of the new King and Queen. It was shared by millions of their people, for the service was broadcast by the B.B.C., an arrangement which had the full support of the King against considerable opposition.

The brilliance of a state visit to France in July 1938 brought a momentary gleam of light in a darkening international situation. The King had full confidence in his prime minister and like Neville Chamberlain believed that every effort must be made to avoid a war. Final disillusionment came in March 1939 when the Munich agreement was swept aside and the Germans finally destroyed Czechoslovakia. Shortly after the return visit to Great Britain by President and Mme Lebrun later in the month there was announced the Anglo-French guarantee of Polish independence against aggression. Two months later came the first occasion on which a reigning British monarch had entered the United States. The visit of the King and Queen to North America in May–June 1939 was a resounding success and gave them an increase of confidence. In Canada the King addressed the members of the Senate and the House of Commons and gave the royal assent to bills passed by the Canadian Parliament. At Hyde Park he was able to discuss with President Roosevelt the help which might be expected from the United States in the event of a European war. The warm regard which the two men felt for one another was thereafter maintained by correspondence. Nevertheless the King chafed in these years at his inability to influence the course of events. His successive suggestions of personal communications to Hitler, to King

Victor Emmanuel, to the Emperor of Japan, were felt to be inadvisable by a Government which did not share his belief in communications between heads of State.

When, inevitably, war with Germany came, the King broadcast to the Empire on the evening of Sunday, 3 September 1939, a simple call to his people to fight for the freedom of the world. Of the issue he was never in doubt and it was no small part of his contribution in the years to come that he was able to transmit this unclouded confidence to more complex and fearful minds.

In October the King visited the Fleet at Invergordon and Scapa Flow and in December he spent some days with the British Expeditionary Force in France. At Christmas he resumed his father's tradition of broadcasting a personal message to the Empire, a custom maintained for the rest of his life despite his dislike of the microphone. When Chamberlain resigned the premiership in May 1940 the King was distressed to see him go and would have liked Lord Halifax to succeed him. But Chamberlain informed him that Halifax, being in the Lords, was 'not enthusiastic' and the King accordingly accepted the advice to send for (Sir) Winston Churchill. By September formal audiences had given way to a weekly informal luncheon and a somewhat guarded relationship had warmed into genuine friendship.

Throughout the war the King and Queen remained in London, sleeping at Windsor during the bombing. Buckingham Palace was hit nine times: in September 1940 it was bombed twice within three days. On the second occasion six bombs were dropped over the Palace by day and the King and Queen had a narrow escape—even the prime minister was not told how narrow. 'A magnificent piece of bombing', remarked a police constable to the Queen; but a tactical error. Prompt and indefatigable in their visits to bombed areas throughout the country the royal pair knew that it was realized that they too had suffered; it was now that they entered into the hearts of their people in a very personal way. It was the King's idea in 1940 to create the George Cross and Medal, primarily for civilian gallantry; and his idea two years later to award the Cross to Malta for heroism under siege. In that year of successive disasters to the Allies the tragedy of war touched the King more closely when his younger brother the Duke of Kent was killed on 25 August 1942 in a flying accident while on active service.

By 1943 the tide of the war had turned and in June the King visited his troops in North Africa where the Axis forces had surrendered. In two weeks he covered some 6,700 miles and although it involved some risk the tour included a visit to Malta, on which he was determined in recognition of the island's gallantry. After the surrender of Italy in September 1943 the

King shared with J. C. Smuts some doubts about the wisdom of opening up a second front in France; they communicated their misgivings to Churchill who made it clear, however, that it was too late to change plans which were already well advanced. On 15 May 1944 the King attended the conference at St. Paul's School at which the preparations for invasion were expounded. Before D-Day (6 June) he had visited all the forces bound for Normandy. Both he and Churchill wanted to witness the assault from one of the ships taking part. The King, on reflection, was able with his usual common sense to see the unwisdom of this course; it was not without difficulty that he prevailed upon Churchill to abandon the idea on his own count. Only ten days after D-Day the King had the satisfaction of visiting General Montgomery's headquarters in Normandy. For eleven days in July–August he was with his armies in Italy, and in October he again visited the 21st Army Group. When the European war ended on 8 May 1945, Londoners crowded towards Buckingham Palace in their rejoicing as they had done on 11 November 1918. In the evening the King broadcast a call to thanksgiving and to work towards a better world. There followed an exhausting fortnight of celebration which left the popularity of the monarchy in no doubt. There were state drives through London and services of thanksgiving at St. Paul's Cathedral (13 May) and at St. Giles' Cathedral, Edinburgh (16 May). On the 17th the King received addresses from both Houses of Parliament in the Great Hall of Westminster. Labour having withdrawn from the coalition, Churchill formed his 'caretaker' government and in July came the first general election of the King's reign. It proved a victory for Labour and, accepting Churchill's resignation, the King invited C. R. (later Earl) Attlee to form a government. When Attlee replied to the King's inquiry that he was thinking of Hugh (later Lord) Dalton as foreign secretary the King suggested that Ernest Bevin might be a better choice. This had indeed been Attlee's first thought but he had allowed himself to be influenced by Bevin's own desire for the Treasury. In the event it was Bevin who went to the Foreign Office.

The King opened Parliament on 15 August 1945, the day of the Japanese surrender, and ten days later he and the Queen left for Balmoral for a much needed rest. On his return to London in October he found that the advent of peace had done little to lighten his, or the nation's, burden. Great Britain, although still beset by austerity, was moving forward into the welfare State; the British Empire was evolving into the British Commonwealth of Nations; and Russian imperialism was on the march. Some of the new ministers lacked experience; while not out of sympathy with Labour there were occasions when the King felt that they were going ahead too fast and that he should exercise the right of the monarch to advise and even to warn. This he was able to do the more easily in that he now had a width of experience and a maturity of judgement which made it natural for people to turn to him for guidance.

In 1947 the King and Queen and the two princesses paid an extensive visit to Southern Africa where the King opened Parliament at Cape Town 21 February, and in Salisbury, Southern Rhodesia, 7 April, and where, also at Cape Town, the Princess Elizabeth celebrated her twenty-first birthday. It was always a matter of regret to the King that he was never able to visit India. The dissolution of the Indian Empire and the emergence of India as a sovereign independent republic within the British Commonwealth brought problems in the relation of the Sovereign to the Commonwealth in which he took great interest; but the necessary legislation had not been completed before he died.

On 20 November 1947 the Princess Elizabeth married Lieutenant Philip Mountbatten, R.N., son of the late Prince Andrew of Greece, whose elevation to the peerage as Duke of Edinburgh was announced on that day. Five months later, 26 April 1948, the King and Queen celebrated their silver wedding and drove in state to St. Paul's Cathedral for a service of thanksgiving. In the following October, for the first time since the war, the King opened Parliament in full state. He had, as usual, a heavy programme of engagements which included a visit to Australia and New Zealand in the spring of 1949. But symptoms of early arteriosclerosis had been apparent for some time and it now seemed that his right leg might have to be amputated. The first announcement of his condition was made on 23 November 1948 when the Australian tour was cancelled. A right lumbar sympathectomy operation was performed at Buckingham Palace 12 March 1949, from which the King made a good recovery although he was not restored to complete activity.

At the general election of February 1950 Labour was returned with but a narrow majority, and to anxiety at home over the uncertainty of government and a precarious economic situation was added anxiety over the outbreak of the Korean war. Both continued into the following year and even the Festival of Britain, opened by the King from the steps of St. Paul's on 3 May 1951, could not dispel the gloom. Towards the end of the month the King succumbed to influenza. There followed convalescence at Sandringham and Balmoral; but he was found to have a malignant growth and on 23 September underwent an operation for the removal of his left lung. Attlee had already asked for a dissolution of Parliament and on 5 October the King was able to give his approval to the act of dissolution. With the return of the Conservatives with a small majority Churchill once more became his prime minister. From the list of government appointments the post of deputy prime minister, which had crept in during the war, was deleted on the King's instructions as being unconstitutional. As he did not fail to observe, it would have restricted his freedom of choice in the event of the death or resignation of the prime minister.

A day of national thanksgiving for the King's recovery was observed on 2 December and there followed a family Christmas at his beloved Sandringham. On the last day of January 1952 the King went to London Airport to see the Princess Elizabeth and the Duke of Edinburgh off on a visit to East Africa, Australia, and New Zealand. But their tour was perforce curtailed for after a happy day's shooting the King died in his sleep at Sandringham early on the morning of 6 February 1952. After lying in state in Westminster Hall he was buried on the 15th in St. George's Chapel, Windsor, where a memorial chapel was built and dedicated in 1969.

Trained to service, although not to the throne, the King had served to the limits of his strength and of the confines of monarchy. Scrupulous in observing his constitutional position, he was nevertheless determined to exercise the role of monarch to the full in the service of his people. It was always an underlying frustration that he could not do more; and a mark of his modest diffidence that he failed to appreciate how much he did by being what he was. The whole of his reign was overshadowed by war and the fears and changes brought about by war. At such a time a nation needs not only the warrior leader which it found in Churchill but also the image of the way of life for which it fights, and this it found in the King. Lithe and handsome, good at sports, an excellent shot and a skilled horseman, he was the country squire, the racehorse owner, the freemason, and above all the family man. His approach to life was one of common sense and humour. He made no claims to brilliance of intellect yet had a questing mind for which the twentieth century held no fears; his keenness of observation and determination to get to the heart of the matter could open up new lines of thought in others. He had few hobbies but was well versed in all that concerned his *métier* as monarch. He was the King *malgré lui* whom the nation had watched grow into kingship with a steadfast courage which had earned him their respect, their gratitude, and their affection.

The King was painted by many of the leading artists of the day, the state portrait of him in his coronation robes being by Sir Gerald Kelly in 1938. There was, in addition, the statue in the Mall by William McMillan which was unveiled by the Queen on 21 October 1955.

[John W. Wheeler-Bennett, *King George VI*, 1958.]

HELEN M. PALMER

published 1971

(1896–1986)

Duchess of Windsor

Wife of the former King Edward VIII, was born 19 June 1896 in Blue Ridge Summit, Pennsylvania, the only child of Teackle Wallis Warfield, an unsuccessful businessman, and his wife, Alice Montague. The Warfields and Montagues were of distinguished Southern stock, but Wallis's parents were poor relations and her father died when she was only five months old. She spent her childhood in cheese-paring poverty, resentfully aware that her friends could afford nicer clothes and more lavish holidays. It seems reasonable to trace to this early deprivation the acquisitive streak which so strongly marked her character.

Though her jaw was too heavy for her to be counted beautiful, her fine violet-blue eyes and petite figure, quick wits, vitality, and capacity for total concentration on her interlocutor ensured that she had many admirers. When only nineteen she fell in love with a naval aviator, Lieutenant Earl Winfield Spencer (died 1950), son of Earl Winfield Spencer, a member of the Chicago Stock Exchange, and married him on 8 November 1916. It proved a disastrous match. Spencer's promising career disintegrated as he took to drink and Wallis, whose tolerance of weakness was never conspicuous, became increasingly alienated. While they were in Washington in 1922 they decided to separate and when Spencer was given command of a gunboat in the Far East, she remained behind, enjoying a flamboyant liaison with an Argentine diplomat.

In 1924 she joined her husband in China, but the reunion was not a success and they divorced in December 1927. By then she had already won the affections of Ernest Aldrich Simpson, whose own marriage was breaking up, the businessman son of an English father (Ernest Simpson, shipbroker and head of the firm of Simpson, Spence, & Young) and an American mother. She joined him in London, where he was managing the office of his family shipping company, and they married on 2 July 1928. Most of their friends were in the American colony in London; among them Benjamin Thaw of the US embassy, his wife Consuelo, and her younger sister Thelma, Viscountess Furness. Lady Furness was at that time mistress of the prince of Wales, and it was in her house at Melton Mowbray that Mrs Simpson, on 10 January 1931, met the man who was to become her third husband—Edward Albert Christian George Andrew Patrick David, the eldest child of King George V. He was called David by his friends and family.

Windsor

The precise nature of Mrs Simpson's appeal to the prince of Wales could only be understood by him; probably he hardly understood it himself. It is sufficient to say that by early 1934 the prince had become slavishly dependent on her and was to remain so until he died. The courtiers at first thought that this was just another of his recurrent infatuations, but throughout 1935 they became increasingly alarmed as her role became more prominent and impinged on the performance of his duties. It seems unlikely that Mrs Simpson seriously entertained the possibility that she might become queen; indeed, all the indications are that she enjoyed her role of *maîtresse en titre* and would have been satisfied to retain it. The prince, however, convinced himself that his happiness depended on securing Mrs Simpson as his wife. From his accession to the throne on 20 January 1936 his main preoccupation was to bring this about.

Edward VIII's reign was marked by swelling scandal as his relationship with Mrs Simpson became more widely known. The cruise which the couple undertook in the yacht *Nahlin* around the eastern Mediterranean in September 1936 attracted keen interest everywhere except in the British Isles, where the press maintained a discreet silence. It was, however, the Simpsons' imminent divorce which convinced the prime minister, Stanley Baldwin (later first Earl Baldwin of Bewdley), that he was faced by a serious constitutional crisis. On 20 October he confronted Edward at the king's country house, Fort Belvedere, but it was only a month later that Edward VIII stated categorically that he intended to marry Mrs Simpson. Baldwin was convinced that this must lead to abdication; the king played with the idea of a morganatic marriage, a solution that would certainly have appealed to Mrs Simpson, but was determined to renounce the throne if that was the price he had to pay.

Once she realized that marriage to her would cost the king his throne, Mrs Simpson tried to change his resolve. Anticipating much hostile publicity when the story broke in the United Kingdom, she retreated first to Fort Belvedere, and then to the South of France. From there, in a series of distraught telephone calls, she tried to persuade Edward not to abdicate, even if this meant giving her up. She accomplished nothing; this was the only subject on which she was unable to dominate her future husband.

On 10 December 1936 Edward VIII abdicated, became duke of Windsor, and went into exile. There followed six months of separation while Mrs Simpson was waiting for her decree absolute (3 May 1937), before, on 3 June 1937, the couple were married at the Château de Candé in Touraine. No member of the royal family was present and the new duchess, on doubtful legal grounds, was denied the title of Her Royal Highness. The refusal of her husband's relations to accept her as part of the family caused embittered and undying resentment in the duchess.

Until the outbreak of war the Windsors lived mainly in Austria and France. The duchess accompanied her husband on his visit to Germany in 1937; it was popularly believed that she had fascist sympathies and it has even been claimed that she worked for German intelligence, but there is no evidence that she held any considered political views, still less indulged in such activities. When war broke out in 1939 she returned with the duke to Britain and then to France. When the Germans overran France in June 1940 the Windsors escaped into Spain and thence to Portugal. From there they left for the Bahamas, where the duke took up the post of governor in August 1940.

The duchess hated their five years in Nassau and made no secret of her views to those close to her, but on the whole she performed the duties of governor's lady conscientiously and well. She entertained stylishly and went through the rituals of opening bazaars and inspecting hospitals with unexpected grace. Her happiest weeks, however, were spent on shopping expeditions in the United States and she was much criticized for irresponsible extravagance at a time when Britain was under assault.

After the war the Windsors settled in France and their life became a dreary—though to her, presumably, satisfying—merry-go-round featuring principally Antibes, Paris, New York, and Palm Beach. The duchess entertained lavishly and was counted among the best dressed and fashionable figures in international society. Some of her friends were raffish, a few even vicious, but it was the sterility of her life that was most remarkable. Though her husband resumed a somewhat cool relationship with his mother and siblings, the duchess was never received by the royal family and remained fiercely hostile to them. In 1956 she published her memoirs, *The Heart Has Its Reasons*, an on the whole good-tempered and balanced book, which was largely ghosted but still reflected fairly her wit and considerable common sense. When the duke died on 28 May 1972 she was invited to Buckingham Palace, but it was too late for the reconciliation to mean much to her. The last fourteen years of her life were spent in increasing decrepitude; during the final five she lived in total seclusion. She died at her home near Paris 24 April 1986 and was buried beside her husband in the royal burial ground at Frogmore.

[Duchess of Windsor, *The Heart Has Its Reasons*, 1956; Michael Bloch, *Wallis and Edward: Letters 1931–1937*, 1986; Ralph G. Martin, *The Woman He Loved*, 1974; private information.]

PHILIP ZIEGLER

published 1996

VICTORIA Alexandra Alice Mary

(1897–1965)

Princess Royal of Great Britain, was born at York Cottage, Sandringham, 25 April 1897, the third child and only daughter of the future King George V and Queen Mary. Among her godparents were Queen Victoria and the Empress Marie of Russia. Known as Princess Mary until her marriage, her education was private. History and geography were her favourite subjects and in languages, like her mother, she acquired a fluency in French. She was brought up quietly at Sandringham, Marlborough House, and later at Buckingham Palace. As an only daughter among five brothers, her childhood interests tended to the outdoor sports which they enjoyed and for some time she shared their lessons. Her reading was frequently boys' adventure stories, her favourite exercise was riding. She became an expert horsewoman and enjoyed hunting, while her lifelong interest in horse-racing was probably partly inherited from her father and after her marriage encouraged by her husband. She developed a natural interest in botany and an enjoyment of music, possessing a pleasant mezzo-soprano voice. She also took an interest in needlework, making dresses and collecting garments for her mother's Needlework Guild.

During the war of 1914–18 the Princess assisted her mother in many activities, such as those for helping the mothers, wives, and children of men serving with the forces. She took a great interest in VAD work, passing the advanced course in nursing with honours. It was a disappointment to her that she was not allowed to serve in France. Another of her great interests was the Girl Guide movement. She helped also in canteen work, insisting on taking her share of the dull routine tasks. It was her own idea after the war to visit the various women's organizations at a number of places in France. She inherited from her paternal grandfather a good memory for names and faces and, like her mother, possessed un-tiring energy.

In 1918 Princess Mary came of age and that year went to the Hospital for Sick Children in Great Ormond Street as a VAD probationer. She had early told her mother she thought nursing was her true vocation and her intense care and interest in the children continued long after she left the hospital in 1920.

On 28 February 1922 she married Henry George Charles Lascelles, Viscount Lascelles, elder son of the fifth and himself later sixth Earl of Harewood. It was the first royal pageant since the war and aroused great public excitement and enthusiasm. After her marriage she was known as

Princess Mary, Viscountess Lascelles, and after her husband's succession to the earldom in 1929 as Princess Mary, Countess of Harewood, until in 1932 she was created Princess Royal. The many interests she shared with her husband included love of horse-racing and hunting, old furniture, interior decoration, and Yorkshire life. During her father-in-law's lifetime their Yorkshire home was Goldsborough Hall and after his death they moved into Harewood House. Their London home was Chesterfield House and they occasionally stayed at Portumna Castle, Galway, which her husband had inherited from his great-uncle, the eccentric Marquess of Clanricarde.

The Princess in 1918 became colonel-in-chief of the Royal Scots (The Royal Regiment), in 1930 of the Canadian Scottish, and in 1935 of the Royal Signals and later of other signal corps in Australia, Canada, India, and New Zealand, and of the Prince of Wales Own Regiment of Yorkshire in 1958, the Royal Regiment of Canada in 1961, and the Royal Newfoundland Regiment in 1963. In 1926 she was appointed commandant-in-chief of the British Red Cross Detachments.

The war of 1939–45 brought many additional duties. In 1940 she was made chief controller and in 1941 controller commandant of the Auxiliary Territorial Service (later the Women's Royal Army Corps). She was energetic in visiting and inspecting these troops; but she never overcame her dislike of inspecting ranks of men, which she regarded as a man's job. In addition, she paid visits to war canteens and similar welfare organizations.

The war brought its personal anxieties to her and her husband. Their elder son George, Viscount Lascelles, who had been born in 1923, was wounded and taken prisoner in Italy when serving with the Grenadier Guards, and their younger son Gerald, born in 1924, was on active service with the Rifle Brigade. However, the end of the war saw the family once more united. The loss of her husband, who died 24 May 1947, a few months after their silver wedding, increased rather than diminished her activities. She became chancellor of Leeds University in 1951, enjoying her work as such and being particularly gratified that among those upon whom she conferred honorary degrees was her elder son.

During the monarch's absences abroad she was a counsellor of state in 1939, 1943, 1944, 1947, 1953, 1954, 1956, and 1957, as also in 1951 during the King's illness. During the last decade of her life she conscientiously carried out many royal duties. In 1956 she visited France, and the next year Nigeria, while in 1960 she toured for four months in the West Indies, two years later representing the Queen at the celebrations on granting independence to Trinidad. In 1964, as colonel-in-chief of the Royal Newfoundland Regiment, she visited them on the fiftieth anniversary of the re-forming of the regiment in 1914. In October the same year she represented the Queen at Lusaka for the independence celebrations when Northern Rhodesia became Zambia. Only shortly before her death she represented the Queen at the funeral in Stockholm of Queen Louise of Sweden. The Princess died suddenly at Harewood House 28 March 1965.

The Princess was appointed CI in 1919, GBE in 1927, GCVO in 1937. She received the honorary degree of DCL from Oxford and the LLD from Cambridge, Leeds, Sheffield, St. Andrews, Manchester, McGill, Laval, and Lille. She became a Dame Grand Cross of the Venerable Order of St. John of Jerusalem in 1926 and an honorary FRCS in 1927.

A conscientious devotion to her royal duties was perhaps the keynote of the Princess's character. Although she never overcame her shyness, which made many of her official duties a trial to her, she never for that reason avoided them or found them a burden. Once she knew people she could talk with them easily and freely, as many senior girl guides and Red Cross members could testify. She was probably happiest in her home life with her family and in the quiet rural life in Yorkshire, to which county she was particularly attached. Sheffield folk always gave her a warm welcome.

A portrait of the Princess with her husband on horseback by Sir Alfred Munnings is at Harewood House, where there are also portraits by Sir Oswald Birley, Frank O. Salisbury, and J. S. Sargent. That by Birley, relaxed and natural, is regarded by the family as particularly good. She is included in a family group by Sir John Lavery, painted in 1913, now in the National Portrait Gallery. At the Royal Signals Officers Mess, Catterick, there is a portrait of her by Sir Gerald Kelly and the Royal Scots Regimental Museum, Edinburgh Castle, has one painted by Simon Elwes in 1933 and another of her with King George V and Queen Mary, painted by Gerald Hudson for the Regimental tercentenary parade the same year. The WRAC Regimental Museum has a portrait by Edward Seago and the WRAC HQ Mess, Guildford, a portrait by A. C. Davidson-Houston.

[Evelyn Graham (Netley Lucas), *Princess Mary, Viscountess Lascelles*, 1930; M. C. Carey, *Princess Mary*, 1922; James Pope-Hennessy, *Queen Mary*, 1959; *The Times*, 29 March 1965; private information.]

G. K. S. HAMILTON-EDWARDS

published 1981

(1900–1974)

Prince of York, and later *Duke of Gloucester*

Was born at York Cottage, Sandringham, 31 March 1900, the fourth of six children and third of five sons of Prince George, Duke of York (later King George V) and Princess (Victoria) Mary ('May') of Teck. The Prince's oppressive upbringing, in which disparagement played a more prominent role than affection, inspired him with feelings of inadequacy. In 1910, the year his father became King, Prince Henry was sent to St. Peter's Court, a preparatory school at Broadstairs. Three years later he passed into Eton where his housemaster, S. G. Lubbock, found him cheerful and unassuming but lacking in self-confidence. In 1918 he entered Sandhurst and was commissioned the following summer. His formal education ended with a year's course at Trinity College, Cambridge (1919–20).

Prince Henry, an outstanding horseman and shot, was attracted by the life of a cavalry officer. His inclinations and talents were those of a country gentleman, and he felt completely at home in the 10th Royal Hussars to which he was posted in 1921. Nothing irritated him more than to discover that as a King's son he was repeatedly prevented from joining his regiment overseas on active duty.

In 1928 Prince Henry was created Duke of Gloucester and began undertaking official engagements, such as his mission to Japan in 1929 to confer the Garter on the Emperor Hirohito, to Abyssinia in 1930 to attend the coronation of Haile Selassie, and to Australia and New Zealand in 1934–5.

In 1935 the Duke of Gloucester married Alice Christabel, the third daughter of John Charles Montagu-Douglas-Scott, seventh Duke of Buccleuch. The wedding took place in the chapel of Buckingham Palace on 6 November. The Gloucesters moved into York House, and in 1938 bought Barnwell Manor, Northamptonshire. They had two sons: Prince William, born in 1941 (see below), and Prince Richard, born in 1944. There were no daughters. The Duke's family life was supremely happy, and Princess Alice gave him the support and confidence he had hitherto lacked.

The death of George V and the abdication of Edward VIII in 1936 left the Duke third in line to the throne. Moreover, until Princess Elizabeth came of age in 1944, he was also regent designate. Under these circumstances he was reluctantly obliged to abandon peacetime soldiering.

Soon after the outbreak of war in 1939 the Duke was appointed chief liaison officer between the British and French armies in Europe. In May he was slightly wounded after his staff car was dive-bombed. In 1941 he was appointed second-in-command of the 20th Armoured brigade. During the war he visited troops throughout the United Kingdom, North Africa, the Middle East, and as far afield as India and Ceylon.

Early in 1945 the Duke succeeded the first Earl of Gowrie as governor-general of Australia, where he wielded greater powers than those of the King in Britain. The country was ravaged by strikes, and several members of the new Labour government proved eager to advertise their disenchantment with royalty. To make matters worse, Prince Henry was infectiously shy and lacked the winning charm and fluent small-talk of his eldest brother (the Duke of Windsor). Nevertheless, he won the hearts of many Australians by his forthright simplicity, his informed interest in farming, and his willingness to visit scattered communities in the remotest parts of their continent. During his two years of office he travelled over seventy-five thousand miles. In 1947 he was summoned back to England to act as senior counsellor of state, while the King, Queen, and two Princesses visited South Africa.

The accession of Elizabeth II in 1952 did nothing to diminish her uncle's duties, nor to shorten the list of institutions to which he gave considerably more than his name: prominent among which were those concerned with hospitals, youth, and farming. In 1953 the Duke represented the Queen at the inauguration of King Faisal II at Baghdad, and of King Hussain in Amman, and in 1957 he conferred independence within the Commonwealth upon the Malayan Federation. The following year he revisited Ethiopia where he was cordially entertained by the Emperor. He returned to Africa in 1959 to represent the Queen at the proclamation of Nigeria's independence.

Early in 1965, while returning to Barnwell from Sir Winston Churchill's funeral, the Duke overturned the Rolls-Royce he was driving. He was not seriously injured in the accident, but his health gradually deteriorated from then onwards. Later that year, he revisited Australia to mark the fiftieth anniversary of Anzac Day, and in 1966 he returned to Malaysia. His strength, however, was failing, and in 1968 he was rendered helpless by two severe stokes. Princess Alice nursed him solicitously, struggling the while to fulfil his public engagements. The Duke died at Barnwell Manor 10 June 1974 and was buried at Frogmore. He was succeeded by his younger son, Prince Richard Alexander Walter George (born 26 August 1944).

During his career Prince Henry acquired a dazzling array of orders. To list but a few, in 1921 he became a Knight of the Garter, in 1933 a Knight of the Thistle, in 1934 a Knight of St. Patrick, and in 1942 Great Master and Knight Grand Cross of the Order of the Bath. He was sworn of the Privy Council in 1925, and received a host of foreign decorations, ranging from the Ethiopian Order of the Seal of Solomon (1930), to the Order of Mohamed Ali (1948). Prince Henry served in virtually every rank of the army, from lieutenant (1919) to field-marshal (1955). The regiments of which he was colonel-in-chief included the 10th Royal Hussars, the Gloucestershire Regiment, the Gordon Highlanders, and the Scots Guards.

Prince Henry's volatile temper, crisp invective, and penetrating stare could be momentarily terrifying, but his wrath was short-lived and soon dispelled by his shrill, staccato laugh. Probably he would have preferred the life of a country gentleman to that of a public figure, but he was sustained in his royal role by the peremptory sense of duty instilled in him by his parents.

[Noble Frankland, *Prince Henry, Duke of Gloucester*, 1980; Princess Alice, Duchess of Gloucester, *Memoirs*, 1983; personal knowledge.]

GILES ST. AUBYN

published 1986

MOUNTBATTEN Louis Francis Albert Victor Nicholas

(1900–1979)

First Earl Mountbatten of Burma

Admiral of the fleet, was born at Frogmore House, Windsor, 25 June 1900 as Prince Louis of Battenberg, the younger son and youngest of the four children of Prince Louis Alexander of Battenberg (later Louis Mountbatten, Marquess of Milford Haven, admiral of the fleet), and his wife, Princess Victoria Alberta Elizabeth Marie Irene, daughter of Louis IV of Hesse-Darmstadt. Prince Louis Alexander, himself head of a cadet branch of the house of Hesse-Darmstadt, was brother-in-law to Queen Victoria's daughter, Princess Beatrice; his wife was Victoria's granddaughter. By both father and mother, therefore, Prince Louis was closely connected with the British royal family. One of his sisters married King Gustav VI of Sweden and the other Prince Andrew of Greece.

Prince Louis, 'Dickie' as he was known from childhood, was educated as befitted the son of a senior naval officer—a conventional upbringing varied by holidays with his German relations or with his aunt, the tsarina, in Russia. At Locker's Park School in Hertfordshire he was praised for his industry, enthusiasm, sense of humour, and modesty—the first two at least being characteristics conspicuous throughout his life. From there in May 1913 he entered the naval training college of Osborne as fifteenth out of eighty-three, a respectable if unglamorous position which he more or less maintained during his eighteen months there. Towards the end of his stay his father, now first sea lord, was hounded from office because of his German ancestry. This affected young Prince Louis deeply, though a contemporary recalls him remarking nonchalantly: 'It doesn't really matter very much. Of course I shall take his place.' Certainly his passionate ambition owed something to his desire to avenge his father's disgrace.

In November 1914 Prince Louis moved on to Dartmouth. Though he never shone athletically, nor impressed himself markedly on his contemporaries, his last years of education showed increasing confidence and ability, and at Keyham, the Royal Naval College at Devonport where he did his final course, he came first out of seventy-two. In July 1916 he was assigned as a midshipman to the *Lion*, the flagship of Admiral Sir David (later Earl) Beatty. His flag captain, (Sir) Roger Backhouse, described him as 'a very promising young officer' but his immediate superior felt he lacked the brilliance of his elder brother George—a judgement which Prince Louis himself frequently echoed. The *Lion* saw action in the eight months Prince Louis was aboard but suffered no damage, and by the time he transferred to the *Queen Elizabeth* in February 1917 the prospects of a major naval battle seemed remote. Prince Louis served briefly aboard the submarine K6—'the happiest month I've ever spent in the service'—and visited the western front, but his time on the *Queen Elizabeth* was uneventful and he was delighted to be posted in July 1918 as first lieutenant on one of the P-boats, small torpedo boats designed primarily for anti-submarine warfare. It was while he was on the *Queen Elizabeth* that his father, in common with other members of the royal family, abandoned his German title and was created Marquess of Milford Haven, with the family name of Mountbatten. His younger son was known henceforth as Lord Louis Mountbatten.

At the end of 1919 Mountbatten was one of a group of naval officers sent to widen their intellectual horizons at Cambridge. During his year at Christ's College (of which he became an honorary fellow in 1946) he acquired a taste for public affairs, regularly attending the Union and achieving the distinction, remarkable for someone in his position, of being elected to the committee. Through his close friend Peter Murphy, he also opened his mind to radical opinions—'We all thought him rather left-wing', said the then president of the Union, (Sir) Geoffrey Shakespeare.

While still at Cambridge, Mountbatten was invited by his cousin, the Prince of Wales, to attend him on the forthcoming tour of Australasia in the *Renown*. Mountbatten's roles were those of unofficial diarist, dogsbody, and, above all, companion to his sometimes moody and disobliging cousin. These he performed admirably—'you will never know', wrote the Prince to Lord Milford Haven, 'what very great friends we have become, what he has meant and been to me on this trip.' His reward was to be invited to join the next royal tour to India and Japan in the winter of 1921–2; a journey that doubly marked his life in that in India he learnt to play polo and became engaged to Edwina Cynthia Annette (died 1960), daughter of Wilfrid William Ashley (later Baron Mount Temple).

Edwina Ashley was descended from the third Viscount Palmerston and the Earls of Shaftesbury, while her maternal grandfather was the immensely rich Sir Ernest Cassel, friend and financial adviser to King Edward VII. At Cassel's death in 1921 his granddaughter inherited some £2.3 million, and eventually also a palace on Park Lane, Classiebawn Castle in Ireland, and the Broadlands estate at Romsey in Hampshire. The marriage of two powerful and fiercely competitive characters was never wholly harmonious and sometimes caused unhappiness to both partners. On the whole, however, it worked well and they established a formidable partnership at several stages of their lives. They had two daughters.

Early in 1923 Mountbatten joined the *Revenge*. For the next fifteen years his popular image was that of a playboy. Fast cars, speedboats, polo, were his delights; above all the last, about which he wrote the classic *Introduction to Polo* (1931) by 'Marco'. Yet nobody who knew his work could doubt his essential seriousness. 'This officer's heart and soul is in the Navy', reported the captain of the *Revenge*, 'No outside interests are ever allowed to interfere with his duties.' His professionalism was proved beyond doubt when he selected signals as his speciality and passed out top of the course in July 1925. As assistant fleet wireless officer (1927–8) and fleet wireless officer (1931–3) in the Mediterranean, and at the signals school at Portsmouth in between, he won a reputation for energy, efficiency, and inventiveness. He raised the standard of signalling in the Mediterranean Fleet to new heights and was known, respected, and almost always liked by everyone under his command.

In 1932 Mountbatten was promoted commander and in April 1934 took over the *Daring*, a new destroyer of 1,375 tons. After only a few months, however, he had to exchange her for an older and markedly inferior destroyer, the *Wishart*. Undiscomfited, he set to work to make his ship the most efficient in the Mediterranean Fleet. He succeeded and *Wishart* was Cock of the Fleet in the regatta of 1935. It was at this time that he perfected the 'Mountbatten station-keeping gear', an ingenious device which was adopted by the Admiralty for use in destroyers but which never really proved itself in wartime.

Enthusiastically recommended for promotion, Mountbatten returned to the Naval Air Division of the Admiralty. He was prominent in the campaign to recapture the Fleet Air Arm from the Royal Air Force, lobbying (Sir) Winston Churchill, Sir Samuel Hoare (later Viscount Templewood), and A. Duff Cooper (later Viscount Norwich) with a freedom unusual among junior officers. He vigorously applauded the latter's resignation over the Munich agreement and maintained a working relationship with Anthony Eden (later the Earl of Avon) and the fourth Marquess of Salisbury in their opposition to appeasement. More practically he was instrumental in drawing the Admiralty's attention to the merits of the Oerlikon gun, the adoption of which he urged vigorously for more than two years. It was during this period that he also succeeded in launching the Royal Naval Film Corporation, an organization designed to secure the latest films for British sailors at sea.

The abdication crisis caused him much distress but left him personally unscathed. Some time earlier he had prepared for the Prince of Wales a list of eligible Protestant princesses, but by the time of the accession he had little influence left. He had been King Edward VIII's personal naval aide-de-camp and in February 1937 King George VI appointed him to the same position, simultaneously appointing him to the GCVO.

Since the autumn of 1938 Mountbatten had been contributing ideas to the construction at Newcastle of a new destroyer, the *Kelly*. In June 1939 he took over as captain and *Kelly* was commissioned by the outbreak of war. On 20 September she was joined by her sister ship *Kingston*, and Mountbatten became captain (D) of the fifth destroyer flotilla.

Mountbatten was not markedly successful as a wartime destroyer captain. In surprisingly few months at sea he almost capsized in a high sea, collided with another destroyer, and was mined once, torpedoed twice, and finally sunk by enemy aircraft. In most of these incidents he could plead circumstances beyond his control, but the consensus of professional opinion is that he lacked 'sea-sense', the quality that ensures a ship is doing the right thing in the right place at the right time. Nevertheless he acted with immense panache and courage, and displayed such qualities of leadership that when *Kelly* was recommissioned after several months refitting, an embarrassingly large number of her former crew clamoured to rejoin. When he took his flotilla into Namsos in March 1940 to evacuate (Sir) Adrian Carton de Wiart and several thousand Allied troops, he conducted the operation with cool determination. The return of *Kelly* to port in May, after ninety-one hours in tow under almost constant bombardment and with a fifty-foot hole in the port side, was an epic of fortitude and seamanship. Feats like this caught Churchill's imagination and thus altered the course of Mountbatten's career.

In the spring of 1941 the *Kelly* was dispatched to the Mediterranean. Placed in an impossible position, Admiral Sir A. B. Cunningham (later Viscount Cunningham of Hyndhope) in May decided to support the army in Crete even though there was no possibility of air cover. The *Kashmir* and the *Kelly* were attacked by dive-bombers on 23 May and soon sunk. More than half the crew of *Kelly* was lost and Mountbatten only escaped by swimming from under the ship as it turned turtle. The survivors were machine-gunned in the water but were picked up by the *Kipling*. The *Kelly* lived on in *In Which We Serve*, a skilful propaganda film by (Sir) Noël Coward, which was based in detail on the achievements of Lord Louis Mountbatten and his ship. Mountbatten was now appointed to command the aircraft-carrier *Illustrious*, which had been severely damaged and sent for repair to the United States. In October he flew to America to take over his ship and pay a round of visits. He established many useful contacts and made a considerable impression on the American leadership: '. . . he has been a great help to all of us, and I mean literally ALL', wrote Admiral Starke to Sir A. Dudley Pound. Before the *Illustrious* was ready, however, Mountbatten was called home by Churchill to take charge of Combined Operations. His predecessor, Sir Roger (later Lord) Keyes, had fallen foul of the chiefs of staff and Mountbatten was initially appointed only as 'chief adviser'. In April 1942, however, he became chief of Combined Operations with the acting rank of vice-admiral, lieutenant-general, and air marshal and with *de facto* membership of the chiefs of staff committee. This phenomenally rapid promotion earned him some unpopularity, but on the whole the chiefs of staff gave him full support.

'You are to give no thought for the defensive. Your whole attention is to be concentrated on the offensive', Churchill told him. Mountbatten's duties fell into two main parts: to organize raids against the European coast designed to raise morale, harass the Germans, and achieve limited military objectives; and to prepare for an eventual invasion. The first responsibility, more dramatic though less important, gave rise to a multitude of raids involving only a handful of men and a few more complex operations such as the costly but successful attack on the dry dock at St. Nazaire. Combined Operations were responsible for planning such forays, but their execution was handed over to the designated force commander, a system which led sometimes to confusion.

The ill results of divided responsibilities were particularly apparent in the Dieppe operation of August 1942. Dieppe taught the Allies valuable lessons for the eventual invasion and misled the Germans about their intentions, but the price paid in lives and material was exceedingly, probably disproportionately, high. For this Mountbatten, ultimately responsible for planning the operation, must accept some responsibility.

Nevertheless the errors which both British and German analysts subsequently condemned—the adoption of frontal rather than flank assault, the selection of relatively inexperienced Canadian troops for the assault, the abandonment of any previous air bombardment, and the failure to provide the support of capital ships—were all taken against his advice or over his head. Certainly he was not guilty of the blunders which Lord Beaverbrook and some later commentators attributed to him.

When it came to preparation for invasion, Mountbatten's energy, enthusiasm, and receptivity to new ideas showed to great advantage. His principal contribution was to see clearly what is now obvious but was then not generally recognized, that successful landings on a fortified enemy coast called for an immense range of specialized equipment and skills. To secure an armada of landing craft of different shapes and sizes, and to train the crews to operate them, involved a diversion of resources, both British and American, which was vigorously opposed in many quarters. The genesis of such devices as Mulberry (the floating port) and Pluto (pipe line under the ocean) is often hard to establish, but the zeal with which Mountbatten and his staff supported their development was a major factor in their success. Mountbatten surrounded himself with a team of talented if sometimes maverick advisers—Professor J. D. Bernal, Geoffrey Pyke, Solly (later Lord) Zuckerman—and was ready to listen to anything they suggested. Sometimes this led him into wasteful extravagances—as in his championship of the iceberg/aircraft carrier Habbakuk—but there were more good ideas than bad. His contribution to D-Day was recognized in the tribute paid him by the Allied leaders shortly after the invasion: '. . . we realize that much of . . . the success of this venture has its origins in developments effected by you and your staff.'

His contribution to the higher strategy is less easy to establish. He himself always claimed responsibility for the selection of Normandy as the invasion site rather than the Pas de Calais. Certainly when Operation Sledgehammer, the plan for a limited re-entry into the Continent in 1942, was debated by the chiefs of staff, Mountbatten was alone in arguing for the Cherbourg peninsula. His consistent support of Normandy may have contributed to the change of heart when the venue of the invasion proper was decided. In general, however, Sir Alan Brooke (later Viscount Alanbrooke) and the other chiefs of staff resented Mountbatten's ventures outside the field of his immediate interests and he usually confined himself to matters directly concerned with Combined Operations.

His headquarters, COHQ, indeed the whole of his command, was sometimes criticized for its lavishness in personnel and encouragement of extravagant ideas. Mountbatten was never economical, and waste there undoubtedly was. Nevertheless he built up at great speed an organization of remarkable complexity and effectiveness. By April 1943 Combined Operations Command included 2,600 landing-craft and over 50,000 men. He almost killed himself in the process for in July 1942 he was told by his doctors that he would die unless he worked less intensely. A man with less imagination who played safe could never have done as much. It was Alan Brooke, initially unenthusiastic about his elevation, who concluded: 'His appointment as Chief of Combined Operations . . . was excellent, and he played a remarkable part as the driving force and main-spring of this organization. Without his energy and drive it would never have reached the high standard it achieved.'

Mountbatten arrived at the Quebec conference in August 1943 as chief of Combined Operations; he left as acting admiral and supreme commander designate, South East Asia. 'He is young, enthusiastic and triphibious', Churchill telegraphed C. R. (later Earl) Attlee, but though the Americans welcomed the appointment enthusiastically, he was only selected after half a dozen candidates had been eliminated for various reasons.

He took over a command where everything had gone wrong. The British and Indian army, ravaged by disease and soundly beaten by the Japanese, had been chased out of Burma. A feeble attempt at counter-attack in the Arakan peninsula had ended in disaster. Morale was low, air support inadequate, communications within India slow and uncertain. There seemed little to oppose the Japanese if they decided to resume their assault. Yet before Mountbatten could concentrate on his official adversaries he had to resolve the anomalies within his own Command.

Most conspicuous of these was General Stilwell. As well as being deputy supreme commander, Stilwell was chief of staff to Chiang Kai-shek and his twin roles inevitably involved conflicts of interest and loyalty. A superb leader of troops in the field but cantankerous, anglophobe, and narrow-minded, Stilwell would have been a difficult colleague in any circumstances. In South East Asia, where his preoccupation was to reopen the road through north Burma to China, he proved almost impossible to work with. But Mountbatten also found his relationship difficult with his own, British, commanders-in-chief, in particular the naval commander, Sir James Somerville. Partly this arose from differences of temperament; more important it demonstrated a fundamental difference of opinion about the supreme commander's role. Mountbatten, encouraged by Churchill and members of his own entourage, believed that he should operate on the MacArthur model, with his own planning staff, consulting his commanders-in-chief but ultimately instructing them on future operations. Somerville, General Sir G. J. Giffard, and Air Marshal Sir R. E. C. Peirse, on the other hand, envisaged him as a chairman of committee, operating like Eisenhower and working through the planning staffs of the commanders-in-chief. The chiefs of staff in London proved reluctant to rule categorically on the issue but Mountbatten eventually abandoned his central planning staff and the situation was further eased when Somerville was replaced by Admiral Sir Bruce Fraser (later Lord Fraser of North Cape).

Mountbatten defined the three principal problems facing him as being those of monsoon, malaria, and morale. His determination that Allied troops must fight through the monsoon, though of greater psychological than military significance, undoubtedly assisted the eventual victories of the Fourteenth Army. In 1943, for every casualty evacuated because of wounds, there were 120 sick, and Mountbatten, by his emphasis on hygiene and improved medical techniques, can claim much credit for the vast improvement over the next year. But it was in the transformation of the soldiers' morale that he made his greatest contribution. By publicity, propaganda, and the impact of his personality, he restored their pride in themselves and gave them confidence that they could defeat the Japanese.

Deciding what campaign they were to fight proved difficult. Mountbatten, with Churchill's enthusiastic backing, envisaged a bold amphibious strategy which would bypass the Burmese jungles and strike through the Andaman Islands to Rangoon or, more ambitious still, through northern Sumatra towards Singapore. The Americans, however, who would have provided the material resources for such adventures, nicknamed South East Asia Command (SEAC) 'Save England's Asiatic Colonies' and were suspicious of any operation which seemed designed to this end. They felt that the solitary justification for the Burma campaign was to restore land communications with China. The ambitious projects with which Mountbatten had left London withered as his few landing-craft were withdrawn. A mission he dispatched to London and Washington returned empty-handed. 'You might send out the waxwork which I hear Madame Tussauds has made', wrote Mountbatten bitterly to his friend (Sir) Charles Lambe, 'it could have my Admiral's uniform and sit at my desk . . . as well as I could.'

It was the Japanese who saved him from so ignoble a role. In spring 1944 they attacked in Arakan and across the Imphal plain into India. The Allied capacity to supply troops by air and their new-found determination to stand firm, even when cut off, turned potential disaster into almost total victory. Mountbatten himself played a major role, being personally responsible at a crucial moment for the switch of two divisions by air from Arakan to Imphal and the diversion of the necessary American aircraft from the supply routes to China. Imphal confirmed Mountbatten's faith in the commander of the Fourteenth Army, General W. J. (later Viscount) Slim and led to his final loss of confidence in the commander-in-chief,

General Giffard, whom he now dismissed. The battle cost the Japanese 7,000 dead; much hard fighting lay ahead but the Fourteenth Army was on the march that would end at Rangoon.

Mountbatten still hoped to avoid the reconquest of Burma by land. In April 1944 he transferred his headquarters from Delhi to Kandy in Ceylon, reaffirming his faith in a maritime strategy. He himself believed the next move should be a powerful sea and air strike against Rangoon; Churchill still hankered after the more ambitious attack on northern Sumatra; the chiefs of staff felt the British effort should be switched to support the American offensive in the Pacific. In the end shortage of resources dictated the course of events. Mountbatten was able to launch a small seaborne invasion to support the Fourteenth Army's advance, but it was Slim's men who bore the brunt of the fighting and reached Rangoon just before the monsoon broke in April 1945.

Giffard had been replaced as supreme commander by Sir Oliver Leese. Mountbatten's original enthusiasm for Leese did not endure; the latter soon fell out with his supreme commander and proved unpopular with the other commanders-in-chief. A climax came in May 1945 when Leese informed Slim that he was to be relieved from command of the Fourteenth Army because he was tired out and anyway had no experience in maritime operations. Mountbatten's role in this curious transaction remains slightly obscure; Leese definitely went too far, but there may have been some ambiguity about his instructions. In the event Leese's action was disavowed in London and he himself was dismissed and Slim appointed in his place.

The next phase of the campaign—an invasion by sea of the Malay peninsula—should have been the apotheosis of Mountbatten's command. When he went to the Potsdam conference in July 1945, however, he was told of the existence of the atom bomb. He realized at once that this was likely to rob him of his victory and, sure enough, the Japanese surrender reduced Operation Zipper to an unopposed landing. This was perhaps just as well; faulty intelligence meant that one of the two landings was made on unsuitable beaches and was quickly bogged down. The invasion would have succeeded but the cost might have been high.

On 12 September 1945, Mountbatten received the formal surrender of the Japanese at Singapore. Not long afterwards he was created a viscount. The honour was deserved. His role had been crucial. 'We did it together', Slim said to him on his deathbed, and the two men, in many ways so different, had indeed complemented each other admirably and proved the joint architects of victory in South East Asia.

Mountbatten's work in SEAC did not end with the Japanese surrender; indeed in some ways it grew still more onerous. His Command was now extended to include South Vietnam and the Netherlands East Indies: 1½ million square miles containing 128 million inhabitants, ¾ million armed and potentially truculent Japanese, and 123,000 Allied prisoners, many in urgent need of medical attention. Mountbatten had to rescue the prisoners, disarm the Japanese, and restore the various territories to stability so that civil government could resume. This last function proved most difficult, since the Japanese had swept away the old colonial regimes and new nationalist movements had grown up to fill the vacuum. Mountbatten's instincts told him that such movements were inevitable and even desirable. Every effort, he felt, should be made to take account of their justified aspirations. His disposition to sympathize with the radical nationalists sometimes led him into naïvely optimistic assessment of their readiness to compromise with the former colonialist regimes—as proved to be the case with the communist Chinese in Malaya—but the course of subsequent history suggests that he often saw the situation more clearly than the so-called 'realists' who criticized him.

Even before the end of the war he had had a foretaste of the problems that lay ahead. Aung San, head of the pro-Japanese Burmese National Army, defected with all his troops. Mountbatten was anxious to accept his co-operation and cajoled the somewhat reluctant chiefs of staff into agreeing on military grounds. Inevitably, this gave Aung San a stronger position than the traditionalists thought desirable when the time came to form Burma's post-war government. Mountbatten felt that, though left wing and fiercely nationalistic, Aung San was honourable, basically rea-sonable, and ready to accept the concept of an independent Burma within the British Commonwealth; '. . . with proper treatment', judged Slim, 'Aung San would have proved a Burmese Smuts'. The governor, Sir Reginald Dorman-Smith, conceded Aung San was the most popular man in Burma but considered him a dangerous Marxist revolutionary. When Aung San was accused of war crimes committed during the Japanese occupation, Dorman-Smith wished to arrest and try him. This Mount-batten forestalled; but the hand-over to civil government in April 1946 and the murder of Aung San the following year meant that the supreme commander's view of his character was never properly tested.

In Malaya the problem was more immediately one of law and order. Confronted by the threat of a politically-motivated general strike, the authorities proposed to arrest all the leaders. 'Naturally I ordered them to cancel these orders', wrote Mountbatten, 'as I could not imagine anything more disastrous than to make martyrs of these men.' Reluctantly he agreed that in certain circumstances Chinese trouble-makers might be deported, but rescinded that approval when it was proposed to deport certain detainees who had not had time to profit by his warnings. His critics maintained that sterner action in 1945–6 could have prevented, or at least mitigated the future troubles in Malaya, but Mountbatten was convinced that the prosperity of Malaya and Singapore depended on the co-operation of Malay and Chinese, and was determined to countenance nothing that might divide the two communities.

In Vietnam and Indonesia Mountbatten's problem was to balance nationalist aspirations against the demands of Britain's Allies for support in the recovery of their colonies. He was better disposed to the French than the Dutch, and though he complained when General (Sir) Douglas Gracey exceeded his instructions and suppressed the Viet Minh—'General Gracey has saved French Indo-China', Leclerc told him—the reproof was more formal than real. In Indonesia Mountbatten believed that Dutch intransigence was the principal factor preventing a peaceful settlement. Misled by Dutch intelligence, he had no suspicion of the force of nationalist sentiment until Lady Mountbatten returned from her brave foray to rescue Allied prisoners of war. His forces could not avoid conflict with the Indonesian nationalists but Mountbatten sought to limit their commitment, with the result that both Dutch and Indonesians believed the British were favouring the other side. He did, however, contrive to keep open the possibility of political settlement; only after the departure of the British forces did full-scale civil war become inevitable.

Mountbatten left South East Asia in mid-1946 with the reputation of a liberal committed to decolonization. Though he had no thought beyond his return to the navy, with the now substantive rank of rear-admiral, his reputation influenced the Labour government when they were looking for a successor to Viscount (later Earl) Wavell who could resuscitate the faltering negotiations for Indian independence. On 18 December 1946 he was invited to become India's last viceroy. That year he had been created first Viscount Mountbatten of Burma.

Mountbatten longed to go to sea again, but this was a challenge no man of ambition and public spirit could reject. His reluctance enabled him to extract favourable terms from the government, and though the plenipotentiary powers to which he was often to refer are not specifically set out in any document, he enjoyed far greater freedom of action than his immediate predecessors. His original insistence that he would go only on the invitation of the Indian leaders was soon abandoned but it was on his initiative that a terminal date of June 1948 was fixed, by which time the British would definitely have left India.

Mountbatten's directive was that he should strive to implement the recommendations of the Cabinet mission of 1946, led by Sir R. Stafford Cripps which maintained the principle of a united India. By the time he arrived, however, this objective had been tacitly abandoned by every major politician of the sub-continent with the important exception of M. K. Gandhi. The viceroy dutifully tried to persuade all concerned of the benefits of unity but his efforts foundered on the intransigence of the Muslim leader Mahomed Ali Jinnah. His problem thereafter was to find some formula which would reconcile the desire of the Hindus for a central India from which a few peripheral and wholly Muslim areas would secede, with Jinnah's aspiration to secure a greater Pakistan including all the Punjab and as much as possible of Bengal. In this task he was supported by Wavell's staff from the Indian Civil Service, reinforced by General H. L. (later Lord) Ismay and Sir Eric Miéville. He himself contributed immense energy, charm and persuasiveness, negotiating skills, agility of mind, and endless optimism.

He quickly concluded that not only was time not on his side but that the urgency was desperate. The run-down of the British military and civil presence, coupled with swelling inter-communal hatred, were intensely dangerous. 'The situation is everywhere electric, and I get the feeling that the mine may go up at any moment', wrote Ismay to his wife on 25 March 1947, the day after Mountbatten was sworn in as viceroy. This conviction that every moment counted dictated Mountbatten's activities over the next five months. He threw himself into a hectic series of interviews with the various political leaders. With Jawaharlal Nehru he established an immediate and lasting rapport which was to assume great importance in the future. With V. J. Patel, in whom he identified a major power in Indian politics, his initial relationship was less easy, but they soon enjoyed mutual confidence. Gandhi fascinated and delighted him, but he shrewdly concluded that he was likely to be pushed to one side in the forthcoming negotiations. With Jinnah alone did he fail; the full blast of his charm did not thaw or even moderate the chill intractability of the Muslim leader.

Nevertheless negotiations advanced so rapidly that by 2 May Ismay was taking to London a plan which Mountbatten believed all the principal parties would accept. Only when the British Cabinet had already approved the plan did he realize that he had gravely underestimated Nehru's objections to any proposal that left room for the 'Balkanization' of India. With extraordinary speed a new draft was produced, which provided for India's membership of the Commonwealth, and put less emphasis on the right of the individual components of British India to reject India or Pakistan and opt for independence. After what Mountbatten described as 'the worst 24 hours of my life', the plan was accepted by all parties on 3 June. He was convinced that any relaxation of the feverish pace would risk destroying the fragile basis of understanding. Independence, he announced, was to be granted in only ten weeks, on 15 August 1947.

Before this date the institutions of British India had to be carved in two. Mountbatten initially hoped to retain a unified army but quickly realized this would be impossible and concentrated instead on ensuring rough justice in the division of the assets. To have given satisfaction to everyone would have been impossible, but at the time few people accused him of partiality. He tackled the problems, wrote Michael Edwardes in a book not generally sympathetic to the last viceroy, 'with a speed and brilliance which it is difficult to believe would have been exercised by any other man'.

The princely states posed a particularly complex problem, since with the end of British rule paramountcy lapsed and there was in theory nothing to stop the princes opting for self-rule. This would have made a geographical nonsense of India and, to a lesser extent, Pakistan; as well as creating a plethora of independent states, many incapable of sustaining such a role. Mountbatten at first attached little importance to the question, but once he was fully aware of it, used every trick to get the rulers to accept accession. Some indeed felt that he was using improper influence on loyal subjects of the Crown, but it is hard to see that any other course would in the long run have contributed to their prosperity. Indeed the two states which Mountbatten failed to shepherd into the fold of India or Pakistan—Hyderabad and Kashmir—were those which were subsequently to cause most trouble.

Most provinces, like the princely states, clearly belonged either to India or to Pakistan. In the Punjab and Bengal, however, partition was necessary. This posed horrifying problems, since millions of Hindus and Muslims would find themselves on the wrong side of whatever frontier was established. The Punjab was likely to prove most troublesome, because 14 per cent of its population consisted of Sikhs, who were warlike, fanatically anti-Muslim, and determined that their homelands should remain inviolate. Partition was not Mountbatten's direct responsibility, since Sir Cyril (later Viscount) Radcliffe was appointed to divide the two provinces. Popular opinion, however, found it hard to accept that he was not involved, and even today it is sometimes suggested he may have helped shape Radcliffe's final conclusions.

Mountbatten had hoped that independence day would see him installed as governor-general of both new dominions; able to act, in Churchill's phrase, as 'moderator' during their inevitable differences. Nehru was ready for such a transmogrification but Jinnah, after some months of apparent indecision, concluded that he himself must be Pakistan's first head of state. Mountbatten was uncertain whether the last viceroy of a united India should now reappear as governor-general of a part of it, but the Indian government pressed him to accept and in London both Attlee and George VI felt the appointment was desirable. With some misgivings, Mountbatten gave way. Independence day in both Pakistan and India was a triumph, tumultuous millions applauding his progress and demonstrating that, for the moment at least, he enjoyed a place in the pantheon with their national leaders. 'No other living man could have got the thing through', wrote Lord Killearn to Ismay; '. . . it has been a job supremely well done.'

The euphoria quickly faded. Though Bengal remained calm, thanks largely to Gandhi's personal intervention, the Punjab exploded. Vast movements of population across the new frontier exacerbated the already inflamed communal hatred, and massacres on an appalling scale developed. The largely British-officered Boundary Force was taxed far beyond its powers and Delhi itself was engulfed in the violence. Mountbatten was called back from holiday to help master the emergency, and brought desperately needed energy and organizational skills to the despondent government. 'I've never been through such a time in my life', he wrote on 28 September, 'The War, the Viceroyalty were jokes, for we have been dealing with life and death in our own city.' Gradually order was restored and by November 1947 Mountbatten felt the situation was stable enough to permit him to attend the wedding of Princess Elizabeth and his nephew Philip Mountbatten in London. He was created first Earl Mountbatten of Burma, with special remainder to his daughter Patricia.

Estimates vary widely, but the best-documented assessments agree that between 200,000 and 250,000 people lost their lives in the communal riots. Those who criticize Mountbatten's viceroyalty do so most often on the grounds that these massacres could have been averted, or at least mitigated, if partition had not been hurried through. Mountbatten's champions maintain that delay would only have made things worse and allowed the disorders to spread further. It is impossible to state conclusively what *might* have happened if independence had been postponed by a few months, or even years, but it is noteworthy that the closer people were to the problem, the more they support Mountbatten's policy. Almost every senior member of the British administration in India and of the Indian government has recorded his conviction that security was deteriorating so fast and the maintenance of non-communal forces of law and order proving so difficult, that a far greater catastrophe would have ensued if there had been further delay.

Mountbatten as governor-general was a servant of the Indian government and, as Ismay put it, 'it is only natural that they . . . should regard themselves as having proprietary rights over you'. Mountbatten accepted this role and fought doughtily for India's interests. He did not wholly abandon impartiality, however. When in January 1948 the Indian government withheld from Pakistan the 55 million crores of rupees owing after the division of assets, the governor-general argued that such conduct was dishonourable as well as unwise. He recruited Gandhi as his ally, and together they forced a change of policy on the reluctant Indian ministers. It was one of Gandhi's final contributions to Indian history. On 30 January he was assassinated by a Hindu extremist. Mountbatten mourned him sincerely. 'What a remarkable old boy he was', he wrote to a friend, 'I think history will link him with Buddha and Mahomet.'

His stand over the division of assets did the governor-general little good in Pakistan where he was believed to be an inveterate enemy and, by persuading Radcliffe to award Gurdaspur to India, to have secured that country access to Kashmir. When, in October 1947, Pathan tribesmen invaded the Vale of Kashmir, Mountbatten approved and helped organize military intervention by India. He insisted, however, that the state must first accede and that, as soon as possible, a plebiscite should establish the wishes of the Kashmiri people. When war between India and Pakistan seemed imminent he was instrumental in persuading Nehru that the matter should be referred to the United Nations.

The other problem that bedevilled Mountbatten was that of Hyderabad. He constituted himself, in effect, chief negotiator for the Indian government and almost brought off a deal that would have secured reasonably generous terms for the Nizam. Muslim extremists in Hyderabad, however, defeated his efforts, and the dispute grumbled on. Mountbatten protested when he found contingency plans existed for the invasion of Hyderabad and his presence was undoubtedly a main factor in inhibiting the Indian take-over that quickly followed his departure.

On 21 June 1948 the Mountbattens left India. In his final address, Nehru referred to the vast crowds that had attended their last appearances and 'wondered how it was that an Englishman and Englishwoman could become so popular in India during this brief period'. Even his harshest critics could not deny that Mountbatten had won the love and trust of the people and got the relationship between India and her former ruler off to a far better start than had seemed possible fifteen months before.

At last Mountbatten was free to return to sea. Reverting to his substantive rank of rear-admiral he took command of the first cruiser squadron in the Mediterranean. To assume this relatively lowly position after the splendours of supreme command and viceroyalty could not have been easy, but with goodwill all round it was achieved successfully. He was 'as great a subordinate as he is a leader', reported the commander-in-chief, Admiral Sir Arthur Power. He brought his squadron up to a high level of efficiency, though not concealing the fact that he felt obsolescent material and undermanning diminished its real effectiveness. After his previous jobs, this command was something of a holiday, and he revelled in the opportunities to play his beloved polo and take up skin-diving. In Malta he stuck to his inconspicuous role, but abroad he was fêted by the rulers of the countries his squadron visited. 'I suppose I oughtn't to get a kick out of being treated like a Viceroy', he confessed after one particularly successful visit, 'but I'd have been less than human if I hadn't been affected by the treatment I received at Trieste.' He was never less, nor more than human.

Mountbatten was promoted vice-admiral in 1949 and in June 1950 returned to the Admiralty as fourth sea lord. He was at first disappointed, since he had set his heart on being second sea lord, responsible for personnel, and found himself instead concerned with supplies and transport. In fact the post proved excellent for his career. He flung himself into the work with characteristic zeal, cleared up many anomalies and outdated practices, and acquired a range of information which was to stand him in good stead when he became first sea lord. On the whole he confined himself to the duties of his department, but when the Persians nationalized Anglo-Iranian Oil in 1951, he could not resist making his opinions known. He felt that it was futile to oppose strong nationalist movements of this kind and that Britain would do better to work with them. He converted the first lord to his point of view but conspicuously failed to impress the bellicose foreign secretary, Herbert Morrison (later Lord Morrison of Lambeth).

The next step was command of a major fleet and in June 1952 he was appointed to the Mediterranean, being promoted to admiral the following year. St. Vincent remarked that naval command in the Mediterranean 'required an officer of splendour', and this Mountbatten certainly provided. He was not a great operational commander like Andrew Cunningham, but he knew his ships and personnel, maintained the fleet at the highest level of peacetime efficiency, and was immensely popular with the men. When 'Cassandra' of the *Daily Mirror* arrived to report on Mountbatten's position, he kept aloof for four days, then came to the flagship with the news that the commander-in-chief was 'O.K. with the sailors'. But it was on the representational side that Mountbatten excelled. He loved showing the flag and, given half a chance, would act as honorary ambassador into the bargain. Sometimes he overdid it, and in September 1952 the first lord, at the instance of the prime minister, wrote to urge him 'to take the greatest care to keep out of political discussions'.

His diplomatic as well as administrative skills were taxed when in January 1953 he was appointed supreme Allied commander of a new NATO Mediterranean Command (SACMED). Under him were the Mediterranean fleets of Britain, France, Italy, Greece, and Turkey, but not the most powerful single unit in the area, the American Sixth Fleet. He was required to set up an integrated international naval/air headquarters in Malta and managed this formidable organizational task with great efficiency. The smoothing over of national susceptibilities and the reconciliation of his British with his NATO role proved taxing, but his worst difficulty lay with the other NATO headquarters in the Mediterranean, CINCSOUTH, at Naples under the American Admiral R. B. Carney. There were real problems of demarcation, but as had happened with Somerville in South East Asia, these were made far worse by a clash of personalities. When Carney was replaced in the autumn of 1953, the differences melted away and the two commands began to co-operate.

In October 1954, when he became first sea lord, Mountbatten achieved what he had always held to be his ultimate ambition. It did not come easily. A formidable body of senior naval opinion distrusted him and was at first opposed to his appointment, and it was not until the conviction hardened that the navy was losing the Whitehall battle against the other services that opinion rallied behind him. 'The Navy wants badly a man and a leader', wrote Andrew Cunningham, who had formerly been Mountbatten's opponent. 'You have the ability and the drive and it is you that the Navy wants.' Churchill, still unreconciled to Mountbatten's role in India, held out longer, but in the end he too gave way.

Since the war the navy had become the Cinderella of the fighting Services, and morale was low. Under Mountbatten's leadership, the Admiralty's voice in Whitehall became louder and more articulate. By setting up the 'Way Ahead' committee, he initiated an overdue rethinking of the shore establishments which were absorbing an undue proportion of the navy's resources. He scrapped plans for the construction of a heavy missile-carrying cruiser and instead concentrated on destroyers carrying the Sea Slug missile: 'Once we can obtain Government agreement to the fact that we are the mobile large scale rocket carriers of the future then everything else will fall into place.' The Reserve Fleet was cut severely and expenditure diverted from the already excellent communications system to relatively underdeveloped fields such as radar. Probably his most important single contribution, however, was to establish an excellent relationship with the notoriously prickly Admiral Rickover, which was to lead to Britain acquiring US technology for its nuclear submarines and, eventually, to the adoption of the Polaris missile as the core of its nuclear deterrent.

In July 1956 Nasser nationalized the Suez canal. Mountbatten was asked what military steps could be taken to restore the situation. He said that the Mediterranean Fleet with the Royal Marine commandos aboard could be at Port Said within three days and take the port and its hinterland. Eden rejected the proposal since he wished to reoccupy the whole canal zone, and it is unlikely anyway that the other chiefs of staff would have approved a plan that might have left lightly armed British forces exposed to tank attack and with inadequate air cover. As plans for full-scale invasion were prepared, Mountbatten became more and more uneasy about the contemplated action. To the chiefs of staff he consistently said that political implications should be considered and more thought given to the long-term future of the Middle East. His views were reflected in the chiefs' recommendations to the government, a point that caused considerable irritation to Anthony Eden, who insisted that politics should be left to the politicians. In August Mountbatten drafted a letter of resignation to the prime minister but, without too much difficulty, was dissuaded from sending it by the first lord, Viscount Cilcennin. He was, however, instrumental in substituting the invasion plan of General Sir Charles Keightley for that previously approved by the Cabinet, a move that saved the lives of many hundreds of civilians. On 2 November, when the invasion fleet had already sailed, Mountbatten made a written appeal to Eden to accept the United Nations resolution and 'turn back the assault convoy before it is too late'. His appeal was ignored. Mountbatten again offered his resignation to the first lord and again was told that it was his duty to stay on. He was promoted admiral of the fleet in October 1956.

With Harold Macmillan (later the Earl of Stockton) succeeding Eden as prime minister in January 1957, Duncan Sandys (later Lord Duncan-Sandys) was appointed minister of defence with a mandate to rationalize the armed services and impose sweeping economies. There were many embittered battles before Sandys's first defence white paper appeared in the summer of 1957. The thirteenth and final draft contained the ominous words: 'the role of the Navy in Global War is somewhat uncertain'. In the event, however, the navy suffered relatively lightly, losing only one-sixth of its personnel over the next five years, as opposed to the army's 45 per cent and the air force's 35 per cent. The role of the navy east of Suez was enshrined as an accepted dogma of defence policy.

In July 1959 Mountbatten took over as chief of defence staff (CDS). He was the second incumbent, Sir William Dickson having been appointed in 1958, with Mountbatten's support but against the fierce opposition of Field-Marshal Sir Gerald Templer. Dickson's role was little more than that of permanent chairman of the chiefs of staff committee but Sandys tried to increase the CDS's powers. He was defeated, and the defence white paper of 1958 made only modest changes to the existing system. Mountbatten made the principal objective of his time as CDS the integration of the three Services, not to the extent achieved by the Canadians of one homogenized fighting force, but abolishing the independent ministries and setting up a common list for all senior officers. During his first two years, however, he had to remain content with the creation of a director of defence plans to unify the work of the three planning departments and the acceptance of the principle of unified command in the Far and Middle East. Then, at the end of 1962, Macmillan agreed that another attempt should be made to impose unification on the reluctant Services. 'Pray take no notice of any obstructions', he told the minister of defence, 'You should approach this . . . with dashing, slashing methods. Anyone who raises any objection can go.'

At Mountbatten's suggestion Lord Ismay and Sir E. Ian Jacob were asked to report. While not accepting all Mountbatten's recommendations—which involved a sweeping increase in the powers of the CDS—their report went a long way towards realizing the concept of a unified Ministry of Defence. The reforms, which were finally promulgated in 1964, acknowledged the supreme authority of the secretary of state for defence and strengthened the central role of the CDS. To Mountbatten this was an important first step, but only a step. He believed that so long as separate departments survived, with differing interests and loyalties, it would be impossible to use limited resources to the best advantage. Admiralty, War Office, Air Ministry—not to mention Ministry of Aviation—should be abolished. Ministers should be responsible, not for the navy or the air force, but for communications or supplies. 'We cannot, in my opinion, afford to stand pat', he wrote to Harold Wilson (later Lord Wilson of Rievaulx) when the latter became prime minister in October 1964, 'and must move on to, or at least towards the ultimate aim of a functional, closely knit, smoothly working machine.' 'Functionalization' was the objective which he repeatedly pressed on the new minister of defence, Denis Healey. Healey was well disposed in principle, but felt that other reforms enjoyed higher priority. Though Mountbatten appealed to Wilson he got little satisfaction, and the machinery which he left behind him at his retirement was in his eyes only an unsatisfactory half-way house.

Even for this he paid a high price in popularity. His ideas were for the most part repugnant to the chiefs of staff, who suspected him of seeking personal aggrandizement and doubted the propriety of his methods. Relations tended to be worst with the chiefs of air staff. The latter believed that Mountbatten, though ostensibly above inter-Service rivalries, in fact remained devoted to the interests of the navy. It is hard entirely to slough off a lifetime's loyalties, but Mountbatten *tried* to be impartial. He did not always succeed. On the long-drawn-out battle over the merits of aircraft-carriers and island bases, he espoused the former. When he urged the first sea lord to work out some compromise which would accommodate both points of view, Sir Caspar John retorted that only a month before Mountbatten had advised him: 'Don't compromise—fight him to the death!' Similarly in the conflict between the TSR 2, sponsored by the air

621

force, and the navy's Buccaneer, Mountbatten believed strongly that the former, though potentially the better plane, was too expensive to be practicable and would take too long to develop. He lobbied the minister of defence and urged his right-hand man, Solly Zuckerman, to argue the case against the TSR 2—'You know why I can't help you in Public. It is *not* moral cowardice but fear that my usefulness as Chairman would be seriously impaired.'

The question of the British nuclear deterrent also involved inter-Service rivalries. Mountbatten believed that an independent deterrent was essential, arguing to Harold Wilson that it would 'dispel in Russian minds the thought that they will escape scot-free if by any chance the Americans decide to hold back release of a strategic nuclear response to an attack'. He was instrumental in persuading the incoming Labour government not to adopt unilateral nuclear disarmament. In this he had the support of the three chiefs of staff. But there was controversy over what weapon best suited Britain's needs. From long before he became CDS, Mountbatten had privately preferred the submarine-launched Polaris missile to any of the airborne missiles favoured by the air force. Though not himself present at the meeting at Nassau between Macmillan and President John F. Kennedy at which Polaris was offered and accepted in exchange for the cancelled Skybolt missile, he had already urged this solution and had made plans accordingly.

Though he defended the nuclear deterrent, he was wholly opposed to the accumulation of unnecessary stockpiles or the development of new weapons designed to kill more effectively people who would be dead anyway if the existing armouries were employed. At NATO in July 1963 he pleaded that 'it was madness to hold further tests when all men of goodwill were about to try and bring about test-banning'. He conceded that tactical nuclear weapons added to the efficacy of the deterrent, but argued that their numbers should be limited and their use subject to stringent control. To use *any* nuclear weapon, however small or 'clean', would, he insisted, lead to general nuclear war. He opposed the 'mixed manned multilateral force' not just as being military nonsense, but because there were more than enough strategic nuclear weapons already. What were needed, he told the NATO commanders in his valedictory address, were more 'highly mobile, well-equipped, self-supporting and balanced "Fire Brigade" forces, with first-class communications, able to converge quickly on the enemy force'.

Mountbatten's original tenure of office as CDS had been for three years. Macmillan pressed him to lengthen this by a further two years to July 1964. Mountbatten was initially reluctant but changed his mind after the death of his wife in 1960. Subsequently he agreed to a further extension to July

1965, in order to see through the first phase of defence reorganization. Wilson would have happily sanctioned yet another year but Healey established that there would be considerable resentment at such a move on the part of the other Service leaders and felt anyway that he would never be fully master of the Ministry of Defence while this potent relic from the past remained in office. Whether Mountbatten would have stayed on if pressed to do so is in any case doubtful; he was tired and stale, and had a multiplicity of interests to pursue outside.

His last few months as CDS were in fact spent partly abroad leading a mission on Commonwealth immigration. The main purpose of this exercise was to explain British policy and persuade Commonwealth governments to control illegal immigration at source. The mission was a success; indeed Mountbatten found that he was largely preaching to the converted, since only in Jamaica did the policy he was expounding meet with serious opposition. He presented the mission's report on 13 June 1965 and the following month took his formal farewell of the Ministry of Defence.

Retirement did not mean inactivity; indeed he was still officially enjoying his retirement leave when the prime minister invited him to go to Rhodesia as governor to forestall a declaration of independence by the white settler population. Mountbatten had little hesitation in refusing: 'Nothing could be worse for the cause you have at heart than to think that a tired out widower of 65 could recapture the youth, strength and enthusiasm of twenty years ago.' However, he accepted a later suggestion that he should fly briefly to Rhodesia in November 1965 to invest the governor, Sir Humphrey Gibbs, with a decoration on behalf of the Queen and generally to offer moral support. At the last minute the project was deferred and never revived.

The following year the home secretary asked him to undertake an enquiry into prison security, in view of a number of recent sensational escapes. Mountbatten agreed, provided it could be a one-man report prepared with the help of three assessors. The report was complete within two months and most of the recommendations were carried out. The two most important, however—the appointment of an inspector-general responsible to the home secretary to head the prison service and the building of a separate maximum security gaol for prisoners whose escape would be particularly damaging—were never implemented. For the latter proposal Mountbatten was much criticized by liberal reformers who felt the step a retrograde one; this Mountbatten contested, arguing that, isolated within a completely secure outer perimeter, the dangerous criminal could be allowed more freedom than would otherwise be the case.

Mountbatten was associated with 179 organizations, ranging alphabetically from the Admiralty Dramatic Society to the Zoological Society. In some of these his role was formal, in many more it was not. In time and effort the United World Colleges, a network of international schools modelled on the Gordonstoun of Kurt Hahn, received the largest share. Mountbatten worked indefatigably to whip up support and raise funds for the schools, lobbying the leaders of every country he visited. The electronics industry, also, engaged his attention and he was an active first chairman of the National Electronic Research Council. In 1965 he was installed as governor of the Isle of Wight and conscientiously visited the island seven or eight times a year, in 1974 becoming the first lord lieutenant when the island was raised to the status of a shire. A role which gave him still greater pleasure was that of colonel of the Life Guards, to which he was also appointed in 1965. He took his duties at Trooping the Colour very seriously and for weeks beforehand would ride around the Hampshire lanes near Broadlands in hacking jacket and Life Guards helmet.

His personal life was equally crowded. The years 1966 and 1967 were much occupied with the filming of the thirteen-part television series *The Life and Times of Lord Mountbatten*, every detail of which absorbed him and whose sale he promoted energetically all over the world. He devoted much time to running the family estates and putting his massive archive in order, involving himself enthusiastically in the opening of Broadlands to the public, which took place in 1978. He never lost his interest in naval affairs or in high strategy. One of his last major speeches was delivered at Strasburg in May 1979, when he pleaded eloquently for arms control: 'As a military man who has given half a century of active service I say in all sincerity that the nuclear arms race has no military purpose. Wars cannot be fought with nuclear weapons. Their existence only adds to our perils because of the illusions which they have generated.'

Some of his happiest hours were spent on tour with the royal family in their official yacht *Britannia*. He derived particular pleasure from his friendship with the Prince of Wales, who treated him as 'honorary grandfather' and attached great value to his counsel. When Princess Anne married, the certificate gave as her surname 'Mountbatten-Windsor'. This was the culmination of a long battle Mountbatten had waged to ensure that his family name, adopted by Prince Philip, should be preserved among his nephew's descendants. He took an intense interest in all the royal houses of Europe, and was a source of advice on every subject. Harold Wilson once called him 'the shop-steward of royalty' and Mountbatten rejoiced in the description.

Every summer he enjoyed a family holiday at his Irish home in county Sligo, Classiebawn Castle. Over the years the size of his police escort increased but the Irish authorities were insistent that the cancellation of his holiday would be a victory for the Irish Republican Army. On 27 August 1979 a family party went out in a fishing boat, to collect lobster-pots set the previous day. A bomb exploded when the boat was half a mile from Mullaghmoor harbour. Mountbatten was killed instantly, as was his grandson Nicholas and a local Irish boy. His daughter's mother-in-law, Doreen Lady Brabourne, died shortly afterwards. His funeral took place in Westminster Abbey and he was buried in Romsey Abbey. He had begun his preparations for the ceremony more than ten years before and was responsible for planning every detail, down to the lunch to be eaten by the mourners on the train from Waterloo to Romsey.

Mountbatten was a giant of a man, and his weaknesses were appropriately gigantic. His vanity was monstrous, his ambition unbridled. The truth, in his hands, was swiftly converted from what it was to what it should have been. But such frailties were far outweighed by his qualities. His energy was prodigious, as was his moral and physical courage. He was endlessly resilient in the face of disaster. No intellectual, he possessed a powerfully analytical intelligence; he could rapidly master a complex brief, spot the essential and argue it persuasively. His flexibility of mind was extraordinary, as was his tolerance—he accepted all comers for what they were, not measured against some scale of predetermined values. He had style and panache, commanding the loyal devotion of those who served him. To his opponents in Whitehall he was 'tricky Dickie', devious and unscrupulous. To his family and close friends he was a man of wisdom and generosity. He adored his two daughters, Patricia and Pamela, and his ten grandchildren. However pressing his preoccupations he would make time to comfort, encourage, or advise them. Almost always the advice was good.

Among Mountbatten's honours were MVO (1920), KCVO (1922), GCVO (1937), DSO (1941), CB (1943), KCB (1945), KG (1946), PC (1947), GCSI (1947), GCIE (1947), GCB (1955), OM (1965), and FRS (1966). He had an honorary DCL from Oxford (1946), and honorary LL Ds from Cambridge (1946), Leeds (1950), Edinburgh (1954), Southampton (1955), London (1960), and Sussex (1963). He was honorary D.Sc. of Delhi and Patna (1948).

Mountbatten was much painted. His head, by John Ulbricht, is held by the National Portrait Gallery, while portraits by Philip de László, Brenda Bury, Derek Hill, and Carlos Sancha are in the possession of the family. His state portrait by Edward Halliday hangs in the former viceroy's house, New Delhi, and by Da Cruz in the Victoria Memorial Building, Calcutta. A memorial statue by Franta Belsky was erected in 1983 on Foreign Office Green in London.

On Mountbatten's death the title passed to his elder daughter, Patricia Edwina Victoria Knatchbull (born 1924), who became Countess Mountbatten of Burma.

[Philip Ziegler, *Mountbatten*, 1985; family papers.]

PHILIP ZIEGLER

published 1986

MOUNTBATTEN Edwina Cynthia Annette

(1901–1960)

Countess Mountbatten of Burma

Was born in London 28 November 1901, the elder daughter of Colonel W. W. Ashley, P.C., M.P., later Baron Mount Temple, of Broadlands, Romsey, and Classiebawn Castle, county Sligo (both inherited from Palmerston), and his first wife, Amalia Mary Maud, only child of Sir Ernest Cassel. On her father's side she was the great-granddaughter of the seventh Earl of Shaftesbury, the social reformer. King Edward VII was her godfather.

She was nearly twenty when Cassel died and left between her and her younger sister the income from an immense fortune. In 1922 she married, at St. Margaret's, Westminster, Lieutenant Lord Louis Mountbatten, Royal Navy, younger son of Admiral of the Fleet the Marquess of Milford Haven, formerly Prince Louis of Battenberg, and his wife, Victoria, a granddaughter of Queen Victoria. As the wife of Lord Louis, who was pursuing a highly successful career in the navy, she had a very full social life, but her energy and inquiring mind led her to undertake world-wide tours and numerous charitable activities on her own account.

The outbreak of war in 1939 provided the real outlet for her talents and aspirations for social welfare work and marked the beginning of a distinguished career of service with the Order of St. John. After undertaking numerous duties for the Order, including work in the east end of London at the time of the intensive raids, she was appointed superintendent-in-chief of the St. John Ambulance Brigade in July 1942. The scope of her operations, involving extensive tours of inspection, widened with the course of the war and her husband's rapid military promotion. When he was appointed chief of Combined Operations in 1942 she organized the Command's welfare branch. But it was after he had become supreme allied commander South East Asia in 1943, and in the wake of the Japanese surrender in 1945, that she was able to make perhaps her greatest contribution to the allied cause. In a gigantic rescue operation covering effectively the whole of South East Asia she inaugurated desperately needed welfare services for the returned allied prisoners of war and internees.

No sooner had this task been completed than another historic role awaited her. She was to be at her husband's side for the decisive period (March 1947 to June 1948) when he was the last viceroy and the first governor-general of independent India. The implementation of his policy for rapid transfer of power involved many acts of social as well as political conciliation in which Lady Mountbatten's insight and initiative were of primary importance in strengthening the ties of friendship between the British and Indian peoples.

Independence, however, brought in its train grave massacres and the migrations of whole populations in the Punjab to which she responded with prodigious efforts to stem the tide of human suffering. Under her chairmanship the United Council for Relief and Welfare was formed which included all the major voluntary organizations and co-ordinated their activities.

On their return from India, Lord Mountbatten's resumption of his Service career meant no diminution of Lady Mountbatten's welfare work. In 1948 she became chairman of the St. John and Red Cross Services Hospitals welfare department and in 1950 superintendent-in-chief of the St. John Ambulance Brigade Overseas, making further long-range tours of inspection and severely taxing her strength in the process. It was on one of these exhausting missions to the Far East on behalf of the Order of St. John that she died in her sleep at Jesselton, North Borneo, on the night of 20–21 February 1960. Her body was flown back to England and buried at sea off Portsmouth with naval honours.

She was actively and officially associated with some hundred organizations. In addition to the St. John Ambulance Brigade she took a special interest in the Save the Children Fund of which she was president, and the Royal College of Nursing, of which she was a vice-president. To enable her work for these three particular causes to be perpetuated the Edwina Mountbatten Trust was formed.

Many dignities and decorations were conferred on the Mountbattens. He was created successively viscount (1946) and earl (1947) for his services in South East Asia and India. She was appointed C.I. (1947), G.B.E. (1947), D.C.V.O. (1946), and G.C.St.J. (1945).

She had two daughters, Patricia, born in 1924, who married the seventh Baron Brabourne in 1946, and Pamela, born in 1929, who married David Hicks in January 1960.

George

Lady Mountbatten was not content to rest on her inheritance of beauty, wealth, and privilege but made her mark on the history of her times as an emancipator, a tough and relentless fighter against poverty and suffering. She had an abundance of charm and compassion which reinforced her powers of leadership. In support of her husband in South East Asia and India her social conscience played a significant part in mitigating the consequences of the political and military crises with which her husband was grappling. She had, as India's prime minister, Jawaharlal Nehru, said of her, 'the healer's touch'.

There are portraits of her by P. A. de László and Salvador Dali (at Broadlands) and by Edward I. Halliday (in New Delhi).

[Private information; personal knowledge.]

ALAN CAMPBELL-JOHNSON

published 1971

GEORGE Edward Alexander Edmund

(1902–1942)

Duke of Kent

The fourth son of King George V and Queen Mary, was born at York Cottage, Sandringham, 20 December 1902. He passed through Dartmouth into the Royal Navy, in which he served until 1929, visiting many parts of the Empire, and he accompanied his brother the Prince of Wales on visits to Canada in 1927 and to South America in 1931. After working at the Foreign Office in 1929 he was attached to the Home Office. In 1934 at the invitation of the Government of the Union he made an extensive tour of South Africa and also visited the territory of Basutoland, the protectorate of Bechuanaland, and Rhodesia, the Belgian Congo, and Portuguese West Africa. Shortly before his marriage in November 1934 to Princess Marina, daughter of Prince Nicholas of Greece, he was created Duke of Kent, Earl of St. Andrews, and Baron Downpatrick. His happy marriage was a turning-point in his life, strengthening his character, and making his purpose in life more definite. In 1935 he was appointed lord high commissioner to the General Assembly of the Church of Scotland, and in 1938 was designated governor-general of Australia, but the outbreak of war prevented his taking up the post. He remained in this country, attached in 1939 to the naval intelligence division of the Admiralty with the rank of captain (later rear-admiral), visiting naval establishments. In April 1940 he was appointed staff officer in the Training Command of the Royal Air Force in which he held the rank of group captain (later air commodore). His duties, the supervision of welfare work for the members of the Royal Air Force, took him not only to stations in Britain but also overseas, including Canada and the United States, which he visited in the summer of 1941. On 25 August 1942 the Duke set out to inspect establishments in Iceland, but was killed when his aircraft crashed at the Eagle's Rock, near Dunbeath in Caithness. He was buried at Windsor. He was survived by his widow and three children, Prince Edward George Nicholas Paul Patrick (born 1935) who succeeded to his titles; Princess Alexandra Helen Elizabeth Olga Christabel (born 1936); and Prince Michael George Charles Franklin (born July 1942).

The Duke was endowed with more than ordinary charm, his wavy brown hair and bright blue eyes contributing to a notably handsome appearance; in maturity he rather exceeded the average height and build of his family. A cheerful and amusing companion, there was no meanness in his nature, and he had many friends; he was fond of sport, hunted in the shires and was a fair game shot, but being devoted to walking, he was perhaps happiest when stalking or playing golf. He shared with his mother an informed interest in furniture and works of art, of which he built up a notable collection. He appreciated music and played the piano with enjoyment; he read intelligently and even widely and would have been accounted a cultured man in any society. He made his home at Coppins, Iver, Buckinghamshire, which he inherited from his aunt, Princess Victoria.

[Private information.]

JOHN GORE

published 1959

MARINA (1906–1968)

Duchess of Kent

Was the youngest of the three daughters of Prince and Princess Nicholas of Greece. Her father was the third son of King George I of Greece and her mother was the Grand Duchess Helen, daughter of the Grand Duke Vladimir, uncle of Tsar Nicholas II. Born in Athens 13 December 1906, she enjoyed a particularly happy early childhood, spent mostly in the Greek capital and at the enchanting palace at Tatoi at the foot of Mount Parnes. Her parents, although for their position not wealthy, provided a comfortable home life, which combined discipline with affection and understanding. A childhood visit to her maternal grandmother gave her glimpses of the splendours of the Russian court, but her own upbringing was simple, the home atmosphere in many ways English; the children's governess, Miss Kate Fox, although firm and at times severe, was held in affection throughout her life by the Princess and her two sisters.

The Princess early acquired fluency in her native language, in English which was habitually spoken within the family, and also in French. She was brought up in the Greek Orthodox Church and her affection for the country of her birth survived all its disturbed history, even though this brought two periods of exile. The first was in 1917, when political upheavals forced Prince Nicholas and his family to seek refuge in Switzerland. Some four years later they returned to Greece, but in 1922 were again driven into exile. The family settled in Paris, where Princess Marina went for a time to a finishing school run by Princess Meshchersky, an old friend of the family.

Their financial position and social life were now greatly altered. Nevertheless their Paris days were happy. Prince Nicholas was able to make profitable use of his artistic talents and Princess Nicholas devoted her time and some of her slender wealth to helping less fortunate Russian refugees. Princess Marina aided her mother, and also developed her good taste in clothes, many of which she made for herself. So began her lifelong reputation as one of the best-dressed women of her time. After her marriage her elegance greatly influenced the style and appearance not only of other members of the British royal family but also of the British public, while her choice of British fabrics, especially cotton, did much to revive home industries.

In 1923 her eldest sister Olga married Prince Paul of Yugoslavia and in 1934 the next sister, Elizabeth, married Count Toerring-Yettenbach of Bavaria. In August of that year Princess Marina became engaged to Prince George, fourth son of King George V and Queen Mary, whom she had met from time to time when she visited London. Princess Marina rapidly won the hearts of the British people. Her attractive beauty and obvious happiness made her wedding in Westminster Abbey on 29 November 1934 a notable event. Prince George had been created Duke of Kent shortly before his marriage and the duchess quickly adapted herself to her new role as a member of the British royal family, fulfilling her varied engagements with graceful conscientiousness. Her home life, as in Greece, was unobtrusive and simple. The duke and duchess particularly enjoyed converting into a pleasant home Coppins, near Iver, Buckinghamshire, the

Victorian house which was left to the duke by his aunt, Princess Victoria. At their London home in Belgrave Square they extended their hospitality to a widely ranging circle of people: artists, authors, actors, besides those associated with the charitable organizations in which the duke and duchess were especially interested.

The death of the duke in a flying accident in Scotland while serving with the Royal Air Force, 25 August 1942, was a cruel blow. The eldest son, Prince Edward, who succeeded as second duke, had been born 9 October 1935; their daughter, Princess Alexandra, on Christmas day the following year; and Prince Michael on 4 July 1942. The duchess did not for long allow her loss to interrupt her war work. She had trained as a VAD, but her principal energies were devoted to the WRNS, of which she had become commandant (later chief commandant) in 1940. She took a detailed and continuing interest in this Service and it was generally accepted that her taste in dress influenced the attractive uniform designed for it. Her other concern was the bringing up of her family in an atmosphere which was well ordered and relaxed.

Her public duties increased with widowhood. She replaced the duke in many of the organizations of which he had been president or patron, and in his work as an unofficial factory inspector. As president of the Royal National Lifeboat Institution she was active in visiting many small harbours; her constant attendance at Wimbledon as president of the All England Lawn Tennis Club was indicative of her genuine interest in the game; and towards the end of her life she took seriously her duties as chancellor of the newly formed university of Kent. Another deep and constant concern was for those suffering from mental illness: manifested in her patronage of the National Association for Mental Health. Nor did she abandon the interest in painting and music which she had so closely shared with her husband.

A number of her duties took her abroad. In 1952 she made an extensive tour of the Far East, beginning and ending at Singapore and including Hong Kong and Sarawak. As colonel-in-chief of the Queen's Own Royal West Kent Regiment she saw some of its troops in operation against the rebels in the Malayan jungle. She represented the Queen in 1957 at the independence celebrations of Ghana and in 1966 at those of Botswana and Lesotho. On these and other tours in Australia, Canada, Mexico, and South America her charm and natural friendliness increased the prestige of British royalty overseas. Although basically shy and diffident she never allowed this to stand in the way of her duties and showed great courage in the adverse events of her life. Her warm-heartedness and generosity made for her strong friendships and she retained from childhood a sense of humour and interest in people which made her an enchanting companion.

During her last years she was happy in the marriages of her eldest son and of her daughter, and found much enjoyment in her grandchildren's progress. After her son's marriage she was known as Princess Marina, Duchess of Kent, and moved to Kensington Palace so that her son might have his independent establishment at Coppins. She had been appointed CI and GBE in 1937 and GCVO in 1948.

Financially the post-war years were far from easy. There was no provision for her in the Civil List and the situation was only partially eased through the sale of many of the art treasures which she and the duke had acquired before the war. She died at Kensington Palace after a short illness 27 August 1968. At the time of his death her husband's body had been placed in the vaults of St. George's Chapel, Windsor, but at her wish they were now buried side by side in the private burial ground at Frogmore.

Two of her three portraits by P. A. de László, portraits by Judy Cassab, and a pair by the Russian artist Sorine of the duke and herself are in family possession. There is also a full-length portrait of her by (Sir) William Dargie, the Australian artist, in the hall of the Clothworkers' Company, of which she was a freewoman, and there are two portraits by Simon Elwes in the possession of the Queen's Regiment, and one by Norman Hepple in the possession of the Corps of Royal Electrical and Mechanical Engineers, of which she was the colonel-in-chief.

[*The Times*, 28 August and 6 September 1968; Arthur S. Gould Lee, *The Royal House of Greece*, 1948; Jennifer Ellis, *The Duchess of Kent*, 1952; J. Wentworth Day, *H.R.H. Princess Marina, Duchess of Kent*, 2nd edn. 1969; Stella King, *Princess Marina*, 1969; private information.]

G. K. S. HAMILTON-EDWARDS

published 1981

ADEANE Michael Edward

(1910–1984)

Baron Adeane

Private secretary to Queen Elizabeth II, was born 30 September 1910 in London, the only son of Captain Henry Robert Augustus Adeane, of the Coldstream Guards, who was killed in action in 1914, and his wife, Victoria Eugenie, daughter of Arthur John Bigge (later Lord Stamfordham). He was educated at Eton and Magdalene College, Cambridge, where he achieved a second class (first division) in part i of the history tripos (1930) and a first class (second division) in part ii (1931). The college made him an honorary fellow in 1971.

He then joined the Coldstream Guards and from 1934 to 1936 was aide-de-camp to two successive governors-general of Canada, the Earl of Bessborough and Lord Tweedsmuir. In 1937 he was appointed equerry and assistant private secretary to King George VI and accompanied the King and Queen on their visit to Canada and the United States in the summer of 1939. On the outbreak of war he rejoined his regiment, being promoted to major in 1941. From 1942 to 1943 he was a member of the joint staff mission in Washington with the acting rank of lieutenant-colonel. From 1943 to 1945 he served with the 5th battalion Coldstream Guards as company commander and second-in-command. In the battle of Normandy he had to take over command of the battalion, was wounded in the stomach, and mentioned in dispatches. In 1945 he returned to Buckingham Palace and for the remainder of the reign served as assistant private secretary to King George VI. In 1947 he was a member of the royal party on their visit to South Africa and in 1952, having been seconded to the staff of Princess Elizabeth, was with her in Kenya at the time of her father's death. The new Queen decreed that he should continue as one of her assistant private secretaries, which he did until, on the retirement of Sir Alan Lascelles on 1 January 1954, he became her principal private secretary, retaining this office until his retirement in 1972. He was also keeper of the Queen's archives (1953–72).

The three main duties of the Queen's private secretary are to be the link between the monarch and her ministers, especially her prime ministers, to make the arrangements for her public engagements and for the numerous speeches which she is called upon to make, and to deal with her massive correspondence.

The first twenty years of the reign were marked by demands for an ever-expanding programme of public engagements at home and abroad, and by an intrusive, and not always charitable, scrutiny of the Queen and her family by the media. It was largely due to Adeane that the monarchy was able to adjust to these pressures, while retaining its essential dignity and mystery. Although some judged his advice to be unduly cautious and the speeches which he drafted for the Queen to be lacking in imagination, he was able to avoid the controversies to which a more adventurous private secretary might have exposed a constitutional sovereign. Adeane had to deal with six British prime ministers and with many more from Commonwealth countries as well as with their governors-general. He treated all with equal courtesy and respect and was invariably well briefed on their personalities and policies. These qualities showed to particular advantage during overseas tours. During these years the Queen visited almost every country in the Commonwealth, several of them more than once, and many foreign countries including most of those in western Europe. Adeane was responsible for the arrangements for all these visits. He also performed a notable service to the royal family by his compelling evidence to the select committee of the House of Commons on the civil list in 1971 outlining the Queen's workload and commitments. This led later to the civil list being reviewed annually and submitted to Parliament in the same way as a departmental budget.

Professor Harold Laski wrote in 1942: 'The Secretary to the Monarch occupies to the Crown much the same position that the Crown itself in our system occupies to the Government; he must advise and encourage and warn ... The Royal Secretary walks on a tight-rope below which he is never unaware that an abyss is yawning ... A bad Private Secretary, who was rash or indiscreet or untrustworthy might easily make the system of constitutional monarchy unworkable' (*Fortnightly Review*, vol. clviii, July–Dec. 1942). By these criteria, Adeane was highly successful.

In his style of work, he closely resembled his grandfather, Lord Stamfordham, of whom it was said (*DNB 1931–40*) that he was 'a man of persistent industry, making it his practice to finish the day's work within the day'. Like him too, he was 'regarded by his colleagues with a love which perhaps never wholly cast out fear'. His wisdom, sense of humour, and discretion endeared him to other members of the royal family and their households, to whom his advice was always available. But he could also be severe on any lack of tact or competence. He was a popular member of several dining clubs, and although he enjoyed conversation, he would never gossip about the royal family. A totally concentrated listener, he rarely came away from such occasions without useful information which he stored in a capacious and accurate memory.

Adeane was at heart a countryman, a fine but unassuming shot and a skilful fisherman. He was an enthusiastic gardener, on the roof of his house in Windsor Castle and in the small gardens of the house in Chelsea and the cottage in Aberdeenshire which he made his homes in his retirement. He also painted in water-colours and was a voracious reader of biography, history, and Victorian novels, especially those of Anthony Trollope. Modest, even spartan in his personal life, he nevertheless appreciated good food and wine and liked to smoke a good cigar. He was entirely free from social, religious, and racial prejudice.

On his retirement in 1972 he acquired several directorships, including those of Phoenix Assurance, the Diners Club, the Banque Belge, and the Royal Bank of Canada. He was also appointed chairman of the Royal Commission on Historical Monuments and served as the Queen's representative on the board of the British Library. He was a fellow of the

Society of Antiquaries and a governor of Wellington College. As a member of the House of Lords he sat on the cross-benches but spoke rarely.

His honours came in a steady progression after the war until his retirement. He was appointed MVO in 1946, CB in 1947, KCVO in 1951, KCB in 1955, GCVO in 1962, GCB in 1968, and, on his retirement in 1972, received the Royal Victorian Chain. He was made a privy councillor in 1953 and a life peer in 1972.

In 1939 he married Helen, elder daughter of Richard Chetwynd-Stapleton, stockbroker, of Headlands, Berkhamsted. They had one daughter, who died in 1953, and one son, Edward, who became private secretary to the Prince of Wales (1979–85). Adeane died in Aberdeen 30 April 1984 of heart failure after enjoying two days' fishing in the Dee. It was characteristic of his modesty that, by his special request, no thanksgiving service was held in his memory. A portrait of him by David Poole, commissioned by the Queen, hangs at Buckingham Palace.

[*The Times*, 2 May 1984; personal knowledge.]

EDWARD FORD

published 1990

WILLIAM Henry Andrew Frederick

(1941–1972)

Prince of Great Britain, the elder son and elder child of Prince Henry and Princess Alice of Gloucester, was born 18 December 1941 in Lady Carnarvon's Home, Barnet, a Hertfordshire nursing home. His schooling began in 1950 at Wellesley House, Broadstairs. Four years later he passed high into Eton, where he proved gregarious, enterprising, and intelligent. Prince William's student days were spent at Magdalene College, Cambridge (1960–3), where he obtained a third class in part i and a second class (2nd division) in part ii of the historical tripos. With his parents' full approval, he shared the unsheltered life of his fellow undergraduates. Indeed, the unprecedented freedom with which he chose his companions, male and female, was seen as a challenging novelty. In 1963–4 he spent a postgraduate year at Stanford, California.

The Prince was a born explorer and in the summer vacation of 1963 made a film for the BBC of a twelve thousand mile safari in Africa. Those who accompanied him on such journeys praised his resource, humour, integrity, and courage. He never wearied of travel, partly because of the opportunities it gave him to fly, drive, climb, ski, shoot, and skin-dive. But he was no mere playboy.

Suspecting that the army might treat him as a 'mascot', Prince William sought a career elsewhere. Possibly the deepest need of his nature was to achieve greatness and not have it thrust upon him. In 1965 he joined the Commonwealth Relations Office as third secretary on the staff of the British high commission at Lagos, from which vantage point he witnessed the Nigerian civil war. Three years later he was transferred to the British embassy in Tokyo as second (commercial) secretary. During his tour of duty he vigorously promoted Anglo-Japanese trade, travelled all over the country, and helped restore friendly relations with the imperial family. His charm, good looks, and informality won Britain many friends.

Prince William returned to England in 1970 to undertake some of his father's public duties. In that year he represented the Queen at the celebrations marking Tonga's independence, and in 1971 at the state funeral of President Tubman of Liberia. The Prince was killed in a flying accident at Halfpenny Green, Staffordshire, 28 August 1972, while competing in an air race.

Prince William was something of a non-conformist, torn between the demands of his inheritance and his love of independence. In struggling to resolve this conflict he pioneered a new style of royalty. He was unmarried.

[Giles St. Aubyn (ed.), *William of Gloucester*, 1977; personal knowledge.]

GILES ST. AUBYN

published 1986

Alphabetical Index

Alphabetical Index